Freedom of Speech in International Law

Freedom of Speech in International Law

AMAL CLOONEY AND DAVID NEUBERGER

Assistant Editor
ALICE GARDOLL

Great Clarendon Street, Oxford, OX2 6DP,
United Kingdom

Oxford University Press is a department of the University of Oxford.
It furthers the University's objective of excellence in research, scholarship,
and education by publishing worldwide. Oxford is a registered trade mark of
Oxford University Press in the UK and in certain other countries

© The multiple contributors 2024

The moral rights of the authors have been asserted

First Edition published in 2024

All rights reserved. No part of this publication may be reproduced, stored in
a retrieval system, or transmitted, in any form or by any means, without the
prior permission in writing of Oxford University Press, or as expressly permitted
by law, by licence or under terms agreed with the appropriate reprographics
rights organization. Enquiries concerning reproduction outside the scope of the
above should be sent to the Rights Department, Oxford University Press, at the
address above

You must not circulate this work in any other form
and you must impose this same condition on any acquirer

Public sector information reproduced under Open Government Licence v3.0
(http://www.nationalarchives.gov.uk/doc/open-government-licence/open-government-licence.htm)

Published in the United States of America by Oxford University Press
198 Madison Avenue, New York, NY 10016, United States of America

British Library Cataloguing in Publication Data

Data available

Library of Congress Control Number: 2023947240

ISBN 978-0-19-889937-2

DOI: 10.1093/law/9780198899372.001.0001

Printed and bound by
CPI Group (UK) Ltd, Croydon, CR0 4YY

Links to third party websites are provided by Oxford in good faith and
for information only. Oxford disclaims any responsibility for the materials
contained in any third party website referenced in this work.

Foreword

The five chapters following the Introduction to this book contain a number of recommendations related to how international law related to freedom of expression should be interpreted, applied and reformed. We are grateful that these recommendations have been reviewed and endorsed by:

- The Committee to Protect Journalists
- Reporters without Borders
- The International Bar Association Human Rights Institute
- The United National Special Rapporteur on Freedom of Expression, Ms. Irene Khan
- The Inter-American Special Rapporteur on Freedom of Expression, Mr. Pedro Vaca Villarreal.
- Patrick Penninckx, Head of Information Society Department, Council of Europe
- Francoise Tulkens, former Vice-President of the European Court of Human Rights and member of the High Level Panel of Legal Experts on Media Freedom[1]
- Baroness Helena Kennedy of the Shaws, KC, barrister, member of the House of Lords and member of the High Level Panel of Legal Experts on Media Freedom
- The Honourable Irwin Cotler, PC, OC, OQ, former Minister of Justice and Attorney-General of Canada and member of the High Level Panel of Legal Experts on Media Freedom
- Hina Jilani, lawyer, former UN Special Representative on Human Rights Defenders and member of the High Level Panel of Legal Experts on Media Freedom
- Judge Chile Eboe-Osuji, former President of the International Criminal Court and member of the High Level Panel of Legal Experts on Media Freedom
- Dario Milo, Partner, Webber Wentzel and member of the High Level Panel of Legal Experts on Media Freedom
- Seong-Phil Hong, Professor at Ewha and Yonsei Law Schools, former member of the UN Working Group on Arbitrary Detention and member of the High Level Panel of Legal Experts on Media Freedom.
- Justice Manuel José Cepeda Espinosa, former Chief Justice of the Constitutional Court of Colombia and member of the High Level Panel of Legal Experts on Media Freedom

---

[1] An independent group of lawyers and judges convened at the request of the governments of the United Kingdom and Canada to 'provide advice and recommendations to promote and protect a vibrant free press'. See IBAHRI, 'High Level Panel of Legal Experts on Media Freedom'.

- Karuna Nundy, Advocate at the Supreme Court of India and member of the High Level Panel of Legal Experts on Media Freedom
- Marietje Schaake, international policy director at Stanford University Cyber Policy Center and member of the High Level Panel of Legal Experts on Media Freedom
- Can Yeginsu, Barrister and Deputy Chair of the High Level Panel of Legal Experts on Media Freedom
- Catherine Amirfar, Partner, Debevoise & Plimpton and Deputy Chair of the High Level Panel of Legal Experts on Media Freedom
- Catherine Anite, human rights lawyer and member of the High Level Panel of Legal Experts on Media Freedom
- Nadim Houry, Executive Director of the Arab Reform Initiative and member of the High Level Panel of Legal Experts on Media Freedom.

All sources and references have been checked for accuracy as of 1 January 2022.

Amal Clooney
David Neuberger
London, 25 October 2023

Acknowledgments

The editors would like to thank the lawyers and academics who have contributed as authors to one or more chapters of this book: Professor Phillipa Webb, Professor Dario Milo, Professor Marko Milanovic, Dr Rosana Garciandia Garmendia and Alice Gardoll. We are grateful for your excellent work and your enduring commitment to this project and to protecting freedom of speech and of the press.

We would like to thank our pool of illustrious legal experts who provided valuable feedback on key elements of the text, despite very demanding schedules. This includes Judge Robert Sack; Baroness Françoise Tulkens, Irwin Cotler PC OC KC, Gail Gove, Sir Michael Tugendhat, Baroness Helena Kennedy KC, Can Yeginsu, Jeanne Sulzer, Jeremy Perelman, Anne Charbord, Nadim Houry, Professor Sarah Cleveland, Professor David Kaye, Professor Evelyn Aswad, Pedro Vaca Villarreal, Inter-American Special Rapporteur on Freedom of Expression, Assistant Professor Vincent Wong, Dougal Hurley, Michael O'Flaherty, Theodore J. Boutrous Jr. and Brandon Silver. We are very grateful for your probing questions and comments as we developed our analysis and recommendations.

Thanks to our excellent team of researchers and reviewers: Alisha Mathew, Emma DiNapoli, Katharina Lewis, Nadine Reiner, Samarth Patel, Patricia Peña-Drilon, Perri Lyons and Vera Padberg. And to those we relied on for their amazing eye for detail in the final stages: Daisy Peterson, James Tanna, Hannah Reid and Tomas Moeremans. We know this was painstaking, but essential, work and we would not have reached the finishing line without them.

There are also many institutions and organizations that have provided excellent research support through their talented students. These include Columbia University; King's College London; National Law University Delhi; Sciences Po Law School Clinic and in particular students who carried extensive research of legislation and jurisprudence into media freedom and counter terrorism; The Institute for Law and Public Policy; Thomson Reuters Foundation; Universidad de los Andes; Ghent University; the University of Pretoria; the University of Toronto and MinterEllison. We have also been greatly assisted by reviews and comments from the High Level Panel of Legal Experts on Media Freedom and the support of legal experts identified by the International Bar Associations Human Rights Institute (IBAHRI). We also thank Myriam Whaibe, Astrid Bendixen Kettis, Anna-Henrikje Buroh and Petra Radetic Baric for their dedicated support.

This book would not have been possible without the many national-law experts who were consulted to verify national law references to legislation and caselaw throughout the drafting process. We are most grateful to these busy practitioners and academics for their time and expertise. They include: Abdoul Mtoka; Aicha Mane, Houda Avocats;

Alejandra Negrete Morayta; Ambreen Qureshi, Barrister at Law, Advocate Lahore High Court; Alexandra Perloff-Giles; Anastasios A. Antoniou, Antoniou McCollum & Co; Andre S. Coore; Professor Andrea Saccucci, University of Campania Luigi Vanvitelli; Ari Yannakogeorgos, Allen & Overy LLP; Berit Reiss-Andersen; Blánaid Ní Chearnaigh; Judge Camelia Bogdan; Carol Yuen, RCL Chambers Law Corporation; Catherine Anite; Chara Daouti, Lambadarios Law Firm; Chapter One Foundation; Charitiano Lwin, Deakin University; Chester Toh; Christine Nkonge; Claire Overman; Debora Dineva, Kinstellar; Desmond Orisewezie; Dieudonné Takam, Cameroon Bar Association; Dmitri Laevski, Belarusian human rights lawyer; Elise Perry; Emily Foale, IBAHRI; Emmanuel Saffe Abdulai (PhD), Head of Department, Department of Law, Faculty of Law, Fourah Bay College, The University of Sierra Leone; Eric Bizimana; Esther-Maureen Appenteng, A B & David Africa; Esther Muigai-Mnaro, Pan African Lawyers Union; Dr Ewelina Ochab, IBAHRI; Fatou Touray, Amie Bensouda; Franka Baica, Croatian Attorney at Law; Ferdaus Rahman, A.S & Associates; Fiona Iliff, Senior Legal Consultant, American Bar Association Center for Human Rights, Justice Defenders Program (Sub-Saharan Africa); Dr Gehan Gunatilleke, Pembroke College, University of Oxford; Dr Gleb Bogush, Research Fellow at the University of Copenhagen; Haby Mballo, Houda Advocats; Hawwa Reena Hassa; Haruki Matsui; Haymanot Belay; Hicham Kantar; Hideaki Roy Umetsu; Ilga Gudrenika-Krebs; Iulia Furtuna; Jan Juroška; Jesper Rothe, Partner, Bech-Bruun Law Firm P/S and President, Association of Danish Law Firm; Joel Osekeny, A B & David Africa; Joia W.S. Reece, Dentons Delany; Julie Steinnes, Master of Laws, Member of the Norwegian Bar Association; Dr Joan Barata, Senior Legal Fellow, Future of Free Speech, Justitia; Katarina Emeršič Polić, Pirc Musar & Partners; Karuna Nundy; Kee Hui Yee, Advocate & Solicitor of the High Court of Malaya and Senior Associate, Messrs Kanesalingam & Co, Malaysia; Khalid Aghaliyev, Media Rights Group; Khine Khine Zin; Kyong Mok Kim, partner at Bae, Kim & Lee LLC; László Detre, Hungarian Helsinki Committee; Laura Bugajová; Judge Ledi Bianku, Associate Attorney, Doughty Street Chambers; Leonidas Erotokritou; Lukáš Ševčík; Magdalena Balcells, DLA Piper; Malick Lo, Houda Advocats; Manel Chibane; Margaux Bia, DLA Piper; Marija Filipovska; Marija Stojanović; Marie Laure Haroun, Houda Advocats; Marina Modi; Marta Pardavi, Hungarian Helsinki Committee; Marta Duch Giménez, advocate at the Brussels Bar; Maya A.L. Carrington, Dentons Delany; Merlin Seeman, Hedman Law Firm; Mesfin Tafesse; Michael Butera; Milica Popović; Molly Norburg; Moriah Yeakula, Counsellor-At-Law; Namrata Maheshwari, Digital Rights Advocate and India-qualified lawyer; Nako Edisherashvili; Nataša Pirc Musar, President of the Republic of Slovenia; Natashka Karova Simonovska; Nicolas Angelet, advocate at the Brussels Bar; Nikolay Gergov, Kinstellar; Professor Ngoc Son Bui, University of Oxford; Oana Grigore; Oksana Legka; Piseth Duch, Founding Lawyer of Business & Human Rights Law Group; Peter Danowsky; Rehnuma Binte Mamun, Research Lead, A.S & Associates; Rindra Rakotonaivo; Sarah Peeters, Pan African Lawyers Union; Serena Sih-Yu Chen, National Taiwan University; Sherzod Sodatkadamov; Sibel Uranues; Subarkah Syafruddin, Columbia Law School '19; Sybil-Marie Agyeman, A B & David Africa; Dr Therese Comodini Cachia, University of

Malta; Associate Professor Dr Tossapon Tassanakunlapan; Toomas Seppel, Hedman Law Firm; Ulf Isaksson; Vafa Fati-zade, Justice for Journalists Foundation; Valerie Bisasur; Vasile Gavrilita; Yevgeniy Zhovtis; Xenia Rivkin, Attorney at Law; and Zara Iqbal, IBAHRI.

Thank you, as well, to our publishers, Oxford University Press, and in particular to Jacqueline Larabee, Matthew Williams and Robert Cavooris for their support through the long journey to publication.

Last but definitely not least: we would like to express our deep gratitude to Alice Gardoll for her outstanding contribution to this book as our Assistant Editor. She has been instrumental in research, drafting, editing and verifying every aspect of this work; indefatigable, creative in her thinking, rigorous in her approach and—always—an absolute pleasure to work with.

Amal Clooney and David Neuberger
5 September 2023

Contents

Table of Cases — xv
Table of International Instruments — xxv
List of Abbreviations — xxxi
List of Contributors — xxxv

1. Introduction — 1
   Amal Clooney
   I. Introduction — 2
   II. International Standards on Freedom of Speech and of the Press — 5
      1. Treaties — 5
         1.1. Treaty language — 5
            1.1.1. Abuses by the state — 5
            1.1.2. Obligation to prevent abuses by others — 10
         1.2. Drafting history — 13
            1.2.1. International treaties — 13
            1.2.2. Regional treaties — 22
         1.3. Reservations — 26
            1.3.1. International treaties — 27
            1.3.2. Regional treaties — 34
         1.4. Derogations — 36
            1.4.1. International treaties — 36
            1.4.2. Regional treaties — 39
      2. Customary International Law — 41
      3. Jurisprudence — 44
         3.1. Key convergences — 47
            3.1.1. Justifications for penalizing speech — 47
            3.1.2. False speech — 48
            3.1.3. Speech related to national security — 49
            3.1.4. Political and public interest speech — 50
            3.1.5. Importance of protecting the press — 50
            3.1.6. Criminal penalties for speech — 53
         3.2. Key divergences — 54
            3.2.1. Denialism — 55
            3.2.2. Blasphemy — 56
            3.2.3. Intent and harm requirements — 57
            3.2.4. Defences — 59
            3.2.5. Relevance of whether the speaker is a journalist — 59
            3.2.6. Criminal penalties for speech — 62
            3.2.7. Remedies — 66
   III. Conclusion — 69

2. Insulting Speech — 71
   Philippa Webb, Dario Milo and Rosana Garciandia
   I. Introduction — 72

II.	State Practice	74
	1. Overview of Laws Regulating Insulting Speech	74
	1.1. Type of speech	75
	1.2. Intent	75
	1.3. Harm	77
	1.4. Exclusions, exceptions and defences	81
	1.5. Penalties	85
	2. Application of National Laws	92
	2.1. Europe	92
	2.2. Asia Pacific	96
	2.3. North and South America	99
	2.4. Middle East and Africa	100
III.	International Legal Standards	101
	1. Legality	101
	2. Legitimacy	104
	3. Necessity	105
	3.1. Intent	105
	3.2. Causal link between the speech and the harm	107
	3.3. Level of harm caused by the speech	108
	4. Exclusions, Exceptions and Defences	114
	4.1. Truth	114
	4.2. Public interest	116
	4.3. Reasonable publication	120
	4.4. Accurate reporting of official documents	124
	4.5. Opinion	125
	5. Right to a Fair Trial	127
	6. Penalties	128
	6.1. Criminal penalties	128
	6.2. Civil penalties	135
IV.	Recommendations	140

3. Hate Speech — 153
Amal Clooney and Alice Gardoll

I.	Introduction	153
II.	State Practice	156
	1. Overview of Hate Speech Laws	156
	1.1. Type of speech	156
	1.2. Harm	158
	1.3. Intent	159
	1.4. Exclusions, exceptions and defences	160
	1.5. Penalties	160
	2. Application of Hate Speech Laws Around the World	161
	2.1. Europe	161
	2.2. Asia Pacific	165
	2.3. North and South America	166
	2.4. Middle East and Africa	171
III.	International Legal Standards	172
	1. Mandatory Restrictions on Hate Speech	173
	1.1. ICCPR Article 20	175
	1.2. CERD Article 4	177
	1.3. Genocide Convention Article 3	178
	1.4. Mandatory restrictions at the regional level	180

			1.5. Summary	182
		2.	Discretionary Restrictions on Hate Speech	183
			2.1. Legality	185
			2.2. Legitimacy	187
			2.3. Necessity	193
			2.4. Exclusions, exceptions and defences	198
			2.5. Penalties	204
	IV.	Key Divergences in International and Regional Guidance		207
	V.	Approach of Private Companies to Online Hate Speech		208
	VI.	Recommendations		211
4.	False Speech			220
	Marko Milanovic and Philippa Webb			
	I.	Introduction		220
	II.	State Practice		223
		1.	Overview of Laws Regulating False Speech Around the World	224
			1.1. Vagueness and overbreadth	224
			1.2. Harm	225
			1.3. Intent	229
			1.4. Exclusions, exceptions and defences	231
			1.5. Penalties	231
		2.	Application of False Speech Laws Around the World	234
			2.1. Europe	234
			2.2. Asia Pacific	235
			2.3. Middle East and Africa	236
	III.	International Legal Standards		237
		1.	Legality	238
		2.	Legitimacy	240
			2.1. States must not restrict false speech for ulterior purposes	241
			2.2. What objectives can justify the penalization of false speech?	242
		3.	Necessity	244
			3.1. Harm	245
			3.2. Intent	249
		4.	Exclusions, Exceptions and Defences	253
			4.1. Truth	253
			4.2. Opinion	254
			4.3. Public interest and 'responsible journalism'	255
		5.	Penalties	257
			5.1. Criminal	257
			5.2. Civil	259
	IV.	Recommendations		260
5.	Speech Related to National Security: Espionage and Official Secrets Laws			277
	Amal Clooney and Alice Gardoll			
	I.	Introduction		277
	II.	State Practice		280
		1.	Overview of Laws Regulating Disclosure of 'Secret' Material	280
			1.1. Type of speech	280
			1.2. Harm	283
			1.3. Intent	284
			1.4. Exclusions, exceptions and defences	285
			1.5. Penalties	287

  2. Application of Espionage and Official Secrets Laws Around the World   288
   2.1. Europe and United Kingdom   288
   2.2. Asia Pacific   293
   2.3. Middle East and Africa   298
   2.4. North and South America   300
 III. International Legal Standards   306
  1. International Standards Related to Speech Affecting National Security   307
  2. Legality   313
  3. Legitimacy   315
  4. Necessity   316
   4.1. Secrecy   318
   4.2. Harm   320
   4.3. Intent   325
  5. Exclusions, Exceptions and Defences   325
   5.1. Public interest defence   325
   5.2. Reasonableness of the publication   329
   5.3. Truth   333
   5.4. Opinion   334
  6. Penalties   334
 IV. Recommendations   337

6. Speech Related to National Security: Terrorism Laws   347
Alice Gardoll
 I. Introduction   347
 II. State Practice   350
  1. Terrorism Laws and Associated Offences   350
   1.1. Type of speech   351
   1.2. Intent   356
   1.3. Harm   357
   1.4. Exclusions, exceptions and defences   358
   1.5. Penalties   359
  2. Application of Terrorism Laws Around the World   360
   2.1. Europe   361
   2.2. Asia Pacific region   365
   2.3. Middle East and Africa   367
   2.4. North and South America   369
 III. International Legal Standards   373
  1. Legality   374
  2. Legitimacy   379
  3. Necessity   382
   3.1. Harm   382
   3.2. Causal link between speech and harm   389
   3.3. Intent   397
  4. Exclusions, Exceptions and Defences   403
   4.1. Public interest   403
   4.2. Truth and opinion   406
  5. Penalties   407
  6. Approach of Private Companies to Online Incitement to Terrorism   411
 IV. Recommendations   414

Index   423

Table of Cases

INTERNATIONAL COURTS AND TRIBUNALS

International Court of Justice (ICJ)
Advisory Opinion on the Legality of the Threat or Use of Nuclear Weapons, 8 July 1996.......... 42
Application of the Convention on the Prevention and Punishment of the Crime
    of Genocide (Croatia v. Serbia), Judgment of 3 February 2015......................... 179
Military and Paramilitary Activities in and against Nicaragua (Nicaragua v.
    United States of America), Judgment of 27 June 1986................................ 43
North Sea Continental Shelf Cases (FRG/Denmark; FRG/Netherlands),
    Judgment of 20 February 1969.. 41

International Criminal Tribunal for Rwanda (ICTR)
Nahimana v. Prosecutor (ICTR-99-52-A), Appeals Judgement, 28 November 2007........... 42, 43
Nzabonimana v. Prosecutor (ICTR-98-44D-A), Judgement, 29 September 2014 .... 179, 180
Prosecutor v. Akayesu (ICTR-96-4-T), Judgement, 2 September 1998........................ 174
Prosecutor v. Kayishema and Ruzindana (ICTR-95-1-T), Trial Judgement, 21 May 1999 163
Prosecutor v. Nahimana et. al. (ICTR-99-52-A), Judgement, 28 November 2007 .... 174, 179–80
Prosecutor v. Nzabonimana (ICTR-98-44D-T), Judgement and Sentence, 31 May 2012 179

UNITED NATIONS

Committee on the Elimination of Racial Discrimination (CERD)
Adan v. Denmark (Comm. no. 43/2008), 13 August 2010................................... 178
The Jewish Community of Oslo v. Norway (Comm. no. 30/2003), 15 August 2005.............. 178

Human Rights Committee (HRC)
Adonis v. Philippines (Comm. no. 1815/2008), 26 October 2011........... 10–11, 66, 104, 109, 115,
                                                           117–18, 132–33, 249–50, 253–54
Aduayom v. Togo (Comm. nos. 422/1990 & others), 12 July 1996............................. 66
Agazade and Jafarov v. Azerbaijan (Comm. no. 2205/2012), 27 October 2016...... 6–7, 104, 183, 380
A.K. and A.R. v. Uzbekistan (Comm. no. 1233/2003), 31 March 2009 .... 53, 188, 204, 257
Akhmedyarov v. Kazakhstan (Comm. no. 2535/2015), 23 July 2020....................... 249–50
Aleksandrov v. Belarus (Comm. no. 1933/2010), 24 July 2014........... 6–7, 104, 183, 240–41, 380
Ballantyne v. Canada (Comm. nos. 359/1989 & 285/1989), 31 March 1993.................... 66
Baytelova v. Kazakhstan (Comm. no. 2520/2015), 22 July 2020.............................. 66
Bodrožić v. Serbia and Montenegro (Comm. no. 1180/2003), 31 October 2005 .. 51, 66, 109, 111, 130
Cacho Ribeiro v. Mexico (Comm. no. 2767/2016), 17 July 2018......................... 132–33
Coleman v. Australia (Comm. no. 1157/2003), 17 July 2006................................. 66
Dissanayake v. Sri Lanka (Comm. no. 1373/2005), 22 July 2008 66
Esergepov v. Kazakhstan (Comm. no. 2129/2012), 29 March 2016 .... 308–9, 320–21
Faurisson v. France (Comm. no. 550/1993), 8 November 1996 .... 53, 55–56, 158, 173, 175, 188,
                                                            194, 196–97, 198–99, 204, 208, 257
Gauthier v. Canada (Comm. no. 633/95), 5 May 1999................................. 50–51, 66
J. R. T. and the W. G. Party v. Canada (Comm. no. 104/1981), 6 April 1983 175
Kim v. Republic of Korea (Comm. no. 968/2001), 27 July 2005 .... 53, 204, 242, 257, 264, 381
Kozlov v. Belarus (Comm. no. 1986/2010), 24 July 2014............. 108, 113, 145, 201, 245, 255, 271
Kurakbaev and Sabdikenova v. Kazakhstan (Comm. no. 2509/2014), 19 July 2021........ 399, 402–3
Lovell v. Australia (Comm. no. 920/2000), 24 March 2004.......... 6–7, 104, 125, 183, 240–41, 380

xvi   TABLE OF CASES

L.T.K. v. Finland (Comm. no. 185/1984), 9 July 1985. 53
Malei v. Belarus (Comm. no. 2404/2014), 23 July 2020 66
Marchant Reyes v. Chile (Comm. no. 2627/2015), 7 November 2017 . . . . 384–85, 389, 415–16
Marques de Morais v. Angola (Comm. no. 1128/2002), 29 March 2005 . . . . 110, 111, 115, 134–35, 140
Mavlonov and Sa'Di v. Uzbekistan (Comm. no. 1334/2004), 19 March 2009 . . . . 12, 66
Mirzayanov v. Belarus (Comm. no. 2434/2014), 25 July 2019. 66
Nepomnyashchiy v. Russian Federation (Comm. no. 2318/2013), 17 July 2018. . . . . 47, 186
Njaru v. Cameroon (Comm. no. 1353/2005), 19 March 2007 111–12
Park v. Republic of Korea (Comm. no. 628/1995), 20 October 1998 . . . . 66, 308–9, 380
Pietraroia v. Uruguay (Comm. no. 44/1979), 27 March 1981 36–37
Praded v. Belarus (Comm. no. 2029/2011), 10 October 2014 36–37
Rabbae v. Netherlands (Comm. no. 2124/2011), 14 July 2016 . . . . 17, 53, 56–57, 58, 64, 154, 155,
173, 175–76, 191–92, 194, 204, 207, 212,
216–17, 245, 257, 265–66, 335,
384–85, 407, 415–16
Ross v. Canada (Comm. no. 736/1997), 18 October 2000 . . . . 9, 58–59, 173, 175, 188, 194, 204,
207, 245, 257, 382–83, 389
Salgar de Montejo v. Colombia (Comm. no. 64/1979), 24 March 1982 36–37
Shin v. Republic of Korea (Comm. no. 926/2000), 16 March 2004 . . . . 48, 58–59, 66, 194, 245,
308–9, 315, 324, 380, 382–83, 389
Shuilina v. Belarus (Comm. no. 2142/2012), 28 July 2017 36–37
Timoshenko v. Belarus (Comm. no. 2461/2014), 23 July 2020 66
Toregozhina v. Kazakhstan (Comm. no. 2688/2015), 25 March 2021 66
Yaker v. France (Comm. no. 2747/2016), 17 July 2018. 349–50
Zhagiparov v. Kazakhstan (Comm. no. 2441/2014), 25 October 2018. 117–18
Zündel v. Canada (Comm. no. 953/2000), 27 July 2003. . . . . 55, 198–99

Working Group on Arbitrary Detention (WGAD)

61 individuals v. United Arab Emirates (Opinion no. 60/2013), 22 November 2013. 306–7
Abdolfattah Soltani v. Iran (Opinion no. 26/2006), 1 September 2006 318
Agnès Uwimana Nkusi v. Rwanda (Opinion no. 25/2012), 29 August 2012 . . . . 109, 309
Alaa Ahmed Seif al Islam Abd El Fattah v. Egypt (Opinion no. 6/2016), 19 April 2016. . . . 385–86, 389
Al-Hawali v. Saudi Arabia (Opinion no. 29/2023), 3 April 2023. 383
Amer v. Egypt (Opinion no. 35/2008), 20 November 2008 . . . . 110, 128–29, 133, 191–92, 212, 258
Chen Shuqing and Lü Gengsong v. China (Opinion no. 76/2019),
    21 November 2019 . . . . 101, 102, 407–8
Chhin v. Cambodia (Opinion no. 3/2019), 24 April 2019 . . . . 296–97, 307, 313–14, 320–21, 338
Dolma Kyab v. China (Opinion no. 36/2007), 30 November 2007 . . . . 320–21, 383, 385–86
Duy Nguyen Huu Quoc v. Vietnam (Opinion no. 8/2019), 25 April 2019. 125
Eskinder Nega v. Ethiopia (Opinion no. 62/2012), 21 November 2012 394–95
Gulmira Imin v. China (Opinion no. 29/2012), 29 August 2012 . . . . .324, 335, 358, 379, 389, 407–8
Hammouri v. Israel (Opinion no. 13/2023), 29 March 2023 383
Iraee v. Islamic Republic of Iran (Opinion no. 33/2019), 12 August 2019 186
Joaquín Forn I Chiariello v. Spain (Opinion no. 12/2019), 26 April 2019 107
Jordi Cuixart I Navarro v. Spain (Opinion no. 6/2019), 25 April 2019 . . . . 92–93, 107
Karma v. Indonesia (Opinion no. 48/2011), 2 September 2011 311–12
Le Dinh Luong v. Vietnam (Opinion no. 45/2019), 15 August 2019 102
Lee Kun-hee v. South Korea (Opinion no. 29/1994), 29 September 1994 . . . . 318, 338–39
Li Hai v. China (Opinion no. 19/1999) 16 September 1999. . . . . 318–19, 339
López Mendoza v. Venezuela (Opinion no. 26/2014), 26 August 2014 389
Maseko v. Swaziland (Opinion no. 6/2015), 22 April 2015 . . . . 119–20, 128–29, 133, 258
Mejri v. Tunisia (Opinion no. 29/2013), 30 August 2013. . . . . 191–92, 212
Mikalai Statkevich v. Belarus (Opinion no. 13/2011), 4 May 2011 109
Mohammed Rashid Hassan Nasser al-Ajami v. Qatar (Opinion no. 48/2016),
    22 November 2016 . . . . 110, 113
Moti Biyya v. Ethiopia (Opinion no. 18/1999), 15 September 1999 309–10

TABLE OF CASES xvii

De Lima v. Philippines (Opinion no. 61/2018), 24 August 2018...........................45–46
Parvez v. India (Opinion no. 8/2023), 28 March 2023 367
Pasko v. Russian Federation (Opinion No. 9/1999), 20 May 1999 ....318–19, 339
Piskorski v. Poland (Opinion no. 18/2018), 20 April 2018................................306–7
Pornthip Munkong v. Thailand (Opinion no. 43/2015), 2 December 2015..................117–18
Rajab v. Bahrain (Opinion no. 13/2018), 19 April 2018...............................239, 264
Rezaian v. Iran (Opinion no. 44/2015), 3 December 2015.......................298, 299, 348–49
Saber Saidi v. Algeria (Opinion no. 49/2012), 26 May 2014 394–95
Sadeghi v. Iran (Opinion no. 19/2008), 20 April 2018 128–29
Sheikh Suliaman al-Rashudi and others v. Saudi Arabia (Opinion no. 38/2015),
    4 September 2015...172, 239, 264
Shi Tao v. China (Opinion no. 27/2006), 1 September 2006 ....318, 320–21
Siraphop Kornaroot v. Thailand (Opinion no. 4/2019), 24 April 2019......................102
Sokha v. Cambodia (Opinion no. 9/2018), 19 April 2018 313–14
Sokhet v. Cambodia (Opinion no. 75/2021) 18 November 2021 379
Somyot Prueksakasemsuk v. Thailand (Opinion no. 35/2012), 30 August 2012......104, 117–18, 133
Sriboonpeng v. Thailand (Opinion no. 44/2016), 21 November 2016 133
Tek Math Rizal v. Bhutan (Opinion no. 48/1994), 1 December 1994......................309–10
Thammavong v. Laos (Opinion no. 61/2017), 25 August 2017..........................128–29
Tri Agus Susanto Siswowihardjo v. Indonesia (Opinion no. 42/1996),
    3 December 1996 ....59–60, 117–18, 125
Van Kham v. Viet Nam (Opinion no. 13/2022), 31 March 2022 383
Waleed Abulkhair v. Saudi Arabia (Opinion no. 10/2018), 19 April 2018..............100, 375–76
Xiyue Wang v. Iran (Opinion no. 52/2018), 23 August 2018............... 48, 308–9, 338–39, 380
Zeinab Jalalian v. Iran (Opinion no. 1/2016), 18 April 2016 309–10
Zhang v. China (Opinion no. 25/2021), 6 September 2021 235
Zhao Yan v. China (Opinion no. 33/2005), 2 September 2005 318
Zhen Jianghua and Qin Yongmin v. China (Opinion no. 20/2019), 1 May 2019 .....102, 324, 389
Ziyuan Ren v. China (Opinion no. 55/2014), 21 November 2014........................324, 389

REGIONAL COURTS AND COMMISSIONS

African Commission on Human and Peoples' Rights (African Commission, ACmHPR)

Amnesty International v. Zambia (Comm. no. 212/98), 5 May 1999..........................42
Article 19 v. Eritrea (Comm. no. 275/2003), 30 May 2007................... 7–8, 40–41, 68–69
Commission Nationale des Droits de l'Homme et des Libertes v.
    Chad (Comm. no. 74/92), 11 October 1995 40–41
Constitutional Rights Project v. Nigeria (Comm. no. 140/1994), 15 November1999 .....8–9, 190–91
Egyptian Initiative for Personal Rights and Interights v. Egypt (Comm. no. 323/2006),
    16 December 2011 10–11
Elgak v. Sudan (Comm. no. 379/09), 7–14 March 2014....................................8–9
Good v. Botswana (Comm. no. 313/2005), 26 May 2010.........7–9, 40–41, 42, 68–69, 120, 190–91,
                                                                            307, 311–12
Law Office of Ghazi Suleiman v. Sudan (Comm. no. 228/99), 29 May 2003 68–69
Malawi African Association and Others v. Mauritania (Comm. no. 54/91 and others),
    11 May 2000 187
Media Rights Agenda v. Nigeria (Comm. nos. 105/93 & others), 31 October 1998 110
Media Rights Agenda v. Nigeria (Comm. no. 224/98),
    23 October–6 November 2000 ....40–41, 48, 308–9
Ouko v. Kenya (Comm. no. 232/99), 23 October– 6 November 2000 134
Scanlen & Holderness v. Zimbabwe (Comm. no. 297/2005), 3 April 2009 ..... 11–12, 59–60, 124–25
Uwimana-Nkusi v. Rwanda (Comm. no. 426/12), 16 April 2021 ....45–46, 68–69
Zegveld v. Eritrea (Comm. no. 250/2002), 20 November 2003...........................68–69
Zimbabwe Lawyers for Human Rights & Associated Newspapers of Zimbabwe v.
    Zimbabwe (Comm. no. 284/03), 3 April 2009 ....106–7, 206–7

xviii   TABLE OF CASES

African Court on Human and Peoples' Rights (African Court, ACtHPR)

Ajavon v. Republic of Benin (App. no. 062/2019), 4 December 2020 . . . . 44–45, 190, 191, 196, 206–7, 208
Beneficiaries of Late Norbert Zongo v. Burkina Faso (App. no. 013/2011),
    28 March 2014. . . . . 44–45, 68–69
Konaté v. Burkina Faso (App. no. 004/2013), 3 June 2016 68–69
Konaté v. Burkina Faso (App. no. 004/2013), 5 December 2014 . . . . 8–9, 44–45, 50, 52, 53–54, 103, 106–7, 110, 112, 120, 131–32, 133–34, 137, 139–40, 152, 184, 187, 190–91, 201, 204, 206–7, 212, 214–15, 247, 257–58, 334–35, 336–37, 383, 385–86, 406, 407, 410, 420
Noudehouenou v. Republic of Benin (App. no. 028/2020), 1 December 2022 44–45
Omary v. Tanzania (App. no. 001/2012), 28 March 2014. . . . . 7–8, 184
Umuhoza v. Rwanda (App. no. 003/2014), 24 November 2017. . . . . 7–8, 44–46, 55–56, 68, 120, 184, 187, 190–91, 200–1, 206–7, 243–44, 314

Court of Justice of the European Union (CJEU)

Proceedings relating to the execution of a European arrest warrant
    against X C-717/18, 3 March 2020 (GC) 362

East African Court of Justice (EACJ)

Burundi Journalists Union v. Attorney General of Burundi (Ref no. 7/2013), 15 May 2015. 13
Media Council of Tanzania and others v. Attorney General of the
    United Republic of Tanzania (Ref no. 2/2017), 28 March 2019 . . . . 103, 240, 247, 249–50, 270

Economic Community of West African States Court of Justice (ECOWAS CCJ)

Federation of African Journalists v. Gambia (Suit no. ECW/CCJ/APP/36/15),
    13 February 2018 . . . . 53–54, 64–65, 68–69, 86, 103, 129, 131–32, 134, 190–91, 239, 240, 247, 258, 336–37, 340–41, 410
Incorporated Trustees of Laws and Rights Awareness Initiatives v. Nigeria
    (Suit no. ECW/CCJ/APP/53/2018), 10 July 2020. . . . . .8–9, 190–91

European Commission of Human Rights (ECmHR)

Temeltasch v. Switzerland (App. no. 9116/80), 5 March 1982. 34–35

European Court of Human Rights (ECtHR)

A v. Norway (App. no. 28070/06), 9 April 2009. . . . . 108–9, 246
Akçam v. Turkey (App. no. 27520/07), 25 October 2011 102–3
Alekhina v. Russia (App. no. 38004/12), 17 July 2018. . . . . 50, 67, 107–8, 194–95, 201–2, 245, 248–49, 257, 324, 376, 404, 406–7, 415
Aliyev v. Azerbaijan (App. nos. 68762/14 & 71200/14), 20 September 2018. 242
Alpay v. Turkey (App. no. 16538/17), 20 March 2018. 66–68, 134–35, 141, 376
Alpha Doryforiki Tileorasi Anonymi Etairia v. Greece (App. no. 72562/10), 22 February 2018. . . . 86, 121
Altintas v. Turkey (App. no. 50495/08), 10 March 2020. . . . . 63, 408
Animal Defenders International v. United Kingdom (App. no. 48876/08), 22 April 2013 (GC). . . . 255–56
Antunes Emídio v. Portugal (App. nos. 75637/13 & 8114/14), 24 September 2019 135
Ärztekammer für Wien and Dorner v. Austria (App. no. 8895/10), 16 February 2016 255
Atamanchuk v. Russia (App. no. 4493/11), 11 February 2020. . . . . . . 9, 48, 58, 134, 188, 194–95, 204–6, 214–15, 391
Axel Springer AG v. Germany (App. no. 39954/08), 7 February 2012 (GC) 108–9, 121, 145, 246
Azevedo v. Portugal (App. no. 20620/04), 27 March 2008. 54
Balaskas v. Greece (App. no. 73087/17), 5 November 2020. 135

Balsytė-Lideikienė v. Lithuania (App. no. 72596/01), 4 November 2008 . . . . .188, 195, 204–5, 207
Barfod v. Denmark (App. no. 11508/85), 22 February 1989 . . . . .63, 64–65
Bédat v. Switzerland (App. no. 56925/08), 29 March 2016 (GC) 51, 59, 118, 201, 258, 272,
325–26, 329–30, 333,
335, 344–45, 404
Belkacem v. Belgium (App. no. 34367/14), 27 June 2017 . . . . 189, 204, 205, 208, 214–15, 387–88
Bergens Tidende v. Norway (App. no. 26132/95), 2 May 2000 . . . . 67, 89–90, 115, 253–54, 270–71
Bladet Tromsø v. Norway (App. no. 21980/93), 20 May 1999 (GC) 59–60, 119, 120–23, 124,
132, 203, 254, 256,
332, 401–2
Błaja News Sp. z o. o. v. Poland (App. no. 59545/10), 26 November 2013 136
Bono v. France (App. no. 29024/11), 15 December 2015 119–20
Brambilla v. Italy (App. no. 22567/09), 23 June 2016 . . . . 60, 332
Brasilier v. France (App. no. 71343/01), 11 April 2006 89
Bucur and Toma v. Romania (App. no. 40238/02), 8 January 2013 . . . . 49–50, 254, 290, 306–7,
316–17, 322, 326–27,
330–31, 333–34, 341–42
Busuioc v. Moldova (App. no. 61513/00), 21 December 2004 112
Castells v. Spain (App. no. 11798/85), 23 April 1992 . . . . . 52–53, 110, 115, 132, 253–54, 258, 404, 406
Chauvy v. France (App. no. 64915/01), 29 June 2004 . . . . 65, 135
Colombani v. France (App. no. 51279/99), 25 June 2002 . . . . .110, 115, 122, 124, 253–54
Correira de Matos v. Portugal (App. no. 56402/12), 4 April 2018 44
Couderc and Hachette Filipacchi Associés v. France (App. no. 40454/07),
10 November 2015 (GC) 50, 60, 116–17, 118, 123, 327, 332
Csánics v. Hungary (App. no. 12188/06), 20 January 2009 115
Cuc Pascu v. Romania (App. no. 36157/02), 16 September 2008 122
Cumhuriyet Vakfı v. Turkey (App. no. 28255/07), 8 October 2013 . . . . .102–3, 138
Cumpănă v. Romania (App. no. 33348/96) 17 December 2004 (GC) 54, 63–64, 67–68, 132,
134, 139–40, 152, 408, 420
Dalban v. Romania (App. no. 28114/95), 28 September 1999 (GC) 124
Dammann v. Switzerland (App. no. 77551/01), 25 April 2006 . . . . .46, 67–68, 330
De Haes v. Belgium (App. no. 19983/92), 24 February 1997 . . . . 120–21, 122–23, 126, 203, 256
Delfi AS v. Estonia (App. no. 64569/09), 16 June 2015, (GC) 136
Demirel v. Turkey (No. 3) (App. no. 11976/03), 9 December 2008 . . . . .400–1, 404, 405
Demirtaş v. Turkey (No. 2) (App. no. 14305/17), 22 December 2020 (GC) 376
Dichand v. Austria (App. no. 29271/95), 26 February 2002 . . . . 126, 147
Dickinson v. Turkey (App. no. 25200/11), 2 February 2021 . . . . 110, 135
Dilipak v. Turkey (App. no. 29680/05), 15 September 2015 102–3
Dink v. Turkey (App. nos. 2668/07 & others), 14 September 2010 . . . . 11, 212
Dmitriyevskiy v. Russia (App. no. 42168/06), 3 October 2018 . . . . .63, 383–84, 404
Dyuldin v. Russia (App. no. 25968/02), 31 July 2007 . . . . 92, 109
E.S. v. Austria (App.no. 38450/12), 25 October 2018 (GC) 57, 163–64, 192–93, 198,
202, 207, 212–13
Éditions Plon v. France (App. no. 58148/00), 18 May 2004 . . . . 46, 51, 62–63, 138, 154–55
Editorial Board of Pravoye Delo v. Ukraine (App. no. 33014/05), 5 May 2011 102–3
Eerikäinen v. Finland (App. no. 3514/02), 10 February 2009 122
Eon v. France (App. no. 26118/10), 14 March 2013 . . . . .111, 126–27, 135
Eood v. Bulgaria (App. no. 14134/02), 11 October 2007 12
Erkizia Almandoz v. Spain (App. no. 5869/17), 22 June 2021 . . . . . 383–85, 397, 404, 405, 415–16, 419
Europapress Holding d.o.o. v. Croatia (App. no. 25333/06), 22 October 2009 . . . . 135, 136
Fatih Taş v. Turkey (no. 3) (App. no. 45281/08), 24 April 2018 63
Fatullayev v. Azerbaijan (App. No. 40984/07), 22 April 2010 . . . . 65, 67–68, 111–12, 134, 376
Fedchenko v. Russia (App. no. 33333/04), 11 February 2010 125
Fedchenko v. Russia (No. 2) (App. no. 48195/06), 11 February 2010 111
Fedchenko v. Russia (No. 5) (App. no. 17229/13), 2 October 2018 125–26
Feldek v. Slovakia (App. no. 29032/95), 12 July 2001 . . . . 126, 255
Féret v. Belgium (App. no. 15615/07), 16 July 2009 . . . . 188, 204–6, 214–15, 386, 391

xx   TABLE OF CASES

Filatenko v. Russia (App. no. 73219/01), 6 December 2007.............................. 107, 115
Flinkkilä v. Finland (App. no. 25576/04), 6 April 2010 .... 135, 136
Flux v. Moldova (No. 6) (App. no. 22824/04), 29 July 2008 .... 61–62, 122–23, 332
Fressoz v. France (App. no. 29183/95), 21 January 1999 (GC) 59–60, 62–63, 120–21, 202, 256
Frisk and Jensen v. Denmark (App. no. 19657/12), 5 December 2017 65
Garaudy v. France (App. no. 65831/01) 24 June 2003............ 55–56, 189, 199–200, 208, 214, 243
Gawlik v. Liechtenstein (App. no. 23922/19), 16 February 2021, (GC) 60–61, 203, 256, 332–33
Ghiulfer Predescu v. Romania (App. no. 29751/09), 27 June 2017 .... 107, 135–36
Giniewski v. France (App. no. 64016/00), 31 January 2006 89
Gîrleanu v. Romania (App. no. 50376/09), 26 June 2018 .... 59–60, 67, 320, 321, 322–23, 330–32,
335, 336, 345–46
Gongadze v. Ukraine (App. no. 34056/02), 8 November 2005 10–11
Goodwin v. United Kingdom (App. no. 17488/90), 27 March 1996, (GC) 12–13
Görmüş v. Turkey (App. no. 49085/07), 19 January 2016 ...... 49–50, 310, 319, 322, 338–39, 341–42
Gözel and Özer v. Turkey (Apps no 43453/04 and 31098/05) 6 July 2010 ..... 399, 401, 403, 404, 418
Guja v. Moldova (App. no. 14277/04), 12 February 2008 (GC)........ 315, 316, 317, 325–27, 329–31,
333, 334–35, 340–41, 343,
345–46, 407, 420
Gündüz v. Turkey (App. no. 35071/97), 4 December 2003 .... 107, 386, 391
Gürbüz and Bayar v. Turkey (App. no. 8860/13), 23 July 2019 63
Hadjianastassiou v. Greece (App. no. 12945/87), 16 December 1992................ 63, 321, 335, 336
Haldimann v. Switzerland (App. no. 21830/09), 24 February 2015 258
Handyside v. United Kingdom (App. no. 5493/72), 7 December 1976 42
Hertel v. Switzerland (App. no. 25181/94), 25 August 1998........................ 242, 246, 271
Hizb Ut-Tahrir v. Germany (App. no. 31098/08), 12 June 2012 .... 63, 185, 189, 387, 388, 416, 418
I.A. v. Turkey (App. no. 42571/98), 13 September 2005............................. 46, 57, 204–5
Ibragimov v. Russia (App. nos. 1413/08 & 28621/11), 28 August 2018 .... 58–59, 63, 189, 194–96,
207, 217, 378, 386,
391, 416, 417–18
Incal v. Turkey (App. no. 22678/93), 9 June 1998, (GC)............................. 132, 258, 408
Independent News and Media v. Ireland (App. no. 55120/00), 16 June 2005 135–36
Independent Newspapers (Ireland) Limited v. Ireland (App. no. 28199/15), 15 June 2017...... 89–90
Informationsverein Lentia v. Austria (App. nos. 13914/88 & others), 24 November 1993 11
Ivanov v. Russia (App. no. 35222/04), 20 February 2007 .... 185, 189, 194–95, 207–8, 214–15, 387
Ivanova v. Bulgaria (App. no. 36207/03), 14 February 2008 .... 65, 132
Janowiec v. Russia (App. nos. 55508/07 & 29520/09),
   21 October 2013 (GC)...48, 308, 310, 338–39, 380
Janowski v. Poland (App. no. 25716/94), 21 January 1999................................. 111
Jersild v. Denmark (App. no. 15890/89), 23 September 1994 (GC) 51, 57–58, 60, 122–23, 148,
188, 197, 201–2, 203,
332, 399, 401–2, 418
Jerusalem v. Austria (App. no. 26958/95), 27 February 2001 .... 126, 255
Kącki v. Poland (App. no. 10947/11), 4 July 2017, (GC)............. 60, 120–22, 135, 203, 256, 332
Karácsony v. Hungary (App. nos. 42461/13 & 44357/13), 17 May 2016, (GC) 111
Karapetyan v. Armenia (App. no. 59001/08), 17 November 2016 381
Karataş v. Turkey (App. no. 23168/94), 8 July 1999 (GC)................................. 384
Karsai v. Hungary (App. no. 5380/07), 1 December 2009 126
Kasabova v. Bulgaria (App. no. 22385/03), 19 April 2011 .... 89, 106, 127, 136, 250, 257
Kasymakhunov and Saybatalov v. Russia (Apps. no. 26261/05 and 26377/06),
   14 March 2013...387, 388, 416, 418
Khadija Ismayilova v. Azerbaijan (App. nos. 65286/13 & 57270/14), 10 January 2019 119
Kilin v. Russia (App. no. 10271/12), 11 May 2021....................................63, 204–5
Le Pen v. France (App. no. 18788/09), 7 May 2010..................................... 214–15
Lehideux and Isorni v. France (App. no. 24662/94), 23 September 1998..................... 243
Lepojić v. Serbia (App. no. 13909/05), 6 November 2007 .... 86, 136
Leroy v. France (App. no. 36109/03), 2 October 2008 .... 57–59, 113–14, 195, 197, 250, 384–85,
391, 393, 395, 399, 415–16

Lešník v. Slovakia (App. no. 35640/97), 11 March 2003......................................112
Lewandowska-Malec v. Poland (App. no. 39660/07), 18 September 2012......................258
Lilliendahl v. Iceland (App. no. 29297/18), 12 May 2020.........55–56, 63–64, 185, 186, 188, 194–95,
    207, 217, 248–49, 387, 417–18
Lindon, Otchakovsky-Laurens and July v. France (App. nos. 21279/02 & 36448/02),
    22 October 2007 (GC)...65, 132, 134, 258
Lingens v. Austria (App. no. 9815/82), 8 July 1986.........118, 119, 125, 244, 254, 255, 271–72, 404
Liu v. Russia (No. 2) (App. no. 29157/09), 26 July 2011...............................48, 308, 380
M'Bala M'Bala v. France (App. no. 25239/13), 20 October 2015...............55–56, 199–200, 243
Macovei v. Romania (App. no. 53028/14), 28 July 2020..............108–9, 115, 127, 253–54, 255
Maestri v. Italy (App. no. 39748/98), 17 February 2004, (GC)................................238
Magyar Helsinki Bizottság v. Hungary (App. no. 18030/11),
    8 November 2016, (GC).....................................60–61, 118, 203, 256, 332–33
Magyar Jeti Zrt v. Hungary (App. no. 11257/16), 4 December 2018 ....113, 121, 203
Magyar Kétfarkú Kutya Párt v. Hungary (App. no. 201/17), 20 January 2020..................74
McVicar v. United Kingdom (App. no. 46311/99), 7 May 2002.........60, 106, 121–22, 127, 138, 250
Medžlis Islamske Zajednice Brčko v. Bosnia and Herzegovina (App. no. 17224/11),
    27 June 2017, (GC)...108–9
Mehmet Hasan Altan v. Turkey (App. no. 13237/17), 20 March 2018...............383–84, 404–5
Mengi v. Turkey (App. nos. 13471/05 & 38787/07), 27 November 2012......................106
Merabishvili v. Georgia (App. no. 72508/13), 28 November 2017 (GC)......................242
MGN Limited v. United Kingdom (App. no. 39401/04), 12 June 2012........................67
MGN Limited v. United Kingdom (App. no. 39401/04), 18 January 2011...................91, 139
Milosavljević v. Serbia (App. no. 57574/14), 25 May 2021..........................102, 111, 122
Molnar v. Romania (App. no. 16637/06), 23 October 2012......58–59, 63–64, 194–95, 204, 205, 208,
    214–15, 217
Morice v. France (App. no. 29369/10), 23 April 2015 (GC).....................5, 112, 119–20, 254
Murphy v. Ireland (App. no. 44179/98), 10 July 2003..................46, 57, 184–85, 192–93, 201
Navalnyy v. Russia (No. 2) (App. no. 43734/14), 9 April 2019..............................242
Nikowitz and Verlagsgruppe News GmbH v. Austria (App. no. 5266/03), 22 February 2007....135, 139
Nikula v. Finland (App. no. 31611/96), 21 March 2002......................106, 111, 119–20
Nilsen v. Norway (App. no. 23118/93), 25 November 1999, (GC)...........................107
Nix v. Germany (App. no. 35285/16), 13 March 2018................57–58, 197, 214–15, 250, 381
Norman v. United Kingdom (App. no. 41387/17), 6 July 2021...............................63
Norwood v. United Kingdom (App. no. 23131/03), 16 November 2004.........189, 194–95, 207–8,
    214–15, 387
Novaya Gazeta v. Russia (App. no. 14087/08), 28 March 2013...........................123–24
Oberschlick v. Austria (App. no. 11662/85), 23 May 1991..................................91
Oberschlick v. Austria (No. 2) (App. no. 20834/92), 1 July 1997........................111, 126
Observer and Guardian v. United Kingdom (App. no. 13585/88),
    26 November 1991 (Plenary Court)...................................49–50, 319, 338–39
OOO Flavus v. Russia (App. nos. 12468/15 & others), 23 June 2020........................242
Orban v. France (App. no. 20985/05), 15 January 2009...................................387
Otegi Mondragon v. Spain (App. no. 2034/07), 15 March 2011..........46, 110, 125, 184–85, 186
Ottan v. France (App. no. 41841/12), 19 April 2018..................................119–20
Otto-Preminger-Institut v. Austria (App. no. 13470/87), 20 September 1994.........204–5, 207
Özgür Gündem v. Turkey (App. no. 23144/93), 16 March 2000..............................10
Öztürk v. Turkey (App. no. 22479/93), 28 September 1999, (GC).......................132, 258
Pakdemirli v. Turkey (App. no. 35839/97), 22 February 2005...........................136–37
Paksas v. Lithuania (App. no. 34932/04), 6 January 2011 (GC)........................185, 387
Paraskevopoulos v. Greece (App. no. 64184/11), 28 June 2018.............................106
Pasko v. Russia (App. no. 69519/01), 22 October 2009.................................335–36
Pastörs v. Germany (App. no. 55225/14), 3 October 2019..................55–56, 185, 189, 198,
    199–200, 243–44
Pedersen and Baadsgaard v. Denmark (App. no. 49017/99),
    17 December 2004 (GC)...............51, 62, 63, 64–65, 107, 112, 120–22, 123, 202, 256, 332
Pentikäinen v. Finland (App. no. 11882/10), 20 October 2015, (GC)...........60, 121, 325–26, 332

xxii   TABLE OF CASES

Perinçek v. Switzerland (App. no. 27510/08), 15 October 2015 (GC) 9, 47, 54, 55–56,
58–59, 63, 67–68, 107–8, 113–14, 185, 186, 189,
194–95, 198, 199, 200, 201, 202, 217, 243,
246, 248–49, 314, 324, 338, 348, 374–75,
380, 381, 383–84, 386, 387,
391, 399, 416, 417–18
Peruzzi v. Italy (App. no. 39294/09), 30 June 2015 119–20
Prager and Oberschlick v. Austria (App. no. 15974/90),
26 April 1995 (GC)... 63, 64–65, 112, 271–72
Radio France v. France (App. no. 53984/00), 30 March 2004 .... 65, 132, 135, 258
Reznik v. Russia (App. no. 4977/05), 4 April 2013 ....115, 253–54
RID Novaya Gazeta v. Russia (App. no. 44561/11), 11 May 2021 401
Rizanov v. Azerbaijan (App. no. 31805/06), 17 July 2012.................................... 10–11
Roj TV A/S v. Denmark (App. no. 24683/14), 17 April 2018....... 185, 189, 387–88, 401–2, 416, 418
Romanov v. Ukraine (App. no. 63782/11), 16 July 2020... 63
Rotaru v. Romania (App. no. 28341/95), 4 May 2000, (GC) 238
Rouillan v. France (App. no. 28000/19), 23 June 2022 ....63, 383–84, 396, 408, 409, 416
Rujak v. Croatia (App. no. 57942/10), 2 October 2012..................................... 106
Rungainis v. Latvia (App. no. 40597/08), 14 June 2018 ....115, 253–54
Ruokanen v. Finland (App. no. 45130/06), 6 April 2010 .... 54, 63–64, 65, 132, 134
Rusu v. Romania (App. no. 25721/04), 8 March 2016... 69
S. and Marper v. United Kingdom (App. Nos. 30562/04 & 30566/04),
4 December 2008, (GC)..238–39
S.A.S. v. France (App. no. 43835/11), 1 July 2014 (GC) 349–50
Salihu v. Sweden (App. no. 33628/15), 10 May 2016............................60, 120–21, 332
Salov v. Ukraine (App. no. 65518/01), 6 September 2005 ....48–49, 57–58, 67, 240–41, 242, 246,
252–53, 257, 259
Salumäki v. Finland (App. no. 23605/09), 29 April 2014 65
Sanchez v. France (App. no. 45581/15), 15 May 2023....................................... 63, 201
Sanoma Uitgevers B.V. v. Netherlands (App. no. 38224/03) 14 September 2010, (GC) 12–13
Satakunnan Markkinapörssi Oy v. Finland (App. no. 931/13),
27 June 2017 (GC) 51, 60–61, 110, 116–17, 143–44, 202, 314, 327, 332–33, 374–75
Savva Terentyev v. Russia (App. no. 10692/09), 28 August 2018............46, 102, 184–85, 186, 201
Scharsach v. Austria (App. no. 39394/98), 13 November 2003 126
Selisto v. Finland (App. no. 56767/00), 16 November 2004.................................. 124
Sipos v. Romania (App. no. 26125/04), 3 May 2011 107
Skałka v. Poland (App. no. 43425/98), 27 May 2003 106
Soulas v. France (App. no. 15948/03), 10 July 2008................................204–5, 214–15
Sousa Goucha v. Portugal (App. no. 70434/12), 22 March 2016 108–9
Standard Verlagsgesellschaft mbH v. Austria (No. 3) (App. no. 39378/15), 7 December 2021 74
Steel v. United Kingdom (App. no. 68416/01), 15 February 2005..........127, 136, 139, 149, 271–72
Stoll v. Switzerland (App. no. 69698/01), 10 December 2007 (GC) 46, 51, 62–63, 120–21, 122–24,
154–55, 203, 258, 307, 310, 315,
321, 325–27, 338–39
Stomakhin v. Russia (App. no. 52273/07), 9 May 2018......... 91, 139–40, 195–96, 203, 207, 379–80
Stubbings v. United Kingdom (App. nos. 22083/93 & 22095/93), 22 October 1996............... 128
Sunday Times v. United Kingdom (App. no. 13166/87), 26 November 1991 (Plenary Court) 319
Sunday Times v. United Kingdom (App. no. 6538/74), 26 April 1979 ....138, 186, 244, 374–75
Sürek v. Turkey (App. nos. 23927/94 and 24277/94), 8 July 1999 (GC) 201, 392–93, 400, 401–2,
403, 404
Sürek v. Turkey (no. 1) (App. no. 26682/95), 8 July 1999, (GC).........63, 188, 197, 379–80, 392–93,
399, 400, 401–2, 408, 418
Sürek v. Turkey (No. 2) (App. no. 24122/94), 8 July 1999 (GC)..... 118, 325–26, 344–45, 379–80, 404
Sürek v. Turkey (No. 3) (App. no. 24735/94), 8 July 1999 (GC)........63, 379–80, 391, 392–93, 395,
400, 408, 417–18
Sürek v. Turkey (No. 4) (App. no. 24762/94), 8 July 1999 (GC)......... 384–85, 391–93, 400, 417–18
Taganrog LRO and Others v. Russia (App. nos. 32401/10 & 19 others), 7 June 2022 378

Tagiyev v. Azerbaijan (App. no. 13274/08), 5 December 2019 . . . . . . .46, 57, 184–85, 192–93, 195–96, 202, 204–5
Terentyev v. Russia (App. no. 25147/09), 26 January 2017. 127
Thoma v. Luxembourg (App. no. 38432/97), 29 March 2001 256
Thorgeirson v. Iceland (App. no. 13778/88), 25 June 1992. 126
Tierbefreier E.V. v. Germany (App. no. 45192/09), 16 January 2014 138
Times Newspapers Ltd (Nos. 1 and 2) v. United Kingdom (App. nos. 3002/03 & 23676/03), 10 March 2009. . . . . 80, 128
Timpul Info-Magazin v. Moldova (App. no. 42864/05), 27 November 2007. 136
Tolstoy Miloslavsky v. United Kingdom (App. no. 18139/91), 13 July 1995. . . . . 89–90, 135–36, 138, 139
Tønsbergs Blad A.S. v. Norway (App. no. 510/04), 1 March 2007. 255
Toranzo Gomez v. Spain (App. no. 26922/14), 20 November 2018 258
Tuşalp v. Turkey (App. nos. 32131/08 & 41617/08), 21 February 2012 106
Üçdağ v. Turkey (App. no. 23314/19), 31 August 2021. 384–85
Unabhängige Initiative Informationsvielfalt v. Austria (App. no. 28525/95), 26 February 2002 . . . . 126, 138
Vajnai v. Hungary (App. no. 33629/06), 8 July 2008. 113
Vejdeland v. Sweden (App. no. 1813/07), 9 February 2012 . . . . . . 58, 63–64, 186, 195,195, 197, 204–5, 207, 208, 214–15, 218, 386, 416
Vereinigung Bildender Künstler v. Austria (App. no. 68354/01), 25 January 2007 126–27
Vereniging Weekblad Bluf! v. Netherlands (App. no. 16616/90), 9 February 1995 . . . . .319, 338–39
Verlagsgruppe Droemer Knaur GmbH & Co. KG v. Germany (App. no. 35030/13), 19 October 2017 . . . . .122, 124–25
Von Hannover v. Germany (No. 2) (App. nos. 40660/08 & 60641/08), 7 February 2012 (GC) 110, 116–17, 118, 143–44, 325–26
Williamson v. Germany (App. no. 64496/17), 8 January 2019 . . . . 189, 207, 243
Wingrove v. United Kingdom (App. No. 17419/90), 25 November 1996. . . . . . 46, 57, 184–85, 192–93, 325–26, 344–45, 404
Witzsch v. Germany (App. no. 7485/03), 13 December 2005 55–56
Wojczuk v. Poland (App. no. 52969/13), 9 December 2021. 65
Yam v. United Kingdom (App. no. 31295/11), 16 January 2020 308
Yavuz and Yaylalı v. Turkey (App. no. 12606/11), 17 December 2013 . . . . .383–84, 395
Yildirim v. Turkey (App. no. 3111/10), 18 December 2012 138
Z.B. v. France (App. no. 46883/15) 2 September 2021 . . . . 63, 393, 396–97, 399–400, 409
Zana v. Turkey (App. no. 18954/91), 25 November 1997, (GC) 46, 62–63, 132, 154–55, 184–85, 195, 204–5, 208, 217, 379–80, 384, 395, 401–2, 408–9
Zemmour v. France (App. no. 63539/19), 20 December 2022. . . . . 63, 189
Ziembiński v. Poland (No. 2) (App. no. 1799/07), 5 July 2016. .126–27, 255

Inter-American Commission of Human Rights (IACmHR)

Asencios Lindo v. Peru (Case 11.182), 13 April 2000. 39–40
Biscet v. Cuba (Case 12.476), 21 October 2006. . . . . 130, 379, 384–85, 389–90
Dogliani v. Uruguay (Petition 228-07) 16 March 2010 105–6
Roca Antúnez v. Cuba (Case 12.127), 24 February 2018 . . . . .103, 130–31, 134, 379, 382, 384–85, 389–90, 406, 415–16

Inter-American Court of Human Rights (Inter-American Court -IACtHR)

Álvarez Ramos v. Venezuela (Series C, no. 380), 30 August 2019. . . . . 118–19, 130, 141, 154, 182, 190, 214–15, 255, 258, 420
Bedoya Lima v. Colombia (Series C, no. 431), 26 August 2021. 10–11
Canese v. Paraguay (Series C, no. 111), 31 August 2004. . . . . . 52, 64–65, 105–6, 109, 118–19, 134–35, 140, 255
Carvajal Carvajal v. Colombia (Series C, no. 365), 13 March 2018. .10–11

TABLE OF CASES

Compulsory Membership in an Association Prescribed by Law for the Practice of
  Journalism (Arts. 13 and 29 American Convention on Human Rights),
  Advisory Opinion OC-5/85 (Series A, no. 5), 13 November 1985 .... 6, 11–12, 48–49, 51,
  183–84, 240–41, 244,
  246–47, 381
Fontevecchia v. Argentina (Series C, no. 238), 29 November 2011 .... 110–11, 116–17, 137
González v. Peru (Series C, no. 289), 20 November 2014 36–37
Granier (Radio Caracas Televisión) v. Venezuela (Series C, no. 293),
  22 June 2015 .... 11, 68, 123–24
Herrera Ulloa Case v. Costa Rica (Series C, no. 107), 2 July 2004 .... 42, 50, 52, 59, 64–65, 68, 116,
  118–19, 134, 181,
  183–84, 201, 406
Ivcher-Bronstein v. Peru (Series C, no. 74), 6 February 2001 68
Judicial Guarantees in States of Emergency (Articles 27(2), 25 and 8 of the American
  Convention on Human Rights), Advisory Opinion OC-9/87 (Series A, no. 9),
  6 October 1987 36–37
Kimel v. Argentina (Series C, no. 177), 2 May 2008 .... 48, 103, 110, 123–24, 127, 131,
  135, 147, 190, 199
'Last Temptation of Christ' (Olmedo-Bustos et al.) v. Chile (Series C, no. 73),
  5 February 2001 .... 6, 138–39, 192, 212
Mémoli v. Argentina (Series C, no. 265), 22 August 2013 .... 53–54, 59–60, 64–65, 106, 123–24,
  131, 132, 134, 202, 206,
  249–50, 257–58, 331–32
Millar Silva v. Chile (Case 12.799), 29 November 2016 52
Moya Chacón v. Costa Rica (Series C, no. 451), 6 September 2022 .... 106, 121–22
Norín Catrimán et al. v. Chile (Series C, no. 279), 29 May 2014 ... 206, 376–77, 398–99, 410, 415, 418
Palacio Urrutia v. Ecuador (Series C, no. 446), 24 November 2021 ...... 94–95, 99–100, 118–19, 130,
  137, 199
Palamara Iribarne v. Chile (Series C, no. 135), 22 November 2005 .... 110, 118–19, 130–31, 204,
  310, 328, 334–35,
  336, 338–39, 407
Ricardo Canese v. Paraguay (Series C, no. 111), 31 August 2004 255
Serrano-Cruz Sisters v. El Salvador (Series C, no. 118), 23 November 2004 35
Tristán Donoso v. Panama (Series C, no. 193), 27 January 2009 .... 68, 106, 107–8, 137, 150–51,
  246–47, 248–50, 254
Usón Ramirez v. Venezuela (Series C, no. 207), 20 November 2009 .... 48, 58, 68, 103, 106,
  109, 111–12, 130–31, 145, 147, 186–87, 212,
  246–47, 249–50, 254, 307, 314, 323,
  324, 334, 340–41, 342
Uzcátegui v. Valenzuela (Series C, no. 249), 3 September 2012 .... 10–11, 68, 111–12
Velez Restrepo v. Colombia (Series C, no. 248), 3 September 2012 10–11

Table of International Instruments

INTERNATIONAL INSTRUMENTS

ACHPR: African Charter on Human
and Peoples' Rights (1981),
1520 UNTS 217 . . . . 1–25, 25, 35–36,
40–41, 129, 153, 172–73,
184, 187, 206–7, 307
   Art 1 10–11
   Art 2 50
   Art 6 7–8
   Art 7(2) 239
   Art 8 7–8
   Art 9 . . . 1–36, 40–41, 52, 68–69, 101, 133–34,
172–73, 187, 190, 191, 247, 307
   Art 9(2) 5, 7–8, 184, 187, 191, 206–7, 238, 307
   Art 10(1) 7–8
   Art 12(2) 7–8, 103
   Art 13(5) 154
   Art 27(2) 8–9, 190–91
   Art 56(7) 44
   Art 60 7–8
ACmHPR, Declaration of Principles
of Freedom of Expression and
Access to Information in Africa
(2019) 8–9, 11–12, 13, 108, 116,
124, 190–91, 197–98, 248–49,
323, 324, 334, 341–42,
389–90, 398–99, 406
   Principle 2 127
   Principle 4 8–9
   Principle 9 . . . . 8–9, 190–91
   Principle 9(2) 269, 270, 274
   Principle 9(4) 266
   Principle 11.3 11
   Principle 14(3) 12
   Principle 17 . . . . 137, 274
   Principle 21 . . . . 116, 124, 253–54, 406
   Principle 21(1) 250, 254, 271–72
   Principle 21(1)(c) 137
   Principle 22 . . . . 108, 324
   Principle 22(2) 64–65, 129, 266
   Principle 22(3) 137
   Principle 22(5) 196, 248–49, 323, 389–90
   Principle 23(2) 58–59
   Principle 23(2)(c) . . . 197–98, 215–16, 398–99
   Principle 23(2)(f) 196, 207–8
   Principle 24 12
   Principle 25 13

   Principle 34 274
   Principle 35 . . . . 254, 329
   Principle 39(4) 274
ACHR: American Convention on
Human Rights (1969), 1144
UNTS 123 . . . 1–24, 25, 35, 39–40, 43, 44,
68, 104, 127, 138–39, 154, 172–73,
174–75, 180–81, 182, 183–84,
216, 307, 313–14, 323, 381, 389–90
   Preamble 41
   Art 1 . . . . 10, 50
   Art 2 10
   Art 8 9
   Art 9 . . . . 239, 314, 323
   Art 12 . . . . 192, 212
   Art 13 . . . . . 1–35, 39–40, 53–54, 101, 118–19,
130–31, 138–39, 172–73,
174–75, 183–84, 192,
212, 257–58, 314,
323, 381, 410
   Art 13(1) 5
   Art 13(2) 6, 116, 138, 151, 183–84, 238
   Art 13(2)(a) 6
   Art 13(2)(b) 307
   Art 13(3) 183–84
   Art 13(4) 6, 138, 183–84
   Art 13(5) 9, 24–25, 39–40, 154, 180–82,
181, 182, 246–47,
384–85, 415–16
   Art 14 . . . . 24, 137
   Art 17 9
   Art 27 36
   Art 27(1) 36–37, 39–40, 307
   Art 27(2) 8–9, 25, 39–40
   Art 29 35
   Art 32(2) 307
   Art 46(1)(c) 44
   Art 60 184
   Art 61(1) 44–45
   Art 75 35
American Declaration of the Rights and
Duties of Man (1948) 379
   Art IV 130
   Art XXVIII 307
Arab Charter on Human Rights
(2004) 5, 172–73
   Preamble 41
   Art 4(1) 36–37

Art 4(2) 36–37
Art 32 . . . . 101, 172–73
ASEAN Human Rights
  Declaration (2012) 5, 172–73, 307
Art 7 172–73
Art 8 307
Art 23 . . . . 101, 172–73, 373
Cairo Declaration on Human
  Rights in Islam (1990) 172–73
Art 22 . . . . 101, 172–73, 373
Camden Principles on Freedom of
  Expression and Equality
Art 19 42
Principle 12.1 176
CERD: International Convention on the
  Elimination of All Forms of Racial
  Discrimination (1965), 660 UNTS
  195 . . . . 5, 9, 13–14, 15, 20, 26,
            28, 30–31, 32, 33, 34,
            39, 154, 162, 174,
            177, 181, 182, 216
Art 1 . . . . 178, 182
Art 4 . . . . . 1–34, 39, 43, 64, 154, 173, 174, 177,
            177–78, 179–80, 182, 213,
            215–16, 217, 218, 278–79
Art 4(a) 20, 21, 177, 178
Art 4(b) 21
Art 5 . . . . 5, 9, 15, 21–22, 32, 39, 174, 177
Art 7 32
Art 9 21
Art 20 34
CERD Committee, General
  Recommendation
  No. 35 (2013) 174, 177–78, 215–16
s 6 . . . . 177, 178, 182
s 12 . . . . 9, 178, 214–15, 420
s 13 . . . . 154, 177–78, 182, 218
s 13(b) 178, 216
s 13(d) 178, 216
s 14 . . . . 199, 213–14
s 15 177
s 16 . . . . 174, 177–78, 215–16, 217
s 17 214–15
s 19 178
s 25 . . . . 154, 178
Convention on the Prevention and
  Punishment of the Crime of
  Genocide (Geneva, 1948) 5, 13–14,
            41, 154, 157–58, 163,
            174, 179, 215–16
Art 3 . . . . 41, 154, 163, 174, 178–79,
            182, 215–16
Art 3(c) 5, 178
Council of Europe Convention on
  the Prevention of Terrorism
  (CETS No. 196) 353, 359, 390–91,
            398, 418, 419

Art 5 . . . . 353, 359, 385, 390–91, 398,
            400, 418, 419
Art 12 359
Council of Europe Declaration of the
  Committee of Ministers on the
  Desirability of International
  Standards dealing with
  Forum Shopping in respect of
  Defamation, "Libel Tourism", to
  ensure Freedom of Expression 149
ECHR: European Convention for the
  Protection of Human Rights and
  Fundamental Freedoms (1950),
  213 UNTS 221 . . . . 1–24, 28–29,
            34–35, 39, 46, 55–56, 62–63,
            64, 66–67, 112, 172–73, 184,
            185, 189, 207, 208–9, 211,
            246, 307, 348, 380,
            408–9, 411
Preamble 22–23, 41
Art 1 . . . . 10–11, 50
Art 7 239
Art 8 . . . . 108–9, 204–5, 246
Art 8(2) 380
Art 9 388
Art 10 . . . . 1–34, 34–35, 39, 47, 48, 49–50,
            55–56, 62–64, 67–68, 89–90, 91, 101,
            104, 106, 108–9, 112, 115, 123, 126–27,
            136, 147, 154–55, 164, 172–73, 183–84,
            189, 193, 195, 197, 204–5, 240–41,
            243, 246, 250, 252–54, 290–91, 304,
            316, 319, 322–23, 326, 330, 336,
            341–42, 374, 376, 380, 383–85, 387–88,
            391–92, 393, 396, 397, 400–1, 405,
            406–7, 409, 419, 420
Art 10(1) 5, 12
Art 10(2) . . . 6, 48, 49–50, 62–63, 154–55, 183,
            184–85, 186, 188, 201, 238, 242,
            264, 307, 315, 322, 329–30,
            376, 380, 386–87
Art 11 388
Art 11(2) 380
Art 15 36
Art 15(1) 36–37, 39–40
Art 15(2) 36–37, 39–40
Art 16 28–29
Art 17 . . . . 55–56, 63–64, 154–55, 185, 189,
            194–96, 199–200, 204, 207–8, 217,
            243, 386–88, 396–97, 401–2,
            409, 416, 417–18
Art 18 . . . . 241, 242
Art 35(2) 44
Art 57 34–35
Art 64 34–35
ECOWAS, Revised Treaty (1993)
art 66(2) 103
art 66(2)(c) 68–69

IACmHR, Declaration of Principles
    on Freedom of Expression
    (2000) 11–12, 120
  Principle 7 .... 116, 253–54
  Principle 8 13
  Principle 10 .... 105–6, 130–31,
                                    249–50
  Principle 11 130–31
ICCPR: International Covenant on Civil
    and Political Rights (1966), 999
    UNTS 171 ..... 1, 5, 6–7, 8–9, 12, 13–14,
      15, 16, 17, 20, 22–24, 26–27, 28, 36–37,
      38, 39, 42, 44, 47, 51, 56–57, 66, 101,
      109, 112, 133, 154, 173, 175, 181, 182,
      185, 188, 198–99, 208–9, 210, 213–14,
      216, 240–41, 265–66, 307, 309–10,
                  313–14, 373, 380, 411
  Art 2 .... 10, 50
  Art 2(3) 10–11, 66
  Art 2(3)(a) 66
  Art 3 26–27
  Art 4 .... 6, 36–37, 38
  Art 4(1) 36–37, 39–40
  Art 4(2) 36–37, 38
  Art 5(1) 241
  Art 6 26–27
  Art 6(1) 17
  Art 7 26–27
  Art 8(1) 17
  Art 10 133
  Art 12 307
  Art 13 .... 133, 307
  Art 14 .... 128–29, 307
  Art 15 239
  Art 16 28–29
  Art 18 26–27
  Art 19 .... 1–2, 4, 5, 6, 9, 14–1, 15, 16–17,
      19–20, 21, 26–27, 28–29, 30, 32, 37,
      38, 41, 42–43, 44–45, 47, 52, 54–55,
          66, 68–69, 101, 116, 128–29, 133,
          145, 172–73, 175, 183–84, 186, 188,
        191–92, 208–10, 211, 212, 213, 215–16,
          218–19, 250, 264, 307, 313–14, 318,
              320–21, 373, 380, 381, 384–85, 389,
                      396–97, 411, 416, 421
  Art 19(1) 6, 15, 37, 134–35
  Art 19(2) 5, 6, 15, 28, 37–38, 47, 103, 125,
                                  245, 308–9
  Art 19(3) 6, 8–9, 16, 17–18, 28,
          30, 48, 49, 101, 104, 111–12, 172–73,
          178, 181, 183–84, 185–86, 187–88,
          190–92, 193, 204, 208–10, 211, 212,
          237, 238–39, 240, 241, 247–48, 307,
              308–9, 311, 318, 320–21, 373,
                  379–80, 381, 382, 411
  Art 19(3)(a) 8–9, 190–91
  Art 19(3)(b) 8–9, 190–91

Art 20 .... 2, 4, 5, 9, 14, 16–17, 18–29, 30,
      32, 38, 39–40, 43, 44–45, 55, 64,
      154, 161, 173–75, 175–76, 177–78,
      179–80, 182, 198–99, 204, 213,
      214, 215–16, 217, 218, 245, 278–79
  Art 20(1) 16, 29–31
  Art 20(2) 29, 30–31, 56–57, 64, 154,
                175–76, 180, 191–92, 209–10
  Art 21 .... 30, 38, 307
  Art 22 307
  Art 25 .... 50–51, 138
  Art 26 .... 154, 218
  Art 41 44–45
  Art 49 13–14
ICESCR: International Covenant on
    Economic, Social and
    Cultural Rights (1966) 25
HRC: Human Rights Committee 12
  General Comment No. 10 (1983)
    s 1 175
  General Comment No. 11 (1983)
    s 2 30–31
  General Comment No. 15 (1986)
    s 2 28–29
  General Comment No. 24 (1994) 43
    s 3 27
    s 5 26–27
    s 12 28
    s 18 26–27
  General Comment No. 29 (2001) 39–40
    s 2 36–37
    s 4 36–37
    s 11 36–37
    s 13 38
    s 15 36–37
  General Comment No. 31 (2004)
    s 8 10
    s 10 28–29
    s 16 66
  General Comment No. 34
    (2011) 6–7, 53, 54–55, 106–7, 117,
                125, 178, 188, 196–97,
            209–10, 217, 308, 311, 324, 325
    s 2 42
    ss 2–3 .... 255, 271
    ss 2–4 153–54
    s 5 .... 6, 37
    ss 5–6 10
    s 7 274
    ss 7–8 153–54
    s 9 .... 6, 132–33, 134–35
    s 13 .... 12, 50–51, 138
    s 14 11
    ss 20–21 8–9
    s 21 .... 187, 307, 415
    ss 21–22 47
    s 22 .... 15, 101, 237, 241, 264–65, 307, 373

ss 22–30 187–88
s 23 241
s 24 185
ss 24–25 101
s 25 . . . . 185, 212, 238, 263, 374–75
s 26 . . . . 307, 415–16
s 27 . . . . 45–46, 188, 307
s 28 . . . . 48, 188
s 30 . . . . . 49, 50, 271, 308, 325, 344, 419–20
s 31 . . . . 6–7, 104, 183, 240–41, 380, 381
s 33 244
s 34 . . . . 183, 193, 238, 261, 262–63, 271–72,
382, 393–94
ss 34–35 . . . . 204, 334–35, 345–46, 407, 420
s 35 . . . . . . 58–59, 107, 145, 194, 207–8, 244,
245, 248, 265–66, 308–9, 315,
320–21, 324, 339, 341–42,
382–83, 389, 415–16
s 36 . . . . 45–46, 154–55, 184–85
s 37 . . . . 53, 242, 264
s 38 . . . . 109, 110, 111, 113, 130,
265–66, 271–72
s 39 . . . . 11, 12, 259–60
s 40 11
s 42 241
s 44 . . . . 11–12, 52
s 45 12
s 46 . . . . . . 63, 348, 377–78, 394, 400–1, 420
s 47 . . . . 57–58, 59, 64–65, 105, 109,
114, 115, 117–18, 125, 128, 132, 135,
147, 198, 214–15, 221–22, 240, 245,
249–50, 253–54, 255, 258, 270, 271,
272–73, 333, 403, 406, 420
s 48 . . . . 56–57, 191–92, 212
s 49 . . . . 48–49, 55, 158, 194, 198–99,
213–14, 240, 243–44
s 50 . . . . 30, 64, 173
ss 50–52 175
General Comment No. 35
(2013) 33, 215–16
s 19 33
Johannesburg Principles on National
Security, Freedom of Expression
and Access to Information . . . 42, 208–9,
311–12, 319–20, 324,
329, 341–42, 411
Preamble 311–12
Principle 1.1 314–15
Principle 1.1(a) 338
Principle 1.3 323
Principle 2 323
Principle 2(a) 339
Principle 2(b) 340
Principle 6 . . . . 311–12, 323, 324, 341–42
Principle 7 . . . . 311–12, 329
Principle 15 311–12
Principle 17 . . . . 319–20, 338–39
Principle 22 337
Nuremberg Charter: Charter of the
International Military Tribunal
(1945), 82 UNTS 279 157–58
Optional Protocol to the International
Covenant on Civil and Political
Rights (1966), 999 UNTS 171 44–45
Art 5(2)(a) 44
OSCE Parliamentary Assembly,
Bucharest Declaration (2000) 129
OSCE Parliamentary Assembly, Paris
Declaration: Resolution on
Freedom of the Media 129
OSCE Parliamentary Assembly, Warsaw
Declaration (1997) 129
Protocol No. 4 of the European
Convention for the Protection of
Human Rights and Fundamental
Freedoms
Art 2(3) 381
Protocol No. 11 of the European
Convention for the Protection of
Human Rights and Fundamental
Freedoms see ECHR: European
Convention for the Protection
of Human Rights and
Fundamental Freedoms (1950),
213 UNTS 221 34–35
Protocol to the African Charter on the
Establishment of an African
Court (ACHPR Protocol)
Art 2 44–45
Art 6 44
Art 34(6) 44
Rabat Plan of Action on the prohibition
of advocacy of national, racial or
religious hatred that constitutes
incitement to discrimination,
hostility or violence (Rabat Plan
of Action) 58, 107, 176, 177,
191–92, 194, 209–10, 213,
215–16, 217, 248, 417
s 19 . . . . 191–92, 213
s 21 215–16
s 29 . . . . 176, 393–94
s 29(c) 176, 215–16
s 29(f) 42, 58, 107, 194,
207–8, 217,
248, 417
s 34 176
Rome Statute: Statute of the
International Criminal Court
(1998), 2187 UNTS 3 . . . . 157–58, 178

Siracusa Principles on the Limitation
 and Derogation Provisions in the
 International Covenant on Civil
 and Political Rights (1984) 311,
  312–13, 382
 ss 29–30 vi
 s 31 vi
 s 32 vi
Statute of the Council of Europe
 (Treaty of London, 1949)
 Ch 1 Art 1(a) 22
Statute of the International Court of
 Justice (1945)
 Art 38(1)(b). 41
Statute of the International Criminal
 Tribunal for Rwanda (1994)
 Art 2(3)(c) 179
Tshwane Principles: Global Principles on
 National Security and the Right to
 Information 42, 279, 306–7,
  312–13, 319–20, 323, 324, 328–29,
  330–31, 334, 337–39, 340–42, 344–46
 Introduction and Preamble. 312
 Principle 3 . . . . 312–13, 314–15, 323, 324
 Principle 3a 314–15, 338
 Principle 4 .312–13, 323
 Principle 9 339
 Principle 10 339
 Principle 10(a)(4) 334
 Principle 11 324
 Principle 11(a)–(c) 319–20
 Principle 35 334
 Principle 37 328–29
 Principle 38 . . . 254, 328–29, 334, 340–41, 344
 Principle 40 340–41
 Principle 40(b) 328–29
 Principle 41 328–29
 Principle 41(e) 328–29
 Principle 43 . . . . 312–13, 328–29, 331, 344
 Principle 45(b)(ii). 323
 Principle 46 337
 Principle 46(b) 337
 Principle 47 . . . . 312–13, 328, 334, 345–46
 Principle 47(b) 328
 Principle 48 328
 Principle 49(b) 319–20, 338–39
UDHR: Universal Declaration of
 Human Rights (1948) 13–15, 18,
  22–23, 25, 32, 41,
  174, 177, 318
 Art 9 133
 Art 10 . . . . .128–29, 133
 Art 19 . . . . . 5, 23, 32, 41, 125–26, 128–29, 133,
  147, 172–73, 174,
  177, 186, 373

Art 29 23
Art 29(2) 21, 23
United Nations Charter (1945) 14–15, 18,
  25, 30–31
 Art 1(3) 14–15
 Art 55 14–15
 Art 56 14–15
United Nations Guiding Principles on
 Business and Human Rights
 (2011) 208–9, 211, 260, 275, 411
 Principle 1 274
 Principle 3(c) 274
 Principle 11 275
United Nations Special Rapporteur on the
 promotion and protection of the
 right to freedom of opinion and
 expression
 Disease Pandemics and the freedom
  of opinion and expression
  (2020) UN Doc.
  A/HRC/44/49. . . . 129, 222, 234, 238–39,
   244–45, 258, 259, 262–63,
   265–66, 341–42
 Disinformation and freedom of
  opinion and expression
  (2021) UN Doc.
  A/HRC/47/25. . . . .240, 248, 262, 265–66
UN Special Rapporteur on Freedom of
 Opinion and Expression, OSCE
 Representative on Freedom
 of the Media, and OAS Special
 Rapporteur on Freedom of
 Expression (International
 Mechanisms for Promoting
 Freedom of Expression)
 Joint Declaration (2000) 137, 150–51,
  311–12
 Joint Declaration on Access to
  Information and Secrecy
  Legislation (2004) 311–12, 314–15,
   320, 329, 345–46
 Joint Statement on Racism and
  the Media (2001) 198, 254, 406
UN Special Rapporteur on Freedom of
 Opinion and Expression, OSCE
 Representative on Freedom of the
 Media, OAS Special Rapporteur
 on Freedom of Expression and the
 ACHPR Special Rapporteur on
 Freedom of Expression and
 Access to Information
 Joint Declaration on Defamation of
  Religions, and Anti-Terrorism
  and Anti-Extremism
  Legislation (2008) 377–78, 395

Joint Declaration on Freedom of Expression
  and 'Fake News', Disinformation and
  Propaganda (2017) ... 147, 237, 238–39,
        241, 261, 263, 264, 269,
        270, 273, 274, 276
Joint Declaration on Freedom of
  Expression and Responses to
  Conflict Situations (2015)...... 270, 274
UN Special Rapporteur on Freedom of
  Opinion and Expression and OAS
  Special Rapporteur on Freedom of
  Expression
Joint Declaration on Surveillance
  Programs and Their Impact
  on Freedom of Expression
  (2013)......................... 337
VCLT: Vienna Convention on the Law of
  Treaties (1969)
  Art 19(c) 26–27
  Art 27............................... 33

List of Abbreviations

ACHPR	African Charter on Human and Peoples' Rights (adopted in 1981), 1520 United Nations Treaty Series 217—see also: African Charter
ACHPR Protocol	See also African Charter Protocol
ACHR	American Convention on Human Rights (adopted in 1969), 1144 United Nations Treaty Series 123—see also: American Convention
ACmHPR	African Commission on Human and Peoples' Rights—see also: African Commission
ACtHPR	African Court on Human and Peoples' Rights—see also: African Court
African Charter	African Charter on Human and Peoples' Rights (adopted in 1981), 1520 United Nations Treaty Series 217—see also: ACHPR
African Charter Protocol	See also ACHPR Protocol
African Commission	African Commission on Human and Peoples' Rights—see also: ACmHPR
African Court	African Court on Human and Peoples' Rights—see also: ACtHPR
American Convention	American Convention on Human Rights (adopted in 1969), 1144 United Nations Treaty Series 123—see also: ACHR
American Declaration	American Declaration of the Rights and Duties of Man (adopted by Organization of American States Resolution XXX in 1948)
Arab Charter	Arab Charter on Human Rights (adopted in 2004)
ASEAN	Association of Southeast Asian Nations
Camden Principles	Camden Principles on Freedom of Expression and Equality
CERD	International Convention on the Elimination of All Forms of Racial Discrimination (adopted in 1966), 660 United Nations Treaty Series 195
CERD Committee	United Nations Committee on the Elimination of Racial Discrimination
CFJ	Clooney Foundation for Justice
Christchurch Call	Christchurch Call to Action to Eliminate Terrorist and Violent Extremist Content Online
CJEU	Court of Justice of the European Union
COE	Council of Europe
COE Committee of Ministers	Committee of Ministers of the Council of Europe
COE Convention on the Prevention of Terrorism	Council of Europe Convention on the Prevention of Terrorism
CPJ	Committee to Protect Journalists

CTED	United Nations Counter-Terrorism Committee Executive Directorate
EACJ	East African Court of Justice
ECHR	European Convention for the Protection of Human Rights and Fundamental Freedoms (adopted in 1950), 213 United Nations Treaty Series 221—see also: European Convention
ECmHR	European Commission of Human Rights—see also: European Commission
ECOWAS	Economic Community of West African States
ECOWAS CCJ	Community Court of Justice of the Economic Community of West African States—see also: ECOWAS Court
ECOWAS Court	Community Court of Justice of the Economic Community of West African States—see also: ECOWAS CCJ
ECtHR	European Court of Human Rights—see also: European Court
European Commission	European Commission of Human Rights—see also: ECmHR
European Convention	European Convention for the Protection of Human Rights and Fundamental Freedoms (adopted in 1950), 213 United Nations Treaty Series 221—see also: ECHR
European Court	European Court of Human Rights—see also: ECtHR
EU	European Union
Genocide Convention	Convention on the Prevention and Punishment of the Crime of Genocide
GNI	Global Network Initiative
HRC	United Nations Human Rights Committee
IACmHR	Inter-American Commission on Human Rights—see also: Inter-American Commission
IACtHR	Inter-American Court of Human Rights—see also: Inter-American Court
IBAHRI	International Bar Association's Human Rights Institute
ICC	International Criminal Court
ICCPR	International Covenant on Civil and Political Rights (adopted in 1966), 999 United Nations Treaty Series 171
ICJ	International Court of Justice
ICJ Statute	Statute of the International Court of Justice (adopted in 1945)
ICTR	International Criminal Tribunal for Rwanda
ILC	International Law Commission
Inter-American Commission	Inter-American Commission on Human Rights—see also: IACmHR
Inter-American Court	Inter-American Court of Human Rights—see also: IACtHR
Johannesburg Principles	Johannesburg Principles on National Security, Freedom of Expression and Access to Information (adopted by a group of experts in international law, national security, and human rights, convened by Article 19, the International Centre Against Censorship, in collaboration with the Centre for Applied Legal Studies of the University of the Witwatersrand, in Johannesburg in 1995)
NGO	Non-Governmental Organization

Nuremberg Charter	Charter of the International Military Tribunal (adopted 1945), 82 United Nations Treaty Series 279
OAS	Organization of American States
OAS Rapporteur	Inter-American Commision on Human Rights Special Rapporteur for Freedom of Expression
OECD	Organization for Economic Co-operation and Development
OHCHR	Office of the United Nations High Commissioner for Human Rights
Optional Protocol to the ICCPR	Optional Protocol to the International Covenant on Civil and Political Rights (adopted in 1966), 999 United Nations Treaty Series 171
OSCE	Organization for Security and Cooperation in Europe
PKK	Kurdistan Workers' Party
Protocol 11	Protocol No. 11 to the Convention for the Protection of Human Rights and Fundamental Freedoms (adopted in 11 May 1994)
Rabat Plan of Action	Rabat Plan of Action on the prohibition of advocacy of national, racial or religious hatred that constitutes incitement to discrimination, hostility or violence
Res.	Resolution
Rome Statute of the ICC	Rome Statute of the International Criminal Court (adopted in 1998), 2187 United Nations Treaty Series 3
Siracusa Principles	Siracusa Principles on the Limitation and Derogation Provisions in the International Covenant on Civil and Political Rights (1984)
Tshwane Principles	Global Principles on National Security and the Right to Information (Tshwane Principles)
UDHR	Universal Declaration of Human Rights (adopted by United Nations General Assembly Resolution 217 A (111) in 1948)
UK	United Kingdom
UN	United Nations
UNGA	United Nations General Assembly
UNSC	United Nations Security Council
UN Special Rapporteur	UN Special Rapporteur on freedom of expression and opinion
UN Special Rapporteur on terrorism	UN Special Rapporteur on counter-terrorism and human rights
UNTS	United Nations Treaty Series
US	United States
USSR	Union of Soviet Socialist Republics
Venice Commission	European Commission for Democracy through Law
WGAD	Working Group on Arbitrary Detention—see also: Working Group
Working Group	Working Group on Arbitrary Detention—see also: WGAD

List of Contributors

Amal Clooney is a leading human rights lawyer who has spent the past two decades defending victims of injustice around the world. She has secured victories in landmark human rights cases including representing victims in the first trial at the International Criminal Court charging a Sudanese militant for crimes against humanity in Darfur and representing a survivor of sexual violence in the world's first trial in which an ISIS member was convicted of genocide. She has also won numerous awards for her work in freeing detained journalists around the globe. Ms Clooney is an Adjunct Professor at Columbia Law School and co-author of *The Right to a Fair Trial in International Law* (OUP 2020), which won the top publishing award at the American Society of International Law 2022 book awards. In 2016, she and her husband George Clooney co-founded the Clooney Foundation for Justice, which has a mission to 'wage justice' for human rights abuses around the world and now operates in over 40 countries.

Alice Gardoll is a human rights lawyer and Chief of Staff to Amal Clooney. She has spent her career defending and amplifying the voices of journalists, victims of human rights abuses, asylum seekers and incarcerated individuals. At the international human rights organization Reprieve, Ms Gardoll specialized in arbitrary and unlawful detention. She has practised as a public defender representing Aboriginal Australians in the Northern Territory and as a refugee lawyer in Australia and Greece. She also sits on the Board of the Refugee Advice & Casework Service. She began her career as a clerk to President of the New South Wales Court of Appeal, Her Excellency the Honourable Margaret Beazley AC KC, the 39th Governor of New South Wales. Ms Gardoll obtained her law degree at the University of Sydney and her Master of Laws as a Fulbright Scholar at Columbia University.

Dario Milo has practised in the area of media law at a leading law firm in South Africa for almost two decades. He lectures in media law, access to information law and privacy law at the University of the Witwatersrand, where he is an Adjunct Professor. Milo is the author of *Defamation and Freedom of Speech* (OUP 2008) and co-author of *A Practical Guide to Media Law* (Lexis-Nexis 2013). He is a global expert in freedom of expression and information at Columbia University's Global Freedom of Expression project, is on the editorial board of the *Journal of Media Law* (United Kingdom) and is a member of the High-Level Panel of Legal Experts on Media Freedom, chaired by Lord Neuberger. In his practice, Milo has acted for the media in numerous high-profile cases, including the defamation case brought by former president Jacob Zuma against the world-famous cartoonist Zapiro, and has been lead attorney in many of the media freedom cases decided by the highest courts in South Africa.

Lord Neuberger After 21 years as a barrister, David Neuberger was appointed a Judge in 1996 and was President of the UK Supreme Court from 2012 to 2017. He has decided cases involving some of the most significant human rights and constitutional law issues, including the admissibility of evidence obtained by torture, the legality of the Government's refusal to publish letters from the Prince of Wales to ministers and the entitlement of ministers to leave the EU without formal Parliamentary sanction. Lord Neuberger has also written and spoken extensively on free speech and privacy issues. Since 2010 he has sat as a Non-Permanent Judge of the Hong Kong Court of Final Appeal, and since 2018 he has also sat as a Judge in Singapore. He is President of the British Institute of International and Comparative Law and the Chair of the High-Level Panel of Legal Experts on Media Freedom, an independent advisory body composed of leading experts in international law established at the request of the international Media Freedom Coalition.

Marko Milanovic is Professor of Public International Law at the University of Reading School of Law. He is co-general editor of the ongoing Tallinn Manual 3.0 project on the application of international law in cyberspace and Senior Fellow, NATO Cooperative Cyber Defence Centre of Excellence. He is also co-editor of EJIL: Talk!, the blog of the European Journal of International Law, as well as a member of the EJIL's Editorial Board. Professor Milanovic was formerly Professor of Public International Law and Co-Director of the Human Rights Law Centre at the University of Nottingham School of Law and served as Vice-President and member of the Executive Board of the European Society of International Law. He is a prolific author in human rights law, public international law, international criminal law and the law of armed conflict with leading publishers and peer-reviewed journals. His publications include one monograph, one edited collection, 26 research articles, 15 book chapters and over 400 blog posts.

Philippa Webb is Professor of Public International Law at King's College London and Director of the Centre for International Governance and Dispute Resolution. She is also a barrister at Twenty Essex, appearing before the International Court of Justice, the European Court of Human Rights, the International Tribunal for the Law of the Sea and the UK Supreme Court. Her publications include: *The Right to a Fair Trial in International Law* (OUP 2020, with Amal Clooney) with the accompanying *travaux préparatoires* to article 14 of the ICCPR (2021), *Oppenheim's International Law: United Nations* (OUP 2017, with Dame Rosalyn Higgins GBE KC & others), *The Law of State Immunity* (OUP 2015, with Lady Hazel Fox KC) and *International Judicial Integration and Fragmentation* (OUP 2015). Her work has been cited by the leading national courts and has twice been awarded the American Society of International Law's Certificate of Merit.

Dr **Rosana Garciandia** is Associate Director of the Centre for International Governance and Dispute Resolution and Lecturer in Public International Law at The Dickson Poon School of Law, King's College London. She conducts research on the international law response to human rights abuses, including torture, racial discrimination, violations of socio-economic rights, labour exploitation and all contemporary forms of slavery. Her focus is on the responsibility of states and businesses, and on the potential of existing mechanisms to ensure their accountability for human rights abuses. She is also a Research Fellow at the British Institute of International and Comparative Law and a Fellow of the Macrocrimes Center of the University of Ferrara. Her publications include: articles on human rights and corruption (EP DROI Subcommittee, September 2021), on state responsibility and positive obligations (*Leiden Journal of International Law*, March 2020) and on state responsibility for modern slavery (*International and Comparative Law Quarterly*, July 2019, with Philippa Webb) among other topics, as well as co-editing the book *Human Dignity and International Law* (Brill 2020, with Philippa Webb and Andrea Gattini), and monographs on fragile states in international law (2013) and on the international law applicable to external debt (2011).

1

Introduction

Amal Clooney

I. Introduction	2	1.3.2.2. American Convention: Article 13	35
II. International Standards on Freedom of Speech and of the Press	5	1.3.2.3. African Charter: Article 9	35
1. Treaties	5	1.4. Derogations	36
1.1. Treaty language	5	1.4.1. International treaties	36
1.1.1. Abuses by the state	5	1.4.2. Regional treaties	39
1.1.2. Obligation to prevent abuses by others	10	2. Customary International Law	41
1.1.2.1. Harassment and violence	10	3. Jurisprudence	44
		3.1. Key convergences	47
1.1.2.2. Media pluralism	11	3.1.1. Justifications for penalizing speech	47
1.1.2.3. Protection of sources	12	3.1.2. False speech	48
1.2. Drafting history	13	3.1.3. Speech related to national security	49
1.2.1. International treaties	13		
1.2.1.1. ICCPR: Article 19	13	3.1.4. Political and public interest speech	50
1.2.1.2. ICCPR: Article 20	22		
1.2.1.3. CERD: Article 4	23	3.1.5. Importance of protecting the press	50
1.2.2. Regional treaties	22		
1.2.2.1. European Convention	22	3.1.6. Criminal penalties for speech	53
1.2.2.2. American Convention	23	3.2. Key divergences	54
1.2.2.3. African Charter	25	3.2.1. Denialism	55
1.3. Reservations	26	3.2.2. Blasphemy	56
1.3.1. International treaties	27	3.2.3. Intent and harm requirements	57
1.3.1.1. ICCPR: Article 19	23	3.2.4. Defences	59
1.3.1.2. ICCPR: Article 20	25	3.2.5. Relevance of whether the speaker is a journalist	59
1.3.1.3. CERD: Article 4	27		
1.3.2. Regional treaties	34	3.2.6. Criminal penalties for speech	62
1.3.2.1. European Convention: Article 10	34	3.2.7. Remedies	66
		III. Conclusion	69

International Covenant on Civil and Political Rights

Article 19

1. Everyone shall have the right to hold opinions without interference.
2. Everyone shall have the right to freedom of expression; this right shall include freedom to seek, receive and impart information and ideas of all kinds, regardless of frontiers, either orally, in writing or in print, in the form of art, or through any other media of his choice.

3. The exercise of the rights provided for in paragraph 2 of this article carries with it special duties and responsibilities. It may therefore be subject to certain restrictions, but these shall only be such as are provided by law and are necessary:
   (a) For respect of the rights or reputations of others;
   (b) For the protection of national security or of public order (*ordre public*), or of public health or morals.

Article 20

1. Any propaganda for war shall be prohibited by law.
2. Any advocacy of national, racial or religious hatred that constitutes incitement to discrimination, hostility or violence shall be prohibited by law.

I. Introduction

Without freedom of speech, all human rights are under threat. As the English 17th century poet John Milton put it: 'give me the liberty to know, to utter, and to argue freely according to conscience, above all liberties'.[1] Yet, today this basic freedom faces unprecedented attacks, as laws related to 'fake news' and 'national security' become more sweeping, penalties of imprisonment are increasingly applied, and technology provides new opportunities to suppress truthful communications.[2]

This global gag on free speech also threatens freedom of the press. Autocratic states now outnumber liberal democracies.[3] The number of journalists dying outside war zones is higher than the number dying in war.[4] Around the world, almost 80 per cent of journalists' murders remain unsolved.[5] Saudi officials were bold enough to kidnap, murder and mutilate a journalist at a foreign consulate.[6] Belarus diverted a commercial airliner in mid-air to kidnap a journalist.[7] And in recent years we have seen journalists murdered in the heart of Europe, from Malta to Slovakia.[8]

---

[1] J. Milton, *Areopagitica* (1644).
[2] 'The new censors: The global gag on free speech is tightening' (The Economist, 17 August 2019). NGOs report the highest rates of imprisonment for speech-related crimes since records began. See, e.g., Reporters Without Borders, 'New record number of journalists jailed worldwide' (14 December 2022); CPJ, 'Attacks on the Press in 2022' (December 2022).
[3] V-Dem Institute, 'Democracy Report 2023: Defiance in the Face of Autocratization' (March 2023), 9 .
[4] Reporters Without Borders, '2022 Round-up: Journalists detained, killed, held hostage and missing' (December 2022), 13, finding that 64.9 per cent of journalists killed between January to December 2022 were killed outside war zones.
[5] J. Dunham, 'Killing with impunity: Vast majority of journalists' murderers go free' (CPJ, 1 November 2022).
[6] 'Saudi Crown Prince is Held Responsible for Khashoggi Killing in U.S. Report' (The New York Times, 26 February 2021).
[7] A. Troianovski & I. Nechepurenko, 'Belarus Forces Down Plane to Seize Dissident; Europe Sees "State Hijacking"' (The New York Times, 23 May 2021).
[8] 'EU to monitor investigations of reporters killed in Malta, Slovakia' (Reuters, 5 June 2018).

Journalists are also being prosecuted and imprisoned at record-breaking rates around the world.[9] States are 'weaponizing' their legal systems by allowing baseless suits against journalists that are expensive to defend.[10] Journalists are being spied on and subjected to smear campaigns sponsored by government officials.[11] Internet shutdowns are becoming more sophisticated, lasting longer and affecting more people.[12] Economic coercion by states is forcing local media outlets to close and local news networks to come off the air.[13] Illiberal governments have withdrawn advertising dollars from independent news channels,[14] imposed restrictions on foreign ownership of media and launched baseless and drawn-out tax investigations.[15] Some states have even starved independent media of ink, paper and printing material after critical reporting.[16]

The repercussions of suppressing truthful reporting have been extreme and in some cases deadly. Reports suggest that up to 130 million Americans consumed false news ahead of the 2016 Presidential elections in the United States.[17] And false claims about treatments for Covid-19 across social media have contributed to many deaths.[18]

International law aims to provide a response to such abuses. More than 170 governments have ratified a treaty, the International Covenant on Civil and Political Rights, that requires them to protect the right to freedom of expression and there is an array of courts and human rights bodies that exist to enforce it.[19] But what does international law have to say about the contours of the right to free speech and to a free press? And are its provisions, developed in the aftermath of the Second World War—before the internet, social media platforms and AI algorithms—still fit for purpose?

Despite the importance of these questions, many academic works focus on a single jurisdiction, leaving the definition of an international standard unclear. Many scholars examine one type of speech, such as defamation, without reference to whether other types of speech should be treated differently. And there is a lack of clear guidance about

---

[9] CPJ, Number of jailed journalists spikes to new global record (14 December 2022).

[10] A prominent example is the Maltese journalist Daphne Caruana Galizia who was facing over 40 defamation and other civil lawsuits at the time of her assassination. See ch. 2 (Insulting Speech), s. II.2.1.3. (SLAPP and libel tourism).

[11] See, e.g., OHCHR, 'Use of spyware to surveil journalists and human rights defenders, Statement by UN High Commissioner for Human Rights Michelle Bachelet' (19 July 2021); COE Platform to Promote the Protection and Safety of Journalists, 'Hands Off Press Freedom: Attacks on Media in Europe Must Not Become A New Normal' (March 2020).

[12] Access Now #KeepItOn, 'Weapons of Control, Shields of Impunity: Internet shutdowns in 2022' (February 2023)(tracking 187 shutdowns which took place in 2022, including 48 shutdowns in 14 countries coinciding with documented human rights abuses).

[13] S. Repucci, 'Key Findings' in Freedom and the Media 2019: A Downward Spiral (Freedom House, 2019), 2.

[14] See, e.g., International Press Institute et al., 'Conclusions of the Joint International Press Freedom Mission to Hungary' (3 December 2019).

[15] Z. Csaky, 'A New Toolbox for Co-opting the Media', in Freedom and the Media 2019: A Downward Spiral (Freedom House, 2019), 17–18; 'Amal Clooney and Caoilfhionn Gallagher KC welcome acquittal of Maria Ressa of spurious tax charges' (Doughty Street Chambers, 18 January 2023).

[16] 'The new censors: The global gag on free speech is tightening' (The Economist, 17 August 2019).

[17] 'How to deal with free speech on social media' (The Economist, 22 October 2020).

[18] See, e.g., 'Iran: Over 700 dead after drinking alcohol to cure coronavirus' (Al Jazeera, 27 April 2020); 'Desperate Bolivians seek out toxic bleach falsely touted as Covid-19 cure' (The Guardian, 17 July 2020). See ch. 4 (False Speech), s. I. (Introduction).

[19] UNTC Depositary, Status of Treaties, ch. IV.4 ICCPR, Status. See, e.g., HRC, CERD Committee, ECtHR, IACtHR, IACmHR, ACtHPR, ACmHPR. See ss II. (International Standards on Freedom of Speech and the Press) and II.2. (Customary International Law).

the circumstances under which international law allows criminal penalties, as opposed to civil sanctions, to be imposed.

This book has two main purposes. First, we intend to clarify what the right to freedom of expression means under international law. Many states are failing to uphold minimum international standards protecting speech, and it is our hope that this book helps efforts to encourage reform, or at least accountability. By making the yardstick clear, we aim to show where governments are failing to measure up. We want to make international law on the right to free speech clear, accessible and meaningful to journalists, legislators, judges and lawyers all over the world. And we want to make it more difficult for state authorities to claim adherence to international law where their laws and practice paint a different picture.

So we explain, in granular detail, how articles 19 and 20 of the ICCPR have been interpreted to date, how these articles compare with the equivalent provisions in regional human rights treaties and how all these provisions have been applied by international bodies. We canvas whether the treaty provisions which enshrine the right to free expression have reached customary international law status and therefore apply to states—such as China, Myanmar and Cuba—that have not ratified these agreements.[20]

Second, this book provides recommendations about how international standards should be interpreted, updated and enforced. We aim to identify the gaps, conflicts and deficiencies that exist in international human rights law and provide best practice recommendations on where the lines should be drawn. These recommendations build on existing international standards and are informed by the expertise of the esteemed group of academics, lawyers and former judges from across the world who have worked on this book and endorsed its recommendations.[21]

Recommendations relevant to the specific types of speech covered in the book—defamatory and insulting speech, hate speech, false speech and speech affecting national security—are set out at the end of each of the chapters that follow. But these recommendations overlap and intersect given common issues that arise. They are intended to inform the actions not only of governments, but also of social media platforms with responsibilities related to their algorithms and resulting content.[22]

---

[20] See s. II.2. (Customary International Law). See also OHCHR, Status of Ratification: Ratification of 18 International Human Rights Treaties.

[21] See Foreword, setting out experts who have endorsed the recommendations in the book. Other experts have contributed as authors of chapters in the book. Those who have endorsed the recommendations contained in this book include the Committee to Protect Journalists; Reporters without Borders; The International Bar Association Human Rights Institute; the United Nations Special Rapporteur on Freedom of Opinion and Expression; the Inter-American Special Rapporteur on Freedom of Expression; Patrick Penninckx, Head of Information Society Department, Council of Europe; Francoise Tulkens, former Vice-President of the European Court of Human Rights; Baroness Helena Kennedy of the Shaws, KC, member of the House of Lords; The Honourable Irwin Cotler, PC, OC, OQ, former Minister of Justice and Attorney-General of Canada; Hina Jilani, former UN Special Representative on Human Rights Defenders; Seong-Phil Hong, Professor at Ewha and Yonsei Law Schools, former member of the UN Working Group on Arbitrary Detention; Justice Manuel José Cepeda Espinosa, former Chief Justice of the Constitutional Court of Colombia and Judge Chile Eboe-Osuji, former President of the International Criminal Court.

[22] See ch. 3 (Hate Speech), s. VI.5. (Recommendations) and ch. 4 (False Speech), s. IV.12. (Recommendations).

II. International Standards on Freedom of Speech and of the Press

This chapter explores the key international and regional human rights treaty provisions that protect freedom of expression, their drafting history and the key jurisprudence interpreting them.[23] It also assesses the scope of customary international law that applies even to states that have not ratified relevant treaties.

1. Treaties

1.1. Treaty language
1.1.1. Abuses by the state
In international law, speech is primarily regulated in two treaties: the International Covenant on Civil and Political Rights and the Convention on the Elimination of Racial Discrimination.[24] There is also a prohibition on 'direct and public incitement to commit genocide' in a third treaty, the Genocide Convention.[25] Freedom of expression is also enshrined in regional human rights treaties including the European Convention on Human Rights, the American Convention on Human Rights and the African Charter on Human and Peoples' Rights.[26]

The right to freedom of expression is defined in a similar manner in these instruments. Most instruments reference two distinct rights, the right to freedom of opinion or thought—a 'purely private matter, belonging to the realm of the mind'—and the right to express those opinions.[27] And almost all the provisions provide broad definitions of the right to not only speak but also to receive and impart 'information and ideas of all kinds, regardless of frontiers... through any media'.[28]

---

[23] This book covers many aspects of the right to freedom of speech, including the rules of international law that apply to insulting speech, hate speech, false speech and speech related to issues of national security. It does not cover, at least in any detail, certain related topics such as the right to information, due process protections, the protection of sources and materials, the right to privacy, the right to be forgotten or remain anonymous or systemic restrictions on the media.
[24] ICCPR Arts 19, 20; CERD Arts 4, 5. See also UDHR Art. 19.
[25] Genocide Convention Art. 3(c).
[26] ECHR Art. 10; ACHR Art. 13; ACHPR Art. 9. There is also the Arab Charter on Human Rights and the ASEAN Declaration of Human Rights but there are no regional courts with jurisdiction to apply the rights enshrined in them.
[27] M. Nowak, *U.N. Covenant on Civil and Political Rights: Nowak's CCPR Commentary* (N.P. Engel 2019), 545. See also ECHR Art. 10(1); ACHPR Art. 9(2). See further ECtHR, *Morice v. France* (App. no. 29369/10), 23 April 2015, §126.
[28] ICCPR Art. 19(2); ECHR Art. 10(1); ACHR Art. 13(1). The exception is the African Charter, although subsequent jurisprudence confirms that the right should nonetheless be interpreted consistently with international standards. See s. II.3. (Jurisprudence).

The text of the American Convention is more protective of speech than other treaties in that it explicitly prohibits prior restraint of speech[29] as well as 'indirect government restrictions' or 'private controls'.[30] The Special Rapporteur of the Organization of American States has found that, as a result, 'the restrictions provided for in other international instruments are not applicable in the American context, nor should such instruments be used to interpret the American Convention restrictively'.[31]

Although the right to freedom of opinion 'permits no exception or restriction',[32] international law is clear that, by contrast, the right to free expression is subject to defined exceptions. Article 19 of the ICCPR provides a small number of exhaustive permissible reasons for restrictions to the right of freedom of expression: (i) 'for respect of the rights or reputations of others' or (ii) 'for the protection of national security or of public order ... or of public health or morals'.[33] These exceptions are mirrored in almost identical terms in article 13 of the American Convention.[34]

Article 10 of the European Convention includes the same permissible restrictions on free speech as article 19(3) of the ICCPR, but also provides additional grounds. These are: 'in the interests of territorial integrity or public safety', to prevent 'disorder or crime', to prevent 'the disclosure of information received in confidence' or 'for maintaining the authority and impartiality of the judiciary'.[35]

Although these specific grounds are not listed in the ICCPR, it is not clear whether European drafters in fact intended to cast a broader net on the type of speech that can be penalized. A committee of experts reporting to the Council of Europe on the 'coexistence of the human rights obligations' under the European Convention and the ICCPR found that at 'first sight, the text of the European Convention seems to be more

---

[29] ACHR Arts 13(2) ('The exercise of the right [to freedom of thought and expression] shall not be subject to prior censorship') and 13(4) ('Notwithstanding the provisions of paragraph 2 above, public entertainments may be subject by law to prior censorship for the sole purpose of regulating access to them for the moral protection of childhood and adolescence'). See also IACtHR, *Compulsory Membership in an Association Prescribed by Law for the Practice of Journalism (Arts 13 and 29 American Convention on Human Rights)*, Advisory Opinion OC-5/85 (Series A, no. 5), 13 November 1985, §38; IACtHR, *'Last Temptation of Christ' (Olmedo Bustos et al.) v. Chile* (Series C, no. 73), 5 February 2001, §70.

[30] IACtHR, *Compulsory Membership in an Association Prescribed by Law for the Practice of Journalism (Arts 13 and 29 American Convention on Human Rights)*, Advisory Opinion OC-5/85 (Series A, no. 5), 13 November 1985, §§45–48.

[31] See the Office of the Special Rapporteur for Freedom of Expression IACmHR, *Inter-American Legal Framework regarding the Right to Freedom of Expression* (2009) OEA/Ser.L/V/II CIDH/RELE/INF. 2/09, §4, citing IACmHR, *Report No. 11/96 Francisco Martorell in Chile* (3 May 1996) Case 11.230, §56 and IACtHR, *Compulsory Membership in an Association Prescribed by Law for the Practice of Journalism (Arts 13 and 29 American Convention on Human Rights)*, Advisory Opinion OC-5/85 (Series A, no. 5), 13 November 1985, §52.

[32] The Human Rights Committee has therefore classified this a non-derogable right despite its absence from the list of such rights in article 4 of the ICCPR. See HRC, General Comment No. 34 (2011), §§5, 9. See also Nowak (n 27) 545–547 for a discussion of the limited Human Rights Committee cases that address article 19(1) as a distinct right. See s. II.1.4. (Derogations).

[33] ICCPR Art. 19 (3).

[34] This language is the same except that in article 13(2)(a) of the American Convention 'public order' is not followed by the French equivalent 'ordre public' in brackets. However, the chapeau to each provision differs: article 19(3) of the ICCPR provides that the exercise of rights in article 19(2) 'carries with it special duties and responsibilities' and may 'therefore be subject to certain restrictions, but these shall only be such as are provided by law and are necessary', whereas article 13(2) states that the right to freedom of thought and expression 'shall not be subject to prior censorship but shall be subject to subsequent imposition of liability, which shall be expressly established by law to the extent necessary'.

[35] ECHR Art. 10 (2).

restrictive in listing more grounds of permissible restrictions, while the text of the UN Covenant apparently affords more protection for the individual by imposing stricter obligations on Contracting States'.[36] However, the experts noted that the additional grounds listed in the European Convention could 'be included in the notion of "public order"' listed in the ICCPR.[37] Although the experts did not reach a firm conclusion either way in their report, the Consultative Assembly of the Council of Europe welcomed the report and in 1971 declared itself 'convinced that the two systems of protection of Human Rights, regional and universal, are not conflicting but complementary'.[38] And the Human Rights Committee has considered 'public order' to encompass the additional aims expressly listed in article 10 of the European Convention.[39]

The right to freedom of expression in the African Charter is framed more restrictively on paper than its counterparts, though African human rights courts have not, so far, found that this creates a different standard of protection.[40] In comparison to other regional bodies, African human rights bodies have tended to more closely mirror the decisions of international bodies such as the Human Rights Committee.[41]

Article 9(2) of the African Charter simply states that '[e]very individual shall have the right to express and disseminate his opinions within the law'.[42] This is in line with the general approach of the Charter to provide less detailed descriptions of rights and include a claw-back clause allowing rights to be limited by 'law'.[43] But the phrase 'within the law' has been interpreted by the African Court and the African Commission on Human Rights as requiring that restrictions must be 'prescribed by law, serve a legitimate purpose and [be] necessary and proportional as may be expected in a democratic society', thereby bringing the provision in line with international and regional equivalents.[44] Article 60 of the African Charter also provides that the Commission shall 'draw inspiration from international law on human and peoples rights' when interpreting

---

[36] COE, *Report of the Committee of Experts to the Committee of Ministers on the problems arising from the co-existence of the UN Covenants on Human Rights and the European Convention on Human Rights* (1970) H(70)7, §175.

[37] Ibid., §177. The report was published in 1970, before the Covenant was in force (in 1976), but based on the final wording that had been adopted (in 1966).

[38] Consultative Assembly of the COE, Recommendation 642 relating to the ratification of the UN Covenants on Human Rights (8 July 1971), §7. See also M. Eissen, 'The European Convention on Human Rights and the United Nations Covenant on Civil and Political Rights: Problems of Coexistence' (1972) 22 *Buffalo Law Review* 181, 214.

[39] See HRC, *Lovell v. Australia* (Comm. no. 920/2000), 24 March 2004, §9.4; HRC, General Comment No. 34 (2011), §31 ('Contempt of court proceedings relating to forms of expression may be tested against the public order (ordre public) ground'); HRC, *Agazade and Jafarov v. Azerbaijan* (Comm. no. 2205/2012), 27 October 2016, §§7.4–7.5; HRC, *Aleksandrov v. Belarus* (Comm. no. 1933/2010), 24 July 2014, §7.4 (holding that Belarus had not explained how the actions of a protestor 'would have violated the rights and freedoms of others or would have posed a threat to public safety or public order (*ordre public*)').

[40] See s. II.3.1. (Key convergences).

[41] See s. II.3.2.6. (Criminal penalties for speech). See also ch. 3 (Hate Speech), s. IV. (Key Divergences in International and Regional Guidance).

[42] ACHPR Art. 9(2).

[43] See Arts 6 (right to liberty and security), 8 (freedom of conscience), 10(1) (freedom of association), 12(2) (freedom of movement); R. Murray, *The African Charter on Human Rights: A Commentary* (OUP 2019), 56.

[44] ACtHPR, *Umuhoza v. Rwanda* (App. no. 3/2014), 24 November 2017, §133. See also ACmHPR, *Good v. Botswana* (Comm. no. 313/2005), 26 May 2010, §188.

the rights contained in it.[45] And the drafting history of the Statute suggests that the phrase 'within the law' was intended to encompass international law,[46] meaning that 'only restrictions on rights which are consistent with the Charter and with State Parties' international obligations should be enacted by the relevant national authorities'.[47] The lawfulness of a state's restriction to speech will thereby be considered against both 'the Charter and other norms of international law'.[48]

African human rights courts and bodies have not, however, 'always consistently cited' the legitimate grounds that can be used to restrict speech under the Charter.[49] Although the African Court and Commission and the Community Court of Justice of the Economic Community of West African States have all held that the aims listed in article 19(3) of the ICCPR are 'legitimate' grounds to restrict speech,[50] it is not clear whether additional grounds are also recognized. Article 27(2) of the African Charter provides that Charter rights generally 'shall be exercised with due regard to the rights of others, collective security, morality and common interest' and the African Commission has cited article 27(2) as the 'only legitimate reasons' for limiting rights.[51] It is therefore unclear whether the aims in article 19(3) of the ICCPR and article 27(2) of the Charter are considered cumulative grounds to validly restrict speech, or whether article 27(2) is to be interpreted as equivalent to article 19(3) in the context of freedom of expression.[52] In addition, the African Commission's 2019 Declaration of Principles on Freedom of Expression adopts the grounds enumerated in article 19(3), but excludes 'morals'.[53] The Commission has also said that 'public interest' can be recognized as a justifiable ground for limiting freedom of expression, even though this does not appear in the text of any of the human rights treaties.[54] But, given that the case law of the African Court interprets the Charter in conformity with the ICCPR when possible, and the fact that the

---

[45] The draft of the African Charter refers to the African Commission only, as the African Court was established in 1998 after the Charter was adopted. The African Court has since interpreted article 60 to grant the Court the same powers: see, e.g., ACtHPR, *Omary v. Tanzania* (App. no. 1/2012), 28 March 2014, §73.

[46] See s. II.1.2. (Drafting history).

[47] See, e.g., ACmHPR, *Article 19 v. Eritrea* (Comm. no. 275/2003), 30 May 2007, §92; ACmHPR, *Good v. Botswana* (Comm. no. 313/2005), 26 May 2010, §188.

[48] ACmHPR, *Article 19 v. Eritrea* (Comm. no. 275/2003), 30 May 2007, §92.

[49] Murray (n 43).

[50] ACtHPR, *Konaté v. Burkina Faso* (App. no. 4/2013), 5 December 2014, §§134–135; ECOWAS CCJ, *The Incorporated Trustees of Laws and Rights Awareness Initiatives v. Nigeria* (Suit no. ECW/CCJ/APP/53/2018), 10 July 2020, §§139–140.

[51] ACHPR Art. 27(2); ACmHPR, *Constitutional Rights Project v. Nigeria* (Comm. no. 140/1994), 15 November 1999, §41; ACtHPR, *Konaté v. Burkina Faso* (App. no. 4/2013), 5 December 2014, §§134–135 ('the Court is of the view that the only legitimate reasons to limit these rights and freedoms are stipulated in Article 27 (2), namely that rights "shall be exercised in respect of the rights of others, collective security, morality and common interest"'. The Court further notes that the legitimate purpose of a restriction is stated in Article 19 (3) (a) and (b) of the Covenant'). See also ACmHPR, *Elgak v. Sudan* (Comm. no. 379/09), 7–14 March 2014, §115 (holding that there was no justifiable reason to limit the impugned speech as it had not 'endangered the lives of others, national security, morality, common interest or caused any other legitimate prejudice').

[52] See, e.g., ACtHPR, *Konaté v. Burkina Faso* (App. no. 4/2013), 5 November 2014, §§134–135, in which the ACtHPR stated that the '*only* legitimate reasons' to limit freedom of expression are stipulated under article 27(2) but went on to observe that 'the legitimate purpose of a restriction' is stated in article 19(3)(a) and (b) of the ICCPR (emphasis added).

[53] ACmHPR, Declaration of Principles of Freedom of Expression and Access to Information in Africa (2019), Principle 9.

[54] ACmHPR, *Good v. Botswana* (Comm. no. 313/05), 26 May 2010, §189.

aims in article 19(3) are intended to be exhaustive,[55] the Court may in due course determine that it is appropriate to adopt the narrower interpretation of 'legitimate' aims—matching the approach under the ICCPR.[56]

A key divergence that emerges from a comparison of the legitimate aims for penalizing speech under the relevant treaties is the extent to which states may (and in some cases must) penalize or criminalize hateful speech.[57] In the ICCPR, article 19 *allows for* a restriction of speech based on certain permissible purposes, but article 20 *requires* penalties for speech that constitutes advocacy of national, racial or religious hatred if it incites 'discrimination', 'hostility' or 'violence'.[58] Article 4 of CERD goes even further than article 20 of the ICCPR in requiring the *criminalization* of racist 'hate speech' even if it does not constitute incitement.[59]

The regional treaties are in tension with these provisions and with each other on this point. The American Convention is the only instrument with a parallel provision to article 20 of the ICCPR, though it is significantly narrower in that it only requires penalization of hateful speech that incites 'lawless violence or ... any other similar action' as opposed to discrimination or hostility.[60] Neither the African Charter nor the European Convention contain an equivalent provision to article 20.[61] Although the European Court of Human Rights has used article 17 of the Convention, which prohibits the 'abuse of rights', as a mechanism to exclude speech that employs 'ends clearly contrary to the values of the Convention' from the scope of protection under the Convention,[62] this does not extend to a positive obligation to prohibit speech as provided in both the ICCPR and CERD.[63]

---

[55] HRC, General Comment No. 34 (2011), §§20–21. See also UN Special Rapporteur D. Kaye, *Report on the promotion and protection of the right to freedom of opinion and expression* (2019) UN Doc. A/74/486, §6.

[56] The African Commission has also provided that '[w]here a conflict arises between any domestic and international human rights law, the most favourable provision for the full exercise of the rights to freedom of expression or access to information shall prevail': ACmHPR, Declaration of Principles of Freedom of Expression and Access to Information in Africa (2019), Principle 4.

[57] See also A. Clooney & P. Webb, 'The Right to Insult in International Law' (2017) 48(2) *Columbia Human Rights Law Review* 1, 44.

[58] ICCPR Arts 19(3), 20. The Human Rights Committee has however clarified that even if a statement complies with article 20 it must also comply with article 19(3). See HRC, *Ross v. Canada* (Comm. no. 736/1997), 18 October 2000, §10.6.

[59] CERD Art. 5. See also CERD Committee, General Recommendation No. 35 (2013), §12, recommending that the criminalization of racist expression be reserved for 'serious cases'. See further UN Special Rapporteur Frank La Rue, *Report on the promotion and protection of the right to freedom of opinion and expression* (2011) UN Doc. A/66/290, §31. See also Clooney & Webb, 'The Right to Insult in International Law' (n 57) 19, 53.

[60] ACHR Art. 13(5).

[61] Article 19, 'Prohibiting incitement to discrimination, hostility or violence: Policy Brief' (December 2012), 14, 16–17.

[62] ECtHR (GC), *Perinçek v. Switzerland* (App. no. 27510/08), 15 October 2015, §114.

[63] ICCPR Art. 20; CERD Art. 4. See also Clooney & Webb 'The Right to Insult in International Law' (n 57) 22. ECtHR (GC), *Perinçek v. Switzerland* (App. no. 27510/08), 15 October 2015, §114. Cf. ECtHR, *Atamanchuk v. Russia* (App. no. 4493/11), 11 February 2020, §70 ('Contracting States are permitted, or even obliged, by their positive obligations under Article 8 of the Convention, to regulate the exercise of freedom of expression so as to ensure adequate protection by law in such circumstances and/or where fundamental rights of others have been seriously impaired').

1.1.2 Obligation to prevent abuses by others

In addition to regulating the penalties that governments can impose on speech, international law enumerates positive duties owed by states to prevent abuses by others.[64] The ICCPR requires in article 2 that states both refrain from violating Covenant rights, and 'ensure' that these rights are protected.[65] This means that a state's positive obligations 'will only be fully discharged if individuals are protected' not just against violations of Covenant rights by a state's 'agents, but also against acts committed by private persons or entities that would impair the enjoyment of Covenant rights'.[66] Although these obligations cannot impose an 'impossible or disproportionate burden on the domestic authorities', states must adopt reasonable measures to prevent a real and immediate risk to a speaker's rights from the acts of a third party.[67] Regional treaties have been interpreted to give rise to similar obligations.[68]

1.1.2.1. Harassment and violence The obligation to 'ensure' compliance with treaty norms applies to freedom of expression in at least two ways. First, international bodies such as the Human Rights Committee have highlighted that states have an obligation to protect journalists from harassment and violence.[69] According to the Inter-American Court, this means that states 'have the obligation to adopt special measures of prevention and protection for journalists subject to special risk owing to the exercise of their profession'.[70] The European Court has held that such measures should include 'effective criminal-law provisions to deter the commission of offences', backed up by 'law enforcement machinery for the prevention, suppression and punishment of breaches of such provisions', as well as in certain circumstances positive obligations to take 'preventive operational measures to protect' journalists or other speakers 'whose lives are at risk from the criminal acts of another individual'.[71] Article 2(3) of the ICCPR and its regional equivalents also generate obligations to effectively investigate violations of

---

[64] ICCPR Art. 2; ECHR Art. 1; ACHR Arts 1, 2; ACPHR Art. 1. See also HRC, General Comment No. 34 (2011), §§7–8; ECtHR, Guide on Article 10 of the Convention, 31 August 2022, §11.
[65] ICCPR Art. 2.
[66] HRC, General Comment No. 31 (2004), §8.
[67] COE, *Factsheet: Positive Obligations on Member States to Protect Journalists and the Freedom of Expression* (2018); ECtHR, *Özgür Gündem v. Turkey* (App. no. 23144/93), 16 March 2000, §43.
[68] See, e.g., ECHR Art. 1; ACHR Arts 1, 2; ACHPR Art. 1; IACtHR, *Carvajal Carvajal v. Colombia* (Series C, no. 365), 21 November 2018, §§176–177.
[69] See, e.g., HRC, *Concluding Observations, Ghana* (2016) UN Doc. CCPR/C/GHA/CO/1, §§39–40; HRC, *Concluding Observations, Mongolia* (2017) UN Doc. CCPR/C/MNG/CO/6, §§37–38; HRC, *Concluding Observations, Russian Federation* (2015) UN Doc. CCPR/C/RUS/CO/7, §18.
[70] IACtHR, *Velez Restrepo v. Colombia* (Series C, no. 248), 3 September 2012, §194. See also IACtHR, *Carvajal Carvajal v. Colombia* (Series C, no. 365), 13 March 2018, §196. The Court has also highlighted the obligation to take into account gender considerations. See IACtHR, *Bedoya Lima v. Colombia* (Series C, no. 431), 26 August 2021, §91: 'States must ... carry out a risk analysis and implement protection measures that consider the ... risk faced by women journalists as a result of violence based on gender').
[71] ECtHR, *Gongadze v. Ukraine* (App. no. 34056/02), 8 November 2005, §§164, 165, 168. Although this reasoning applies to all persons, not just journalists, the European Court noted that prosecutors should be aware of the 'vulnerable position in which a journalist who covered politically sensitive topics placed himself/herself vis-à-vis those in power'.

human rights when they do take place, as well as to prevent similar violations occurring in the future.[72]

1.1.2.2. Media pluralism Second, international bodies recognize that states, as the 'ultimate guarantor[s]' of freedom of speech, have an obligation to encourage pluralism in media[73] and 'to create ... a favourable environment for participation in public debate by everyone ... without fear'.[74] The Human Rights Committee has highlighted that, as a result, states 'should take particular care to encourage an independent and diverse media'.[75] This means that systemic restrictions on the media by way of arbitrary or abusive accreditation, licensing or financing practices may violate international human rights standards.[76] States 'should not have monopoly control over the media' and should take appropriate action 'to prevent undue media dominance or concentration by privately controlled media groups ... that may be harmful to a diversity of sources and views'.[77]

The Human Rights Committee has also held that accreditation schemes 'are permissible only where necessary to provide journalists with privileged access to certain places and/or events', and should be applied in a non-discriminatory manner 'based on objective criteria and taking into account that journalism is a function shared by a wide range of actors'.[78] And international bodies have expressed concern about accreditation schemes that restrict the freedom of movement of journalists, impose prohibitive fees or do not include sufficient procedural safeguards.[79] This principle is reiterated in the Declaration of Principles on Freedom of Expression in Africa, which provides that 'any registration system for media shall be for administrative purposes only, and shall not impose excessive fees or other restrictions on the media'.[80] Similarly the Inter-American Commission has stated that '[c]ompulsory membership or the requirements

---

[72] See, e.g., HRC, *Adonis v. Philippines* (Comm. no. 1815/2008), 26 October 2011, §9. See also ECHR Art. 1; ACHPR Art. 1; ECtHR, *Rizanov v. Azerbaijan* (App. no. 31805/06), 17 July 2012, §55; IACtHR, *Uzcátegui v. Valenzuela* (Series C, no. 249), 3 September 2012, operative paragraph 1; ACmHPR, *Egyptian Initiative for Personal Rights and Interights v. Egypt* (Comm. no. 323/2006), 16 December 2011, §274, operative paragraph v.
[73] ECtHR, *Informationsverein Lentia v. Austria* (App. nos. 13914/88 & others), 24 November 1993, §38. See also IACtHR, *Granier v. Venezuela* (Series C, no. 293), 22 June 2015, §141; ACmHPR, Declaration of Principles on Freedom of Expression (2019), Principle 11.3.
[74] ECtHR, *Dink v. Turkey* (App. nos. 2668/07 & others), 14 September 2010, §137.
[75] HRC, General Comment No. 34 (2011), §14. See also, HRC, *Concluding Observations, Kuwait* (2011) UN Doc CCPR/C/KWT/CO/2, §25 ('The State party should also protect media pluralism'); HRC, *Concluding Observations, Lebanon* (1997) UN Doc. CCPR/C/79/Add.7, §24 (noting with concern that Lebanon's media laws regarding licensing of television and radio stations 'do not appear to be consistent with the guarantees enshrined in article 19 of the Covenant ... The licensing process has had the effect of restricting media pluralism and freedom of expression').
[76] HRC, General Comment No. 34 (2011), §§39, 40, 44.
[77] Ibid., §40. See, e.g., the European Media Freedom Act, which was adopted by the European Commission in September 2022 to protect media pluralism and independence in the European Commission, 'European Media Freedom Act: Commission proposes rules to protect media pluralism and independence in the EU' (16 September 2022).
[78] HRC, General Comment No. 34 (2011), §44.
[79] IACtHR, *Compulsory Membership in an Association Prescribed by Law for the Practice of Journalism*, Advisory Opinion OC-5/85 (Series A, no. 5), 13 November 1985, §46; ACmHPR, *Scanlen & Holderness v. Zimbabwe* (Comm. no. 297/2005), 3 April 2009, §97.
[80] ACmHPR, Declaration of Principles on Freedom of Expression and Access to Information in Africa (2019), §12(2).

of a university degree for the practice of journalism constitute unlawful restrictions of freedom of expression. Journalistic activities must be guided by ethical conduct, which should in no case be imposed by the State'.[81]

Although licensing regimes are not per se in conflict with international law,[82] a number of guiding principles have been developed by international and regional bodies to limit their use against the media.[83] The criteria for broadcast licensing applications and fees should be 'reasonable and objective, clear, transparent, non-discriminatory and otherwise in compliance' with the ICCPR.[84] And, according to the Human Rights Committee, licensing regimes should be overseen by an independent media or licensing authority independent of the executive.[85] Finally, government funding, subsidies and advertising should not be used in a way which impedes freedom of expression or acts as a mechanism to punish dissent and criticism.[86]

1.1.2.3. Protection of sources The duty of states to protect a free press in international law extends to protection for their sources.[87] This has been recognized by the United Nations as an incident of the right to 'a free, uncensored and unhindered press or other media'.[88] The UN General Assembly and Human Rights Council have, for instance, both called on states to accord to journalists 'their rights to freedom of expression ... including ... to protect the confidentiality of their sources'.[89]

Similarly, the European Court considers the protection of journalistic sources to be 'one of the basic conditions for press freedom' and that the disclosure of a source 'cannot be compatible with Article 10 ... of the Convention unless it is justified by an overriding requirement in the public interest'[90] following 'review by a judge or other

---

[81] IACmHR, Declaration of Principles on Freedom of Expression, §6.
[82] ECHR Art. 10(1) expressly provides that that article 'shall not prevent States from requiring the licensing of broadcasting, television or cinema enterprises'.
[83] HRC, General Comment No. 34 (2011), §39. See also HRC, *Mavlonov and Sa'Di v. Uzbekistan* (Comm. no. 1334/2004), 19 March 2009, §8.3; Office of the Special Rapporteur for Freedom of Expression IACmHR, *Freedom of Expression Standards for Free and Inclusive Broadcasting* (2010) OEA Ser.L/V/II CIDH/RELE/INF. 3/09.
[84] HRC, General Comment No. 34 (2011), §39.
[85] Ibid.; HRC, *Concluding Observations, Kyrgyzstan* (2000) UN Doc. CCPR/CO/69/KGZ, §21. See also ECtHR, *Eood v. Bulgaria* (App. no. 14134/02), 11 October 2007, §§45–46; ACmHPR Declaration of Principles on Freedom of Expression in Africa (2019), Principle 14(3).
[86] HRC, *Concluding Observations, Ukraine* (2001) UN Doc. CCPR/CO/73/UKR, §22; *Concluding Observations, Lesotho* (1999) UN Doc. CCPR/C/79/Add. 106, §22. See also Declaration on the Principles of Freedom of Expression in Africa (2019), Principle 24; IACmHR, Principles on the Regulation of Government Advertising and Freedom of Expression (2012) OEA/Ser.L/V/II.CIDH/RELE/INF.6/12, §§10–11.
[87] HRC, General Comment No. 34 (2011), §45. See also HRC, *Concluding Observations, Kuwait* (2000) UN Doc. CCPR/CO/69/KWT, §20. UN Special Rapporteur, *Report on the promotion and protection of the right to freedom of opinion and expression* (2015) UN Doc. A/70/361, §15.
[88] HRC, General Comment No. 34 (2011), §13. The UN Special Rapporteur on the promotion and protection of freedom of opinion and expression has recognized that the principles regarding source confidentiality are also derived from the corollary right to seek, receive and impart information in article 19 of the ICCPR: UN Special Rapporteur, *Report on the promotion and protection of the right to freedom of opinion and expression* (2015) UN Doc. A/70/361, §§14–15.
[89] UNGA Resolution 'The safety of journalists and the issue of impunity' (13 November 2017) A/C.3/72/L.35/Rev.1, §14; UN Human Rights Council, Resolution 33 'The safety of journalists' (26 September 2016) A/HRC/33/L.6, §§12–13.
[90] ECtHR (GC), *Goodwin v. United Kingdom* (App. no. 17488/90), 27 March 1996, §39.

independent and impartial decision-making body'.[91] The Council of the European Union and European Parliament have also encouraged states to protect the right of journalists not to disclose their sources or materials.[92]

To much the same effect, the Declaration of Principles on Freedom of Expression in Africa provides that journalists 'and other media practitioners' should not be required to reveal confidential sources of information 'except where disclosure has been ordered by a court after a full and fair public hearing', and where (a) the identity of the source is necessary 'for the investigation or prosecution of a serious crime or the defence of a person accused of a criminal offence'; (b) information leading to the same result cannot be obtained elsewhere and (c) the 'public interest in disclosure outweighs the harm to freedom of expression'.[93] The East African Court of Justice has also adopted the European Court's reasoning when striking down a Burundian law seeking to force journalists to reveal their sources of information relating to 'state security, public order, defence secrets'.[94] In the Americas, the right to protection of sources is also explicitly recognized as extending beyond journalists and those working as 'media practitioners' to 'every social communicator', who has 'the right to keep his/her source of information, notes, personal and professional archives confidential'.[95]

1.2. Drafting history
1.2.1. International treaties

International human rights treaties governing free expression were adopted in the aftermath of the Second World War, along with other key treaties related to genocide and war crimes adopted as the United Nations system was being established.[96] The first human rights instrument of this era was the 1948 Universal Declaration, adopted by the General Assembly a day after it adopted the Genocide Convention, while the Nuremberg trials of the Nazis were still ongoing.[97] Two years later, in 1950, the European Convention was adopted.[98] The next wave of treaties, providing 'flesh on the

---

[91] ECtHR (GC), *Sanoma Uitgevers B.V. v. Netherlands* (App. no. 38224/03) 14 September 2010, §§88–90. The Court also held that this independent body should be 'invested with the power to determine whether a requirement in the public interest overriding the principle of protection of journalistic sources exists': §90.

[92] European Parliament, Resolution 2017/2209(INI) on media pluralism and media freedom in the European Union, 3 May 2018, §§14, 28, 41; Council of the European Union, EU Human Rights Guidelines on Freedom of Expression Online and Offline, §31.

[93] ACmHPR Declaration of Principles on Freedom of Expression in Africa (2019), Principle 25.

[94] EACJ, *Burundi Journalists Union v. Attorney General of Burundi* (Ref no. 7/2013), 15 May 2015, §§107–108. This law also required journalists to reveal their sources relating to 'the moral and physical integrity of one or more persons'.

[95] IACmHR Declaration of Principles on Freedom of Expression, Principle 8. European soft law instruments that encourage the protection of journalist's sources also advocate for an expansive definition of journalism: see European Parliament, Resolution 2017/2209(INI) on media pluralism and media freedom in the European Union, 3 May 2018; Council of the European Union, EU Human Rights Guidelines on Freedom of Expression Online and Offline, §5; CoM Recommendation No. R (2000) 7 on the right of journalists not to disclose their sources of information, 8 March 2000, Definitions.

[96] C. Tomuschat, 'International Covenant on Civil and Political Rights' (UN AVIL Historic Archives), 1; W.A. Schabas, 'Convention for the Prevention and Punishment of the Crime of Genocide' (UN AVIL Historic Archives), 1; UN AVIL Historic Archives, 'Charter of the United Nations'.

[97] Genocide Convention; UNGA, Resolution 260 A (III), 9 December 1948; UDHR; UNGA, Resolution 217 A (III), 10 December 1948.

[98] ECHR (adopted on 4 November 1950), 213 United Nations Treaty Series 221.

bones' of specific rights in the Universal Declaration of Human Right, came almost two decades later, when the ICCPR, CERD and American Convention were adopted.[99] And finally, and another decade later, in 1981, the African Charter was agreed.[100]

For the most part, these treaties were drafted by state representatives and diplomats rather than by lawyers or experts in the 'new' field of human rights.[101] The ICCPR and CERD were drafted over the course of two decades, first by a small committee of drafters led by Eleanor Roosevelt as the chairperson of the Commission on Human Rights, with other state representatives contributing to the negotiations, until both texts were submitted to the UN General Assembly for adoption.[102] The European Convention was similarly drafted by representatives of the Council of Europe, then a grouping of Western European representatives;[103] the American Convention was drafted by representatives of almost all of the active members of the OAS, with human rights experts and other observers invited to attend;[104] and the African Charter was drafted by state representatives and jurists, with early drafting by Kéba M'Baye, a Senegalese jurist who was then President of the International Court of Justice.[105] The history of the drafting process for each of the key international provisions governing speech—articles 19 and 20 of the ICCPR and article 4 of CERD—helps to explain their focus and meaning.

1.2.1.1. ICCPR: Article 19 The Charter of the United Nations, adopted in 1945, defines one of the purposes of the UN as 'promoting and encouraging respect for human rights and for fundamental freedoms for all without distinction as to race, sex, language, or religion'.[106] However, the UN Charter did not 'impose any concrete human

---

[99] CERD (adopted 21 December 1965); ICCPR (adopted 16 December 1966); ACHR (adopted 22 November 1969).

[100] Adopted on 27 June 1981. Each of the dates in this paragraph reflects when these treaties were adopted and their terms were agreed in final form, which differs from the date at which each of these treaties was ratified by a sufficient number of states to enter into force. For example, the ICCPR entered into force on 23 March 1976, in accordance with article 49, after the 35th ratification was received.

[101] Cf. F. Viljoen, 'The African Charter on Human and Peoples' Rights: The *Travaux Préparatoires* in the Light of Subsequent Practice' (2004) 25(9–12) *Human Rights Law Journal* 313, 314–315 on the participation of notable jurists, including President M'baye of the ICJ; IACtHR *Basic Documents Pertaining to Human Rights in the Inter-American System*, OEA/Ser.L.V/II.82 doc.6 rev.1 at 13(1992) on the participation of the Inter-American Council of Jurists in the drafting of the American Convention.

[102] The ICCPR was initially drafted on the basis that an additional convention, the Convention on Freedom of Information, would be adopted, but debate on this draft Convention was postponed and ultimately abandoned. The drafters of the ICCPR considered whether, 'since a separate convention on freedom of expression was being drafted, the covenant on human rights should include an article on freedom of expression and information at all'. However, 'the consensus of opinion was that the covenant could not ignore freedom of information which the General Assembly, in resolution 59 (I), had declared to be "a fundamental human right" and the "touchstone of all the freedoms to which the United Nations is consecrated"': Draft International Covenants on Human Rights, prepared by the Secretary-General (1 July 1955) UN Doc. A/2929, 144–145. See also Tomuschat, 'International Covenant on Civil and Political Rights' (n 96), 1; T. McGonagle & Y. Donders (eds) *The United Nations and Freedom of Expression: Critical Perspectives* (CUP 2015), ch. 1, 11–15.

[103] An early draft of the Convention has been credited to three well-known jurists: Pierre-Henri Teitgen (France), Sir David Maxwell-Fyfe (United Kingdom) and Fernand Dehousse (Belgium). E. Bates, *The Evolution of the European Convention on Human Rights* (OUP 2010), 52.

[104] See W. Landry, 'The Ideals and Potential of the American Convention on Human Rights' (1975) 4 (3) *Human Rights* 395, 398.

[105] Viljoen (n 101) 314–315. However, deliberations by the OAU-mandated 'highly qualified experts' on Mr. M'Baye's draft 'culminated into the adoption of a vastly different proposal': 314.

[106] UN Charter Art. 1(3).

rights obligations on the UN member states'.[107] Nor did the Universal Declaration of Human Rights, proclaimed by the UN General Assembly in December 1948, have any 'legally binding force'.[108]

It was not until the ICCPR came into force in 1976 that the right to free speech became enshrined in an international treaty.[109] Articles 19(1) and (2) of the ICCPR set out the general right to freedom of expression in similar terms to the Universal Declaration of Human Rights.[110] The drafters recognized the importance of the right, describing it as 'the touchstone of all the freedoms to which the United Nations are dedicated'.[111] The United States also argued that few freedoms were 'in greater jeopardy in contemporary times than freedom of information', which they described as 'one of the first freedoms to be stamped out when undemocratic regimes seized power'.[112]

But freedom of expression is not an absolute right: from the outset, drafting negotiations were dominated by a discussion of possible restrictions to freedom of expression.[113] Two schools of thought on the issue of restrictions developed during negotiations, the first advocating a 'brief statement of general limitations' and the second a 'full catalogue of specific limitations', so as to avoid equivocal language.[114] Advocates for the first approach included the United States, United Kingdom and Canada, which argued that extensive limitations 'would weaken the article and run the risk of making it an instrument for the suppression of the very freedom the Committee was seeking to preserve'.[115] The second school of thought nonetheless ultimately prevailed, with the final draft focusing on a list of broad permissible purposes for any restriction of speech that was intended to be exhaustive.[116]

The amount of controversy surrounding the inclusion of each of the permissible restrictions varied.[117] Almost all of the early drafts of article 19 included restrictions on speech based on the need to protect reputation and to protect national security, topics on which there was limited debate.[118] Concerns were however raised as to 'vague and flexible' restrictions which related to 'the protection of public safety, health or morals', which the Yugoslavian delegate noted 'might give rise to differing interpretations'.[119]

---

[107] T. Buergenthal, 'The Evolving International Human Rights System' (2006) 100 *American Journal of International Law* 783, 786. The Charter does however include two broad human rights provisions: Arts 55 and 56.
[108] A. Martin, 'Human Rights and World Politics' (1951) 5 *Yearbook of World Affairs* 37, 40, cited in E. Bates, *The Evolution of the European Convention on Human Rights* (OUP 2010), 38.
[109] Although the 'right to freedom of opinion and expression' is guaranteed in article 5 of CERD, which was adopted and came into force before the ICCPR, it was only upon the adoption of the ICCPR that the right—and its exceptions—were fleshed out in an international treaty in detailed form.
[110] See M. O'Flaherty, 'Freedom of Expression: Article 19 of the International Covenant on Civil and Political Rights and the Human Rights Committee's General Comment No 34' (2012) 12(4) *Human Rights Law Review* 627, 633–634.
[111] (1948) UN Doc. E/CN.4/80, 9.
[112] (1950) UN Doc. E/CN.4/SR.160, §33.
[113] W.L. Timmermann, *Incitement in International Law* (Routledge 2016), 72.
[114] (1955) UN Doc. A/2929, 148. See also O'Flaherty (n 110) 634–635.
[115] (1961) UN Doc. A/C.3/SR.1074, 31.
[116] Timmermann (n 113), 72. See also Nowak (n 27) 562; HRC, General Comment No. 34 (2011), §22; (1961) UN Doc. A/C.3/SR.1072, §9.
[117] See, e.g., Timmermann (n 113), 72. See also Nowak (n 27) 562–564; (1950) UN Doc. E/CN.4/SR.161, §92.
[118] Timmermann (n 113), 72.
[119] (1950) UN Doc. E/CN.4/SR.161, §92.

Of the final list of permissible restrictions,[120] the 'public order' exception was the most controversial. The United Kingdom pushed to rephrase the restriction to 'the prevention of disorder or crime', consistently with article 10 of the European Convention of Human Rights as 'public order' was an overly broad limitation that could 'cloak many abuses' and serve as 'a loophole for arbitrary action by the Government'.[121] However, a number of states agreed that the concept of public order was wider than that. France, for instance, stressed that the United Kingdom's proposal would limit restrictions to the realm of criminal law and would not capture other conduct that 'nevertheless threatened public order and which might necessitate a restriction on freedom of information'.[122] This has led some experts to consider that the ICCPR formulation of this restriction is broader than the formulation 'prevention of disorder or crime' in the European Convention.[123] Although the United Kingdom's proposal was narrowly defeated, concerns about the inclusion of the 'public order' as a limitation remained, with delegates arguing that the term was overly vague and that '[t]here was nothing, for instance, to prevent South Africa from pursuing its policy of "apartheid" on the grounds of public order'.[124]

Many states also considered that incitement to discrimination, hatred and violence could have been listed as legitimate bases to penalize speech, but this was ultimately considered redundant given that it appeared to be expressly covered in article 20.[125] Similarly, certain states, in particular the Soviet Union, pushed for the inclusion of a limitation to 'war propaganda' in article 19, which ultimately was shifted to article 20(1).[126] The United Kingdom also proposed to add limitations that were included in the European Convention but this suggestion was rejected by other states.[127] For instance, the United States considered that a limitation on the basis of 'maintaining the authority and impartiality of the judiciary' was unclear,[128] and that a limitation based on 'preventing the disclosure of information received in confidence' was inappropriate as it 'would compel a government to undertake to prevent the publication of any information received by its officials in the course of their duties, whereas normally the public was entitled to such information, except when it might endanger national security'.[129]

A common thread apparent from the *travaux* for both articles 19 and 20 is the then-recent experience of Nazi Germany and the desire to prevent the dissemination of racist and totalitarian propaganda.[130] Even though the United States represented a strong voice against the more extensive limits to speech proposed by Soviet bloc nations, the US delegate also emphasized that 'the methodical defamation by which the

---

[120] ICCPR Art. 19(3), encompassing 'respect of the rights or reputations of others ... the protection of national security, public order ... public health or morals'.
[121] (1950) UN Doc. E/CN.4/SR.162, §30.
[122] (1950) UN Doc. E/CN.4/SR.166, §60.
[123] Nowak (n 27) 570. See also O'Flaherty (n 110) 627, 652. Cf. s. II.1.1.1. (Abuses by the State).
[124] (1961) A/C.3/SR.1073, §59.
[125] Clooney & Webb 'The Right to Insult in International Law' (n 57) 16.
[126] See, e.g., (1954) UN Doc. E/CN.3/SR.565, §31; (1954) UN Doc. E/CN.3/SR.571, §16 (Polish delegate).
[127] (1950) UN Doc. E/CN.4/SR.160, 27 April 1950, §39.
[128] Ibid.
[129] (1952) UN Doc. E/CN.4/SR.321, 8.
[130] UN Doc. E/C.3/SR.1074, §20.

Nazis had come to power had not been forgotten in her country, any more than it had in other parts of the world.[131]

1.2.1.2. ICCPR: Article 20 Article 20 is a rare provision within the ICCPR that establishes a positive obligation for states to prohibit speech.[132] Although it does not require criminalization, it mandates that speech 'shall be prohibited by law' if it constitutes 'propaganda for war' or 'advocacy of national, racial or religious hatred' that amounts to 'incitement to discrimination, hostility or violence'.[133] This *requirement* that certain speech should be penalized puts hate speech laws on a different footing to other types of speech such as defamatory speech, false speech and speech related to issues affecting national security.[134]

The earliest version of this provision was proposed by a Soviet representative in 1947 as part of the drafting of a 'general prohibition of discrimination', which provided that any 'advocacy of national, racial and religious hostility or of national exclusiveness, or hatred and contempt, as well as any action establishing a privilege or a discrimination ... constitute a crime and shall be punishable under the law of the State'.[135] Unlike the final version, this original wording did not require 'incitement' to violence or other harm, and mandated criminalization rather than prohibition.[136]

The Soviet Union pushed for the inclusion of this language on the basis that it was 'a powerful weapon ... to restrict the dissemination of Nazi-Fascist propaganda'.[137] A number of Eastern European, African and South American delegates—including Poland, Brazil, Cameroon, Chile and Mali—also supported broad formulations of what became article 20.[138] Among the nations that opposed or questioned the need for such a provision or sought to limit it were the United States, Japan, the United Kingdom, certain Western European nations, Saudi Arabia, and South American states such as Ecuador and Colombia.[139]

The United States considered article 19(3) a sufficient regulation of hateful speech and cautioned that 'any criticism of public or religious authorities might all too easily be described as incitement to hatred and consequently prohibited' and that 'it was difficult to draw a distinction between advocacy and incitement'.[140] Similarly, the United

---

[131] UN Doc. E/C.3/SR.1074, §20; (1954) UN Doc. A/C.3/SR.576, §31.
[132] Nowak (n 27) 580. Cf. HRC, *Rabbae v. Netherlands* (Comm. no. 2124/2011), 14 July 2016, Individual Opinion (concurring) of Committee members Sarah Cleveland and Mauro Politi, §3: 'the obligation to prohibit conduct by law is not unique under the Covenant. Other articles likewise obligate State parties to prohibit certain conduct, including article 8(1) (obligating States ... to prohibit slavery) ... and article 6(1) (requiring protection by law of the right to life). Article 20 is unique, however, in that it requires prohibition of conduct in an area that otherwise is highly protected freedom of expression'.
[133] ICCPR Art. 20.
[134] Cf. ch. 3 (Hate Speech), ch. 4 (False Speech), ch. 5 (Espionage and Official Secrets Laws), ch. 6 (Terrorism Laws).
[135] Timmermann (n 113) 109–110; (1947) UN Doc E/CN.4/Sub.2/21.
[136] Timmermann (n 113) 109–110; (1947) UN Doc E/CN.4/Sub.2/21.
[137] (1948) UN Doc. E/CN.4/AC.1/SR.28, 3.
[138] Timmermann (n 113), 115.
[139] (1961) UN Doc. A/C.3/SR.1080, §20; (1961) UN Doc. A/CN.4/SR.1083, §§14, 119–120; (1961) UN Doc. A/C.3/SR.1084, §§22–24; (1961) UN Doc. E/CN.4/SR.1079, §§21–22.
[140] (1950) UN Doc. E/CN.4/SR.174, §§25–26.

Kingdom objected to vague terms such as 'hatred' that are difficult to define as a penal offence and bore too great a risk of abuse.[141] The UK delegate noted that the expression 'incitement to hatred' in particular 'could be used by unscrupulous Governments to suppress the very freedoms and rights which the draft Covenant set out to preserve'.[142] As to 'hostility', the US delegate noted that '[w]hile most members would condemn the advocacy of hostility of any kind, such a prohibition would entail acceptance of the principle of totalitarian control over all forms of expression'.[143] Japan was also concerned with definitional difficulties, querying how words like 'hatred', 'incitement' and 'hostility' could be 'objectively defined'.[144] The Cambodian delegate, in contrast, observed that 'he did not think it could be said that the word "hatred" was too vague, for in that case the same criticism could be applied to such words as "freedom", "justice" or "equality"'.[145]

Delegates also disagreed about whether the provision should reference discrimination. Some argued that such an inclusion would be superfluous, 'since any advocacy of national, racial or religious hostility generally involved discriminatory measures'.[146] Others, such as Mali, argued that '[t]he evils of discrimination were well established in history', pointing to 'the racist frenzy that led to "apartheid"—a crime against humanity as great as the crimes of the Hitlerite fascists'.[147] There was limited discussion of the rationale for choosing 'national, racial or religious' grounds to hate as the basis for the provision, with delegates particularly focused on the 'racial' element in light of the context of the drafting process.[148] At an early juncture, the Soviet representative stressed the need for an express provision 'for preventing propaganda by nazis or fascists or propaganda based on racial or religious discrimination'.[149] Eastern European states argued that '[t]he sufferings caused by the racial theories of Nazi criminals were well known, and the world had already paid too dearly for the so-called freedom of expression'.[150] A Brazilian proposal to include 'class prejudice' was rejected by other states, with Romania warning that this language was not found in the UN Charter or Declaration of Human Rights.[151]

A central point of disagreement was whether article 20 should be restricted to incitement to violence. Some delegates argued that this restriction 'instead of going to the root of the evil, merely tackled its consequences', reasoning that there are 'some forms of propaganda which, while in appearance unaggressive' are 'so insidious as to constitute a very serious danger in the long run'.[152] These arguments were motivated by

---

[141] Ibid., §63; (1961) UN Doc. A/C.3/SR/.1078, §§6, 17.
[142] (1961) UN Doc. A/C.3/SR.1078, §17.
[143] (1954) UN Doc A/C.3/SR.568, §15.
[144] (1961) UN Doc. A/C.3/SR.1079, §22.
[145] (1961) UN Doc. A/C.3/SR.1081, §64.
[146] Ibid., §18 (Congo). See also (1961) UN Doc. A/C.3/SR.1083, §8 (France).
[147] (1961) UN Doc. A/C.3/SR.1080, §5, see also §§11–12 (Czechoslovakia).
[148] (1961) UN Doc. A/C.3/SR.1080, §5, see also §§11–12 (Czechoslovakia); (1948) UN Doc. E/CN.4/AC.1/SR.26, 5–6.
[149] (1948) UN Doc. E/CN.4/AC.1/SR.26, 5–6.
[150] (1954) UN Doc. A/C.3/SR.576, §31.
[151] (1961) UN Doc. A/C.3/SR.1074, §14.
[152] (1953) UN Doc E/CN.4/SR.377, 4–5, cited in Timmermann (n 113) 113.

a belief that a prohibition of incitement to violence alone was not sufficient to prevent the recurrence of Nazi-style crimes.[153] Others, such as Japan, were concerned about encroaching on freedom of expression, arguing that since '[a]dvocacy of national, racial or religious hostility did not always lead to violence', 'should it nevertheless be forbidden? And would such a ban not be very detrimental to freedom of expression?'.[154] And the Philippines considered the concept of 'incitement to hatred' to be 'subjective by nature and difficult to define', whereas the concept of 'hatred inciting to violence' was 'a legally valid one'.[155] The nations in support of prohibiting only incitement to violence stressed that this did not mean 'there must be violence before the prohibition could be enforced'; it could be propaganda 'likely to lead to violence' or 'of a nature to incite violence'.[156] But not all Western nations supported this position, the Netherlands, for instance, arguing that confining the provision to inciting violence 'limited unduly the article's scope'.[157]

There was also considerable debate on whether and how war 'propaganda' should be sanctioned, given the recent experience of the Nazi propaganda machine and the looming threat of a Cold War.[158] The Israeli delegate argued that in a 'time of unprecedented technical capacity for propaganda, such sufferings as had recently befallen the Jews might be experienced by other groups unless advocacy of such hostility was nipped in the bud'.[159] Bulgaria stressed that 'it was the Committee's duty categorically to prohibit any war propaganda as a contribution to saving the world from thermo-nuclear catastrophe'.[160] In contrast, the Scandinavian countries were concerned that these provisions 'lent themselves to conflicting interpretations and contradictory applications—for what was condemned in one country as war propaganda might be welcomed in another as laudable activity of a positive policy'.[161] Similarly the Australian delegate expressed concern that the concept of propaganda for war 'was not clearly related to any right of the individual, was not defined and opened the way to stringent limitations on freedom of speech'.[162]

The text was ultimately amended to move the reference to 'propaganda for war' into a separate paragraph, which the Yugoslavian delegate explained 'brought it to the foreground and, at the same time, met the objections of those delegations which had regarded the linking of war propaganda with incitement to violence as implying the possibility of war propaganda which did not incite to violence'.[163] The requirement

---

[153] Timmermann (n 113) 142.
[154] (1961) UN Doc. A/C.3/SR.1079, §22.
[155] (1961) UN Doc. A/C.3/SR.1081, §21.
[156] (1961) UN Doc. A/C.3/SR.1080, §20; (1961) UN Doc. A/C.3/SR.1081, §21.
[157] (1961) UN Doc. A/C.3/SR.1081, §16.
[158] (1948) UN Doc. E/CN.4/AC.1/SR.28, 3; (1961) UN Doc. A/C.3.SR.1083, 116–117; Timmermann (n 113) 110–113.
[159] (1961) UN Doc. A/C.3/SR.1080, §8.
[160] (1961) UN Doc. A/C.3/SR.1074, §6.
[161] (1961) UN Doc. A/C.3/SR.1084, §5.
[162] Ibid., §9. Brazil's delegate felt that the term 'propaganda' was not difficult to define: 'What it in fact meant was the repeated and insistent expression of an opinion for the purpose of creating a climate of hatred and lack of understanding between the peoples of two or more countries, in order to bring them eventually to armed conflict': (1961) UN Doc. A/C.3/SR.1079, §2.
[163] (1961) UN Doc. A/C.3/SR.1082, §10.

to criminalize speech was also removed from article 20 and the provision was shifted so that it immediately followed article 19 in order to emphasize the link between the two.[164] The contentious nature of the provision is reflected in the voting on its adoption, with 52 votes in favour, 19 votes against and 12 abstentions.[165]

1.2.1.3. CERD: Article 4 The Convention on the Elimination of Racial Discrimination was adopted in 1965, a year before the ICCPR, although both treaties took years to come into force.[166] The key provision relating to speech is article 4, which provides that states '[s]hall declare an offence punishable by law all dissemination of ideas based on racial superiority or hatred, incitement to racial discrimination, as well as all acts of violence or incitement to such acts against any race or group of persons of another colour or ethnic origin'.[167] It was the subject of lengthy drafting negotiations and remains a contentious provision to this day.[168]

The drafting history of article 4 reveals three key debates.[169] First, and consistently with the drafting history of article 20 of the ICCPR, states disagreed about whether the provision should be limited to incitement to violence or also extend to incitement to other harms.[170] The initial proposal for article 4 recommended by the Commission on Human Rights provided that 'all incitement to racial discrimination *resulting in acts of violence*' should be punishable.[171] This narrow formulation was supported overwhelmingly by Western democratic nations, with the United Kingdom arguing, for example, that the inclusion of the words 'resulting in acts of violence' were indispensable, as '[s]peech should be free, but incitement to violence should be repressed'.[172] The UK delegate claimed that amendments which broadened the scope of the provision risked the Convention becoming 'just a list of exhortations—a document demanding legislation which few could put into effect', with the result that 'all the Committee's efforts would have been wasted'.[173]

However, the Soviet Union, Eastern European states and a broad coalition of developing, post-colonial and other nations including Israel, Senegal and Uruguay, argued for a more expansive provision, on the basis that incitement to acts of violence 'in most countries were already punishable by penal law regardless of their motivation' and that appeals to acts of racial discrimination 'should also be held punishable in order to ... prevent such acts from gaining strength to create circumstances which would

---

[164] (1961) UN Doc. A/C.3/SR.1072, §19.
[165] (1961) UN Doc. A/C.3/SR.1083, 120.
[166] CERD came into force in 4 January 1969 and the ICCPR entered into force in 23 March 1976.
[167] CERD Art. 4 (a).
[168] See, e.g., Clooney & Webb, 'The Right to Insult in International Law' (n 57) 53.
[169] Another debate related to whether the treaty should prohibit racist organizations, as opposed to their activities. See, e.g., E/CN.4/SR.792, 10. P. Thornberry, *The International Convention on the Elimination of All Forms of Racial Discrimination: A Commentary* (OUP 2016), 274.
[170] (1965) UN Doc. A/C.3/SR.1315, §§2, 8, 20.
[171] Draft International Convention on the Elimination of All Forms of Racial Discrimination, UN Doc. A/5921, 4 (emphasis added).
[172] (1965) UN Doc. A/C.3/SR.1315, §2 (United Kingdom).
[173] Ibid., §3 (United Kingdom).

result in acts against any given race'.[174] The Yugoslavian delegate similarly expressed support for the inclusion of a prohibition on the 'dissemination of ideas' on the basis that it would require states 'to take action against incitement to racial discrimination without waiting until it resulted, as it inevitably must, in acts of violence'.[175]

The second key debate on the scope of article 4 of CERD centred on the question of appropriate penalties for the speech it covered. Delegates from states including Brazil, the Soviet Union, Czechoslovakia, Burundi, Mali and Chile insisted that speech sanctioned by article 4 must be 'punishable under criminal law' and that organizations that engaged in such activities be prohibited.[176] In contrast, nations including the United States, Denmark, the United Kingdom, Australia, Saudi Arabia and Japan sought to limit article 4 to a *condemnation* of racist speech and organizations, rather than the imposition of criminal penalties.[177] The Danish delegate argued that the proposed wording on criminal penalties was 'so sweeping a statement that it clearly imperilled' the principles of freedom of association and expression.[178] The UK delegate argued that the proposal 'went so far that [it] might easily be interpreted as an endorsement of the persecution of unpopular minority groups'.[179] Australia urged that '[r]acial propaganda was best combated by open discussion, which was liable to expose the intellectual bankruptcy of the advocates of discrimination'.[180] But the Israeli delegate countered that while in 'some cases legislation might infringe rights and freedoms', that 'was not ... a new issue either nationally or internationally' and that '[r]estrictions on freedom had been accepted at both levels'.[181] The nations in favour of mandatory criminal penalties ultimately prevailed, though the reference to condemnation of propaganda was shifted to the introductory section of the provision.[182]

The third main debate that took place during the drafting process was about the scope of exceptions. The Nordic countries submitted that in enacting such new offences, states must have 'due regard' to 'other equally fundamental human rights' as

---

[174] (1964) UN Doc. E/CN.4/874, §162.See also (1965) UN Doc. A/C.3/SR.1318, §§23 (Uruguay), 48 (Israel); see further §31 (Senegal), critiquing an earlier draft of article 4 on the basis that 'it took too timid an approach on the very important question of the dissemination of racist ideas'.

[175] (1965) UN Doc A/C.3/SR.1315, §20; see also §4 (recording similar views expressed by Czechoslovakia).

[176] (1963) UN Doc. A/5603, §§118–119 on Brazil's proposal, co-sponsored by the USSR, Yugoslavia, Burundi, Ceylon, Chile, Mali and Tanganyika, which provided that 'all propaganda based on ideas or theories of the superiority of one race or group of persons of one colour or ethnic origin with a view to justifying or promoting racial discrimination in any form, and all incitement of hatred and violence against any race or group of persons of another colour or ethnic origin, should be punishable under criminal law. All organizations engaged in such activities should be prohibited and disbanded'. At the time, this was contained in article 9 of the Draft Declaration on the Elimination of All Forms of Racial Discrimination, the basis for article 4 of ICERD.

[177] (1963) UN Doc. A/5603, §§123, 124, 128; (1963) UN Doc. A/C.3/SR.1227, §§3, 5, 17, 21, 30.

[178] (1963) UN Doc. A/C.3/SR.1227, §3 (Denmark).

[179] Ibid., §5 (United Kingdom).

[180] Ibid.; §17; see also §21 (Saudi Arabia: 'It was difficult to draw the line between propaganda and sincere expression of opinion, and the adoption of the amendments might lead to interference with such activities as ethnological research, or comparative studies of culture'); §30 (Japan: 'endorsed the principle that persons disseminating propaganda or forming organizations of the kind referred to in article 9 should not be punished for that reason alone, however detestable their ideas might be to the majority').

[181] Ibid., §§10–15 (Israel) (citing the limitations set out in article 29(2) of the Universal Declaration, articles 19 and 20 of the ICCPR and the European Convention as well as in a number of penal laws of Western European nations). CERD Arts 4, 4(a), 4(b).

[182] CERD Arts 4, 4(a), 4(b).

well as article 5 of CERD, which sets out certain human rights including the right to freedom of expression.[183] This amendment was intended to act as a compromise between states with competing views, although doubts persisted as to the appropriateness of any criminalization of the 'dissemination of ideas'.[184] States also held divergent views on the meaning of the 'due regard' clause, with certain delegations considering the clause an appropriate balance between freedom of expression and the creation of a new criminal offence, while the United States interpreted its inclusion to mean that article 4 'did not impose on a State party the obligation to take any action impairing the right to freedom of speech or freedom of association'.[185] Article 4 was ultimately adopted by 88 votes to none, with five abstentions.[186]

1.2.2. Regional treaties

1.2.2.1. European Convention Like the ICCPR, the European Convention's drafting process began in the wake of World War II, when the crimes of Nazi Germany—propelled by a powerful propaganda regime—had shown the importance of both enshrining human rights and stemming the spread of totalitarian ideas.[187] At the time of the Convention's drafting, the 'iron curtain' was also descending, with communist regimes coming to power across eastern Europe.[188] As a result, 'ideas for a European Convention were dominated by the need to prevent the rise of another Hitler and the fear that Europe was in danger of being overrun by communists'.[189] The Convention was viewed by some as a mechanism to unite Europe against these threats, and coincided with the establishment of the Council of Europe, at that time a group of 10 Western European states aiming to 'achieve a greater unity between its members' and safeguard the 'ideals and principles which are their common heritage'.[190]

At the time the European Convention was drafted, global consensus on an international human rights covenant was a distant prospect.[191] The drafters recognized this in the Convention's preamble, describing member states as 'resolved ... to take the first steps for the collective enforcement of certain of the rights stated in the Universal

---

[183] (1965) UN Doc A/C.3/SR.1315, §18 (known as the 'five-Power Amendment' ((1965) UN Doc. A/C.3/L.1245), proposed by Denmark, Finland, Iceland, Norway and Sweden). Article 5 of the Convention provides that states must guarantee to everyone, without distinction, the enjoyment of a number of rights including the right to freedom of opinion and expression. See also (1965) UN Doc A/C.3/SR.1318, 150; (1965) UN Doc. A/C.3/L.1250: Nigeria later on proposed an amendment to include the phrase 'with due regard *to the principles embodied in the Universal Declaration*' to article 4.

[184] (1965) UN Doc A/C.3/SR.1315, §18 (Finland) ('Article IV was designed to safeguard certain human rights and fundamental freedoms, but that objective should not be achieved at the expense of other equally fundamental rights. Accordingly, the five-Power amendment would introduce a reference to the rights set forth in article V... in order to make the amendment more acceptable to delegations known to be favourably disposed towards it').

[185] (1965) UN Doc. A.C.3/SR.1318, §§52, 59; Thornberry (n 169) 277.

[186] The 'due regard' clause was adopted by 76 votes to 1 with 14 abstentions; the words 'all dissemination of ideas based on racial superiority or hatred' in paragraph (a) were adopted by 57 votes to none, with 35 abstentions: (1965) UN Doc. A.C.3/SR.1318, §46.

[187] Bates (n 108), 44–45, 53.

[188] Ibid., 46.

[189] Ibid., 44.

[190] Chapter I of the Statute, Art. 1(a); the Council of Europe was set up by 10 member states (Belgium, Denmark, France, Ireland, Italy, Luxembourg, Netherlands, Norway, Sweden, United Kingdom); see COE, 'Map & Members'.

[191] See, e.g., Buergenthal (n 107) 783, 792.

Declaration'.[192] So the Convention was adopted relatively quickly, within two years of the Universal Declaration and 16 years before the ICCPR text was finally concluded.[193]

In this context, initial drafts of the Convention sought urgently to enshrine agreed fundamental rights without defining such rights in detail, on the basis that a supplementary agreement could follow if further clarity was required.[194] An early draft provided a pithy list of rights including 'freedom of opinion and expression, in accordance with article 19 of the United Nations Declaration'.[195] This list was accompanied by a general limitation clause similar to article 29 of the Universal Declaration, which provided that limitations could only be imposed when established by law, 'with the sole object of ensuring the recognition and respect for the rights and freedoms of others, or with the purpose of satisfying the just requirements of public morality, order and security in a democratic society'.[196]

But some states like the United Kingdom pushed for more detailed definitions of rights with a view to reducing the power that would be given to a European Court.[197] A split formed between those nations that wanted to precisely define rights, and those that preferred a broader formulation and were more receptive to the establishment of a regional Court.[198]

During drafting negotiations, the UK representative submitted an amendment to article 10 similar to the text it had proposed at that time in the drafting process for the ICCPR, including a set of permissible restrictions modelled on article 29(2) of the Universal Declaration.[199] This text was ultimately adopted with minimal changes that included the addition of 'territorial integrity' as a legitimate aim for speech restrictions suggested by Turkey, and adding 'in a democratic society' after 'necessary'.[200] The reference to 'a democratic society' was originally added to the phrase 'for the protection of health or morals', but was ultimately shifted by the Drafting Committee to apply more generally to all permissible restrictions on speech.[201]

1.2.2.2. American Convention The American Convention was adopted after the ICCPR and the European Convention. It is modelled on their provisions but adapted

---

[192] Preamble to European Convention; see Bates (n 108) 40.
[193] The European Convention was adopted on 4 November 1950. The ICCPR was adopted on 16 December 1966.
[194] Bates (n 108) 62.
[195] Ibid., 64.
[196] Ibid., 65.
[197] Ibid., 83–84, 88.
[198] Ibid., 90. Belgium and Luxembourg were in favour of a broader enumeration of rights if a Court was created, but against this if one was not.
[199] ECmHR, Preparatory Work on article 10 of the European Convention on Human Rights, DH (56) 15, §12; W. Schabas, *The European Convention on Human Rights: A Commentary* (OUP 2021), 445.
[200] The Turkish proposal was made 'in order to make provision for the need of States to be able to defend themselves against all activities which might lead to the disintegration of the nation, although the drafters of the Convention emphasized that this restriction was only accepted 'on the clear understanding that it did not permit a restriction on the rights of national minorities to advocate their views by democratic means': ECmHR, Preparatory Work on article 10 of the European Convention on Human Rights, DH (56) 15, §14–19. The third sentence of article 10(1) regarding licensing was added at a late stage in the drafting process.
[201] ECmHR, Preparatory Work on article 10 of the European Convention on Human Rights, DH (56) 15, §16.

to the unique experiences of the Americas.[202] Although a binding Inter-American treaty was suggested as early as 1945, it was not until 1969 that a convention enshrining human rights and establishing an Inter-American Court was adopted, and it entered into force almost a decade later.[203] The permissible restrictions to the right to free expression are set out in article 13 of the Convention in very similar terms to the ICCPR and European Convention, though in some key ways the Inter-American Convention is more protective of speech.[204]

Drafters of the American Convention also included a separate and distinct provision, article 14, which provides a 'right of reply' to defamed persons.[205] This was suggested by countries including Colombia, Argentina and Honduras but led to objections. The United States argued that it was unduly vague, liable to abuse and a burden on media outlets, and the Dominican Republic deemed the article unnecessary and impracticable.[206] Similarly, Chile considered the right of a 'second order' without widespread international support.[207] Nevertheless it was ultimately adopted and incorporated into the treaty.

Unlike other regional treaties, but consistently with article 20 of the ICCPR, article 13(5) of the American Convention mandates restrictions to certain hateful speech and propaganda.[208] The United States had advocated against mandatory restrictions to 'propaganda for war', arguing that such a restriction covered 'a series of classical texts, such as Homer's Iliad, lots of plays by Shakespeare and [works by] Thomas Aquinas'.[209] But this language remained in the final text.[210] The United States was however successful in limiting the provision.[211] Initial drafts were similar to article 20 of the ICCPR, which requires penalties for speech that incites 'discrimination' or 'hostility' as well as violence.[212] But this was significantly narrowed in the final version of article 13 to speech that incites 'lawless violence or to any other similar action', with the US delegate noting that this amendment was very important to his delegation to ensure consistency

---

[202] See, e.g., J. Pasqualucci, 'The Inter-American Human Rights System: Establishing Precedents and Procedure in Human Rights Law' (1994–1995) 26(2) *Inter-American Law Review* 304.
[203] OAS, Basic documents pertaining to human rights in the Inter-American System.
[204] See s. II.1.1. (Treaty language).
[205] IACtHR, *Enforceability of the Right to Reply or Correction (Arts. 14(1), 1(1) and 2 of the American Convention on Human Rights)*, Advisory Opinion OC-7/86 (Series A, no. 7), 29 August 1986, §33. See also Pasqualucci (n 202) 352–353.
[206] OAS, Documents of the 1969 Inter-American Conference on Human Rights: 'Observation Presented by the Government of Dominican Republic to the Draft Convention on Human Rights' (1969) Doc. 9, 61; OAS, Documents of the 1969 Inter-American Conference on Human Rights: 'Minutes of the Ninth Session of Commission 1' (1969) Doc. 50, 220.
[207] OAS, Documents of the 1969 Inter-American Conference on Human Rights: 'Observations by the Government of Chile to the Draft Convention on Human Rights' (1969) Doc. 7, 40.
[208] ACHR Art. 13(5) prohibits 'any propaganda for war and advocacy of national, racial, or religious hatred that constitutes incitements to lawless violence or to any other similar action'.
[209] OAS, Documents of the 1969 Inter-American Conference on Human Rights: 'Minutes of the 8th meeting of the First Committee (Summary Version)' (1969) Doc. 48, 215.
[210] ACHR Art. 13(5).
[211] OAS, Documents of the 1969 Inter-American Conference on Human Rights: 'Observation Presented by the US Delegate to the Draft Convention on Human Rights' (1969) Doc. 86, 444.
[212] OAS, Documents of the 1969 Inter-American Conference on Human Rights: 'Draft Articles 1 to 33 of the Inter-American Convention on the Protection of Human Rights', First Committee (1969) Doc. 65, 314.

with the constitutional guarantee to free speech enshrined within the First Amendment to the US Constitution.[213]

1.2.2.3. African Charter

The Charter establishing the Organization of African Unity (OAU)—adopted in 1963—did not include any explicit human rights obligations.[214] It was not until 1979 that an expert committee was convened by the OAU to draft a human rights instrument.[215] The Committee prepared an initial draft of the Charter based on a working document by Kéba M'Baye, then President of the ICJ, which drew from the provisions of the International Covenant on Economic, Social and Cultural Rights and American Convention.[216] It was agreed at a conference in Banjul, The Gambia, adopted by the OAU assembly in 1981 and came into force in 1986.[217]

Although the African Charter 'substantially followed the lead of other international instruments in respect of its provisions protecting civil and political rights', it has a number of unique characteristics.[218] It includes civil and political rights as well as economic, social and cultural rights, references 'people's rights' and incorporates obligations on individuals as well as states.[219] It also adopts a more high-level approach to drafting than equivalent treaties when it comes to both the definition of the rights and exceptions to them.[220] There is however limited information about the rationale for this approach in the drafting history of the Charter.[221]

It is reported that one of the earliest working versions of the Charter, known as the M'Baye draft, did not include an express right to freedom of expression.[222] But by the time the next key draft—known as the Dakar draft—was finalized, article 9 enshrined the right to 'express and disseminate' opinions 'within the law', subject to 'the respect of others' honour and reputation' as well as the 'rights of others', 'collective security' and 'morals and common interest'.[223]

---

[213] OAS, Documents of the 1969 Inter-American Conference on Human Rights: 'Observation Presented by the US Delegate to the Draft Convention on Human Rights' (1969) Doc. 86, 444.

[214] The OAU Charter did, however, lay foundations for the future protection of human rights in Africa, for example by providing that one of its purposes was to promote international cooperation having 'due regard' to the UN Charter and UDHR and by promoting self-determination of peoples under colonial domination: M. Ssenyonjo (ed), *The African Regional Human Rights System: 30 years after the African Charter on Human and Peoples' Rights* (Martinus Nijhoff Publishers 2012), 6.

[215] Viljoen (n 101) 313–314.

[216] Ibid.

[217] This conference took place after an earlier meeting was scheduled that did not occur for want of quorum. 'According to some, this was due to deliberate attempts to derail the process by some states that were not prepared to openly oppose the creation of a Charter: Viljoen (n 101) 313–315; ACmHPR, History: Introduction. See also Murray (n 43) 2–3.

[218] O. Amao, 'Chapter 2: Civil and Political Rights in Africa', in M. Ssenyonjo (ed), *The African Regional Human Rights System: 30 Years after the African Charter on Human and Peoples' Rights* (Martinus Nijhoff Publishers 2012), 29.

[219] Murray (n 43) 8.

[220] See s. II.1.1.1. (Abuses by the state) regarding African Charter language. This was described during the drafting process as providing a 'relatively simple form' of rights 'so as to enable the future users of the legal instrument to apply and interpret them with some flexibility': see CAB/LEG/67/Draft Rapt. Rpt (II) Rev.4, §13.

[221] See Murray (n 43) 3. See also Viljoen (n 101) 313, 325.

[222] See draft for the Meeting of Experts in Dakar, Senegal from 28 November to 8 December 1979, by Kéba Mbaye, CAB/LEG/67/1.

[223] Preliminary draft of the African Charter prepared during the Dakar Meeting of Experts at the end of 1979, CAB/LEG/67/3/Rev. 1.

It is not clear why the limitations included in article 9 of the Dakar draft were ultimately stripped away when the text was finalized.[224] But the understanding of the phrase 'within the law' evolved from the initial M'Baye draft, which contemplated limits to rights only on the basis of national law.[225] For example, provisions of the M'Baye draft limited rights by reference to conditions 'established beforehand by the constitution of the State Party concerned or by a law established pursuant thereto', but any explicit reference to the national system was later removed, 'enabl[ing] the African Commission to interpret the [word] "law" more broadly than merely [by reference to] "national legislation"'.[226]

1.3. Reservations

International human rights treaties such as the ICCPR and CERD have been widely ratified.[227] However, a considerable number of states have entered reservations to the articles on freedom of expression in these treaties.[228] The scope and status of reservations is important for understanding not only whether the right, or part of it, has reached customary status but also to ascertain whether and to what extent a 'reserving state' has modified its obligations under the treaty as a matter of international law.[229]

A reservation must be compatible with the object and purpose of a treaty, meaning that it cannot affect 'an essential element of the treaty that is necessary to its general tenor, in such a way that the reservation impairs the raison d'être of the treaty'.[230] There have been no objections by states or determinations by courts providing that reservations relating to freedom of expression are incompatible with the treaty on this basis, with one exception: Pakistan's initial reservation to article 19 of the ICCPR, which garnered 23 objections.[231] Pakistan had declared that article 19 and other provisions of the treaty 'shall be applied to the extent they are not repugnant to the Provisions of the Constitution of Pakistan and the Sharia laws'.[232] A number of states such as Canada objected to the 'general, indeterminate scope' of Pakistan's reservation, arguing that the reservation 'makes it impossible to identify the modifications to obligations under the Covenant that each reservation purports to introduce'.[233] The United States objected in

---

[224] See Rapporteur's Report, CAB/LEG/67/Draft Rapt. Rpt (II) Rev.4, §43 (suggesting that the words 'subject to the respect of others' honour and reputation' were deleted during the Ministerial Meeting in Banjul, The Gambia).
[225] See s. II.1.1. (Treaty language) regarding the African Charter; see also draft for the Meeting of Experts in Dakar, Senegal from 28 November to 8 December 1979, by Kéba Mbaye, CAB/LEG/67/1, Arts 20(2), 29; Viljoen (n 101) 322.
[226] Viljoen (n 101) 322.
[227] CERD has been ratified by 182 states, while the ICCPR has been ratified by 173 states: See UNTC, Status of Treaties, IV.2 and IV.4.
[228] For a list of declarations and reservations to CERD and ICCPR made upon ratification, accession or succession, see UNTC, Status of Treaties, IV.2 and IV.4: Declarations and Reservations.
[229] See s. II.2. (Customary International Law).
[230] ILC Guide to Practice on Reservations to Treaties (2011) §3.1.5 (*Incompatibility of a reservation with the object and purpose of the treaty*) 32. See also Vienna Convention on the Law of Treaties (1969) Art. 19(c); HRC, General Comment No. 24 (1994), §5.
[231] Australia, Austria, Belgium, Canada, Czech Republic, Denmark, Estonia, Finland, France, Germany, Hungary, Ireland, Italy, the Netherlands, Norway, Poland, Portugal, Slovakia, Spain, Sweden, Switzerland, the United Kingdom and the United States.
[232] The other provisions were articles 3, 6, 7, 18 of the ICCPR.
[233] See, for example, Australia, Austria, Belgium, Czech Republic, Denmark, Estonia, Finland, France, Germany, Hungary, Italy, the Netherlands, Poland, the United Kingdom and the United States.

similar terms and concluded that the reservation was incompatible with the object and purpose of the ICCPR.[234] Others objected that a state cannot rely on its internal law to justify the failure to perform a treaty.[235] Belgium also noted that Pakistan's reservation 'may contribute to undermining the bases of international human rights treaties' more generally.[236] However, a number of states specified in their objections that the ICCPR should still enter into force between the relevant parties despite their objections as they would simply consider the reservation to be severable from Pakistan's otherwise valid assumption of obligations under the treaty.[237] And Pakistan ultimately withdrew it.[238]

Objections to reservations to the ICCPR are not, in any case, dispositive of the question of whether a state has successfully altered its obligations under a treaty through a reservation.[239] The Human Rights Committee has stated that, in relation to the ICCPR, it 'necessarily falls to the Committee to determine whether a specific reservation is compatible with the object and purpose of the Covenant'.[240] The Committee has also highlighted that 'the pattern [of objections to reservations to the ICCPR] is so unclear that it is not safe to assume that a non-objecting State thinks that a particular reservation is acceptable', and that '[t]he absence of protest by States cannot imply that a reservation is either compatible or incompatible with the object and purpose of the Covenant'.[241]

1.3.1. International treaties

1.3.1.1. ICCPR: Article 19 There are 173 state parties to the ICCPR,[242] and currently eight reservations[243] and three declarations[244] to article 19 of the treaty.[245]

---

[234] The conclusion regarding incompatibility with the 'object and purpose' of the treaty was also reached by Australia, Austria, Belgium, Canada, Czech Republic, Denmark, Estonia, Finland, France, Germany, Hungary, Ireland, Italy, the Netherlands, Norway, Poland, Portugal, Slovakia, Spain, Sweden and the United States. See also United Kingdom ('a reservation should clearly define for the other States Parties to the Covenant the extent to which the reserving State has accepted the obligations of the Covenant').
[235] Australia, Belgium, Czech Republic, Denmark, Finland, Hungary and Poland.
[236] See also, e.g., Ireland and Czech Republic.
[237] See, e.g., United States ('This objection does not constitute an obstacle to the entry into force of the Covenant between the United States and Pakistan, and the aforementioned articles shall apply between our two states, except to the extent of Pakistan's reservations'). See also objections by Czech Republic, Finland, Norway, Slovakia, Sweden: UNTC Depositary, Status of Treaties, ch. IV. 4 ICCPR, Declarations and Reservations. The United Kingdom did not clearly specify its position on this.
[238] See C.N.604.2011.Treaties-41 (Depositary Notification), 21 September 2011 (withdrawing its reservations to article 19 as well as other articles). This withdrawal occurred after the European Union indicated that Pakistan would be ineligible for Generalized Scheme of Preferences Plus (GSP+) status, which removes tariffs for developing nations in certain circumstances: See '*Pakistan decides to withdraw most of reservations on ICCPR, UNCAT*' (The Nation, 23 June 2011).
[239] HRC, General Comment No. 24 (1994), §18.
[240] Ibid., §18.
[241] Ibid., §17.
[242] And six signatories who have not acceded or ratified the treaty: China, Comoros, Cuba, Nauru, Palau, Saint Lucia.
[243] By Austria, Belgium, France, Germany, India, Luxembourg, Malta and the Netherlands: UNTC Depositary, Status of Treaties, ch. IV. 4 ICCPR, Declarations and Reservations. Three additional countries had such reservations but withdrew them: France (withdrawn in part on 22 March 1988), Ireland (withdrawn on 15 December 2011), Pakistan (withdrawn on 20 September 2011).
[244] By Italy, Monaco and the United States: UNTC Depositary, Status of Treaties, ch. IV. 4 ICCPR, Declarations and Reservations.
[245] Austria, Belgium, France, Germany, India, Luxembourg, Malta and the Netherlands have made reservations that remain in force: UNTC Depositary, Status of Treaties, ch. IV. 4 ICCPR, Declarations and Reservations. Australia, France, Ireland and Pakistan all previously had entered reservations or declarations to Article 19 that they have since withdrawn. The United Kingdom made a number of general reservations to the ICCPR, including

28 FREEDOM OF SPEECH IN INTERNATIONAL LAW

Of these reservations, only two seek to restrict the key scope of protections under article 19—from India and Malta—both by reference to constitutional and national law.[246] India's reservation states that article 19(3) would 'be so applied as to be in conformity with the provisions of article 19 of the Constitution of India', which provides a wider set of permissible justifications for penalizing speech including on the basis of 'decency and morality', 'the interests of the sovereignty and integrity of India', the 'security of the State' and 'friendly relations with foreign States'.[247] Malta's reservation sought to preserve the ability to restrict speech by public officials on a broader basis than article 19 based on the Maltese constitution and other provisions of national law.[248] Although the status of the two reservations is undetermined,[249] the Human Rights Committee has criticized the reservation entered by Malta[250] and has, in the past, found sweeping references to national law similar to India's reservation to article 19 to be incompatible with the object and purpose of the ICCPR.[251] The Human Rights Committee has also indicated that a 'general' reservation to article 19(2), which is inextricably linked to sub-paragraph (3), 'would be' incompatible with the Covenant.[252]

Five European states also entered reservations to article 19 stating that they would only recognize article 19 to the extent that its provisions were aligned with those of article 10 of the European Convention.[253] Four of these states—Austria, France, Germany and Malta—all referenced article 16 of the European Convention, which provides that states should not be prevented from 'imposing restrictions on the political activity of aliens'.[254] However, the Human Rights Committee in its General Comment No. 15 has since found that 'each one

some that could apply to Article 19, such as 'reserv[ing] the right' not to apply provisions to 'members of and persons serving with the armed forces' or to prisoners. Whether they are termed 'declaration' or 'reservation' is not determinative and does not guarantee that they will have the desired effect of altering a state's legal obligations: '[r]egard will be had to the intention of the State, rather than the form of the instrument', and a statement which 'purports to exclude or modify the legal effect of a treaty ... constitutes a reservation': HRC, General Comment No. 24 (1994), §3.

[246] UNTC Depositary, Status of Treaties, ch. IV. 4 ICCPR, Declarations and Reservations.

[247] India, UNTC Depositary, Status of Treaties, ch. IV.2 CERD, Declarations and Reservations. As provided at the time India ratified both CERD and the ICCPR on 10 April 1979. Pakistan entered a similar reservation that has since been withdrawn.

[248] Malta, UNTC Depositary, Status of Treaties, ch. IV. 4 ICCPR, Declarations and Reservations.

[249] Both India and Malta are yet to withdraw their reservations despite the Human Rights Committee calling for their withdrawal: see HRC, *Concluding Observations, Malta* (2014) UN Doc. CCPR/C/MLT/CO/2, §6; HRC, *Concluding Observations, India* (1997) UN Doc. CCPR/C/79/Add.81, §14; HRC, *List of issues prior to submission of the fourth periodic report of India* (2019) UN Doc. CPPR/C/IND/QPR/4, §4.

[250] HRC, *Concluding Observations, Malta* (2014) UN Doc. CCPR/C/MLT/CO/2, §6 stating that the reservation is 'obsolete' and that Malta's reservations 'in general' have an 'adverse effect on the effective implementation of the Covenant'.

[251] See, e.g., HRC, *Concluding Observations, Kuwait* (2000) UN Doc. CCPR/CO/69/KWT, §4; HRC, *Concluding Observations, Kuwait* (2016) UN Doc. CCPR/C/KWT/CO/3, §8.

[252] HRC, General Comment No. 34 (2011), §§5–6; HRC, General Comment No. 24 (1994), §12 ('Of particular concern are widely formulated reservations which essentially render ineffective all Covenant rights which would require any change in national law to ensure compliance with Covenant obligations'), §19 ('Nor should interpretative declarations or reservations seek to remove an autonomous meaning to Covenant obligations, by pronouncing them to be identical, or to be accepted only insofar as they are identical, with existing provisions of domestic law').

[253] Austria, France, Germany, Malta, Belgium: UNTC Depositary, Status of Treaties, ch. IV. 4 ICCPR, Declarations and Reservations.

[254] Belgium did not specify any articles of the European Convention, and France's reservation has since been withdrawn: UNTC Depositary, Status of Treaties, ch. IV. 4 ICCPR, Declarations and Reservations.

of the rights of the Covenant must be guaranteed without discrimination between citizens and aliens'.[255] In addition, four countries—Luxembourg, the Netherlands, Italy and Monaco—have made reservations or declarations to article 19 in order to protect their domestic licensing scheme for radio, TV broadcasting and film.[256]

Finally, there is a declaration by the United States, but this seeks to *increase* the scope of protection of the right to free expression under article 19 in compliance with the First Amendment to the US constitution. In the words of the declaration:

> [I]t is the view of the United States that States Party to the Covenant should wherever possible refrain from imposing any restrictions or limitations on the exercise of the rights recognized and protected by the Covenant, even when such restrictions and limitations are permissible under the terms of the Covenant. For the United States, article 5, paragraph 2, which provides that fundamental human rights existing in any State Party may not be diminished on the pretext that the Covenant recognizes them to a lesser extent, has particular relevance to article 19, paragraph 3 which would permit certain restrictions on the freedom of expression. The United States declares that it will continue to adhere to the requirements and constraints of its Constitution in respect to all such restrictions and limitations.[257]

1.3.1.2. ICCPR: Article 20 Since article 20 creates a state obligation to limit the right to freedom of expression set out in the preceding article, some commentators have referred to article 20 as 'practically a fourth paragraph to Article 19' which has to be 'read in close connection' with it.[258] This has created an unusual scenario whereby states have sought to use a treaty reservation to reduce the restriction contained in article 20 and thereby to *expand* the scope of the right to freedom of expression under article 19.[259] Fifteen reservations and three declarations are currently in place in relation to article 20, many of which seek to alter the core meaning of the provision.[260]

Six states—the Nordic countries[261] and the Netherlands—entered reservations specific to article 20(1) which prohibits 'propaganda for war'—with Finland and Iceland's

---

[255] HRC, General Comment No. 15 (1986), §2. See also HRC, General Comment No. 31 (2004), §10 (Covenant rights must be 'available to all individuals, regardless of nationality or statelessness, such as asylum seekers, refugees, migrant workers and other persons, who may find themselves in the territory or subject to the jurisdiction of the State Party').

[256] See, e.g., Netherlands (article 19 'shall not prevent the Kingdom from requiring the licensing of broadcasting, television or cinema enterprises'): UNTC Depositary, Status of Treaties, ch. IV. 4 ICCPR, Declarations and Reservations.

[257] United States, UNTC Depositary, Status of Treaties, ch. IV. 4 ICCPR, Declarations and Reservations.

[258] T. McGonagle, 'The International and European legal standards for combating racist expression: selected current conundrums', in Expert Seminar: *Combating racism while respecting freedom of expression* (ECRI 2007), 40, 41.

[259] See, e.g., Iceland's reservation which referred to the fact that 'a prohibition against propaganda for war *could limit the freedom of expression*'. Iceland, UNTC Depositary, Status of Treaties, ch. IV. 4 ICCPR, Declarations and Reservations (emphasis added).

[260] Reservations: Australia, Denmark, Finland, Iceland, Ireland, Liechtenstein, Luxembourg, Malta, the Netherlands, New Zealand, Norway, Sweden, Switzerland, the United Kingdom and the United States. Declarations: Belgium, Thailand and France: UNTC Depositary, Status of Treaties, ch. IV. 4 ICCPR, Declarations and Reservations. Liechtenstein and Switzerland have both withdrawn their reservations to article 20 (2) while their reservations to article 20 (1) stand.

[261] Denmark, Finland, Iceland, Norway and Sweden: UNTC Depositary, Status of Treaties, ch. IV. 4 ICCPR, Declarations and Reservations.

reservations expressly stating that such a prohibition could 'limit' or 'endanger' freedom of expression.[262]

In addition, the United States entered a reservation by reference to its domestic laws providing that 'article 20 does not authorize or require legislation or other action by the United States that would restrict the right of free speech and association protected by the Constitution and laws of the United States'.[263] Like its reservation to article 19, the United States' reservation seeks to ensure that free speech cannot be curtailed beyond the speech-protective parameters of the First Amendment.[264]

Nine states also entered reservations and declarations to article 20 indicating that the signatory state did not need to or could not easily introduce further legislative provisions to implement article 20.[265] For instance, Australia, the United Kingdom and New Zealand's reservations alluded to legislation already in place that complied with the obligations set out in article 20.[266] Belgium's declaration and Luxembourg's reservation state that they did not consider themselves obliged to adopt legislation on the issues covered by article 20(1).[267] And Ireland's reservation reserved the right to postpone the introduction of legislative measures having 'regard to the difficulties in formulating a specific offence capable of adjudication at a national level'.[268]

Five of these states—Australia, Belgium, Luxembourg, Malta and the United Kingdom—also clarified their understanding that article 20 would be interpreted or applied in a manner that did not conflict with other rights in the Covenant, including the right to freedom of expression.[269] The United Kingdom, for instance, stated that it interpreted article 20 'consistently with the rights conferred by articles 19 and 21 of the Covenant and ... reserve[s] the right not to introduce any further legislation'.[270] This would likely be considered acceptable by the Human Rights Committee since it has itself stated that articles 19 and 20 are 'compatible with and complement each other', and that any limitation 'justified on the basis of article 20 must also comply with article 19, paragraph 3'.[271]

Finally, France and Thailand made declarations to article 20(1) on the basis that each has interpreted 'war' to mean war in 'contravention of international law'.[272] The Human Rights Committee has since indicated that article 20(1) extends to 'all forms of propaganda threatening or resulting in an act of aggression or breach of the peace contrary to

---

[262] Denmark's reservation also makes reference to 'the preceding article concerning freedom of expression': UNTC Depositary, Status of Treaties, ch. IV. 4 ICCPR, Declarations and Reservations.
[263] UNTC Depositary, Status of Treaties, ch. IV. 4 ICCPR, Declarations and Reservations: United States.
[264] UNTC Depositary, Status of Treaties, ch. IV. 4 ICCPR, Declarations and Reservations: United States (Declaration 2).
[265] Australia, Belgium, Ireland, Liechtenstein, Luxembourg, Malta, New Zealand, Switzerland and the United Kingdom: UNTC Depositary, Status of Treaties, ch. IV. 4 ICCPR, Declarations and Reservations.
[266] Although both Liechtenstein's and Switzerland's reservations do not go so far as to state that they had already complied with article 20, both reserve the right 'not to adopt *further* measures to ban propaganda for war' (emphasis added). UNTC Depositary, Status of Treaties, ch. IV. 4 ICCPR, Declarations and Reservations: Liechtenstein, Switzerland.
[267] UNTC Depositary, Status of Treaties, ch. IV. 4 ICCPR, Declarations and Reservations: Belgium, Luxembourg.
[268] Ireland: UNTC Depositary, Status of Treaties, ch. IV. 4 ICCPR, Declarations and Reservations.
[269] Australia, Belgium, Luxembourg, Malta, United Kingdom: UNTC Depositary, Status of Treaties, ch. IV. 4 ICCPR, Declarations and Reservations.
[270] United Kingdom: UNTC Depositary, Status of Treaties, ch. IV. 4 ICCPR, Declarations and Reservations.
[271] HRC, General Comment No. 34 (2011), §50.
[272] France, Thailand: UNTC Depositary, Status of Treaties, ch. IV. 4 ICCPR, Declarations and Reservations.

the Charter of the United Nations', and does not prohibit 'advocacy of the sovereign right of self-defence or the right of peoples to self-determination and independence in accordance with the Charter of the United Nations'.[273] These declarations would therefore not be likely to be considered reservations.[274]

1.3.1.3. CERD: Article 4

There are 182 state parties to the International Convention on the Elimination of All Forms of Racial Discrimination.[275] Nineteen states have a current reservation or declaration to article 4.[276] How these have been described varies, with a small number expressly referred to as reservations,[277] a higher percentage described as 'interpretative declarations' or using the word 'interprets' or 'declares',[278] and some adopting both sets of terminology.[279] This lack of clarity is compounded by the CERD Committee using both terms—reservation and declaration—to describe Austria,[280] Belgium,[281] France,[282] Ireland,[283] Italy[284] and Monaco's responses to article 4.[285]

---

[273] HRC, General Comment No. 11 (1983), §2.

[274] Liechtenstein and Switzerland initially entered a reservation to reserve the right to adopt a criminal provision taking into account the requirements of article 20(2) once they had acceded to the Convention on the Elimination of All Forms of Racial Discrimination 1966. Both of these reservations have now been withdrawn following those states' accession to the Convention and implementation of relevant legislation. See Switzerland's second report to the HRC (6 September 1999, UN Doc. CCPR/C/CH/98/2), §174; Liechtenstein's initial report to the HRC (8 July 2003, UN Doc. CCPR/C/LIE/2003/1), §151.

[275] There are also three signatories who have not yet acceded: Bhutan, Nauru and Palau: See UNTC Depositary Status of Treaties, ch. IV.2 CERD.

[276] Antigua and Barbuda, Australia, Austria, the Bahamas, Barbados, Belgium, France, Grenada, Ireland, Italy, Japan, Malta, Monaco, Nepal, Papua New Guinea, Switzerland, Tonga, the United Kingdom and the United States: UNTC Depositary, Status of Treaties, ch. IV.2 CERD, Declarations and Reservations. Fiji has since withdrawn its declaration on 10 August 2012 and Thailand withdrew its reservation on 7 October 2017.

[277] Japan, Monaco, Papua New Guinea, United States and Switzerland: UNTC Depositary, Status of Treaties, ch. IV.2 ICERD, Declarations and Reservations.

[278] See, e.g., Antigua and Barbuda ('declaration'); Australia ('declares'); Bahamas ('wishes to state its understanding'); Barbados ('interprets'); Belgium ('wishes to emphasize'); France ('interprets'); Grenada ('declaration' and 'interprets'); Italy ('declaration'); Malta ('declaration' and 'interprets'); Nepal ('interprets') and Tonga ('declaration' and 'interprets'): UNTC Depositary, Status of Treaties, ch. IV. 2, ICERD: Reservations and Declarations. The representative for Malta has referred to the Maltese statement as a 'reservation' (but the Committee on the Elimination of Racial Discrimination has referred to it as a 'declaration' and has noted there is a 'divergence of opinion' between the Committee and Malta: Committee's Report, General Assembly Official Records: Forty-Sixth Session, Supplement No. 18 (1992) UN Doc. A/46/18, §§153, 156; CERD, *Concluding Observations, Malta* (1996) UN Doc. CERD/C/304/Add.14, §9).

[279] Ireland ('reservation/interpretative declaration') and the United Kingdom ('reservation and interpretative statements'): UNTC Depositary, Status of Treaties, ch. IV. 2, ICERD: Reservations and Declarations.

[280] CERD referred to it as a 'declaration': CERD, *Concluding Observations, Austria* (1999) UN Doc. CERD/C/304/Add.64, §16, but then later as a 'reservation' CERD, *Concluding Observations, Austria* (2012) UN Doc. CERD/C/AUT/CO/18-20, §10.

[281] CERD refers variously to it as a 'declaration': CERD, *Concluding Observations, Belgium* (1997) UN Doc. CERD/C/304/Add.26, §10 and CERD, *Concluding Observations, Belgium* (2008) UN Doc. CERD/C/BEL/CO/15, §23; and a 'reservation': CERD, *Concluding Observations, Belgium* (2002) UN Doc. CERD/C/60/CO/2, §14.

[282] The only reference in concluding observations by CERD is as a 'reservation': CERD, *Concluding Observations, France* (2015) UN Doc. CERD/C/FRA/CO/20-21, §7. Notwithstanding that France had clarified that it considered it to be an interpretative declaration.

[283] CERD initially refers to it as a 'declaration': CERD, *Concluding Observations, Ireland* (2005) UN Doc. CERD/C/IRL/CO/2, §10 but then continues to refer to it as a 'reservation/interpretative declaration': CERD, *Concluding Observations, Ireland* (2011) UN Doc. CERD/C/IRL/CO/3-4, §17 and CERD, *Concluding Observations, Ireland* (2019) UN Doc. CERD/C/IRL/CO/5-9, §§9–10.

[284] CERD has variously referred to this as a 'reservation': CERD, *Report to the General Assembly* (1995) UN Doc. A/50/18, §82; and a 'declaration': CERD, *Concluding Observations, Italy* (1999) UN Doc. CERD/C/304/Add.68, §20 and CERD, *Concluding Observations, Italy* (2012) UN Doc. CERD/C/ITA/CO/16-18, §10.

[285] CERD, *Concluding Observations, Monaco* (2010) UN Doc. CERD/C/MCO/CO/6, §7.

The reservations to article 4 can be classified into three key categories: those stating that legislation will only be introduced to enact article 4 where 'necessary', those that interpret article 4 in manner that is compatible with other rights, and those that refer to domestic or constitutional law.

The first and most significant reservations restrict the application of the Convention by reference to the state's law or constitution, with the effect of enhancing protections for free speech.[286] The United States provided that 'the Constitution and laws of the United States contain extensive protections of individual freedom of speech, expression and association' and that accordingly, the United States did 'not accept any obligation under this Convention, in particular under articles 4 and 7, to restrict those rights, through the adoption of legislation or any other measures, to the extent that they are protected by the Constitution and laws of the United States'.[287] The CERD Committee recorded its concern with this reservation, however, noting that the 'prohibition of dissemination of all ideas based upon racial superiority or hatred is compatible with the right to freedom of opinion and expression, given that a citizen's exercise of this right carries special duties and responsibilities, among which is the obligation not to disseminate racist ideas'.[288] Like the United States, Japan stated that it would fulfil its obligations under article 4 to the extent 'compatible with the guarantee of the rights to freedom of assembly, association and expression and other rights under the Constitution of Japan'.[289]

Secondly, twelve states—including France, Italy and the United Kingdom—stated that they interpreted article 4 as being in compliance with other human rights.[290] Each referred to the 'due regard' provision of article 4, which references freedom of expression, as well as other rights, and some explicitly mentioned articles 19 and 20 of the ICCPR and article 19 of the Universal Declaration.[291] For instance, Austria, Ireland and Italy all stated that the obligations derived from article 4 do not 'jeopardize' the right to freedom of expression laid down in articles 19 of the ICCPR and article 5 of CERD.[292] Belgium stated that the 'obligations imposed by article 4 must be reconciled with the right to freedom of opinion and expression'.[293] And France and Monaco stated that the reference in the due process clause to the UDHR and article 5 of CERD had the effect of 'releasing' states from the 'obligation to enact anti-discrimination legislation which is incompatible with the freedom of opinion and expression' guaranteed by those texts.[294]

---

[286] Antigua and Barbuda, the Bahamas, Barbados, Grenada, Guyana, Jamaica, Nepal, Papua New Guinea, Thailand and the United States: UNTC Depositary, Status of Treaties, ch. IV. 2, ICERD: Reservations and Declarations.
[287] United States: UNTC Depositary, Status of Treaties, ch. IV. 2, ICERD: Reservations and Declarations.
[288] CERD, *Report to the General Assembly* (2001) UN Doc. A/56/18, §391.
[289] Japan (also noting the 'due regard' clause): UNTC Depositary, Status of Treaties, ch. IV. 2, ICERD: Reservations and Declarations.
[290] The 12 states are: Austria, Bahamas, Belgium, France, Ireland, Italy, Malta, Monaco, Nepal, Papua New Guinea, Tonga and the United Kingdom: UNTC Depositary, Status of Treaties, ch. IV. 2, ICERD: Reservations and Declarations.
[291] Ibid.
[292] Austria, Ireland, Italy: UNTC Depositary, Status of Treaties, ch. IV.2, ICERD, Declarations and Reservations.
[293] Belgium: UNTC Depositary, Status of Treaties, ch. IV.2 ICERD, Declarations and Reservations.
[294] Monaco's reservation is worded as 'repressive laws' rather than 'anti-discrimination laws'. France, Monaco: UNTC Depositary, Status of Treaties, ch. IV.2, ICERD: Reservations and Declarations.

These declarations would be likely to be considered compatible with the Treaty since the Committee has since itself commented in similar terms on the relationship between articles 4 and other rights, stating in its General Comment No. 35 that:

> The phrase due regard implies that, in the creation and application of offences, as well as fulfilling the other requirements of article 4, the principles of the Universal Declaration of Human Rights and the rights in article 5 must be given appropriate weight in decision-making processes. The due regard clause has been interpreted by the Committee to apply to human rights and freedoms as a whole, and not simply to freedom of opinion and expression, which should however be borne in mind as the most pertinent reference principle when calibrating the legitimacy of speech restrictions.[295]

A third group of 10 states, including various Caribbean States, Malta, Switzerland and the United Kingdom, made reservations and declarations concerning the extent to which new legislation is required by this provision.[296] Some states indicated they would adopt legislation only where necessary to attain the 'end' or 'ends' specified in article 4,[297] or only 'where it is considered the need arises'.[298]

Beyond the 19 reservations made specifically to article 4, twelve states made general reservations to CERD that could affect the scope of article 4.[299] Two reservations—Saudi Arabia and Thailand—sought to provide less, rather than more, protection for speech, and both invoked national law as a basis for this.[300] Saudi Arabia stated that it would implement the Convention's provisions provided 'these do not conflict with the precepts of the Islamic Shariah', and Thailand limited its obligations by reference to its constitution and domestic laws as well as its obligations under other treaties.[301] Turkey also provided a reservation stating that it would implement the provisions of the Convention 'only to the States Parties with which it has diplomatic relations' and only 'with regard to the national territory where the Constitution and the legal and administrative order of the Republic of Turkey are applied'.[302]

---

[295] HRC, General Comment No. 35 (2013), §19.
[296] Antigua and Barbuda, Bahamas, Barbados, Grenada, Malta, Nepal, Papua New Guinea, Switzerland, Tonga, United Kingdom: UNTC Depositary, Status of Treaties, ch. IV.2, ICERD: Reservations and Declarations. This list overlaps with the second category of reservations—being the 'due regard' references—as some states combined both sets of reservations.
[297] Nepal, Tonga, the United Kingdom and Papua New Guinea: UNTC Depositary, Status of Treaties, ch. IV.2, ICERD: Reservations and Declarations.
[298] Antigua and Barbuda, Barbados and Grenada and similarly, Malta: UNTC Depositary, Status of Treaties, ch. IV.2, ICERD: Reservations and Declarations.
[299] Antigua and Barbuda, Bahamas, Barbados, Grenada, Guyana, Jamaica, Nepal, Papua New Guinea, Saudi Arabia, Thailand, Turkey and the United States: UNTC Depositary, Status of Treaties, ch. IV. 2, ICERD: Reservations and Declarations. Most of these reservations restricted the application of the Convention by reference to that state's constitution.
[300] However, national law cannot be a reason not to comply with international treaty obligations: Vienna Convention on the Law of Treaties Art. 27 ('A party may not invoke the provisions of its internal law as justification for its failure to perform a treaty'). See also CERD, *Concluding Observations, Thailand* (2021) UN Doc. CERD/C/THA/CO4-8, §§7–8; CERD, *Concluding Observations, Saudi Arabia* (2018) UN Doc. CERD/C/SAU/CO/4-9, §§5–6.
[301] Thailand and Saudi Arabia: UNTC Depositary, Status of Treaties, ch. IV. 2, ICERD: Reservations and Declarations.
[302] Turkey: UNTC Depositary, Status of Treaties, ch. IV. 2, ICERD: Reservations and Declarations.

Although no states have objected to specific reservations made to article 4, a number of objections were expressed against the general reservations made by states to the Convention as a whole. Both the United Kingdom and France objected to the 'general and indeterminate scope' of Grenada's reservation seeking to restrict Grenada's obligations to those in its constitution.[303] Similarly, Thailand's reservation was objected to by France, Germany, Romania, Sweden and the United Kingdom on the basis of its 'general and indeterminate scope', which France suggested made the provisions of the Convention 'completely ineffective'.[304] Cyprus, Sweden and the United Kingdom objected to Turkey's reservation.[305] And a number of European states objected to Saudi Arabia seeking to limit its obligations based on Sharia law,[306] raising concerns as to the general and unspecified nature of this reservation, which created 'doubts' as to Saudi Arabia's commitment to the object and purpose of the Convention.[307] However, most of these objecting states indicated that they did not object to the Convention entering into force or the reserving state becoming a party, emphasizing that the Convention would apply 'in its entirety' without the reserving state being able to rely on its reservation.[308]

1.3.2. Regional treaties

1.3.2.1. European Convention: Article 10 There are 46 state parties to the European Convention. Three states—Azerbaijan, Malta and Monaco—have current reservations to article 10 and Spain has a current declaration regarding article 10.[309]

Article 57 of the European Convention provides that '[r]eservations of a general character shall not be permitted' and that states seeking to 'make a reservation in respect of any particular provision of the Convention' must provide 'a statement of the law' that is 'in force in its territory' which 'is not in conformity with the provision'.[310] The Court has also held that 'the necessity of including a statement of the law is much greater where a very wide provision of the Convention is concerned, e.g. Article 10'.[311]

---

[303] See objections of France and the United Kingdom: UNTC Depositary, Status of Treaties, ch. IV.2, CERD: Objections.

[304] See Objections of France, Germany, Romania, Sweden and the United Kingdom to Thailand's reservation: UNTC Depositary, Status of Treaties, ch. IV.2, CERD, Objections.

[305] See Objections of Cyprus, Sweden and the United Kingdom to Turkey's reservation: UNTC Depositary, Status of Treaties, ch. IV.2, CERD, Objection.

[306] Austria, Finland, Germany, the Netherlands, Norway, Spain and Sweden: UNTC Depositary, Status of Treaties, ch. IV.2 CERD, Objection.

[307] Austria, Finland, Germany and Sweden: UNTC Depositary, Status of Treaties, ch. IV.2 CERD, Objection.

[308] However, Tonga and the United Kingdom made declarations regarding article 20 of ICERD, which provides that 'a reservation incompatible with the object and purpose of this Convention shall not be permitted, nor shall a reservation the effect of which would inhibit the operation of any of the bodies established by this Convention be allowed. A reservation shall be considered incompatible or inhibitive if at least two thirds of the States Parties to this Convention object to it'. The United Kingdom and Tonga both declared that they interpret article 20 as meaning that if a reservation is not accepted, the State making the reservation will not become a party to the Convention. Fiji had made a declaration to the same effect, but this was withdrawn on 10 August 2012. Fiji, Tonga, United Kingdom: UNTC Depositary, Status of Treaties, ch. IV.2 CERD, Reservations and Declarations.

[309] Portugal withdrew its reservation to article 10 on 11 May 1987 and France withdrew its reservation on 29 March 1988. See COE, Reservations and Declarations for Treaty No. 005 – Convention for the Protection of Human Rights and Fundamental Freedoms, Article number 10.

[310] ECHR Art. 57. Prior to Protocol 11, this was article 64 of the European Convention.

[311] ECmHR, *Temeltasch v. Switzerland* (App. no. 9116/80), 5 March 1982, §90.

Consequently, although a number of states have made broadly worded reservations to the Convention as a whole that might on their face apply to article 10, they are unlikely to comply with article 57.[312]

Most reservations and declarations pertaining to article 10 concern the regulation and licensing of media and broadcasting services.[313] In addition, Malta declared that 'public officers in Malta' are constitutionally precluded 'from taking an active part in political discussions or other political activity during working hours or on official premises'. And Monaco entered a reservation based on constitutional and other domestic provisions that ensure respect for privacy and create criminal offences for insulting the Monégasque Prince and his Family.[314] There have been no objections to reservations or declarations relating to article 10 or decisions by the Court on their validity.[315]

1.3.2.2. American Convention: Article 13 Twenty-five states have ratified or acceded to the American Convention on Human Rights.[316] There have been no reservations or declarations made to article 13 of the Convention specifically.[317] Bolivia and El Salvador have both made general reservations that seek to apply the Convention consistently with their constitutions that may indirectly impact the right to freedom of expression enshrined by article 13.[318] There were no objections to these reservations and the Inter-American Court has not had occasion to opine on them.[319]

1.3.2.3. African Charter: Article 9 Fifty-four states have ratified the African Charter on Human and Peoples' Rights.[320] Three reservations and declarations have been made to the Charter, and only one, by Egypt, concerns article 9, which governs freedom of speech. This states that 'as far as the Arab Republic of Egypt is concerned, the [right to

---

[312] See, e.g., Andorra's reservation, which seeks to 'emphasize that the fact that it forms a State with limited territorial dimensions requires it to pay special attention to problems of residence, work and other social measures in respect of foreigners'; San Marino's almost identical reservation; Azerbaijan's reservation that 'it is unable to guarantee the application of the provisions of the Convention in the territories occupied by the Republic of Armenia until those territories are liberated from that occupation'.

[313] See, e.g., reservations of France, Portugal, Azerbaijan, Monaco, Spain in COE, Reservations and Declarations for Treaty No. 005 – Convention for the Protection of Human Rights and Fundamental Freedoms, Article number 10.

[314] Malta, Ratification with Reservations and Declarations, 590 UNTS 300, 301; Monaco, Ratification with Reservations and Declarations, 2361 UNTS 21, 22.

[315] Multiple states did object to the Turkish declaration regarding the power of the former European Commission of Human Rights to receive individual petitions: See COE, Reservations and Declarations for Treaty No. 005 (Türkiye), Declaration registered on 28 January 1987; COE, Reservations and Declarations for Treaty No. 005 (Türkiye), Communication registered on 29 June 1987 acknowledging receipt of letters from Sweden, Luxembourg, Greece, Denmark and Norway objecting to the conditions laid down by Turkey in accepting the competence of the European Commission.

[316] See ACHR, Signatories and Ratifications. Trinidad and Tobago denunciated the Convention in 1991. Venezuela also denunciated the Convention on 10 September 2012, but the Guaidó government has ratified the treaty again on 31 July 2019.

[317] Articles 75 and 29 of the Convention provide guidance as to the permissible scope of reservations and interpretation of the Convention.

[318] Letter of the Government of Bolivia dated 22 July 1993 (OAS/262/93); Reservation made by El Salvador at the time of ratification, 1144 UNTS 143, 209 (1979).

[319] See IACtHR, *Serrano-Cruz Sisters v. El Salvador* (Serie C, no. 118), 23 November 2004, §§57–96 (opining on El Salvador's reservation but only in relation to whether it can reserve the Court's jurisdiction).

[320] ACHPR, State Parties to the African Charter.

receive information] should be [confined] to such information as could be obtained within the limits of the Egyptian laws and regulations'.[321] The African Commission has urged Egypt to withdraw this reservation.[322]

1.4. Derogations

In addition to reservations, which seek to redefine the obligations a state owes under a treaty during peacetime, a state can derogate from a treaty in times of emergency.[323] Derogations, if valid, suspend the application of treaty obligations for the derogating state for a defined period of time while the emergency exists.[324] State practice on derogations can also be an indication of whether a provision in a treaty has reached the status of customary international law and whether such an obligation can, therefore, apply to a state that has not signed or ratified the treaty.[325]

1.4.1. International treaties

Article 4 of the ICCPR provides that 'in time of public emergency which threatens the life of the nation and the existence of which is officially proclaimed', states may derogate from their obligations under the Covenant.[326] However, a state cannot 'evade the obligations' of the ICCPR 'by merely invoking the existence of a state of siege'; rather, the state must be able to provide a 'sufficiently detailed account' of the particular facts constituting an emergency to the Human Rights Committee.[327] And even when a right is derogable, any derogation must be of an exceptional and temporary nature, and persist only 'to the extent strictly required by the exigencies of the situation'.[328] States may not derogate from a right in a manner that would compromise a non-derogable right, such as freedom of religion[329] and states may 'in no circumstances invoke article 4 of

---

[321] By Egypt, South Africa and Zambia: see AU Legal Division, 'Regional Protection of Human Rights in Africa: Reservations, Interpretive Declarations and Objections' (2004) 1 *Human Rights Law in Africa Online* 97, 108.
[322] ACmHPR, Concluding Observations and Recommendations on the Seventh and Eighth Periodic Report of the Arab Republic of Egypt, Thirty-Seventh Ordinary Session, 27 April–11 May 2005, §25.
[323] ICCPR Art. 4; ECHR Art. 15; ACHR Art. 27. Although beyond the scope of this book, a separate body of jurisprudence, international humanitarian law, overlaps with human rights law in times of armed conflict. See, e.g., O. Ben-Naftali (ed), *International Humanitarian Law and International Human Rights Law* (OUP 2011), Introduction.
[324] ICCPR Art. 4; ECHR Art. 15; ACHR Art. 27.
[325] See s. II.2. (Customary International Law). The number of derogations reflects how widespread state practice is in relation to a particular treaty provision, and therefore there is less likelihood that a treaty provision has attained customary international law status if there are a large number of substantive derogations to it. See International Law Commission, *Draft conclusions on identification of customary international law with commentaries* (2018) UN Doc. A/73/10, Conclusion 8, Commentary (5) which states that 'where the relevant acts are divergent to the extent that no pattern of behaviour can be discerned, no general practice (and thus no corresponding rule of customary international law) can be said to exist'. See also International Law Commission, *Second Report on identification of customary international law* (2014) UN Doc. A/CN.4.672, §78.
[326] ICCPR Art. 4(1).
[327] HRC, *Salgar de Montejo v. Colombia* (Comm. no. 64/1979), 24 March 1982, §10.3. See also HRC, *Pietraroia v. Uruguay* (Comm. no. 44/1979), 27 March 1981, §14; HRC, *Shuilina v. Belarus* (Comm. no. 2142/2012), 28 July 2017, §§3.5, 6.5–6.7; HRC, *Praded v. Belarus* (Comm. no. 2029/2011), 10 October 2014, §§3.2, 7.8–7.9, 8.
[328] ICCPR Art. 4(1). See also ECHR Art. 15(1); ACHR Art. 27(1); Arab Charter Art. 4(1). HRC, General Comment No. 29, §§2, 4. See further IACtHR, *González v. Peru* (Series C, no. 289), 20 November 2014, §117.
[329] See, e.g., ICCPR Art. 4(2); ACHR Art. 27(1); Arab Charter Art. 4(2). Cf. ECHR Art. 15(2) (permitting derogations from the right to life 'in respect of deaths resulting from lawful acts of war'). HRC, General Comment No.

the Covenant as justification for acting in violation of humanitarian law or peremptory norms of international law'.[330]

Freedom of expression under article 19 of the ICCPR is not listed as a non-derogable right under article 4(2) of the treaty. But the Human Rights Committee has indicated that freedom of opinion, protected under article 19(1), is non-derogable because 'it can never become necessary to derogate from [the obligation to respect freedom of opinion] during a state of emergency'.[331] The Committee has not made a similar statement about article 19(2)—relating to speech—and the UN Special Rapporteur on Freedom of Opinion and Expression has noted that 'the ICCPR permits derogations from freedom of expression (but not opinion) during declared states of emergency'.[332]

Prior to the COVID-19 pandemic, nineteen states lodged declarations to derogate from article 19, varying widely in breadth.[333] Some states, including El Salvador, Nepal, Nicaragua, Serbia, Sri Lanka and Turkey, provided limited details, asserting that a state of emergency has been declared and that article 19 was one of a number of articles of the ICCPR that would be derogated from.[334] States have sometimes been more specific. For instance, in 1990 the Soviet Union stated that 'issuance of certain newspapers has been temporarily suspended and control of press media has been imposed' in the 'Nagorno-Karabakh autonomous region and certain other areas'.[335]

Certain derogations specify particular regions,[336] and others set a time period—from 14 days provided for in Jamaica's derogation in 2018 to six months stipulated by Nicaragua in 1982.[337] In other instances, the derogation was declared to apply to the entire nation with vague time limits, for example in the case of Panama's 1987 derogation which purported to stay in place 'as long as reasons for the disruption of law and order remain'.[338] Most of these derogations refer generally to article 19 or to article 19(2) specifically, with the exception of Armenia which expressly derogated from both articles 19 (1) and (2) in 2008.[339]

---

29 (2001), §15, see also §11; IACtHR, *Judicial Guarantees in States of Emergency (Articles 27(2), 25 and 8 of the American Convention on Human Rights)*, Advisory Opinion OC-9/87 (Series A, no. 9), 6 October 1987, §25.

[330] HRC, General Comment No. 29 (2001), §11. See also IACmHR, *Report on Terrorism and Human Rights* (2002) OEA/Ser.L/V/II.116, §20.

[331] HRC, General Comment No. 34 (2011), §5.

[332] UN Special Rapporteur, 'Preliminary Conclusions and Observations by the UN Special Rapporteur on the Right to Freedom of Opinion and Expression to his Visit to Turkey' (OHCHR, 2016).

[333] Nowak (n 27) 544, n. 20–21, citing C.N.155.1991.Treaties-10 (Algeria); C.N.185-2008.Treaties-6 (Armenia); C.N. 424.1994.Treaties-13 (Azerbaijan); C.N. 306.1976.Treaties-9 (Chile); C.N.68.1984.Treaties-5 (Ecuador); C.N.9.1984.Treaties-1 (El Salvador); C.N.347.2009.Treaties-8 (Guatemala); C.N.51.2018.Treaties-IV.4 (Jamaica); C.N.271.2005.Treaties-5 (Nepal); C.N.244.1982.Treaties-9 (Nicaragua); C.N.141.1987.Treaties-11 (Panama); C.N.37.1982.Treaties-2 (Poland); C.N.24.1990.Treaties-2 (Russian Federation); C.N.274.2003.Treaties-3 (Serbia); C.N.373.2000.Treaties-5 (Sri Lanka); C.N.49.2014.Treaties-IV.4 (Thailand); C.N.580.2016.Treaties-IV.4 (Turkey); C.N.193.1976.Treaties-6 (United Kingdom); C.N.98.1989.Treaties-5 (Venezuela). See also C.N.403.2019.Treaties-IV-4 (Ecuador), C.N.148.2019-Treaties-IV.4 (Burkina Faso).

[334] C.N.9.1984.Treaties-1 (El Salvador); C.N.271.2005.Treaties-5 (Nepal); C.N.244.1982.Treaties-9 (Nicaragua); C.N.274.2003.Treaties-3 (Serbia); C.N.373.2000.Treaties-5 (Sri Lanka); C.N.580.2016.Treaties-IV.4 (Turkey).

[335] CN.24.1990.Treaties-2 (Russian Federation). See also C.N.155.1991.Treaties-10 (Algeria).

[336] See, e.g., C.N.51.2018.Treaties-IV.4 (Jamaica); C.N.68.1984.Treaties-5 (Ecuador); CN.24.1990.Treaties-2 (Russian Federation), C.N.49.2014.Treaties-IV.4 (Thailand).

[337] C.N.51.2018.Treaties-IV.4 (Jamaica); C.N.244.1982.Treaties-9 (Nicaragua).

[338] C.N.141.1987.Treaties-11 (Panama).

[339] C.N.185-2008.Treaties-6 (Armenia). Nowak (n 27) 554.

The United Kingdom declared a particularly wide derogation in 1976, citing 'campaigns of organized terrorism related to Northern Irish affairs' that led the United Kingdom 'to take powers, to the extent strictly required by the exigencies of the situation, for the protection of life, for the protection of property and the prevention of outbreaks of public disorder, and including the exercise of powers of arrest and detention and exclusion'.[340] It then declared that, to the extent these measures were inconsistent with article 19(2), the United Kingdom derogated from its obligations under the provision.[341]

The COVID-19 pandemic has seen a high number of derogations from the ICCPR, but these have largely pertained to article 21 (freedom of assembly) rather than article 19. Colombia is the only state that has explicitly proclaimed a 'power to temporarily suspend' article 19 due to the Covid-19 pandemic.[342] The Human Rights Committee also released a statement in response to derogations to rights under the Covenant in connection with the pandemic acknowledging that states 'confronting the threat of widespread contagion may, on a temporary basis, resort to exceptional emergency powers and invoke their right of derogation ... provided that it is required to protect the life of the nation'.[343] However, the Committee emphasized that states should not derogate from rights 'when they are able to attain their public health or other public policy objectives by invoking the possibility of restrict[ing] certain rights, such as ... article 19 (freedom of expression) ... in conformity with the provision for such restrictions set out in the Covenant'.[344]

Article 20 of the ICCPR is not listed as a non-derogable right in the treaty. However, the Human Rights Committee has said that '[n]o declaration of a state of emergency made pursuant to article 4 ... may be invoked as justification for a State party to engage itself, contrary to law, in propaganda for war, or in advocacy of national, racial or religious hatred that would constitute incitement to discrimination, hostility or violence'.[345] The UN High Commissioner for Human Rights has also referred to the prohibition enshrined in article 20 as a right or freedom 'under customary international law (which is applicable to all States) that may not be derogated from even if not listed in article 4(2)' of the ICCPR.[346] There have been no attempted derogations from article 20 by states.[347]

---

[340] C.N.193.1976.Treaties-6 (United Kingdom).
[341] C.N.193.1976.Treaties-6 (United Kingdom).
[342] C.N.131.2020.Treaties-IV.4 (Colombia). Guatemala has also notified the Secretary General that 'measures have been taken' that 'restrict' the application of article 19 on the basis of a state of emergency due to the influx of migrants who do not comply with 'public health measures'. See C.N.47.2021.Treaties-IV.4 (Guatemala).
[343] HRC, Statement on derogations from the Covenant in connection with the COVID-19 pandemic (30 April 2020), CCPR/C/128/2, §2.
[344] Ibid., §2(c).
[345] HRC, General Comment No. 29 (2001), §13.
[346] OHCHR, 'Human Rights, Terrorism and Counter-Terrorism: Fact Sheet No. 32' (June 2008), 28. See also the Paris Minimum Standards of Human Rights Norms in a State of Emergency (reproduced in the American Journal of International Law, 70 Am. J. Int'l. 1072) which also include this prohibition as a non-derogable right.
[347] See Nowak (n 27) 577. See also UN Treaty Collection website listing no derogations or notifications concerning article 20 from 2019–February 2022.

Unlike the ICCPR, CERD does not have a provision restricting the right to derogate from its provisions,[348] and no state has registered an intention to derogate from articles 4 or 5.

1.4.2. Regional treaties

The European Convention does not list article 10 as a non-derogable right,[349] and prior to 2020 no derogations had been registered pertaining to this article.[350] However, three states registered derogations from article 10 between 2020 and 2021 on the basis of states of emergencies.[351] Armenia and Azerbaijan respectively declared martial law in September 2020 due to the Nagorno-Karabakh conflict and each derogated—with few details as to scope—from article 10.[352] Armenia and Azerbaijan terminated their derogations in April 2021 and December 2020 respectively.[353] The Republic of Moldova also declared a state of emergency on 3 November 2021 due to a shortage of gas, stating that restrictions such as 'coordinating the work of the media, in particular on the introduction of special rules for the use of telecommunications' would be required.[354] It withdrew the derogation in December 2021.[355]

No countries derogated from article 10 of the European Convention on the basis of the COVID-19 pandemic, although a number did make derogations to article 11 governing the right to free assembly.[356]

The American Convention does not list the right to freedom of expression—or the mandatory restrictions to hateful speech under article 13(5), the Convention's equivalent of article 20 of the ICCPR—as a non-derogable right.[357] However, both the ICCPR and the

---

[348] G. McDougall, 'The International Convention on the Elimination of All Forms of Racial Discrimination' (UN AVL 2001), Introduction.

[349] ECHR Art. 15(2).

[350] However, both Albania and Georgia have made declarations under the Convention which reference, but do not expressly derogate from article 10. In 1997 Albania declared a state of public emergency and prohibited the '[p]ublication … of reports which stir up and call for violent actions against national security, the constitutional law, public security and the life of the individual', but noted 'we do not prohibit the freedom of the press' (Note Verbale from the Ministry of Foreign Affairs of Albania to the COE Secretariat General dated 4 March 1997). In 2007 Georgia declared a 15-day state of emergency and noted that limits had been imposed on freedom of expression but assured that restrictions to rights would 'be applied in good faith and only within the margin of appreciation give to the State Parties by the' European Convention (Letter of the Minister of Foreign Affairs of Georgia to the COE Secretariat General dated 7 November 2007).

[351] Armenia (Note Verbale No. 3201/C-308/2020 dated 29 September 2020), Azerbaijan (Note Verbale no. 5/11-3238/01/20 dated 28 September 2020), Moldova (Note Verbale No. FRA-CoE/352/536 dated 3 November 2021).

[352] Derogation contained in the Note verbale No. 3201/C-308/2020 from the Permanent Representation of the Republic of Armenia, dated 29 September 2020, registered at the Secretariat General on 29 September 2020; Derogation contained in the Note verbale No. 5/11-3283/01/20 from the Ministry of Foreign Affairs of Azerbaijan, dated 28 September 2020, registered at the Secretariat General on 28 September 2020.

[353] Note verbale No. 3201/C-124/2021 from the Permanent Representation of the Republic of Armenia, dated 12 April 2021, registered at the Secretariat General on 14 April 2021; Note Verbale no. 5/11-4331/01/20 dated 15 December 2020.

[354] Derogation contained in the Note verbale No. FRA-CoE/352/536 of the Permanent Representation of Moldova, dated 3 November 2021, registered at the Secretariat General on 3 November 2021.

[355] Note verbale no. FRA-CoE/352/591 dated 6 December 2021.

[356] Albania, Armenia, Estonia, Georgia, Latvia, North Macedonia, Moldova, Romania, San Marino, Serbia. See COE, 'Derogations Covid-19'. Human Rights Watch has reported that, of 83 countries found to have breached freedom of expression or assembly rights during the COVID-19 pandemic, only 44 had declared a state of emergency and none had registered derogations relating to freedom of expression: see Human Rights Watch, 'Covid-19 Triggers Wave of Free Speech Abuse' (11 February 2021).

[357] ECHR Art. 15(2); ACHR Art. 27(2).

American Convention provide that states may only take measures derogating from rights to the extent that these are consistent with the state's other obligations under international law.[358] As a result, the Human Rights Committee's position that no derogation can justify a state party engaging in propaganda for war, or in 'advocacy of national, racial or religious hatred that would constitute incitement to discrimination, hostility or violence' may also apply to article 13 of the American Convention.[359]

A number of states have attempted to derogate from the guarantee of free expression under the American Convention.[360] Most of the recent derogations have been time limited, spanning from six days to three months, and while some were limited geographically, others covered the entire nation.[361] Many of the derogations refer to limiting protests, demonstrations or the right to assembly but are vague as to the scope of the derogation from article 13.[362] A striking example is Ecuador's 2016 derogation, which provided a general suspension of article 13 on the basis that 'some media have served as a platform to instigate and provoke ... acts of aggression and violence' against the police and armed forces.[363] Since the outbreak of the COVID-19 pandemic, Bolivia, Suriname and Guatemala have all issued derogations to the American Convention under article 13.[364] Bolivia and Guatemala's derogations focused on limiting public demonstrations and protests.[365] Suriname's derogation did not explicitly reference article 13 but authorized the government to 'take measures with regard to those who intentionally distribute false messages or information that is harmful to society in connection with the COVID-19 pandemic'.[366]

The African Charter does not contain a derogation clause, and the African Commission has consistently interpreted this to mean that the '[t]he African Charter, unlike other human rights instruments, does not allow for state parties to derogate from their treaty obligations during emergency situations'.[367] The Commission has also found violations of

---

[358] ICCPR Art. 4(1); ECHR Art. 15(1).
[359] HRC, General Comment No. 29 (2001). ACHR Art. 27(1). IACmHR, *Second Report on the Situation of Human Rights in Peru* (2000) OEA/Ser.L/V/II.106, Ch. II, §72; IACmHR, *Asencios Lindo v. Peru* (Case 11.182), 13 April 2000, §71 (observing that 'suspension of given rights must be consistent with all other obligations imposed by other international instruments ratified by the country').
[360] Between 2000 and January 2021, 35 derogations were made to article 13 of the American Convention. See OAS Department of International Law, 'Suspension of Guarantees under article 27 of the American Convention on Human Rights'.
[361] See, e.g., Guatemala (Decree 1-2020 of 16 January 2020) (6 days); Suriname (COVID-19 State of Emergency Act, 9 April 2020) (three months); Guatemala (Gubernatorial Decree 10-2011, 18 October 2011) covering the whole Guatemalan territory.
[362] See, e.g., Guatemala: Decree 2-2017 of May 10th 2017; Guatemala: Decree 1-2019 of September 4th 2019; Ecuador: Decree 884 of October 3rd 2019; Guatemala: Decree 1-2020 of January 16th 2020.
[363] Ecuador: Decree 1276 of December 14th 2016.
[364] Bolivia: Decree 4200 of March 25th 2020; Suriname: Act No. 83 of 9 April 2020; Guatemala: Decree 1-2021 of January 11th 2021. Guatemala likewise derogated from article 13 in May and August 2020, although it did not explicitly mention COVID-19. See Guatemala: Decree 10-2020 of May 29th 2020; Guatemala: Decree 16-2020 of 13th August 2020.
[365] Bolivia: Decree 4200 of March 25th 2020; Guatemala: Decree 1-2021 of January 11th 2021.
[366] This derogation applied to the whole of Suriname for three months: Suriname: Act No. 83 of 2020, Art. 5(3).
[367] ACmHPR, *Commission Nationale des Droits de l'Homme et des Libertes v. Chad* (Comm. no. 74/92), 11 October 1995, §21. See also ACmHPR, *Good v. Botswana* (Comm. no. 313/05), 26 May 2010, §118; ACmHPR, *Article 19 v. Eritrea* (Comm. no. 275/2003), 30 May 2007, §87.

freedom of expression under article 9 of the Charter even where states have sought to justify their conduct on the basis of an emergency situation.[368]

2. Customary International Law

There has been limited analysis of the degree to which the right to freedom of expression has achieved the status of customary international law and can therefore be binding even on states—like China, Myanmar and Saudi Arabia—that have not ratified any of the relevant treaties.[369] There is, however, a solid basis for finding that article 19 of the ICCPR has achieved customary status, given the existence of widespread and representative state practice as well as *opinio juris*, meaning 'evidence of a belief that this practice is rendered obligatory by the existence of a rule of law requiring it'.[370]

First, the right to freedom of expression is enshrined in article 19 of the Universal Declaration of Human Rights, and—over the course of over seven decades since its adoption—it has been repeatedly affirmed and referenced in international instruments.[371] This has led legal commentators to conclude that it reflects customary international law.[372] One of the original drafters of the Declaration, Professor John Humphrey, who served as Director of the UN Human Rights Division during the drafting of the Declaration, affirmed as far back as 1979 that 'articles two to twenty-one' of the Declaration, including the right to freedom of expression, had 'certainly ... acquired the force of law as part of the customary law of nations'.[373] And according to the US Third Restatement of Foreign Relations Law, '[p]ractice of states that is accepted as building customary human rights law includes: ... virtually universal and frequently reiterated acceptance of the Universal Declaration of Human Rights'.[374]

---

[368] See, e.g., ACmHPR, *Article 19 v. Eritrea* (Comm. no. 275/2003), 30 May 2007, §87; ACmHPR, *Media Rights Agenda v. Nigeria* (Comm. no. 224/98), 6 November 2000, §73. For an analysis of derogations in the African system, see, B.K. Kombo, 'A Missed Opportunity? Derogation and the African Court Case of APDF and IHRDA v Mali' (2020) 20 *African Human Rights Law Journal*, 756–776.

[369] An important exception is article III of the Genocide Convention, as the entirety of the Genocide Convention constitutes both customary international law and an *erga omnes* obligation: ICJ, *Application of the Convention on the Prevention and Punishment of the Crime of Genocide* (1996), §31.

[370] ICJ, *North Sea Continental Shelf Cases (FRG/Denmark; FRG/Netherlands)*, Judgment of 20 February 1969, §77. See also ICJ Statute Art. 38(1)(b); ILC Conclusions on *Identification of customary international law* (2018) UN Doc A/73/10, Conclusions 2, 4, 6, 11 (2). Cf. H. Hannum, 'The Status of the Universal Declaration of Human Rights in International Law' (1995) 25 *Georgia Journal of International and Comparative Law* 287, 340, 348 (stating that while 'there would seem to be little argument that many of the provisions of the [UDHR] today do reflect customary international law', the 'widespread restrictions on freedom of opinion and expression ... make it difficult to conclude that this provision is now part of customary international law, unless one accepts that the restrictions to freedom of expression which states believe are permissible can be so broad as to swallow the right itself').

[371] See, e.g., ECHR Preamble §1; Arab Charter Preamble §5; ACHR Preamble §4.

[372] See, e.g., J. Oster, *European and International Media Law* (CUP 2017), 25 (citing De Schutter, observing that 'the rights enumerated in the Declaration have acquired the status of customary international law'). See also B. Simma & P. Alston, 'The Sources of Human Rights Law: Custom, Jus cogens, and General Principles', 12 *Australian Year Book of International Law* 82, 84, 90–96.

[373] B.D. Lepard, *Customary International Law: A New Theory with Practical Applications* (CUP 2010), 318; 'Universal Declaration of Human Rights (1948): Drafting History' (United Nations Library).

[374] Third Restatement of Foreign Relations Law, 1987, §701, 154 (adding 'even if only in principle') (§701 was not covered in the Fourth Restatement of Foreign Relations Law: see Fourth Restatement of Foreign Relations Law, 498 [Table 2: Section Numbers from Restatement Third to Restatement Fourth]).

Second, the fact that a rule is set forth in a number of treaties may 'indicate that [it] reflects a rule of customary international law'.[375] There is widespread adoption of international and regional treaties as well as soft law instruments that enshrine the right to freedom of expression and opinion in similar and overlapping terms.[376] This is strong evidence of extensive state practice as well as *opinio juris*.[377] And international bodies interpreting and supervising states' performance under these treaties have regularly reiterated the right and its importance to the protection of other human rights in a democratic society.[378] African jurisprudence similarly considers freedom of expression a 'fundamental human right, essential to ... individual personal development, political consciousness and participation in the public affairs of a country'.[379] And a number of legal commentators consider that the substantive rights included in the ICCPR have attained customary status.[380]

Third, state practice on reservations does not 'reveal profound disagreement' or division among parties that may undermine the conclusion that the protection of freedom of expression as expressed in article 19 of the ICCPR has achieved customary status.[381] Indeed, given that only two reservations to article 19 seek to clearly dilute the key protection provided by it, with others seeking to *increase* the level of protection, there cannot be said to be either widespread or profound disagreement about its core provisions.[382]

Finally, the fact that there are 'widespread restrictions on freedom of opinion and expression' in national practice does not necessarily negate the existence of a customary international norm.[383] The International Law Commission has observed that violations do not necessarily prevent a rule from attaining customary international law status, especially when the breaching state 'denies the violation or expresses support for the rule' and justifies the breach by pointing to exceptions contained in the rule itself.[384] The fact that the restrictions frequently cited by states in derogating from the right to freedom

---

[375] UNGA Resolution 73/203, Identification of customary international law, (2019) UN Doc. A/Res/73/203, Conclusion 11(2).
[376] See s. II.1.1. (Treaty language). See, e.g., Johannesburg Principles; Tshwane Principles; Camden Principles. Cf. Rabat Plan of Action.
[377] UNGA, Resolution 73/203, Identification of customary international law, (2019) UN Doc. A/Res/73/203, Conclusions, 10, 11(2). See also S. Coliver, *The Article 19 Freedom of Expression Handbook* (Article 19 1993), 26.
[378] See, e.g., ECtHR, *Handyside v. United Kingdom* (App. no. 5493/72), 7 December 1976, §49; IACtHR, *Herrera Ulloa Case v. Costa Rica* (Series C, no. 107), 2 June 2004, §116. See also HRC, General Comment No. 34 (2011), §2.
[379] ACmHPR, *Good v. Botswana* (Comm. no. 313/2005), 26 May 2010, §197, citing ACmHPR, *Amnesty International v. Zambia* (Comm. no. 212/98), 5 May 1999, §46.
[380] See, e.g., Lepard (n 373) 327–330; Coliver (n 377) 26.
[381] See, e.g., s. II.1.3. (Reservations). UN Special Rapporteur Sir M. Wood, *Second report on identification of customary international law* (2014) UN Doc. A/CN.4/672, 64. Cf. ICTR, *Nahimana v. Prosecutor* (ICTR-99-52-A), Appeals Judgment, 28 November 2007, Partly Dissenting Opinion of Judge Meron, §5; ICJ, *Advisory Opinion on the Legality of the Threat or Use of Nuclear Weapons*, 8 July 1996, §67 (where the Court held it was not able to find *opinio juris* in circumstances where 'the members of the international community are profoundly divided').
[382] See s. II.1.3. (Reservations); International Law Commission, *Second report on identification of customary international law* (2014) UN Doc. A/CN.4/672, 64.
[383] See, e.g., Hannum (n 370) 348.
[384] See International Law Commission, *Draft conclusions on identification of customary international law with commentaries* (2018) UN Doc. A/73/10, Conclusion 8, Commentaries (7), (8).

of expression are permissible restrictions under article 19 reaffirms the existence of the right as a rule of customary international law.[385]

As the International Court of Justice has affirmed:

> [F]or a rule to be established as customary, the corresponding practice [need not] be in absolutely rigorous conformity with the rule. In order to deduce the existence of customary rules, the Court deems it sufficient that the conduct of States should, in general, be consistent with such rules, and that instances of State conduct inconsistent with a given rule should generally have been treated as breaches of that rule, not as indications of the recognition of a new rule. If a State acts in a way prima facie incompatible with a recognized rule, but defends its conduct by appealing to exceptions or justifications contained within the rule itself, then whether or not the State's conduct is in fact justifiable on that basis, the significance of that attitude is to confirm rather than to weaken the rule.[386]

There is, on the other hand, no sufficient basis to conclude that the provisions *requiring* the prohibition or criminalization of certain speech—article 20 of the ICCPR and 4 of CERD—have achieved customary international law status. Unlike article 19, whose provisions are reflected in all human rights treaties, only one regional treaty, the American Convention, contains such a provision.[387] And the number and scope of the reservations to these provisions are extensive. Eighteen states have made a reservation or declaration in relation to article 20, many of which seek to limit the key meaning of this provision in favour of greater freedom of expression.[388] Nineteen states have entered a reservation to article 4 of CERD, many of which are sweeping and suggest that they will only apply article 4 when they consider it 'necessary', when compatible with the right to freedom of expression or by reference to their own law.[389] As Judge Meron concluded in a case at the International Criminal Tribunal for Rwanda involving speech that was alleged to have incited genocide:

> The number and extent of the reservations [to the speech-related provisions in international treaties] reveal that profound disagreement persists in the international community as to whether mere hate speech is or should be prohibited, *indicating that Article 4 of the CERD and Article 20 of the ICCPR do not reflect a settled principle.* Since a consensus among states has not crystallized, there is clearly no norm under customary international law criminalising mere hate speech.[390]

---

[385] International Law Commission, *Second report on identification of customary international law* (2014) UN Doc. A/CN.4/672, 78: '[T]he practice that is not in accordance with a rule may be an occasion that reaffirms an *opinio juris* if the action is justified in terms that support that customary rule'.
[386] ICJ, Military and Paramilitary Activities in and against Nicaragua (*Nicaragua v. United States of America*), Judgment of 27 June 1986, §186.
[387] See s. II.1.1.1. (Abuses by the state) regarding the American Convention.
[388] See s. II.1.3.1.2. (ICCPR: Article 20).
[389] See s. II.1.3.1.3. (CERD: Article 4).
[390] ICTR, *Nahimana v. Prosecutor* (ICTR-99-52-A), Appeals Judgment, 28 November 2007, Partly Dissenting Opinion of Judge Meron, §5. Cf. HRC, General Comment No. 24 (1994) ('provisions in the Covenant that represent customary international law (and a fortiori when they have the character of peremptory norms) may not be the subject of reservations. Accordingly, a State may not reserve the right ... to permit the advocacy of national, racial or religious hatred'; this phrasing suggests that article 20 has customary international law status).

3. Jurisprudence

International treaties that protect speech are interpreted by a number of different international courts and human rights bodies. And many states are subject to more than one international instrument and institutional regime for monitoring and holding states accountable for violations of the right to freedom of expression. For instance, the 46 states that come within the jurisdiction of the European Court of Human Rights and the 21 states that have accepted the Inter-American Court's contentious jurisdiction have also ratified the ICCPR.[391] All eight of the states that recognize the competence of the African Court to receive cases from NGOs and individuals are also ICCPR states parties.[392] And the Working Group on Arbitrary Detention—as a non-treaty-based mechanism whose mandate expressly provides for consideration of individual complaints—can act on petitions from individuals anywhere in the world.[393]

Although international bodies have admissibility rules designed to limit scope for duplication,[394] claims concerning similar issues of law and fact do come before multiple jurisdictions. The European Court has observed that 'even where the provisions of the Convention and those of the ICCPR are almost identical, the interpretation of the same fundamental right by the HRC and by this Court may not always correspond'.[395]

International bodies interpreting, applying and developing the right to freedom of expression have diverse mandates, are embedded in different institutional regimes, have their own governing instruments, and employ varied procedures for fact-finding, decision-making and enforcement. At one end of the spectrum, there is the longstanding European Court of Human Rights, the 'human rights hegemon'[396] with a corpus of more than 1,000 judgments on free speech issues.[397] At the other end, the African Court has delivered less than 10 judgments on free speech issues since its inception.[398] The Inter-American Court has issued fewer than 40 decisions relating to

---

[391] Russia having ceased to be a party to the European Convention on Human Rights on 16 September 2022: Council of Europe, 'Russia ceases to be party to the European Convention on Human Rights' (16 September 2022). This does not include Trinidad and Tobago which has since denounced the American Convention effective 26 May 1999. UNTC Status of Treaties, Chapter IV.4 (ICCPR); COE, Chart of signatures and ratifications of Treaty 005; ACHR, 'Recognition of the Jurisdiction of the Court'.
[392] Burkina Faso, The Gambia, Ghana, Guinea Bissau, Malawi, Mali, Niger, Tunisia. This count does not include Benin, Côte d'Ivoire, Rwanda and Tanzania who have previously deposited declarations under article 34(6) of the Protocol to the African Charter on the Establishment of an African Court, recognizing the competence of the African Court to hear cases from individuals and NGOs but have since withdrawn their declarations. See ACtHPR, 'The Republic of Guinea Bissau becomes the eighth country to deposit a declaration under Article 34(6) of the Protocol establishing the Court' (3 November 2021); ACHPR, 'Declarations'.
[393] OHCHR, 'Revised Fact Sheet No. 26: The Working Group on Arbitrary Detention'.
[394] Optional Protocol to the ICCPR Art. 5(2)(a); ECHR Art. 35(2); ACHR Art. 46(1)(c); African Charter Protocol Art. 6, read with African Charter Art. 56(7); Methods of Work of the Working Group on Arbitrary Detention (2017) UN Doc. A/HRC/36/38, Section VII, §33.
[395] ECtHR, *Correira de Matos v. Portugal* (App. no. 56402/12), 4 April 2018, §135.
[396] S. Vasiliev, 'International Criminal Tribunals in the Shadow of Strasbourg and Politics of Cross-fertilisation' (2015) 84(3) *Nordic Journal of International Law* 371, 380.
[397] ECtHR, *Annual Report 2021* (2022), 189 ; ECtHR, *Annual Report 2022* (2023) (which identify 1,067 violations between 1959 and 2022). This count includes only decisions on the merits.
[398] ACtHPR, *Beneficiaries of Late Norbert Zongo v. Burkina Faso* (App. no. 13/2011), 28 March 2014; ACtHPR, *Konaté v. Burkina Faso* (App. no. 4/2013), 5 December 2014; ACtHPR, *Umuhoza v. Rwanda* (App. no. 3/2014),

freedom of expression over four decades, and a number of these relate to the right to information or violence against journalists rather than an assessment of restrictions to speech.[399] Both the Inter-American and African Court have cases referred to them by their respective Commissions, which can also examine individual complaints and issue their own decisions.[400] And within the UN system, since 1976, the Human Rights Committee has issued over 260 decisions on article 19 and only a handful relate to article 20 of the ICCPR.[401] The Human Rights Committee is a body of independent experts that meets on a sessional basis, and, like the Working Group on Arbitrary Detention, requests or recommends rather than orders states to remedy a violation.[402] Unlike the regional courts, it almost never hears oral argument.[403]

The fragmented legal landscape of international bodies can lead to freedom of expression being interpreted differently according to international and regional sources. Divergences on certain categories of speech—such as denial and blasphemy laws—have arisen, as well as diverging approaches to issues such as the proportionality of criminal penalties and remedies.[404]

International bodies also accord different degrees of deference when assessing whether states have 'demonstrate[d] the legal basis for any restrictions imposed on freedom of expression'.[405] The Human Rights Committee 'reserves to itself an assessment of whether, in a given situation, there may have been circumstances which made a restriction of freedom of expression necessary', has expressly rejected allowing a margin of appreciation to national courts.[406] The Working Group on Arbitrary Detention,[407] the Inter-American Court and Commission,[408] and the African Court

---

24 November 2017; ACtHPR, *Sébastien Germain Marie Aïkoue Ajavon v. Benin* (App. no. 62/2019), 4 December 2020; ACtHPR, *Noudehouenou v. Republic of Benin* (App. no. 028/2020), 1 December 2022. See also PULP, African Court Law Report Volumes 1–3 (2019, 2020, 2021) reporting on judgments, advisory opinions, and other decisions of the African Court from 2006–2016 (Vol. 1), 2017–2018 (Vol. 2), 2019 (Vol. 3). See further ACtHPR, 'Finalised Cases', reporting finalised cases from 2009 to 09 January 2022. This count includes only decisions on the merits. This count likewise excludes a small number of cases on the right to information.

[399] IACtHR, 'Digesto Themis' (concerning decisions on the merits).
[400] ACHR Art. 61(1); ACHPR Protocol Art. 2.
[401] OHCHR, 'Jurisprudence Database' (identifying decisions on the merits).
[402] ICCPR Art. 41; WGAD Revised Factsheet No. 26 (8 February 2019), 8.
[403] HRC, Fact Sheet no. 15 (Rev. 1), 26 ('No oral evidence is submitted' in the consideration of individual complaints under the Optional Protocol to the ICCPR).
[404] See s. II.3.2. (Key divergences).
[405] HRC, General Comment No. 34 (2011), §27. Although beyond the scope of this book, international bodies have variable standards of proof: see, e.g., A. Clooney & P. Webb, *The Right to a Fair Trial at International Law* (OUP 2020), 49–56.
[406] HRC, General Comment No. 34 (2011), §36.
[407] WGAD, *De Lima v. Philippines* (Opinion no. 61/2018), 24 August 2018, §45 (stating that WGAD will apply 'a heightened standard of review in cases in which the rights to freedom of ... opinion and expression ... are involved').
[408] IACmHR, *Report on Terrorism and Human Rights* (2002) OEA/Ser.L/V/II.116/Doc.5 Rev.1 corr., §§54–55 saying that freedom of expression, among other rights, may only be restricted subject to the strict and rigorous review by the supervisory bodies of the Inter-American system and that any action affecting the right 'cannot be subject to the discretion of a government or its officials'; B. Duhaime, 'Subsidiarity in the Americas: What Room is There for Deference in the Inter-American System', in L. Gruszczynski & W. Werner (eds), *Deference in International Courts and Tribunals, Standard of Review and Margin of Appreciation* (OUP 2014), 307–308, 314; J. Contesse, 'Contestation and Deference in the Inter-American Human Rights System' (2016) 79 *Law and Contemporary Problems* 123, 127.

and Commission have adopted a similar approach, although the African Court will account for 'the margin of appreciation that [a] State enjoys in defining and prohibiting some criminal acts in its domestic legislation'.[409]

In contrast, the European Court considers that states 'have a certain margin of appreciation' in assessing whether a 'pressing social need' makes a speech-restriction 'necessary' under the European Convention[410] and this doctrine has become 'the central conceptual doctrine in the ... jurisprudential architecture' of the Court.[411] Although the European Court applies a narrow margin when speech relates to a matter of public concern,[412] it has stated that it affords governments a particularly wide margin of appreciation when expression is 'liable to offend intimate personal convictions within the sphere of morals or, especially, religion',[413] and 'where such remarks incite violence against an individual, a public official or a sector of the population'.[414] This doctrine has contributed to the European Court's diverging jurisprudence on denial and blasphemy laws.[415]

Such differences in the approach of international bodies are exacerbated by the emergence of panels of international experts convened by technology companies to issue decisions on behalf of companies applying the same treaty standards that were developed for states.[416] And there is no single principle for resolving conflicts of interpretation, nor a hierarchy or avenue of appeal among them.[417]

Yet, despite this significant potential for fragmentation, there is far more convergence than divergence on the meaning of freedom of expression and the elements which must be proven before speech can be restricted. These convergences span various categories of speech—false speech, speech related to national security, political and public interest speech—as well as recognition of the need to protect the press and limit criminal penalties for speech.[418] There is an international legal *system*, 'albeit one that is diffuse and

---

[409] ACtHPR, *Umuhoza v. Rwanda* (App. no. 3/2014), 24 November 2017, §138; ACmHPR, *Uwimana-Nkusi v. Rwanda* (Comm. no. 426/12), 16 April 2021, §182 ('the failure of a State Party to justify in explicit terms the relationship between the imposition of limitations and public order or national security interests, would amount to a violation of Article 9').

[410] See, e.g., ECtHR, *Zana v. Turkey* (App. no. 18954/91), 25 November 1997, §51. However, this margin is more 'limited' when freedom of the press is at stake: See s. II.3.1.5. (Importance of protecting the press); ECtHR (GC), *Stoll v. Switzerland* (App. no. 69698/01), 10 December 2007, §105, citing ECtHR, *Éditions Plon v. France* (App. no. 58148/00), 18 May 2004, §44; ECtHR, *Dammann v. Switzerland* (App. no. 77551/01), 25 April 2006, §51.

[411] D. McGoldrick, 'A Defence of the Margin of Appreciation and An Argument for Its Application by the Human Rights Committee' (2016) 65 *International & Comparative Law Quarterly* 21, 21.

[412] See, e.g., ECtHR, *Otegi Mondragon v. Spain* (App. no. 2034/07), 15 March 2011, §51; ECtHR, *Tagiyev v. Azerbaijan* (App. no. 13274/08), 5 December 2019, §39.

[413] ECtHR, *Murphy v. Ireland* (App. no. 44179/98), 10 July 2003, §67. See also ECtHR, *Wingrove v. United Kingdom* (App. No. 17419/90), 25 November 1996, §53; ECtHR, *I.A. v. Turkey* (App. no. 42571/98), 13 September 2005, §25.

[414] ECtHR, *Savva Terentyev v. Russia* (App. no. 10692/09), 28 August 2018, §65.

[415] See s. II.3.2.1. (Denialism) and s. II.3.2.2. (Blasphemy). See also ch. 3 (Hate Speech), s. III.2. (Discretionary Restrictions on Hate Speech).

[416] See, e.g., Oversight Board, 'The Purpose of the Board'.

[417] For a summary of interpretative principles that international bodies have used to resolve or reduce conflicting human rights norms to maximize protection for the defendant, see Clooney & Webb, *The Right to a Fair Trial at International Law* (n 405), 60–65.

[418] See s. II.3.1. (Key convergences).

decentralized',[419] as well as general agreement on both the existence and content of the right to freedom of expression[420] and increasing interaction between international bodies as well as with national courts.[421]

3.1. Key convergences

The broad parameters for regulating speech are framed in similar terms in the ICCPR and regional treaties, and much of the jurisprudence interpreting these treaty standards is consistent and mutually reinforcing. This includes jurisprudence relating to the legitimate justifications for restricting speech, the approach to defamation and other false speech, speech related to national security and, broadly speaking, standards of protection for political speech and the press.

3.1.1. Justifications for penalizing speech

Although the list of justifications for imposing penalties on speech differ slightly across treaties—with article 10 of the European Convention containing grounds additional to those listed in article 19 of the ICCPR—international and regional human rights bodies have adopted a similar approach to the question of which objectives can be legitimate bases for penalizing speech.[422]

First, the jurisprudence of human rights bodies has focused on whether a particular penalty imposed on speech is 'necessary' and 'proportionate', rather than considering whether the objective being advanced through the penalty is legitimate. The Human Rights Committee's discussion of legitimate aims 'tends to be rather perfunctory', and it is 'exceedingly rare for the Committee to find a violation of Art. 19(2) because of a failure to provide a justifiable ground' for restricting speech.[423] The European Court of Human Rights has taken a similar approach.[424] And each international and regional human rights body recognizes that the legitimate aims articulated in article 19 of the ICCPR and regional equivalents are intended to be exhaustive, and cannot be used pretextually to curtail speech.[425]

---

[419] P. Webb, *International Judicial Integration and Fragmentation* (OUP 2015), 4.

[420] See s. II.2. (Customary International Law).

[421] See Clooney & Webb, *The Right to a Fair Trial in International Law* (n 405), 60, citing J. Martinez, 'Towards an International Judicial System' (2003) 56 *Stanford Law Review* 429, 443.

[422] See s. II.1.1. (Treaty language) regarding the scope of protection.

[423] Nowak (n 27) 567. An exception to this is the Committee's decisions relating to Russian laws criminalizing 'propaganda of homosexuality among minors', which Russia argued were justified on the basis of the 'morals' of minors. However, the Committee reasoned that given 'the principle of non-discrimination', Russia had 'failed to establish that the ban on propaganda of homosexuality among minors ... was based on reasonable and objective criteria and in pursuit of an aim that is legitimate under the Covenant': HRC, *Nepomnyashchiy v. Russian Federation* (Comm. no. 2318/2013), 17 July 2018, §7.5.

[424] ECtHR, Guide on Article 10 of the Convention (31 August 2022), §61 ('The Court ... analyses whether the interference was "prescribed by law" and whether it "pursued one of the legitimate aims" within the meaning of Article 10 §2, and lastly whether the interference was "necessary in a democratic society"; in the majority of cases, this is the question which determines the Court's conclusion in a given case'). See, e.g., ECtHR (GC), *Perinçek v. Switzerland* (App. no. 27510/08), 15 October 2015, §§146–154.

[425] HRC, General Comment No. 34 (2011), §§21–22; Office of the Special Rapporteur for Freedom of Expression IACmHR, *Inter-American Legal Framework Regarding the Right to Freedom of Expression* (2009) OEA/Ser.L/V/II CIDH/RELE/INF.2/09, 28, §74.

Defamation and hate speech laws will generally be considered to be pursuing a legitimate aim of respecting 'the rights or reputation of others',[426] with the European Court noting that this justification is 'by far' the one 'most frequently relied on in the Article 10 cases brought before the Court'.[427] The 'rights' of others have been interpreted broadly by international bodies to include 'human rights as recognized ... in international human rights law", and 'others' encompassing both 'other persons individually or as members of the community'.[428]

Espionage, official secrets and terrorism laws will generally be justified on the basis that they advance the objective of 'the protection of national security or of public order' under the other arm of article 19(3).[429] A state's assertion that national security interests are at stake will be given considerable deference by international bodies.[430] The European Court, for example, 'seldom challenges the legitimate national security aim adduced by the state'.[431] However, international bodies will not simply accept a state's bald assertion that national security is implicated without reaching their own view that a specific threat makes the restriction on speech necessary and proportionate.[432]

3.1.2. False speech

Although prohibitions on false speech have existed for over a century, most laws criminalizing it have been introduced much more recently.[433] As a result, international jurisprudence assessing these laws is still developing, but so far indicates a degree of harmonization across international and regional human rights bodies. The Human Rights Committee, Working Group on Arbitrary Detention, East African Court of Justice and ECOWAS Court have each criticized misinformation laws on the basis that they are impermissibly vague, including in circumstances where these laws incorporate

---

[426] See ch. 3 (Hate Speech), s. III.2.2. (Legitimacy) and ch. 2 (Insulting Speech), s.III.2. (Legitimacy). Cf. ch. 4 (False Speech), s. III.2. (Legitimacy).
[427] ECtHR, Guide on Article 10 of the Convention (31 August 2022), §123.
[428] HRC, General Comment No. 34 (2011), §28. See also ECtHR, *Atamanchuk v. Russia* (App. no. 4493/11), 11 February 2020, §42; IACtHR, *Kimel v. Argentina* (Series C, no. 177), 2 May 2008, §71; IACtHR, *Usón Ramirez v. Venezuela* (Series C, no. 207), 20 November 2009, §64: See ch. 3 (Hate Speech), s. III.2.2. (Legitimacy).
[429] See ch. 5 (Espionage and Official Secrets Laws), s. III.3. (Legitimacy); See also ch. 6 (Terrorism Laws), s. III.2. (Legitimacy). Article 10 also includes the additional aims of territorial integrity, public safety and the prevention of disorder or crime, but these are 'frequently invoked in combination' along with national security: ECHR Art. 10.2; ECtHR, Guide on Article 10 of the Convention (31 August 2022), §539.
[430] See, e.g., ECtHR (GC), *Janowiec v. Russia* (App. nos. 55508/07 & 29520/09), 21 October 2013, §213; ECtHR, *Liu v. Russia (No. 2)* (App. no. 29157/09), 26 July 2011, §85.
[431] ECtHR Research Division, National security and European case-law (2013), §46.
[432] HRC, *Shin v. Republic of Korea* (Comm. no. 926/2000), 16 March 2004, §7.3 (holding that while the national courts 'identified a national security basis as justification' for the penalty imposed 'the State party must demonstrate in specific fashion the precise nature of the threat to any of the enumerated purposes caused by the author's conduct'); WGAD, *Xiyue Wang v. Iran* (Opinion no. 52/2018), 23 August 2018, §75; ACmHPR, *Media Rights Agenda v. Nigeria* (Comm. no. 224/98), 23 October–6 November 2000, §53 (stating that there must be more than an 'omnibus statement' from the state authorities claiming a security threat); ECtHR (GC), *Janowiec v. Russia* (App. nos. 55508/07 & 29520/09), 21 October 2013, §213 (stating that while the Court is 'not well equipped to challenge' a state's claim of national security consideration, the state must make available an avenue for 'challenging effectively the executive assertion that national security was at stake'). See ch. 5 (Speech Related to National Security: Espionage and Official Secrets Laws), s. III.1. (International Standards Related to Speech Affecting National Security).
[433] See ch. 4 (False Speech), s. I. (Introduction).

harm requirements such as 'damag[ing] the national interest'.[434] And across the board, human rights bodies have been clear that speech cannot be restricted for the sole purpose of preventing falsehoods. In the words of the Inter-American Court, '[a] system that controls the right of expression in the name of a supposed guarantee of the correctness and truthfulness of the information that society receives can be the source of great abuse and, ultimately, violates the right to information that this same society has'.[435]

3.1.3. Speech related to national security
Another developing area of jurisprudence which shows signs of convergence is the publication of government-controlled information, including so-called 'official secrets'. The Human Rights Committee has cautioned that 'extreme care must be taken' by states to ensure that 'provisions relating to national security', whether 'described as official secrets or sedition laws', 'treason laws' or 'otherwise' are crafted and applied in conformity with the 'strict requirements' of article 19(3) and has cautioned against use of such laws to prosecute those who disseminate information of public interest.[436]

Although article 10(2) of the European Convention explicitly incorporates 'preventing the disclosure of information received in confidence' as a ground for restricting speech, whereas other treaties do not, the European Court has also applied a strict approach to penalties for this type of speech.[437] The Court has, for instance, taken a rigorous approach to the requirement that information is in fact confidential, and has found violations of article 10 where domestic courts did not examine a 'confidential' classification on the merits, or where information had lost such status.[438] And in key cases, including a decision regarding a Romanian whistleblower who has been compared to Edward Snowden in the United States, the Court found that a criminal conviction violated the right to free expression because the public interest in speech outweighed the potential damage that could be caused by its publication.[439] The Court noted that the revelation of illegality within the Romanian Intelligence Services 'was so important in a democratic society that it prevailed over the interest in maintaining public confidence in that institution'.[440] The European Court's approach in these cases is in line with pronouncements from the Human Rights Committee, the Inter-American

---

[434] See ch. 4 (False Speech), s. II.1.1. (Vagueness and overbreadth).
[435] IACtHR, *Compulsory Membership in an Association Prescribed by Law for the Practice of Journalism (Arts 13 and 29 American Convention on Human Rights)*, Advisory Opinion OC-5/85 (Series A, no. 5), 13 November 1985, §77. See also HRC, General Comment No. 34 (2011), §49; ECtHR, *Salov v. Ukraine* (App. no. 65518/01), 6 September 2005, §113.
[436] HRC, General Comment No. 34 (2011), §30.
[437] ECHR Art. 10 (2). This contrasts with the European Court's lack of tolerance for 'hate speech' including blasphemy and denialism. See s. II.3.2.1. (Denialism) and s. II.3.2.2. (Blasphemy).
[438] See ch. 5 (Espionage and Official Secrets Laws), s. III.4.1. (Secrecy); ECtHR, *Görmüş v. Turkey* (App. no. 49085/07), 19 January 2016, §§62, 64–66, 76; ECtHR, *Observer and Guardian v. United Kingdom* (App. no. 13585/88), 26 November 1991, §§66–70.
[439] ECtHR, *Bucur and Toma v. Romania* (App. no. 40238/02), 8 January 2013, §115. In 2013, Edward Snowden, formerly a contractor at the US National Security Agency, provided journalists classified documents revealing a 'global surveillance system' that allowed the NSA to 'sweep in the telephone, Internet and location records of whole populations' in the name of national security. B. Gellman, 'Edward Snowden, after months of NSA revelations, says his mission's accomplished' (Washington Post, 23 December 2013). See ch. 5 (Espionage and Official Secrets Laws).
[440] ECtHR, *Bucur and Toma v. Romania* (App. no. 40238/02), 8 January 2013, §115.

Court and international instruments that highlight the importance of weighing the public interest in speech in an assessment of whether it is necessary and proportionate to penalize it, particularly through criminal penalties.[441]

3.1.4. Political and public interest speech

International human rights bodies consistently recognize that a particularly high level of protection should be afforded to 'political' or 'public interest' speech by international human rights bodies. Across the board, such bodies recognize that when speech addresses a matter of public interest, this should be a factor favouring a higher degree of protection, and that 'very strong reasons' are required to 'justif[y] [any] restrictions on political debate'.[442] While there is no consistent definition of what constitutes political or public interest speech, nor a consistent approach to how additional protection should be reflected in national law (e.g., as a defence or a factor for courts to consider), human rights bodies have consistently recognized that such speech deserves particular protection and should be penalized only under very narrow circumstances, even when the 'rights of others', 'national security' or 'public order' are implicated.[443]

3.1.5. Importance of protecting the press

International bodies have also taken a broadly consistent approach to the importance of protecting the press. The starting point is that all speakers have the same right to speak, as international standards protect freedom of opinion and expression by all persons without distinction.[444]

International bodies have, however, consistently highlighted the link between the right to free speech, the right to a free press and democracy. As the Human Rights Committee has recognized, a 'free, uncensored and unhindered press ... is essential in any society to ensure freedom of opinion and expression and the enjoyment of other Covenant rights. It constitutes one of the cornerstones of a democratic society'.[445] The Committee has also recognized that 'the right to take part in the conduct of public affairs, as laid down in article 25 of the Covenant ... "implies a free press"'.[446] The UN

---

[441] See ch. 5 (Espionage and Official Secrets Laws), s. III.5.1. (Public interest defence). Cf. s. II.3.1.6. (Criminal penalties for speech).

[442] ECtHR, *Alekhina v. Russia* (App. no. 38004/12) 17 July 2018, §212. See also HRC, General Comment No. 34 (2011), §30 ('It is not compatible with paragraph 3, for instance, to invoke such laws to suppress or withhold from the public information of legitimate public interest that does not harm national security or to prosecute journalists ... or others, for having disseminated such information'); IACtHR, *Herrera-Ulloa v. Costa Rica* (Series C, no. 107), 2 July 2004, §127 ('there should be a reduced margin for any restriction on political debates or on debates on matters of public interest'); ACtHPR, *Konaté v. Burkina Faso* (App. no. 4/2013), 5 December 2014, §155 ('freedom of expression in a democratic society must be the subject of a lesser degree of interference when it occurs in the context of public debate relating to public figures').

[443] See, e.g., ECtHR (GC), *Couderc and Hachette Filipacchi Associés v. France* (App. no. 40454/07), 10 November 2015, §§114–115. See also ch. 2 (Insulting Speech), s. III.4.2. (Public interest).

[444] ICCPR Art. 2; ECHR Art. 1; ACHR Art. 1; ACHPR Art. 2. Cf. D. Tambini, 'What is Journalism? The Paradox of Media Privilege' (2021) 5 *European Human Rights Law Review*, 523–539. See s. II.3.1.5. (Importance of protecting the press).

[445] HRC, General Comment No. 34 (2011), §13.

[446] HRC, *Gauthier v. Canada* (Comm. no. 633/95), 5 May 1999, §13.4.

Rapporteur has similarly opined that 'without respect for freedom of expression, and in particular freedom of the press, an informed, active and engaged citizenry is impossible. An attack against a journalist is therefore an attack against the principles of transparency and accountability... which are essential for democracy'.[447]

Regional bodies have also highlighted the connection between freedom of expression, a free press and democracy.[448] The Inter-American Court considers freedom of expression to be 'a cornerstone upon which the very existence of a democratic society rests', and stated that '[w]ithin this context, journalism is the primary and principal manifestation of freedom of expression of thought'.[449] Accordingly, the 'practice of professional journalism cannot be differentiated from freedom of expression', and 'both are obviously intertwined'.[450] Similarly, a 'constant thread running through' the European Court's case law is 'the insistence on the essential role of a free press in ensuring the proper functioning of a democratic society' by being a 'public watchdog'.[451]

In addition, as international and regional human rights bodies provide heightened protection for speech concerning the public interest or political debate, journalists—in light of their function—are often the beneficiaries of these greater protections. The Human Rights Committee has recognized this connection, observing that 'in circumstances of public debate in a democratic society, especially in the media, concerning figures in the political domain, the value placed by the Covenant upon uninhibited expression is particularly high'.[452] Similarly, the European Court has held that, where 'freedom of the press' is at stake, the authorities only have a limited margin of appreciation to decide whether a 'pressing social need' exists.[453] It has highlighted that it is not for the Court 'nor for the national courts for that matter, to substitute their own views for those of the press as to what technique of reporting should be adopted by journalists'[454] since journalistic freedom provides for a recourse to 'a degree of exaggeration, even provocation'.[455] And it has recognized that the 'punishment of a journalist for assisting in the dissemination of statements made by another person in an interview would seriously hamper the contribution of the press to discussion of matters of public interest and should not be envisaged unless there are particularly strong reasons for doing so'.[456]

---

[447] UN Special Rapporteur Frank La Rue, *Report on the promotion and protection of the right to freedom of opinion and expression* (2012) UN Doc. A/HRC/20/17, §54.

[448] ACmHPR, Resolution on the Adoption of the Declaration of Principles of Freedom of Expression in Africa, ACHPR/Res.62, 23 October 2002, Preamble.

[449] IACtHR, *Compulsory Membership in an Association Prescribed by Law for the Practice of Journalism (Arts 13 and 29 American Convention on Human Rights)*, Advisory Opinion OC-5/85 (Series A, no. 5), 13 November 1985, §§70–71.

[450] Ibid., §74.

[451] ECtHR (GC), *Pedersen v. Denmark* (App. no. 49017/99), 17 December 2004, §71.

[452] HRC, *Bodrožić v. Serbia* (Comm. no. 1180/2003), 31 October 2005.

[453] ECtHR (GC), *Stoll v. Switzerland* (App. no. 69698/01) 10 December 2007, §105, citing *Éditions Plon v. France* (App. no. 58148/00), 18 May 2004, §44.

[454] ECtHR (GC), *Jersild v. Denmark* (App. no. 15890/89), 23 September 1994, §31. See also ECtHR (GC), *Satakunnan Markkinapörssi Oy v. Finland* (App. no. 931/13), 27 June 2017, §127.

[455] ECtHR, *Bédat v. Switzerland* (App. no. 56925/08), 29 March 2016, §58.

[456] ECtHR (GC), *Jersild v. Denmark* (App. no. 15890/89), 23 September 1994, §35. One point of divergence is the European Court's responsible journalism doctrine. See s. II.3.2. (Key divergences).

The Inter-American Court also considers it 'essential that journalists who work in the media should enjoy the necessary protection and independence to exercise their functions to the fullest, because it is they who keep society informed, an indispensable requirement to enable society to enjoy full freedom and for public discourse to become stronger'.[457] And both the Inter-American Commission and Court conceive of the right to freedom of expression as having two dimensions: 'an individual and a societal dimension', entailing not just the right to communicate but the 'right of all persons to freely learn of opinions, accounts and news'.[458]

International bodies have also taken a consistently broad, functional approach to who can be classified as a 'journalist'.[459] The Human Rights Committee has declared that '[j]ournalism is a function shared by a wide range of actors, including professional full-time reporters and analysts, as well as bloggers and others who engage in forms of self-publication in print, on the internet or elsewhere'.[460] The UN Rapporteur has similarly stated that journalism is 'the regular gathering of information, with or without formal training, accreditation or other government acknowledgment, with the intent to disseminate one's findings in any form'.[461] The African Court has taken a similar view. For example, in one case before the African Court, Burkina Faso sought to argue that a journalist was 'not even a Journalist' on the basis he had 'no Press Card and is not registered with ... administrative authorities'.[462] Noting that 'Articles 9 of the Charter and 19 of the Covenant guarantee the right of freedom of expression to anyone regardless and not only to journalists', the African Court took a functional approach, stating that the speaker had been targeted for journalistic work and had the '*de facto* status of a Journalist' despite any administrative requirements.[463]

In line with this functional approach, '[i]nternational bodies increasingly use terms more general than "journalist", such as "media professionals" or "media workers".[464] The UN Rapporteur has also noted that 'those who most closely reflect the professional engagement in collection and dissemination' of information include academics, freelance writers and NGOs publishing content, as well as 'citizen journalists' and bloggers and other media 'non-professionals'.[465] The European Court has extended the notion of a 'public watchdog' beyond the press to NGOs, academic researchers, authors of literature and

---

[457] IACtHR, *Herrera-Ulloa v. Costa Rica* (Series C, no. 107), 2 July 2004, §119.

[458] IACmHR, *Millar Silva v. Chile* (Case 12.799), 29 November 2016, §41; IACtHR, *Canese v. Paraguay* (Series C, no. 111), 31 August 2004, §79.

[459] Tambini (n 444) 523–539 (arguing that this avoids a 'centralised, top-down definition of journalism to determine who will access the privileges and protections that attach to the role', which would in itself be a 'threat to media freedom' but noting that there 'remains', however, 'a role for accreditation and professional gatekeeping' that is not controlled by private media interests or the state).

[460] HRC, General Comment No. 34 (2011), §44.

[461] UN Special Rapporteur D. Kaye, *Report on Freedom of Opinion and Expression to the General Assembly on the contemporary challenges to freedom of expression* (2016) UN Doc. A/71/373, §35.

[462] Burkina Faso alleged this was relevant to admissibility issues as the applicant had not furnished the Court with 'all the particulars concerning him in his Application': ACtHPR, *Konaté v. Burkina Faso* (App. no. 4/2013), 5 December 2014, §§49, 54.

[463] Ibid., §§57–58.

[464] UN Special Rapporteur D. Kaye, *Report on Freedom of Opinion and Expression to the General Assembly on the Protection of Sources and Whistleblowers* (2015) UN Doc A/70/361, §18.

[465] Ibid., §§19–20.

'bloggers and popular users of the social media'.[466] And UNESCO has argued for a definition of 'acts of journalism' rather than having the status of journalists determine access to source protection.[467]

3.1.6. Criminal penalties for speech

One of the consistent themes that emerges from international and regional jurisprudence relating to freedom of speech is the recognition that speech almost never warrants the imposition of criminal penalties, especially if they include a term of imprisonment. This is evident from statements of principle as well as the outcomes of their jurisprudence: the Human Rights Committee, African Court and Inter-American Court have rarely, if ever, found criminal penalties compatible with freedom of expression.

The Human Rights Committee's jurisprudence demonstrates that it has exercised 'great caution in the imposition of criminal penalties that punish speech', to the point that a term of imprisonment has *never* been found an appropriate restriction on speech.[468] The Committee has only found criminal penalties for speech permissible in a very limited number of cases: its now 'overturned' decision on France's Holocaust-denial laws which involved an approximately 57,000 Euro criminal fine,[469] and a case in which a journalist was subject to a criminal fine of approximately $445 US dollars in Korea for publishing polling data too close to an election.[470] And in both of these cases the criminal punishment in question—convictions and fines—were less severe than imprisonment.[471]

Similarly, the African Court has never found a term of imprisonment to be compatible with freedom of expression, and it has opined on the 'serious and very exceptional circumstances' in which it considers such a punishment might be appropriate, which it has defined as 'incitement to international crimes, public incitement to hatred, discrimination or violence or threats against a person or a group of people, because of

---

[466] ECtHR (GC), *Magyar Helsinki Bizottság v. Hungary* (App. no. 18030/11), 8 November 2016, §168. The European Court has also found that other categories of speaker are entitled to heightened protections: see, e.g., ECtHR, *Castells v. Spain* (App. no. 11798/85), 23 April 1992, §42 ('While freedom of expression is important for everybody, it is especially so for an elected representative of the people ... interferences with the freedom of expression of an opposition member of parliament ... call for the closest scrutiny').

[467] UNESCO, 'Protecting Journalism Sources in the Digital Age' (2017), 18.

[468] HRC, *Rabbae v. Netherlands* (Comm. no. 2124/2011), 14 July 2016, Individual Opinion (concurring) of Committee members Sarah Cleveland and Mauro Politi, §7.

[469] HRC, *Faurisson v. France* (Comm. no. 550/1993), 8 November 1996: The criminal fine was applied to two defendants, Faurisson and a magazine editor, in the amount of approximately 57,000 EUR, payable to the plaintiff associations made up of French resistance fighters and deportees to German camps. However this ruling was essentially overturned in the Committee's General Comment No. 34: See ch. 3 (Hate Speech), s. III.2.3.1. (Harm).

[470] HRC, *Kim v. Republic of Korea* (Comm. no. 968/2001), 27 July 2005. See also HRC, *A.K. v. Uzbekistan* (Comm. no. 1233/2003), 31 March 2009; HRC, *L.T.K. v. Finland* (Comm. no. 185/1984), 9 July 1985.

[471] HRC, *Kim v. Republic of Korea* (Comm. no. 968/2001), 27 July 2005, §8.3 ('The Committee also notes that the sanction visited on the author, albeit one or criminal law [sic], cannot be categorized as excessively harsh'). This case elicited dissenting opinions from seven Committee members, who argued that Korea had 'failed to demonstrate the reality of the threat which it contends the exercise of the author's freedom of expression posed'; Individual Opinion (dissenting) by Committee members, Ms. Christine Chanet and Messrs. Abdelfattah Amor, Prafullachandra Natwarlal Bhagwati, Alfredo Castillero Hoyos, Ahmed Tawfik Khalil and Rajsoomer Lallah. See also Individual Opinion (dissenting) by Committee Member Ms. Ruth Wedgewood. And more recent Committee statements have criticized other laws penalizing such speech during election campaigns. See, e.g., HRC, General Comment No. 34 (2011), §37; HRC, *Concluding Observations, Tunisia* (2008) UN Doc CCPR/C/TUN/CO/5, §19.

specific criteria'.[472] And the Inter-American Court has only found a term of imprisonment compatible with article 13 once, in a decision considered to be an outlier.[473]

The European Court of Human Rights has allowed comparatively greater restrictions to speech, including allowing terms of imprisonment for speech by journalists and others.[474] But the Court has stressed that any criminal sanction is liable to have a chilling effect on speech[475] and that 'the imposition of a prison sentence for a press offence will be compatible with journalists' freedom of expression ... only in exceptional circumstances, notably where other fundamental rights have been seriously impaired'.[476] As the Court has explained, 'expression on matters of public interest is in principle entitled to strong protection',[477] and the Court will 'exercise the utmost caution where the measures taken or sanctions imposed by the national authorities are such as to dissuade the press from taking part in the discussion of matters of legitimate public concern'.[478]

3.2. Key divergences

Despite the relative similarity of the key treaty provisions,[479] and consistency on many key issues in the interpretation of these provisions,[480] there are also substantial divergences among international bodies on some topics. These divergences have not generally been justified as resulting from wording differences in the relevant treaty provisions—they have instead emerged from the application of similar standards differently, including on issues such as hate speech, the applicability of criminal penalties and the remedies granted to speakers whose rights have been violated.

In some areas, the Human Rights Committee has been more protective of speech than the European Court,[481] with its codification of relevant standards in General Comment No. 34 representing a high-water mark for free-speech standards. Although

---

[472] ACtHPR, *Konaté v Burkina Faso* (App. no. 4/2013), 5 December 2014, §165; ECOWAS CCJ, *Federation of African Journalists v. Gambia* (Suit no. ECW/CCJ/APP/36/15), 13 February 2018 (where the ECOWAS CCJ held that the practice of imposing criminal sanctions for sedition, defamation and false news publication has a chilling effect that may unduly restrict journalists' freedom of expression).

[473] IACtHR, *Mémoli v. Argentina* (Series C, no. 265), 22 August 2013. See ch. 2 (Insulting speech). The judgment has been described as a 'regression' by Catalina Botero-Marino, Special Rapporteur for Freedom of Expression for the Commission from 2008 to 2014: see C. Botero-Marino, 'The Role of the Inter-American Human Rights System in the Emergence and Development of Global Norms on Freedom of Expression', in L. Bollinger & A. Callamard (eds), *Regardless of Frontiers* (Columbia University Press 2021), 193–194. See also Media Defence, 'Setbacks and Tension in the Inter-American Court of Human Rights' (1 December 2013) (deeming the decision a 'serious and notable setback').

[474] See s. II.3.2.6. (Criminal penalties for speech); see also s.3.2.2 (Blasphemy). However, this still represents a small fraction of speech-related cases that come before the Court.

[475] ECtHR, *Cumpănă v. Romania* (App. no. 33348/96) 17 December 2004, §§113–114. See also ECtHR, *Azevedo v. Portugal* (App. no. 20620/04), 27 March 2008, §33.

[476] ECtHR (GC), *Cumpănă v. Romania* (App. no. 33348/96), 17 December 2004, §115; ECtHR, *Ruokanen v. Finland* (App. no. 45130/06), 6 April 2010, §50.

[477] ECtHR, *Perinçek v. Switzerland* (App. no. 27510/08), 15 October 2015, §230.

[478] ECtHR (GC), *Cumpănă v. Romania* (App. no. 33348/96), 17 December 2004, §111.

[479] See s. II.1.1. (Treaty language).

[480] See s. II.3.1. (Key convergences).

[481] See, e.g., HRC, *Annual Report to the UNGA* (1994) UN Doc. A/49/40, §76. See also A. Buyse, 'Tacit Citing: The Scarcity of Judicial Dialogue Between the Global and the Regional Human Rights Mechanisms in Freedom of Expression Cases', in McGonagle & Donders (eds) (n 102) 446–449.

it is ten years old, the General Comment is cited frequently by the Committee and legal scholars, with one scholar describing it as having 'a similar centrifugal influence at an interpretative level as Article 19 ICCPR has had at the norm-setting level'.[482]

The divergent practice between the Human Rights Committee and the Strasbourg court is evidenced on a number of issues: (1) hate speech in the form of 'denialism' of certain events; (2) hate speech in the form of blasphemous speech; (3) intent and harm requirements for speech to be penalized; (4) the relevance of whether the speaker is a journalist; (5) defences that speakers should be able to invoke to protect speech; (6) the question of what speech can legitimately attract criminal penalties; and (7) remedies for violations of the right to freedom of speech.

3.2.1. Denialism

The Human Rights Committee has held that opinions that deny or call into question genocides or historical narratives cannot be penalized.[483] The Committee has concluded in its 2011 'General Comment' that laws 'that penalize the expression of opinions about historical facts are incompatible' with 'respect for freedom of ... expression'.[484] This position represents a deliberate reversal of the Committee's earlier approach, in which it had held that a French professor's conviction and fine for denying the existence of the Holocaust did not violate article 19 as 'the denial of the existence of the Holocaust' is a 'principle vehicle for anti-semitism'.[485] And since its General Comment, the Committee has criticized so-called 'denial laws' in a number of countries.[486] The Human Rights Committee has suggested that some restrictions to expression regarding historical facts could be permitted if they constitute speech that *must be* penalized under article 20 of the ICCPR (on the basis that it incites 'discrimination, hostility or violence').[487] But it has not yet identified any legislation that meets this threshold.

The European Court has taken a different approach and consistently held that stating certain opinions—such as a belief that the Holocaust did not take place—*cannot* be protected speech.[488] The Court has repeatedly struck out claims relating to such speech on

---

[482] T. McGonagle, 'The development of freedom of expression and information within the UN: leaps and bounds or fits and starts?', in McGonagle & Donders (eds) (n 102) 31.

[483] HRC, General Comment No. 34 (2011), §49. See also HRC, *Concluding Observations, Hungary* (2010) UN Doc. CCPR/C/HUN/CO/5, §19 ('The Committee is concerned that the evolution of the so-called "memory laws" in the State party risks criminalizing a wide range of views on the understanding of the post-World War II history of the State party. The State party should review its "memory laws" so as to ensure their compatibility with articles 19 and 20 of the Covenant').

[484] HRC, General Comment No. 34 (2011), §49. See also HRC, *Concluding Observations, Hungary* (2010) UN Doc. CCPR/C/HUN/CO/5, §19.

[485] HRC, *Faurisson v. France* (Comm. no. 550/1993), 8 November 1996, §9.7. See O'Flaherty (n 110) 653 ('the Committee adjusted the provision on "memory" laws, or "laws that penalise the expression of opinions about historical facts", to the effect that they are never compatible with the ICCPR (thus overruling *Faurisson*)'). Cf. HRC, *Zündel v. Canada* (Comm. no. 953/2000), 27 July 2003, §8.5.

[486] See, e.g., HRC, *Concluding Observations, Lithuania* (2018) UN Doc. CCPR/C/LTU/CO/4, §§27–28 (expressing concern 'at reports of recently proposed legislative amendments that would ban the sale of material that 'distorts historical facts' about the nation'). See ch. 3 (Hate Speech).

[487] HRC, General Comment No. 34 (2011), §49.

[488] See, e.g., ECtHR, *Pastörs v. Germany* (App. no. 55225/14), 3 October 2019, §48. The European Court's approach is however consistent with the position of the African Court on denial laws: See ACtHPR, *Umuhoza v. Rwanda* (App. no. 3/2014), 24 November 2017.

the basis that they run counter to the 'fundamental values' of the Convention.[489] Such rulings are made under the admissibility provisions of article 17 of the Convention, which prohibits 'any act aimed at the destruction of any of the rights and freedoms' contained in the treaty, thereby by-passing any balancing exercise that would be required under article 10.[490] Statements of historical untruths about the Holocaust have been construed by the European Court as 'one of the most acute forms of racial defamation of Jews and of incitement to hatred of them'.[491] For this reason such language has consistently been held to reach article 17's 'high threshold',[492] that applies 'on an exceptional basis and in extreme cases'.[493] And the Court has, on this basis, allowed restrictions to speech constituting Holocaust-denial even when it was uttered in a national parliament or during a comedy sketch, and even when the penalty for such speech has included a prison term.[494]

3.2.2. Blasphemy

Another major divergence that has developed between the Human Rights Committee and the European Court relates to the question of blasphemy: speech that insults religious ideas, icons, places or the feelings of religious communities.[495] After a long debate at the UN about whether 'defamation of religions' was speech that could legitimately be penalized,[496] the Human Rights Committee has made clear that all '[p]rohibitions of displays of lack of respect for a religion or other belief system, including blasphemy laws, are incompatible with the Covenant, except in the specific circumstances envisaged in

---

[489] See, e.g., ECtHR, *Witzsch v. Germany* (App. no. 7485/03), 13 December 2005, §3: 'The applicant's statement that the opinion expressed by W. was part of the war propaganda and after-war atrocity propaganda combined with the denial of Hitler's and the national Socialists' responsibility in the extermination of the Jews showed the applicant's disdain towards the victims of the Holocaust [...] ran counter to the text and the spirit of the Convention. Consequently, he cannot, in accordance with Article 17 of the Convention, rely on the provisions of Article 10 as regards his statements at issue.'
[490] ECHR Art. 17.
[491] ECtHR, *Garaudy v. France* (App. no. 65831/01) 24 June 2003, §29. See, e.g., ECtHR, *M'Bala M'Bala v. France* (App. no. 25239/13), 20 October 2015, §40 ('the blatant display of a hateful and anti-Semitic position disguised as an artistic production is as dangerous as a fully-fledged and sharp attack'). This is consistent with the HRC's position in the Faurisson case, before this reasoning was rejected.
[492] ECtHR, *Lilliendahl v. Iceland* (App. no. 29297/18), 12 May 2020, §25.
[493] Ibid. See also ECtHR, *Perinçek v. Switzerland* (App. no. 27510/08), 15 October 2015, §114.
[494] ECtHR, *Pastörs v. Germany* (App. no. 55225/14), 3 January 2020; ECtHR, *M'Bala M'Bala v. France* (App. no. 25239/13), 20 October 2015; ECtHR, *Witzsch v. Germany* (App. no. 7485/03), 13 December 2005. The European Court has however refused to extend its reasoning on Holocaust denial to denial of the Armenian genocide, creating a 'speculative hierarchy between the Holocaust and other twentieth-century mass atrocities'. A. Cherviatsova, 'Memory as a battlefield: European memorial laws and freedom of speech' (2021) 25(4) *The International Journal of Human Rights* 675, 684. See also ECtHR, *Perinçek v. Switzerland* (App. no. 27510/08), 15 October 2015.
[495] See ch. 3 (Hate Speech), s. II.1.1. (Type of speech) and s. III.2.2. (Legitimacy). See USCIRF, 'Violating Rights: Enforcing the World's Blasphemy Laws' (2020).
[496] For over a decade beginning in the late 1990s, the Organization of Islamic Cooperation (OIC) pushed for the adoption of a number of resolutions in the UN Human Rights Council and at the UNGA that recognized the concept of 'defamation of religions' and sought to either prohibit or criminalize speech disrespectful of religion, while Western nations consistently rejected the concept and the resolutions that sought to entrench it. In 2011, a consensus was reached by way of the Human Rights Council's Resolution 16/18, which moved away from a legal prohibition regarding the defamation of religions and instead 'presents an action-oriented approach to combat religious intolerance through practical steps that states should take, such as enforcing anti-discrimination laws and speaking out against intolerance, while also protecting freedoms of speech and religion': see E. Aswad & others, 'Why the United States Cannot Agree to Disagree on Blasphemy Laws' (2014) 32 *Boston University International Law Journal*, 144–145.

article 20, paragraph 2' (which penalizes incitement to 'discrimination, hostility or violence').[497] The Committee has consequently repeatedly recommended that states repeal blasphemy provisions in their national laws.[498] And in the case of *Rabbae v. The Netherlands,* the Committee emphasized that 'criticism of even the most deeply-held convictions of the adherents of a religion is protected by freedom of expression.'[499]

The European Court has taken a different view by considering that blasphemy laws can constitute legitimate restrictions on speech. The Court has recognized a 'wider margin of appreciation ... when regulating freedom of expression in relation to matters liable to offend intimate personal convictions within the sphere of ... religion' and has held that, because what 'is likely to cause substantial offence to persons of a particular religious persuasion will vary significantly from time to time and place to place ... State authorities are in principle in a better position than an international judge to give an opinion' on the need for such a restriction.[500] Although a 'religious group must tolerate the denial by others of their religious beliefs and even the propagation by others of doctrines hostile to their faith', the Court has held that this does not extend to statements that 'incite to hatred or religious intolerance'.[501] Applying this approach, the European Court has approved a criminal conviction for 'disparaging religious doctrines' in Austria after a woman referred to the 56-year-old Prophet Muhammad's marriage to his wife Aisha as 'paedophilia', even though it was accepted that the marriage began when she was six years old.[502]

3.2.3. Intent and harm requirements

Although all international and regional courts and human rights bodies recognize that restrictions to speech must be both necessary and proportionate, there is some variation in how these bodies interpret the integral components of necessity, namely the level of mental culpability the speaker should have (negligence, recklessness or malice) and the type, seriousness, imminence and foreseeability of harm required before speech can be penalized or even criminalized.

There is minimal guidance from international and regional human rights bodies as to the requisite level of intent that should be required by law before speech can be sanctioned, and existing guidance is somewhat divergent. This is most apparent for defamatory speech: the Human Rights Committee and the Inter-American bodies favour the 'actual malice' test, derived from the seminal US Supreme Court decision in *New York Times v. Sullivan,* which decided that untrue statements about public officials should not

---

[497] HRC, General Comment No. 34 (2011), §48.
[498] See HRC, *Concluding Observations, Kuwait* (2016) UN Doc. CCPR/C/KWT/CO/3, §§39, 41; HRC, *Concluding Observations, Russian Federation* (2015) UN Doc. CCPR/C/RUS/CO/7, §19; HRC, *Concluding Observations, Ireland* (2014) UN Doc. CCPR/C/IRL/CO/4, §22.
[499] HRC, *Rabbae v. Netherlands* (Comm. no. 2124/2011), 18 November 2016, §10.5.
[500] ECtHR, *Murphy v. Ireland* (App. no. 44179/98), 10 July 2003, §67. See also ECtHR, *Wingrove v. United Kingdom* (App. No. 17419/90), 25 November 1996, §53; ECtHR, *I.A. v. Turkey* (App. no. 42571/98), 13 September 2005, §25.
[501] ECtHR, *Tagiyev v. Azerbaijan* (App. no. 13274/08), 5 December 2019, §44; ECtHR (GC), *E.S. v. Austria* (App. no. 38450/12), 25 October 2018, §52.
[502] ECtHR (GC), *E.S. v. Austria* (App. no. 38450/12), 25 October 2018. See ch. 3 (Hate Speech), s. II.2.1.2. (Austria) and III.2.2. (Legitimacy).

be sanctioned if published 'in error but without malice',[503] whereas European and African courts have declined to adopt this standard.[504] And the European Court has generally applied a lenient approach to intent across the spectrum of speech offences. While the Court considers intent a relevant factor in determining the necessity of restrictions to a range of different types of speech,[505] in a number of cases and even in the criminal context, it has allowed convictions without a clear showing of intent or simply by inferring intent on the basis of the offensive content of the speech.[506]

The European Court has also adopted a more lenient approach than its counterparts when it comes to defining the harm that is required before hate speech can be penalized. For instance, members of the Human Rights Committee have suggested that criminal penalties for hate speech should be limited to 'speech that incites the commission of criminal offences or acts of violence'[507] and the UN-approved Rabat Plan of Action requires 'a *reasonable probability* that the speech would succeed in *inciting actual action* against the target group'.[508] The European Court has, on the other hand, held that hateful speech does not need to 'involve an explicit call for an act of violence, or other criminal acts' and that states may choose to validly restrict speech 'insulting, holding up to ridicule or slandering specific groups of the population'.[509]

This less exacting harm threshold is also coupled with a more lenient causation standard at the European Court. The Human Rights Committee has determined that a state 'must demonstrate in specific and individualized fashion the precise nature of the threat' caused by speech and establish a 'direct and immediate connection between the expression and the threat'.[510] And the Inter-American and African bodies have taken a similar approach.[511] The European Court, by contrast, considers as a relevant, but not

---

[503] Since *New York Times v. Sullivan,* US courts have extended this principle to public figures, and then to private figures suing on a matter of public concern where presumed or punitive damages are sought: US Supreme Court, *Curtis Publishing Co v. Butts* 388 US 130, 12 June 1967; US Supreme Court, *Gertz v. Welch Inc* 418 US 323, 25 June 1974; US Supreme Court, *Dun & Bradstreet Inc v Greenmoss Builders Inc* 472 US 749, 26 June 1985. See ch. 2 (Insulting Speech), s. III.3.1. (Intent of the speaker). HRC, General Comment No. 34 (2011), §47. Inter-American bodies have not applied a consistent test but have generally formulated intent standards by reference to an 'actual malice' or at least 'gross negligence' requirement: See ch. 2 (Insulting Speech), s. III.3.1. (Intent of the speaker).

[504] See ch. 2 (Insulting Speech), s. III.3.1. (Intent of the speaker).

[505] See, e.g., ECtHR (GC), *Jersild v. Denmark* (App. no. 15890/89), 23 September 1994, §33 (in the context of hate speech); ECtHR, *Salov v. Ukraine* (App. no. 65518/01), 6 September 2005, §113 (in the context of misinformation).

[506] See, e.g., ECtHR, *Leroy v. France* (App. no. 36109/03), 2 October 2008, §43; ECtHR, *Nix v. Germany* (App. no. 35285/16), 13 March 2018, §51. See ch. 3 (Hate Speech).

[507] HRC, *Rabbae v. Netherlands* (Comm. no. 2124/2011), Individual opinion (concurring) of Committee members Sarah Cleveland and Mauro Politi, §7. See ch. 3 (Hate Speech), s. II.1.2. (Harm). See also, ACmHPR Declaration of Principles on Freedom of Expression in Africa (2019), Principle 23(2). See further, IACtHR, *Usón Ramírez v. Venezuela* (Series C, no. 207), 20 November 2009, §§73–75.

[508] Rabat Plan of Action on the prohibition of advocacy of national, racial or religious hatred that constitutes incitement to discrimination, hostility or violence, §29(f) (emphasis added).

[509] ECtHR, *Atamanchuk v. Russia* (App. no. 4493/11), 11 February 2020, §52; see also ECtHR, *Vejdeland v. Sweden* (App. no. 1813/07), 9 February 2012, §55.

[510] HRC, General Comment No. 34 (2011), §35, citing HRC, *Shin v. Republic of Korea* (Comm. no. 926/2000), 16 March 2004. See also HRC, *Ross v. Canada* (Comm. no. 736/1997), 18 October 2000, §11.5.

[511] See, e.g., Declaration of Principles on Freedom of Expression in Africa (2019), Principle 23(2); IACmHR, *Violence Against Lesbian, Gay, Bisexual, Trans and Intersex Persons in the Americas* (2015) OEA/Ser.L/V/II. Doc.36/15 Rev.2, §235. Although in the context of defamatory speech the Inter-American Court assumes the harm exists and does not analyse the causal link: See ch. 2 (Insulting Speech), s. III.3.2. (Causal link between the speech and the harm).

determinative, factor whether speech is 'capable of' or 'could... be seen as a call for' the requisite harm,[512] or in some cases circumvents any detailed analysis of this issue entirely.[513]

3.2.4. Defences

Some defences, such as the defence of truth, are recognized across international and regional courts and human rights bodies.[514] But the impact of speech dealing with a matter of public interest is treated somewhat differently depending on the human rights body and the category of speech in question.[515] The Human Rights Committee has suggested 'a public interest in the subject matter of the criticism should be recognized as a defence' for defamatory speech,[516] but regional human rights bodies state that this should be a factor favouring a higher degree of protection, not a defence.[517] The European Court has also declined to apply this higher degree of protection if such speech constitutes a call for 'hatred' or 'intolerance'.[518]

3.2.5. Relevance of whether the speaker is a journalist

Despite a high degree of convergence in the approach of international bodies about the importance of protecting the press,[519] a key point of difference in jurisprudence is the European Court's application of what it describes as a 'responsible journalism' doctrine.

According to the European Court, the 'protection' afforded to the press is 'subject to the proviso that they act in good faith in order to provide accurate and reliable information in accordance with the tenets of responsible journalism'.[520] But no other international body has used a 'responsible journalism' doctrine to determine the outcome of cases involving speech by the press. The Inter-American Court has held that journalists 'must, when exercising their duties, abide by the principles of responsible journalism, namely to act in good faith, provide accurate and reliable information, objectively reflect the opinions of those involved in a public debate, and refrain from pure

---

[512] See, e.g., ECtHR, *Ibragimov v. Russia* (App. nos. 1413/08 & 28621/1128 August 2018, §98; ECtHR, *Perinçek v. Switzerland* (App. no. 27510/08) 15 October 2015, §§206–207, 240. See ch. 6 (Terrorism Laws), s.III.3.2. (Causal link between speech and harm).

[513] See, e.g., ECtHR, *Molnar v. Romania* (App. no. 16637/06), 23 October 2012, §23; ECtHR, *Leroy v. France* (App. no. 36109/03), 2 October 2008, §45.

[514] See ch. 2 (Insulting Speech), s. III.4.1. (Truth); ch. 3 (Hate Speech), s. III.2.4.1. (Truth) and ch. 4 (False Speech), s. III.4.1. (Truth).

[515] There is a degree of consistency as to the minimum floor of protection for public interest speech: See s. II.3.1.4. (Political and public interest speech).

[516] See ch. 2 (Insulting Speech), s. III.4.2. (Public Interest); HRC, General Comment No. 34 (2011), §47.

[517] See ch. 2 (Insulting Speech), s. III.4.2. (Public interest). See, e.g., ECtHR (GC), *Bédat v. Switzerland* (App. no. 56925/08), 29 March 2016, §49. See also IACtHR, *Herrera-Ulloa v. Costa Rica* (Series C, no. 107), 2 July 2004, §§128–129.

[518] See, e.g., ECtHR (GC), *Perinçek v. Switzerland* (App. no. 27510/08), 15 October 2015, §§230–231. See ch. 3 (Hate Speech), s. III.2.4.3. (Public interest).

[519] See s. II.3.1.5. (Importance of protecting the press).

[520] ECtHR, *Gîrleanu v. Romania* (App. no. 50376/09), 26 June 2018, §84. This passage is sometimes written as 'in accordance with the *ethics of journalism*', rather than the 'tenets of responsible journalism': see, e.g., ECtHR, *Fressoz v. France* (App. no. 29183/95), 21 January 1999, §54; ECtHR (GC), *Bladet Tromsø v. Norway* (App. no. 21980/93), 20 May 1999, §65.

sensationalism'.[521] But the doctrine does not appear to be dispositive of cases before the Court.[522] Indeed, Inter-American bodies have adopted the 'actual malice' standard of culpability for all speech relating to public figures, which sets a high standard for protection of all political speech regardless of the speaker's profession.[523] Neither the African Court, nor the UN bodies—the Human Rights Committee and the Working Group on Arbitrary Detention—have used the doctrine in their decisions.[524]

The European Court applies the doctrine by addressing three questions. First, it considers whether a journalist has acted unlawfully in 'the manner in which the information was obtained' since journalists are not supposed to be above the law.[525] Secondly, 'responsible journalism requires that the journalists check the information provided to the public to a reasonable extent': 'special grounds' are required before the media can be dispensed from their 'ordinary obligation to verify factual statements'.[526] And finally, the Court considers the manner of presentation of the speech, recognizing that although a court should not seek to determine 'what technique of reporting should be adopted by journalists', and journalistic freedom allows 'recourse to a degree of exaggeration, or even provocation', this deference is not 'unlimited'.[527]

While these questions—essentially relating to whether the speaker was negligent or reckless as to the falsity of the speech—are in themselves unobjectionable, and indeed the issue of intent or mental fault is relevant to an analysis of all speech under international standards,[528] the relevance of the profession of the speaker is not clear. Is the Court saying that it provides *heightened* protection for journalists—separate from the higher protection (or, in its terms, narrowed margin of appreciation) applied to political and public interest speech if the speech meets the test of 'reasonableness'? Or is it *reducing* the standard level protection available when journalists do not act responsibly? The Court has applied this doctrine even in circumstances where it does not consider that an impugned publication could be regarded as 'contributing to a debate of public interest' or as constituting 'political speech' so in these cases at least it seems to be establishing a

---

[521] IACtHR, *Mémoli v. Argentina* (Series C, no. 265), 22 August 2013, §122.
[522] See ch. 2 (Insulting Speech), s. III.4.3. (Reasonable publication).
[523] See ch. 2 (Insulting Speech), s. III.3.1. (Intent of the speaker).
[524] Cf. WGAD, *Tri Agus Susanto Siswowihardjo v. Indonesia* (Opinion no. 42/1996), 3 December 1996, §8 ('The integrity, or lack of it, of Tri Agus in violating the code of ethics of journalism is again not germaine to the issue'). See also ACmHPR, *Scanlen & Holderness v. Zimbabwe* (Comm. no. 297/05), 3 April 2009, §120.
[525] ECtHR (GC), *Pentikäinen v. Finland* (App. no. 11882/10), 20 October 2015, §90. See also ECtHR, *Brambilla v. Italy* (App. no. 22567/09), 23 June 2016, §64 ('The Court reiterates that the concept of responsible journalism requires that whenever a journalist's conduct flouts the duty to abide by ordinary criminal law, the journalist has to be aware that he or she is liable to face legal sanctions, including of a criminal character'); ECtHR, *Salihu v. Sweden* (App. no. 33628/15), 10 May 2016, §59 (where journalists purchased a firearm to demonstrate the ease of doing so, and the Court held this 'could have been illustrated by other means').
[526] ECtHR (GC), *Kącki v. Poland* (App. no. 10947/11), 4 July 2017, §52. See also ECtHR, *McVicar v. United Kingdom* (App. no. 46311/99), 7 May 2002, §84; ECtHR (GC), *Bladet Tromsø v. Norway* (App. no. 21980/93), 20 May 1999, §66.
[527] ECtHR (GC), *Jersild v. Denmark* (App. no. 15890/89), 23 September 1994, §31. See also ECtHR (GC), *Bladet Tromsø v. Norway* (App. no. 21980/93), 20 May 1999, §§59, 63; ECtHR (GC), *Couderc and Hachette Filipacchi Associés v. France* (App. no. 40454/07), 10 November 2015, §144.
[528] See ss II.3.2.3. (Intent and harm requirements) and II.3.2.4. (Defences).

separate standard based on the speaker, and not the subject matter of the speech.[529] But the doctrine has also been applied to non-journalists, such as human rights activists, NGOs and whistleblowers who engage in public debate and are also considered 'watchdogs'.[530] This means that the responsible journalism doctrine, although in many cases applied in a manner that is protective of journalists, adds unnecessary confusion.

In addition, in some cases, the application of the doctrine appears to have resulted in the application of stricter standards to a journalist, and has led to questionable outcomes that have inspired strong dissents.

In one case, the dissenting judges recognized that the 'responsible journalism' doctrine was originally 'shorthand for judicial respect for journalistic ethics' and was used to emphasize that journalists do not get immunity if they commit a crime simply because they are journalists.[531] But the judges observe that 'the fact that journalists cannot claim unlimited protection in criminal cases in the name of freedom of expression is now increasingly understood as imposing special duties on journalists in reporting in general in the civil context' and that this 'results in undermining freedom of the press'.[532]

In one case, a newspaper in Moldova had quoted a letter from parents alleging that the principal at their children's public school had taken bribes.[533] The principal asked the newspaper to publish a reply, but it refused.[534] He then successfully sued the newspaper for civil damages, despite the newspaper producing three independent witnesses who testified that they had paid bribes to the principal.[535] The majority found that such penalties were appropriate in light of the newspaper's 'flagrant disregard of the duties of responsible journalism', noting the journalist 'made no attempt to contact' the principal ahead of publication, did not publish his reply, and wrote a further article whose 'tone ... indicate[d] a degree of mockery'.[536] But the dissenting judges argued that the Court had placed undue weight on perceived unprofessional conduct rather than recognizing that the allegations constituted either 'true' statements, 'value judgments' regarding the use of public spending or 'issues of serious public interest', namely the pervasiveness of corruption in the public educational system.[537] The dissent took issue with the Court's focus on the principal not being contacted to—presumably—deny allegations against him, lamenting that if journalists '[d]on't ask a stupid question ... you're in trouble in Strasbourg'.[538] And they concluded that the Court should

---

[529] ECtHR, *Satakunnan Markkinapörssi Oy v. Finland* (App. no. 931/13), 27 June 2017, §§174–178. Cf. Dissenting Opinion of Judges Sajo and Karakas.
[530] ECtHR (GC), *Magyar Helsinki Bizottság v. Hungary* (App. no. 18030/11), 8 November 2016, §159; ECtHR (GC), *Gawlik v. Liechtenstein* (App. no. 23922/19), 16 February 2021, §77.
[531] Ibid., Joint Dissenting Opinion of Judges Sajo and Tsotsoria.
[532] Ibid., Joint Dissenting Opinion of Judges Sajo and Tsotsoria.
[533] ECtHR, *Flux v. Moldova (No. 6)* (App. no. 22824/04), 29 July 2008, Dissenting Opinion of Judge Bonello, Joined by Judges Davíd Thór Björgvinsson and Šikuta, §5. The journalist concerned knew the identity of the authors of the letter but had not disclosed them to protect their children: §18.
[534] Ibid., §6.
[535] Ibid., §20. The domestic court concluded that the statements of three witnesses 'were not sufficient to overturn the presumption of innocence enjoyed by the principal': §11.
[536] Ibid., §§29–34.
[537] Ibid., Joint Dissenting Opinion of Judge Bonello, Joined by Judges David Thor Bjorgvinsson and Sikuta, §§3–6.
[538] Ibid., §14.

not be 'attach[ing] more value to [the] professional[ism] [of] behaviour than to the unveiling of corruption' in the way in which they applied 'the concept of responsible journalism' to speech by the press.

In another case, two journalists in Denmark were convicted and forced to pay over 13,000 Euros for alleging in a television program that a man convicted in a murder trial was innocent and questioning whether a police chief had concealed witness statements. The majority found the conviction appropriate based on the lack of 'responsible journalism'.[539] The Court considered the allegation against the police chief to be insufficiently verified, as the journalists had relied on one witness to make their allegation, and did not check whether there was an objective basis for the witness' evidence.[540] And the allegations ran at peak viewing time, 'in a programme devoted to objectivity and pluralism' and were communicated via audiovisual media, which has 'a much more immediate and powerful effect than the print media'.[541] In light of this, and despite the fact the program dealt with topics 'of serious public interest', the Court considered that the conviction and penalty was proportionate.[542] Eight judges dissented from the Court's reasoning on this point, finding that '[t]he fact that a person who had been sentenced to twelve years' imprisonment for murder and spent almost ten years of his life behind bars was later acquitted on a trial, serves at least to confirm the high degree of public interest involved in the television programme in its endeavour to alert the public to a possible miscarriage of justice'.[543]

The forceful dissents in these cases highlight the problematic use of the doctrine of responsible journalism. Although the issue of verification of sources is clearly relevant, it would be clearer if the European Court had in each case considered the intent or culpability of the speaker, the harm that would likely be caused by the speech and whether it involved matters of public interest, rather than focusing on the profession of the speaker and undefined associated ethical rules. Such an approach also avoids the risk of abuse by authoritarian governments seeking to define 'responsible' content; and it would bring the European Court's approach in line with that of the Human Rights Committee and other international bodies.[544]

3.2.6. *Criminal penalties for speech*
The jurisprudential schism between international and regional bodies on specific types of speech, such as denialism and blasphemy, are representative of a broader divergence

---

[539] ECtHR (GC), *Pedersen and Baadsgaard v. Denmark* (App. no. 49017/99), 17 December 2004, §§10–23, 78.
[540] Ibid., §83.
[541] Ibid., §79.
[542] Ibid., §§71, 78.
[543] Ibid., Joint Partly Dissenting Opinion of Judges Rozakis, Türmen, Strážnická, Bîrsan, Casadevall, Zupančič, Maruste and Hajiyev, §§4–8.
[544] Although the UN-approved Rabat Standards recommend that '[t]he speaker's position or status in the society should be considered, specifically the individual's or organization's standing in the context of the audience to whom the speech is directed', this relates to the harm that is likely to be created by the speech rather than the speaker's profession. See also Meta, 'Our approach to newsworthy content' (Meta Transparency Center, 25 August 2022), 'While the speaker may factor into the balancing test, we do not presume that any person's speech is inherently newsworthy, including politicians'.

on the issue of appropriate penalties for speech. In general, the European Court has allowed criminal penalties more broadly than its counterparts, which have only allowed such penalties for speech in extremely limited circumstances.[545] This is in part a result of the Court's 'margin of appreciation' doctrine, under which the Court gives states significant leeway to define whether restrictions on speech are 'necessary' under article 10(2) of the European Convention.[546] Its approach is also consistent with the history of the Convention, drafted shortly after World War II with a focus on stemming the spread of totalitarian ideology.[547] As a result of this, unlike the Human Rights Committee and other regional bodies, the European Court has found criminal penalties compatible with the right to free speech in dozens of cases, including cases involving terms of imprisonment and speech by journalists.[548]

The cases in which the European Court has allowed criminal penalties cover various types of speech including speech considered 'capable of' or 'liable to' incite violence,[549] speech allegedly advocating, glorifying or justifying terrorism,[550] speech that 'could' be 'seen as a call' for 'hatred or intolerance',[551] speech disclosing state secrets[552] and defamatory speech.[553]

Even though the Court has held that the imposition of a custodial sentence for a media-related offence will be compatible with article 10 of the Convention 'only in exceptional circumstances', it classifies 'hate speech' as constituting such circumstances.[554]

---

[545] See s. II.3.1.6. (Criminal penalties for speech). Although the European Court has accepted that article 10 'protects journalists' rights to divulge information on issues of general interest provided they are acting in good faith and on an accurate factual basis': ECtHR, *Fressoz and Roire v. France* (App. no. 29183/95), 21 January 1999.

[546] See, e.g., ECtHR, *Zana v. Turkey* (App. no. 18954/91), 25 November 1997, §51. However, this margin is more 'limited' when freedom of the press is at stake: see s. II .3.1.5 (Importance of protecting the press), ECtHR (GC), *Stoll v. Switzerland* (App. no. 69698/01), 10 December 2007, §105, citing ECtHR, *Éditions Plon v. France* (App. no. 58148/00), 18 May 2004, §44.

[547] See s. II.1.2.2.1 (European Convention).

[548] See s. II.3.1.6. (Criminal penalties for speech).

[549] See ch. 6 (Terrorism Laws), s. III.3.1. (Harm). See, e.g., ECtHR (GC), *Sürek v. Turkey (No. 1)* (App. no. 26682/95), 8 July 1999, §§62–64; ECtHR, *Zana v. Turkey* (App. no. 18954/91), 25 November 1997. See also ECtHR, *Sürek v. Turkey (No. 3)* (App. no. 24735/94), 8 July 1999; ECtHR, *Altıntaş v. Turkey* (App. no. 50495/08), 10 March 2020, §34; ECtHR, *Gürbüz and Bayar v. Turkey* (App. no. 8860/13), 23 July 2019, §43; ECtHR, *Fatih Taş v. Turkey (No. 3)* (App. no. 45281/08), 24 April 2018, §34.See also ECtHR, *Roj TV A/S v. Denmark* (App. no. 24683/14), 17 April 2018, §31; ECtHR, *Hizb Ut-Tahrir v. Germany* (App. no. 31098/08), 12 June 2012, §§73–74; ECtHR, *Romanov v. Ukraine* (App. no. 63782/11), 16 July 2020, §164.

[550] See ch. 6 (Terrorism Laws), s. III.3.1. (Harm). See, e.g., ECtHR, *Leroy v. France* (App. no. 36109/03), 2 October 2008; ECtHR, *Dmitriyevskiy v. Russia* (App. no. 42168/06), 2 October 2017, §100. Cf. the position of the Human Rights Committee: HRC, General Comment No. 34 (2011), §46 ('Such offences as "encouragement of terrorism" and "extremist activity" as well as offences of "praising", "glorifying" or "justifying" terrorism, should be clearly defined to ensure that they do not lead to unnecessary or disproportionate interference with freedom of expression'). See also ECtHR, *Z.B. v France* (App. no. 46883/15), 2 September 2021, §§63–68; ECtHR, *Rouillan v. France* (App. no. 28000/19), 23 June 2022, §71.

[551] See, e.g., ECtHR, *Ibragimov v. Russia* (App. nos. 1413/08 & 28621/11), 28 August 2018, §§94–98; ECtHR, *Perinçek v. Switzerland* (App. no. 27510/08), 15 October 2015, §207; ECtHR, *Kilin v. Russia* (App. no. 10271/12), 11 May 2021, §§84–89. See also ECtHR (GC), *Sanchez v. France* (App. no. 45581/15), 15 May 2023, §189; ECtHR, *Zemmour v. France* (App. no. 63539/19), 20 December 2022, §§64–67.

[552] See, e.g., ECtHR, *Norman v. United Kingdom* (App. no. 41387/17), 6 July 2021, §89; ECtHR, *Hadjianastassiou v. Greece* (App. no. 12945/87), 16 December 1992.

[553] See, e.g., ECtHR, *Barfod v. Denmark* (App. no. 11508/85), 22 February 1989; ECtHR (GC), *Pedersen and Baadsgaard v. Denmark* (App. no. 49017/99), 17 December 2004; ECtHR, *Prager and Oberschlick v. Austria* (App. no. 15974/90), 26 April 1995.

[554] ECtHR (GC), *Cumpănă v. Romania* (App. no. 33348/96), 17 December 2004, §115; ECtHR, *Ruokanen v. Finland* (App. no. 45130/06), 6 April 2010, §50.

In the context of hate speech, the Court has accepted custodial sentences as appropriate penalties for speech when leaflets distributed to school children described homosexuality as having a 'morally destructive effect'[555] and when posters were found at the home of a far-right sympathizer containing slogans such as 'Romania needs children, not homosexuals'.[556] In cases like the Romanian one, the Court dismissed the application challenging the conviction based on the 'content of the expression and the manner of its delivery',[557] even though the harm that might be caused by such speech was merely hypothetical.[558]

The European Court's readiness to accept criminal penalties for hateful speech in contrast to some other international bodies is ironic given that article 20(2) of the ICCPR expressly requires penalties for speech in certain circumstances,[559] while no equivalent provision exists in the European Convention.[560] However, article 20 does not require *criminal* penalties, and the Human Rights Committee's jurisprudence on article 20 requires higher intent and harm requirements than the European Court before criminal sanctions can apply.[561] Members of the Committee in the leading decision of *Rabbae v. The Netherlands* also held that article 20(2) of the ICCPR sets 'a high bar' that requires not only 'advocacy' of national, racial or religious hatred, but 'incitement' to prohibited harms.[562] The Committee members also suggested that criminal penalties may only be permissible for speech that incites 'criminal offences or acts of violence' (rather than 'discrimination' or 'hostility') given the Committee's 'great caution' in allowing 'the imposition of criminal penalties' to punish speech.[563]

The European Court has also approved of criminal penalties for defamatory speech (i.e., speech that is harmful to reputation), whereas the Human Rights Committee and African bodies have not.[564] The Committee has consistently argued that '[s]tates parties should consider the decriminalization of defamation and, in any case, the application

---

[555] ECtHR, *Vejdeland v. Sweden* (App. no. 1813/07), 9 February 2012 (finding no violation of article 10 for suspended sentences and fines, as well as one defendant being sentenced to probation).

[556] ECtHR, *Molnar v. Romania* (App. no. 16637/06), 23 October 2012 (where an application challenging a six-month term of imprisonment was found inadmissible under article 17).

[557] See, e.g., ECtHR, *Lilliendahl v. Iceland* (App. no. 29297/18), 12 May 2020, §36.

[558] See ch. 3 (Hate Speech), s. II.1.2. (Harm).

[559] See also CERD Art. 4 (mandating states to declare racist propaganda, incitement and acts of racial violence 'offence[s] punishable by law').

[560] See s. II.1.1. (Treaty language) and ch. 3 (Hate Speech), s. III.1. (Mandatory Restrictions on Hate Speech). The CERD Committee has also accepted and indeed mandated such penalties, although its stance has softened in recent years. See ch. 3 (Hate Speech), III.1.2. (CERD Article 4).

[561] See ch. 3 (Hate Speech), s. III.1.1. (ICCPR Article 20). See also HRC, General Comment No. 34 (2011), §50; HRC, *Rabbae v. Netherlands* (Comm. no. 2124/2011), 14 July 2016, Individual Opinion (concurring) of Committee members Sarah Cleveland and Mauro Politi.

[562] HRC, *Rabbae v. Netherlands* (Comm. No. 2124/2011), 14 July 2016, Individual Opinion (concurring) of Committee members Sarah Cleveland and Mauro Politi, §4.

[563] Ibid., Individual Opinion (concurring) of Committee members Sarah Cleveland and Mauro Politi, §7, see also §5 ('it is well established under the Committee's jurisprudence that no individual is entitled to secure the *prosecution* of a particular person' and that the 'Committee has made equally clear, *ipso facto*, that no person is entitled to secure the criminal *conviction* of another person').

[564] See, e.g., ECtHR, *Barfod v. Denmark* (App. no. 11508/85), 22 February 1989; ECtHR (GC), *Pedersen and Baadsgaard v. Denmark* (App. no. 49017/99), 17 December 2004; ECtHR, *Prager and Oberschlick v. Austria* (App. no. 15974/90), 26 April 1995.

of the criminal law should only be countenanced in the most serious of cases and imprisonment is *never* an appropriate penalty'.[565] Other bodies have gone further: the ECOWAS Court has stated that '[t]he existence of criminal defamation and insult or sedition laws are ... inacceptable instances of gross violation of free speech and freedom of expression' and the African Commission called for the repeal of criminal defamation laws across Africa.[566] The African Court and the Working Group on Arbitrary Detention have also consistently found criminal penalties in defamation laws to be disproportionate.[567] Similarly, although the Inter-American Court has allowed criminal penalties for defamatory speech in one outlier judgment,[568] in all other cases it found such measures disproportionate.[569]

The European Court's position on criminal defamation laws is more equivocal. The Court has stated that it will apply 'utmost caution' to such a sanction[570] and has repeatedly found terms of imprisonment to be disproportionate responses to defamatory speech.[571] Nonetheless, the Court has found that 'a criminal measure as a response to defamation cannot, as such, be considered disproportionate to the aim pursued',[572] and it has allowed criminal fines for defamatory speech on a number of occasions: against the author and publisher of a book casting doubt on the innocence of two French resistance members;[573] against an employee who sent anonymous letters containing allegations of corruption and incompetence of his employer;[574] against journalists who produced a documentary insinuating that a doctor had treated patients with a particular drug after being paid by its manufacturer to do so;[575] and against Finnish journalists who implied that a well-known businessman was connected to a homicide.[576]

---

[565] HRC, General Comment No. 34 (2011), §47 (emphasis added), citing HRC, *Concluding Observations, Italy* (2006) UN Doc. CCPR/C/ITA/CO/5; HRC, *Concluding Observations, the Former Yugoslav Republic of Macedonia* (2008) UN Doc. CCPR/C/MKD/CO/2. See also HRC, *Concluding Observations, Portugal* (2020) UN Doc. CCPR/C/PRT/CO/5, §43; *Concluding Observations, Senegal* (2019) UN Doc. CCPR/C/SEN/CO/5, §45; *ConcludingOobservations, Czech Republic* (2019) UN Doc. CCPR/C/CZE/CO/4, §35. See ch. 2 (Insulting Speech), s. III.6.1. (Criminal penalties).
[566] See, e.g., ECOWAS CCJ, *Federation of African Journalists v. Gambia* (Suit no. ECW/CCJ/APP/36/15), 13 February 2018, 37; ACmHPR, Resolution 169(XLVIII)10 on Repealing Criminal Defamation Laws in Africa, 24 November 2010. See also ACmHPR, Declaration of Principles on Freedom of Expression and Access to Information in Africa, Principle 22(2).
[567] See ch. 2 (Insulting Speech), s. III.6.1. (Criminal penalties).
[568] IACtHR, *Mémoli v. Argentina* (Series C, no. 265), 22 August 2013.
[569] See, e.g., IACtHR, *Herrera Ulloa v. Costa Rica* (Series C, no. 107), 2 July 2004, §135; IACtHR, *Canese v. Paraguay* (Series C, no. 111), 31 August 2004, §§105–106.
[570] T. McGonagle, *Freedom of Expression and Defamation: A Study of the Case law of the European Court of Human Rights* (COE 2016), 57.
[571] See, e.g., ECtHR, *Fatullayev v. Azerbaijan* (App. No. 40984/07), 22 April 2010, §103. See ch. 2 (Insulting Speech), s. III.6.1.1.2. (Applicability of penalty of imprisonment for defamatory or insulting speech).
[572] ECtHR (GC), *Lindon, Otchakovsky-Laurens and July v. France* (App. nos. 21279/02 & 36448/02), 22 October 2007, §59; ECtHR, *Radio France v. France* (App. no. 53984/00), 30 March 2004, §40; ECtHR, *Ivanova v. Bulgaria* (App. no. 36207/03), 14 February 2008, §68; ECtHR, *Ruokanen v. Finland* (App. no. 45130/06), 6 April 2010, §50; McGonagle (n 570) 18.
[573] ECtHR, *Chauvy v. France* (App. no. 64915/01), 29 June 2004.
[574] ECtHR, *Wojczuk v. Poland* (App. no. 52969/13), 9 December 2021.
[575] ECtHR, *Frisk and Jensen v. Denmark* (App. no. 19657/12), 5 December 2017.
[576] ECtHR, *Salumäki v. Finland* (App. no. 23605/09), 29 April 2014. See also ECtHR, *Radio France v. France* (App. no. 53984/00), 30 March 2004; ECtHR, *Barfod v. Denmark* (App. no. 11508/85), 22 February 1989; ECtHR (GC), *Prager and Oberschlick v. Austria* (App. no. 15974/90), 26 April 1995.

3.2.7. Remedies

As with other human rights, international bodies adopt a very different approach when it comes to awarding remedies for violations of the right to free speech. According to the Human Rights Committee, an 'effective' remedy for human rights violations as provided by article 2(3)(a) of the ICCPR 'can involve restitution, rehabilitation and ... changes in relevant laws and practices, as well as bringing to justice the perpetrators of human rights violations'.[577]

In the context of violations of article 19 of the ICCPR, the Human Rights Committee will generally award 'adequate' or 'appropriate' compensation or reimbursement to a successful applicant rather than specifying a sum,[578] reimbursement for legal costs or fees[579] and sometimes calls upon states to 'revise', 'amend' or 'review' their legislation.[580] For example, where the Committee found a violation of article 19 of the ICCPR after a journalist was convicted under criminal libel laws in the Philippines for reporting on a politician's alleged extramarital affair, the Committee held that the Philippines was 'under an obligation to take steps to prevent similar violations occurring in the future, including by reviewing the relevant libel legislation'.[581]

In some cases, including one involving fair-trial violations, the Committee has also called for convictions based on speech to be quashed or reviewed.[582] The Committee has also recommended restoration of rights lost due to a conviction, for example where a parliamentarian's right to vote and be elected to office was removed due to a contempt of court conviction that the Committee found had violated article 19.[583] In that case, the Committee considered the 'restoration of his right to vote and to be elected' as part of an adequate remedy.[584] The Committee has also called on states to comply with remedies such as reconsidering an application for a newspaper's registration; returning a painting seized in violation of article 19 in its original condition; and reviewing an application for access to parliamentary press facilities.[585]

In contrast to the Human Rights Committee, the European Court has consistently taken the position that 'its judgments are essentially declaratory in nature and that,

---

[577] HRC, General Comment No. 31 (2004), §16; ICCPR Art. 2(3).
[578] See, e.g., HRC, *Timoshenko v. Belarus* (Comm. no. 2461/2014), 23 July 2020, §9; HRC, *Baytelova v. Kazakhstan* (Comm. no. 2520/2015), 22 July 2020, §11; HRC, *Park v. Republic of Korea* (Comm. no. 628/1995), 20 October 1998, §12; HRC, *Aduayom v. Togo* (Comm. nos. 422/1990 & others), 12 July 1996, §9.
[579] See, e.g., HRC, *Timoshenko v. Belarus* (Comm. no. 2461/2014), 23 July 2020, §9; HRC, *Toregozhina v. Kazakhstan* (Comm. No. 2688/2015) 25 March 2021, §10.
[580] See, e.g., HRC, *Malei v. Belarus* (Comm. no. 2404/2014), 23 July 2020, §11 ('the State party should revise its normative framework on public events'); HRC, *Ballantyne v. Canada* (Comm. nos. 359/1989 & 285/1989), 31 March 1993, §13 ('The Committee calls upon the State party to remedy the violation of article 19 of the Covenant by an appropriate amendment to the law').
[581] HRC, *Adonis v. Philippines* (Comm. no. 1815/2008), 26 October 2011, §9.
[582] See, e.g., HRC, *Mirzayanov v. Belarus* (Comm. no. 2434/2014), 25 July 2019, §10; HRC, *Coleman v. Australia* (Comm. no. 1157/2003), 17 July 2006, §9 ('the State party is under an obligation to provide the author with an effective remedy, including quashing of his conviction'); HRC, *Shin v. Republic of Korea* (Comm. no. 926/2000), 16 March 2004, §9; HRC, *Bodrožić v. Serbia and Montenegro* (Comm. no. 1180/2003), 31 October 2005, §9.
[583] See HRC, *Dissanayake v. Sri Lanka* (Comm. no. 1373/2005), 22 July 2008, §10.
[584] Ibid. (ordering compensation and recommending Sri Lanka 'make such changes to the law and practice, as are necessary to avoid similar violations in the future').
[585] See, e.g., HRC, *Mavlonov and Sa'di v. Uzbekistan* (Comm. no. 1334/2004), 19 March 2009, §10; HRC, *Shin v. Republic of Korea* (Comm. no. 926/2000), 16 March 2004, §9; HRC, *Gauthier v. Canada* (Comm. no. 633/1995), 5 May 1999, §15.

in general, it is primarily for the State concerned to choose the means to be used in its domestic legal order to discharge its legal obligations ... provided that such means are compatible with the conclusions set out in the Court's judgment'.[586] Over the first four decades of its practice, the Court made declarations about whether the European Convention had been violated in individual cases, but refused to order a state to remedy those violations in specific ways, except through compensation.[587] This changed in 2004 when the Committee of Ministers of the Council of Europe, the political body charged with supervising enforcement of the Court's judgments, asked the Court to provide states with greater guidance on the necessary measures to remedy the violation.[588] But the Court's practice directions still state that '[o]nly in extremely rare cases can the Court consider a consequential order aimed at putting an end [to] or remedying the violation in question'.[589]

The result of this approach is that the European Court will usually order damages or costs in cases involving violations of article 10, rather than broader non-monetary remedies or an explicit order that legislation should be reformed.[590] Most awards for breaches of article 10 are less than approximately 20,000 Euros,[591] although in rare decisions—usually relating to defamation—the Court has ordered higher amounts.[592]

In a small proportion of its article 10 cases, the Court has found that a declaration that there has been a violation of article 10 constitutes 'just satisfaction' for any damage suffered.[593] This approach has been described as relying 'on the persuasive power of its ruling', in expectation that each judgment by the Court 'identifies the underlying problem so clearly that states are able to undertake the necessary actions to prevent further breaches at home'.[594] Only in very rare circumstances has the European Court ordered the release of a journalist from custody, for example in a case where a journalist had been sentenced to over eight years' imprisonment after serious due process

---

[586] See, e.g., ECtHR, *Alpay v. Turkey* (App. no. 16538/17), 20 March 2018, §193.
[587] L.R. Helfer, 'Redesigning the European Court of Human Rights: Embeddedness as a Deep Structural Principle of the European Human Rights Regime' (2008) 19(1) *European Journal of International Law* 125, 146.
[588] CoM Resolution Res(2004)3 on judgments revealing an underlying systemic problem, 12 May 2004.
[589] ECtHR, Practice direction on Just Satisfaction claims, 28 March 2007, §23 (emphasis added).
[590] See D. Shelton, *Remedies in International Human Rights Law* (OUP 2015), 384–385 (describing the evolution of the European Court's interpretation of 'just satisfaction' and its impact on remedies).
[591] See, e.g., ECtHR, *Alekhina v. Russia* (App. no. 38004/12), 17 July 2018 (ordering approximately 21,000 EUR for the three applicants, and nearly 12,000 EUR in costs and expenses) See ch. 6 (Terrorism Laws), s. III.4.2. (Truth and opinion); ECtHR, *Gîrleanu v. Romania* (App. no. 50376/09), 26 June 2018 (4,500 EUR of non-pecuniary damages and nearly 3,700 EUR in costs); see ch. 5 (Espionage and Official Secrets Laws), III.5.5. (Penalties); ECtHR, *Salov v. Ukraine* (App. no. 65518/01), 6 September 2005 (ordering 10,000 EUR in non-pecuniary damages plus interest); see ch. 4 (False Speech).
[592] See, e.g., ECtHR, *Bergens Tidende v. Norway* (App. no. 26132/95), 2 May 2000 (awarding approximately 600,000 EUR based on an amount ordered in the domestic court judgment); ECtHR, *MGN Limited v. United Kingdom* (App. no. 39401/04), 12 June 2012 (awarding approximately 286,700 EUR based on success fees paid as part of the settlement of the claimant's appeal).
[593] See, e.g., ECtHR, *Perinçek v. Switzerland* (App. no. 27510/08), 15 October 2015, §295; ECtHR, *Cumpănă v. Romania* (App. no. 33348/96), operative paragraph 2; ECtHR, *Dammann v. Switzerland* (App. no. 77551/01), 25 April 2006, operative paragraph 2.
[594] V. Fikfak, 'Changing State Behaviour: Damages before the European Court of Human Rights' (2019) 29(4) *The European Journal of International Law* 1091, 1093.

violations, with the Court noting that, in certain cases 'the nature of the violation found is such as to leave no real choice as to measures required to remedy it'.[595]

In contrast to the European Court, the Inter-American Court has not traditionally awarded mere declaratory relief plus compensation, but instead has awarded sweeping remedies that seek to restore victims' rights and prevent future violations.[596] Orders annulling convictions are relatively commonplace for the Inter-American Court,[597] as well as orders that states revise laws contravening freedom of expression.[598] And its orders of compensation have often been higher than its European counterpart.[599]

Like the Inter-American Court, African regional human rights bodies have tended to adopt a more generous approach to remedies, providing damages in amounts higher than their European counterparts, ordering legal reform of laws incompatible with freedom of expression and the quashing of unfair convictions.[600] For example, the African Court ordered over $1 million US dollars in damages to a murdered journalist's family members.[601] The African Commission, African Court and ECOWAS Community Court of Justice have all ordered states to decriminalize defamation laws, or to release those who have been detained because of the exercise of freedom of expression. The African Commission has also ordered legal reform where laws allowed impunity for security forces who violated freedom of expression, or were used to deport

---

[595] See, e.g., ECtHR, *Alpay v. Turkey* (App. no. 16538/17), 20 March 2018, §194; ECtHR, *Fatullayev v. Azerbaijan* (App. no. 40984/07), 22 April 2010, §174.

[596] See, e.g., IACtHR, *Ivcher-Bronstein v. Peru* (Series C, no. 74), 6 February 2001, operative paragraph 8 (ordering the State to facilitate the conditions to recover the use and enjoyment of Mr. Ivcher-Bronstein's rights to his company); IACtHR, *Granier (Radio Caracas Televisión) v. Venezuela* (Series C, no. 293), 22 June 2015, operative paragraph 15 (ordering the State to re-establish the concession of the frequency corresponding to the relevant television channel); IACtHR, *Kimel v. Argentina* (Series C, no. 177), 2 May 2008, operative paragraph 11 (ordering the State to bring its laws into conformity with the American Convention to prevent future violations of freedom of expression).

[597] See, e.g., IACtHR, *Kimel v. Argentina* (Series C, no. 177), 2 May 2008, §123; IACtHR, IACtHR, *Herrera Ulloa v. Costa Rica* (Series C, no. 107), 2 July 2004, §195; IACtHR, *Tristán Donoso v. Panama* (Series C, no. 193), 27 January 2009, §195; IACtHR, *Usón Ramírez v. Venezuela* (Series C, no. 207), 20 November 2009, §168.

See, e.g., IACtHR, *Kimel v. Argentina* (Series C, no. 177), 2 May 2008, §140.11 ('To order the State to bring within a reasonable time its domestic legislation into conformity with the provisions of the Inter-American Convention on Human Rights, so that the lack of accuracy acknowledged by the State ... be amended in order to comply with the requirements of legal certainty so that, consequently, they do not affect the exercise of the right to freedom of thought and expression').

[598] The IACtHR has regularly awarded pecuniary damages ranging from approximately 6,000 EUR to 54,000 EUR, non-pecuniary damages from 11,000 EUR to 40,000 EUR, and costs ranging from approximately 3,000 to 44,000 EUR. See, e.g., IACtHR, *Uzcátegui v. Venezuela* (Series C, no. 249), 3 September 2012, §§276–279 (awarding pecuniary damages in the amount of approximately 54,000 EUR, and non-pecuniary damages in the amount of 39,000 EUR for Luis Uzcátegui, the applicant whose right to freedom of expression has been violated); IACtHR, *Tristán Donoso v. Panamá* (Series C, no. 193), 27 January 2009, §191 (awarding non-pecuniary damages in the amount of approximately 11,000 EUR); IACtHR, *Ivcher-Bronstein v. Peru* (Series C, no. 74), 6 February 2001, operative paragraph 10 (awarding costs in the amount of approximately 44,000 EUR).

[599] See ACtHPR, *Konaté v. Burkina Faso* (App. no. 4/2013), 3 June 2016, §§21–23 (where convictions for criminal defamation charges were expunged). Cf. ACtHPR, *Umuhoza v. Rwanda* (App. no. 3/2014), 24 November 2014, §31.

[600] See ACtHPR, *Beneficiaries of Late Norbert Zongo v. Burkina Faso* (App. no. 13/2011), 5 June 2015, operative paragraph ii. See also C. Odinkalu, 'African Court Orders Remedies and Damages in Case of Murdered Journalist' (Open Society Justice Initiative, 9 June 2015).

[601] See, e.g., ACtHPR, *Konaté v. Burkina Faso* (App. no. 4/2013), 3 June 2016, operative paragraph 8 ('orders the Respondent State to amend its legislation on defamation in order to make it compliant with article 9 of the Charter, article 19 of the Covenant and article 66(2)(c) of the Revised ECOWAS Treaty: —by repealing custodial sentences for acts of defamation'); ACmHPR, *Uwimana-Nkusi v. Rwanda* (Comm. no. 426/12), 16 April 2021, §228(iv); ACmHPR, *Article 19 v. Eritrea* (Comm. no. 275/2003), 30 May 2007, operative paragraphs; ECOWAS CCJ, *Federation of African Journalists v. Gambia* (Suit no. ECW/CCJ/APP/36/15), 13 February 2018, operative paragraph 3.

a journalist for his political opinions.⁶⁰² And in a case in which 18 journalists were detained incommunicado and without trial, the Commission ordered their release or a speedy trial.⁶⁰³

III. Conclusion

This book charts the minimum protections for speech enshrined in international human rights law, and illustrates examples where states, through unfair laws or unfair application of their laws, are falling short. Examples throughout the book demonstrate the ways that state practice is sometimes wildly at odds with what governments have committed to doing in international treaties. It also details the new legislative tools relied on by states to quash dissent—not just sedition, treason and criminal defamation laws that have traditionally targeted speech but, increasingly, terrorism, 'false news' and other vague laws that autocrats use to protect themselves against unflattering press.⁶⁰⁴

An analysis of the various international treaties that protect free speech—as well as the reservations and declarations that states have made to them, and the jurisprudence interpreting them—reveals broad convergence on key issues, and a solid basis for concluding that the right to free speech is recognized under customary international law. As a result, states have an obligation to respect the right even if they have not ratified the ICCPR or a regional human rights treaty.

But there are some divergences and challenges that emerge from an analysis of international standards on freedom of speech. A central question is how best to protect freedom of the press. On the one hand, international bodies have recognized that the media plays a unique role in a democratic society. But legal doctrines that attempt to set journalists apart from other speakers threaten to lower the bar for 'ordinary' speakers. They also embolden states to crack down on any speaker who may not fit the conventional mould of a journalist.⁶⁰⁵ Endowing journalists or media workers with rights that are different from other speakers 'potentially opens a door to censorship by offering whoever defines the status of journalist control of access to the privileges necessary for journalism',⁶⁰⁶ creating a framework for abuse by authoritarian states.⁶⁰⁷

A better approach is the one adopted by the Human Rights Committee, which states that all speakers are entitled to the same freedoms, and that the right to free expression

---

⁶⁰² ACmHPR, *Law Office of Ghazi Suleiman v. Sudan* (Comm. no. 228/99), 29 May 2003; ACmHPR, *Good v. Botswana* (Comm. no. 313/05), 26 May 2010, §§195, 244(ii).
⁶⁰³ ACmHPR, *Article 19 v. Eritrea* (Comm. no. 275/2003), 30 May 2007. See also ACmHPR, *Zegveld v. Eritrea* (Comm. no. 250/2002), 20 November 2003 (ordering Eritrea to release 11 detainees who had neither been charged nor brought to court).
⁶⁰⁴ See ch. 2 (Insulting Speech), s. II. (State Practice); ch. 3 (Hate Speech), s. II. (State Practice); ch. 4 (False Speech), s. II. (State Practice) and ch. 5 (Speech Related to National Security: Espionage and Official Secrets Laws), s. II. (State Practice) and ch. 6. (Terrorism Laws), s. II. (State Practice).
⁶⁰⁵ R.C. Paddock, 'Myanmar Soldiers, Aiming to Silence Protests, Target Journalists' (New York Times, 1 April 2021).
⁶⁰⁶ Tambini (n 444) 523–539. See also A. Lewis, 'A Preferred Position for Journalism' (1979) 7(3) *Hofstra Law Review* 595–628, 608. Cf. P. Stewart, 'Or of the Press' (1975) 26 *Hastings Law Journal* 631.
⁶⁰⁷ See ECtHR (GC), *Rusu v. Romania* (App. no. 25721/04), 24 November 2017, Dissenting Opinion of Judges Sajó and Tsotsoria.

should only be curtailed under stringent conditions related to intent, harm, causation and proportionate penalties.[608] Speech should also benefit from certain exemptions or protections based on the type of speech in question (as opposed to the identity of the speaker or the viewpoint expressed by the speaker) such as a higher 'intent' requirement when speech relates to a matter of public interest, and protection for statements that are true or expressions of opinion.[609]

A second challenge is that the treaties that govern free speech were drafted decades ago, in a specific post-war context that influenced the text that was adopted. The drafters clearly had in mind the dangers of the Nazi propaganda machine and the capacity of speech to incite fascism. The outcome consists of prohibitions that are in some ways too narrow – by being limited to speech that is hateful on 'national', 'racial' or 'religious' grounds but not others. In other ways the language that was adopted was too broad, allowing speech to be targeted based on vague harms such as potential 'contempt' and 'discrimination' untethered to criminal or violent consequences. The standards are therefore both under-inclusive of certain groups that may be targeted, and under-protective of speech. And they are not addressed to the technology and social media companies that are principal gatekeepers of speech in the modern day.

Finally, there is the question of penalties. The Human Rights Committee, African and Inter-American human rights bodies have largely rejected restrictions on speech through criminal penalties, and terms of imprisonment have almost never been found compatible with the right to freedom of expression. Generally speaking, these bodies correctly find that speech itself should not be criminal, but that it can be a *mode* of committing a criminal offence and that even when speech is abhorrent it is best for courts to walk the 'difficult path of denouncing the bigot's hateful ideas ... yet at the same time challenging any community's attempt to suppress hateful ideas by force of law'.[610] So far, however, the European Court of Human Rights has developed a unique body of jurisprudence that is more permissive of criminal sanctions against speakers, particularly when it comes to hate speech such as Holocaust denial and blasphemy. This sets a dangerous precedent whereby speech can be criminalized based on content, at the discretion of a government or court.

This book aims to distil the minimum protections for speech enshrined in international law and—where there is a divergence or gap—set out a recommended policy endorsed by global experts. Codifying international standards can help to guide both governments and private companies navigating the contemporary challenges of protecting freedom of expression. And enforcing these global standards would reduce the ability of autocratic regimes to weaponize the law to silence journalists and other independent voices. The hope is that this text can be used in courtrooms and newsrooms around the world by those working to protect our right to freedom of speech, and to bring to justice those who violate it.

---

[608] But this approach does not detract from a state's positive obligations to encourage an independent and diverse media and protect them from abuse: See s. II.1.1.2. (Obligation to prevent abuses by others).
[609] See s. II.3.2.5. (Relevance of whether the speaker is a journalist).
[610] US Supreme Court, *Virginia v. Black* 538 U.S. 343, 7 April 2003.

2

Insulting Speech

Philippa Webb, Dario Milo and Rosana Garciandia

I. Introduction	72	
II. State Practice	74	
1. Overview of Laws Regulating Insulting Speech	74	
1.1. Type of speech	75	
1.2. Intent	75	
1.3. Harm	77	
1.3.1. Causal link between the speech and the harm	77	
1.3.2. Level of harm caused by the speech	78	
1.3.2.1. Measuring harm: identity of the speaker	79	
1.3.2.2. Measuring harm: the extent to which the speech is public	79	
1.4. Exclusions, exceptions and defences	81	
1.4.1. Truth	81	
1.4.2. Public interest	81	
1.4.3. Reasonable publication	83	
1.4.4. Fair and accurate reporting of official documents	83	
1.4.5. Opinion	84	
1.5. Penalties	85	
1.5.1. Criminal penalties	85	
1.5.2. Civil penalties	89	
1.5.3. Other penalties	91	
2. Application of National Laws	92	
2.1. Europe	92	
2.1.1. Spain	92	
2.1.2. Turkey	93	
2.1.3. SLAPP and libel tourism	94	
2.2. Asia Pacific	96	
2.2.1. Thailand	96	
2.2.2. India	97	
2.2.3. Philippines	97	
2.3. North and South America	99	
2.3.1. Ecuador	99	
2.4. Middle East and Africa	100	
2.4.1. South Africa	100	
2.4.2. Saudi Arabia	100	
III. International Legal Standards	101	
1. Legality	101	
2. Legitimacy	104	
3. Necessity	105	
3.1. Intent	105	
3.2. Causal link between the speech and the harm	107	
3.3. Level of harm caused by the speech	108
3.3.1. Measuring harm: subject matter of speech or identity of the target	109
3.3.1.1. Statements about public officials including heads of state or government	110
3.3.1.2. Statements about the military, police or security forces	111
3.3.1.3. Statements about the judiciary	112
3.3.1.4. Statements about national symbols	113
3.3.2. Measuring harm: the extent to which the speech is public	113
4. Exclusions, Exceptions and Defences	114
4.1. Truth	114
4.2. Public interest	116
4.3. Reasonable publication	120
4.3.1. Lawfulness of journalist's conduct	121
4.3.2. Verification of facts	121
4.3.3. Form and manner of the speech and its presentation	122
4.4. Accurate reporting of official documents	124
4.5. Opinion	125
5. Right to a Fair Trial	127
6. Penalties	128
6.1. Criminal penalties	128
6.1.1. Criminalization	128
6.1.1.1. Applicability of criminal penalties to defamatory or insulting speech	128
6.1.1.2. Applicability of penalty of imprisonment for defamatory or insulting speech	132
6.2. Civil penalties	135
6.2.1. Damages	135
6.2.2. Injunctions	138
6.2.3. Costs	139
6.2.4. Deprivation of other rights	139
IV. Recommendations	140

I. Introduction

Speech about a nation's leaders is at the heart of the democratic process, allowing voters to understand and challenge the actions of elected officials and other powerful figures such as judges, military officers or parliamentarians. [1] But there is a long history of stifling such speech by way of insult, defamation, sedition and similar laws.[2] The infamous Star Chamber in England began to enforce criminal libel laws at the beginning of the 17th century to control the press during the reigns of James I and Charles I and suppress political and religious discussion.[3] Colonial sedition laws used to silence critics and minority voices, including Gandhi in India and Mandela in South Africa, are still in steady use today.[4] Although insult and defamation laws may serve the legitimate function of protecting a person's reputation, in practice these laws can present a threat to freedom of the press and to anyone seeking to express their political views.

Today, more than 160 countries have criminal defamation laws on their books, and many of these—instead of providing extra protection for political speech—include aggravated punishment for speech that criticizes public officials, heads of state, state bodies and the State itself.[5] Civil defamation laws can also result in damages awards so high that they can bankrupt individuals, including journalists and media outlets.[6] And

---

[1] The authors would like to thank the following: King's College London students in the Media Freedom Seminar (2019–2021) (Olivia Arana Figueroa, Marah Badran, Ezgi Nur Baytok, Laura Bertagnoli, Cai Cherry, Gabriela Commateo, Phoebe Cook, Aya Dardari, Aleksandra Dobrzynska, Misha English-McBeth, Tara Fiechter, Chloe Gershon, Lili Grosser, Carla Hibbert, Celine Hou, Ines Infante, Tanya Joon, Karen Kandelman, Hanna Lehmonen, Isha Murugkar, Andreea M Popovici, Lucia Saborio, Angeliki Salichou, Isabelle Standen, Matthew Tang, Alessandra Thomas, Ilinca Tuvene); student researchers, Emma Montoya and Drishti Suri; expert commentators, including Catherine Anite, Galina Arapova, Matthew Caruana Galizia, Gabriela Cuevas, Karen Eltis, Peter Feeney, Gail Gove, Dougal Hurley, Peter Bartlett, Peter Jacobsen, David Kaye, Marko Milanovic, Michael O'Flaherty, Professor Kate O'Regan, Advocate Gilbert Marcus SC, Maria Ressa, Jennifer Robinson, Judge Robert Sack, Michael Tugendhat, Francoise Tulkens, Nik Williams, Can Yeginsu; the outstanding editorial team of Alice Gardoll, Perri Lyons, Patricia Peña-Drilon, and Nadine Reiner; and the editors Amal Clooney and Lord David Neuberger for their wise guidance and enduring commitment to this important project.

[2] This chapter uses the terms 'insult' and 'defamation' laws interchangeably, to describe the set of laws that impose criminal or civil liability on speech on the grounds that it harms the reputation, honour or dignity of the subject. This includes speech captured by *lèse-majesté* laws, which prohibit insult of the monarchy, as well as 'sedition', an archaic offence criminalizing the incitement of rebellion against the government: see CFJ, *TrialWatch Fairness Report: The Crime of Sedition: At the Crossroads of Reform and Resurgence* (April 2022). Some scholars have articulated a theoretical distinction between defamation and insult laws: 'that the former focus only on the false assertion of fact, while the latter are meant to penalize the truth', or that insult laws protect a person's feelings whereas defamation laws seek to protect their reputation. However, vague and poorly worded defamation laws mean that this distinction is often not clear in practice: see, e.g., E. Yanchukova, 'Criminal Defamation and Insult Laws: An Infringement on the Freedom of Expression in European and Post-Communist Jurisdictions' (2003) 41 *Columbia Journal of Transnational Law* 861, 863–864; see s. II. (State practice).

[3] V.V. Veeder, 'The History and Theory of the Law of Defamation' (1903) 3 *Columbia Law Review* 546, 567–568.

[4] See s. II.2.2.2. (India); B.T. Balule, 'Insult Laws: A Challenge to Media Freedom in the SADC's Fledgling Democracies?' (2008) 41(3) *The Comparative and International Law Journal of Southern Africa* 404, 408–409; J. Bahkle, 'Savarkar (1883–1966), Sedition and Surveillance: The Rule of Law in a Colonial Situation' (2010) 35 *Social History* 51, 53.

[5] UNESCO, *Journalism is a public good: World Trends in Freedom of Expression and Media Development: Global Report 2021/2022: Highlights* (2021), 12 . See s. II.1.5. (Penalties).

[6] See, e.g., OSCE, *Defamation and Insult Laws in the OSCE Region: A Comparative Study* (2017), 209. See s. II.1.5.2. (Civil penalties).

many countries still have sedition and similar laws that allow for the penalization and even criminalization of political speech.[7]

States are not shy about using such laws to suppress insulting political speech. Over 9,000 people were imprisoned for insulting President Erdoğan between 2014 and 2020.[8] In the world's largest democracy, India, more than 7,000 people have faced sedition charges since Narendra Modi was elected prime minister in 2014.[9] Alexei Navalny, the Russian opposition figure, was charged with criminal slander.[10] Maria Ressa, a Nobel Prize-winning Filipino journalist, has faced a string of libel prosecutions that expose her to decades behind bars.[11] And before she was murdered in 2017, Maltese journalist Daphne Caruana Galizia was facing more than 40 libel claims filed by government officials, companies and individuals that her son Matthew described as a 'never-ending type of torture' in response to her reporting on government corruption.[12]

Such practices violate the obligation of states to protect freedom of speech under international law. International standards require states to provide extra protection for speech about matters of public interest, and mandate that they do not penalize speech that is true or expresses an opinion.[13] And these standards strictly restrict the circumstances under which it is ever permissible to impose criminal penalties for speech.[14]

More needs to be done to enforce international standards that exist to protect freedom of speech. But international standards also need clarification or development. For instance, international bodies generally agree that imprisonment is not an appropriate penalty in defamation laws or similar laws used to target insults to public officials.[15] However, some bodies permit criminalization in exceptional cases and the European Court of Human Rights allows states a 'margin of appreciation' to do so.[16] In addition, international standards are not sufficiently clear about the requisite level of culpability required of a speaker before particular penalties can be imposed.[17] And the standards related to speech on matters of 'public interest'—as well as the definition of this term—are yet to be determined in concrete terms by international courts.[18]

---

[7] Some treason and sedition laws also cover non-speech activities such as the use of force: see, e.g., 18 U.S.C. §2381 (codifying the offence of treason against anyone owing allegiance to the United States who 'levies war against them or adheres to their enemies, giving them aid and comfort within the United States or elsewhere'). Other forms of sedition, including words that offend national security laws, fall outside of the scope of this chapter. Likewise, insults that amount to hate speech or blasphemy are not dealt with in this chapter. See ch. 3 (Hate Speech) and ch. 6 (Terrorism Laws).

[8] Stockholm Center for Freedom, '128,872 people have faced criminal investigation for insulting President Erdoğan in five years' (29 March 2021).

[9] K. Purohit, 'Our New Database Reveals Rise In Sedition Cases In The Modi Era' (Article 14, 2 February 2021).

[10] T. Merz, 'Alexei Navalny accuses state of orchestrating war veteran slander case' (The Guardian, 12 February 2021).

[11] See s. II.2.2.3. (Philippines).

[12] G. Phillips, 'How the free press worldwide is under threat' (The Guardian, 28 May 2020). See s. II.2.1.3. (SLAPP and libel tourism).

[13] See s. III.4. (Exclusions, Exceptions and Defences).

[14] See s. III.6.1.1. (Criminalization).

[15] See s. III. 6.1.1. (Criminalization).

[16] See s. II.2.1.3. (SLAPP and libel tourism).

[17] See s. III.3.1. (Intent).

[18] See s. III. 4.2. (Public Interest).

International human rights bodies are also yet to seriously grapple with some of the most pressing contemporary phenomena that threaten free speech, such as 'libel tourism', the use of vexatious suits to silence journalists (known as 'strategic litigation against public participation' or SLAPPs), and the concept of continuous or multiple publication in the digital age.[19] This chapter assesses the current state of the law and proposes recommendations based on international standards and best practices to address gaps or inconsistencies in international human rights law related to political speech.

II. State Practice

1. Overview of Laws Regulating Insulting Speech

A survey of state practice[20] illustrates the range of laws that are used to penalize political speech, including a broad use of defamation laws as well as laws penalizing insult, sedition, contempt and treason. In places like Thailand, so-called *lèse-majesté* laws prohibit insult of the monarchy.[21] And 'cyber libel' laws are used worldwide to target online speech.[22] In assessing the way in which laws can stifle legitimate political speech, a number of elements must be assessed: the type of speech covered by the wording of the law, the mental culpability required of a speaker before punishment can be imposed, the harm that must or might be caused by such speech, the exemptions or defences available under the law and the penalties that can be prescribed. These elements are inter-related and must be assessed as a whole when evaluating national law and practice.

---

[19] This concept is that each individual publication of speech, even if it is the same (or substantially the same) as that previously published, accrues a cause of action in defamation, and each cause of action has its own separate limitation period.

[20] This survey of state practice does not purport to be comprehensive but rather to identify significant examples and trends. Therefore, where the language of a statute is set out, this does not necessarily include an analysis of all case law interpreting that language in the jurisdiction under review. We have selected the following jurisdictions based on diversity of legal systems and regions: Albania, Algeria, Argentina, Austria, Australia, Azerbaijan, Bahrain, Bangladesh, Barbados, Bulgaria, Belarus, Bolivia, Botswana, Burkina Faso, Burundi, Canada, Cambodia, Chile, Costa Rica, Croatia, Cyprus, Denmark, Ecuador, Ethiopia, England, Wales and Northern Island, Kingdom of Eswatini, France, The Gambia, Germany, Ghana, Greece, Guatemala, Honduras, Hong Kong, Hungary, India, Indonesia, Iran, Iraq, Ireland, Israel, Italy, Japan, Jamaica, Republic of Korea, Liberia, Madagascar, Maldives, Malawi, Malta, Mauritius, Mauritania, Montenegro, Morocco, Myanmar, North Macedonia, New Zealand, Nigeria, the Netherlands, Norway, Pakistan, Russia, Rwanda, Romania, Serbia, Sierra Leone, Singapore, South Africa, Slovakia, Slovenia, Spain, Sri Lanka, Sweden, Switzerland, Peru, Paraguay, Philippines, Qatar, Saudi Arabia, Turkey, Thailand, Tajikstan, Uganda, Ukraine, Uruguay, Yemen, Zimbabwe.

[21] See s. II.2.2.1. (Thailand).

[22] There is a debate about the extent to which it is permissible under international human rights law to hold a publisher, host or other intermediary liable in a criminal or civil case for the words of an author, or to require a host provider to disclose the personal data of its users. See, e.g., ECtHR (GC), *Magyar Kétfarkú Kutya Párt v. Hungary* (App. no. 201/17), 20 January 2020, §87; ECtHR, *Standard Verlagsgesellschaft mbH v. Austria (No. 3)* (App. no. 39378/15), 7 December 2021. However, intermediary liability for such speech is beyond the scope of this chapter.

1.1. Type of speech

Many domestic laws penalizing political speech by way of defamation and insult laws are exceptionally vague, making it difficult to know what speech is covered and facilitating potential abuse of government critics. A prominent example is the Turkish offence of public speech that 'degrad[es]' the Turkish 'nation', 'government', 'judicial bodies' or 'military and security organisations'.[23] The Council of Europe's Venice Commission considered this language 'not specific enough to meet the requirements of predictability'.[24] Other states which criminalize insult of the state or state officials with vaguely worded laws include Austria, Germany, Spain, India, Iran and Kazakhstan.[25]

1.2. Intent

States' laws vary as to what level of fault (or intent) is required in order to penalize or recover damages for defamatory speech, both when it comes to the falsity of the speech and its likely impact.

Perhaps the most protective legal standard is the 'actual malice' test established by the US Supreme Court in the seminal *Sullivan* case. This provides that if a statement relates to a public official,[26] that official must demonstrate that the speaker acted with 'actual malice' to recover damages for defamation.[27] 'Actual malice' means that the speaker knew the statement was false or acted with a 'high degree of awareness of [its] probable falsity'.[28] This is a high bar:[29] 'failure to investigate'[30] or reliance on 'statements made by a single source' that 'reflect only one side of the story' will not alone support a finding of actual malice[31] as there is 'no duty to corroborate [a] defamatory

---

[23] Turkish Penal Code Art. 301, see for a translation provided by Council of Europe, CDL-REF(2016)011. See s. III.1. (Legality).

[24] Venice Commission, *Opinion on Articles 216, 299, 301 and 314 of the Penal Code of Turkey* (2015) CDL-AD(2016)002, §§86–87.

[25] Austrian Criminal Code Art. 248(1) ('publicly and in a hateful manner insulting or disparaging the Republic of Austria or one of its provinces'); German Criminal Code s. 90a ('insulting or maliciously expressing contempt toward Germany or one of its states or its constitutional order'); Spanish Criminal Code Arts 491, 496, 504, 556, and 543 (Art. 543 criminalizing any 'offense or insult, by parole, in writing or through actions, against Spain, its Autonomous Communities, or their symbols or emblems when made publicly'); Indian Penal Code 1860 s. 124A (sedition committed by 'whoever, by words, either spoken or written, or by signs, or by visible representation, or otherwise, brings or attempts to bring into hatred or contempt, or excites or attempts to excite disaffection towards, the Government established by law in [India]'); Iranian Islamic Penal Code 2013 Art. 514; Kazakhstani Criminal Code 2014 Arts 373, 375, 376 and 378.

[26] Later extended to public figures, and then to private figures suing on a matter of public concern where presumed or punitive damages are sought: US Supreme Court, *Curtis Publishing Co v. Butts* 388 U.S. 130, 12 June 1967; US Supreme Court, *Gertz v. Robert Welch Inc* 418 U.S. 323, 25 June 1974; US Supreme Court, *Dun & Bradstreet Inc v. Greenmoss Builders* 472 U.S. 749, 26 June 1985.

[27] See US Supreme Court, *New York Times v. Sullivan* 376 U.S. 254, 9 March 1964. See also R. D. Sack, 'New York Times Co. v. Sullivan–50-year Afterwords' (2014) 66 *Alabama Law Review* 273, 283. Although there have been suggestions that the US Supreme Court would reconsider *New York Times v. Sullivan*, in a recent case concerning 'true threats', the Court (with the exception of Justice Thomas in dissent) affirmed *Sullivan's* reasoning: See A. Liptak, 'Two Justices Say Supreme Court Should Reconsider Landmark Libel Decision' (The New York Times, 2 July 2021); US Supreme Court, *Counterman v. Colorado* 600 U.S. 66, 18 April 2023. See ch. 3 (Hate Speech), s. II.2.3.2. (United States).

[28] US Supreme Court, *Garrison v. Louisiana* 379 U.S. 64, 23 November 1964, 271–272.

[29] See s. IV.B.3. (Recommendations). See, e.g., US Supreme Court, *Berisha v. Lawson* 594 US (2021), 2 July 2021, Gorsuch J, dissenting ('over time the actual malice standard has evolved from a high bar to recovery into an effective immunity from liability').

[30] US Supreme Court, *Harte-Hanks Communications v. Connaughton* 491 U.S. 657, 22 June 1989, 692.

[31] US Court of Appeals, Fifth Circuit, *New York Times Co. v. Connor* 365 F.2d 567, 4 August 1966, 576.

allegation'[32] and 'no obligation to seek comment' from the subject.[33] And the subjectivity of the standard, confirmed in subsequent cases, remains one of the biggest obstacles to plaintiff victories in defamation suits as damages cannot be recovered in the absence of a finding that the defendant 'in fact ... entertained serious doubts' about the truthfulness of their statement.[34]

The *Sullivan* test has been followed, at least on paper, in jurisdictions including Argentina, Hungary, South Korea and the Philippines.[35] However, it has not been adopted by other states, such as Australia, New Zealand, South Africa and England and Wales.[36] These countries' courts and legislators have instead emphasized the 'vital importance'[37] of the protection of reputation[38] and the availability of defences or exemptions related to opinion,[39] fair comment,[40] qualified privilege,[41] reasonable publication[42] and public interest.[43]

Some states impose an objective intent requirement relating to falsity of the speech, such as in Thailand, where the law provides that a speaker can be penalized if they ought to have known about the falsity of the information.[44]

Other states impose an intent requirement related to the *impact* of the statement. For instance, the penal codes of India, Bangladesh, Malaysia and Myanmar require that the speaker intended to harm the reputation of the plaintiff, or knew or had reason to believe the statement would harm their reputation.[45] In South Africa, for non-media

---

[32] US Court of Appeals, District of Columbia Circuit, *Jankovic v. International Crisis Group* 822 F.3d 576, 10 May 2016, 590.

[33] US Court of Appeals, 10th Circuit, *Spacecon Specialty Contractors, LLC v. Bensinger* 713 F.3d 1028, 15 April 2013, 1043.

[34] US Supreme Court, *St. Amant v. Thompson* 390 U.S. 727, 29 April 1968, 731.

[35] See Argentine Supreme Court, *Patitó v. Diario La Nación*, 24 June 2008; Constitutional Court of Hungary, *Decision 36/1994 on Defamation of Public Officials and Politicians*, 24 June 1994 (although *Sullivan* is not explicitly cited by the Constitutional Court); Supreme Court of South Korea, 2013 Da 74837, 24 April 2014; Supreme Court of South Korea, 2011 Da 40373, 23 August 2012; Philippine Supreme Court, *Borjal v. Court of Appeals* [1999] 301 SCRA 1, 14 January 1999.

[36] High Court of Australia, *Lange v. Australian Broadcasting Corporation* [1997] HCA 25, 8 July 1997 (relating to civil defamation claims in Australia); *Australian Broadcasting Corporation v. O'Neill* (2006) 227 CLR 57, 28 September 2006, 95–96 (Kirby J); Canadian Supreme Court, *Grant v. Torstar Corporation* 2009 SCC 61, 22 December 2009; New Zealand Court of Appeal, *Lange v. Atkinson* [1998] 3 NZLR 424 (CA), 25 May 1998, reaffirmed in New Zealand Court of Appeal, *Lange v. Atkinson* [2000] 3 NZLR 385 (CA), 21 June 2000 (the Court said the common law test for malice still applied); South Africa Constitutional Court, *Khumalo v. Holomisa* [2002] ZACC 12, 14 June 2002; UK House of Lords, *Reynolds v. Times Newspapers Ltd* [2001] 2 AC 127, 28 October 1999, 168.

[37] Canadian Supreme Court, *Hill v. Church of Scientology of Toronto* [1995] 2 SCR 1130, 20 July 1995, 1332 (Cory J).

[38] Canadian Supreme Court, *Grant v. Torstar Corporation* 2009 SCC 61, 22 December 2009, §86 (McLachlin CJ); Canadian Supreme Court, *Hill v. Church of Scientology of Toronto* [1995] 2 SCR 1130, 20 July 1995, §137 (Cory J); South African Constitutional Court, *Khumalo v. Holomisa* [2002] ZACC 12, 14 June 2002, §27.

[39] See, e.g., England and Wales Defamation Act 2013 s. 3.

[40] See s. II.1.4.5. (Opinion).

[41] See, e.g., Canadian Supreme Court, *Hill v. Church of Scientology of Toronto* [1995] 2 SCR 1130, 20 July 1995, §§137, 209.

[42] See, e.g., South African Constitutional Court, *Khumalo v. Holomisa* [2002] ZACC 12, 14 June 2002, §43.

[43] See, e.g., England and Wales Defamation Act 2013 s. 4.

[44] Thai Civil and Commercial Code 1925 s. 423.

[45] Indian Penal Code 1860 s. 499; Bangladeshi Penal Code 1860 s. 499; Myanmar Penal Code 1861 s. 499; Malaysian Penal Code s. 499. See also Botswanan Penal Code ss 192, 193; Moroccan Penal Code 1962 Arts 263, 265; Algerian Penal Code Art. 144. See also laws requiring an intention to share information that insults, defames or slanders: Indonesian Penal Code 1999 Art. 207; Ethiopian Criminal Code Arts 244(1), 613, 614, 615 and 618.

defendants,[46] a speaker is only liable if they had subjective foresight of the possibility that they would actionably defame the plaintiff.[47]

At the lower end of the spectrum are states that impose a negligence standard. This includes US defamation cases not involving public officials or public figures, where at least negligence is required regarding the impact of the statement, but precise standards vary by state,[48] and the South African standard in defamation cases against the media, where negligence is the test (albeit that it is for the media to prove they did not act negligently).[49]

In other jurisdictions, no mental element is required at all either as to the falsity or impact of the statement. Countries such as Russia and Malta[50] have civil defamation laws that do not contain an intent requirement as to the impact of the statement at all. And in England and Wales, no mental element must be proved to establish a cause of action for defamation, the mental element being relevant only to certain defences.[51] And even laws that impose criminal penalties for defamation can be silent or ambiguous on intent, such as in Thailand and Ecuador.[52] Certain criminal sedition laws—for example in India,[53] Bangladesh[54] and Iran[55]—also do not contain an intent requirement.

1.3. Harm

1.3.1. *Causal link between the speech and the harm*

Some states' laws require that an insulting statement be *capable of* or *likely to* cause harm, such as Australia, Canada and England and Wales for civil defamation,[56] and Botswana, Canada, Nigeria, South Africa, Tanzania and Uganda for criminal

---

[46] South African Supreme Court of Appeal, *Economic Freedom Fighters v. Manuel* [2020] ZASCA 172, 17 December 2020. See s. II.1.3.2.1. (Measuring harm: identity of the speaker).

[47] D. Milo, *Defamation and Freedom of Speech* (OUP 2008), 187–188.

[48] See US Supreme Court, *Gertz v. Robert Welch Inc* 418 U.S. 323, 25 June 1974. The Ninth Circuit found that 'liability for a defamatory blog post involving a matter of public concern cannot be imposed without proof of fault and actual damages': US Court of Appeals, Ninth Circuit, *Obsidian Finance Group, LLC v. Cox* 740 F.3d 1284, 17 January 2014, 1291–1292.

[49] Milo (n 47) 195–196. See also South African Supreme Court of Appeal, *National Media Ltd v. Bogoshi* [1998] ZASCA 94, 29 September 1998. See also Rwandan Penal Code 2012 Art. 588; Costa Rican Penal Code Art. 153.

[50] Russian Civil Code Art. 152(1); Russian Code of Administrative Offences No. 195-FZ 2001 Arts 5.61, 20.1; Maltese Media and Defamation Act 2018 Art. 3.

[51] UK Committee on Defamation, *Report of Committee on Defamation* (1975) Cmnd 5909, 53–55; UK House of Lords, *Reynolds v. Times Newspapers Ltd* [2001] 2 AC 127, 28 October 1999, §168; UK Supreme Court Procedure Committee, *Report on Practice and Procedure in Defamation* (1991), 164.

[52] Thai Penal Code Arts 326–332; Ecuadorian Criminal Code Arts 182, 396.1.

[53] Indian Penal Code 1860 s. 124A.

[54] Bangladeshi Penal Code 1860 Art. 124A.

[55] Iranian Islamic Penal Code 2013, Book 5, Art. 500.

[56] Australian Defamation Act 2005 (NSW) s. 10A ('has caused, or is likely to cause, serious harm'). Defamation actions in Australia are governed by substantially uniform defamation law. The relevant legislation is as follows: Defamation Act 2005 (NSW); Defamation Act 2005 (Qld); Defamation Act 2005 (SA); Defamation Act 2005 (Tas); Defamation Act 2005 (Vic); Defamation Act 2005 (WA); Civil Law (Wrongs) Act 2002 (ACT) and Defamation Act 2006 (NT). A number of the Australian examples included in this chapter relate only to NSW. For a summary of the uniform defamation law and recent amendments thereto, see P. Bartlett & D. Hurley, 'Australian Media Law' in C. Glasser Jr. (ed), *International Libel and Privacy Handbook* (LexisNexis 2022–2023); Canadian Supreme Court, *Botiuk v. Toronto Free Press* [1995] 3 SCR 3, 21 September 1995, §62; Canadian Supreme Court, *Bou Malhab v. Diffusion Métromédia CMR inc.*, 2011 SCC 9, [2011] 1 S.C.R. 214, 17 February 2011 (although civil law varies across Canadian provinces); England and Wales Defamation Act 2013 s. 1(1); UK Supreme Court, *Lachaux v. Independent Print Ltd* [2020] AC 612, 12 June 2019, §§12–16.

defamation.[57] In England and Wales, for instance, claimants must show that the publication of a statement 'has caused or is likely to cause serious harm' to their reputation.[58] The occurrence of actual harm as a result of the speech is required in jurisdictions such as Thailand[59] and the United States[60] for civil defamation and in Madagascar for criminal defamation.[61]

1.3.2. Level of harm caused by the speech

In many jurisdictions, a showing of harm must be made by a plaintiff or prosecutor in a defamation case. In England and Wales, '[a] statement is not defamatory unless its publication has caused or is likely to cause serious harm to the reputation of the claimant',[62] to be determined by reference to the actual impact of the statement.[63] This approach has been followed in jurisdictions such as Malta and Australia.[64]

In the United States, a court will consider whether a publication 'tends ... to harm the reputation of another as to lower him in the estimation of the community or to deter third persons from associating or dealing with him' when deciding whether to uphold a claim for damages.[65] And in South Africa, a statement is considered defamatory 'if it is likely to injure the good esteem in which he or she is held by the reasonable or average person to whom it had been published'.[66] But no demonstration of actual harm is required.[67]

Some jurisdictions do not require any showing of actual or potential harm to establish that speech is insulting or defamatory. This includes jurisdictions in which criminal

---

[57] Botswanan Penal Code, Chapter 08:01, ss 192, 193; Canadian Criminal Code s. 298(1); Nigerian Penal Code (Northern States) Federal Provisions Act (1960) Cap. (P3) Laws of the Federation of Nigeria 2004 s. 391(1); South African Supreme Court of Appeal, *Hoho v. The State* (493/05) [2008] ZASCA 98, 17 September 2008, §23; Tanzanian Media Services Act 2016 s. 35; Ugandan Penal Code Act s. 180 (although a statement will also be defamatory if it has the effect of 'exposing the person to hatred, contempt or ridicule').
[58] England and Wales Defamation Act 2013 s. 1(1).
[59] Thai Civil and Commercial Code 1925, Obligations, Title V, Torts, Chapter 1, s. 423. *But see* s. III.1. (Legality).
[60] US District Court (Western District of Washington), *Hennick v. Bowling* 115 F. Supp. 2d 1204, 14 September 2000; US Supreme Court of Washington, *Mark v. Seattle Times* 96 Wn. 2d 473, 12 November 1981. Cf. US Supreme Court, *Gertz v. Robert Welch Inc*, 418 U.S. 323, 25 June 1974, 350; US Supreme Court, *Dun & Bradstreet, Inc. v. Greenmoss Builders, Inc.*, 472 U.S. 749, 26 June 1985. Further, some categories of statements are defamatory *per se*, meaning that the plaintiff is not required to prove actual damages, such as (1) accusing the plaintiff of a crime; (2) injuring the plaintiff in his or her business; (3) claiming the plaintiff has a 'loathsome disease'; or (4) imputing unchastity to a woman or, later, serious sexual misconduct allegations in relation to either a man or woman: see, e.g., Restatement (Second) of Torts §§569 – 574 (1977).
[61] Madagascar Presidence de la Republique Loi n° 2016–029 Portant Code de la Communication Mediatisee Art. 23. Madagascar requires 'personal and direct damages to the person or body concerned' for a successful prosecution for defamation.
[62] England and Wales Defamation Act 2013 s. 1(1).
[63] UK Supreme Court, *Lachaux v. Independent Print Ltd* [2020] AC 612, 12 June 2019, §14. It is permissible, however, for a claimant to advance an inferential case as to serious harm: §22.
[64] Maltese Media and Defamation Act 2018 s. 3(4); Australian New South Wales Defamation Amendment Act 2020 s. 10(a).
[65] American Law Institute, American (Second) Restatement of Torts, Sec. 559. See, e.g., US Texas Court of Appeals, *Means v. ABCABCO, Inc* 315 S.W.3d 209, 3 June 2010, 215 (requiring 'an element of disgrace'); V. R. Johnson, 'Comparative Defamation Law: England and the United States' (2016) 24 *University of Miami International and Comparative Law Review* 1, 83.
[66] South African Constitutional Court, *Le Roux v. Dey* [2011] ZACC 4, 8 March 2011, §§89, 91; South African Supreme Court of Appeal, *Independent Newspapers Holdings Ltd v. Suliman* [2004] ZASCA 57, 28 May 2004, §31.
[67] Milo (n 47) 227.

penalties may be applied to such speech such as Ecuador,[68] Iran[69] and Thailand (for *lèse-majesté*).[70]

1.3.2.1. Measuring harm: identity of the speaker Defamation and similar laws are used to target political speech by journalists as well as other speakers. Some states have adopted laws that provide *less protection* for defamation emanating from the media, reflecting a view that the media should be held to a higher or different standard than other speakers. That is the case in Spain, Peru, Chile and (in respect of the fault requirement) South Africa.[71]

At the other end of the spectrum, some jurisdictions provide *more protection* to journalists than other speakers who defame others. In South Africa, the media is afforded greater protection than non-media defendants in that the defence of reasonable publication is generally available to the media and not to others.[72] In some jurisdictions, 'secondary publishers' are also entitled to special defences.[73]

In other jurisdictions the identity of the speaker is irrelevant. For example, in US courts, the protections of the First Amendment do not turn on whether the defendant was a trained journalist, or formally affiliated with traditional news entities (although the public profile of the person who is being talked about is).[74] Similarly, Canadian courts have provided defamation defences to 'anyone who publishes material of public interest in any medium'.[75]

1.3.2.2. Measuring harm: the extent to which the speech is public Domestic jurisdictions may require 'publication' of statements for a claim of defamation to be triggered. 'Publish' tends to be broadly understood as 'received in a communicable form'.[76] England and Wales, the United States, Canada, South Africa, Australia, and the Philippines, for example, require the claimant to establish that the defamatory

---

[68] See, e.g., Ecuadorian Criminal Code Art. 182.
[69] Iranian Islamic Penal Code 2013, Book 5, Arts 514, 609.
[70] Thai Penal Code Art. 112.
[71] Spanish Criminal Code Art. 211; Italian Penal Code Art. 595(3); Peruvian Penal Code Art. 132; Chilean Law No. 19733 Art. 29; In South Africa, non-media defendants benefit from greater protection in that they escape liability if they did not intend to defame the plaintiff; for media defendants, the relevant fault element is negligence: see South African Supreme Court of Appeal, *Economic Freedom Fighters v. Manuel* [2020] ZASCA 172, 17 December 2020, §65.
[72] There are, however, conflicting decisions as to whether the defence should be extended to non-media defendants. See South African High Court, Gauteng Local Division, *Gqubule-Mbeki v. Economic Freedom Fighters* [2020] ZAGPJHC 2, 24 January 2020, §§72–73; cf. South African High Court, Gauteng Local Division, *Manuel v. Economic Freedom Fighters* [2019] ZAGPJHC 157, 30 May 2019, §67. The South African Supreme Court of Appeal in the appeal in *Economic Freedom Fighters v. Manuel* [2020] ZASCA 172, 17 December 2020 left the question open.
[73] Milo (n 47) 212–215. See England and Wales Defamation Act 1996 s. 1(2).
[74] US Court of Appeals, Ninth Circuit, *Obsidian Finance Group, LLC v. Cox* 740 F.3d 1284, 17 January 2014, 1291; see also cases collected at R. D. Sack, *Sack on Defamation: Libel, Slander, and Related Problems* (5th edn, vol 1, PLI Press 2017), chapter 5, n. 399.
[75] Canadian Supreme Court, *Grant v. Torstar Corporation* 2009 SCC 61, 22 December 2009, §96 (McLachlin CJ)—quoting Lord Hoffmann in UK House of Lords, *Jameel v. Wall Street Journal Europe (No.2)* [2006] UKHL 44, 11 October 2006, §54.
[76] See, e.g., Australia: publication occurs when it is received in a communicable form by at least one third party (High Court of Australia, *Dow Jones and Company Inc v. Gutnick* [2002] HCA 56, 10 December 2002, 600). See also Canadian Criminal Code Art. 299.

statement was published to at least one party other than the person defamed—it need not be more public than that.[77] Turkish criminal law requires that the defamatory statement must be communicated to at least three people to find a person guilty in the absence of the victim, but does not require a third party when the victim is present.[78] The penalty for defamation is aggravated if it is committed in public in states such as Slovenia, Turkey, Spain and Russia.[79] States including Russia and Honduras provide for increased penalties, or further standalone offences, when defamation is conducted online.[80]

For identifying when 'publication' occurs, there are a variety of rules. Under the single publication rule (applied, for example, in US courts[81]), 'a plaintiff's cause of action accrues only once, at the time of publication, and thus later publications do not give rise to additional defamation causes of action'.[82] Under the multiple publication rule (Canada,[83] the Philippines[84] and Australia[85]), each individual publication of a defamatory statement gives rise to a separate cause of action in law.[86] In England and Wales, a 'new cause of action in libel proceedings' 'accrues each time defamatory material on the Internet is accessed',[87] but for limitation purposes there is a single publication rule with claims barred after 12 months from the date of first publication, provided certain conditions are met.[88]

---

[77] See, e.g., US Bankruptcy Court, S.D. New York, *In re Food Management Group LLC* 359 B.R. 543, 13 February 2007, 560; US District Court (Western District of Washington), *Hennick v. Bowling* 115 F.Supp.2d 1204, 14 September 2000, 1209; Canadian Criminal Code Art. 299; South African Constitutional Court, *Le Roux v. Dey* [2011] ZACC 4, 8 March 2011; Supreme Court of the Philippines, *Yuchengco v. Manila Chronicle Publishing Corporation* G.R. No. 184315, 25 November 2009; *Pullman v. Walter Hill & Co Ltd* [1891] QB 524 (CA), 19 December 1980, 527, 529, 530; *Jones v. Amalgamated Television Services Pty Ltd* (1991) 23 NSWLR 364, 18 May 1991, 367. In England and Wales, the serious harm requirement under s. 1 of the Defamation Act 2013 (as well as other tools such as abuse of process as in UK House of Lords, *Jameel v. Wall Street Journal Europe (No. 2)* [2006] UKHL 44, 11 October 2006) mean that claims founded on limited publication may face difficulties.
[78] Turkish Penal Code Art. 125.
[79] Slovenian Criminal Code 2008 (amended 2011) Art. 160(1); Turkish Penal Code, Law No. 5237 Art. 125(4); Spanish Criminal Code Arts 211, 209, 206 (if commited 'with publicity', being diffusion via print, broadcast or other media); Russian Penal Code Art. 128.1(1) (with 'online' speech explicitly included in the definition of public); Italian Penal Code Art. 595(3).
[80] Honduran Penal Code Decree No. 130-2017 Art. 232: for insult and slander 'carried out using collective disclosure websites or social networks through the Internet, the respective penalties will be increased from one sixth (1/6) to one half (1/2)'; Russian Code of Administrative Offences No. 195-FZ 2001 Art. 20.1(3) 'Dissemination via information and telecommunication networks, including the internet... shall entail the imposition of an administrative fine in the amount of thirty thousand to one hundred thousand rubles'.
[81] American Law Institute, American (Second) Restatement of Torts, §577A; US Court of Appeals, New York. *Gregoire v. GP Putnam's Sons* 298 N.Y.119, 16 July 1948, referred to and cited in ECtHR, *Times Newspapers Ltd (Nos. 1 and 2) v. United Kingdom* (App. nos. 3002/03 & 23676/03), 10 March 2009, §24.
[82] US Court of Appeals, Sixth Circuit, *Milligan v. United States* 670 F.3d 686, 5 March 2012, 698. See also US Court of Appeals, New York, *Firth v. State of New York* 98 N.Y.2d 365, 2 July 2002.
[83] Canadian Ontario Court of Appeal, *John v. Ballingall* 2017 ONCA 579, 7 July 2017, §35.
[84] Philippines Regional Trial Court, *People of the Philippines v. Santos, Ressa, and Rappler* R-MNL-19-01141-CR, 15 June 2020, 16. The court referred to Supreme Court of the Philippines, *Brillante v. Court of Appeals* G.R. Nos. 118757 & 121571, 19 October 2004, which held that a 'single defamatory statement, if published several times, gives rise to as many offenses as there are publications'.
[85] Australian Model Defamation Amendment Provisions 2020; Australian Supreme Court of Western Australia, *Rayney v. Western Australia (No. 9)* [2017] WASC 367, 15 December 2017, §§822, 824.
[86] UK High Court of England and Wales, Queen's Bench Division, *Duke of Brunswick v. Harmer* (1849) 14 QB 185, 2 November 1849, referred to and cited in ECtHR, *Times Newspapers Ltd (Nos. 1 and 2) v. United Kingdom* (App. nos. 3002/03 & 23676/03), 10 March 2009, §20.
[87] England and Wales Defamation Act 2013 s. 8. The Delhi High Court has reached the same result: Indian High Court, Delhi, *Khawar Butt v. Asif Nazir Mir* CS(OS) 290/2010, 7 November 2013, §14.
[88] See England and Wales Defamation Act 2013 Chapter 26 s. 8.

1.4. Exclusions, exceptions and defences

1.4.1. Truth

The defence of truth is available in many domestic defamation laws, although its scope differs across jurisdictions.[89] Truth is an absolute defence in jurisdictions in which libel carries civil penalties such as Australia, England and Wales, the United States and Russia,[90] and in jurisdictions in which it is also a crime such as Spain, Nigeria, Turkey and Uganda.[91] In some jurisdictions such as Bangladesh, Malaysia and South Africa, it is a partial defence, for example, when the truthful statement was made 'for the public good' or when 'it was for the public benefit that the matter should be published'.[92]

Some states have a narrow version of the truth defence available when a defamatory statement relates to a criminal offence committed by a public official in the course of their duties.[93] Finally, in some jurisdictions, such as Thailand,[94] truth is not a defence because falsity is part of the cause of action.[95] And in Sweden, a court will first decide whether the alleged defamation was 'justifiable' before considering whether it is true or not,[96] meaning that criminal liability can be enlivened even for truthful statements.[97]

1.4.2. Public interest

The public interest in the subject matter of speech may provide some protection from defamation or insult claims, but the nature and extent of that protection varies amongst states. Public interest may be a self-standing defence, an essential ingredient for another defence such as 'reasonable publication', or a justification for imposing a more onerous culpability requirement.[98]

The laws of many jurisdictions have a public interest defence—sometimes expressed as a defence of 'public good' or 'public benefit', or a speaker acting under a 'legal,

---

[89] See ch. 4 (False Speech).

[90] England and Wales Defamation Act 2013 s. 2; US Supreme Court, *New York Times v. Sullivan* 376 U.S. 254, 9 March 1964; Russian Civil Code Art. 152(1); Australia has a statutory defence of justification: New South Wales Defamation Act 2005 s. 25. It is also a defence at common law that the imputations complained of are true in substance and in fact: High Court of Australia, *Howden v. Truth and Sportsman Ltd* [1937] HCA 74, 15 December 1937.

[91] Spanish Criminal Code Art. 207. The defence of truth is also available for insult against public officials in the exercise of their functions (Art. 210 of the Spanish Criminal Code), and therefore not as an absolute defence; Nigerian Criminal Code Act (1916) Cap (C.38) Laws of the Federation of Nigeria 2004 s. 391; Turkish Penal Code, Law No. 5237 Art. 127; Turkish Constitution Art. 39. See also D. Tezcan & others, *Teorik ve Pratik Ceza Özel Hukuku* (Seçkin Yayınları 2017), 596; Ugandan Penal Code Act of 1950 (cap 120), s. 180.

[92] Bangladeshi Penal Code 1860 s. 499, Malaysian Penal Code s. 499 ('It is not defamation to impute anything which is true concerning any person, if it be for the public good that the imputation should be made or published. Whether or not it is for the public good is a question of fact'). See also South African Criminal Procedure Act s. 107; South African Supreme Court of Appeal, *Hoho v. The State* (493/05) [2008] ZASCA 98, 17 September 2008, §24.

[93] See, e.g., Italian Penal Code Art. 596 (Truth is relevant only in defamation cases where offended person is a public official and the fact at issue related to his exercise of duties; where criminal proceedings are ongoing or initiated against the offended person as a result of the fact at issue; or where the claimant requests the judgment to ascertain the truth/falsity of the allegation. In such cases, it is for the defendant to prove the truth of the allegation).

[94] Thai Civil and Commercial Code 1925 s. 423.

[95] Ibid. (the statement must be 'contrary to the truth').

[96] An example of 'justifiable' speech (also translated as 'defensible') is if it is in the public interest: U. Isaksson, 'Sweden Media Law Guide: Defamation and Privacy Laws in Sweden' (Carter-Ruck).

[97] Swedish Penal Code Chapter 5 s. 1; J. Nordberg, 'The Case that Killed #MeToo in Sweden' (The New York Times, 15 March 2022); H. Jemal, 'Truth not a defence against defamation, says law professor' (Sverige Radio, 13 July 2021).

[98] See s. III.3.1. (Intent).

moral or social duty'. This includes criminal defamation laws in Denmark, India, Iraq, Japan, Korea, Malawi, Malaysia, the Netherlands, Nigeria, Singapore, Switzerland and Uganda,[99] and civil defamation laws in Australia, Barbados, Israel and Mauritius.[100]

Despite its importance, the concept of 'public interest' is rarely defined in legislation or case law.[101] In England and Wales, however, judges have made clear that it does not mean 'what the public is interested in' or what is 'newsworthy', nor—at the other end of the spectrum—what the public 'need to know'; but rather that 'there must be some real public interest in having this information in the public domain'.[102]

The US approach reflects a focus on the person rather than the issue. Speech about a public official or public figure is protected by a high intent requirement ('actual malice').[103] And the Supreme Court has explicitly decided 'not to fully extend the *Sullivan* protection to all communications about matters of public interest'.[104]

The criminal laws of certain states including India, Bangladesh, Malaysia and Myanmar similarly suggest that there should be a higher tolerance for insulting speech that is directed at public officials.[105] In South Africa[106] and in England and Wales,[107] government bodies cannot sue for defamation.[108] And in Canada, while sedition laws exist, 'seditious intention' does *not* include communications made in good faith to criticize measures taken by the government or monarch.[109]

---

[99] Danish Criminal Code No. 1719 2018 s. 269; Indian Penal Code 1860 s. 499; Iraqi Penal Code Law No. 111 1969 Art. 433; Japanese Penal Code (1907, as amended in 2022) Arts 230–232; South Korean Penal Code Art. 310; Malawian Penal Code Chapter 7:01 of the Laws of Malawi s. 205; Malaysian Penal Code s. 499; Dutch Criminal Code (1881, as amended in 2014) Art. 266, §2; Nigerian Penal Code (Northern States) Federal Provisions Act (1960) Cap. (P3) Laws of the Federation of Nigeria 2004 s. 391(2); Singaporean Penal Code Art. 499; Swiss Criminal Code Art. 173 (although this defence is only applicable to statements that the speaker had reason to believe were true); Ugandan Penal Code Act of 1950 (cap 120) ss 182, 184.

[100] New South Wales Defamation Act 2005 s. 29A; Barbados Defamation Act Chapter 199 s. 8(1) (see also s. 34(2) in relation to criminal defamation); Israeli Defamation Law 5725-1965 s. 14 (but the media defendant must also prove that the statement was true, depending on the seriousness of the defamation): I. Zamir & S. Colombo (eds), *The Law of Israel: General Surveys* (Harry and Michael Sacher Institute for Legislative Research and Comparative Law, the Hebrew University of Jerusalem 1995), 385). See also T. Gidron, 'Defamation Law in Turbulence: Does Israel Need 'Libel Reform'?' (2013) 46 *Israel Law Review* 95; Mauritian Criminal Code 1838 Art. 288(4)(a)–(c), (e), (g)–(j); Mauritian Supreme Court, *Soornack Nandanee v. Le Mauricien ltd* 2013 SCJ 58, 6 February 2013.

[101] Canadian Supreme Court, *Grant v. Torstar Corporation* 2009 SCC 61, 22 December 2009, §105 (internal citations omitted).

[102] UK House of Lords, *Jameel v. Wall Street Journal Europe (No. 2)* [2006] UKHL 44, 11 October 2006, §147.

[103] See s. III.3.1. (Intent).

[104] Sack (n 27) 273, 291, citing US Supreme Court, *Gertz v. Robert Welch Inc* 418 U.S. 323, 25 June 1974. Whether a plaintiff is a public figure may depend, though, on the relationship, if any, between them and a matter of public interest. The US Supreme Court in *Gertz v. Robert Welch Inc* 418 U.S. 323, 25 June 1974, said, for example, that public figures ordinarily 'have assumed roles of especial prominence in the affairs of society' at 345, and to have 'assume[d] special prominence in the resolution of public questions' at 351. The Court has imposed the 'actual malice' standard on private plaintiffs suing for presumed or punitive damages on matters of public concern: See s. III.3.1. (Intent) and s. IV.2. (Recommendations).

[105] Indian Penal Code 1860 s. 499 (which carves out an exception for any 'good faith' expression of opinion on the 'conduct of a public servant in the discharge of his public functions'); Bangladeshi Penal Code 1860 Art. 499; Malaysian Penal Code s. 499 (cf. Federal Court of Malaysia, *Chong Chieng Jen v. Government of State of Sarawak & Anor* [2019] 3 MLJ 300, 26 September 2018); Myanmar Penal Code 1861 Art. 499 Second Exception.

[106] Milo (n 47) 67–68.

[107] England and Wales House of Lords, *Derbyshire County Council v. Times Newspapers Limited* [1993] UKHL 18, [1993] AC 534, 18 February 1993.

[108] There is, however, no prohibition on individual officials suing for defamation. See UK House of Lords, *Derbyshire County Council v. Times Newspapers Limited* [1993] UKHL 18, [1993] AC 534, 18 February 1993, 550; *Spoorland v. South African Railways* 1946 (AD) 999, Separate Concurring Opinion of Schreiner, JA, 1012–1013.

[109] Canadian Criminal Code ss 59–61.

At the other end of the spectrum, in states like Thailand, the approach is inverted: there is a *lower* tolerance for insulting speech directed at public officials.[110] Singaporean law provides lesser protection to speech about the judiciary.[111] Symbols are protected from insulting speech in Russia,[112] India,[113] and Burundi,[114] and Hong Kong Law prohibits certain uses of the national flag and national emblem.[115] Increased penalties for defamation of public officials as compared to private individuals is a feature of the criminal laws in Italy,[116] Spain,[117] and Turkey.[118]

1.4.3. Reasonable publication

In some jurisdictions, a defence, sometimes labelled 'reasonable publication', allows a standard of care displayed by a speaker to provide protection from defamation claims. In Canada, for example, a defence to civil defamation is 'responsible communication on matters of public interest'; this allows 'publishers to escape liability if they can establish that they acted responsibly in attempting to verify the information on a matter of public interest'.[119] A similar approach is also adopted in Austria, Australia, England and Wales, Ethiopia, Ireland and New Zealand.[120]

1.4.4. Fair and accurate reporting of official documents

The defence of fair and accurate reporting protects the speaker who relied on an official public document or statement by a public official, made clear that the document or

---

[110] Thai Penal Code ss 393, 136.

[111] Singaporean Administration of Justice (Protection) Act 2016 s. 3 (which defines the offence of contempt of court as including any person who 'scandalises the court' by publishing or doing anything that 'imputes improper motives to or impugns the integrity, propriety or impartiality of any court' or 'poses a risk that public confidence in the administration of justice would be undermined').

[112] Russian Code of Administrative Offences No. 195-FZ 2001 Art. 20.1(3); Russian Penal Code Art. 354.1(3) (insulting 'symbols of military glory').

[113] Indian Prevention of Insults to National Honour (Amendment) Act 2005 ss 2, 3 (protecting 'the Indian national flag, the Constitution of India and the national anthem').

[114] Burundian Penal Code Art. 383.

[115] Hong Kong National Flag and National Emblem Ordinance 1997 (2021 Amendment) s. 4.

[116] Italian Penal Code Art. 595(4) (defamation). See also Italian Penal Code Arts. 278, 290–292 (regarding defamation committed against the President, the Republic, the constitutional institutions, the Army, the Italian nation, the flag or other symbols of the state).

[117] Spanish Criminal Code Arts 496, 504(1), 504(2) (serious defamation of public officials); cf. Art. 209 (defamation of anyone).

[118] See paragraph 3(a) of Turkish Penal Code Art. 125 (insult), determining one years' imprisonment as the minimum punishment for insulting public officials due to their performance of their duty, while the minimum punishment under paragraph one is three months of imprisonment. See also Turkish Penal Code, Law No. 5237 Art. 299 (insult to the president), providing for a punishment with a higher minimum and maximum term of imprisonment than that of Art. 125 and excluding fine as an alternative punishment, which is provided for under Art. 125.

[119] Canadian Supreme Court, *Grant v. Torstar Corporation* 2009 SCC 61, 22 December 2009, §85 (emphasis added).

[120] Austrian Federal Act on the Press and other Publication Media (Media Act) 1981 Art. 29; New South Wales Defamation Amendment Act 2020 s. 29; England and Wales Defamation Act 2013 s. 4. See ch. 5 (Espionage and Official Secrets Laws), s. II.2.1.1. (United Kingdom). See also Ethiopian Civil Code Arts 2046, 2049; Irish Defamation Act 2009 ss 16, 18, 20, 26. The defences of truth, qualified privilege and honest opinion are also available; New Zealand Court of Appeal, *Durie v. Gardiner* [2018] NZCA 278, 31 July 2018. Other jurisdictions do not explicitly tie the defence to public interest speech. See, e.g., South Africa (South African Supreme Court of Appeal, *National Media Ltd v. Bogoshi* [1998] ZASCA 94, 29 September 1998, 1212–1213); Sierra Leonean Public Order Act 1965 s. 30(e) in particular.

statement was the source, and fairly and accurately used the source. It typically covers copies, extracts and summaries of certain official publications.[121]

The defence is recognized in many states with civil defamation laws, especially common law jurisdictions including Australia, England and Wales, Canada, South Africa and the United States,[122] as well as jurisdictions that have criminal libel laws such as Bangladesh, Kenya, Malaysia, Nigeria and Uganda.[123]

In England and Wales, absolute privilege covers a contemporaneous fair and accurate report of words spoken in public legal proceedings.[124] Qualified privilege attaches to fair and accurate copies, extracts or summaries of public speech by or on behalf of a legislature or government anywhere in the world.[125] US courts have taken a less global view than the UK courts, so far refusing to apply the defence to speech by foreign governments.[126]

In South Africa, there is a defence in civil proceedings of qualified privilege for fair and accurate reports of legal, quasi-legal or parliamentary proceedings.[127] Bangladeshi[128] and Indian[129] penal codes also provide that the crime of defamation exempts 'substantially true' reports of court proceedings.

1.4.5. Opinion

Whereas the defence of truth relates to the facts in a statement, the defence of opinion is concerned with value judgements. In the United States, for example, the plaintiff in a civil defamation case usually has to show that a statement is *not* an opinion in order for liability to attach.[130]

In Australia,[131] Singapore,[132] Hong Kong[133] and Kenya,[134] civil defamation laws refer to a defence of 'fair comment' or 'honest opinion' that protects against liability for an

---

[121] See, e.g., UK Defamation Act 1996 Schedule 1.
[122] See, e.g., Australian New South Wales Defamation Act 2005 ss 27, 29, 30; see ch. 5 (Espionage and Official Secrets Laws), s. II.2.2.2. (Australia); UK Defamation Act 1996 ss 14–15; Canadian Ontario Libel and Slander Act s. 3; Civil: Canadian Ontario Superior Court of Justice, *1522491 Ontario Inc v. Stewart, Esten Professional Corporation* [2010] ONSC 727, 6 January 2010; Ontario Court of Appeal, *Soliman v. Bordman*, 2021 ONSC 7023; Canadian Criminal Code s. 60; South African Appellate Division (as it then was), *Borgin v. De Villiers* 1980 3 SA 556 (A); US California Civil Code s. 47; US Florida Statutes Chapter 836 Defamation, Libel, Threatening Letters and Similar Offenses s. 836.08; US Ohio Revised Code ss 2317.04, 2317.05; US Michigan Compiled Laws s. 600.2911(3); US Texas Civil Practice and Remedies Code s. 73.002.
[123] Bangladeshi Penal Code 1860 Art. 499; Kenyan Penal Code ss 198–199; Kenyan Defamation Act 2010 ss 10–12; Malaysian Penal Code s. 499; Nigerian Criminal Code Act (1916) Cap (C.38) Laws of the Federation of Nigeria 2004 s. 379; Ugandan Penal Code Act of 1950 (cap 120) ss 182, 183.
[124] This covers national and international courts: England and Wales Defamation Act 2013 s. 7 amending s. 14 of UK Defamation Act 1996.
[125] England and Wales Defamation Act 1996 Schedule 1, s. 9(1).
[126] Johnson (n 65) 95.
[127] D. Milo & P. Stein, *A Practical Guide to Media Law* (Lexis Nexis-Butterworths 2013), 42–43.
[128] Bangladeshi Penal Code 1860 Art. 499.
[129] Indian Penal Code 1860 Chapter XXI s. 499.
[130] Johnson (n 65) 38. See also US Court of Appeals, Ninth Circuit, *Herring Networks, Inc. v. Maddow* 8 F.4th 1148, 17 August 2021 (in which a talk show host's comments that a US news network 'really literally is paid Russian propaganda' were considered protected 'opinion' in furtherance of her constitutional right to free speech on a public issue, rather than 'an assertion of objective fact').
[131] New South Wales Defamation Amendment Act 2020 s. 31. In Australia, the common law defence of fair comment operates alongside the statutory defence of honest opinion: see, e.g., Federal Court of Australia, *Dutton v. Bazzi* [2021] FCA 1474, 24 November 2021, [180].
[132] Singaporean Defamation Act 1975 s. 9.
[133] Hong Kong Defamation Ordinance Cap 21 s. 27 (providing for the defence of fair comment).
[134] Kenyan Defamation Act 2010 s. 15.

expression of opinion. Under Australian statutory law, the defence is limited to a subset of opinions that are 'based on proper material'.[135]

In England and Wales, the common law defence of 'fair comment' was replaced by a statutory defence of 'honest opinion', which applies when the statement is a statement of opinion,[136] indicates the basis of the opinion and 'an honest person' could have held the opinion given the facts existing at the time the allegedly defamatory statement was made.[137]

In some jurisdictions, there is a defence to criminal defamation focused on opinions about public officials, a 'public question' or for the 'public good', such as in Bangladesh, India, Malaysia, Uganda and Nigeria.[138] In South Africa, a defence of 'protected comment' applies to opinions expressed without malice based on facts that are true and in relation to matters of public interest.[139] In Chile,[140] 'personal opinions' and criticism of 'politics, literature, history, art, science and sports' cannot be considered insult or defamation, unless 'their tenor reveals the *purpose* of insulting, in addition to criticizing'. States such as Iran and Mauritania, on the other hand, provide no defence related to opinions at all.[141]

1.5. Penalties
1.5.1. *Criminal penalties*

Over 160 states allow criminal penalties for defamatory speech[142] and many states have specific laws criminalizing sedition and the insult of heads of state, although decriminalization of defamation has taken place in some regions.

Many European states with criminal defamation laws allow for imprisonment as a possible punishment for defamation.[143] Prison sentences tend to range between two months and two years, but can be longer (e.g., three years in Greece, Italy,[144] and

---

[135] New South Wales Defamation Amendment Act 2020 s. 31. Being 'based on proper material' may be satisfied by material that is substantially true, published on an occasion or absolute or qualified privilege, or published on an occasion that attracts the defence of honest opinion, 'publication of public documents' or 'fair report of proceedings of public concern'.

[136] England and Wales Defamation Act 2013 s. 3(2).

[137] This also extends to anything said to be a fact in a privileged statement published before the impugned statement was made. See England and Wales Defamation Act 2013 s. 3(4) ('an honest person could have held the opinion on the basis of (a) any fact which existed at the time the statement complained of was published; (b) anything asserted to be a fact in a privileged statement published before the statement complained of ').

[138] Bangladeshi Penal Code 1860 Art. 499; Indian Penal Code 1860 s. 499; Malaysian Penal Code s. 499; Ugandan Penal Code Act 1950 (cap 120), ss 183, 184; Nigerian Criminal Code Act (1916) Cap (C.38) Laws of the Federation of Nigeria 2004 s. 377. See s. III.4.2. (Public interest).

[139] South African Constitutional Court, *The Citizen 1978 (Pty) Ltd v. McBride* [2011] ZACC 11, 8 April 2011, §83.

[140] Chilean Law No. 19,733 Art. 29 (emphasis added). Cf. Costa Rican Criminal Code Art. 151.

[141] Article 19, 'Islamic Republic of Iran: Computer Crimes Law' (2012), 3, 25–26, 35; No defences for defamation, insult or libel are provided in the Iranian Islamic Penal Code 2013 Arts 513–514, 608–609, 697–700. Mauritanian Penal Code 1983 Art. 348.

[142] UNESCO, *Journalism is a public good: World Trends in Freedom of Expression and Media Development: Global Report 2021/2022: Highlights* (2021).

[143] With the exception of countries including Russia, Albania, Croatia and Bulgaria.

[144] Italian Penal Code Art. 595(3) (which provides higher penalties for defamation emanating from the press or advertising).

Switzerland for wilful defamation[145] and up to five years in Germany).[146] Even so, in Europe, it is rare that a conviction for defamation will result in a prison sentence.[147]

In the Asian states that retain criminal defamation laws, prison sentences generally range from one to three years, with higher sentences available for example in Indonesia (six years).[148] Bangladesh, India, Iraq and Pakistan allow life imprisonment for sedition.[149] In Thailand, defamation of the King can result in imprisonment for 15 years per count.[150]

In some states, criminal fines can be imposed, as in Greece,[151] Serbia,[152] Italy[153] and The Gambia.[154] Under the Russian Penal Code, defamation, combined with the accusation of a person of a grave or especially grave crime, is punishable by a fine of over $60,000 US dollars, three years of the convicted person's salary or income, or by compulsory labour for up to 480 hours.[155] Some states, such as the United States, retain such defamation laws on their books but prosecutors seldom, if ever, apply them in practice.[156]

There is a trend towards decriminalization of defamation laws, though the momentum has been uneven. In Africa, Liberia, Kenya and Burkina Faso have abolished prison sentences for defamation or insult.[157]

In Europe, Norway,[158] Romania,[159] Ireland,[160] England and Wales, Malta,[161] Montenegro, North Macedonia,[162] and Serbia[163] have each repealed criminal

---

[145] Swiss Criminal Code Art. 174(1).
[146] German Criminal Code s. 187 (for public defamatory statments that are capable of damaging a person's reputation or jeopardizing their creditworthiness).
[147] CPJ, 'Explore CPJ's database of attacks on the press' (2019).
[148] Indonesian Law No. 11 on Electronic Information and Transactions 2008 Art. 45(1).
[149] Bangladeshi Penal Code 1860 Art. 124A; Indian Penal Code 1860 s. 124A; Iraqi Penal Code Law No. 111 1969 Art. 160; Pakistani Penal Code 1860 Art. 124A.
[150] Thai Penal Code §112. In some cases, an even longer prison term is imposed: see s. II.2.2.1. (Thailand).
[151] ECtHR, *Alpha Doryforiki Tileorasi Anonymi Etairia v. Greece* (App. no. 72562/10), 22 February 2018.
[152] ECtHR, *Lepojić v. Serbia* (App. no. 13909/05), 6 November 2007.
[153] Italian Penal Code Art. 595(1)–(3).
[154] ECOWAS CCJ, *Federation of African Journalists v. The Gambia* (Suit no. ECW/CCJ/APP/36/15), 13 February 2018, 4 (fine of approximately 4,200 USD for sedition and the publication of false news, payable within two hours). The criminal law on defamation is under review by The Gambia's National Assembly (at a committee level) and The Gambia's sedition provision remains in place.
[155] Russian Penal Code Art. 128.1(5).
[156] Sack (n 74), §3.2, n. 17.1. citing US Court of Appeals, Eighth Circuit, *Tollett v. United States* 485 F.2d 1087, 2 October 1973, §§1094–1099.
[157] Liberian Kamara Abdullah Kamara (KAK) Act of Press Freedom 2019; Burkinabe Law 057-2015/CNT; UNESCO, 'African Court's landmark decision to ensure prosecution of crimes against journalists' (12 March 2021); Constitutional and Human Rights Division of the High Court of Kenya, *Jacqueline Okuta & another v. Attorney General & 2 others* [2017] eKLR, 6 February 2017.
[158] Norwegian Penal Code s. 185 still envisages fines or imprisonment, but in practice the Supreme Court does not award immediate custodial punishments for defamation and insult (Norwegian Supreme Court Judgment 29 January 2020, HR-2020-184-A).
[159] The decriminalization of the defamation offence (domestically regulated as the offence of slander and/or the offence of insult) occurred with the adoption of the new Romanian Criminal Code (adopted in 2009, through Law no. 286/2009), effective since 1 February 2014.
[160] Irish Defamation Act 2009 s. 35.
[161] Maltese Media and Defamation Act 2018 Art. 25.
[162] In 2012, North Macedonia adopted the Law on Civil Liability for Insult and Defamation and repealed Arts 172, 176, and 184 of the Criminal Code, thereby decriminalizing defamation. COE Committee of Ministers, *Action Report: Makraduli v. North Macedonia* (12 June 2019). Planned reform of the North Macedonian Law on Civil Liability for Insult and Defamation which will hopefully see fines reduced has been delayed by Covid-19; N. Georgievski, 'The coronavirus crisis postpones the drafting of new Law on Civil Liability for Insult and Defamation until September' (Meta, 24 May 2020).
[163] Reform of the Serbian Criminal Code in 2012 abolished criminal defamation, but insult remains a criminal offence (Serbian Criminal Code Art. 170).

defamation laws and Croatia has removed custodial penalties.[164] Norway also repealed its *lèse-majesté* law in 2015[165] and Cyprus has decriminalized defamation with a few exceptions.[166] But some European states such as Hungary have actually strengthened or reintroduced legislation on criminal defamation.[167] Russia decriminalized defamation in 2011 only to reintroduce the offence one year later.[168]

In the Americas, states have increasingly adopted reforms decriminalizing defamation or limiting enforcement of defamation laws.[169] Jamaica was the first independent Caribbean state to have no criminal defamation laws, including seditious libel.[170] In 2020, Honduras removed criminal sanctions for *desacato*, 'a class of legislation that criminalizes expression which offends, insults or threatens a public official in the performance of his or her duties', but maintains criminal penalties for so-called 'crimes against honor', including insult and slander.[171] Uruguay and Guatemala have also decriminalized *desacato*.[172]

In Asia, decriminalization of defamation has been limited. Although states such as Sri Lanka[173] and the Maldives[174] have decriminalized defamation, 38 of 44 states retain criminal defamation laws[175] and states such as Bangladesh and Myanmar have strengthened criminal provisions on defamation.[176] States with notorious *lèse-majesté*

---

[164] OSCE, 'OSCE media watchdog praises Croatia's abolition of prison sentences for defamation' (29 June 2006).
[165] Norwegian Penal Code 1902 s. 135 was repealed with the Norwegian Penal Code 2005.
[166] Criminal defamation was repealed in 2003 by Cyprus Law 84(I)/2003, which amended the Criminal Code, Cap. 154. However, insulting the armed forces of the Republic of Cyprus, defaming foreign heads of state, and insulting the memory of the deceased remain criminal offences. A. Spaic & others, 'Decriminalization of Defamation—The Balkans Case a Temporary Remedy or a Long Term Solution?' (2016) 47 *International Journal of Law, Crime and Justice* 21. 'Decriminalisation of Defamation' (Centre for Media Pluralism and Media Freedom, January 2019). Civil defamation operates under the Cyprus Civil Wrongs Law. Defamation is defined under s. 17(1) of the Cyprus Civil Wrongs Law, Cap. 148.
[167] Hungarian Criminal Code s. 226A. See also s. 226B (punishes making such a recording accessible to the public). Cf. P. Judit & A.H. Kávai, 'No imprisonment for defamatory or libellous articles in the press, Hungarian Parliament votes' (Telex, 23 May 2023). Similarly, the Republika Srpska of Bosnia and Herzegovina re-criminalized defamation: see OHCHR, 'Bosnia and Herzegovina: UN experts alarmed by re-criminalisation of defamation in the Republika Srpska entity' (25 July 2023).
[168] Russian Penal Code Art. 128.1 (although defamation with respect to judges and some other public officials remained throughout this period); V. Khachatryan & P. Roudik, 'Russia: Defamation is Criminalized Again' (Law Library of Congress, 20 August 2012). It also adopted the so-called 'Disrespect for Authority' Law in 2019: S. Kiselyov, 'Russia Passes Legislation Banning "Disrespect" of Authorities and "Fake News"' (The Moscow Times, 7 March 2019).
[169] L. Holt & others, 'Decriminalizing Defamation: A Comparative Law Study' (*GW Law International Law and Policy Brief*, March 2022). See also J. Simon & others, 'Weaponizing the Law: Attacks on Media Freedom' (Thomson Reuters and Tow Centre for Digital Journalism, April 2023), 43: noting that *desacato* laws have been repealed or declared unconstitutional in many countries in Latin America.
[170] Jamaican Defamation Act 2013 s. 7.
[171] CPJ, 'La Corte Suprema de Justicia deroga el delito de desacato' (26 May 2005). *Desacato* remained in the Honduran Penal Code until it was amended in 2020; CPJ, 'Honduras enacts penal code maintaining "crimes against honor"' (26 June 2020).
[172] Although exceptions to decriminalization of *desacato* apply under Uruguayan law, such as when the claimant can 'demonstrate the existence of real malice': Uruguayan Criminal Code Art. 336. CPJ & others, 'Critics Are Not Criminals: Comparative Study of Criminal Defamation Laws in the Americas' (2016), 47; Guatemalan Constitutional Court, *Partial Judgment of General Unconstitutionality*, Case file 1122-205, 1 February 2006, 3.
[173] 'Sri Lanka abolishes criminal defamation' (Zee News, 18 June 2002).
[174] 'Anti-defamation law repealed' (Maldives Independent, 14 November 2018).
[175] UNESCO, 'Defamation laws and SLAPPs increasingly "misused" to curtail freedom of expression' (8 December 2022).
[176] Amnesty International, 'Bangladesh: New Digital Security Act is attack on freedom of expression' (12 November 2018); OHCHR, *The Invisible Boundary—Criminal prosecutions of journalism in Myanmar* (11 September 2018), 9–11; OHCHR, 'Myanmar: UN report details silencing by law of independent journalism' (11 September 2018).

laws such as Thailand and Turkey maintain such laws in force and use them often.[177] Cambodia also introduced a new *lèse-majesté* provision to the Penal Code in 2018.[178]

Abolition of sedition laws has followed a similar mixed trajectory. The crime of sedition—defined in English common law as the oral or written publication of words with seditious intent—was abolished in the England, Wales and Northern Ireland in 2010[179] and denounced as an 'arcane' offence.[180] Eight Commonwealth states have abolished these laws over the past 25 years: Kenya, Ghana, New Zealand, England, Wales and Northern Ireland, Jamaica, Sierra Leone, Maldives and most recently in October 2021, Singapore.[181] Courts in Uganda and the Kingdom of Eswatini have declared those countries' sedition laws unconstitutional.[182]

Yet it remains a colonial legacy in some Commonwealth states. Sometimes it is a dead letter—Canada has not prosecuted anyone for sedition since 1951.[183] In the United States, sedition carries a potential sentence of 20 years in prison but this offence has long since developed from its origins as a speech-related offence to a rarely charged crime of 'threatened or actual use of force' against the US Government.[184]

---

[177] '903 minors among thousands tried or jailed for insulting Turkey's ruler Erdogan' (Arab News, 19 December 2020). See Turkish Penal Code, Law No. 5237 Art. 299; 'Thailand jails man for 35 years for insulting the monarchy on Facebook' (The Independent, 12 June 2017); 'Lese-majeste explained: How Thailand forbids insult of its royalty' (BBC, 6 October 2017).

[178] Cambodian Criminal Code Art. 437bis. P. Chan Thul, 'Cambodia parliament adopts lese-majeste law, prompting rights concerns' (Reuters, 14 February 2018). The law provides for imprisonment between one and five years' and a fine between 500 and 2,500 USD.

[179] Abolished in UK Coroners and Justice Act 2009 s. 73. J.C. Smith & B. Hogan, *Criminal Law* (3rd edn, Butterworths 1973), 646, cited in Law Commission of England and Wales, Working Paper No. 72 Second Programme, Item XVIII: Codification of the Criminal Law—Treason, Sedition and Allied Offences (1977), 41. Although in 1951 the Canadian Supreme Court noted that 'probably no crime has been left in such vagueness of definition' as the offence of sedition, the classical definition of seditious intent is an 'intention to bring into hatred or contempt, or to excite disaffection against the person of, Her Majesty, her heirs or successors, or the government and constitution of the United Kingdom ... or to incite any person to commit any crime in disturbance of the peace, or to raise discontent or disaffection amongst Her Majesty's subjects, or to promote feelings of ill-will and hostility between different classes of such subjects': CFJ, TrialWatch Fairness Report (n 2) 4, citing J.F. Stephen, *A Digest of the Criminal Law* (4th edn, MacMillan and co. 1887), 66 (Art. 93). However, UK and Canadian authorities have added that seditious intent must also 'be founded in an intention to incite to violence or to create public disturbance or disorder against His Majesty or the institutions of government': UK Divisional Court, *R v. Chief Metropolitan Stipendiary Magistrate ex parte Choudhury* [1991] 1 QB 429, 9 April 1990, 453; Canadian Supreme Court, *Boucher v. R* [1951] SCR 265, 18 December 1950, 315 (Kellock J).

[180] UK Minster Claire Ward's words were quoted in a senate hearing in Canada: Senate of Canada, Proceedings of the Standing Senate Committee on Legal and Constitutional Affairs Issue No. 47 (14 June 2018).

[181] CFJ, TrialWatch Fairness Report (n 2). Ghanaian Repeal of the Criminal and Seditious Laws (Amendment) Act 2001, July 2001. Jamaica has abolished the criminal offence of seditious libel, but retained other offences for which elements of the crime include seditious intent: see, e.g., Jamaican Seditious Meetings Act.

[182] CFJ, TrialWatch Fairness Report (n 2) 11, citing Ugandan Constitutional Court, *Mwenda v. Attorney General* [2010] UGSC 5, 25 August 2010; Swazi High Court, *Maseko v. The Prime Minister of Swaziland* (2180/2009) [2016] SZHC 180, 16 September 2016. But the Eswatini Supreme Court has reinstated the state's appeal against this decision: P. Fabricius, 'Historic Swazi court judgment striking down parts of sedition and terrorism laws is under threat' (Daily Maverick, 29 September 2022).

[183] Canadian Supreme Court, *Boucher v. R* [1951] SCR 265, 18 December 1950, §288.

[184] US Code Title 18 Crimes and Criminal Procedure ss 2384–2385; Sack (n 27) 273, 276 ('the early American Republic did adopt the English statutory and common laws of sedition, criminalizing certain criticism of government. These gave way, by the time of Sullivan, to well-settled doctrine, expressly recognized in Sullivan, that sedition laws—in particular ours of 1798—were generally barred by the First Amendment'). See also Sack (n 74) §3.2 ('Criminal libel lives on in American law, but barely; prosecutions for criminal libel ... appear to be rare'); M. Alfaro, 'What is sedition?' (The Washington Post, 13 January 2022).

But countries like Malaysia, Hong Kong, India and Pakistan[185] still have such laws on their books.[186] And although Australia amended its Criminal Code to remove 'sedition' offences it reintroduced them as new classes of offences under anti-terrorism laws.[187]

1.5.2. Civil penalties

Civil penalties in national defamation laws mainly consist of damages for injury to reputation and costs of legal proceedings. Some jurisdictions award nominal damages, such as the 'one franc in symbolic compensation' awarded by French courts.[188] Others award damages that are relatively low but can still have serious consequences for some speakers.[189]

Some states award damages that are objectively large. Extremely high defamation awards have been secured in the United States in recent years and the mere risk of such substantial claims is in itself a potential chilling factor. Three defamation trials against a radio host named Alex Jones brought by the families of 10 victims of a massacre at Sandy Hook school that Jones had denied resulted in total damages of nearly $1.5 billion US dollars.[190] In one trial, a jury handed down $965 million US dollars in compensatory damages against Mr. Jones, described as the 'largest defamation verdict in US history', at least for compensatory damages.[191] Fox News and its parent company, Fox Corp, faced a $1.6 billion US dollars defamation suit filed by Dominion Voting Systems, a technology company, following claims aired on Fox News that Dominion rigged its voting machines to steal the 2020 Presidential election from Donald Trump.[192] The case was ultimately settled by Fox News paying Dominion $787.5 million.[193]

Large damages awards used to be a feature of the system in England and Wales, when the assessment of damages for defamation was the province of the jury with no upper limit. This led, for instance, to an award of approximately $1.8 million US dollars against a historian who wrote a pamphlet in the mid-1990s alleging that Lord

---

[185] See s. II.2. (Application of national laws).
[186] See, e.g., Malaysia: Human Rights Watch, 'Malaysia: End Use of Sedition Act' (17 July 2019); CFJ, TrialWatch Fairness Report (n 2) 13–14. However, the Lahore High Court has struck Pakistan's sedition law as unconstitutional, a decision which remains subject to review by the Supreme Court: 'Pakistani court strikes down sedition law in win for free speech' (Al Jazeera, 30 March 2023).
[187] Australian Anti-Terrorism Act (No. 2) 2005 Schedule 7. In 2010 the term 'sedition' was replaced by the phrase 'urging violence': Australian National Security Legislation Amendment Act 2010 Schedule 1.
[188] See ECtHR, *Brasilier v. France* (App. no. 71343/01), 11 April 2006; ECtHR, *Giniewski v. France* (App. no. 64016/00), 31 January 2006, 55 (the Court still emphasized the chilling effect of the sanction). French Code of Criminal Procedure Art. 475-1 (relating to civil proceeding following a conviction).
[189] See, e.g., ECtHR, *Kasabova v. Bulgaria* (App. no. 22385/03), 19 April 2011, $71 (sum awarded against Bulgarian journalist that was made up of fines, costs and damages and amounted to 35 times her actual monthly salary).
[190] E. Williamson, 'With New Ruling, Sandy Hook Victims Win Over $1.4 Billion From Alex Jones' (The New York Times, 10 November 2022).
[191] S. S. Ali, 'Alex Jones unlikely to escape 'historically high' defamation award, legal experts say' (NBC, 14 October 2022). In June 2023, Alex Jones appealed the $1.4 billion verdict: R. Chumney, 'Conspiracy theorist Alex Jones appeals $1.4 billion defamation verdict awarded to Sandy Hook victims' (newstimes, 3 June 2023).
[192] C. McGreal, 'Is Dominion's $1.6 bn defamation lawsuit a death blow for Murdoch and Fox News?' (The Guardian, 12 December 2022);
[193] S. Levine & K. Lerner, 'Fox and Dominion settle for $787.5m in defamation lawsuit over US election lies' (The Guardian, 18 April 2023).

Aldington, a member of Parliament, was a war criminal.[194] But awards are now in practice made by judges and typically are not greater than the equivalent of approximately $300,000 US dollars in a defamation case.[195] However Irish defamation law still leaves the decision on damages to the jury.[196] Norway also has a track record of their courts awarding large damages in civil proceedings of tens, if not hundreds, of thousands of Euros.[197] And the Singapore High Court ordered a blogger to pay Prime Minister Lee Hsien Loong 100,441 US dollars for sharing an article on Facebook that falsely linked the Prime Minister to a corruption scandal.[198]

Some states seek to control damages through judicial assessment or statutory caps. In South Africa, the quantum of damages is generally not substantial, with the overarching principle being that the purpose of a damages award is to compensate the plaintiff for their impaired reputation and vindicate the plaintiff in the eyes of the public—not to punish the defendant.[199] A number of factors are taken into account, including the seriousness of the defamation, the breadth of distribution, the motivation and conduct of the defendant and the public profile of the plaintiff.[200] This is the principle in England and Wales as well.[201] In Australia, New South Wales recently amended defamation law provides for a statutory cap on non-economic loss approximately $292,000, noting the maximum amount will be awarded only in 'a most serious case'.[202] Prior to this amendment, the actor Geoffrey Rush was awarded a record amount of $2 million US dollars in his case against a newspaper that published an article portraying him as a sexual predator.[203]

---

[194] ECtHR, *Tolstoy Miloslavsky v. United Kingdom* (App. no. 18139/91), 13 July 1995. The case remains relevant today, as it would make it difficult for a claimant to obtain enforcement in England of the very high awards of damages which are still awarded in other jurisdictions, including the United States (UK High Court of England and Wales, *Adelson v. Anderson* [2011] EWHC 2497 (QB), 7 October 2011, §§85–86).

[195] A. Mullis & C. Doley, *Carter-Ruck on Libel and Privacy* (6th edn, LexisNexis 2010), §§15.26–15.33.

[196] For claims over 75,000 EUR. See, e.g., over 10 million EUR order reduced to 250,000 EUR on appeal: Irish Court of Appeal, *Kinsella v. Kenmare Resources PLC* [2019] IECA 54, 28 February 2019. See also ECtHR, *Independent Newspapers (Ireland) Limited v. Ireland* (App. no. 28199/15), 15 June 2017, §§105, 129 (a jury awarded 1,872,000 EUR for damages. The Supreme Court found it excessive and reduced it to 1,250,000 EUR and the ECtHR found a violation of article 10, considering that 'relevant and sufficient reasons' need to be given for such a high award). There have also been recent proposals to remove juries from defamation trials: Irish Draft General Scheme of the Defamation (Amendment) Bill (28 March 2023). A recent report by the Oireachtas justice committee called for keeping juries in Irish High Court defamation actions: 'Keep juries for defamation – Oireachtas committee' (Law Society Gazette Ireland, 3 October 2023).

[197] See, e.g., ECtHR, *Bergens Tidende v. Norway* (App. no. 26132/95), 2 May 2000, 4.7 million Norwegian Kroner is approximately 391,503.86 EUR.

[198] Singaporean High Court, *Lee Hsien Loong v. Leong Sze Hian* [2021] 4 SLR 1128 (HC), 24 March 2021 (75,520 USD in general damages, 24,921 USD in aggravated damages).

[199] Milo & Stein (n 127) 43–44.

[200] See, e.g., South African High Court, Gauteng Local Division, *Manuel v. Economic Freedom Fighters* [2019] ZAGPJHC 157, 30 May 2019, §§31–37.

[201] Since the England and Wales Defamation Act 2013 reversed the presumption that defamation cases be tried by jury: England and Wales Defamation Act 2013 s. 11. Judges now assess damages with the current notional cap on general damages set at around 305,000 USD (See, e.g., UK High Court of England and Wales, *Gilham v. MGN Limited* [2020] EWHC 2217 (QB), 12 August 2020, §32).

[202] New South Wales Defamation Amendment Act 2020 Schedule 1, §34, amending s. 35 of the Australian New South Wales Defamation Act 2005. The court may order aggravated damages, to which the cap does not apply, that exceed the cap if it 'is satisfied that the circumstances of the publication of the defamatory matter to which the proceedings relate are such as to warrant an award of aggravated damages'. New South Wales Defamation Act 2005 s. 35(2B) and (2A).

[203] Australian Federal Court, *Nationwide News Pty Limited v. Rush* [2020] FCAFC 115, 2 July 2020 (the amount included 659,651 USD in non-economic loss and aggravated damages and one million in past economic loss).

Apart from damages, the order to pay legal costs may lead to huge financial burdens on journalists in some jurisdictions. In one case, supermodel Naomi Campbell sued a newspaper after it published a photograph of her attending a Narcotics Anonymous clinic.[204] She ultimately won her claim in the English courts and was awarded only approximately 4,000 Euros in damages. However, under the conditional fee agreement, if the appeal succeeded (which it did), her solicitors and counsel were entitled to base costs as well as success fees amounting to approximately 1,256,562.94 Euros.[205] England and Wales later abolished such 'success fees' in defamation and privacy cases.[206]

1.5.3. Other penalties

States have placed restrictions on journalism licences or publications or limited other civil liberties following convictions for defamation. Politicians may be barred from holding positions in public office as a result of convictions for criminal defamation.[207] Criminal defamation laws may ban work as a journalist permanently or for a specific period of time. There is precedent for this penalty in nations such as the Netherlands,[208] Indonesia,[209] Iran[210] and Yemen.[211] In Russia, the withdrawal of the right to hold certain posts for a specific period of time has been imposed on bloggers[212] and journalists.[213] Courts have seized or permanently blocked publication of information in defamation proceedings in Austria[214] and Russia.[215] The banning or closure of media outlets is a penalty in Bahrain,[216] Ukraine,[217] and Qatar.[218] And an injunction of publication or republication can, for example, be sought in Austria[219] and South Africa.[220]

---

[204] The case was for breach of confidence but the law on defamation was discussed at length. See also UK Supreme Court, *Times Newspapers Ltd v. Flood* [2017] UKSC 33, 11 April 2017.
[205] ECtHR, *MGN Limited v. United Kingdom* (App. no. 39401/04), 18 January 2011 (finding a breach of Art. 10 and chilling effect of costs).
[206] UK Legal Aid, Sentencing and Punishment of Offenders Act 2012 (Commencement No. 13) Order 2018 SI/2018/1287.
[207] J. Reed, 'Rahul Gandhi barred from India's parliament following conviction over Modi remarks' (Financial Times, 25 March 2023).
[208] Dutch Criminal Code Art. 271, §3 (which penalizes insults concerning a deceased person and provides that if the offender commits this offence 'in his profession' he may 'be deprived of the exercise from that profession').
[209] Indonesian Penal Code 1999 Arts 137, 155(2). Indonesia recently passed a new criminal code that will enter into force in 2025, which contains 'dozens' of 'online and offline criminal defamation' provisions: Human Rights Watch, 'Indonesia: New Criminal Code Disastrous for Rights' (8 December 2022).
[210] Iranian Press Law 2002 Art. 27 (criminalizing insults against the 'Leader of the Islamic Republic of Iran or the true Sources of Emulation').
[211] Yemeni Press and Publications Law No. 25 1990 Art. 106.
[212] Reporters Without Borders, 'Jailed journalist to spend total of three years in prison camp' (23 January 2015).
[213] ECtHR, *Stomakhin v. Russia* (App. no. 52273/07), 9 May 2018, §128.
[214] ECtHR, *Oberschlick v. Austria* (App. no. 11662/85), 23 May 1991, §26.
[215] See Russian Federal Law No. 149-FZ on Information, Information Technologies and the Protection of Information 2006 Art. 15.1.1.
[216] Bahraini Decree-by-law No. 47 Art. 19 (the ministerial decision to ban an outlet can be challenged before a civil court within 15 days of the decision).
[217] The Law of Ukraine 'On Media' No. 2849-IX 2022 Art. 99.
[218] Qatari Law No. 8 of 1979 on Publications and Publishing Art. 84.
[219] Austrian Civil Code Art. 1330 (2).
[220] See, e.g., South African Supreme Court of Appeal, *Economic Freedom Fighters v. Manuel* [2020] ZASCA 172, 17 December 2020.

Other forms of punishment for defamation include correctional labour (Belarus)[221] and loss of the right to hold office or serve in the army (the Netherlands).[222] A requirement to 'rectify' publications to declare their falsity or to publish a judgment is also a civil penalty available in Russia.[223]

2. Application of National Laws

Across the world, governments and other powerful actors have sought to chill political speech through a range of civil and criminal laws, from defamation to *lèse-majesté* provisions or sedition charges. How these laws are misused varies widely: from lengthy terms of imprisonment handed down for social media posts or legitimate journalism,[224] to powerful plaintiffs harassing journalists with an onslaught of civil charges that are cripplingly expensive to defend.[225]

According to a report by the Committee to Protect Journalists, 'over two-thirds of the governments' in the Americas 'routinely use [criminal defamation] laws to silence dissent and to deprive citizens of information on matters of public interest'.[226] These laws are also alive and well in Asia. Thailand is using *lèse-majesté* laws regularly against students and protesters.[227] India deploys criminal defamation laws—as well as sedition laws—to devastating effect on citizens and the media.[228] And Hong Kong has revived sedition laws that have been dormant for five decades for use against those who criticize the state.[229] Some striking cases are surveyed below, and illustrate how such practices are developing across each region.

2.1. Europe
2.1.1. Spain
A prominent European case involving a restriction on political speech in recent years has been the trial of Catalonia independence leaders in Spain. In October 2019, Spain's Supreme Court unanimously convicted nine Catalan leaders of sedition and other crimes—such as embezzlement of public funds—sentencing them to between nine

---

[221] Belarusian Criminal Code Art. 188 (meaning deductions are made from the earnings of a convicted person at his place of work and provided to the state).
[222] Dutch Criminal Code Art. 262 §2.
[223] Russian Civil Code Art. 152; ECtHR, *Dyuldin v. Russia* (App. no. 25968/02), 31 July 2007. See also Russian Federal Law No. 149-FZ on Information, Information Technologies and the Protection of Information 2006 Art. 15.1.1. See further South Africa and Slovakia: South African Supreme Court of Appeal, *Economic Freedom Fighters v. Manuel* [2020] ZASCA 172, 17 December 2020; Slovak Civil Code Art. 11 et ss.
[224] See, e.g., s. II.2.2.1. (Thailand). See, e.g., R. Ratcliffe, 'Woman jailed for record 43 years for insulting Thai monarchy' (The Guardian, 19 January 2021).
[225] See s. II.2.1.3. (SLAPP and libel tourism).
[226] CPJ & others, 'Critics Are Not Criminals: Comparative Study of Criminal Defamation Laws in the Americas' (2016), 9; see, e.g., s. II.2.3.1. (Ecuador).
[227] CFJ TrialWatch Fairness Report: (n 2), 18–19.
[228] Freedom House, *Freedom in the World 2023 Country Report: India* (2023). US Department of State, *Country Reports on Human Rights Practices: India* (2022), 1, 10: In 2022, the Supreme Court of India suspended the application of their colonial-era sedition law while it undergoes judicial review.
[229] CFJ, TrialWatch Fairness Report (n 2) 13–14.

and 13 years' imprisonment.[230] The Working Group on Arbitrary Detention found that their peaceful 'calls for the organization of processes that promote public participation' had been 'legitimate expressions of the exercise of freedom of opinion and expression' that should not have been criminalized.[231] And Amnesty International commented that the 'Supreme Court's interpretation of the crime of sedition' had been 'overly broad and resulted in criminalising legitimate acts of protest'.[232]

In January 2023, an amendment to the Criminal Code entered into force, eliminating the crime of sedition (article 544)[233] and incorporating instead the crime of aggravated public disorder. It envisages prison sentences of three to five years, lower than those associated with sedition (10 to 15 years).[234]

Spain has also been urged to amend the provisions of its Criminal Code on 'insult to the crown' and 'exhaulting terrorism', given the growing number of convictions of artists for controversial expressions on social media.[235]

2.1.2. Turkey

Since President Erdoğan took office, tens of thousands of prosecutions have taken place under Turkish laws related to insulting speech.[236] This includes article 299 of the Turkish Penal Code, which criminalizes insult to the President by up to four years' imprisonment.[237] In 2014, the year of President Erdoğan's election, 132 prosecutions were instigated under this provision.[238] These figures have sharply increased, with over 6,000 prosecutions filed in 2017 alone.[239]

Prominent convictions include a 14-month suspended prison sentence handed down to a former Miss Turkey for insulting the president on Instagram after she posted

---

[230] Catalonia's former vice-president Oriol Junqueras, various officials and civil society activists were also sentenced to prison terms. See Spanish Supreme Court, *Judgment No. 459/2019*, Special Proceedings No. 20907/2017, 14 October 2019. The various convictions included in this decision were confirmed by the Constitutional Court when deciding on separate appeals filed by the defendants. See also Spanish Supreme Court, *Judgment No. 459/2019*, Special Proceedings No. 20907/2017, 14 October 2019, 78–97.

[231] WGAD, *Jordi Cuixart I Navarro v. Spain* (Opinion no. 6/2019), 25 April 2019, §§110, 120. Although none of the convictions related solely to speech, in its bill of indictment committing the defendants to trial, the Supreme Court observed that the defendants had the 'ability to mobilise hundreds of thousands of followers from the prosovereignty organisations, from their speeches in the media and multiple messages on digital platforms', through which, the Court alleged, they 'encouraged a massed force to clash with the police and prevented voting'. Spanish Supreme Court, *Judgment No. 459/2019*, Special Proceedings No. 20907/2017, 14 October 2019.

[232] Amnesty International, 'Spain's conviction for sedition of Jordi Sànchez and Jordi Cuixart threatens rights to freedom of expression and peaceful assembly' (19 November 2019). In June 2021, Spain issued partial pardons for all nine defendants, releasing all from prison but retaining their ban on a return to public office for the duration of their original sentences. And in December 2022, Spain repealed the crime of sedition, replacing it with an 'aggravated public disorder' offence carrying between three and five years' imprisonment. C. Giles, 'Spanish govt reforms sedition law in nod to Catalan allies' (Associated Press, 22 December 2022).

[233] Spanish Organic Law 14/2022 Art. 1.20, derogating Art. 544 of the Spanish Criminal Code.

[234] Spanish Criminal Code Art. 557.

[235] Spanish Criminal Code Arts 578, 490, 491; COE Commissioner for Human Rights, Letter to the Spanish Minister of Justice dated 11 March 2021; OHCHR, ' "Two legal reform projects undermine the rights of assembly and expression in Spain"—UN experts' (23 February 2015). See ch. 6 (Terrorism Laws), s. II. 2.1.1. (Spain).

[236] Turkey has been characterized in this chapter as a European nation because it is a member of the Council of Europe, state party to the European Convention on Human Rights and is subject to the jurisdiction of the European Court of Human Rights.

[237] See s. III.4.2. (Public Interest).

[238] Human Rights Watch, 'Turkey: End Prosecutions for "Insulting President"' (17 October 2018).

[239] Ibid.

a satirical poem adapting the national anthem and referencing a corruption scandal.[240] Even public officials have been charged under these offences. For example, the mayor of Istanbul, Ekrem Imamoğlu, was sentenced to more than two and a half years' imprisonment for insulting members of the Supreme Electoral Council in December 2022.[241] Mr. Imamoğlu, seen as a key opponent to the President, was sentenced for 'insult' after he told the media that those who cancelled the 2019 Istanbul mayoral election that he won were 'fools'.[242] The Court has also banned Mr. Imamoğlu from holding political office.[243]

2.1.3. SLAPP and libel tourism

Strategic Litigation Against Public Participation (SLAPP)[244] refers to frivolous charges filed by powerful subjects against individuals who have expressed a critical position on an issue of public significance, aimed at silencing their voices. Because of the time and costs involved in such litigation, such cases present a serious threat to journalists, activists, academics or bloggers who are forced to defend themselves from such libel charges. The problem of SLAPP suits and libel tourism in Europe in particular is growing, but is emblematic of a broader global trend, and has resulted in the Council of Europe making specific recommendations to reduce SLAPP suits.[245]

The case of investigative journalist Daphne Caruana Galizia illustrates the problem of SLAPP suits in Malta. At the time Galizia was murdered, her assets had been frozen in conjunction with four libel suits brought by Maltese Economy Minister Chris Cardona and his consultant.[246] Galizia described the lawsuits against her at the time as 'an intimidation strategy'.[247] At the time of her murder, she was facing 43 civil and five criminal libel suits filed by a range of prominent politicians and businessmen.[248] Her lawsuits have now been passed on to her family.[249]

In the *El Universo* decision, the Inter-American Court recently held that the recourse by 'public officials to judicial channels to file lawsuits for crimes of slander or insult, not with the objective of obtaining a rectification, but to silence the criticisms made

---

[240] 'Ex-Miss Turkey sentenced for Erdogan poem' (DW, 31 May 2016).
[241] 'Istanbul mayor sentenced to prison for insulting public officials' (Al Jazeera, 14 December 2022).
[242] Human Rights Watch, 'Turkey: Court Convicts Istanbul Mayor Ekrem Imamoğlu' (14 December 2022).
[243] Pursuant to Turkish Penal Code Art. 53. Human Rights Watch, 'Turkey: Court Convicts Istanbul Mayor Ekrem Imamoğlu' (14 December 2022).
[244] The term 'anti-SLAPP' ('Strategic Lawsuits Against Public Participation') was first used by Professors George Pring and Penelope Canan of the University of Denver in the 1980s. See G. Pring & P. Canan, *SLAPPS: Getting Sued for Speaking Out* (Temple University Press 1996); see also J.W. Beatty, 'The Legal Literature on SLAPPS: A Look Behind the Smoke Nine Years After Pring and Canan First Yelled "Fire"' (1997) 9 *University of Florida Journal of Law & Public Policy* 85, 87, n. 11. The term 'anti-SLAPP' can be somewhat unhelpful insofar as the anti-SLAPP laws may relate, e.g., to 'a party's exercise of the right of free speech, right to petition, or right of association', US Texas Civil Practice and Remedies Code §27.003(a), not merely 'public participation'.
[245] See, e.g., CASE Coalition Against SLAPPs in Europe, 'SLAPPs'; Article 19, 'Europe: ARTICLE 19 welcomes Council of Europe anti-SLAPPs initiatives' (30 March 2022).
[246] E. Allaby, 'After journalist's murder, efforts to combat SLAPP in Europe' (Columbia Journalism Review, 24 April 2019).
[247] D. Caruana Galizia, 'We're the ones who should be suing them for the disaster they've brought to Malta' (Running Commentary: Daphne Caruana Galizia's Notebook, 12 May 2017).
[248] Daphne Caruana Galizia Foundation, 'Defence against frivolous and vexatious libel suits'; Allaby (n 246).
[249] Allaby (n 246).

regarding their actions in the public sphere, constitutes a threat to freedom of expression'; '[t]his type of process, known as "SLAPP"', the Court said, 'constitutes an abusive use of judicial mechanisms that must be regulated and controlled by the States'.[250] UN Special Rapporteurs have also expressed concern at the practice.[251] And the Council of Europe (COE) Rapporteur has explained that 'the risk of being drawn into costly and time-consuming legal proceedings can create a climate of fear and self-censorship'.[252]

The COE Rapporteur has recommended 15 good practices, including 'the prohibition of abuse of rights' and the use of the *forum non conveniens* doctrine to address cases of abusive forum shopping.[253]

Anti-SLAPP legislation has also been introduced in the United States and Canada, allowing the person sued to file a motion to strike out the case on the basis that it involves speech on a matter of public concern.[254] Costs sustained by the defendant can be recouped and there are measures in place to penalize abuse, such as fining the plaintiff. In the United States, anti-SLAPP laws currently exist in 32 states and the District of Columbia,[255] but these may not protect against lawsuits brought in federal courts.[256] In South Africa, a SLAPP defence was recognized under common law through the doctrine of abuse of court process.[257]

The problem of frivolous suits by powerful defendants is magnified when such cases can be filed all over the world, posing a threat to journalists in jurisdictions far from where they live and work. In England and Wales, although effective common law means were available for a defendant to obtain early dismissal of frivolous claims[258] and the Defamation Act 2013 brought forward a number of reforms, SLAPP and libel tourism remain a threat to journalists and other speakers. Although the entry into force of the UK Defamation Act resulted in a 40 per cent reduction in defamation claims in one year,[259] foreign journalists and news outlets continue to face claims in English courts.[260]

---

[250] IACtHR, *Palacio Urrutia v. Ecuador* (Series C, no. 446), 24 November 2021, §95. See also IACtHR, *Baraona Bray v. Chile* (Series C, no. 481), 24 November 2022, §91; See s. IV.13 (Recommendations).

[251] UN Special Rapporteur M. Sekaggya, *Report of the Special Rapporteur on the situation of human rights defenders* (2013) UN Doc. A/HRC/25/55, §§59, 70; COE Special Rapporteur E. Prévost, *Liability and Jurisdictional Issues in Online Defamation Cases* (2019) DGI(2019)04, 9.

[252] ≤IBT≥COE Rapporteur E. Prévost, *Liability and Jurisdictional Issues in Online Defamation Cases* (2019) DGI(2019)04, 8.

[253] Ibid., 35–36.

[254] In Canada, Ontario, British Columbia and Quebec have such laws: Ontario Protection of Public Participation Act, 2015, S.O. 2015 c. 23 (resulting in the addition of sections 137.1 to 137.5 of Ontario's Courts of Justice Act, RSO 1990 c. C-43); British Columbia Protection of Public Participation Act, SBC 2019 c. 3; Quebec: Code of Civil Procedure CQLR c C-25 Arts 51–54.

[255] A. Vining & S. Matthews, 'Overview of Anti-SLAPP Laws' (Reporters Committee for Freedom of the Press).

[256] See, e.g., US Court of Appeals, Second Circuit, *La Liberte v. Reid* 966 F.3d 79, 15 July 2020, 85–89 (California anti-SLAPP statute held inapplicable in federal case pending in New York-based federal court inasmuch as procedures established by the statute conflict with those applied under the Federal Rules of Civil Procedure).

[257] South African Constitutional Court, *Mineral Sands Resources (Pty) Ltd v Reddell* [2022] ZACC 37, 14 November 2022.

[258] This includes early rulings on meanings and striking out, in particular for abuse of process (UK Court of Appeal, *Jameel v. Dow Jones* [2005] EWCA Civ 75, 3 February 2005). See Mullis & Doley (n 195), chapter 28.

[259] 227 in 2014 down to 135 in 2015: UK Ministry of Justice, *Civil Justice Statistics Quarterly, England and Wales (Incorporating The Royal Courts of Justice 2015)* (2016).

[260] A report including a survey of over 60 journalists in 41 countries investigating cross-border financial crime and corruption has concluded that 31 per cent had been threatened with court action in London, mainly for defamation or privacy claims, with the United Kingdom as the most common jurisdiction for legal threats after a

And despite commitments to 'moving decisively to stamp out SLAPPs', the UK Government has yet to do so.[261]

The Defamation Act established a serious harm threshold for actionable claims[262] and a defence of publication on matters of public interest.[263] It also requires that, if a defendant is domiciled outside of the United Kingdom, the court will not have jurisdiction to hear and determine an action unless England and Wales is 'clearly the most appropriate place' in which to bring an action.[264] A similar shift has been observed in Canada, though there the initiative was largely taken by the courts not the legislature.[265] In the United States some provisions that could discourage libel tourism seem to have limited effects.[266] France has also attracted libel tourism as libel is a criminal offence and therefore provides a powerful threat against the speaker.[267]

2.2. Asia Pacific
2.2.1. Thailand

In Asia, Thailand's *lèse-majesté* law is used to suppress insult of 'the King, the Queen, the Heir-apparent or the Regent' and provides for 'imprisonment of three to fifteen years' per count that is charged. Because a count often relates to one statement, cases often carry the threat of multiple decades in prison.[268]

Thailand experienced a wave of *lèse-majesté* prosecutions following the 2014 coup d'état, with at least 127 individuals charged between 2014 and 2018.[269] After the 2020 pro-democracy protests, hundreds more were charged and many have been subjected to decades long sentences.[270] A sentence of 70 years (reduced to 35 years on a guilty plea) was imposed on one person for posting content on Facebook that allegedly exposed the King, Rama IX, and other members of the royal family to 'public hatred and humiliation'.[271] And a former civil servant was sentenced to 87 years in prison (reduced

---

journalist's home country: S. Coughtrie & P. Ogier, 'Unsafe for Scrutiny: Examining the pressures faced by journalists uncovering financial crime and corruption around the world' (The Foreign Policy Centre, 2 November 2020), 6.

[261] UK Ministry of Justice, 'Consultation Outcome: Strategic Lawsuits Against Public Participation (SLAPPs)' (17 March 2022).
[262] England and Wales Defamation Act 2013 s. 1(1).
[263] Ibid., s. 4(1).
[264] Ibid., s. 9(2).
[265] Canadian Supreme Court, *Éditions Écosociété Inc. v. Banro Corp.*, 2012 SCC 18, 18 April 2012; Canadian Supreme Court, *Haaretz.com v. Goldhar* 2018 SCC 28, 6 June 2018 following Canadian Supreme Court, *Club Resorts Ltd v. Van Breda* 2012 SCC 17, 18 April 2012.
[266] US Code Title 28 Judiciary and Judicial Procedure s. 4102(a)(l)(A); US Securing the Protection of our Enduring and Established Constitutional Heritage Act (2010) which bars US courts from recognizing foreign libel judgments, unless it finds that the foreign judgment does not infringe the First Amendment rights: US Code Title 28 Judiciary and Judicial Procedure §4102(a)(l)(A); J. Larkin, 'False Havens: Assessing New Developments in the Libel Tourism Debate' (2019) 11 *Journal of Media Law* 82.
[267] D. Sullivan, *Libel Tourism: Silencing the Press Through Transnational Legal Threats* (Center for International Media Assistance, 2010), 21.
[268] Thai Penal Code s. 112. See CFJ, 'Thailand Should Dismiss Charges Against 22 Protest Leaders' (16 January 2023).
[269] In early 2018 a policy shift resulted in a brief moratorium halting use of this provision. International Federation for Human Rights & others, *Second Wave: The return of lèse-majesté in Thailand* (2021) (reporting 124 individuals were charged under Art. 112 between November 2020 and August 2021), 4–5.
[270] Ibid.
[271] See Columbia Global Freedom of Expression, 'Public Prosecutor v. Wichai'.

to 43 years and six months upon pleading guilty) for posting 'audio clips to Facebook and YouTube with comments critical of the monarchy'.[272] UN experts have criticized Thailand's use of *lèse-majesté* and sedition laws to suppress speech, calling on the government to 'stop the repeated use of such serious criminal charges against individuals for exercising their rights to freedom of peaceful expression'.[273]

2.2.2. India

In India, there is increasing use of colonial-era sedition laws to stifle criticism. The vast majority of sedition cases filed against Indian journalists, students, academics and opposition politicians for criticizing governments and politicians over the last decade were registered after 2014, when Prime Minister Modi took power, and more than 7,000 individuals have been charged since.[274] In January 2021, eight journalists who reported on protests by farmers regarding agricultural reform were charged with sedition and 'making statements inimical to national integration'.[275] An investigative news magazine, Caravan, has had 10 sedition cases brought against its senior editorial staff for a story and tweet relating to a protester's death.[276] Sedition charges are among the myriad charges levelled against Indian journalist Rana Ayyub,[277] whose reporting on issues affecting Indian Muslims and vulnerable individuals in the Covid-19 pandemic has seen her subjected to what the UN has called 'judicial harassment' by Indian authorities.[278]

A report by Freedom House warned that 'India, the world's most populous democracy, is … sending signals that holding the government accountable is not part of the press's responsibility'.[279] India's Law Commission has called for reform, noting 'instances where people have been charged with sedition for making statements that in no manner undermine the security of the nation'.[280] And recent developments evince the potential for the law to be overturned: in May 2022, the Indian Supreme Court urged the government to refrain from bringing any new sedition cases pending a review of the law, and the Modi Government informed the Court that it will review it.[281]

2.2.3. Philippines

Perhaps the most high-profile application of libel laws to silence political speech in the Philippines has been the case of Maria Ressa, veteran journalist, CEO of Rappler Inc. and

---

[272] R. Ratcliffe, 'Woman jailed for record 43 years for insulting Thai monarchy' (The Guardian, 19 January 2021).
[273] 'Thailand: UN rights office deeply troubled by treason charges for protestors' (UN News, 18 December 2020).
[274] Purohit (n 9).
[275] S. Biswas, 'Why journalists in India are under attack' (BBC News, 4 February 2021).
[276] Ibid.
[277] C. Cadwalladr, 'Reviled, harassed, abused: Narendra Modi's most trenchant critic speaks out' (The Guardian, 27 February 2022).
[278] 'Halt all retaliation attacks against Indian journalist Rana Ayyub—UN experts' (UN News, 21 February 2022).
[279] S. Repucci, 'Freedom and the Media 2019: Media Freedom: A Downward Spiral' (Freedom House, 2019).
[280] U. Trivedi, 'India Top Court to Consider Quashing Colonial-Era Sedition Law' (Bloomberg, 15 July 2021); Law Commission of India, Consultation Paper on 'Sedition' (2018), §7.3.
[281] 'India's top court puts colonial-era sedition law on hold for review' (Reuters, 11 May 2022). In August 2023, a new law introduced in Parliament proposed to replace the sedition law with a provision criminalizing 'acts endangering sovereignty, unity and integrity of India': A. Sharma, 'India moves to replace British colonial-era sedition law with its own version' (AP News, 12 August 2023).

winner of the 2021 Nobel Peace Prize. On 15 June 2020, a Manila Regional Trial Court Judge found Ressa guilty of cyberlibel for allegedly defaming a businessman, Wilfredo Keng, following Rappler's publication of an article written by another journalist alleging that there were 'shady' dealings between Mr Keng and a former Chief Justice of the Supreme Court.[282] She was sentenced to approximately six years' imprisonment for this offence and ordered to pay approximately $7,100 US dollars in damages.[283] The decision, affirmed by the Court of Appeals, has been considered a death knell for democracy in the Philippines and the UN has repeatedly called on the Philippines to repeal the criminal penalties attached to its defamation laws.[284]

Ressa was convicted even though cyberlibel was not a crime at the time of the publication and the article related to alleged corruption by a justice facing impeachment at that time: a matter of clear public interest.[285] And instead of relying on the one-year limitation period prescribed for 'the crime of libel and other similar offences',[286] prosecutors relied on a general limitation period of 12 years[287] even though the Supreme Court had declared 'cyberlibel is ... not a new crime'.[288]

As a result, Ressa was convicted for an article she did not write, based on a law that did not exist when the article was written, and by way of a prosecution initiated six years after the limitation period had expired.[289] The verdict in this case comes after a long line of politically motivated allegations against Ressa, including additional libel charges,[290] exposing her to a cumulative sentence of over 50 years in prison.[291] Multiple

---

[282] Philippine Regional Trial Court, *People of the Philippines v. Santos, Ressa, and Rappler* R-MNL-19-01141-CR, 15 June 2020; Philippine Cybercrime Prevention Act of 2012 s. 4(c)(4).

[283] Philippine Regional Trial Court, *People of the Philippines v. Santos, Ressa, and Rappler* R-MNL-19-01141-CR, 15 June 2020, 36 (ordering 200,000 Philippine pesos (approximately 3,500 USD) for moral damages and 200,000 pesos (approximately 3,500 USD) for exemplary damages).

[284] The trial court sentenced her to a maximum of six years' imprinsonment. On appeal, the Philippine Court of Appeals imposed a longer maximum sentence of six years, eight months and 20 days upon Ressa and her co-accused: see OHCHR, 'Philippines: UN expert slams court decision upholding conviction of Maria Ressa and shutdown of media outlets' (14 July 2022).

[285] Ibid.

[286] Philippine Revised Penal Code Art. 90.

[287] Philippine Commonwealth Act No. 3326 s. 1(d) (which provides a 12-year limitation period for offences that are silent as to their limitation period and are punishable by over six years' maximum imprisonment); Philippine Cybercrime Prevention Act of 2012 s. 6.

[288] Philippine Revised Penal Code Art. 353, in relation to Art. 355 of the Revised Penal Code already punishes it; Philippine Supreme Court, *Disini v. Secretary of Justice* G.R. No. 203335, 11 February 2014.

[289] The article was published on Rappler.com on 29 May 2012 and a typographical error was corrected changing one letter on 19 February 2014. The Philippine Cybercrime Prevention Act was signed into law on 12 September 2012. Between 9 October 2012 and 22 April 2014, the Cybercrime Prevention Act was the subject of a temporary restraining order imposed by the Supreme Court: Supreme Court of the Philippines, *Disini, et al. v. Secretary of Justice, et al.*, G.R. Nos. 203335, 203299, 203306, 203359, 203378, 203391, 203407, 203440, 203453, 203454, 203469, 203501, 203509, 203515 & 203518, 18 February 2014. Ms. Ressa was charged for the alleged cyberlibel offence in 2019.

[290] See, e.g., Doughty Street Chambers, 'Maria Ressa's Legal Team Welcome Dismissal of Libel Charge against Maria Ressa in the Philippines' (12 August 2021).

[291] R. Ratcliffe, 'Journalist Maria Ressa found guilty of "cyberlibel" in Philippines' (The Guardian, 15 June 2020). Ressa was acquitted of four tax charges in January 2023: J. Gutierrez & M. Ives, 'Maria Ressa, Philippine Journalist and Nobel Laureate, Is Acquitted of Tax Evasion' (The New York Times, 17 January 2023). In September 2023, Ressa was aquitted of her final tax charge: A. France-Presse, 'Philippine Nobel prize winner Maria Ressa acquitted of tax charges' (The Guardian, 12 September 2023).

governments, the UN and the European Parliament have called on the Philippines to drop the charges.[292]

2.3. North and South America
2.3.1. Ecuador
Like in the Philippines, many countries in the Americas allow private citizens to file a complaint seeking to have prosecutors institute criminal proceedings.[293] A high-profile example in Ecuador concerns former President Rafael Correa's defamation complaint against the opinion editor, Emilio Palacio, and three executives of the El Universo daily paper.[294] Palacio's column referred to Correa as 'the dictator' and suggested he had ordered the army to shoot at civilians during a police uprising in 2010, and that his actions may have amounted to crimes against humanity.[295] Correa argued that the defendants should be punished with a prison term of three years and 80 million US dollars in damages.[296]

The judge convicted the defendants of criminal defamation of an authority and sentenced them to three years in prison and a fine of $30 million US dollars.[297] He ordered El Universo to pay an additional 10 million US dollars in damages.[298] The Inter-American Commission and Court of Human Rights, reviewing the case, held that such criminal sanctions violated the right to freedom of expression and condemned the conviction.[299] While the Court stopped short of expressly saying criminal penalties or even imprisonment could never be appropriate for defamation, a position that had been urged by parties intervening in the case, the Court arguably went further than previous cases in concluding that, within a reasonable period of time, Ecuador must adopt legislative measures to 'prevent public officials from resorting to judicial channels to file lawsuits for slander and insult with the aim of silencing criticism of their actions in the public sphere'.[300] The Court also held that to uphold 'media pluralism and diversity' 'requires … on the part of the State' to 'establish, for the protection of the honor of public

---

[292] See, e.g., Doughty Street Chambers, 'Amal Clooney and Caoilfhionn Gallagher QC condemn court decision affirming Maria Ressa's conviction and sentence for 'cyber libel'' (11 July 2022).

[293] See, e.g., s. II.2.2.3. (Philippines); American Bar Association and CFJ, 'Peru: A Preliminary Report on Proceedings Against Journalist Paola Ugaz' (25 October 2020)('In the Peruvian system, private citizens can file complaints regarding certain offenses, including criminal defamation, without the participation of a public prosecutor').

[294] E. Palacio, 'NO a las mentiras' (NO to lies) (El Universo, 6 February 2011).

[295] CPJ, 'Ecuadorian editor and executives sentenced to prison' (21 July 2011).

[296] Ibid.

[297] Ibid; Ecuadorian Criminal Code Art. 493.

[298] CPJ, 'Ecuadorian editor and executives sentenced to prison' (21 July 2011). CPJ, 'El Universo verdict bad precedent for free press in Americas' (16 February 2012). In 2012, President Correa announced that he would pardon the defendants. According to El Universo, the sentences have not been executed, but they have also not been declared invalid. 'Correa Forgives But Does not Forget' (Ecuador Times, 27 February 2012); P. Nalvarte, 'I/A Court HR admits case from newspaper EL Universo against the State of Ecuador after criminal sentence for defamation in 2012' (Knight Center LatAm Journalism Review, 26 February 2020).

[299] IACtHR, *Palacio Urrutia v. Ecuador* (Series C, no. 446), 24 November 2021, §127; IACmHR, *Merits Report No. 29/19* (March 2019) OEA/Ser.L/V/II. Doc. 34; OAS, Press Release R20/12 (12 February 2012).

[300] IACtHR, *Palacio Urrutia v. Ecuador* (Series C, no. 446), 24 November 2021, §182.

2.4. Middle East and Africa

2.4.1. South Africa

In South Africa, former students were held liable under defamation laws for a computer-created image they created and circulated in which the face of a 'deputy principal of the school was super-imposed alongside that of the school principal on an image of two naked men sitting in a sexually suggestive posture'.[302] The Constitutional Court confirmed that the applicants were liable for defamation, but lowered the damages awarded from approximately $2,500 to $1,400 US dollars given the young age of the speakers.[303] This case is significant because the photoshopped image was crude, so that the reasonable person would not believe it to be a true image of the principal.[304] The case therefore sets a precedent for the potential suppression of satirical artworks.

2.4.2. Saudi Arabia

In Saudi Arabia, defamation laws are applied regularly to silence political criticism by journalists. In 2018, newspaper columnist Saleh al-Shehi was sentenced to five years in prison for 'insulting the royal court', with a five-year travel ban going into effect after release.[305] His arrest followed his appearance on a television show in which he said that any Saudi citizen who has a contact within the royal court or someone associated with it 'automatically has an advantage in buying strategically located land otherwise not available to the public'.[306]

Similarly, human rights activist and lawyer Waleed Abulkhair was sentenced to 15 years in prison, a 15-year overseas travel ban and a fine of over $50,000 US dollars for seeking to discredit state legitimacy, inciting public opinion and insulting the judiciary.[307] The convictions stem from his peaceful activism, 'including statements to news media and tweets criticizing human rights abuses in Saudi Arabia'.[308]

---

[301] Ibid., §96; M. Cepeda & D. Milo, 'The Beginning of the End for Criminal Defamation in the Americas? The El Universo Case' (Just Security, 3 May 2022). The El Universo case is part of a string of similar cases stifling political dissent in Ecuador. In 2014, an Assembly member, a former union leader, and a journalist were convicted of slandering former President Rafael Correa, resulting in up to 18 months' imprisonment, the obligation to issue a public apology and an order to pay reparations of 140,000 USD (18 months' imprisonment for the journalist, and six months for the union leader): IACmHR, *Fernando Alcibíades Villavicencio Valencia et al.* (Ecuador) (Precautionary Measures 30-14), 24 March 2014.

[302] South African Constitutional Court, *Le Roux v. Dey* [2011] ZACC 4, 8 March 2011, 1.

[303] South African Constitutional Court, *Le Roux v. Dey* [2011] ZACC 4, 8 March 2011.

[304] Ibid., 89.

[305] CPJ, 'Saudi journalist jailed for five years for insulting royal court' (8 February 2018). Saleh al-Shehi was released from prison on 19 May 2020 and died, reportedly from illness, approximately two months later: Reporters Without Borders, 'RSF calls for probe into Saudi journalist's death after release from prison' (24 July 2020).

[306] CPJ, 'Saudi Arabian authorities arrest local journalist following critical commentary' (5 January 2018).

[307] WGAD, *Waleed Abulkhair v. Saudi Arabia* (Opinion no. 10/2018), 19 April 2018, §§15, 17, 26–27; J. El-Hage & C. Assaf Boustani, 'Waleed Abulkhair sits in a Saudi jail for speaking out' (Human Rights Foundation, 12 July 2016). Saudi Arabian Anti-Cyber Crime Law and the Saudi Arabian Penal Law concerning Crimes of Terrorism and its Financing.

[308] Human Rights Watch, 'Saudi Arabia: 15-Year Sentence for Prominent Activist' (7 July 2014).

III. International Legal Standards

The right to freedom of expression is enshrined in article 19 of the Universal Declaration of Human Rights, article 19 of the International Covenant on Civil and Political Rights (ICCPR) and its regional equivalents.[309] In addition, the right to a fair trial applies to any defendant in a criminal or civil case, and a journalist or speaker who has suffered an unfair trial may bring a claim for violation of that right.[310]

Under article 19(3) of the ICCPR, a state is permitted to restrict speech if the state can prove that the restriction is (1) 'provided by law' (legality requirement); (2) pursues one of the following legitimate objectives: (i) 'for respect of the rights or reputations of others' or (ii) 'for the protection of national security or of public order ... or of public health or morals' (legitimacy requirement); and (3) is 'necessary' to achieve that aim (necessity requirement).[311] An analysis of necessity includes an assessment of proportionality, namely that restrictions are 'appropriate to achieve their protective function', 'the least intrusive instrument amongst those which might achieve their protective function', and 'proportionate to the interest to be protected'.[312] And given that the right to freedom of expression has likely crystallized into customary international law, even those few states who have not ratified the ICCPR or regional treaties are nonetheless bound to give effect to the right under international law, and to treat article 19 of the ICCPR as a floor, not a ceiling, for the protection of the right.[313] In addition, while these treaty provisions were drafted to bind states, today, all the major technology companies involved in speech-regulation have recognized the relevance of international human rights standards to their policies on content-moderation.[314]

1. Legality

International human rights bodies agree that laws restricting freedom of expression must be precise and that states must ensure that citizens can access the law and understand what conduct is proscribed.[315] This is a requirement for the rule of law.[316]

---

[309] ECHR Art. 10; ACHR Art. 13; ACHPR Art. 9; Arab Charter Art. 32; ASEAN Human Rights Declaration Art. 23; Cairo Declaration on Human Rights in Islam Art. 22. See ch. 1 (Introduction), s. II.1.1. (Treaty language).
[310] See A. Clooney & P. Webb, *The Right to a Fair Trial in International Law* (OUP 2021).
[311] See also HRC, General Comment No. 34 (2011), §22.
[312] Ibid., §34.
[313] See ch. 1 (Introduction), s. II.2. (Customary International Law).
[314] See, e.g., Twitter, 'Defending and respecting the rights of people using our service'; @jack, 'Tweet dated 10 August 2018'; Meta, 'Corporate Human Rights Policy'; Meta, 'Facebook Community Standards'. See also R. Allan, 'Hard Questions: Where Do We Draw the Line on Free Expression?' (Meta Newsroom, 9 August 2018); Global Network Initiative, GNI Principles on Freedom of Expression and Privacy. See ch. 3 (Hate Speech), s. IV (Approach of private companies to online hate speech).
[315] HRC, General Comment No. 34 (2011), §§24–25; Art. 19(3) of the ICCPR requires that any restriction be 'provided by law'; WGAD, *Chen Shuqing and Lü Gengsong v. China* (Opinion no. 76/2019), 21 November 2019, §43.
[316] Venice Commission, *Report on the Rule of Law* (2011) CDL-AD(2011)003rev, §41.

In its country reports, the Human Rights Committee has called on various states to 'clarify the vague and broad definition of key terms' contained in their laws relating to defamation, insult and sedition.[317]

The Working Group on Arbitrary Detention similarly criticized certain Chinese laws as 'vague' and in violation of international human rights law, for instance those that refer to 'incit[ing] others by spreading rumours ... to subvert State power or overthrow the socialist system'.[318] And it has criticized Thailand's *lèse-majesté* law on the basis that it 'leaves the determination of whether an offence has been committed entirely to the discretion of the authorities', which rendered the provision 'so vague as to be inconsistent with international human rights law'.[319]

The European Court of Human Rights provides that restrictions to speech 'must be formulated with sufficient precision to enable the persons concerned ... to foresee, to a degree that is reasonable in the circumstances, the consequences which a given action may entail'.[320] The Court's assessment focuses on whether laws are 'interpreted and applied by the domestic courts in a rigorous and consistent manner'.[321] And it has held that the meaning of the words used by a speaker should be determined by judges objectively, on the basis of how the words would have been understood by reasonable members of the audience of the speech and not based on the subjective understanding of the audience in question.[322]

The Court has typically chosen to examine claims regarding freedom of expression under the necessity ('necessary in a democratic society') prong,[323] and very few have resulted in a violation being found on the basis of overbroad and vague legislation or interpretation alone.[324] The leading case on legality relates to a Turkish politician (who later became a history professor) who published an editorial criticizing the prosecution of the editor of a newspaper for 'denigrating Turkishness'.[325] He requested, 'in an expression of solidarity, to be prosecuted on the same ground for his opinions' that the events in 1915–1919 could be described as the Armenian genocide.[326] He was subsequently investigated for 'insulting Turkishness'.[327] The Court considered that the

---

[317] See, e.g., HRC, *Concluding Observations, Kazakhstan* (2016) UN Doc. CCPR/C/KAZ/CO/2, §§49–50; see Kazakshtani Criminal Code Art. 373; HRC, *Concluding Observations, Algeria* (2018) UN Doc. CCPR/C/DZA/CO/4, §43; HRC, *Concluding Observations, Kuwait* (2016) UN Doc. CCPR/C/KWT/CO/3, §§40–41.

[318] WGAD, *Chen Shuqing and Lü Gengsong v. China* (Opinion no. 76/2019), 21 November 2019, §44. See Chinese Criminal Code Art. 10. See also WGAD, *Zhen Jianghua and Qin Yongmin v. China* (Opinion no. 20/2019), 1 May 2019, §73.

[319] WGAD, *Siraphop Kornaroot v. Thailand* (Opinion no. 4/2019), 24 April 2019, §55; Thai Penal Code s. 112. See also WGAD, *Anchan v. Thailand* (Opinion no. 64/2021), 17 November 2021, §66. WGAD, *Le Dinh Luong v. Vietnam* (Opinion no. 45/2019), 15 August 2019, §§54–58; Vietnamese Penal Code Art. 79.

[320] ECtHR, *Akçam v. Turkey* (App. no. 27520/07), 25 October 2011, §87.

[321] ECtHR, *Savva Terentyev v. Russia* (App. no. 10692/09), 28 August 2018, §55.

[322] ECtHR, *Milosavljević v. Serbia* (App. no. 57574/14), 25 May 2021, §64 (objective meaning of 'rapist').

[323] See, e.g., ECtHR, *Dilipak v. Turkey* (App. no. 29680/05), 15 September 2015, §60. See also ECtHR, *Cumhuriyet Vakfı v. Turkey* (App. no. 28255/07), 8 October 2013, §54.

[324] See ECtHR, *Akçam v. Turkey* (App. no. 27520/07), 25 October 2011, §93; ECtHR, *Editorial Board of Pravoye Delo v. Ukraine* (App. no. 33014/05), 5 May 2011, §§56–59.

[325] ECtHR, *Akçam v. Turkey* (App. no. 27520/07), 25 October 2011, §7; The crime of 'denigrating Turkishness' is under Turkish Penal Code, Law No. 5237 Art. 301.

[326] ECtHR, *Akçam v. Turkey* (App. no. 27520/07), 25 October 2011, §§7–10.

[327] Ibid., §72.

provision did not meet the 'quality of law' required 'since its unacceptably broad terms result in a lack of foreseeability as to its effects'.[328] And the scope of law, as interpreted by the Turkish judiciary, was 'too wide and vague', failing to enable 'individuals to regulate their conduct or to foresee the consequences of their acts'.[329]

The Inter-American Court also requires that restrictions on freedom of expression 'must be established by law', and in particular that criminal sanctions be formulated in 'an express, accurate, and restrictive manner' that sets out the elements of the offense and clearly limits punishable conduct.[330] Similarly, the Inter-American Commission held that a Cuban law on sedition contained 'ambiguous concepts that invite[d] arbitrary judicial interpretation', was 'not specific in terms of the punishable conduct and ... use[d] vague and indeterminate concepts ... making it impossible to know in advance what conduct is punishable'.[331]

The African human rights courts have aligned their approach with that of the Human Rights Committee, requiring that laws be 'drafted with sufficient clarity to enable an individual to adapt his behaviour to the rules'.[332] The East African Court of Justice determined that the 'broad and imprecise wording' of Tanzanian legislation meant that it was unclear 'what exactly is prohibited, such that [citizens] may regulate their actions'.[333] The ECOWAS Court similarly assessed that The Gambia's criminal laws on defamation, libel, false news and sedition were not prescribed by law.[334] In the case of sedition, the Court held that '[the] vagueness with which these laws have been framed and the *mens rea* ambiguity of the (seditious intention), makes it difficult to discern with any certainty what constitutes seditious offence'.[335]

The UN Special Rapporteur on Freedom of Expression has also expressed concerns about cases in which journalists have been charged with vague offences such as 'incitement to violation' (Iran), 'instigating hatred and disrespect against the ruling regime' (Bahrain), 'incitement to offences that damage public tranquillity' (Myanmar) and 'misrepresenting events' (Somalia).[336]

---

[328] Ibid., §95. This was despite government amending the legislation to replace 'Turkishness' and 'Republic' with 'Turkish Nation' and 'State of the Republic of Turkey'. The Court held that 'there seems to be no change or major difference in the interpretation of these concepts because they have been understood in the same manner by the Court of Cassation': §§90–91.

[329] ECtHR, *Akçam v. Turkey* (App. no. 27520/07), 25 October 2011, §93.

[330] See, e.g., IACtHR, *Kimel v. Argentina* (Series C, no. 177), 2 May 2008, §63; IACtHR, *Usón Ramírez v. Venezuela* (Series C, no. 207), 20 November 2009, §§55–57.

[331] IACmHR, *Roca Antúnez v. Cuba* (Case 12.127), 24 February 2018, §91.

[332] ACtHPR, *Konaté v. Burkina Faso* (App. no. 4/2013), 5 December 2014, §128; EACJ, *Media Council of Tanzania and others v. Attorney General of the United Republic of Tanzania* (Ref no. 2/2017), 28 March 2019, §66.

[333] EACJ, *Media Council of Tanzania and others v. Attorney General of the United Republic of Tanzania* (Ref no. 2/2017), 28 March 2019, §73. The media services legislation referred, inter alia, to 'unwarranted invasion of privacy', 'hinder or cause substantial harm to the Government to manage the economy', and 'damage the information holder's position': §§64, 66.

[334] ECOWAS CCJ, *Federation of African Journalists v. The Gambia* (Suit no. ECW/CCJ/APP/36/15), 13 February 2018, 50–51.

[335] Ibid., 43; The provision on seditious intent defined it by reference to, amongst others, 'any action likely (a) to bring hatred or contempt or to excite disaffection against the person of the President, or the Government of The Gambia as by law established' (Gambian Criminal Code s. 51). The Court found that the prosecution of journalists under the law on sedition violated the right to free speech under Art. 12(2) of the ACHPR, Art. 19(2) of the ICCPR, and Art. 66(2) of the Revised ECOWAS Treaty: 56.

[336] UN Special Rapporteur F. La Rue, *Promotion and protection of the right to freedom of opinion and expression* (2012) UN Doc. A/67/357, §51.

2. Legitimacy

International law provides a list of objectives that permit the penalization of speech.[337] Under article 19(3), speech can be legitimately restricted when this is necessary for the 'respect of the rights or reputations of others' as well as to protect 'national security or of public order' or 'public health or morals'.[338] The Human Rights Committee has held that this list is exhaustive.[339]

Regional human rights treaties contain a similar list.[340] And even though article 10 of the European Convention on Human Rights enumerates some 'aims' that are not listed in the ICCPR and other treaties, the Human Rights Committee has considered 'public order' to encompass the additional aims expressly listed in article 10 of the European Convention.[341] And both treaties, as well as the American Convention on Human Rights, include the 'rights' or 'reputation' of individuals as a listed ground.[342] The African Court on Human and Peoples' Rights does not specifically list grounds but has accepted in its case law that the grounds listed in article 19(3) of the ICCPR contain legitimate grounds for restrictions.[343]

Defamation and insult laws are usually justified by states on the basis of protection of the 'rights of others', namely their reputational rights,[344] whereas sedition and *lèse-majesté* generally purport to protect national security and public order.[345] Although some cases have held that the aim being advanced by the state did not in fact correspond to these categories,[346] most cases turn on whether the advancement of this aim is necessary and proportionate to the measures restricting speech.[347]

---

[337] See ch. 1 (Introduction), s. II.1.1. (Treaty language).
[338] Ibid.
[339] Ibid.
[340] Ibid.
[341] See HRC, *Lovell v. Australia* (Comm. no. 920/2000), 29 March 2004, §9.4; HRC, General Comment No. 34 (2011), §31 ('Contempt of court proceedings relating to forms of expression may be tested against the public order (ordre public) ground'); HRC, *Agazade and Jafarov v. Azerbaijan* (Comm. no. 2205/2012), 27 October 2016, §7.5; HRC, *Aleksandrov v. Belarus* (Comm. no. 1933/2010), 24 July 2014, §7.4 (holding that Belarus had not explained how the actions of a protestor 'would have violated the rights and freedoms of others or would have posed a threat to public safety or public order (*ordre public*)'). See also COE, *Report of the Committee of Experts to the Committee of Ministers on the problems arising from the co-existence of the UN Covenants on Human Rights and the European Convention on Human Rights* (1970) H(70)7, 2, §§175–177. See ch. 1 (Introduction), s. II.1.1. (Treaty language).
[342] See ch. 1 (Introduction), s. II.1.1. (Treaty language).
[343] Ibid.
[344] See, e.g., ECtHR, Guide on Article 10 of the European Convention on Human Rights—Freedom of Expression, 31 August 2022, §123 ('The protection of the reputation or rights of others is, by far, the legitimate aim most frequently relied on in the Article-10 cases brought before the Court'); HRC, *Adonis v. The Philippines* (Comm. no. 1815/2008), 26 October 2011, §4.2.
[345] See, e.g., UN Special Rapporteur D. Kaye, *Promotion and protection of the right to freedom of opinion and expression* (2016) UN Doc. A/71/373, §§19, 31–32 ('Political and human rights activists have been especially targeted by such rules against criticism [as sedition and treason], often under the pretext of protecting public order'); WGAD, *Somyot Prueksakasemsuk v. Thailand* (Opinion no. 35/2012), 30 August 2012, §15 (Thai authorities arguing that 'views or unfair criticisms that are disrespectful of the monarchy ... can generate spontaneous actions ... and could cause the country to disintegrate into factions' and that the 'lèse majesté law is therefore legitimate and indispensable for national security').
[346] ECtHR, Guide on Article 10 of the European Convention on Human Rights—Freedom of Expression, 31 August 2022, §85 ('The Court may find that an interference does not serve to advance the legitimate aim relied on ... or choose to retain only one of the legitimate aims relied on by the State, while dismissing others').
[347] See, e.g., ibid., §61. See s. III.1. (Legality).

3. Necessity

Most of the case law at the international level concerns whether a restriction on speech that advances a legitimate aim is 'necessary'.[348] This in turn has been held to depend on a number of factors including (i) the intent of the speaker; (ii) the causal link between the speech and the harm suffered by the target and (iii) the type and level of harm suffered by the target of the speech. An assessment of the level of harm depends on the context which may include the identity of the speaker and the target, the subject matter of the speech and an assessment of whether and to what extent the speech is made public.

3.1. Intent

International human rights bodies have not taken a consistent approach to the type of intent (or *mens rea*) required for defamation to constitute a necessary restriction on speech. While the Human Rights Committee and Inter-American bodies formulate intent by reference to the United States' 'actual malice' test, the European and African human rights bodies have not endorsed this test.

The 'actual malice' test is derived from the seminal US Supreme Court decision in *New York Times v. Sullivan*,[349] in which the Supreme Court held that a speaker is liable in defamation if they knew the statement about a public official was false or acted with 'reckless disregard' as to the statement's truth.[350] The Human Rights Committee has endorsed this standard for speech about public figures, considering that '[a]t least with regard to comments about public figures, consideration should be given to avoiding penalizing or otherwise rendering unlawful untrue statements that have been published in *error but without malice*'.[351] The Committee also recommended that the United Kingdom 'consider the utility of a so-called "public figure" exception, requiring proof by the plaintiff of actual malice in order to go forward on actions concerning reporting on public officials and prominent public figures'.[352]

The Inter-American Commission has also taken the position that 'actual malice' or at least 'gross negligence' is required to justify civil liability for defamation in cases involving 'a public official, a public person or a private person who has voluntarily become involved in matters of public interest'.[353] In such cases 'it must be proven that in disseminating the news, the social communicator *had the specific intent to inflict harm, was fully aware that false news was disseminated, or acted with gross negligence* in

---

[348] ECtHR, Guide on Article 10 of the European Convention on Human Rights—Freedom of Expression, 31 August 2022, §61.
[349] US Supreme Court, *New York Times v. Sullivan* 376 U.S. 254, 9 March 1964, 376. See s. II.1.2. (Intent).
[350] US Supreme Court, *New York Times v. Sullivan* 376 U.S. 254, 9 March 1964, 376. Under US jurisprudence, 'recklessness' for these purposes means not some degree of extreme negligence, but 'subjective awareness of probable falsity', US Supreme Court, *Gertz v. Robert Welch Inc* 418 U.S. 323, 25 June 1974, 335, n. 6 (citing US Supreme Court, *St. Amant v. Thompson* 390 U.S. 727, 29 April 1968, 731: 'There must be sufficient evidence to permit the conclusion that the defendant in fact entertained serious doubts as to the truth of his publication').
[351] HRC, General Comment No. 34 (2011), §47 (emphasis added).
[352] HRC, *Concluding Observations, The United Kingdom of Great Britain and Northern Ireland* (2008) UN Doc. CCPR/C/GBR/CO/6, §25.
[353] IACmHR, Declaration of Principles on Freedom of Expression (2000), Principle 10 (emphasis added), §46.

efforts to determine the truth or falsity of such news'.[354] And in another case the Inter-American Commission welcomed a Uruguayan law that eliminated criminal sanctions for 'divulging opinion or information on public officials or regarding matters of public interest, *except* when the allegedly affected person can demonstrate the existence of *true malice*'.[355]

In cases in which the Inter-American Court has assessed criminal penalties for defamatory speech, the Court has required 'intent' or some form of 'malicious intent', which was translated as 'actual malice' in one case.[356] The Court noted that it would consider 'the extreme seriousness of the conduct of the individual who expressed the opinion, *his actual malice*, the characteristics of the unfair damage caused, and other information which shows the absolute necessity to resort to criminal proceedings as an exception'.[357] The Court has not explicitly adopted 'actual malice' as the standard to be applied in all cases involving public interest speech but has required a 'specific intention of inflicting harm on the person or persons affected by the article' in such cases.[358]

The European Court has also declined to set a single standard for the intent requirement for insulting speech that states seek to penalize. In the cases in which it does articulate a standard, however, it is not that of 'actual malice'.[359] In cases involving 'denigration' of a person or authority, the Court has stated that the speech may be unprotected where 'the sole intent of the offensive statement is to insult'.[360] But such cases appear to conflate intent and motive and differ from the 'actual malice' standard by not considering whether the speaker knew of or was reckless to the falsity of the statement. At the other end of the intent spectrum, the Court has found that convicting a person for defamation for 'negligent' criticism of a public prosecutor violated article 10 and had a 'chilling effect'.[361]

The position of the African Court on intent is not clear. It has found the right to freedom of speech to be violated when a journalist was prosecuted for defamation and Burkina Faso 'failed to prove' that the journalist's use of the name 'People's Democratic Republic' was 'for the purpose of poisoning the minds of the public … or that it is

---

[354] IACmHR, Declaration of Principles on Freedom of Expression (2000), Principle 10 (emphasis added). See also IACmHR, *The Inter-American Legal Framework regarding the Right to Freedom of Expression* (2009) OEA/Ser.L/V/II/CIDH/RELE/INF. 2/09, §115 (emphasis added); IACtHR, *Canese v. Paraguay* (Series C, no. 111), 31 August 2004, §72(h).

[355] IACmHR, *Dogliani v. Uruguay* (Petition 228-07), 16 March 2010, §16 (emphasis added).

[356] See IACtHR, *Tristán Donoso v. Panama* (Series C, no. 193), 27 January 2009, §120. See also IACtHR, *Usón Ramírez v. Venezuela* (Series C, no. 207), 20 November 2009, §56; IACtHR, *Mémoli v. Argentina* (Series C, no. 265), 22 August 2013, §§139, 141.

[357] IACtHR, *Tristán Donoso v. Panama* (Series C, no. 193), 27 January 2009, §§119–120, 125 (emphasis added).

[358] See, e.g., IACtHR, *Moya Chacón v. Costa Rica* (Series C, no. 451), 6 September 2022, §88.

[359] ECtHR, *McVicar v. United Kingdom* (App. no. 46311/99), 7 May 2002, §§27, 65, 73; ECtHR, *Kasabova v. Bulgaria* (App. no. 22385/03), 19 April 2011, §§48, 63–68.

[360] ECtHR, *Tuşalp v. Turkey* (App. nos. 32131/08 & 41617/08), 21 February 2012, §48; the Court held that the 'use of vulgar phrases in itself is not decisive in the assessment of an offensive expression' for these purposes. See also ECtHR, *Skałka v. Poland* (App. no. 43425/98), 27 May 2003, §34; ECtHR, *Rujak v. Croatia* (App. no. 57942/10), 2 October 2012, §29; ECtHR, *Mengi v. Turkey* (App. nos. 13471/05 & 38787/07), 27 November 2012, §58.

[361] ECtHR, *Nikula v. Finland* (App. no. 31611/96), 21 March 2002, §54. See also ECtHR, *Paraskevopoulos v. Greece* (App. no. 64184/11), 28 June 2018, §40 (domestic courts 'are asked to consider whether the context of the case, the public interest and the intention of the author of the impugned article justified the possible use of a dose of provocation or exaggeration').

intended to subvert the integrity and status of Burkina Faso or to bring it to disrepute. Furthermore, it has not shown that such designation is used in bad faith by the Applicant'.[362] Similarly, the African Commission has stated that speech regarding the judiciary can only be restricted if it is 'aimed at unlawfully and intentionally violating the dignity, reputation or integrity of a judicial officer or body and whether it is used in a manner calculated to pollute the minds of the public'.[363] But on other matters, the African bodies have followed the approach of the Human Rights Committee, including its General Comment No. 34 which applies the 'malice' test.[364]

When assessing the intent of a speaker, the context—including whether the speech was oral or written, spontaneous or premeditated, can be relevant. For instance, the European Court has also accorded protection to 'statements [that] were made orally during a live television broadcast, so that [the journalist] had no possibility of reformulating, refining or retracting them before they were made public'.[365] The Court has also recognized that the reporting of oral statements by the press can leave little or no opportunity for a journalist to reformulate, perfect or retract their statements before publication.[366]

3.2. Causal link between the speech and the harm

A state seeking to justify restrictions on speech should establish a causal link between the defamatory or insulting speech and concrete harms that are said to result from it, but international human rights bodies have not settled on a common description of the required causal link.

According to the Human Rights Committee, a state 'must demonstrate ... the necessity and proportionality of the specific action taken, in particular by establishing a *direct and immediate connection* between the expression and the threat'.[367]

The European Court has, as part of its context-specific approach to cases involving freedom of expression, considered whether speech had the 'capacity—*direct or indirect*—to lead to harmful consequences'.[368] But the Inter-American Court's case law

---

[362] ACtHPR, *Konaté v. Burkina Faso* (App. no. 4/2013), 5 December 2014, §72.
[363] ACmHPR, *Zimbabwe Lawyers for Human Rights & Associated Newspapers of Zimbabwe v. Zimbabwe* (Comm. no. 284/03), 3 April 2009, §91.
[364] See, e.g., ch. 1 (Introduction), s. II.3.1.6. (Criminal penalties for speech) (regarding the similar approach taken by the HRC and African bodies to criminal penalties for defamatory speech).
[365] ECtHR, *Gündüz v. Turkey* (App. no. 35071/97), 4 December 2003, §49. See also ECtHR, *Ghiulfer Predescu v. Romania* (App. no. 29751/09), 27 June 2017, §52; ECtHR, *Filatenko v. Russia* (App. no. 73219/01), 6 December 2007, §47 (noting the 'obvious constraints of a live television show where time was of essence'). Cf. ECtHR, *Sipos v. Romania* (App. no. 26125/04), 3 May 2011, §32. See further ECtHR (GC), *Pedersen & Baadsgaard v. Denmark* (App. no. 49017/99), 17 December 2004, §79 (allegations made during peak viewing time on television have a more 'powerful effect' than print).
[366] ECtHR (GC), *Nilsen v. Norway* (App. no. 23118/93), 25 November 1999, §48.
[367] HRC, General Comment No. 34 (2011), §35 (emphasis added). See also WGAD, *Jordi Cuixart I Navarro v. Spain* (Opinion no. 6/2019), 25 April 2019, §§111–115, 119; WGAD, *Joaquín Forn I Chiariello v. Spain* (Opinion no. 12/2019), 26 April 2019, §§100–102, 109. In the context of incitement to violence, the UN-approved Rabat Plan of Action provides that in restricting speech 'the courts will have to determine that there was a reasonable probability that the speech would succeed in inciting actual action against the target group, *recognizing that such causation should be rather direct*'. Rabat Plan of Action, §29(f).
[368] ECtHR, *Alekhina v. Russia* (App. no. 38004/12), 17 July 2018, §220 (emphasis added). See also ECtHR (GC), *Perinçek v. Switzerland* (App. no. 27510/08), 15 October 2015, §207. See ch. 3 (Hate Speech).

on defamation has generally appeared to assume that harm occurs and does not directly address causation.[369]

Similarly, the African Commission's 2019 Declaration of Principles of Freedom of Expression only speaks of 'a close causal link between the risk of harm and the expression' in the context of restricting speech on public order or national security grounds, although this should presumably be transferable to other contexts.[370]

3.3. Level of harm caused by the speech

International human rights law requires the existence of a requisite level of harm to the target of defamatory speech to justify a restriction on speech, but the definition of the required harm varies among human rights bodies.[371]

The Human Rights Committee has not set out a requisite level of harm to reputation in defamation cases, but it has found a violation of freedom of expression in a case in which the damage to the public servant's reputation was 'only of a limited nature' because the speaker sent his letter criticizing state officials to the Minister of Finance of Belarus without making it public through media.[372]

The European Court has held that insulting or defamatory speech must 'attain a certain level of seriousness and be in a manner causing prejudice to personal enjoyment of' the rights of the target of the speech.[373] The requisite level of seriousness was found to have been met in a case in which a public servant working at a multi-ethnic radio station was accused of 'being disrespectful in regard to another ethnicity and religion', as this was 'not only capable of tarnishing her reputation, but also of causing her prejudice in both her professional and social environment'.[374] The threshold was also met in a case in which a politician was accused of 'a typical act of corruption by political influence' by working as a member of parliament while also practising as a lawyer.[375] However, the level of seriousness was *not* attained when a joke was made

---

[369] It considers causation in determining damages and reparations: see IACtHR, *Tristán Donoso v. Panamá* (Series C, no. 193), 27 January 2009, §120. For speech alleged to have incited violence, the Court requires that the imposition of sanctions 'must be backed up by actual, truthful, objective and strong proof that the person was not simply issuing an opinion (even if that opinion was hard, unfair or disturbing), but that the person had the clear intention of committing a crime and the actual, real and effective possibility of achieving this objective': IACmHR, *Inter-American Legal Framework Regarding the Right to Freedom of Expression* (2009) OEA/Ser.L/V/II, CIDH/RELE/INF. 2/09, §58. See ch. 3 (Hate Speech).

[370] ACmHPR, Declaration of Principles of Freedom of Expression and Access to Information in Africa (2019), Principle 22.

[371] Certain jurisdictions impose a requirement that 'serious harm' to reputation or a likelihood of it must result from the publication of the words complained of filter out weak or frivolous defamation claims. See s. II.1.3.2. (Level of harm caused by the speech). See England and Wales Defamation Act 2013 s. 1(1) and New South Wales Defamation Act 2005 s. 10A.

[372] HRC, *Kozlov v. Belarus* (Comm. no. 1986/2010), 24 July 2014, §7.6. See s. III.3.3.2. (Measuring harm: the extent to which the speech is public). The former UN Special Rapporteur on Freedom of Expression has also observed that a defamatory statement must be 'injurious' because 'there is no defamation without injury', but did not specify a threshold. UN Special Rapporteur A. Ligabo, *Implementation of General Assembly Resolution 60/251 of March 2006 Entitled "Human Rights Council"* (2007) UN Doc. A/HRC/4/27, §47.

[373] ECtHR (GC), *Axel Springer AG v. Germany* (App. no. 39954/08), 7 February 2012, §83; ECtHR, *A v. Norway* (App. no. 28070/06), 9 April 2009, §64 (in the context of Art. 8, not 10).

[374] ECtHR (GC), *Medžlis Islamske Zajednice Brčko v. Bosnia and Herzegovina* (App. no. 17224/11), 27 June 2017, §79.

[375] ECtHR, *Macovei v. Romania* (App. no. 53028/14), 28 July 2020, §85.

about a well-known television host in the context of a television comedy show, taking into account 'the playful and irreverent style' of the show.[376]

Similarly, the Inter-American Court has found that, when it comes to criminal penalties, defamation must constitute a 'serious attack' or do 'serious damage' to the right to have one's reputation protected.[377] For civil liability to be imposed on the speaker, the Court's case law suggests that the right to reputation must be 'clearly harmed or threatened'.[378]

3.3.1. Measuring harm: subject matter of speech or identity of the target

The European Court has held that 'a fundamental requirement of the law of defamation is that in order to give rise to a cause of action the defamatory statement must refer to a particular person'.[379] It found a violation of article 10 in a case in which a newspaper was ordered to pay damages to members of a regional government after it had published an 'open letter' criticizing the regional authority but did not name any of the government officials who had sued.[380]

International human rights bodies have also considered that even though public figures have the right to protect their reputation, 'the interest of public officials being free from insult pales in comparison to the societal interests facilitated by the freedom of expression'.[381] According to the Human Rights Committee, 'in circumstances of public debate concerning public figures in the political domain and public institutions, the value placed by the Covenant upon uninhibited expression is particularly high'.[382] This is in line with the position of the Working Group[383] as well as certain national laws imposing a higher intent requirement of 'actual malice' for speech about a public figure[384] and why speech about matters of public interest is often exempt from or a recognized defence under laws that penalize insulting speech.[385]

---

[376] ECtHR, *Sousa Goucha v. Portugal* (App. no. 70434/12), 22 March 2016, §§26, 52–55.

[377] IACtHR, *Usón Ramírez v. Venezuela* (Series C, no. 207), 20 November 2009, §§73–75.

[378] IACmHR, *The Inter-American Legal Framework regarding the Right to Freedom of Expression* (2009) OEA/Ser.L/V/II/CIDH/RELE/INF. 2/09, §§77, 107; IACtHR, *Canese v. Paraguay* (Series C, no. 111), 31 August 2004, §72(f).

[379] ECtHR, *Dyuldin v. Russia* (App. no. 25968/02), 31 July 2007, §43. This point does not appear to have been addressed by other international human rights bodies.

[380] Ibid. See also ECtHR, *OOO Memo v. Russia* (App. no. 2840/10), 15 March 2022, §47 ('civil defamation proceedings brought, in its own name, by a legal entity that exercises public power may not, as a general rule, be regarded to be in pursuance of the legitimate aim of "the protection of the reputation ... of others" under Article 10 § 2 of the Convention', but 'this does not exclude individual members of a public body' from bringing such claims).

[381] E.L. Carter, 'Error but Without Malice" in Defamation of Public Officials: The Value of Free Expression in International Human Rights Law' (2016) 21 *Communication Law and Policy* 301, 321. See also HRC, General Comment No. 34 (2011), §38; see HRC, *Bodrožić v. Serbia and Montenegro* (Comm. no. 1180/2003), 31 October 2005; HRC, *Adonis v. The Philippines* (Comm. no. 1815/2008), 26 October 2011.

[382] HRC, General Comment No. 34 (2011), §38. See also HRC, *Adonis v. The Philippines* (Comm. no. 1815/2008), 26 October 2011, §7.9, n. 12, citing HRC, General Comment No. 34 (2011), §47; HRC, *Bodrožić v. Serbia and Montenegro* (Comm. no. 1180/2003), 31 October 2005, §7.2. See also WGAD, *Agnès Uwimana Nkusi v. Rwanda* (Opinion no. 25/2012), 29 August 2012, §58.

[383] WGAD, *Mikalai Statkevich v. Belarus* (Opinion no. 13/2011), 4 May 2011, §9. See also WGAD, *Farah v. Somalia* (Opinion no. 17/2022), 31 May 2022, §58; WGAD, *Anchan v. Thailand* (Opinion no. 64/2021), 17 November 2021, §61 (holding that '[t]he mere fact that forms of expression are considered to be insulting to a public figure is not sufficient to justify the imposition of penalties').

[384] See s. III.3.1. (Intent).

[385] See s. III.4.2. (Public interest).

In assessing whether the test of necessity is satisfied, the European Court has considered whether the speech makes a contribution to a debate of general interest; how well known the target of the speech is and the subject matter of the speech.[386] The Inter-American and African courts similarly take into account that speech related to public officials is 'afforded greater protection'[387] and the African Court agrees that 'freedom of expression in a democratic society must be the subject of a lesser degree of interference when it occurs in the context of public debate relating to public figures'.[388]

3.3.1.1. Statements about public officials including heads of state or government
International human rights bodies have considered that laws that afford a head of state or government greater protection from insults or which stipulate heavier penalties violate the right to freedom of expression. The Human Rights Committee has stated that 'all public figures, including those exercising the highest political authority *such as heads of state and government*, are legitimately subject to criticism and political opposition'.[389] In a case in which a journalist was successfully prosecuted for defamation and slander after writing articles that were critical of the Angolan President, the Committee found that 'the severity of the sanctions imposed ... cannot be considered as a proportionate measure to protect public order or the honour and the reputation of the President, a public figure who, as such, is subject to criticism and opposition'.[390] The Working Group on Arbitrary Detention has taken the same view.[391]

The European Court has also consistently held that heads of state are not shielded from criticism 'solely on account of their function or status, irrespective of whether the criticism is warranted'; such a 'special privilege ... cannot be reconciled with modern practice and political conceptions'.[392] This applies to both foreign heads of state and the heads of the state itself. For example, a collage by a British artist depicting the then Turkish Prime Minister Erdoğan as a dog held on a leash decorated with the colours of the US flag was considered protected speech because a politician must show greater tolerance towards criticism, especially when it takes the form of satire.[393]

The Inter-American Court has reached the same result. It held that reporting regarding 'the elected public official of the highest-ranking position in the country

---

[386] ECtHR (GC), *Von Hannover v. Germany (No. 2)* (App. nos. 40660/08 & 60641/08), 7 February 2012, §§62, 108–113 (in the context of balancing freedom of expression with the right to private life). See also ECtHR, *Satakunnan Markkinapörssi Oy v. Finland* (App. no. 931/13), 27 June 2017, §165.
[387] IACtHR, *Fontevecchia v. Argentina* (Series C, no. 238), 29 November 2011, §47. See also IACtHR, *Palamara Iribarne v. Chile* (Series C, no. 135), 22 November 2005, §84; IACtHR, *Kimel v. Argentina* (Series C, no. 177), 2 May 2008, §86.
[388] ACtHPR, *Konaté v. Burkina Faso* (App. no. 4/2013), 5 December 2014, §155. See also ACmHPR, *Media Rights Agenda v. Nigeria* (Comm. nos. 105/93 & others), 31 October 1998, §74.
[389] HRC, General Comment No. 34 (2011), §38 (emphasis added); HRC, *Marques de Morais v. Angola* (Comm. no. 1128/2002), 29 March 2005, §6.8. See also UN Special Rapporteur F. La Rue, *Report of the Special Rapporteur on the promotion and protection of the right to freedom of opinion and expression* (2012) UN Doc. A/HRC/20/17, §88.
[390] HRC, *Marques de Morais v. Angola* (Comm. no. 1128/2002), 29 March 2005, §6.8.
[391] WGAD, *Amer v. Egypt* (Opinion no. 35/2008), 20 November 2008, §§32–33; WGAD, *Mohammed Rashid Hassan Nasser al-Ajami v. Qatar* (Opinion no. 48/2016), 22 November 2016, §42.
[392] ECtHR, *Colombani v. France* (App. no. 51279/99), 25 June 2002, §68; ECtHR, *Castells v. Spain* (App. no. 11798/85), 23 April 1992, §46; ECtHR, *Otegi Mondragon v. Spain* (App. no. 2034/07), 15 March 2011, §55.
[393] ECtHR, *Dickinson v. Turkey* (App. no. 25200/11), 2 February 2021, §55.

involved matters of public interest, which were in the public domain,[394] with a lower standard of protection applying to officials, especially those who were elected, and to information concerning matters of public interest.[395] The Court considers that public officials voluntarily expose themselves to 'the scrutiny of society'[396] and their activities 'enter the realm of a public debate'.[397]

International human rights bodies have also considered that public officials and civil servants should not benefit from laws that 'protect their honour' that are used to suppress reporting about the performance of their duties.[398] The European Court has suggested that civil servants acting in an official capacity are subject to a wider limit of acceptable criticism than private individuals, though not as wide as speech about politicians,[399] when defamatory speech relates to claims of inappropriate or unlawful exercise of official duties.[400]

The European Court also gives an 'elevated level of protection' to freedom of expression in Parliament because '[p]arliament is a unique forum for debate in a democratic society, which is of fundamental importance'.[401] According to the European Court, greater tolerance should also to be shown when allegedly defamatory statements are made *in response* to statements by politicians that were 'clearly intended to be provocative and consequently to arouse strong reactions'.[402]

3.3.1.2. Statements about the military, police or security forces

Wider limits of permissible criticism may also apply to the military, police, armed forces or security forces.[403] International human rights bodies have found reports about the military to be in the public interest, thereby granting them special protection. For example, the European Court has held that 'limits of journalistic freedom' were not crossed by reports with 'certain exaggerated or provocative assertions' about, *inter alia*, members of the Azerbaijani armed forces.[404] The Inter-American Court has also found that criminal sanctions imposed on reporting critical of the military violate the right to freedom of expression.[405] The Human Rights Committee has

---

[394] IACtHR, *Fontevecchia v. Argentina* (Series C, no. 238), 29 November 2011, §71.
[395] Ibid., §59.
[396] Ibid., §60.
[397] Ibid., §47.
[398] See, e.g., HRC, General Comment No. 34 (2011), §38; HRC, *Concluding Observations, Costa Rica* (2007) UN Doc. CCPR/C/CRI/CO/5, §11; HRC, *Marques de Morais v. Angola* (Comm. no. 1128/2002), 29 March 2005; HRC, *Bodrožić v. Serbia and Montenegro* (Comm. no. 1180/2003), 31 October 2005.
[399] ECtHR, *Janowski v. Poland* (App. no. 25716/94), 21 January 1999, §33; ECtHR, *Nikula v. Finland* (App. no. 31611/96), 21 March 2002, §48. Cf. ECtHR, *Fedchenko v. Russia (No. 2)* (App. no. 48195/06), 11 February 2010, §60.
[400] ECtHR, *Milosavljević v. Serbia* (App. no. 57574/14), 25 May 2021, §61.
[401] ECtHR (GC), *Karácsony v. Hungary* (App. nos. 42461/13 & 44357/13), 17 May 2016, §138.
[402] ECtHR, *Oberschlick v. Austria (No. 2)* (App. no. 20834/92), 1 July 1997, §31; ECtHR, *Eon v. France* (App. no. 26118/10), 14 March 2013.
[403] See ch. 5 (Espionage and Official Secrets Laws) and ch. 6 (Terrorism Laws).
[404] ECtHR, *Fatullayev v. Azerbaijan* (App. no. 40984/07), 22 April 2010, §100. It was pertinent that there was an ongoing debate about what had happened in the Khojaly massacre and therefore public interest in discussing the event.
[405] IACtHR, *Usón Ramírez v. Venezuela* (Series C, no. 207), 20 November 2009, §84; IACtHR, *Uzcátegui v. Venezuela* (Series C, no. 249), 3 September 2012, §192.

also noted that 'there can be no legitimate restriction under article 19, paragraph 3 [of the ICCPR], which would justify the arbitrary arrest, torture, and threats to life' of a journalist who accused security forces of corruption and abuse.[406]

3.3.1.3. Statements about the judiciary Prosecutors and law enforcement officials, including judges, may need to be protected from unfounded accusations to be able to exercise their functions.[407] In a case concerning alleged defamatory comments about a member of the judiciary in Burkina Faso, the African Court held that laws 'with respect to dishonouring or tarnishing the reputation of public figures, such as the members of the judiciary, should therefore not provide more severe sanctions than those relating to offenses against the honor or reputation of an ordinary individual'.[408]

Article 10 of the European Convention expressly permits restrictions on freedom of expression 'for maintaining the authority and impartiality of the judiciary',[409] and the European Court recognizes that the judiciary '[a]s the guarantor of justice' must 'enjoy public confidence if it is to be successful in carrying out its duties'.[410] As a result, the European Court will 'protect the judiciary against gravely damaging attacks that are essentially unfounded, bearing in mind that judges are prevented from reacting by their duty of discretion'.[411] For example, the Court found no violation of article 10 when a journalist was convicted of defamation for alleging bullying and poor treatment of defendants by judges sitting on Austrian criminal courts.[412] The Court held the 'extremely serious' allegations were insufficiently researched, as the journalist had not attended a single criminal trial before a judge he had defamed, and 'thus not only damaged [the impugned judges'] reputation, but also undermined public confidence in the integrity of the judiciary as a whole'.[413] But the European Court has also held that 'this cannot have the effect of prohibiting individuals from expressing their views, through value judgments with a sufficient factual basis, on matters of public interest related to the functioning of the justice system'.[414]

---

[406] HRC, *Njaru v. Cameroon* (Comm. no. 1353/2005), 19 March 2007, §6.4.
[407] ECtHR, *Lešník v. Slovakia* (App. no. 35640/97), 11 March 2003, §54 (public prosecutors); ECtHR (GC), *Pedersen & Baadsgaard v. Denmark* (App. no. 49017/99), 17 December 2004, §80 (Chief Superintendent of Police). Cf. ECtHR, *Busuioc v. Moldova* (App. no. 61513/00), 21 December 2004.
[408] ACtHPR, *Konaté v. Burkina Faso* (App. no. 004/2013), 5 December 2014, §156.
[409] A committee of experts reporting to the Council of Europe on the 'co-existence of the human rights obligations' under the European Convention and the ICCPR suggested that a restriction cannot be imposed on this ground under the ICCPR unless it could be included within the notion of 'public order', but that they could not confirm this position: COE, *Report of the Committee of Experts to the Committee of Ministers* (1970) H(70)7, §§176–177.
[410] ECtHR, *Prager and Oberschlick v. Austria* (App. no. 15974/90), 26 April 1995, §34.
[411] ECtHR (GC), *Morice v. France* (App. no. 29369/10), 23 April 2015, §168.
[412] ECtHR, *Prager and Oberschlick v. Austria* (App. no. 15974/90), 26 April 1995.
[413] Ibid., §§36–39.
[414] ECtHR (GC), *Morice v. France* (App. no. 29369/10), 23 April 2015, §168. See also ECtHR, *Benitez Moriana and Iñigo Fernandez v. Spain* (App. nos. 36537/15 & 36539/15), 9 March 2021, §50. See ss II.1.4. (Exclusions, exceptions and defences) and II.1.4.2. (Public interest).

3.3.1.4. Statements about national symbols

The Human Rights Committee has expressed concern regarding laws which prohibit or punish 'disrespect for flags and symbols'.[415] Then UN Special Rapporteur Frank La Rue has explained that defamation is intended to protect the rights and reputation of others and should not be used to protect abstract or subjective notions or concepts such as the state, national symbols, national identity, cultures, schools of thought, religions, ideologies or political doctrines.[416] And the European Court reached a similar conclusion when assessing a Hungarian law that banned the red star, a symbol of the international workers' movement, noting its chilling effect on freedom of expression.[417]

3.3.2. Measuring harm: the extent to which the speech is public

In considering the harm caused by speech,[418] international human rights bodies may consider whether a statement was made in public or private and the extent of its publication and dissemination.[419] For example, the Human Rights Committee observed that damage to a person's reputation was 'only of a limited nature' when the author sent his letter regarding that person to the Minister of Finance only 'without making it public through media or otherwise'.[420] And when a managing director of a company sent a document critical of an employee to her, and received a suspended sentence of five months' imprisonment for slanderous defamation, the European Court held that a 'private dispute' which 'did not reach the public' presented 'no justification for the imposition of a prison sentence'.[421]

A speaker may be responsible for the 'publishing' of speech by republishing an allegation made by a third party. However, the European Court has clarified that liability does not arise from posting a hyperlink because the person 'does not exercise control over the content of the website to which a hyperlink enables access, and which might be changed after the creation of the link'.[422]

Timing and location of speech may also be relevant to an assessment of the harm caused by its publication. Insults in the aftermath of an event may be judged differently by a court than an insult made at a less volatile time. The European Court has held that

---

[415] HRC, General Comment No. 34 (2011), §38.

[416] UN Special Rapporteur F. La Rue, *Report of the Special Rapporteur on the promotion and protection of the right to freedom of opinion and expression* (2010) UN Doc. A/HRC/14/23, §84. See also Article 19, *Defining Defamation: Principles on Freedom of Expression and Protection of Reputation* (2017), Principle 2(c).

[417] ECtHR, *Vajnai v. Hungary* (App. no. 33629/06), 8 July 2008, §54. The US Supreme Court has taken the same approach: see US Supreme Court, *Texas v. Johnson* 491 U.S. 397, 21 June 1989, 417 (finding that a criminal conviction for flag desecration for publicly burning an American flag as a means of political protests was inconsistent with the First Amendment as '[t]here is ... no indication—in the text of the Constitution or in our cases interpreting it—that a separate juridical category exists for the American flag alone').

[418] Whether it was private, public or leaked, spontaneous or pre-meditated, may also be relevant to the question of intent. See s. III.3.1. (Intent).

[419] A. Clooney & P. Webb, 'The Right to Insult in International Law' (2017) 48(2) *Columbia Human Rights Law Review* 1, 30.

[420] HRC, *Kozlov v. Belarus* (Comm. no. 1986/2010), 24 July 2014, §7.6. Cf. WGAD, *Mohammed Rashid Hassan Nasser al-Ajami v. Qatar* (Opinion no. 48/2016), 22 November 2016, §§5, 7, 16, 45 (the fact that poem insulting Qatar's Emir, originally recited to seven people in a private apartment, was later uploaded to YouTube did not change the fact that it was protected artistic expression).

[421] ECtHR, *Matalas v. Greece* (App. no. 1864/18), 25 March 2021, §60.

[422] ECtHR, *Magyar Jeti Zrt v. Hungary* (App. no. 11257/16), 4 December 2018, §§75–77.

passage of time may mean that such insults come to be viewed as part of a historical debate, and protected from criminalization on this basis.[423]

4. Exclusions, Exceptions and Defences

International human rights law recognizes at least five defences or exceptions to liability for speech that are of particular importance for political speech. These include: (i) truth, (ii) public interest, (iii) reasonable publication (also known as 'responsible journalism'), (iv) fair and accurate reporting of official proceedings and (v) opinion including artistic expression.

Truth and reasonable publication are alternative bases to avoid liability—if either of them applies, the defendant should not be liable for their speech. 'Reasonable publication' can be less exacting to establish than truth, as its focus is on the journalistic *process* as opposed to the *outcome*: if the speaker acted reasonably, it does not matter that they cannot prove the statement to be true. On the other hand, while issues such as tone, balance and right of reply are relevant to showing a reasonable publication, they are not necessary to establish the truth of a statement. Fair and accurate reporting is a powerful defence—again not dependent on the truth of the statement—but it tends to apply in the narrow context of, for instance, contemporaneous reporting of judicial and legislative proceedings or reporting official documents. The defence of opinion (also known as fair comment) is also available—and extends to artistic speech such as cartoons and satire—but its contours, in particular the extent to which an opinion must be based on verifiable facts, are not clear.

4.1. Truth

The defence of truth is an essential and absolute defence to insult and defamation laws in international law.[424] And rightly so: there can be no greater travesty than punishing a speaker for speaking the truth. This is particularly important in a democracy when the speaker is a journalist reporting on a matter of public interest. And from the perspective of reputation, 'disseminating a true statement should not be actionable since one cannot defend a reputation one does not deserve in the first place'.[425] It is therefore no surprise that international bodies prioritize the importance of the truth of factual statements, either as a defence or by requiring that the plaintiff must prove falsity (for instance as part of proving 'actual malice').[426] But not all international bodies explicitly explain the role of truth as an exemption or defence. Nor do they explain whether the standard expected in relation to publishing truth is one of *substantial* or *exact* truth.[427]

---

[423] ECtHR (GC), *Perinçek v. Switzerland* (App. no. 27510/08), 15 October 2015, §249; ECtHR, *Leroy v. France* (App. no. 36109/03), 2 October 2008, §§6, 45. See ch. 3 (Hate Speech), ss III.2.4.2. (Opinion) and VI. (Recommendations).
[424] HRC, General Comment No. 34 (2011), §47.
[425] Article 19, *Defining Defamation* (n 416) 10.
[426] See s. III.3.1. (Intent).
[427] See ch. 4 (False Speech), s. III.4.1. (Truth).

According to the Human Rights Committee, '[d]efamation laws ... in particular penal defamation laws, should include such defences as the defence of truth'.[428] The Committee has therefore criticized the approach of Angolan courts in a case where the journalist's 'proposed truth defence against the libel charge was ruled out by the courts' in his attempt to prove his allegations of corruption against the President of Angola.[429] And it has been critical of a narrow approach to a truth defence, 'not[ing] with concern' that South Korean defamation law allowed for criminal prosecution 'even for making statements that [are] true, except when such statements are made solely for the public interest'.[430]

The European Court also regards a truth defence as critical to the protection of freedom of expression in defamation cases.[431] For example, the Court held that article 10 had been violated because a lawyer and politician had been deprived by Spanish courts of the opportunity of establishing the truth of the statements he had published regarding the government.[432] A violation was also found in a case in which the editor-in-chief of Le Monde and a journalist at the newspaper were not able to rely on a defence of truth in a prosecution for a report insulting the King of Morocco.[433]

The European Court appears to accept that 'substantial truth', as opposed to 'exact truth', is a sufficient basis to avoid liability in civil defamation cases. In one case, a Norwegian newspaper published a number of accounts of patients who were dissatisfied with their cosmetic surgery.[434] In finding a violation of article 10, the European Court emphasized that it placed 'considerable weight' on the fact that the patient's accounts of their treatment was 'essentially correct'.[435] The 'general tenor' or 'common sting' of the articles lay in the 'true allegation that Dr. R had failed in his duties as a cosmetic surgeon'.[436]

Along the same lines, when allegations of corrupt practices 'contain a combination of value judgments and statements of fact', the Court has held that in order to avoid liability there must be a 'sufficiently accurate and reliable factual basis proportionate to the nature and degree of the ... statements and allegations'.[437]

---

[428] HRC, General Comment No. 34 (2011), §47.
[429] HRC, *Marques de Morais v. Angola* (Comm. no. 1128/2002), 29 March 2005, §6.8; HRC, *Adonis v. The Philippines* (Comm. no. 1815/2008), 26 October 2011.
[430] HRC, *Concluding Observations, Republic of Korea* (2015) UN Doc. CCPR/C/KOR/CO/4, §46.
[431] Closely linked to the availability of defences to defamation is the ability to present defences and supporting evidence before the Court, which can be of 'decisive importance' in determining whether the right to freedom of expression has been violated: ECtHR, *Castells v. Spain* (App. no. 11798/85), 23 April 1992, §48. See, e.g., ECtHR, *Filatenko v. Russia* (App. no. 73219/01), 6 December 2007, §47 (finding a violation of article 10 when a Russian court determined the falsity of a journalist's statement solely on the basis that no criminal proceedings had been initiated against the subject of the speech).
[432] ECtHR, *Castells v. Spain* (App. no. 11798/85), 23 April 1992, §48.
[433] ECtHR, *Colombani v. France* (App. no. 51279/99), 25 June 2002, §66. The court also noted that the defence of 'justification' ('that is to say proving the truth of the allegation') should have been allowed. See also ECtHR, *Csánics v. Hungary* (App. no. 12188/06), 20 January 2009, §§41, 43.
[434] ECtHR, *Bergens Tidende v. Norway* (App. no. 26132/95), 2 May 2000.
[435] Ibid., §56.
[436] Ibid.
[437] ECtHR, *Macovei v. Romania* (App. no. 53028/14), 28 July 2020, §89; ECtHR, *Reznik v. Russia* (App. no. 4977/05), 4 April 2013, §46; ECtHR, *Rungainis v. Latvia* (App. no. 40597/08), 14 June 2018, §63. It is also important that journalists not be compelled to reveal their sources as a requirement of proving the truth defence: see COE, Recommendation No. R(2000)7 of the Committee of Ministers to member states on the right of journalists not to

The Inter-American Court and Commission also consider that truth should be an exemption or defence in defamation laws.[438] The Inter-American Court has stated that requiring a journalist to prove the veracity of the facts contained in passages from other news reports he reproduced and failing to accept the defence of truth (*exceptio veritatis*) 'is an excessive limitation on freedom of expression that does not comport with Article 13.2 of the [American] Convention'.[439] The Inter-American Commission's Declaration of Principles on Freedom of Expression also provides that 'prior conditioning of expressions, such as truthfulness, timeliness or impartiality is incompatible with the right to freedom of expression recognized in international instruments'.[440] This suggests that falsity should be an element of any civil wrong or criminal offence based on speech.

While the African Court has not yet pronounced on the need for defamation or insult laws to ensure that a defence of truth is available,[441] the African Commission has made clear that '[n]o one shall be found liable for true statements', suggesting that laws could either provide that falsity should be an element that must be shown to establish liability for speech or at a minimum that truth should be a defence that a speaker can seek to establish,[442] and the African Court has generally followed the approach of the Human Rights Committee on article 19 of the ICCPR.[443]

4.2. Public interest

International human rights law sources are in agreement on the importance of the public interest when considering whether restrictions on free speech are necessary. Public interest is treated as a factor governing the permissibility of restricting speech, as an element of defences to defamation including reasonable publication and fair comment, as a stand-alone defence or as a justification for a more onerous standard of intent for a speaker.[444]

International bodies have not clearly defined the term 'public interest', including whether this is an objective test.[445] But the European Court has held that the definition will 'depend on the circumstances of each case' and that 'the public interest relates to matters which affect the public to such an extent that it may legitimately

---

disclose their sources of information (2000), Principle 4. However this in principle position depends on the facts of any specific case and the corroborative evidence available.

[438] The standard is protective because the plaintiff must prove 'malicious intent' (akin to 'actual malice' which protects even against untruthful statements issued in good faith: see s. III.3.1. (Intent)).
[439] IACtHR, *Herrera-Ulloa v. Costa Rica* (Series C, no. 107), 2 July 2004, §132.
[440] IACmHR, Declaration of Principles on Freedom of Expression (2000), Principle 7 (emphasis added).
[441] See, e.g., B. Herskovitz, 'Speaking Truth to Power: Criminal Defamation Before the African Court of Human and Peoples' Rights' (2018) 50 *George Washington International Law Review* 899, 913–915.
[442] ACmHPR, Declaration of Principles on Freedom of Expression and Access to Information in Africa (2019), Principle 21.
[443] See s. III.1. (Legality).
[444] See ss II.1.4.2. (Public interest) and III.3.1. (Intent).
[445] Cf. UK Law Commission, *Protection of Official Data Report (Law Com No. 395)* (September 2020) HC 716 §§11.76–81, which provides that there should be a public interest defence under the UK Official Secrets Act if a person 'proves, on the balance of probabilities, that: (a) it was in the public interest for the information disclosed to be known by the recipient; and (b) the manner of the disclosure was in the public interest'. However, the Law Commission decided to 'make no further recommendation beyond this in respect of the form of the defence', acknowledging that 'there are various ways such a defence could be drafted'.

take an interest in them, which attract its attention or which concern it to a significant degree ... especially in that they affect the well-being of citizens or the life of the community'.[446] According to the Court, it also covers matters 'capable of giving rise to considerable controversy, which concern an important social issue ... or which involve a problem that the public would have an interest in being informed about'.[447] The Court has therefore made clear that 'the press's contribution to a debate of public interest cannot be limited merely to current events or pre-existing debates', as the press can also be a vector for bringing issues to light.[448] Similarly, the Inter-American Court considers that greater protection can be applied not only to speech that relates to the official activities of public officials, but also to information that could be linked to their private lives but has 'revealed matters of public interest'.[449]

The Human Rights Committee has suggested that there should be a self-standing public interest defence in its General Comment No. 34:

> Defamation laws must be crafted with care to ensure that they ... do not serve, in practice, to stifle freedom of expression ... At least with regard to comments about public figures, consideration should be given to avoiding penalizing or otherwise rendering unlawful untrue statements that have been published in error but without malice. *In any event, a public interest in the subject matter of the criticism should be recognized as a defence.*[450]

Stated in this way, this suggests that the Committee endorses a public interest defence in defamation cases purely based on the subject matter of the story. Accordingly, a public interest defence may be invoked regardless of the conduct or culpability of the journalist, meaning that a malicious or grossly negligent article could still qualify for protection if it was on a subject matter of public interest.[451] The reference to 'comments about public figures' does not appear intended to limit the scope of 'public interest'.[452] It appears to have been motivated by the Committee's specific concern about libel tourism and a desire that states such as the United Kingdom discourage cases being brought in

---

[446] ECtHR (GC), *Couderc and Hachette Filipacchi Associés v. France* (App. no. 40454/07), 10 November 2015, §§101–103; see also §98, citing ECtHR (GC), *Von Hannover v. Germany (No. 2)* (App. nos. 40660/08 & 60641/08), 7 February 2012, §109; ECtHR (GC), *Satakunnan Markkinapörssi Oy v. Finland* (App. no. 931/13), 27 June 2017, §171.

[447] ECtHR (GC), *Couderc and Hachette Filipacchi Associés v. France* (App. no. 40454/07), 10 November 2015, §§101–103; see also §98, citing ECtHR (GC), *Von Hannover v. Germany (No. 2)* (App. nos. 40660/08 & 60641/08), 7 February 2012; ECtHR (GC), *Satakunnan Markkinapörssi Oy v. Finland* (App. no. 931/13), 27 June 2017, §171.

[448] ECtHR (GC), *Couderc and Hachette Filipacchi Associés v. France* (App. no. 40454/07), 10 November 2015, §114. See ch. 5 (Espionage and Official Secrets Laws), s. II. 5.1. (Public interest defence).

[449] IACtHR, *Fontevecchia v. Argentina* (Series C, no. 238), 29 November 2011, §60 (holding the publication of articles revealing the existence of then-president Carlos Saul Menem's previously unacknowledged son with a congresswoman to be in the public interest due to allegations of economic and political favours and gifts granted to the son and mother).

[450] HRC, General Comment No. 34 (2011), §47 (emphasis added).

[451] However, the conduct of a speaker is relevant to an assessment of their intent and is relevant to 'reasonable publication' defences in defamation law that have developed in a number of jurisdictions around the world. See s. II.1. (Overview of laws regulating insulting speech). It is also relevant to the European Court's 'responsible journalism' doctrine. See s. III.4.3. (Reasonable publication).

[452] HRC, General Comment No. 34 (2011), §47 citing HRC, *Concluding Observations, United Kingdom* (2008) UN Doc. CCPR/C/GBR/CO/6.

local courts by foreign public figures by introducing a malice test.[453] This is consistent with the Committee's case law on defamation, which focuses on the public interest in the subject matter of the speech[454] as well as comments from the Working Group.[455]

The European Court has stated that speech about matters of public interest should get additional protection.[456] The Court has held that there is 'little scope' for restrictions on free speech 'in two fields, namely political speech and matters of public interest',[457] and has clarified that 'public interest' encompasses, and extends beyond, political speech.[458] According to the Court, 'a particularly narrow margin of appreciation' will be accorded where remarks 'concern matters of the public interest'.[459] It has also recognized that protection for such speech is particularly important in cases involving journalists since their 'task is ... to impart—in a manner consistent with its obligations and responsibilities—information and ideas on all matters of public interest'.[460]

Similarly, the Inter-American Court considers the public interest relevant to whether it is permissible to restrict speech in a manner compatible with article 13 of the American Convention. The Court has held that 'individuals who have an influence on matters of public interest have laid themselves open voluntarily to a more intense public scrutiny and ... are subject to a higher risk of being criticized, because their activities go beyond the private sphere and belong to the realm of public debate'.[461] The Court has also observed that domestic courts should take into account when a journalist has spoken 'in the context of an electoral campaign for the presidency of the Republic and with regard to matters of public interest', which is when 'opinions and criticisms are issued in a more open, intense and dynamic way, according to the principles of democratic pluralism'.[462] In a case concerning statements by an environmental activist accusing a senator of exerting political pressure on authorities to carry out illegal logging, the Court found that 'access to information ... that could have an impact on the environment is a matter of clear public interest, and therefore enjoys special protection due to its importance in a democratic society'.[463] And it has made clear that speech on

---

[453] HRC, *Concluding Observations, United Kingdom* (2008) UN Doc. CCPR/C/GBR/CO/6, §25.
[454] HRC, *Adonis v. The Philippines* (Comm. no. 1815/2008), 26 October 2011, §7.9; HRC, *Zhagiparov v. Kazakhstan* (Comm. no. 2441/2014), 25 October 2018, §5.3.
[455] WGAD, *Somyot Prueksakasemsuk v. Thailand* (Opinion no. 35/2012), 30 August 2012, §20 (concurring with the Special Rapporteur on the right to freedom of opinion and expression); WGAD, *Pornthip Munkong v. Thailand* (Opinion no. 43/2015), 2 December 2015, §18; WGAD, *Tri Agus Susanto Siswowihardjo v. Indonesia* (Opinion no. 42/1996), 3 December 1996, §8.
[456] See s. III.3.3.1. (Measuring harm: subject matter of speech or identity of the target).
[457] ECtHR (GC), *Bédat v. Switzerland* (App. no. 56925/08), 29 March 2016, §49. See, similarly, ECtHR (GC), *Sürek v. Turkey (No. 2)* (App. no. 24122/94), 8 July 1999, §34.
[458] See ECtHR, *Lingens v. Austria* (App. no. 9815/82), 8 July 1986, §41: 'Whilst the press must not overstep the bounds set, inter alia, for the "protection of the reputation of others", it is nevertheless incumbent on it to impart information and ideas on *political issues just as on those in other areas of public interest*' (emphasis added).
[459] ECtHR (GC), *Bédat v. Switzerland* (App. no. 56925/08), 29 March 2016, §49. ECtHR, Guide on Article 10 of the European Convention on Human Rights—Freedom of Expression, 31 August 2022, §488; ECtHR (GC), *Von Hannover v. Germany (No. 2)* (App. nos. 40660/08 & 60641/08), 7 February 2012, §§109–113, §119. See also ECtHR, *Magyar Helsinki Bizottság v. Hungary* (App. no. 18030/11), 8 November 2016, §§161–162.
[460] ECtHR (GC), *Couderc and Hachette Filipacchi Associés v. France* (App. no. 40454/07), 10 November 2015, §89.
[461] IACtHR, *Herrera-Ulloa v. Costa Rica* (Series C, no. 107), 2 July 2004, §129.
[462] IACtHR, *Canese v. Paraguay* (Series C, no. 111), 31 August 2004, §105.
[463] IACtHR, *Baraono Bray v. Chile* (Series C, no. 481), 24 November 2022, §108.

matters 'of public interest concerning a public official' cannot under any circumstances be sanctioned by criminal penalties.[464]

The European Court has also considered a speaker's status as a member of the press or a lawyer as part of its assessment of the public value of speech.[465] The Court applies its 'most careful scrutiny' to any penalties on speech that 'are capable of discouraging the participation of the press in debates over matters of legitimate public concern'[466] because the press should not be hindered in 'performing its task as purveyor of information and public watchdog'.[467] And states have a positive obligation to create a favourable environment for participation in public debate, including allowing the press to express opinions and ideas 'without fear, even if these run counter to those defended by the official authorities or by a significant part of public opinion, or even if they are irritating or shocking'.[468]

Similarly, the European Court has held that although lawyers' criticisms cannot overstep 'certain bounds' set out in their national codes of conduct,[469] lawyers have a 'specific status' that warrants a narrow margin of appreciation for interference to speech, in light of the right to a fair trial and the public interest in the functioning of the judiciary.[470] This means that, when a lawyer is representing a client, especially in a criminal case, there must be 'a free and even forceful exchange of argument between the parties'.[471] For example, the European Court found a violation of the right to freedom of speech in a case in which a lawyer, in written pleadings, accused French judges of being complicit in the torture of his client by Syrian secret services, and was issued with a five-year disqualification.[472] The Court focused on the fact that the remarks were made in a 'judicial context' and that the remarks directly contributed to the lawyer's task of defending his client.[473] Penalizing speech outside of the courtroom will be subject to less protection (or, for the Court a greater 'margin of appreciation'[474]), but even then

---

[464] See IACtHR, *Álvarez Ramos v. Venezuela* (Series C, no. 380), 30 August 2019, §§121–123, 129. See also IACtHR, *Baraono Bray v. Chile* (Series C, no. 481), 24 November 2022, §109 (finding that the 'use of criminal law to impose subsequent liability for statements made in the media on matters of public interest would ... constitute intimidation which, ultimately, would limit freedom of expression'); IACtHR, *Palamara Iribarne v. Chile* (Series C, no. 135), 22 November 2005, §85 (finding that the question of whether restrictions are a 'necessary' and therefore a lawful restriction on speech 'will depend on whether they are designed to fulfil an overriding public interest'). Cf. IACtHR, *Palacio Urrutia v. Ecuador* (Series C, no. 446), 24 November 2021, Concurring Opinion of Judge Humberto Antonio Sierra Porto, §16 (disagreeing with 'the tendency to establish an absolute rule regarding the impossibility of establishing criminal sanctions in cases such as this one'). See also s. II.2.3.1. (Ecuador). High-Level Panel of Legal Experts on Media Freedom, Amicus Curiae Brief in the case of Palacio Urrutia v. Ecuador (2021), §73.
[465] See s. III.4.3. (Reasonable publication).
[466] ECtHR (GC), *Bladet Tromsø v. Norway* (App. no. 21980/93), 20 May 1999, §64.
[467] ECtHR, *Lingens v. Austria* (App. no. 9815/82), 8 July 1986, §44. See s. III.4.3. (Reasonable publication) and ch. 1 (Introduction), s. II.3.2.5. (Relevance of whether the speaker is a journalist).
[468] ECtHR, *Khadija Ismayilova v. Azerbaijan* (App. nos. 65286/13 & 57270/14), 10 January 2019, §158. See also IACmHR, *Inter-American Legal Framework Regarding the Right to Freedom of Expression* (2009) OEA/Ser.L/V/II, CIDH/RELE/INF. 2/09, §165.
[469] ECtHR (GC), *Morice v. France* (App. no. 29369/10), 23 April 2015, §134.
[470] Ibid., §§132–148; ECtHR, *Ottan v. France* (App. no. 41841/12), 19 April 2018, §57. See also ECtHR, *Nikula v. Finland* (App. no. 31611/96), 21 March 2002, §45.
[471] ECtHR (GC), *Morice v. France* (App. no. 29369/10), 23 April 2015, §137.
[472] ECtHR, *Bono v. France* (App. no. 29024/11), 15 December 2015.
[473] Ibid., §§48–56.
[474] See ch. 1 (Introduction), s. II.3. (Jurisprudence).

the European Court has held that lawyers cannot be penalized for everything published in an interview where the press has edited certain statements.[475]

In line with other regional human rights bodies, African jurisprudence provides that a 'higher degree of tolerance is expected' for political speech, and 'an even higher threshold is required' when such speech relates to the actions of the government and government officials.[476] The Declaration of Principles of Freedom of Expression in Africa also provides that public figures 'shall be required to tolerate a degree of criticism'.[477]

4.3. Reasonable publication

Many national systems include 'reasonable publication' as a defence to speech-related liability.[478] This provides a lower level protection for speech than the *NYT v. Sullivan* approach which requires that speech about public officials be made with 'actual malice'—as it requires negligence but not 'knowledge' of falsity or 'reckless disregard' to the truth before speech can be punishable.[479] International bodies have not specifically addressed whether such a defence is a requirement under international human rights law, although the Human Rights Committee has embraced 'actual malice' as the relevant standard for public-interest speech, and other bodies have stated that a minimum level of intent or fault should be required before speech can be penalized.[480]

The European Court has taken a unique approach among international bodies by establishing a rule that applies to certain speakers rather than certain speech.[481] According to the European Court, there should be 'increased protection' afforded to speech by 'public watchdogs' and including in particular the press.[482] The Court has also found that when freedom of the press is at stake, authorities have a limited margin of appreciation to decide that a 'pressing social need' for restrictions exist.[483] But the Court has also made clear that the press must not 'overstep certain bounds', in

---

[475] ECtHR (GC), *Morice v. France* (App. no. 29369/10), 23 April 2015, §§137–138. The Court has construed this distinction strictly, holding that comments made to a journalist while inside the court building after an acquittal did not form part of 'conduct in the courtroom'. See, e.g., ECtHR, *Ottan v. France* (App. no. 41841/12), 19 April 2018, §55. Cf. ECtHR, *Peruzzi v. Italy* (App. no. 39294/09), 30 June 2015, §§60–63. See also WGAD, *Maseko v. Swaziland* (Opinion no. 6/2015), 22 April 2015, §28 (finding that lawyers have 'the right to take part in public discussions on matters concerning the law and the administration of justice').

[476] ACmHPR, *Good v. Botswana* (Comm. no. 313/05), 26 May 2010, §198. See also ACtHPR, *Konaté v. Burkina Faso* (App. no. 4/2013), 5 December 2014, §§155–156; ACtHPR, *Umuhoza v. Rwanda* (App. no. 3/2014), 24 November 2017, §161.

[477] ACmHPR, *Good v. Botswana* (Comm. no. 313/05), 26 May 2010, §198.

[478] See s. II.1.4.3. (Reasonable publication). See also s. III.3.1. (Intent). Milo (n 47) 108–114.

[479] US Supreme Court, *New York Times v. Sullivan* 376 U.S. 254, 9 March 1964, 279–280. See s. III.3.1. (Intent). The Inter-American Court does not consider the responsible journalism standard as opposing, qualifying or modifying in any meaningful way the 'actual malice' requirement; it has invoked the responsible journalism standard as a way to develop doctrine, but on its own it has not played a meaningful role in the adjudication process.

[480] See s. III.3.1. (Intent).

[481] See ch. 1 (Introduction), s. II.3.2.5. (Relevance of whether the speaker is a journalist). See also s. III.4.3.3 (Form and manner of the speech and its presentation).

[482] ECtHR, Guide on Article 10 of the European Convention on Human Rights—Freedom of Expression, 31 August 2022, §§298–304. See also ECtHR (GC), *Fressoz v. France* (App. no. 29183/95), 21 January 1999, §45(ii); ECtHR (GC), *Pedersen & Baadsgaard v. Denmark* (App. no. 49017/99), 17 December 2004, §71; ECtHR, *Salihu v. Sweden* (App. no. 33628/15), 10 May 2016, §52.

[483] ECtHR, Guide on Article 10 of the European Convention on Human Rights—Freedom of Expression, 31 August 2022, §299.

particular the reputation and rights of others and the need to prevent the disclosure of information received in confidence.[484] The Court has made clear that being engaged in journalistic activities does not create an unfettered right to claim immunity from criminal liability.[485] The protection offered to the press is therefore '*subject to the condition that* they comply with the duties and responsibilities connected with the function of journalist, and the consequent obligation of "responsible journalism" '.[486]

The European Court has held, in a case involving a journalist, that the Court 'will examine whether the journalist ... *acted in good faith in accordance with the tenets of responsible journalism*'.[487] Whether or not a journalist acted 'responsibly' is in turn assessed based on the content of the information which is collected and disseminated by journalistic means as well as the process of publication. More specifically, the Court has applied this doctrine by addressing three factors: (1) 'the lawfulness of the *conduct* of a journalist', (2) whether appropriate efforts were made to verify facts, and (3) the form and manner in which the speech was written and presented.[488]

4.3.1. Lawfulness of journalist's conduct

The European Court interprets the fact that a journalist has breached the law by publishing their speech or through 'the manner in which the information was obtained' as 'a most relevant, albeit not decisive, consideration when determining whether he or she has acted responsibly'.[489] This analysis includes an assessment of the journalists' interaction with governmental authorities when exercising journalist functions and whether they complied with relevant laws.[490]

4.3.2. Verification of facts

Second, the European Court considers the extent to which journalists have verified information in determining whether speech constitutes 'responsible journalism'.[491] According to the Court, 'responsible journalism requires that the journalists check the

---

[484] ECtHR, *De Haes v. Belgium* (App. no. 19983/92), 24 February 1997, §37; ECtHR (GC), *Bladet Tromsø and Stensaas v. Norway* (App. no. 21980/93), 20 May 1999, §62.
[485] ECtHR (GC), *Stoll v. Switzerland* (App. no. 69698/01), 10 December 2007, §91.
[486] ECtHR, Guide on Article 10 of the European Convention on Human Rights—Freedom of Expression, 31 August 2022, §305 (emphasis added). See, e.g., ECtHR, *Kącki v. Poland* (App. no. 10947/11), 4 July 2017, §49.
[487] ECtHR, *Kącki v. Poland* (App. no. 10947/11), 4 July 2017, §49 (emphasis added). The Court has also asked whether the journalist 'act[ed] in good faith, respect[ed] the ethics of journalism and perform[ed] the due diligence expected in responsible journalism?': ECtHR, *Magyar Jeti Zrt v. Hungary* (App. no. 11257/16), 4 December 2018, §77.
[488] See s. III.4.3.1 (Lawfulness of journalist's conduct), s. III.4.3.2 (Verification of facts), and s. III.4.3.3 (Form and manner of the speech and its presentation).
[489] ECtHR, *Alpha Doryforiki Tileorasi Anonymi Etairia v. Greece* (App. no. 72562/10), 22 February 2018, §59; ECtHR (GC), *Pentikäinen v. Finland* (App. no. 11882/10), 20 October 2015, §90; ECtHR (GC), *Axel Springer AG v. Germany* (App. no. 39954/08), 7 February 2012, §93.
[490] See ch. 5 (Espionage and Official Secrets Laws), s. II.5.2.3. ('Responsible journalism'). See, e.g., ECtHR (GC), *Fressoz v. France* (App. no. 29183/95), 21 January 1999, §§52–53 (concerning a journalist who published income details obtained from a confidential tax file).
[491] ECtHR (GC), *Pedersen & Baadsgaard v. Denmark* (App. no. 49017/99), 17 December 2004, §78. See also IACtHR, *Moya Chacón v. Costa Rica* (Series C, no. 451), 6 September 2022, §76 ('for investigative journalism to exist in a democratic society, journalists must be allowed "room for error" because, without this margin of error, neither independent journalism nor the possibility of the necessary democratic scrutiny that results from this can exist').

information provided to the public to a reasonable extent'.[492] This inquiry includes the extent to which the media can reasonably regard their sources as reliable, to be assessed in light of the situation as it presented itself to the journalist at the material time, rather than with the benefit of hindsight.[493]

The Court has noted that the press 'should normally be entitled, when contributing to public debate on matters of legitimate concern, to rely on the content of official reports without having to undertake independent research'.[494] The Court has also held that reporting 'based on interviews, whether edited or not, constitutes one of the most important means whereby the press is able to play its vital role of "public watchdog" '[495] and that 'a journalist cannot always be reasonably expected to check all the information provided in an interview'.[496]

But in a case in which a journalist made various offensive statements about a member of parliament, accusing him of fraud and plagiarism, the Court found that it was defensible for him to be convicted of defamation by a Romanian court and required to pay approximately 2,000 Euros in damages on the basis that he did not verify the content of the article before publication.[497] The Court noted that where a report concerns criminal allegations, 'it has to be kept in mind that the suspect has a right to be presumed innocent of any criminal offence until proven guilty and that the courts are the proper forum for the determination of a person's guilt or innocence on a criminal charge' and that the publication had not been 'responsible' in this context.[498]

4.3.3. Form and manner of the speech and its presentation

Third, the European Court considers the way in which the speech was drafted and communicated.[499] The Court considers that it is not for it, 'nor for the national courts for that matter, to substitute their own views for those of the press as to what technique of reporting should be adopted by journalists'.[500] And it

---

[492] ECtHR, Kącki v. Poland (App. no. 10947/11), 4 July 2017, §52. See also ECtHR, McVicar v. United Kingdom (App. no. 46311/99), 7 May 2002, §84; ECtHR (GC), Bladet Tromsø v. Norway (App. no. 21980/93), 20 May 1999, §66; ECtHR (GC), Pedersen & Baadsgaard v. Denmark (App. no. 49017/99), 17 December 2004, §78.

[493] ECtHR, McVicar v. United Kingdom (App. no. 46311/99), 7 May 2002, §84; ECtHR (GC), Bladet Tromsø v. Norway (App. no. 21980/93), 20 May 1999, §66.

[494] ECtHR, Colombani v. France (App. no. 51279/99), 25 June 2002, §65. See s. III.4.4. (Accurate reporting of official documents).

[495] ECtHR (GC), Jersild v. Denmark (App. no. 15890/89), 23 September 1994, §35. See also ECtHR (GC), Pedersen & Baadsgaard v. Denmark (App. no. 49017/99), 17 December 2004, §77.

[496] ECtHR, Kącki v. Poland (App. no. 10947/11), 4 July 2017, §52. But in certain circumstances, a journalist can be required to systematically and formally distance themselves from the content of information that might display a conflict between public interest and an individual's right. See ch. 3 (Hate Speech).

[497] ECtHR, Cuc Pascu v. Romania (App. no. 36157/02), 16 September 2008, §31.

[498] ECtHR, Verlagsgruppe Droemer Knaur GmbH & Co. KG v. Germany (App. no. 35030/13), 19 October 2017, §54. See also ECtHR, Eerikäinen v. Finland (App. no. 3514/02), 10 February 2009, §60; ECtHR, Milosavljević v. Serbia (App. no. 57574/14), 25 May 2021, §64. See also IACtHR, Moya Chacón v. Costa Rica (Series C, no. 451), 6 September 2022, §76: 'for investigative journalism to exist in a democratic society, journalists must be allowed "room for error" because, without this margin of error, neither independent journalism nor the possibility of the necessary democratic scrutiny that results from this can exist'.

[499] See ECtHR, Flux v. Moldova (No. 6) (App. no. 22824/04), 29 July 2008, §26; ECtHR (GC), Stoll v. Switzerland (App. no. 69698/01), 10 December 2007, §104.

[500] T. McGonagle, Freedom of Expression and Defamation: A study of the case law of the European Court of Human Rights (COE 2016), 44; ECtHR (GC), Jersild v. Denmark (App. no. 15890/89), 23 September 1994, §31; ECtHR (GC), Bladet Tromsø v. Norway (App. no. 21980/93), 20 May 1999, §63.

acknowledges that 'methods of objective and balanced reporting may vary considerably, depending among other things on the media in question'.[501] The Court also recognizes that journalistic freedom allows 'recourse to a degree of exaggeration, or even provocation' or harshness.[502] But it has also held that this judicial deference is not 'unlimited'.[503]

Applying this standard, the Court has found it permissible to impose a conviction and fine on a journalist for writing articles that were 'reductive and truncated' and 'liable to mislead the reader', thereby 'considerably detract[ing] from the importance of their contribution to the public debate'.[504]

On the other hand, the Court found a violation of the right to free expression where a French weekly magazine published an interview whose 'tone ... appeared to be measured and non-sensationalist' and where readers could 'easily distinguish' between the factual material and the interviewee's perception of events.[505] Although the Court noted that the interview was 'accompanied by graphic effects and headlines which were intended to attract the reader's attention and provoke a reaction', these were held to be matters of 'editorial decision' and the presentation of the material, as a whole, did 'not distort the content of the information'.[506] It was therefore held to be inappropriate for French courts to fine the magazine 50,000 Euros and order that they display text regarding the judgment in the magazine.[507]

The Inter-American Court has quoted and approved the approach of the European Court in stating that journalists 'must, when exercising their duties, abide by the principles of responsible journalism, namely to act in good faith, provide accurate and reliable information, objectively reflect the opinions of those involved in a public debate, and refrain from pure sensationalism'.[508] More specifically, the Court considers that 'journalists have an obligation to verify, reasonably although not necessarily exhaustively, the facts on which they base their opinions'[509] and that journalists should 'take a critical distance from their sources and compare them with other relevant information'.[510] However, the contours of any doctrine of 'responsible journalism' are not clear and it appears to be used by the Court as a relevant factor in assessing intent when

---

[501] ECtHR (GC), *Jersild v. Denmark* (App. no. 15890/89), 23 September 1994, §31.
[502] ECtHR (GC), *Bladet Tromsø v. Norway* (App. no. 21980/93), 20 May 1999, §59; ECtHR, *De Haes v. Belgium* (App. no. 19983/92), 24 February 1997, §46.
[503] ECtHR (GC), *Bladet Tromsø v. Norway* (App. no. 21980/93), 20 May 1999, §58.
[504] ECtHR (GC), *Stoll v. Switzerland* (App. no. 69698/01), 10 December 2007, §152. The Court found that there was no violation of article 10, in circumstances where the published articles had been so inaccurate and misleading that it was clearly the intention of the journalist 'not to inform the public on a topic of general interest' but to make the subject of the article 'the subject of needless scandal': §§151–152.
[505] ECtHR (GC), *Couderc v. France* (App. no. 40454/07), 10 November 2015, §141.
[506] Ibid., §144.
[507] Ibid., §152. See ch. 1 (Introduction), s. II.3.2.5. (Relevance of whether speaker is a journalist) discussing ECtHR (GC), *Pedersen & Baadsgaard v. Denmark* (App. no. 49017/99), 17 December 2004.
[508] IACtHR, *Mémoli v. Argentina* (Series C, no. 265), 22 August 2013, §122, citing at length the European Court decisions on *Novaya Gazeta v. Russia* (App. no. 14087/08), 28 March 2013 and ECtHR (GC), *Stoll v. Switzerland* (App. no. 69698/01), 10 December 2007; IACtHR, *Granier v. Venezuela* (Series C, no. 293), 22 June 2015, §139. See also IACtHR, *Kimel v. Argentina* (Series C, no. 177), 2 May 2008, §79.
[509] IACtHR, *Mémoli v. Argentina* (Series C, no. 265), 22 August 2013, §122.
[510] Ibid., §122.

weighing the necessity of restrictions on speech rather than specifically recognized as a defence.[511]

The African Commission's 2019 Declaration of Principles on Freedom of Expression directs states to ensure that in defamation cases, publishers may not be found liable for statements which are 'reasonable to make in the circumstances'.[512] The Commission has also observed (in a compulsory accreditation case) that 'while accurate reporting is the goal to which all journalists should aspire', in some circumstances 'it is sufficient if journalists have made a reasonable effort to be accurate and have not acted in bad faith'.[513]

4.4. Accurate reporting of official documents

The most detailed jurisprudence on the defence of fair and accurate reporting emanates from the European Court. In a leading case, the Court examined the civil liability of a newspaper and its editor for defamation for articles alleging that seal hunters had skinned harp seals alive.[514] The Court found a violation of article 10 because the newspaper had directly quoted from an official report drawn up by an inspector appointed by the Norwegian Ministry of Fisheries to monitor the seal hunt.[515] It concluded that 'the press should normally be entitled, when contributing to public debate on matters of legitimate concern, to rely on the contents of official reports without having to undertake independent research'.[516]

In other cases, the European Court has found a violation of article 10 for criminal defamation proceedings when the press had relied on reports by Romania's Fraud Squad for allegations of bribery,[517] quoted extracts from a confidential French government report alleging a foreign head of state was involved in cannabis trafficking[518] and based reporting on the alleged unprofessional conduct of a Finnish surgeon on a publicly available police pre-trial record.[519]

The extent to which different sources may be relied upon by journalists was explained by the European Court in a case in which an injunction and damages were sought against a publisher for a book that referred to a person as a presumed member of the mafia.[520] The Court held that the press was entitled to rely on the content of public official reports and official press releases without undertaking independent research.[521] However, the Court criticized reliance on *internal* official reports' that indicated

---

[511] Ibid., §122–123.
[512] ACmHPR, Declaration of Principles of Freedom of Expression and Access to Information in Africa (2019), Principle 21.
[513] ACmHPR, *Scanlen & Holderness v. Zimbabwe* (Comm. no. 297/05), 3 April 2009, §120.
[514] ECtHR (GC), *Bladet Tromsø v. Norway* (App. no. 21980/93), 20 May 1999, §§12–13. The domestic court had decided that the newspaper had to pay each of the plaintiffs approximately 850 EUR (10,000 Norwegian Kroner) and the editor 85 EUR(1,000 Norwegian Kroner).
[515] ECtHR (GC), *Bladet Tromsø v. Norway* (App. no. 21980/93), 20 May 1999, §§66–68.
[516] Ibid., §68; see also §72 noting the newspaper had acted in good faith.
[517] ECtHR (GC), *Dalban v. Romania* (App. no. 28114/95), 28 September 1999, §§13–14, 17–19, 46–50.
[518] ECtHR, *Colombani v. France* (App. no. 51279/99), 25 June 2002, §§13, 65.
[519] ECtHR, *Selisto v. Finland* (App. no. 56767/00), 16 November 2004, §§60–63.
[520] ECtHR, *Verlagsgruppe Droemer Knaur Gmbh & Co KG v. Germany* (App. no. 35030/13), 19 October 2017.
[521] Ibid., §§46, 48.

only 'vague suspicious circumstances' whereas the book 'exaggerated the level of suspicion'.[522]

Other international human rights bodies have provided limited comment on the fair and accurate reporting defence but the Human Rights Committee has found that an author was exercising his right to impart information under article 19(2) of the ICCPR when he published documents that were referred to in open court, implicitly recognizing the validity—though not expressly articulating the necessity—of this defence.[523]

4.5. Opinion

The defence of opinion is also recognized in international law.[524] The Human Rights Committee has stated in its General Comment No. 34 that defamation laws 'should not be applied with regard to those forms of expression that are not, of their nature, subject to verification'.[525] This suggests that opinions should not even be caught in the net of speech-restriction laws, and not just that opinion should be a defence for the speaker to prove.

The Working Group has similarly held that statements of opinion should not be punished because 'the right to hold an opinion and expressing it freely is the core of the right to freedom of expression. Even if the opinion of [the speaker] is erroneous, he has the right to believe in it and to express it'.[526]

International bodies also acknowledge that a truth defence cannot apply where opinions have been expressed because opinions by their very nature are not capable of verification: they are the subjective viewpoint of the speaker. And since truth is a necessary defence, this means that opinions should not be penalized through defamation or similar laws.[527]

In the words of the European Court:

> A careful distinction needs to be made between facts and value-judgments. The existence of facts can be demonstrated, whereas the truth of value-judgments is not susceptible of proof...[528]

The concept of a 'value judgment' is wider than a mere comment; it includes assessment and analysis of facts as well as the expression of an opinion. The Court has emphasized that where national legislation or courts make no distinction between value judgments and statements of fact, which amounts to requiring proof of the truth of a value

---

[522] Ibid., §§47–48 (emphasis added). The Court also noted that it 'agrees with the domestic courts that a distinction has to be made between public official reports or official press releases and internal official reports. While journalists may rely on the former without further research, the same cannot be held for the latter'.

[523] HRC, *Lovell v. Australia* (Comm. no. 920/2000), 29 March 2003, §9.2 (finding that the contempt conviction was permissible under Art. 19 for documents that were *not* read aloud in court, §9.4). See s. IV.8. (Recommendations).

[524] Many states protect opinions through 'fair comment' defences. See s. II. (State Practice).

[525] HRC, General Comment No. 34 (2011), §47.

[526] WGAD, *Tri Agus Susanto Siswowihardjo v. Indonesia* (Opinion no. 42/1996), 3 December 1996, §8; WGAD, *Duy Nguyen Huu Quoc v. Vietnam* (Opinion no. 8/2019), 25 April 2019, §55.

[527] See s. III.4.1. (Truth).

[528] ECtHR, *Lingens v. Austria* (App. no. 9815/82), 8 July 1986, §46; ECtHR, *Fedchenko v. Russia* (App. no. 33333/04), 11 February 2010, §37; ECtHR, *Otegi Mondragon v. Spain* (App. no. 2034/07), 15 March 2011, §53.

judgment as a defence to libel, this is an indiscriminate approach to the assessment of speech and is per se incompatible with freedom of opinion, a fundamental element of freedom of expression.[529]

For example, in a case that concerned the use of the term 'closet Nazi' to describe a politician, the national courts considered the term to be a statement of fact but never examined the question as to whether it could be considered a value judgment. In the European Court's view, this was instead a 'permissible value judgment', and the 'body of facts available [to the journalist] constituted sufficient factual basis for the contested factual statement'.[530] In response to the argument put forward by Austrian authorities that calling someone a 'Nazi' was a very serious reproach close to a criminal charge, the European Court noted that the 'degree of precision' for establishing criminality can 'hardly be compared to that which ought to be observed by a journalist when expressing his opinion on a matter of public concern, in particular when expressing his opinion in the form of a value judgment'.[531]

When an opinion or 'value judgment' is concerned, the European Court will consider the adequacy of the factual basis for a value judgment, though the weight given to the factual basis will vary depending on the nature of the statement.[532] The Court has found that 'even where a statement amounts to a value judgment, the proportionality of an interference may depend on whether there exists a sufficient factual basis for the impugned statement, since even a value judgment without any factual basis to support it may be excessive'.[533]

In some cases, the requirement of a sufficient factual basis will be relaxed,[534] such as when the article relates to an important matter of public interest or is satirical. For instance, the Court did not require a journalist to prove the factual basis of his statements regarding police brutality when he was 'essentially reporting what was being said by others' and it was 'a matter of serious public concern'.[535]

The European Court takes a similarly protective stance towards artistic expression and satire, on the basis that satire 'by its inherent features of exaggeration and distortion of reality, naturally aims to provoke and agitate'.[536] Accordingly, 'any interference

---

[529] ECtHR, *Fedchenko v. Russia (No. 5)* (App. no. 17229/13), 2 October 2018, §37.
[530] ECtHR, *Scharsach v. Austria* (App. no. 39394/98), 13 November 2003, §41. The Court noted that 'the assessment of whether a certain statement constitutes a value judgment or a statement of fact might in many cases be difficult. However, since under the Court's case-law a value judgment must be based on sufficient facts in order to constitute a fair comment under Article 10 ... their difference finally lies in the degree of factual proof which has to be established'.
[531] Ibid., §43.
[532] ECtHR, *Unabhängige Initiative Informationsvielfalt v. Austria* (App. no. 28525/95), 26 February 2002, §40. See also ECtHR, *Karsai v. Hungary* (App. no. 5380/07), 1 December 2009, §§32–33; ECtHR, *Feldek v. Slovakia* (App. no. 29032/95), 12 July 2001, §86.
[533] ECtHR, *Jerusalem v. Austria* (App. no. 26958/95), 27 February 2001, §43, citing ECtHR, *De Haes v. Belgium* (App. no. 19983/92), 24 February 1997, §47, and ECtHR, *Oberschlick v. Austria* (App. no. 20834/92), 1 July 1997, §33; ECtHR, *Dichand v. Austria* (App. no. 29271/95), 26 February 2002, §§42–43; ECtHR, *Scharsach v. Austria* (App. no. 39394/98), 13 November 2003, §§39–40.
[534] McGonagle (n 500) 45.
[535] ECtHR, *Thorgeirson v. Iceland* (App. no. 13778/88), 25 June 1992, §65.
[536] ECtHR, *Eon v. France* (App. no. 26118/10), 14 March 2013, §60.

with the right of an artist—or anyone else—to use this means of expression should be examined with particular care'.[537] The Court has held that the 'use of sarcasm and irony is perfectly compatible with the exercise of a journalist's freedom of expression,'[538] and has found violations of article 10 in a range of instances involving satirical expression, including waving a placard during a Presidential visit stating 'Get lost, you sad prick';[539] a newspaper article describing local government officials as 'numbskulls' and 'posers';[540] and a lewd painting of Austrian politicians.[541]

The approach of the Inter-American Court is similar to that of the other international bodies: there is a clear recognition that a distinction needs to be drawn between fact and opinion, with the latter being protected from liability. The Commission stated that '*desacato*' laws violate the American Convention by failing to distinguish between facts and value judgments, requiring the speaker to prove the veracity of all his statements.[542] The Inter-American Court has also suggested that opinions should be protected speech. It held that opinions expressed by a journalist 'can neither be deemed to be true nor false. As such, an opinion cannot be subjected to sanctions, even more so where it is a value judgment on the actions of a public official in the performance of his duties'.[543]

Similarly, the African Commission requires that states ensure that laws relating to defamation do not impose liability for expressions of opinions.[544]

5. Right to a Fair Trial

International human rights bodies have recognized that criminal and civil proceedings for defamation or insult must comply with certain due process requirements. This includes requirements related to the burden and standard of proof,[545] the need for a reasoned decision by domestic courts,[546] reasonable limitation periods,[547] and respect for the equality of arms.

---

[537] Ibid.
[538] ECtHR, *Ziembiński v. Poland (No. 2)* (App. no. 1799/07), 5 July 2016, §44.
[539] ECtHR, *Eon v. France* (App. no. 26118/10), 14 March 2013.
[540] ECtHR, *Ziembiński v. Poland (No. 2)* (App. no. 1799/07), 5 July 2016.
[541] ECtHR, *Vereinigung Bildender Künstler v. Austria* (App. no. 68354/01), 25 January 2007.
[542] IACmHR, *The Inter-American Legal Framework regarding the Right to Freedom of Expression* (2009) OEA/Ser.L/V/II, CIDH/RELE/INF. 2/09, §138. See ss II.1.5.1. (Criminal penalties) and III.6.1. (Criminal penalties).
[543] IACtHR, *Kimel v. Argentina* (Series C, no. 177), 2 May 2008, §93.
[544] ACmHPR, Declaration of Principles on Freedom of Expression and Access to Information in Africa (2019), Principle 2. Cf. McGonagle (n 500) 45 (suggesting limits to the defence).
[545] See, e.g., ECtHR, *Kasabova v. Bulgaria* (App. no. 22385/03), 19 April 2011; ECtHR, *McVicar v. United Kingdom* (App. no. 46311/99), 7 May 2002, §87; ECtHR, *Steel v. United Kingdom* (App. no. 68416/01), 15 February 2005, §§93, 95.
[546] See, e.g., ECtHR, *Macovei v. Romania* (App. no. 53028/14), 28 July 2020, §88 (criticizing Romanian appellate courts for the 'limited scope of their reasoning', and for not providing 'convincing reasons' for concluding that a corruption allegation against Romanian politicians was an 'untruthful statement of fact'). See also ECtHR, *Terentyev v. Russia* (App. no. 25147/09), 26 January 2017, §22.
[547] The jurisdictions considered in this chapter tend to impose limitation periods for defamation of one to three years, although there are a few outliers with periods of five to 20 years: see s. II. (State Practice).

Lengthy limitation periods may have a chilling effect on freedom of expression, with the possibility of prosecution or lawsuit hanging over the journalist for many years.[548] According to the European Court, states cannot fix a limitation period that is arbitrary or impairs 'the very essence of the applicants' right to access' to a court, and the restrictions must pursue a legitimate aim and be proportionate.[549]

6. Penalties

In international law, the analysis of whether penalties are appropriate is typically undertaken in the context of whether a particular penalty is a necessary restriction on the right to freedom of expression, which in turn triggers a proportionality test. However, international law makes clear that criminal penalties—or at least imprisonment—are *never* appropriate for some types of speech.

6.1. Criminal penalties
6.1.1. Criminalization
International human rights bodies agree that criminal law should only be used in exceptional circumstances to penalize speech and that the penalty of imprisonment should not be used under any circumstances to punish speech that is defamatory or insulting.[550] But some bodies have gone further, and consider that *all* criminal penalties are impermissible under international standards.

6.1.1.1. Applicability of criminal penalties to defamatory or insulting speech UN Special Rapporteurs on freedom of expression, the UN Working Group, the ECOWAS Court, the African Commission, the OSCE and the Council of Europe take the position that criminalization of defamation violates the right to freedom of expression. According to these sources, *any* criminal penalty—even penalties short of imprisonment such as a criminal fine—would violate international law if imposed as a penalty for such speech.

The Working Group on Arbitrary Detention has consistently held that criminal sanctions are not proportionate penalties for defamation.[551] In one case, a blogger was sentenced to one year in prison for insulting the president after blogging about sectarian riots in Egypt.[552] The Working Group found that the 'use of criminal law is particularly

---

[548] Defamation trials must themselves be swift: see HRC, General Comment No. 34 (2011), §47 (providing that it is 'impermissible for a State party to indict a person for criminal defamation but then not to proceed to trial expeditiously').

[549] ECtHR, *Stubbings v. United Kingdom* (App. nos. 22083/93 & 22095/93), 22 October 1996, §§55–56. Cf. ECtHR, *Times Newspapers Ltd (Nos. 1 and 2) v. United Kingdom* (App. nos. 3002/03 & 23676/03), 10 March 2009.

[550] See, e.g., HRC, General Comment No. 34 (2011), §47.

[551] See WGAD, *Maseko v. Swaziland* (Opinion no. 6/2015), 22 April 2015, §§29–30 (finding contravention of articles 14 and 19 ICCPR and articles 10 and 19 UDHR, §36); WGAD, *Amer v. Egypt* (Opinion no. 35/2008), 20 November 2008, §33; WGAD, *Sadeghi v. Iran* (Opinion no. 19/2008), 20 April 2018; WGAD, *Thammavong v. Laos* (Opinion no. 61/2017), 25 August 2017.

[552] WGAD, *Amer v. Egypt* (Opinion no. 35/2008), 20 November 2008, §§5, 15, 25.

inappropriate for alleged defamation against public officials' and 'ha[s] an inhibiting effect on the exercise of the right to freedom of opinion and expression in discussions of matters of public concern'.[553]

The UN Special Rapporteur has also commented that '[c]riminal law should be used only in very exceptional and most egregious circumstances of incitement to violence, hatred or discrimination. Criminal libel is a relic of the colonial past and should be abolished'.[554]

Africa's ECOWAS Court also considers criminalization of insulting speech inappropriate. In one case, three journalists were arrested for insulting the government and the president of the Gambia.[555] One was ordered to pay a fine of roughly $4,000 US dollars within two hours or face a four-year prison term and another was held in custody for 17 months before being acquitted.[556] The ECOWAS Court concluded that '[t]he existence of criminal defamation and insult or sedition laws are indeed inacceptable instances of gross violation of free speech and freedom of expression. It restricts the right of access to public information.'[557] It directed the Gambia to review and decriminalize its legislation on sedition, criminal libel, defamation and false news publication.[558] And in 2010, the African Commission passed resolution 169 entitled 'Repealing Criminal Defamation Law in Africa', which calls on states parties to the African Charter to 'repeal criminal defamation laws or insult laws which impede freedom of speech'.[559]

The OSCE and the Council of Europe have also called for decriminalization of laws like criminal libel or sedition that target insulting speech. The OSCE has, for example, urged states to repeal 'laws which provide criminal penalties for the defamation of public figures, or which penalize the defamation of the State, State organs or public officials as such'.[560] And in 2020 Professor David Kaye, then UN Special Rapporteur, stated that it is 'critical that States repeal any laws criminalizing journalism, including those adopted under the guise of addressing ... defamation.'[561]

---

[553] Ibid., §33. See also UN Special Rapporteur F. La Rue, *Promotion and Protection of the Right to freedom of opinion and expression* (2012) UN Doc. A/67/357, §47 (UN Special Rapporteur referred to only 'serious and extreme instances of incitement to hatred' as offences that 'should be criminalised').

[554] OHCHR, 'Statement by Irene Khan, Special Rapporteur on the promotion and protection of freedom of expression at the 47th Session of the Human Rights Council' (2 July 2021).

[555] ECOWAS CCJ, *Federation of African Journalists v. The Gambia* (Suit no. ECW/CCJ/APP/36/15), 13 February 2018, 3.

[556] Ibid., 3–4 (the penalty was 250,000 Gambian Dalasi, equivalent to approximately 4,897 USD).

[557] Ibid., 40.

[558] Ibid., 48.

[559] ACmHPR, Resolution 169 (XLVIII)10 on Repealing Criminal Defamation Laws in Africa, 24 November 2010. See also ACmHPR, Declaration of Principles on Freedom of Expression and Access to Information in Africa (2019), Principle 22(2) (calling on states to repeal laws that criminalize sedition, insult, and publication of false news).

[560] OSCE Parliamentary Assembly, Warsaw Declaration (1997), §140; OSCE Parliamentary Assembly, Bucharest Declaration (2000), §80. See also OSCE Parliamentary Assembly, Paris Declaration: Resolution on Freedom of the Media (2001), 29–31. See also M. Haraszti, 'Statement at the Fourth Winter Meeting of the OSCE Parliamentary Assembly' (OSCE, 25 February 2005).

[561] UN Special Rapporteur D. Kaye, *Disease pandemics and the freedom of opinion and expression* (2020) UN Doc. A/HRC/44/49, §40. This stance is consistent with his predecessors: UN Special Rapporteur A. Hussain, *Civil and Political Rights Including The Question of Freedom of Expression* (2000) UN Doc. E/CN.4/2000/63, §52; UN Special Rapporteur F. La Rue, *Promotion and protection of the right to freedom of opinion and expression* (2011) UN Doc. A/66/290, §40.

Some international bodies have found that criminal penalties are not appropriate specifically for defamatory or insulting speech that relates to public persons or issues of public interest.

The Human Rights Committee has called on states parties to decriminalize insult of leaders and public officials.[562] In a case in which a journalist and editor were convicted of 'criminal insult' for publishing an article on a former member of the Socialist Party of Serbia, the Human Rights Committee found a violation of freedom of expression.[563] Given that the subject of the article was a 'prominent public and political figure', the Committee did not find any unjustified infringement of his rights and reputation, 'much less one calling for the application of criminal sanction'.[564]

The Inter-American Court and Commission have reached the same conclusion.[565] The Inter-American Court has stated that 'in the case of a speech protected because it concerns matters of public interest, such as the conduct of public officials in the performance of their duties, the State's punitive response through criminal law is not conventionally appropriate, to protect the honor of an official'.[566] The Inter-American Court has recognized the punitive and exceptional nature of criminal prosecution for speech, holding that 'criminal prosecution is the most restrictive measure to freedom of expression, therefore its use in a democratic society must be exceptional and reserved for those eventualities in which it is strictly necessary to protect the fundamental legal interests from attacks that damage or endanger them, since to do otherwise would mean an abusive exercise of the punitive power of the State'.[567] The Court has therefore encouraged states to 'establish, for the protection of the honor of public officials, alternatives to the criminal process' such as 'rectification or response' and civil procedures.[568]

The Commission and the Court have also declared *desacato* laws as incompatible with freedom of expression in article 13 of the American Convention.[569] The

---

[562] HRC, *Concluding Observation, Tajikistan* (2019) UN Doc. CCPR/C/TJK/CO/3, §48. See also HRC, *Concluding Observations, Democratic Republic of the Congo* (2017) UN Doc. CCPR/C/COD/CO/4, §§39–40; HRC, *Concluding Observations, Bahrain* (2018) UN Doc. CCPR/C/BHR/CO/1, §54; HRC, *Concluding Observations, Lebanon* (2018) UN Doc. CCPR/C/LBN/CO/3, §46; HRC, *Concluding Observations, Venezuela* (2015) UN Doc. CCPR/C/VEN/CO/4, §19; HRC, *Concluding Observations, Thailand* (2017) UN Doc. CCPR/C/THA/CO/2, §37. See also HRC, *Concluding Observations, Monaco* (2015) UN Doc. CCPR/C/MCO/CO/3, §10. See further HRC, General Comment No. 34 (2011), §38.
[563] HRC, *Bodrožić v. Serbia and Montenegro* (Comm. no. 1180/2003), 31 October 2005, §§2.1, 2.2, 7.2.
[564] Ibid., §7.2.
[565] IACtHR, *Álvarez Ramos v. Venezuela* (Series C, no. 380), 30 August 2019, §§120–121 (criminal prosecution for the potential abusive exercise of the right to freedom of expression 'will only be appropriate in exceptional cases where it is strictly necessary to protect a pressing social need'); IACtHR, *Palacio Urrutia v. Ecuador* (Series C, no. 446), 24 November 2021, §§118–119 ('the protection of honor through criminal law, which may be legitimate in other cases, is not in accordance with the Convention' with respect to 'speech protected by public interest, such as those referring to the conduct of public officials in the exercise of their duties': High-Level Panel of Legal Experts on Media Freedom, *Amicus Curiae Brief in the case of Palacio Urrutia v. Ecuador* (2021));. See also IACtHR, *Baraona Bray v. Chile* (Series C, no. 481), 24 November 2022, §§109–110; IACmHR, *Inter-American Legal Framework regarding the Right to Freedom of Expression* (2009) OEA/Ser.L/V/II, CIDH/RELE/INF. 2/09, Chapter I, §111. See further IACmHR, *Elías Biscet v. Cuba* (Case 12.476), 21 October 2006 (violation of Art. IV American Declaration for prosecutions of journalists for, inter alia, 'defamatory campaigns intended to harm the integrity of the Cuban State', §113).
[566] IACtHR, *Álvarez Ramos v. Venezuela* (Series C, no. 380), 30 August 2019, §121.
[567] IACtHR, *Palacio Urrutia v. Ecuador* (Series C, no. 446), 24 November 2021, §117.
[568] Ibid., §96.
[569] See ss III.6.1. (Criminal penalties) and III.4.5. (Opinion). IACmHR Special Rapporteur E. Bertoni, *Annual Report of the Special Rapporteur for Freedom of Expression 2002* (2003) OEA/Ser.L/V/II.117 Doc. 1 rev. 1, Chapter

Inter-American Commission has also condemned the criminalization of sedition, which by definition relates to political speech.[570] Similarly, Principle 10 of the Inter-American Commission's Declaration, a soft law instrument which applies to OAS member states, provides that '[t]he protection of a person's reputation should only be guaranteed through civil sanctions in those cases in which the person offended is a public official, a public person or a private person who has voluntarily become involved in matters of public interest'.[571]

This has led the Inter-American Court to condemn criminal penalties, including imprisonment, in such cases. In one case, a journalist published a book criticizing how Argentinian authorities, including a judge, had investigated the murder of five clergymen.[572] The judge sued the journalist for criminal libel and the journalist was sentenced to one year imprisonment.[573] The Inter-American Court found that this violated freedom of expression and was 'overtly disproportionate in relation to the alleged impairment of the right to have one's honour respected in the instant case'.[574]

But in another case that is considered an outlier, and did not relate to speech about a matter of public interest, the Inter-American Court approved short prison terms (suspended sentences of 1–5 months) for two people who had 'publicly denounced the supposedly irregular sale of burial niches in the local cemetery by the executive officers of a mutual association' in a small Argentinian town.[575] They were convicted in relation to statements considered to be 'defamatory or derogatory to the reputation' of members of the association.[576] In the Court's view, 'the punishments ... were not excessive or manifestly disproportionate in a way that affected their right to freedom of expression'[577] especially since 'the information contained in the statements' did not relate to 'public interest' issues.[578]

The African Court also considers criminal sanctions for defamation generally not to be permissible in cases concerning reporting in the public interest[579] and African

---

V, §5; IACmHR, *Inter-American Legal Framework Regarding the Right to Freedom of Expression* (2009) OEA/Ser.L/V/II, CIDH/RELE/INF. 2/09, Chapter I, §134. See IACmHR, Declaration of Principles on Freedom of Expression (2000), Principle 11; IACtHR, *Palamara Iribarne v. Chile* (Series C, no. 135), 22 November 2005, §88; IACtHR, *Usón Ramírez v. Venezuela* (Series C, no. 207), 20 November 2009, §§37, 67, 68.

[570] IACmHR, *Roca Antúnez v. Cuba* (Case 12.127), 24 February 2018, §§117, 122.
[571] IACmHR, Declaration of Principles on Freedom of Expression (2000), Principle 10.
[572] IACtHR, *Kimel v. Argentina* (Series C, no. 177), 2 May 2008, §§2, 42.
[573] Ibid., §2. He was also subjected to a small fine amounting to approximately 90 USD.
[574] Ibid., §94.
[575] IACtHR, *Mémoli v. Argentina* (Series C, no. 265), 22 August 2013, §§1, 84, 131, 144. The judgment has been described as a 'regression' by Catalina Botero-Marino, Special Rapporteur for Freedom of Expression for the Commission from 2008 to 2014: see C. Botero-Marino, 'The Role of the Inter-American Human Rights System in the Emergence and Development of Global Norms on Freedom of Expression', in L. Bollinger & A. Callamard (eds), *Regardless of Frontiers* (Columbia University Press 2021), 193–194. See also E. Bertoni, 'Setbacks and Tension in the Inter-American Court of Human Rights' (Media Defence, 1 December 2013) (deeming the decision a 'serious and notable setback'). See ch. 1 (Introduction), s. II.3.1.6. (Criminal penalties for speech).
[576] IACtHR, *Mémoli v. Argentina* (Series C, no. 265), 22 August 2013, §§ 74, 117.
[577] Ibid., §§144, 149.
[578] Ibid., §147. See s. III.4.2. (Public interest).
[579] ACtHPR, *Konaté v. Burkina Faso* (App. no. 004/2013), 5 December 2014, §165. See s. III.6.1.1.2 (Applicability of penalty of imprisonment for defamatory or insulting speech).

courts have condemned the criminalization of sedition, which by definition relates to political speech.[580]

The European Court's position on criminalization of defamation and insult relies on the margin of appreciation that member states enjoy within the European system, in which the Court defers to individual nations' laws in a number of respects.[581] The Court has repeatedly expressed that in view of this deference, 'a criminal measure as a response to defamation cannot, as such, be considered disproportionate to the aim pursued'.[582] It has however applied 'strict scrutiny', 'most careful scrutiny' and 'utmost caution' to criminal sanctions imposed for defamation in the context of speech on matters of public interest[583] and noted more generally that 'the dominant position which the Government occupies makes it necessary for it to display restraint in resorting to criminal proceedings' in matters of freedom of expression.[584]

6.1.1.2. Applicability of penalty of imprisonment for defamatory or insulting speech
Even when international bodies—including the Human Rights Committee and African Court—have found that criminal penalties may be appropriate for defamatory or insulting speech in some circumstances, these bodies have been clear that imprisonment is never an appropriate penalty.[585] Although they consider that criminal penalties may apply to speech that does not concern matters of public interest, they agree that imprisonment is incompatible with international standards under any circumstances.

According to the Human Rights Committee, '[s]tates parties should consider the decriminalization of defamation and, in any case, the application of criminal law should only be countenanced in the most serious of cases and *imprisonment is never an appropriate penalty*'.[586]

In one case, a journalist published a book exposing a child exploitation ring in Mexico.[587] She was violently detained by armed men and prosecuted for 'defamation and calumny', but the case was eventually dismissed for lack of jurisdiction.[588] The Human Rights Committee found a violation of her right to freedom of expression and considered that Mexico was under an obligation to, *inter alia*, 'take all steps

---

[580] ECOWAS CCJ, *Federation of African Journalists v. The Gambia* (Suit no. ECW/CCJ/APP/36/15), 13 February 2018, 40–43.

[581] See ch. 1 (Introduction), s. II.3. (Jurisprudence). See, e.g., ECtHR (GC), *Zana v. Turkey* (App. no. 18954/91, 25 November 1997, §51 (holding that states 'have a certain margin of appreciation' in assessing whether a 'pressing social need' makes a speech-restriction 'necessary').

[582] ECtHR (GC), *Lindon v. France* (App. nos. 21279/02 & 36448/02), 22 October 2007, §59; ECtHR, *Radio France v. France* (App. no. 53984/00), 30 March 2004, §40; ECtHR, *Ivanova v. Bulgaria* (App. no. 36207/03), 14 February 2008, §68; ECtHR, *Ruokanen v. Finland* (App. no. 45130/06), 6 April 2010, §50; McGonagle (n 500) 18.

[583] ECtHR (GC), *Cumpǎnǎ v. Romania* (App. no. 33348/96), 17 December 2004, §118; ECtHR, *Bladet Tromsø v. Norway* (App. no. 21980/93), 20 May 1999, §64. See also McGonagle (n 500) 57.

[584] See, e.g., ECtHR, *Castells v. Spain* (App. no. 11798/85), 23 April 1992, § 46; ECtHR (GC), *Incal v. Turkey* (App. no. 22678/93), 9 June 1998, §54; ECtHR (GC), *Öztürk v. Turkey* (App. no. 22479/93), 28 September 1999, §66.

[585] See IACtHR *Memoli* case that allowed imprisonment but in very specific circumstances not involving public officials: IACtHR *Mémoli v. Argentina* (Series C, no. 265), 22 August 2013.

[586] HRC, General Comment No. 34 (2011), §47 (emphasis added), citing HRC, *Concluding Observations, Italy* (2006) UN Doc. CCPR/C/ITA/CO/5; HRC, *Concluding Observations, the Former Yugoslav Republic of Macedonia* (2008) UN Doc. CCPR/C/MKD/CO/2.

[587] HRC, *Cacho Ribeiro v. Mexico* (Comm. no. 2767/2016), 17 July 2018, §2.1.

[588] Ibid., §§2.7–2.8.

necessary to ... ensure that all journalists and human rights defenders are able to exercise their right to freedom of expression in their activities, including by decriminalizing the offences of defamation and calumny in all the federated states'.[589] In another case the Committee found a violation of freedom of expression when a radio broadcaster in the Philippines was sentenced to a penalty ranging from five months to over four years for a report on a Filipino congressman's purported 'illicit' relationship with a married television personality and called on the Philippines to 'provide the [broadcaster] an effective remedy' and to 'take steps to prevent similar violations occurring in the future, including by reviewing the relevant libel legislation'.[590] The Committee has also expressed concern that criticism of the royal family in Thailand is punishable by 3–15 years' imprisonment and Thailand's 'extreme sentencing practices' under this provision, with UN experts concluding that such laws 'have no place in a democratic society'.[591] Similarly, in its country reports, the Committee has recommended that states parties to the ICCPR 'should consider decriminalizing defamation and, in any case, resorting to criminal law only in the most serious cases, bearing in mind that imprisonment is never an appropriate penalty for defamation'.[592]

The Working Group has similarly observed that 'criminal sanctions, in particular imprisonment, for alleged libel or defamation are not proportional to the effective exercise of the right to freedom of opinion and expression'.[593] It has also consistently found Thailand's *lèse-majesté* criminal laws to violate freedom of expression on this basis.[594]

Similarly, the African Court has noted that '[a]part from serious and very exceptional circumstances for example, incitement to international crimes, public incitement to hatred, discrimination or violence or threats against a person or a group of people, because of specific criteria such as race, colour, religion or nationality, ... the violations of the laws on freedom of speech and the press cannot be sanctioned by custodial

---

[589] Ibid., §11, n 3. The relevant provisions under Mexican law defined 'calumny' as an offence committed by '(i) [a]nyone who imputes to another a specific act defined as an offence under law, if such act did not occur or if the person to whom it is imputed is innocent; [or] (ii) anyone who presents false claims, accusations or complaints, such being understood as those in which the perpetrator imputes an offence to a person knowing that such person is innocent or that the offence has not been committed'. Defamation is defined as an act of speech falsely imputing to another person or entity 'an act that can cause dishonour, discredit, prejudice, or expose that person or entity to the contempt of another'. See s. I. (Introduction).

[590] HRC, *Adonis v. The Philippines* (Comm. no. 1815/2008), 26 October 2011, §§2.3, 7.9–7.10 (citing HRC, General Comment No. 34 (2011)), 9. See also HRC, *Cacho Ribeiro v. Mexico* (Comm. no. 2767/2016), 17 July 2018, §§10.8–10.9 on the inappropriateness of detention.

[591] OHCHR, 'Thailand: UN experts alarmed by rise in use of lèse-majesté laws' (8 February 2021); HRC, *Concluding Observations, Thailand* (2017) UN Doc. CCPR/C/THA/CO/2, §37. See also HRC, *Concluding Observations, Monaco* (2015) UN Doc. CCPR/C/MCO/CO/3, §10.

[592] See, e.g., HRC, *Concluding Observations, Portugal* (2020) UN Doc. CCPR/C/PRT/CO/5, §43; HRC, *Concluding Observations, Senegal* (2019) UN Doc. CCPR/C/SEN/CO/5, §45; HRC, *Concluding Observations, Czech Republic* (2019) UN Doc. CCPR/C/CZE/CO/4, §35; HRC, *Concluding Observations, Cabo Verde* (2019) UN Doc. CCPR/C/CPV/CO/1/Add.1, §38; HRC, *Concluding Observations, Nigeria* (2019) UN Doc. CCPR/C/NGA/CO/2, §47. Cf. Country Report on Dominica saying the state 'should continue to ensure that no one is imprisoned for defamation' but not mentioning decriminalization: HRC, *Concluding Observations, Dominica* (2020) UN Doc. CCPR/C/DMA/COAR/1, §42.

[593] WGAD, *Maseko v. Swaziland* (Opinion no. 6/2015), 22 April 2015, §27 (quoting the UN Special Rapporteur); WGAD, *Amer v. Egypt* (Opinion no. 35/2008), 20 November 2008, §§37, 41 (finding contravention of Arts 9, 10, 19 UDHR and Arts 10, 13, 19 ICCPR).

[594] WGAD, *Somyot Prueksakasemsuk v. Thailand* (Opinion no. 35/2012), 30 August 2012, §§6, 7, 21, 26; WGAD, *Sriboonpeng v. Thailand* (Opinion no. 44/2016), 21 November 2016, §§5, 25, 29.

sentences'.[595] In a case in which a journalist had been sentenced to 12 months in prison in Burkina Faso for 'defamation, public insult and contempt of Court' following an article implicating public officials in money laundering, the Court held the custodial sentence was 'a disproportionate interference in the exercise of the freedom of expression by journalists'.[596] The Court also unanimously ordered Burkina Faso to 'amend its legislation on defamation in order to make it compliant with article 9 of the Charter ... by repealing custodial sentences for acts of defamation'.[597]

The Inter-American and European courts have however left the door open to imprisonment as a permissible penalty in defamation and insult cases in some cases/instances.[598] Both courts, however, have emphasized the exceptional nature of imprisonment as a penalty.[599] The Inter-American Court has generally concluded that criminal sanctions (both imprisonment and fines) for defamation were disproportionate[600] and the Commission considered a Cuban law under which people had been sentenced to jail terms violated freedom of expression.[601]

Similarly, the European Court has observed that 'the imposition of a prison sentence for a press offence will be compatible with journalists' freedom of expression ... only in exceptional circumstances, notably where other fundamental rights have been impaired, as, for example, in the case of hate speech or incitement to violence'.[602] It found a violation when a newspaper editor was convicted of defamation of a cabinet minister and sentenced to two and a half years' imprisonment.[603] The Court noted that the sanction 'was undoubtedly very severe, especially considering that the applicant had already been sued for the exact same statements' and 'paid a substantial amount in damages'.[604]

International human rights bodies have also found a violation of freedom of expression in cases in which speakers have been arrested and detained pre-trial, whether or not a trial or conviction followed thereafter.[605] According to the Human Rights

---

[595] ACtHPR, *Konaté v. Burkina Faso* (App. no. 004/2013), 5 December 2014, §165.
[596] Ibid., §164.
[597] Ibid., §176 (8).
[598] See IACtHR, *Mémoli v. Argentina* (Series C, no. 265), 22 August 2013 (that allowed imprisonment but in very specific circumstance not involving public official); ECtHR (GC), *Lindon v. France* (App. nos. 21279/02 & 36448/02), 22 October 2007, §59 (noting that 'a criminal measure as a response to defamation cannot, as such, be considered disproportionate to the aim pursued'). See s. III.6.1.1.1. (Applicability of criminal penalties to defamatory or insulting speech).
[599] ACtHPR, *Konaté v. Burkina Faso* (App. no. 004/2013), 5 December 2014, §165. See s. III.6.1.1.1. (Applicability of criminal penalties to defamatory or insulting speech) discussing IACtHR and IACmHR jurisprudence on imprisonment.
[600] IACtHR, *Herrera-Ulloa v. Costa Rica* (Series C, no. 107), 2 July 2004, §135 (journalist was convicted of defamation and ordered to pay a fine, §3); IACtHR, *Canese v. Paraguay* (Series C, no. 111), 31 August 2004, §§ 2, 105–106 (journalist convicted of slander and sentenced to two months' imprisonment, restrictions on leaving the country for over eight years and a fine of 1400 USD). See s. II.6.1.1.1. (Applicability of criminal penalties to defamatory or insulting speech).
[601] IACmHR, *Roca Antúnez v. Cuba* (Case 12.127), 24 February 2018, §122; Cuban Penal Code Arts 100, 125.
[602] See, e.g., ECtHR (GC), *Cumpănă v. Romania* (App. no. 33348/96), 17 December 2004, §115; ECtHR, *Ruokanen v. Finland* (App no. 45130/06), 6 April 2010, §50; ECOWAS CCJ, *Federation of African Journalists v. The Gambia* (Suit no. ECW/CCJ/APP/36/15), 13 February 2018, 44; ACmHPR, *Ouko v. Kenya* (Comm. no. 232/99), 23 October–6 November 2000, §28.
[603] ECtHR, *Fatullayev v. Azerbaijan* (App. no. 40984/07), 22 April 2010, §§8–9, 103.
[604] Ibid., §103. 'Two further sets of criminal proceedings were brought against the defendant after his conviction': §9. Cf. ECtHR, *Atamanchuk v. Russia* (App. no. 4493/11), 11 February 2020, §72.
[605] See, e.g., HRC, *Marques de Morais v. Angola* (Comm. no. 1128/2002), 29 March 2005, §§6.8, 2.12; IACtHR, *Canese v. Paraguay* (Series C, no. 111), 31 August 2004, §128.

Committee, the 'harassment, intimidation or stigmatization of a person, including arrest, detention, trial or imprisonment for reasons of the opinions they may hold, constitutes a violation of article 19, paragraph 1'.[606] And in the words of the European Court, '[t]he pre-trial detention of anyone expressing critical views ... will inevitably have a chilling effect on freedom of expression by intimidating civil society and silencing dissenting voices ... [and] a chilling effect of this kind may be produced even when the detainee is subsequently acquitted'.[607]

In some cases, even modest[608] or suspended[609] sentences or fines have been found to be disproportionate by international human rights bodies.[610] The Human Rights Committee has also found a violation of the right to freedom of expression in a case in which a journalist was given a six months' suspended sentence alongside other penalties for criticism of Angola's President, noting that it was disproportionate.[611] And the European Court has considered that a prison sentence 'by its very nature, will inevitably have a chilling effect on public discussion, and the notion that the applicant's sentence was in fact suspended does not alter that conclusion particularly as the conviction itself was not expunged'.[612]

6.2. Civil penalties

The Human Rights Committee has warned that 'care should be taken by States parties to avoid excessively punitive measures and penalties' in cases involving defamatory speech.[613] And other international bodies have taken a similar approach.

6.2.1. Damages

International human rights bodies have emphasized that an award of damages as compensation for defamation or insulting speech must not be so high as to have a chilling effect on the exercise of freedom of expression. The UN Special Rapporteur has recommended that financial sanctions must be proportionate and may not be so high and disproportionate that they bankrupt small and independent media, thereby resulting in adverse consequences on media freedom.[614] The European Court has found that 'an award of damages for defamation must bear a reasonable relationship of proportionality

---

[606] HRC, General Comment No. 34 (2011), §9.
[607] ECtHR, Şahin Alpay v. Turkey (App. no. 16538/17), 20 March 2018, §182.
[608] See, e.g., ECtHR, Radio France v. France (App. no. 53984/00), 30 March 2004, §40; ECtHR, Chauvy v. France (App. no. 64915/01), 29 June 2004, §78. Cf. ECtHR, Europapress Holding d.o.o. v. Croatia (App. no. 25333/06), 22 October 2009. See also IACtHR, Kimel v. Argentina (Series C, no. 177), 2 May 2008, §85.
[609] See, e.g., ECtHR, Eon v. France (App. no. 26118/10), 14 March 2013, §§30, 60–61; ECtHR, Nikowitz and Verlagsgruppe News GmbH v. Austria (App. no. 5266/03), 22 February 2007, §§25, 27; Cf. ECtHR, Flinkkilä v. Finland (App. no. 25576/04), 6 April 2010, §89; ECtHR, Kącki v. Poland (App. no. 10947/11), 4 July 2017, §57.
[610] Cf. ECtHR, Antunes Emídio v. Portugal (App. nos. 75637/13 & 8114/14), 24 September 2019, §64 (referring to a 'high' fine of 18,000 EUR).
[611] HRC, Marques de Morais v. Angola (Comm. no. 1128/2002), 29 March 2005, §6.8.
[612] ECtHR, Balaskas v. Greece (App. no. 73087/17), 5 November 2020, §61. See also ECtHR, Dickinson v. Turkey (App. no. 25200/11), 2 February 2021, §58 (duration of the criminal proceedings over nearly four years and a five-year suspended conviction had a chilling effect on the journalist's willingness to express his views on matters of public interest).
[613] HRC, General Comment No. 34 (2011), §47.
[614] UN Special Rapporteur F. La Rue, Report of the Special Rapporteur on the promotion and protection of the right to freedom of opinion and expression (2012) UN Doc. A/HRC/20/17, §§85, 87.

to the injury to reputation suffered'.[615] It has also observed that 'it is not necessary to rule on whether [a] damages award had, as a matter of fact, a chilling effect on the press [in a particular case]: as a matter of principle, unpredictably large damages[] awards in libel cases are considered capable of having such an effect and therefore require the most careful scrutiny'.[616]

The Court asserted that '[t]he competent national authorities are better placed than the European Court to assess the matter [of damages] and should therefore enjoy a wide margin of appreciation' as 'perceptions as to what would be an appropriate response by society to speech which does not or is not claimed to enjoy the protection of Article 10 ... of the Convention [that protects freedom of speech] may differ greatly from one Contracting State to another'.[617] However, it noted in the case of an approximately 1.7 million euros damages order made against a historian who accused a British Lord of being a war criminal that the sum 'was three times the size of the highest libel award previously made in England ... and no comparable award has been made since'.[618] It found a violation of the right to freedom of expression, 'having regard to the size of the award ... in conjunction with the lack of adequate and effective safeguards at the relevant time against a disproportionately large award'.[619]

In assessing damages awards, the European Court considers a number of factors including average monthly salaries,[620] the average damages award for other types of harm,[621] and the means of the defendant. In the 'McLibel' litigation, in which two environmental protesters were sued by McDonalds for defamation, the European Court held that awards of approximately 45,000 Euros were very substantial 'when compared to the modest incomes and resources' of the protesters.[622] Conversely, a damages award of nearly 8,000 Euros against the biggest newspaper publisher in Croatia was acceptable and was found to bear a reasonable relationship of proportionality to the injury to reputation suffered.[623]

The European Court has also emphasized that civil damages should not be punitive. In the case of a Turkish history professor and former politician, the Court found a

---

[615] ECtHR, *Tolstoy Miloslavsky v. United Kingdom* (App. no. 18139/91), 13 July 1995, §49. In this case, a jury in the United Kingdom awarded the plaintiff approximately 1,746,239 EUR in damages: §48. See also the opinion of the COE that in civil proceedings, compensation should be proportionate so as to avoid a chilling effect on freedom of expression: COE, *Defamation and Freedom of Expression Selected Documents* (2003) H/ATCM (2003) 1, 3.
[616] ECtHR, *Independent News and Media v. Ireland* (App. no. 55120/00), 16 June 2005, §114. See also ECtHR, *Ghiulfer Predescu v. Romania* (App. no. 29751/09), 27 June 2017, §62.
[617] ECtHR, *Tolstoy Miloslavsky v. United Kingdom* (App. no. 18139/91), 13 July 1995, §48.
[618] Ibid., §49. See s. II.1.5.2. (Civil penalties).
[619] Ibid., §§49–51.
[620] ECtHR, *Lepojić v. Serbia* (App. no. 13909/05), 6 November 2007, §77; ECtHR, *Kasabova v. Bulgaria* (App. no. 22385/03), 19 April 2011, §71. In *Kasabova*, the fines and damages together were equivalent of 35 monthly salaries of the journalist and almost 70 minimum monthly salaries.
[621] ECtHR, *Flinkkilä v. Finland* (App. no. 25576/04), 6 April 2010, §89.
[622] ECtHR, *Steel v. United Kingdom* (App. no. 68416/01), 15 February 2005, §96. See also ECtHR, *Timpul Info-Magazin v. Moldova* (App. no. 42864/05), 27 November 2007, §39 where the Court commented that it 'takes note of its chilling effect on the applicant newspaper ... by silencing a dissenting voice altogether'. Cf. ECtHR, *Błaja News Sp. z o. o. v. Poland* (App. no. 59545/10), 26 November 2013, §71 (quantum of the damages had not been argued to threaten defendant's economic foundations).
[623] ECtHR, *Europapress Holdings d.o.o. v. Croatia* (App. no. 25333/06), 22 October 2009, §73; ECtHR (GC), *Delfi AS v. Estonia* (App. no. 64569/09), 16 June 2015, §160. Cf. ECtHR, *Błaja News Sp. z o. o.* (App. no. 59545/10), 26 November 2013, §71.

violation where the domestic court had ordered him to pay over 87,000 Euros in damages after making a speech at a press conference criticizing Turkey's President Erdoğan. The Court found that the damages awarded had been turned into a form of fine, with the domestic court impermissibly substituting itself for a criminal court.[624]

The Inter-American bodies have reached a similar position. The Inter-American Commission has held that, as a general matter, public debate is served by more speech rather than less, making the exercise of the right of reply set out in article 14 of the American Convention the favoured possibility. But the Commission acknowledges that when that is not sufficient, civil defamation suits are permissible as long as they impose proportionate penalties.[625] The Inter-American Court has similarly observed that 'the fear of a disproportionate civil sanction may clearly be as or more intimidating and inhibiting for the exercise of freedom of expression than a criminal sanction', resulting in potential self-censorship.[626] As a result, it found a violation of freedom of expression even in cases involving relatively modest amounts.[627] And the OAS Rapporteur has said that 'a climate of guarantees for the freedom to report acts of corruption' includes 'ensuring the proportionality of penalties in civil proceedings'.[628] According to the 2000 Joint Declaration, 'pecuniary awards should be strictly proportionate to the actual harm caused and the law should prioritize the use of a range of non-pecuniary remedies'.[629]

African human rights bodies also emphasize the need for proportionality of civil damages in defamation cases. In one case, the African Court held that the Burkina Faso Government had failed to show that the cumulative payment of a fine, damages, interests and costs ordered against a journalist 'does not excessively exceed the income of the [speaker]'.[630] And the African Commission stipulates that states should abolish criminal offences 'in favour of civil offences with sanctions which must themselves be necessary and proportionate'.[631] It adds that 'sanctions shall never be so severe as to inhibit the right to freedom of expression'.[632]

---

[624] ECtHR, *Pakdemirli v. Turkey* (App. no. 35839/97), 22 February 2005, §§51, 53, 58. See also ECtHR, *SIC - Sociedade Independente de Comunicação v. Portugal* (App. no. 29856/13), 27 July 2021, §69 (holding that it was 'difficult to accept' that injury to the reputation of a politician allegedly involved in a paedophile network 'was of such a level of seriousness as to justify' an almost 146,000 EUR award, an amount that the Court considered to be 'capable of discouraging the participation of the press in debates over matters of legitimate public concern').

[625] IACmHR, *Inter-American Legal Framework Regarding the Right to freedom of Expression* (2009) OEA/Ser.L/V/II, CIDH/RELE/INF. 2/09, §79.

[626] IACtHR, *Fontevecchia v. Argentina* (Series C, no. 238), 29 November 2011, §74; IACtHR, *Palacio Urrutia v. Ecuador* (Series C, no. 446), 24 November 2021, §125. See also IACtHR, *Tristán Donoso v. Panama* (Series C, no. 193), 27 January 2009, §129

[627] IACtHR, *Fontevecchia v. Argentina* (Series C, no. 238), 29 November 2011, §72 (a case in which the editor and director of magazine were ordered to pay approximately 600 USD plus legal expenses for an article alleging the President of Argentina had a child out of wedlock).

[628] IACmHR Resolution 1/18 on Corruption and Human Rights, 16 March 2018, 5.

[629] UN Special Rapporteur on Freedom of Opinion and Expression & others, International Mechanisms for Promoting Freedom of Expression: Joint Declaration (2000).

[630] ACtHPR, *Konaté v. Burkina Faso* (App. no. 4/2013), 5 December 2014, §171. It also noted the amount was 'all the more excessive' because the applicant was deprived of revenue from publishing the weekly, due to its suspension for a period of six months.

[631] ACmHPR, Declaration of Principles of Freedom of Expression and Access to Information in Africa (2019), Principles 22(3), 17.

[632] Ibid., Principles 21(1)(c), 17.

6.2.2. Injunctions

Injunctions in defamation and insult cases are permissible if there is a proportionate relationship between the injunction and the aim it pursues.[633] This applies to both prior restraints on publication and injunctions designed to prevent future publication.[634]

The European Court has provided the most detailed guidance on the compatibility of injunctions with freedom of expression in defamation cases at the international level. Final injunctions granted after a full hearing are more likely to be proportionate.[635] On the other hand, the dangers inherent in prior restraints 'call for the most careful scrutiny'.[636]

For instance, a violation was found when Turkish courts granted an injunction in a defamation case against a newspaper about to report a quotation contested by a politician poised to become President. Once he became President, he withdrew the case and the interim injunction was lifted, but 10 months had passed. The Court held that although freedom of expression does not prohibit interim injunctions in all cases, they are subject to careful scrutiny 'including a close examination of the procedural safeguards embedded in the system to prevent arbitrary encroachments upon the freedom of expression'[637] and ensure that injunctions do not extend beyond a 'reasonable period'.[638] In this case, the Court found that Turkish domestic courts had violated freedom of expression by not imposing such procedural safeguards, including by failing to establish a specific time-limit for the injunction's duration, 'coupled with the lack of a periodic review as to its continuing necessity or a prompt determination on the merits'.[639] The Court also noted that the domestic court failed to 'provide any reasoning for its decision, either when granting the injunction or when refusing the ensuing request for it to be lifted', and highlighted delays in affording the applicants an opportunity to present relevant counter-arguments in a timely manner.[640]

However, the Inter-American bodies have taken a different approach to prior restraints due to the unique wording of article 13 of the American Convention, which prohibits prior restraints of speech, 'indirect government restrictions' and 'private controls' in almost all circumstances.[641] As the Inter-American Court has held, the Convention establishes 'an exception to prior censorship ... to regulate access for the

---

[633] Except in the Inter-American system. See ACHR Arts 13(2) and 13(4). In addition, prior restraints may be available to protect the public interest in the right to free and fair elections (ICCPR Art. 25). See, e.g., UK Representation of the People Act 1983 s. 106(3).

[634] HRC, General Comment No. 34 (2011), §13 notes that a 'free press and other media [must be] able to comment on public issues without censorship or restraint and to inform public opinion'.

[635] ECtHR, *Tolstoy Miloslavsky v. United Kingdom* (App. no. 18139/91), 13 July 1995, §54. See also ECtHR, *McVicar v. United Kingdom* (App. no. 46311/99), 7 May 2002, §82; ECtHR, *Tierbefreier E.V. v. Germany* (App. no. 45192/09), 16 January 2014, §§58–59. Cf. ECtHR, *Unabhängige Initiative Informationsvielfalt v. Austria* (App. no. 28525/95), 26 February 2002, §§46, 48.

[636] ECtHR, *Yildirim v. Turkey* (App. no. 3111/10), 18 December 2012, §47.

[637] ECtHR, *Cumhuriyet Vakfı v. Turkey* (App. no. 28255/07), 8 October 2013, §61.

[638] Ibid., §66.

[639] Ibid., §64.

[640] Ibid., §66. See also ECtHR, *Sunday Times v. United Kingdom* (App. no. 6538/74), 26 April 1979, §67. Cf. (in a privacy context) ECtHR, *Éditions Plon v. France* (App. no. 58148/00), 18 May 2004, §47.

[641] See ch. 1 (Introduction), s. II.1.1.1. (Abuses by the state).

moral protection of children and adolescents' but in 'all other cases, any preventive measures implies the impairment of freedom of thought and expression'.[642]

6.2.3. Costs

Domestic courts may require defendant journalists or newspapers to bear the costs of defamation or insult proceedings as a form of sanction. But the European Court has provided clear guidance that unreasonably disproportionate monetary penalties in cases of defamatory statements violate the right to freedom of expression.[643] For instance in one case that came before the European Court, model Naomi Campbell was awarded the equivalent of over 4,000 Euros in damages against a newspaper that published a series of stories about her drug addiction therapy.[644] The UK court also held the newspaper liable for Campbell's legal fees, which included a 'success fee' that almost doubled the base legal costs to over 1.3 million Euros.[645] The European Court ruled that the success fee scheme constituted a 'disproportionate' interference with the right to freedom of expression by discouraging newspapers and other media organizations from publishing legitimate information or promoting the early settlement of defendable claims—and 'exceeded even the broad margin of appreciation accorded to the government in such matters'.[646] It has also emphasized that the cumulative effect of penalties must 'show moderation in interfering with rights'.[647] Similarly, the African Court on Human and Peoples' Rights has ruled that the cumulative effect of 'the payment of a fine, damages, interests and costs' must not 'excessively exceed the income' of the speaker.[648]

6.2.4. Deprivation of other rights

The European and African Courts have considered that deprivation of the right to practise journalism may be an impermissible restriction on freedom of expression. The European Court considered a one-year ban on working as a journalist in a defamation and insult case was 'particularly severe and could not in any circumstances have been justified by the mere risk of the applicants' reoffending'.[649] And the African Court considered in a defamation case that the suspension of a weekly newspaper for six months

---

[642] IACtHR, *'The Last Temptation of Christ' (Olmedo-Bustos et al.) v. Chile* (Series C, no. 73), 5 February 2001, §70 (finding a violation of article 13 where Chile had established a system of prior censorship of films and a film was censored for and in the name of Jesus Christ and the Catholic Church).

[643] ECtHR, *Tolstoy Miloslavsky v. United Kingdom* (App. no. 18139/91), 13 July 1995, §35; ECtHR, *Steel v. United Kingdom* (App. no. 68416/01), 15 February 2005, §96.

[644] ECtHR, *MGN Limited v. United Kingdom* (App. no. 39401/04), 18 January 2011, §§18–19.

[645] Ibid., §56. See s. II.1.5.2. (Civil penalties).

[646] Ibid., §§217, 219. To give effect to the *MGN Limited* decision, in April 2013 the United Kingdom reformed its domestic laws to ensure that lawyers' success fees would no longer be recoverable from losing parties in most civil litigation; in November 2018, the UK Government announced the abolishment of the recoverable success fee regime in respect of defamation and privacy claims. Lord Keen of Elie, 'Statement made on 29 November 2018' (UK Parliament, 29 November 2018).

[647] ECtHR, *Nikowitz and Verlagsgruppe News GmbH v. Austria* (App. no. 5266/03), 22 February 2007, §27.

[648] ACtHPR, *Konaté v. Burkina Faso* (App. no. 4/2013), 5 December 2014, §171.

[649] ECtHR (GC), *Cumpǎnǎ v. Romania* (App. no. 33348/96), 17 December 2004, §118. See also ECtHR, *Stomakhin v. Russia* (App. no. 52273/07), 9 May 2018, §129 (three-year ban coupled with a five-year prison term for a journalist convicted of glorifying terrorism and advocating violence and hatred 'cannot but be regarded as an extremely harsh measure warranting very convincing considerations'). See ch. 6 (Terrorism Laws).

was not necessary to protect the rights and reputation of the prosecutor who had been criticized in its articles.[650]

Deprivation of other rights, such as the right to vote or travel, have also been considered unnecessary and excessive.[651] In a defamation and insult case, the European Court held that depriving convicted journalists of certain rights including the right to vote, to practice a profession, and parental rights was 'inappropriate ... and not justified by the nature of the offences for which the applicants had been held criminally liable'.[652] Similarly, the Human Rights Committee and Inter-American Court have found that travel bans imposed on journalists during criminal defamation proceedings constituted unnecessary and excessive punishment and contributed to a violation of freedom of expression.[653]

IV. Recommendations

The following conclusions and recommendations are based on the standards established by one or more international human rights bodies that best strike the balance between the right to freedom of expression and competing rights, in particular the right to reputation. On issues that have limited, divergent or no international practice, we have based our recommendations on best practices in domestic jurisdictions, emerging standards, and/or cogent recommendations by experts and civil society. The recommendations apply to defamation and similar laws such as insult laws, *lèse-majesté* laws, and sedition or treason laws where these laws seek to target insulting speech.[654] The recommendations are intended to be cumulative: they should all be implemented to ensure that restrictions to political speech comply with minimum international standards.

The topline recommendation is that states should decriminalize these laws and impose proportionate civil liability only. This is at odds with the current state of laws around the world, which still—in 160 countries—provide for such penalties, and many—particularly in Asia—are in regular use against opposition figures and the media.[655]

A second key recommendation is that public interest speech (including speech about public officials and public authorities) should receive greater protection from defamation liability than other speech—something that is also at odds with the laws and practices of states around the world that provide *less* instead of *more* protection for speech about political leaders and state institutions. We propose that plaintiffs suing on matters of public interest should bear the burden of showing that the allegations are false and that the speaker was at fault. Similarly, states should consider requiring that

---

[650] ACtHPR, *Konaté v. Burkina Faso* (App. no. 4/2013), 5 December 2014, §169.
[651] See s. II.1.5.3. (Other penalties).
[652] ECtHR (GC), *Cumpănă v. Romania* (App. no. 33348/96), 17 December 2004, §117.
[653] HRC, *Marques de Morais v. Angola* (Comm. no. 1128/2002), 29 March 2005, §6.8; IACtHR, *Canese v. Paraguay* (Series C, no. 111), 31 August 2004, §106.
[654] See ch. 1 (Introduction).
[655] See s. II (State Practice).

a plaintiff prove a higher degree of fault on the part of the speaker in matters of public interest speech. These additional burdens should apply because speech on matters of public interest lies at the heart of democracy, and is therefore deserving of the greatest protection. We also recommend that 'public interest speech' be broadly defined.

A. Overarching recommendation

1. States should decriminalize offences such as criminal defamation, insult (including *lèse-majesté* laws) and seditious libel. There should be no criminal penalties imposed for defamatory or insulting political speech, and imprisonment is never justifiable in response to such speech.

We recommend that defamation laws should be civil only, and that laws imposing criminal sanctions for harm to reputation should be abolished.[656] This recommendation is consistent with the emerging consensus among international human rights bodies, and the broad trend in certain regions, to decriminalize defamation.[657] And international human rights bodies generally agree that imprisonment is never an appropriate penalty under defamation or insult laws.[658] The OSCE Representative has suggested that 'de-prisonment' of defamation can be an intermediary step on the way to 'de-criminalisation' and 'de-harshening' of criminal and civil defamation laws; this is a possible incremental approach.[659]

The invocation of the criminal process itself for public interest speech is objectionable. When journalists face the prospect of being arrested and detained for political speech, this has a deterrent effect on the investigation and reportage of critical, investigative journalism on matters of public interest.[660] Indeed, even in jurisdictions in which prosecutors rarely make use of such laws, their mere existence has a deterrent and corrosive effect on freedom and democracy.[661]

Although our recommendation is that all states should decriminalize defamation, in states that nevertheless maintain some form of offence for insulting or defamatory language (in violation of international law), it is recommended that any prosecution of a journalist for speech related to political matters should be subject to authorization at a high-level, such as by a specially-appointed independent commissioner, the Attorney-General or an equivalent official in the domestic system, taking into account

---

[656] This includes for laws on *lèse-majesté, desacato,* disrespect for authority, disrespect for flags and symbols, defamation of the head of state or public institutions (such as the army or judiciary), the protection of the honour of public officials, and sedition.
[657] See ss III. (International Standards) and II.1.5.1. (Criminal penalties).
[658] See s. III. (International Standards).
[659] M. Haraszti, 'Preface', in A. Karlsreiter & H. Vuokko (eds), *Ending the Chilling Effect—Working to Repeal Criminal Libel and Insult Laws* (OSCE 2004), 9. OSCE, Communique by the OSCE Representative on Freedom of the Media on criminal defamation laws protecting foreign heads of state (2016) Communiqué No.5/2016; OSCE, *Defamation and Insult Laws in the OSCE Region: A Comparative Study* (2017).
[660] See e.g., ECtHR, *Şaphin Alpay v. Turkey* (App. no. 16538/17), 20 March 2018, §182; IACtHR, *Álvarez Ramos v. Venezuela* (Series C, no. 380), 30 August 2019, §§121–122. See s. III.6. (Penalties).
[661] See s. III.6.1.1.2 (Applicability of penalty of imprisonment for defamatory or insulting speech).

the public interest pre-charge.[662] This may help to reduce abuses by lower-level police or prosecutors.

Our remaining recommendations are premised on the basis that defamation laws are decriminalized and apply to statements which give rise to *civil* liability.

B. Defining elements of a civil wrong

2. Laws prohibiting defamatory, insulting or seditious speech must be public and accessible and drafted with sufficient precision such that their requirements are understandable and that the consequences of law are foreseeable to the public.

Defamation laws should:

- provide clear definitions of what constitutes a civil wrong, whether enshrined in statute, case law or legal doctrine (depending on the legal system involved);
- strictly delineate the elements of the civil wrong including by specifying the intent or fault that is required by the speaker to trigger liability, the type and degree of harm that must be proven by the plaintiff and the causal link between the speech and the harm; and
- specify that the meaning of the words used by the speaker is to be determined objectively, i.e., how the words would have been understood by reasonable members of the audience of the speech and not the subjective understanding of the audience.[663]

Vague concepts and ambiguous terms such as 'seditious intention' are unlikely to satisfy the requirement that restrictions on speech must be 'prescribed by law'.[664]

3. States should adopt an objective standard of fault equivalent to at least a negligence standard in laws that impose civil remedies for defamatory, insulting or seditious speech and a standard of at least gross negligence in cases of speech relating to matters of public interest.

International standards mandate that laws protecting reputation from being harmed by a false allegation must require an element of fault on the part of the speaker to qualify as a necessary restriction on freedom of expression.[665] The requirement of fault should extend to all the elements of a plaintiff's cause of action in cases involving such speech, including the falsity of the speech and the harm caused by the speech.[666]

---

[662] UNESCO & International Association of Prosecutors, *Guidelines for Prosecutors on Cases of Crimes Against Journalists* (2020), 8.
[663] See s. III.1. (Legality).
[664] See s. III.1. (Legality).
[665] See s. III.3.1. (Intent).
[666] We also recommend that the plaintiff bears the burden of proving falsity and fault as well as the other elements of the cause of action on the part of the defendant in public interest cases. Laws that proceed on the presumption of falsity may lead to a chilling effect on freedom of expression on matters of public interest: see Milo (n

At one end of the spectrum, there are laws that punish the speaker regardless of fault. These are commonly referred to as strict liability laws and are antithetical to freedom of expression. Laws which hold the speaker strictly liable for what is written or said on a matter of public interest are clearly incompatible with international standards.[667]

At the other end of the spectrum is the 'actual malice' rule adopted by the US Supreme Court.[668] The rule, as developed in subsequent cases, requires that in relation to claims brought by public officials and figures, the plaintiff must show that the speaker acted with knowledge of the falsity of the statement, or with 'reckless disregard' for the possibility of falsity.[669] This threshold is subjective—relating to what was in the mind of the speaker[670]— and is often very difficult to prove.[671] 'In effect, public officials and public figures must establish that publishers lied and they must do so to a standard of proof higher than the balance of probabilities'.[672]

While *Sullivan* has rightly been celebrated around the world as a landmark freedom of expression case, and the 'actual malice' standard has been recommended as the appropriate standard for public interest speech by the UN Human Rights Committee, international law recognizes that there are also other ways of providing a protective threshold for speech.[673]

Our recommendation is that states should adopt an objective standard of fault, which is at least negligence, and consider a higher objective standard of fault such as gross negligence in cases involving speech relating to matters of public interest.[674] This should be an element of the claim that the plaintiff has to establish. A higher objective *mens rea* standard—such as gross negligence—for public interest speech ensures that priority is given to such speech, consistently with international standards which emphasize its protection given its importance in a democracy.[675] This means

---

47) 164–183. See also Article 19, *Defining Defamation* (n 416) Principle 10; J. Rowbottom, *Media Law* (Hart 2018), 53; T. Weir, *Tort Law* (OUP 2002), 168.

[667] See s. II.3.1. (Intent). See also the rejection of strict liability for the media by the South African Supreme Court of Appeal in *National Media Ltd v. Bogoshi* [1998] ZASCA 94, 29 September 1998.

[668] US Supreme Court, *New York Times v. Sullivan* 376 U.S. 254, 9 March 1964.

[669] Moreover, 'actual malice' must be proved by the plaintiff with clear and convincing evidence (US Supreme Court, *New York Times v. Sullivan* 376 U.S. 254, 9 March 1964, 254–255). For a useful summary of the post-*Sullivan* developments and its application, see R. L. Weaver & others, *The Right to Speak Ill: Defamation, Reputation and Free Speech* (Carolina Academic Press 2006), 49–74. The 'actual malice' rule applies to the falsity element of the plaintiff's cause of action. US defamation cases not involving public figures require at least negligence as to the impact of the statement, although precise standards vary by state: See s. III.1.2. (Intent).

[670] The standard has been described as 'subjective awareness of probable falsity': US Supreme Court, *Gertz v. Robert Welch Inc* 418 U.S. 323, 25 June 1974, 335, n. 6. The speaker must have 'in fact entertained serious doubts' as to the truth of the allegations: US Supreme Court, *St. Amant v. Thompson* 390 U.S. 727, 29 April 1968, 731.

[671] C. J. Glasser Jr., *International Libel and Privacy Handbook: A Global Reference for Journalists, Publishers, Webmasters, and Lawyers* (Bloomberg 2006), 52.

[672] A. Kenyon, 'Defamation Law, *Sullivan* and the Shape of Free Speech' in A. Stone & F. Schauer (eds), *The Oxford Handbook of Freedom of Speech* (OUP 2021), 272.

[673] Milo (n 47) 188–199; see also J. Campbell, 'The law of defamation in flux: Fault and the contemporary Commonwealth accommodation of the right to reputation with the right of free expression' in A. Koltay (ed), *Media Freedom and Regulation in the New Media World* (Wolters Kluwer Ltd 2014), 260–261.

[674] Negligence is required in a number of jurisdictions, typically in the form of a reasonable publication defence: see s. III.4.3. (Reasonable publication).

[675] An example of the gross negligence approach is the standard adopted in New York state in defamation matters where private plaintiffs sue on matters of public concern: see Kenyon (n 672) 277, n. 51. It also was proposed to be the appropriate fault standard in South African law in non-media cases: *Marais v. Groenewald* 2001 (1) SA 634 (T), 646. See s. III.4.2. (Public interest).

speech concerning matters of public interest, objectively defined and regardless of whether they concern public officials, authorities, public figures or private persons.[676] For speech on matters of public interest, there is a higher value placed on 'uninhibited, robust and wide-open public debate' and a desire to avoid a chilling effect that would dampen the vigour of that debate.[677] 'Public interest' speech should be defined broadly and independent courts should determine whether the speech at issue qualifies, against the background of the broad interpretation.[678] Public interest speech includes but goes beyond political speech—speech about government bodies, any of the branches of government and concerning the conduct of public officials.[679]

This approach is an alternative to the 'actual malice' standard, which sets a high subjective bar, and the negligence standard, which sets a lower objective one. It is also an alternative to the European Court's approach to the 'responsible journalism' standard, which focuses on the identity of the speaker and has led to conflicting jurisprudence.[680] And these objective standards—negligence and gross negligence—protect freedom of expression, provided the speaker does not act negligently, but also provides some protection for reputation by encouraging the speaker to take reasonable steps to ascertain the accuracy of the allegations being published.

4. If states do not follow the recommendation that they should require negligence or gross negligence as an element of the civil wrong, they should at least provide a defence of 'reasonable publication' for statements of fact.

If states do not follow the recommendation that they should require negligence or gross negligence as an element of the civil wrong (see recommendation 3, above), states should at least provide the defence of reasonable publication for all defamation laws, pursuant to which a speaker will not be liable if she acted reasonably in publishing the allegation in all the circumstances at the time of publication.[681] This should include a review of steps

---

[676] See definitions of 'public interest' in ECtHR (GC), *Satakunnan Markkinapörssi Oy v. Finland* (App. no. 931/13), 27 June 2017, §171; UK House of Lords, *Jameel v. Wall Street Journal Europe (No. 2)* [2006] UKHL 44, 11 October 2006, §147; US Supreme Court, *Snyder v. Phelps* 562 U.S. 443, 2 March 2011, 6–7; Independent Press Standards Organisation, *Editor's Code of Practice* (2021), 'The Public Interest'. On the relevant of public nature of persons involved, see Brennan J in US Supreme Court, *Rosenbloom v. Metromedia* 403 U.S. 29, 7 June 1971, 43; Canadian Supreme Court, *Grant v. Torstar Corporation* 2009 SCC 61, 22 December 2009, §102; South African Supreme Court of Appeal, *National Media Ltd v. Bogoshi* [1998] ZASCA 94, 29 September 1998, 29; ECtHR (GC), *Von Hannover v. Germany (No. 2)* (App. nos. 40660/08 & 60641/08), 7 February 2012, §§108–113. See also Milo (n 47), Chapter IV.

[677] Kenyon (n 672) 269, 272. See s. IV.B.9. (Recommendations).

[678] UK House of Lords, *Reynolds v. Times Newspapers Ltd* [2001] 2 AC 127, 28 October 1999, 203 (Lord Nicholls: '[t]he court has the advantage of being impartial, independent of government, and accustomed to deciding disputed issues of fact and whether an occasion is privileged. No one has suggested that some other institution would be better suited for this task').

[679] Milo (n 47) 144.

[680] See ch. 1 (Introduction), s. II.3.2.5. (Relevance of whether the speaker is a journalist).

[681] This is akin to the responsible or reasonable journalism defences found in a number of domestic jurisdictions: see s. II.1.4.3. (Reasonable publication). England and Wales Defamation Act 2013 s. 4; Australian New South Wales Defamation Amendment Act 2020 s. 29A(1)(a)(b); New Zealand Court of Appeal, *Durie v. Gardiner* [2018] NZCA 278, 31 July 2018; Canadian Supreme Court, *Grant v. Torstar Corporation* 2009 SCC 61, 22 December 2009, §98; South African Supreme Court of Appeal, *National Media Ltd v. Bogoshi* [1998] ZASCA 94, 29 September 1998, 30. The term 'reasonable' is preferred to 'responsible' as it is arguable that 'responsible' threshold is higher: Australia's Right to Know (ARTK), Submission To The Council Of Attorneys-General Defamation Working Party Regarding The Model Defamation Amendment Provisions 2020 (Consultation Draft) (2020), 12.

taken collectively by journalists, editors and publishers in the case of a joint publication, rather than requiring that all persons separately satisfy the defence.[682] It should not be a requirement to invoke the defence that the speech is on a matter of public interest but if public interest speech is involved a court may require a lower threshold to be met.[683]

Such a defence (or its inverse—liability based on negligence as one of the elements of the claim)[684] serves to promote responsibility on the part of speakers while respecting freedom of expression. This defence is also consistent with the European Court's 'responsible journalism' principle, but avoids the Court's confusing jurisprudence which rests on the identity of the speaker, and in some cases has resulted in lower levels of protection for those acting as the 'public watchdog'.[685]

5. **Only statements that are likely to or have caused direct, immediate and serious harm to reputation should be capable of giving rise to liability.**

The plaintiff should be required to prove it is objectively likely that the statement will cause serious harm to reputation before it can result in legal liability. Although international human rights bodies have not settled on a consistent harm formulation, a 'serious harm' requirement reflects the UN Human Rights Committee, European Court and Inter-American bodies' existing jurisprudence.[686] This threshold is also found in the Defamation Act 2013 of England and Wales,[687] and has been followed in recent amendments to Australian defamation laws.[688] The Human Rights Committee has also made clear that states should ensure that there is a 'direct and immediate' causal link between serious harm and the speech.[689]

Lawmakers may include factors for a court to take into account when determining whether it is objectively likely that the publication will cause direct and immediate serious harm, including:

- 'seriousness of the imputation or imputations conveyed by the matter;
- extent of the publication;
- audience of the publication; and
- circumstances of the publication'.[690]

---

[682] See, along these lines: UK High Court of England and Wales, Queen's Bench Division, *Economou v. de Freitas* [2017] EMLR 4 (upheld by the Court of Appeal, [2019] EMLR 7); *Hays Plc v. Hartley* [2010] EWHC 1068 (QB), 17 May 2010.

[683] See s. IV.B.3. (Recommendations).

[684] Requiring negligence or a higher standard of intent is the preferred course—See s. IV.B.3. (Recommendations).

[685] See ch. 1 (Introduction), s. II.3.2.5. (Relevance of whether the speaker is a journalist); see s. III.4.3. (Reasonable publication).

[686] See s. III.3.3. (Level of harm caused by the speech). See, e.g., HRC, *Kozlov v. Belarus* (Comm. no. 1986/2010), 24 July 2014, §7.6 (finding a violation of Art. 19 of the ICCPR where harm to reputation was 'only of a limited nature'); ECtHR (GC), *Axel Springer AG v. Germany* (App. no. 39954/08), 7 February 2012, §83 (holding that an attack on reputation must 'attain a certain level of seriousness'); IACtHR, *Usón Ramírez v. Venezuela* (Series C, no. 207), 20 November 2009, §§73–75.

[687] England and Wales Defamation Act 2013 s. 1(1). See s. II. (State Practice). The statute allowed both parties to introduce evidence outside of the allegedly defamatory statement to show (or rebut) this level of harm.

[688] New South Wales Defamation Act 2005 s. 10A. Although harm to reputation is traditionally presumed to arise on publication of defamatory statement in many common law-based systems: See s. III.3.3. (Level of harm caused by the speech).

[689] HRC, General Comment No. 34 (2011), §35. See s. III.3.2. (Causal link between the speech and the harm).

[690] Law Council of Australia, Review of Model Defamation Provisions (2019) 3622, §218.

A 'serious harm' threshold 'discourages frivolous, vexatious or trivial claims'.[691] Without such a threshold, filtering of spurious claims where there is no real harm to reputation does not occur until trial—by which point significant time and costs may have been incurred.[692] The 'serious harm' threshold could be combined with pre-trial procedures to have a bifurcated process where evidence of actual or objectively likely harm should be proved before a case can proceed, in appropriate cases. This should not exclude the possibility of the question of harm being raised later in the proceedings, on the initiative of the judge or on a party's application.

Finally, defamatory or insulting speech must be published to at least one-third party (i.e., not the speaker and not the subject of the speech) to attract liability. A speaker may also be responsible for the republication of an allegation which they have caused or authorized.[693]

6. **States should provide a defence of substantial truth or require that falsity be proved as an element of the claim in any law allowing civil penalties for defamatory, insulting or seditious speech.**

International human rights law requires national laws should provide for a defence of truth for the publication of defamatory or insulting statements of fact or alternatively require falsity to be proved as an element of the claim.[694] States should provide that it is a defence to an action for defamation or insult for the defendant to show that 'the imputation conveyed by the statement complained of is substantially true' or alternatively require falsity to be proved as an element of the claim.[695] Errors that do not impact on the main thrust or sting of the statement should not result in liability: what is required is proof of substantial truth, namely that the thrust of the publication or its sting is true.

The truth of the statement should be assessed on all evidence that the defendant discloses at the time of the trial, and not only what was known to be true at the time of publication. Evidence of post-publication facts and events should be available to support a truth defence. The basis for this is that a plaintiff who does not deserve a good reputation should not be entitled to vindication merely because the defendant did not at the time of publication have the necessary evidence to prove truth.[696] If the defendant is able to gather that evidence after publication, the defendant should be permitted to argue that the plaintiff should not succeed because he does not deserve his good reputation.

---

[691] Ibid., §207.
[692] See P. Bartlett & others, 'National defamation law reform: Changes considered' (Minter Ellison, 12 August 2020).
[693] See s. III.3.3.2. (Measuring harm: the extent to which the speech is public).
[694] See s. III.4.1. (Truth). See also Article 19, *Defining Defamation* (n 416) 21; COE, *Recommendation CM/Rec(2016)4 of the Committee of Ministers to members States on the protection of journalism and safety of journalists and other media actors* (2016), 6. The burden of proving falsity should rest with the plaintiff in cases involving public interest speech: see s. III.4.1. (Truth) and s. III.4.5. (Opinion).
[695] England and Wales Defamation Act 2013 s. 2(1).
[696] Milo (n 47) 58.

The defence of truth (or failure to prove falsity as an element of the claim) should be a complete bar to liability for the publication of defamatory statements of fact, and questions such as whether the publication was in the public interest should not be relevant to this defence. A truth defence should also be available to a defendant even if they acted with malice (i.e., spite/ill-will or recklessly as to whether the statement was true or false).[697]

7. States should exempt opinions from liability in any law allowing civil penalties for defamatory, insulting or seditious speech; this can be done by requiring that a statement be 'factual' to be actionable; or at least be providing a defence of opinion.

The defence of opinion, referred to in a number of jurisdictions as 'fair comment',[698] is recognized in international law[699] and in multiple jurisdictions.[700]

It is best practice to include this defence in national laws so that defamation and similar laws do not penalize speech that is an expression of opinion and not a factual statement.[701] The purpose is 'to give the widest scope possible for the freedom of expression in relation to opinions and to allow for comment on a wide range of public as opposed to private matters'.[702] As the UN Human Rights Committee has framed it, defamation laws 'should not be applied with regard to those forms of expression that are not, of their nature, subject to verification'.[703]

The opinion defence (or a requirement to show that a statement is factual) should be available to a speaker who is at least able to show that the relevant statement is an opinion rather than a statement of fact. This assessment is based on the understanding of the reasonable person.[704]

---

[697] M. Socha, 'Double Standard: A Comparison of British and American Defamation Law' (2004) 23 *Penn State International Law Review* 471, 476.

[698] McGonagle (n 500) 45; IACmHR Special Rapporteur E. Lanza, *Annual Report of the Office of the Special Rapporteur for Freedom of Expression: Volume II* (2015) OEA/Ser.L/V/II, Doc. 48/15, §289 (noting similarity of the Canadian fair comment defence with the opinion defence). Some jurisdictions have a related good faith defence or good faith element: see, e.g., Indian Penal Code 1860 Chapter XXI s. 499 (Defamation); Israeli Defamation Law 5725-1965 Art. 15 (1964–1965) (Isr.), ss 4, 10.

[699] UDHR Art. 19; ECHR Art. 10 includes freedom to hold opinions in the right to freedom of expression; ECtHR, *Dichand v. Austria* (App. no. 29271/95), 26 February 2002, §42. The Inter-American Court has held that an 'opinion cannot be the object of any sanction': IACtHR, *Usón Ramírez v. Venezuela* (Series C, no. 207), 20 November 2009, §86, citing IACtHR, *Kimel v. Argentina* (Series C, no. 177), 2 May 2008, §93.

[700] See s. II. (State Practice). It is more accurate to refer to the defence as 'opinion' and not 'fair comment'. As the South African Constitutional Court has put it, 'the defence "fair comment" is misleading ... Criticism is protected even if extreme, unjust, unbalanced, exaggerated and prejudiced, so long as it expresses an honestly held opinion, without malice, on a matter of public interest on facts that are true'. South African Constitutional Court, *The Citizen 1978 (Pty) Ltd v. McBride* [2011] ZACC 11, 8 April 2011, §§82–83.

[701] UN Special Rapporteur on Freedom of Opinion and Expression, OSCE Representative on Freedom of the Media, OAS Special Rapporteur on Freedom of Expression and ACmHPR Special Rapporteur on Freedom of Expression and Access to Information, *Joint Declaration on Freedom of Expression and "Fake News", Disinformation and Propaganda* (2017) FOM.GAL/3/17, §2b; COE, *Recommendation CM/Rec(2016)4 of the Committee of Ministers to members States on the protection of journalism and safety of journalists and other media actors* (2016), 6; Article 19, *Defining Defamation* (n 416) Principle 13.

[702] McGonagle (n 500) 45.

[703] HRC, General Comment No. 34 (2011), §47.

[704] England and Wales Defamation Act 2013 Explanatory Notes s. 3, §21; UK High Court of England and Wales, Queen's Bench Division, *Koutsogiannis v. The Random House Group Ltd* [2020] 4 WLR 25, §16(iii).

Many common law jurisdictions require, in addition, that to be protected, the opinion must relate to a matter of public interest; and must be based on proper material or foundation.[705] But these two elements of the defence should not necessarily be absolute requirements for the defence to apply; in the European Court of Human Rights, for instance, the requirement that a proper foundation must exist for the opinion is sometimes relaxed.[706] Mixed statements of fact and opinion may give rise to defences of opinion and substantial truth or fair and accurate reporting.

When an opinion or 'value judgment' is concerned, international standards recognize that a court can consider the adequacy of the factual basis for a value judgment, though the weight given to the factual basis will vary depending on the nature of the statement.[707] For instance, statements that are satirical or relate to matters of public interest should be given additional protection.[708]

8. States should exempt accurate reports of official proceedings from any liability.

International human rights law recognizes that reports of official proceedings such as parliamentary or judicial proceedings should generally constitute protected speech.[709] There should also be protection for reports of parliamentary and judicial proceedings and similar proceedings. Some states also recognize a defence of 'neutral reportage' in cases 'where the publisher has neutrally and disinterestedly reported in an even-handed way attributed allegations which are of legitimate and topical interest to the readers of the publication but has not adopted those allegations as being true or otherwise embellished them'.[710] This mirrors the European court's helpful decision in the leading *Jersild v. Denmark* case and reflects the principles set out in these recommendations.[711]

9. In order to be legally actionable, the impugned statement must refer to the person who seeks to sue.

In accordance with international standards, in order to be an action in defamation, insult, seditious libel or similar laws, the statement must refer to a particular person, whether a corporate person or an individual.[712]

10. There should be no special protection for public officials or authorities—on the contrary, speech should benefit from greater protection when it is on a matter of public interest.

Laws that afford greater protection from defamation or insult for any public official or authority to protect their reputation (or 'honour') are not consistent with international

---

[705] C. J. Glasser Jr., *International Libel and Privacy Handbook: A Global Reference for Journalists, Publishers, Webmasters, and Lawyers* (LexisNexis 2020), 7.01[9].
[706] See s. III. (International Standards).
[707] See s. III.4.5. (Opinion).
[708] See s. III.4.5. (Opinion).
[709] See s. III.4.4. (Accurate reporting of official documents). See also Glasser Jr. (n 705), 7.01 [7].
[710] See s. II.1.4.4. (Fair and accurate reporting of official documents). UK Court of Appeal, *Charman v. Orion Books* [2008] 1 All ER 750, 11 October 2007, §43; Defamation Act 2013 s. 4(3).
[711] ECtHR (GC), *Jersild v. Denmark* (App. no. 15890/89), 23 September 1994.
[712] See s. III.3.3.1. (Measuring harm: subject matter of speech or identity of the target).

law.[713] Instead, the general rule is that such officials and authorities must have a high tolerance of criticism, and no special protections for their reputations should apply under the law.

C. Procedural Recommendations

11. Claims seeking civil remedies for defamation, insult and seditious libel should have a strong link with the jurisdiction of the forum in which the plaintiff sues in order to proceed.

'Libel tourism' can create unpredictability and risk journalists being drawn into costly legal proceedings abroad, particularly in a world of electronic communications and online media. It is exacerbated if the 'single publication rule' does not apply.[714] As the Council of Europe has recommended, claims should only be brought where there is a strong link between the jurisdiction (or jurisdictions) where the plaintiff sues and the plaintiff's reputation.[715] A strong link exists if the plaintiff has a meaningful reputation in the jurisdiction and the plaintiff's reputation has suffered substantial harm in that jurisdiction.[716] Personal jurisdiction over the defendant also needs to be established according to the laws of the relevant state.

12. Defamation claims should have a limitation period of no longer than one year from the date of publication, unless the plaintiff can show that they were not in fact aware of the publication and a reasonable person would not have been aware of it. The single publication rule should apply.

Limitation periods vary considerably among states, from three months to as long as 20 years.[717] It is recommended that a 12-month limitation period should be a maximum to strike a balance between allowing plaintiffs enough time to prepare a claim while not creating a chilling effect on speech.[718]

To be effective and avoid uncertainty, this limitation period should be combined with the single publication rule. The rule—which is a feature of US law—provides that 'the publication of a book, periodical or newspaper containing defamatory matter gives rise to but one cause of action for libel, which accrues at the time of the original publication, and that the statute of limitations runs from that date. It is no longer the law that every sale or delivery of a copy of the publication creates a new cause of action'.[719]

---

[713] See s. III.4.2. (Public interest).
[714] See s. IV.C.12. (Recommendations).
[715] COE, *Study on forms of liability and jurisdictional issues in the application of civil and administrative defamation laws in Council of Europe member states* (2019) DGI(2019)04, 14.
[716] COE, Declaration of the Committee of Ministers on the Desirability of International Standards dealing with Forum Shopping in respect of Defamation, 'Libel Tourism', to ensure Freedom of Expression (2012); COE, *Study on forms of liability and jurisdictional issues in the application of civil and administrative defamation laws in Council of Europe member states* (2019) DGI(2019)04, 36–37; Article 19, *Defining Defamation* (n 416) 17, 26.
[717] See s. II. (State Practice) and s. III.5. (Right to a fair trial).
[718] See, e.g., ECtHR, *Steel v. United Kingdom* (App. no. 68416/01), 15 February 2005.
[719] US District Court (District of Columbia), *Ogden v. Association of the United States Army* 177 F.Supp. 498, 14 October 1959, 502. The single publication rule only applies to the original publisher, of course, and not to third

Applied to internet publication, the effect is that the cause of action accrues when the publication is first published online.

13. States should enact anti-SLAPP legislation to allow speakers to strike out defamation/insult claims brought to silence speech relating to matters of public interest. This legislation should include provisions on early dismissal, allowing speakers to file an application to strike out unsubstantiated claims.

Speakers should be able to ask a court to dismiss claims that are clearly unsubstantiated, frivolous and are brought with a view to silencing public debate at an early stage.[720] Best practices in anti-SLAPP legislation include dismissal of a SLAPP as early as possible in the pre-trial process, such as allowing a speaker to file an application to strike out the complaint within 30 days of service,[721] and access to legal representation, ideally pro bono or via legal aid.

D. Permissible Civil Penalties

14. Proportionate civil sanctions in defamation, insult and seditious libel cases requires that damages should not be excessively high, relative to the means of the defendant, and any form of punitive or exemplary damages should be abolished.

Excessive civil penalties for defamatory or insulting speech are inconsistent with the right to freedom of expression and should be modified.[722] According to international instruments, 'pecuniary awards should be strictly proportionate to the actual harm caused and the law should prioritize the use of a range of non-pecuniary remedies'.[723] And there should never be higher penalties for speech about public officials or

---

parties who repeat the publication. Although the single publication rule is state-specific, the majority of US states follow it: see, e.g., US Court of Appeals Seventh Circuit, *Pippen v. NBCUniversal Media, LLC* 724 F.3d 610, 21 August 2013, 615.

[720] States should also allow for case management mechanisms, such as offer of amends procedures, to assist in resolving cases before they reach a substantive trial or other hearing in the courts, thus avoiding expensive and time-consuming litigation. Such pre-trial procedures are consistent with states' positive freedom of expression obligations and will assist in reducing the chilling effect of litigation on media freedom. See, e.g., US California Civil Code Div 1 Part 2 s. 48a; Canadian Nova Scotia Defamation Act RSNS 1989 c 122; UK Court of Appeal, *Warren v. Random House Group Ltd* (Nos 1–3) [2009] QB 600, 16 July 2008; UK High Court of England and Wales, Queen's Bench Division, *Tesco Stores Ltd v. Guardian News & Media Ltd* and Rusbridger [2009] EMLR 5, 29 July 2008. See, e.g., the offer of amends procedure reduced damages from £85,000 to £49,000 (approximately 107,000 USD to 62,000 USD) in UK High Court of England and Wales, *Gilham v. MGN Limited* [2020] EWHC 2217 (QB), 12 August 2020.
[721] US California Code of Civil Procedure s. 425.16.
[722] See s. III.6.2 (Civil penalties). See, e.g., HRC, General Comment No. 34 (2011), §47; IACtHR, *Tristán Donoso v. Panama* (Series C, no. 193), 27 January 2009, §129.
[723] UN Special Rapporteur on Freedom of Opinion and Expression & others, International Mechanisms for Promoting Freedom of Expression: Joint Declaration (2000).

authorities: such speech should receive additional protection, not penalties.[724] States should also consider providing for a maximum amount of damages (both compensatory and aggravated) for non-economic loss in laws on defamation, insult and seditious libel.[725] In determining quantum, courts should take into account the means of the speaker and, in the case of a journalist, whether the damages would bankrupt small and independent media.[726]

15. States should adopt measures to prohibit prior restraints on publication to protect public interest speech. Interim injunctions pending the hearing of the case should only be granted exceptionally. Final injunctions imposed after hearings on the merits should be narrowly tailored to prevent the harm caused by the publication.

With the exception of the Inter-American human rights system, international human rights bodies do not generally categorically prohibit prior restraints, but they acknowledge they are unlikely to be proportionate and call for the most careful scrutiny,[727] particularly in cases of public interest speech.[728] Interim injunctions imposed after publication while hearings on the merits are pending should only be available on an exceptional basis and provided the hearing takes place within a reasonable period after the injunction is granted.[729] Final injunctions after a full and fair hearing on the merits should be 'limited in application to the specific statements found to be defamatory and to the specific people found to have been responsible for the publication of those statements. It should be for the defendant to decide how to prevent further publication, for example by removing ... particular statements from a book';[730] and the injunctions should be proportionate in their timeframe.

---

[724] See s. III. (International Standards).
[725] Australian New South Wales Defamation Amendment Act 2020 s. 33 (however, there is no cap on awards for aggravated damages, which must be awarded separately to the amount of damages for non-economic loss: s. 35(2B). See also Article 19, *Defining Defamation* (n 416) 38.
[726] UN Special Rapporteur F. La Rue, *Report of the Special Rapporteur on the promotion and protection of the right to freedom of opinion and expression* (2012) UN Doc. A/HRC/20/17, §85. See also UN Special Rapporteur A. Hussain, *Civil and Political Rights Including The Question of Freedom of Expression* (2000) UN Doc. E/CN.4/2000/63, §52.
[727] But see ACHR Art. 13(2); see s. III.6.2.2. (Injunctions).
[728] See s. III. (International Standards).
[729] Article 19, *Defining Defamation* (n 416), Principle 20, providing that interim injunctions should only be applied where: (i) 'the plaintiff can show they would suffer irreparable damage—which could not be compensated—should further publication take place'; (ii) 'can demonstrate virtual certainty of success'; (iii) 'the statement was unarguably defamatory; and (iv) any potential defences are manifestly unfounded'.
[730] Ibid., Principle 21.

16. States should permit courts to grant other non-pecuniary remedies in appropriate cases such as, for example, alternatives to damages awards.

The law should allow courts to consider remedies that are non-pecuniary.[731] In appropriate cases, corrections, retractions, declarations of falsity and orders requiring rights of reply,[732] and publication of summaries of rulings, may be considered by courts—provided they are not disproportionate.[733] It would generally not be appropriate to ban someone from the practice of journalism.[734]

---

[731] UN Special Rapporteur F. La Rue, *Report of the Special Rapporteur on the promotion and protection of the right to freedom of opinion and expression* (2010) UN Doc. A/HRC/14/23, §83. See s. III.6.2.1 (Damages).

[732] The right of reply should apply only when publishing a correction is not sufficient to redress the damage suffered to the plaintiff's reputation. The reply should receive 'similar, but not necessarily identical, prominence to the original article' and it should not be used to introduce new issues or to comment on correct facts. Article 19, *Defining Defamation* (n 416), Principle 18.

[733] Milo (n 47) 267–278; cf. R. Carroll, 'Apologies and Corrections as Remedies for Serious Invasions of Privacy', in J.N.E. Varuhas & N.A. Moreham (eds), *Remedies for Breach of Privacy* (1st edn, Hart Publishing 2018), 224–231.

[734] A penalty involving a deprivation of the right to practice journalism is an inappropriate restriction on freedom of expression. ECtHR (GC), *Cumpănă v. Romania* (App. no. 33348/96), 17 December 2004, §§117–118; ACtHPR, *Konaté v. Burkina Faso* (App. no. 4/2013), 5 December 2014, §169. See s. III.6. (Penalties).

3

Hate Speech

Amal Clooney and Alice Gardoll

I. Introduction	153	1.3. Genocide Convention Article 3	178
II. State Practice	156	1.4. Mandatory restrictions at the regional level	180
1. Overview of Hate Speech Laws	156	1.5. Summary	182
1.1. Type of speech	156	2. Discretionary Restrictions on Hate Speech	183
1.2. Harm	158	2.1. Legality	185
1.3. Intent	159	2.2. Legitimacy	187
1.4. Exclusions, exceptions and defences	160	2.2.1. Human Rights Committee	187
1.5. Penalties	160	2.2.2. European Court of Human Rights	188
2. Application of Hate Speech Laws Around the World	161	2.2.3. Inter-American Court and Commission	190
2.1. Europe	161	2.2.4. African Charter	190
2.1.1. The Netherlands	161	2.3. Necessity	193
2.1.1.1. Wilders	161	2.3.1. Harm	194
2.1.1.2. Basebya	162	2.3.2. Intent	196
2.1.2. Austria	163	2.4. Exclusions, exceptions and defences	198
2.2. Asia Pacific	165	2.4.1. Truth	198
2.2.1. Indonesia	165	2.4.2. Opinion	198
2.2.2. Myanmar	165	2.4.3. Public interest	201
2.2.3. Pakistan	166	2.4.4. 'Responsible journalism'	202
2.3. North and South America	166	2.5. Penalties	204
2.3.1. Canada	166	IV. Key Divergences in International and Regional Guidance	207
2.3.2. United States	168		
2.4. Middle East and Africa	171	V. Approach of Private Companies to Online Hate Speech	208
2.4.1. Tunisia	171		
2.4.2. Saudi Arabia	172	VI. Recommendations	211
III. International Legal Standards	172		
1. Mandatory Restrictions on Hate Speech	173		
1.1. ICCPR Article 20	175		
1.2. CERD Article 4	177		

I. Introduction

States must protect individuals from violence and discrimination, including when such harm is triggered by hateful speech.[1] And this is increasingly urgent: hate speech spreads faster and wider than ever before; hate-motivated crimes have risen to their highest levels in more than a decade in the United States, and an upsurge in hate crimes

---

[1] The authors and editors would like to thank Professor Evelyn Aswad, Professor Sarah Cleveland and Professor David Kaye for their expert advice on an earlier version of this chapter and for their invaluable respective contributions to this field.

has been recorded across the world.[2] But the right to speak freely is an essential right, the foundation of a free and democratic society and a prerequisite 'for the full enjoyment of' our other human rights.[3] How should these rights be balanced?

International law provides an answer to this question in three human rights treaties—the International Covenant on Civil and Political Rights, the Convention on the Elimination of All Forms of Racial Discrimination and the Convention on the Prevention and Punishment of the Crime of Genocide—as well as regional human rights treaties covering Europe, Africa and the Americas. But unlike other types of speech, states can be *required* rather than simply permitted to penalize hate speech. Mandatory requirements to punish such speech—at least when it rises to the level of 'incitement'—are contained in article 20 of the ICCPR, article 4 of CERD, article 3 of the Genocide Convention, as well as in one regional treaty, article 13(5) of the American Convention on Human Rights.[4] But the harms that the speech must potentially incite vary, with 'violence', 'discrimination', or 'hostility' prohibited in the ICCPR; 'violence', 'discrimination', 'hatred' or 'contempt' prohibited under CERD;[5] and 'lawless violence' or 'other similar action' outlawed in the American Convention provision.

The targeted group also diverges, with CERD only applying to hatred based on racial, national or ethnic origin, as opposed to broader discriminatory grounds recognized in other treaties.[6] Finally, the penalties mandated by each treaty provision differ, with CERD, the Genocide Convention and the American Convention[7] requiring criminalization, and the ICCPR requiring civil sanctions only.[8] Many states have ratified more than one of these treaties, creating a web of obligations that adds to the complexity of states' compliance with these standards.

These treaties also regulate the circumstances under which states can, but are not required to, penalize hateful speech. Although these standards are phrased in similar terms in the treaties, there has been some divergence in practice in this area.[9] While the Human Rights Committee and the African and Inter-American regional human rights bodies have adopted similarly high standards to govern the permissible restrictions

---

[2] See, e.g., S. Haynes, 'This Isn't just a Problem for North America'. The Atlanta Shooting Highlights the Painful Reality of Rising Anti-Asian Violence Around the World' (Time, 22 March 2021). See also M. Yang, 'Hate crimes in US rise to highest level in 12 years, says FBI report' (The Guardian, 31 August 2021).

[3] HRC, General Comment No. 34 (2011), §§2–4.

[4] See ss III.1. (Mandatory Restrictions on Hate Speech) and III.1.4. (Mandatory restrictions at the regional level).

[5] Although 'contempt' does not appear in the text of the treaty, it has been interpreted by the CERD Committee, the body with jurisdiction to interpret and apply the treaty, as being encompassed by its provisions. See CERD Committee, General Recommendation No. 35 (2013), §§13, 25. See s. III.1.2. (CERD Article 4).

[6] See s. III.1.2. (CERD Article 4). See CERD Committee, General Recommendation No. 35 (2013), §13. Cf. ACHPR Art. 13(5); ICCPR Art. 20(2). See also ICCPR Art. 26.

[7] The Inter-American Court has rejected the use of criminal law in cases involving public interest speech but has not ruled on cases of hate speech specifically. See IACtHR, *Álvarez Ramos v. Venezuela* (Series C, no. 380), 30 August 2019, §§120–122; s. III.2.5. (Penalties).

[8] See s. III.1.1. (ICCPR Article 20), s. III.1.2. (CERD Article 4), s. III.1.4. (Mandatory restrictions at the regional level). See also HRC, *Rabbae v. The Netherlands* (Comm. no. 2124/2011), 14 July 2016, §10.4 ('article 20 (2) [ICCPR] does not expressly require the imposition of criminal penalties').

[9] E. Aswad & D. Kaye, 'Convergence & Conflict: Reflections on Global and Regional Human Rights Standards on Hate Speech' (2022) 20(3) *Northwestern Journal of Human Rights* 165, 186–209.

to speech, including stringent harm and intent requirements, the European Court of Human Rights has provided less protection to speech that is hateful.[10] This divergent approach can be attributed in part to the European Court's 'margin of appreciation' doctrine, which provides states with discretion to determine whether a 'pressing social need' makes a speech restriction 'necessary' to promote one of the objectives listed in article 10(2) of the European Convention on Human Rights.[11] And article 17 of the European Convention, which bars abusive claims, has been construed as a 'guillotine provision' that treats speech that is 'apt to destroy the fundamental values of the Convention' as being outside the scope of protection by the Court.[12] In other words, if the Court makes a threshold assessment that the speech at issue violates article 17, it will refuse to even consider whether it should be protected under the balancing test set out in article 10.

Around the world, laws regulating the punishment of hate speech are often vague and fail to address key elements such as the harm caused by the speech, the intent of the speaker and acceptable penalties for the speech. And yet such laws are usually criminal in nature.[13] This creates an unclear level of protection for targets of hate speech and makes such laws particularly susceptible to abuse by authoritarian regimes that use them to silence dissent.

This chapter sets out the minimum international standards that apply to states drafting, interpreting and applying hate speech laws. It also recommends which approach is preferable from a policy perspective where there has been an omission or international bodies have taken divergent views. It recommends that European Court jurisprudence should move closer to the international, more speech-protective approach to hate speech, particularly when criminal laws apply. It also proposes that hate speech should only be subject to criminal penalties where it 'incites the commission of criminal offences or acts of violence' or 'similar action',[14] ensuring that in other circumstances offensive and reprehensible speech is addressed using alternative means.[15] And the chapter concludes that a more unified approach would make the international human rights framework a more practical guide to both states and private companies operating in this area.

---

[10] See s. III.2. (Discretionary Restrictions on Hate Speech).
[11] See, e.g., ECtHR, *Zana v. Turkey* (App. no. 18954/91), 25 November 1997, §51; ECtHR (GC), *Stoll v. Switzerland* (App. no. 69698/01), 10 December 2007, §105, citing ECtHR, *Éditions Plon v. France* (App. no. 58148/00), 18 May 2004, §44; HRC, General Comment No. 34 (2011), §36.
[12] Article 17 provides that nothing in the Convention 'may be interpreted as implying ... any right to engage in any activity or perform any act aimed at the destruction of any of the rights and freedoms set forth herein'. See ECtHR, 'Factsheet—Hate Speech' (September 2023).
[13] See s. II.1.5. (Penalties).
[14] HRC, *Rabbae v. The Netherlands* (Comm. no. 2124/2011), 14 July 2016, Individual Concurring Opinion of Committee members Sarah Cleveland and Mauro Politi, §§4, 7. See s. III.1.4. (Mandatory restrictions at the regional level).
[15] The conclusion that certain offensive speech should not be penalized through criminal or other laws is not intended to discourage robust action by both governments and private companies—including social media platforms—to ensure that racist, misogynistic, homophobic or other deplorable language is addressed, nor does it in any way condone this type of speech. See ch. 1 (Introduction).

II. State Practice

Broadly speaking, hate speech[16] refers to speech that 'attacks or uses pejorative or discriminatory language with reference to a person or a group on the basis of who they are': 'in other words, based on their religion, ethnicity, nationality, race, colour, descent, gender or other identity factor'.[17] But 'hate speech' and 'hate' are not defined terms under international law—indeed, no human rights treaty uses this term.[18] Many national laws also fail to provide a definition of the speech that is covered by legislation in this area. This is despite the fact that approximately 95 per cent of hate speech laws allow for the imposition of criminal penalties.[19]

1. Overview of Hate Speech Laws

Hate speech laws around the globe protect speech to very different degrees, both on paper and in practice. At one end of the spectrum, there are criminal offences proscribing speech without requiring any harm to have been intended or to have been likely to occur. At the other end are laws that require specific intent to cause genocide or violence as a direct result of the speech and either proof that such harm occurred or an objective likelihood that such harm was likely and imminent. Many states fail to define 'hate',[20] or to address the required mental state of the speaker, the harmful consequences of the speech or the foreseeable causal link between the two, resulting in overbroad statutes that chill speech and are susceptible to abuse by authorities seeking to stifle debate or dissent.

1.1. Type of speech
Some laws punish expression of a particular viewpoint, most commonly racism, without requiring any showing of culpability, criminal intent or foreseeable harm, or are unclear as to whether such elements must be established.[21] Some states also proscribe the 'display', 'dissemination', 'glorification' or 'promotion' of hateful ideas without requiring any *mens rea* or showing of resulting harm. Examples include France criminalizing the

---

[16] The review of state laws and practice on hate speech contained in this chapter does not aim to be comprehensive but rather to identify significant examples and trends. Therefore, where the language of a statute is set out, this does not necessarily include an analysis of all case law interpreting that language in the jurisdiction under review.
[17] UN Strategy and Plan of Action on Hate Speech (2019), 2.
[18] See s. III. (International Legal Standards).
[19] See N. Alkiviadou, J. Mchangama & R. Mendiratta, *Global Handbook on Hate Speech Laws* (The Future of Free Speech 2020) (this figure is based on a survey of hate speech laws across 115 nations). The laws discussed in this State Practice section are all criminal unless otherwise indicated.
[20] See, e.g., Kenyan Constitution Art. 33(2); The European Union adopts a tautological definition: '[h]atred should be understood as referring to hatred based on race, colour, religion, descent or national or ethnic origin' European Council Framework Decision 2008/913/JHA of 28 November 2008 on combating certain forms and expressions of racism and xenophobia by means of criminal law Chapeau §9. See s. II.2.3.1. (Canada).
[21] See, e.g., Botswanan Penal Code Chapter 08:01 Art. 92 (fine-only offence).

display of Nazi badges, emblems or uniforms, with strict exemptions,[22] and Austria penalizing anyone who 'glorifies or extols the objectives' of the Nazi party or 'its institutions or actions'.[23]

Case Study: Blasphemy Laws

At least 95 states have criminal laws that punish blasphemy: expression that insults or criticizes 'religious doctrines, deities, symbols' or the 'feelings' of religious communities.[24] Although decriminalized in many Western countries, blasphemy remains an offence in around 40 per cent of the world's states and carries the death penalty in at least five countries.[25]

The crime of blasphemy is often expressed in vague terms that cast a wide net over speech that may insult religious ideas or groups. Broad blasphemy laws include the criminalization of 'contempt of heavenly religions',[26] speech that 'provide[s] an opinion or disperse[s] information' on a matter 'which has conflicting opinions among Islamic Scholars' and words that 'preach or spread any religion other than Islam'.[27]

Other states include religious grounds within a broader hate speech law. For instance, Brazil criminalizes 'injuring someone, offending their dignity or decorum' with additional penalties '[i]f the injury consists in the use of elements referring to race, color, ethnicity, *religion*, origin or condition of elderly or disabled person[s]'.[28]

Case Study: 'Denial laws'

Denial laws prohibit speech denying the truth of historical facts related to genocide, crimes against humanity or other international crimes. Several European

---

[22] French Penal Code R. 645-1 (except for purposes of a film, show or exhibition involving historical invocation, punishable by fine, and additional penalty including the ban to carry an arm, the confiscation of one's arm and community service).

[23] Austrian National Socialism Prohibition Act Art. 3d (punishable by up to 10 years' imprisonment, or if 'the activity should pose a particularly grave danger', up to 20 years' imprisonment).

[24] See United States Commission on International Religious Freedom, 'Legislation Factsheet: Blasphemy' (September 2023).

[25] Ibid. (citing Mauritania, Brunei, Iran and Pakistan). Saudi Arabia does not have a written penal code and relies on judges' interpretation of Sharia law, with judges previously interpreting apostasy as a capital offence: see, e.g., Human Rights Watch, 'Saudi Arabia: Poet Sentenced to Death for Apostasy' (23 November 2015). See IBAHRI, *On Religious Freedom and Discontent: Report on International Standards Relating to Blasphemy Laws and Media Freedom* (2023). In Pakistan, s. 295-C of the Penal Code 1860 was introduced in 1986 which criminalizes blasphemy against the Holy Prophet, punishable by death or life imprisonment. In 1990, the Federal Shariat Court declared that the only penalty under s. 295-C would be the death penalty. Although no executions have taken place under the law, suspects are often killed by vigilantes on the way to court. See s. II.2.2.3. (Pakistan). See also Pew Research Center, 'Four-in-ten countries and territories worldwide had blasphemy laws in 2019' (25 January 2022).

[26] Egyptian Criminal Code s. 98(f) (punishable by up to five years' imprisonment).

[27] Maldivian Regulation on Protecting Religious Unity of Maldives Citizens (2011/R-40) ss 5, 6.

[28] Brazilian Decree-Law No. 2.848 of 1940 Penal Code Art. 140 (punishable by up to three years' imprisonment).

states as well as Israel proscribe expression denying the Holocaust,[29] and certain denial laws are also combined with broader 'memory laws' that compel adherence to a particular historical narrative.[30] This is the case, for instance, in Russia, where it is an offence to 'deny facts recognized by the international military tribunal that judged and punished the major war criminals of the European Axis countries, to approve of the crimes this tribunal judged, and to spread intentionally false information about the Soviet Union's activities during World War II'.[31] An EU directive has sought to harmonize such laws by requiring that EU states punish the 'public condoning, denying, and grossly trivializing' crimes described in the Rome Statute of the International Criminal Court (genocide, war crimes and crimes against humanity) and the Nuremberg Charter (Holocaust denial) wherever they occur.[32]

These laws are usually content-based, criminalizing 'denialism' without further requirements to establish any harmful consequences.[33] Some states do require additional elements, however. This includes Croatia, which punishes public approval, denial or gross trivialization of genocide, crimes against humanity, war crimes, or crimes of aggression when 'directed ... in a manner likely to incite to violence or hatred against such a group or a member of such a group',[34] and Germany, which proscribes the denial of specific crimes 'in a manner suitable for causing a disturbance of the public peace'.[35]

1.2. Harm

States' hate speech laws differ based on the nature of the harm required, if any, and the likelihood or imminence of any harm that may result from the speech. At one end of the spectrum, some states' laws require that speech directly incites genocide in order to be criminalized. Other laws recognize a broader range of harms or omit a harm requirement altogether. For instance, some nations punish speech that incites any 'violence',[36]

---

[29] See, e.g., French Law of 13 July 1990 providing for the punishment of all racist, anti-Semitic, and xenophobic acts, also known as the Gayssot Act and amending French Law of 29 July 1881 on the Freedom of the Press with a new Art. 24bis (punishing the denial of the Holocaust by up to one year imprisonment and/or a fine of 45,000 Euros). See s. III.2.4.2. (Opinion); Belgian Act of 23 March 1995 Art. 1 (concerning the denial, gross minimization, justification or approval of the genocide, in the sense of the Geneva Convention of 9 December 1948, by the German National Socialist Regime during the Second World War (punishable by up to one year imprisonment and a fine up to 5,000 EUR)); see generally M. Whine, 'Expanding Holocaust Denial and Legislation Against It' (2008) 20(1–2) *Jewish Political Studies Review* 1. Israeli Denial of Holocaust (Prohibition) Law 5746-1986 ss 2, 4 (denial must be accompanied by 'intent to defend the perpetrators of those acts or to express sympathy or identification with them', punishable by up to five years' imprisonment).

[30] See, e.g., four different memory laws currently in force in France: (i) the 1990 Gayssot Act, (ii) the Law No. 2001-70 of 29 January 2001 relating to the recognition of the Armenian Genocide of 1915, (iii) the Law No. 2001-434 of 21 May 2001 recognizing the slave trade and slavery as a crime against humanity (also known as the Taubira Act) and (iv) Law No. 2005-158 of 23 February 2005 on the recognition of the Nation and national contribution in favour of repatriated French people.

[31] See Russian Penal Code Art. 354.1 (punishable by up to three years' imprisonment).

[32] European Council Framework Decision 2008/913/JHA of 28 November 2008 on combating certain forms and expressions of racism and xenophobia by means of criminal law Art. 1. See also Art. 1(4).

[33] However, for at least some of these laws, the harmful consequence is presumed to result per se from the content of the speech. See HRC, *Faurisson v. France* (Comm. no. 550/1993), 8 November 1996 (where the HRC upheld France's rationale for the Gayssot Act). Cf. HRC, General Comment No. 34 (2011), §49 (which appears to overrule *Faurisson*): see s. III.2.4.2 (Opinion).

[34] Croatian Penal Code Art. 325(4) (punishable by up to three years' imprisonment).

[35] German Criminal Code Art. 130 (punishable by up to three years' imprisonment).

[36] See, e.g., Malta Criminal Code Chapter 9, Art. 82A (punishable by up to 18 months' imprisonment).

or promotes 'hostility'.[37] And Canada provides criminal liability for a defendant who 'advocates or promotes genocide'—without a separate showing of harm.[38]

Some states have a stringent requirement relating to both the likelihood that harm will occur as the result of 'hate speech' and how imminent that harm is likely to be. For instance, US law only allows criminalization of speech that is 'directed to inciting or producing imminent lawless action and is likely to incite or produce such action'.[39] Latvian law requires that substantial harm *has been caused*.[40] And Estonian law criminalizes incitement to 'hatred, violence or discrimination on the basis of nationality, race, colour, sex, language, origin, religion, sexual orientation, political opinion, or financial or social status' only '*if this results* in danger to the life, health or property of a person'.[41] But many states' laws are vague as to both likelihood and imminence, place the bar very low or fail to address these issues entirely.[42]

1.3. Intent

The EU regulation on hate speech states that the legal prohibition of hate speech should 'ensure that ... *intentional* conduct is punishable'.[43] But it is not clear what form of intent is required and significant variation exists in hate speech laws, even within Europe. For instance, Ireland's law penalizes words that are 'threatening, abusive or insulting *and are intended or, having regard to all the circumstances, are likely to stir up hatred*'.[44] The United Kingdom,[45] Kenya and Malta also have laws that refer to intent.[46] Other states, like the Netherlands, use a knowledge test, requiring that the person makes public a

---

[37] Malawian Preservation of Public Security Act Chapter 14:02 Arts 4(c), 14; Ugandan Penal Code Act 1950 s. 41(1); Act of 10 May 2007 aimed at combating certain forms of discriminations Art. 20; French Law on the Freedom of the Press of 29 July 1881 Art. 24(5).

[38] Canadian Criminal Code s. 318. See also Australian Criminal Code Act 1995 s. 80.2D (punishable by up to seven years' imprisonment).

[39] US Supreme Court, *Brandenburg v. Ohio* 395 U.S. 444, 9 June 1969, 477. See also other limited cases in which speech may be restricted: See s. II.2.3.2. (United States).

[40] Latvian Criminal Law s. 150 (punishable by up to four years' imprisonment in certain circumstances).

[41] Estonian Penal Code RT I 2001, 61, 364 s. 151 (emphasis added) (punishable by a fine or detention of up to three years if the act causes death, damages to health or serious consequences, or is committed by someone previously punished for such an act).

[42] See, e.g., Greek Law No. 4285/2014, amending Law No. 927/1979, Art. 1.1 (speech that '*may lead* to violence, hatred [or] discrimination ... in a way that *may endanger* public order') (punishable by up to three years' imprisonment) (emphasis added). See also Greek Law No. Law 4491/2017.

[43] European Council Framework Decision 2008/913/JHA of 28 November 2008 on combating certain forms and expressions of racism and xenophobia by means of criminal law, Art. 1(1) (emphasis added).

[44] Irish Prohibition of Incitement to Hatred Act 1989, ss 2, 3, 6(b) (punishable by up to two years' imprisonment and a fine of 11,650 EUR when charged on indictment) (emphasis added). The proposed Criminal Justice (Incitement to Violence or Hatred and Hate Offences) Bill 2022 would—if it is enacted—repeal the Irish Prohibition of Incitement to Hatred Act 1989, and introduce a new hate crime offence. The proposed offence introduces a recklessness standard and increases the maximum custodial sentence on indictment from two to five years. See Coalition Against Hate Crime, 'Coalition Against Hate Crime Second Stage Briefing Note for Senators on the Criminal Justice (Incitement to Violence or Hatred and Hate Offences) Bill 2022' (8 June 2023).

[45] Unless otherwise indicated, references to the United Kingdom and the UK refer to England and Wales, Scotland and Northern Ireland. Although many of the same laws apply across these jurisdictions, these laws can vary and Scotland has a separate legal system.

[46] UK Public Order Act 1986 s. 18(1) (punishable by up to seven years' imprisonment when charged on indictment). See also UK Public Order Act 1986, ss 19, 20, 21, 22. The Hate Crime and Public Order (Scotland) Act 2021 will repeal ss 18–22 of the UK Public Order Act 1986 with respect to Scotland—once the relevant provisions are brought into force—and create a broader hatred offence which also refers to intent. See also Kenyan National Cohesion and Integration Act 2008 s. 13 (punishable by up to three years' imprisonment), Maltese Criminal Code Chapter 9 Art. 82A.

statement 'which he knows or should reasonably suspect to be insulting to a group of persons because of their race', or omit a culpability requirement entirely.[47]

1.4. Exclusions, exceptions and defences

Some states have a number of alternative defences available to hate speech crimes; others have one or none. Canada provides defences to the charge of wilful promotion of hatred where a defendant establishes that the statements were (a) 'true', related to 'a religious subject or text' and disseminated in 'good faith'; or (b) were in the 'public interest', for the 'public benefit' and the speaker had 'reasonable grounds to believe the truthfulness' of the statement.[48] The United Kingdom has a limited good faith defence, whereby the defendant will not be guilty of an offence 'if he did not intend his words... to be, and was not aware that [they] might be, threatening, abusive or insulting'.[49] Other laws do not apply to academic debate or news reports that are published to criticize the underlying hatred.[50]

1.5. Penalties

A survey of 115 countries' hate speech laws revealed that over 95 per cent of states use criminal—instead of or in addition to civil—penalties for hate speech.[51] The range of criminal penalties, however, varies considerably across jurisdictions. For instance, although some laws have hate speech offences that result only in fines or carry very short custodial sentences,[52] many others provide for substantial sentences of up to five years' imprisonment,[53] or even lengthier sentences,[54] and at least five authorize capital punishment for blasphemous speech.[55]

Some penalties for hate speech are specific to media companies and online content. In nations such as Bolivia, publication of discriminatory ideas can also result in the suspension of a media company's operating licence.[56] Elsewhere, states impose liability or

---

[47] See, e.g., Dutch Criminal Code s. 137(e) (punishable by up to one year imprisonment). Dutch law also criminalizes intentional hate speech: see Dutch Criminal Code s. 137(c).

[48] A final defence from prosecution arises if 'in good faith', the speaker referred to hate speech 'for the purpose of removal' of such speech: Canadian Criminal Code s. 319(3).

[49] UK Public Order Act 1986 s. 18(5). This defence only applies if the person 'is not shown to have intended to stir up racial hatred'. See also ss 19(2), 20(2), 21(3), 22(5) and (6); Irish Prohibition of Incitement to Hatred Act 1989 s. 2(a).

[50] See, e.g., Montenegrin Law on Media, Official Gazette of Montenegro 82/2020 dated 6 August 2020; Dutch Criminal Code s. 137(e) (excluding culpability when the speech is made 'for any reason other than the provision of factual information').

[51] See Alkiviadou, Mchangama, & Mendiratta (n 19).

[52] See, e.g., Rwandan Law Determining Offences and Penalties in General No. 68 2018 Art. 154 (punishable by three months' imprisonment).

[53] See, e.g., Canadian Criminal Code Art. 318 (five years' imprisonment for advocating or promoting genocide) and Art. 319 (two years' imprisonment for hate speech); Brazilian Law 9459 Art. 20 (five years' imprisonment when committed through media or publishing).

[54] Austrian National Socialism Prohibition Act Art. 3d. Austria has since passed other hate speech provisions with less stringent penalties, such as Art. 188 of the Criminal Code, which provides for up to six months' imprisonment for insulting religion.

[55] Mauritania, Brunei, Iran, Pakistan and Saudi Arabia (see United States Commission on International Religious Freedom, 'Legislation Factsheet: Blasphemy' (September 2023) and Human Rights Watch, 'Saudi Arabia: Poet Sentenced to Death for Apostasy' (23 November 2015)). See s. II.1.1. (Type of speech) (Case Study: Blasphemy Laws).

[56] Bolivian Law Against Racism and All Forms of Discrimination 2010 Art. 16 (punishable by suspension of operating licence or financial penalties). See also German Civil Code ss 823(2), 826 (providing civil remedies where a

hefty penalties for internet intermediaries when hate speech is found on their platform. A controversial example is Germany's 2017 Network Enforcement Act (commonly known as NetzDG) which compels social media platforms to remove unlawful content, including hate speech, from accounts that have more than two million users.[57] Under this law, removal must take place for 'manifestly unlawful' content within 24 hours, and for all other unlawful content within seven days, failing which penalties of up to 50 million Euros can be imposed.[58] UN and media freedom groups have expressed concern about the breadth and severity of this law, noting that companies have 'little incentive to err on the side of free expression'.[59] And more than a dozen countries, including Russia and Turkey, have since passed similar laws.[60]

2. Application of Hate Speech Laws Around the World

Trends in the implementation of hate speech laws vary across geographic regions. Many European hate speech cases have involved balancing a desire to prevent the rise of racist right-wing sentiment with the need to protect freedom of expression and political debate. In the Asia Pacific and Middle Eastern context, certain repressive governments have used vague hate speech provisions and blasphemy laws as a pretext to chill political dissent. American jurisprudence has traditionally reflected a high watermark of free speech in this space, where courts will accept the regulation of hateful speech only in very limited circumstances, namely where such speech is likely to incite imminent violence or unlawful action.[61]

2.1. Europe

2.1.1. The Netherlands

2.1.1.1. Wilders A series of high-profile cases against Geert Wilders, leader of the Dutch far-right 'Party for Freedom', illustrates where Dutch courts draw the line in balancing the right to speak and the right not to be the target of racist and xenophobic sentiment.[62]

In the first case, criminal charges were brought for statements Wilders made during media interviews and on his party website related to Muslim immigrants and

---

person 'commits a breach of a statute that is intended to protect another person' or 'intentionally inflicts damage on another person', including incitement offences).

[57] German Network Enforcement Act 2017 ss 1, 3. This entered into force on 1 October 2017.
[58] Ibid., s. 3; Human Rights Watch, 'Germany: Flawed Social Media Law' (14 February 2018).
[59] Human Rights Watch, 'Germany: Flawed Social Media Law' (14 February 2018); UN Special Rapporteur D. Kaye, Promotion and protection of the right to freedom of opinion and expression (2019) UN Doc. A/74/486, §32.
[60] 'Censorious governments are abusing "fake news" laws' (The Economist, 13 February 2021). Cf. EU Digital Services Act (directly applicable from early 2024, including fines up to six per cent of the global turnover of a service provider).
[61] See s. II.2.3.2. (United States).
[62] See s. III.1.1. (ICCPR Article 20).

Moroccan residents in the Netherlands. In 2011, the Amsterdam District Court acquitted Wilders of five charges including insult and 'incitement to hatred and discrimination' on grounds of religion and race.[63] The Court considered statements like '[w]e have to stop the tsunami of Islamization' to be criticisms of Islam as a religion, rather than a particular group of people, and held that the 'mere circumstance that offensive statements about a religion also offend the adherents of that religion is ... not sufficient' to make out the offence.[64]

In contrast, in a second case, Wilders was convicted for asking an audience at a televised election rally: 'do you want more or less Moroccans in this city and the Netherlands?' and, in compliance with earlier instructions, the audience chanted back 'less, less, less', following which Wilders replied 'well, then we'll arrange that'. The Dutch courts[65] held that he could be convicted for 'insult' but that a prison term or fine was not an appropriate punishment.[66] It also held that he could not be convicted of incitement to racial discrimination because there was no evidence that he intended to incite others to hate or discriminate against Moroccans or that he 'knowingly accepted the significant chance that the public ... would be moved to do so'.[67] The court considered that Wilders was instead seeking 'political gain' from his statement and as a result should be acquitted of this charge.[68]

2.1.1.2. Basebya

In 2013, Yvonne Basebya became the first Dutch citizen to be convicted of incitement to genocide and was sentenced to nearly seven years' imprisonment.[69] At trial, the prosecution presented evidence that Basebya was a member of

---

[63] Dutch Court of Amsterdam, *Judgment of the District Court of Amsterdam in the criminal case against Geert Wilders* Case Number 13-425046-09, 23 June 2011.

[64] Dutch Court of Amsterdam, *Judgment of the District Court of Amsterdam in the criminal case against Geert Wilders* Case Number 13-425046-09, 23 June 2011, §4.2; de Rechtspraak, 'Verdict of the Amsterdam district court as regards the Wilders trial' (23 June 2011). The Court also held that incitement to hatred and discrimination on grounds of 'race' could not apply to speech directed to Moroccans or non-Western immigrants. Dutch Court of Amsterdam, *Judgment of the District Court of Amsterdam in the criminal case against Geert Wilders* Case Number 13-425046-09, 23 June 2011, §4.4. The Dutch Public Prosecution Service had refused to prosecute Wilders because it did not consider his statements illegal, but was later ordered by the Court of Appeal upon a complaint to pursue the prosecution. During the process, the Public Prosecution Service argued that Wilders should be acquitted on all counts and did not appeal the acquittal.

[65] The first instance court found Wilders guilty on two counts of insult and inciting racial discrimination: Dutch District Court of the Hague, *State of the Netherlands v. Wilders* Case Number 09/837304-15, 9 December 2016, §5.4.3. The Court came to a different decision on the legal definition of race than in Wilders' earlier proceedings, interpreting the term consistently with the CERD to encompass persons linked by their 'common Moroccan descent'. Ibid., §5.4.2. Wilders was acquitted of two separate counts which related to statements made on another day saying that people should hope for 'if possible, less Moroccans' in Dutch cities, as the Court found that these statements were made spontaneously at a market and he 'did not have the (conditional) intent to insult people of Moroccan descent or to incite discrimination or hatred': §5.4.4.

[66] Dutch Court of Appeal in The Hague, *Wilders v. State of the Netherlands* Case Number 22-000007-17, 4 September 2020, §8.4. The Appeals Court agreed with the lower Court that a conviction was sufficient punishment (even though a maximum two-year prison term was available) and this judgment was upheld by the Supreme Court. Ibid., §13; Dutch Supreme Court: *Wilders v. State of the Netherlands* Case Number 20/03005, 6 July 2021.

[67] Dutch Court of Appeal in The Hague, *Wilders v. State of the Netherlands* Case Number 22-000007-17, 4 September 2020, §8.5.

[68] Ibid. The District Court had already ruled that incitement to hatred required an additional reinforcing component, beyond merely strong rhetoric, which instigates people to take action that Wilders lacked: Dutch District Court of The Hague, *State of the Netherlands v. Wilders* Case Number 09/837304-15, 9 December 2016, §5.4.3.2.

[69] 'Rwandan-born Dutch woman jailed for inciting genocide' (The Guardian, 1 March 2013); Dutch District Court of The Hague, *The Prosecutor v. Yvonne Basebya* Case Number 09/748004-09, 1 March 2013.

an extremist pro-Hutu political party, and a wealthy and well-respected member of her community. She was alleged to have acted as an 'animator' at meetings where she 'aggressively instilled hatred against the Tutsis and ... encouraged members to kill Tutsis', for example by leading the singing of an extremist anti-Tutsi song entitled 'Tubatsembatsembe', meaning 'let's exterminate them all'.[70] The court heard evidence that following these meetings, Tutsis felt it was dangerous to be on the streets in Basebya's neighbourhood in Kigali, and that they would remain at home.[71]

The District Court of The Hague held that for this conduct to amount to incitement to genocide, the prosecution must prove that there was intent to 'entirely or partially exterminate the Tutsi-population group'; and that the impugned speech was a 'direct' call for genocide.[72] The District Court considered that 'such intent must be 'firmly established' with 'no other explanation ... possible'.[73] In light of the circumstances, namely the 'political framework in which the accused's remarks were made', the violent attacks against Tutsis at the time, Basebya's social standing in the community and the repeated nature of her conduct, the District Court considered that 'no other conclusion' was possible than that Basebya 'had the aim to destroy the Tutsi-population group', by leading the singing of the song at the meetings.[74] In addition, the element of directness was held to be satisfied on the basis that '[i]n view of the nature of the meetings and the public that attended them, this form of expression could not be explained in any other way than that it was an explicit call for the extermination of the local Tutsi-population'.[75] Basebya was sentenced to the maximum sentence of six years and eight months' imprisonment for incitement to genocide.[76]

2.1.2. Austria

In 2013, Austria's Supreme Court confirmed the conviction of a woman known as 'E.S.', for disparaging religious doctrines on the basis of her description of Prophet Muhammad as a paedophile during a seminar.[77]

E.S. had held a number of seminars at the Freedom Party Education Institute, open to members of the Freedom Party, guests and the public. During some of these seminars, attended by an undercover journalist, E.S. stated that 'one of the biggest problems

---

[70] Dutch District Court of The Hague, *The Prosecutor v. Yvonne Basebya* Case Number 09/748004-09, 1 March 2013, §12(8) and (10).

[71] Ibid., §12(16).

[72] Ibid., §12(8). The Court also held that two other factors must be proved: (1) that the Tutsi population was a protected group and (2) that the speech was made publicly. The Court relied on the Rwandan Tribunal's finding that the Tutsi population group can be regarded as an ethnic group within the meaning of the Genocide Convention, citing ICTR, *Prosecutor v. Kayishema and Ruzindana* (ICTR-95-1-T), Trial Judgement, 21 May 1999, §§522–526.

[73] Dutch District Court of The Hague, *The Prosecutor v. Yvonne Basebya* Case Number 09/748004-09, 1 March 2013, §12(10), (12).

[74] Ibid., §12(13)–(20). See s. III.1.3. (Genocide Convention Article 3).

[75] Ibid., §12(24). The District Court determined that the speech was 'public', as the meetings did not have a 'closed character', could be heard from inside witnesses' homes and seen from the public road. Ibid., §12(29). She was acquitted of the remaining charges including committing genocide.

[76] Both the prosecutor as well as the defendant initially appealed the decision, but later withdrew their appeals which made the District Court's judgment final. In May 2015 the Supreme Court rejected Basebya's request for revision; see Dutch Supreme Court, *Revision* Case Number 14/05251, 13 May 2015.

[77] Austrian Supreme Court, *Decision on request for renewal* Reference Number 15Os52/12d, 11 December 2013.

we are facing today is that Muhammad is seen as the ideal man, the perfect human, the perfect Muslim ... [but] he was a warlord, he had many women ... and liked to do it with children'. She also stated: '[a] 56-year-old and a six-year-old? ... What do we call it, if it is not paedophilia?'[78] These comments referred to the Prophet Muhammad's marriage to a child named Aisha who, according to religious tenets, was six at the time of the marriage and nine at the time it was consummated.[79]

E.S. was convicted of an offence on the basis that her speech 'publicly disparages or insults a person who ... is an object of veneration of a ... religious community' in circumstances where their 'behaviour is likely to arouse justified indignation', a crime punishable by up to six months' imprisonment in Austria.[80] E.S. argued that her speech 'merely criticized the notion that an adult had had sexual intercourse with a nine-year-old and questioned whether this amounted to paedophilia' and should be protected.[81] However, three levels of Austrian courts—including the Supreme Court of Austria—disagreed, finding that such speech was not protected by article 10 of the European Convention on Human Rights. E.S. was ordered to pay costs and a fine of 480 Euros, with 60 days' imprisonment in default.

Austria's Supreme Court held that this law had a legitimate aim that was 'the protection of religious peace and the religious feelings of others', and that a criminal conviction may be necessary to pursue this aim.[82] The court held that the speech was likely to arouse 'justified indignation' as it was neither 'a factual criticism of religion' nor a contribution to the public debate on questions of child marriage or Islam, but rather was 'insulting' and made 'deliberately degrading remarks about the Prophet Mohammed'.[83] Although the Supreme Court accepted the lower court's finding that 'criticising child marriages was justifiable', it highlighted that E.S. had improperly disregarded the fact that 'the marriage had continued until the Prophet's death, when Aisha had already turned eighteen'.[84] The Supreme Court also considered a criminal conviction to be 'proportionate'.[85] This decision, and its endorsement by the European Court of Human Rights, has been the subject of extensive criticism on the basis that it was poorly reasoned and insufficiently protective of speech.[86]

---

[78] ECtHR, *E.S. v. Austria* (App. no. 38450/12), 25 October 2018, §13.
[79] Ibid., §14.
[80] Austrian Criminal Code Art. 188. Charges were originally brought against E.S. for inciting hatred, pursuant to Art. 283(1) of Austria's Criminal Code (punishable by fine or imprisonment of up to two years).
[81] ECtHR, *E.S. v. Austria* (App. no. 38450/12), 25 October 2018, §16.
[82] Austrian Supreme Court, *Decision on request for renewal* Reference Number 15Os52/12d, 11 December 2013.
[83] The Court of Appeal also held that there was a distinction between a child marriage and paedophilia and that there was no reliable evidence to suggest that Muhammad's 'primary sexual interest in Aisha had been her not yet having reached puberty'. ECtHR, *E.S. v. Austria* (App. no. 38450/12), 25 October 2018, §18. See also Austrian Supreme Court, *Decision on request for renewal* Reference Number 15Os52/12d, 11 December 2013, 4, 13, 14.
[84] ECtHR, *E.S. v. Austria* (App. no. 38450/12), 25 October 2018, §§14, 22; Austrian Supreme Court, *Decision on request for renewal* Reference Number 15Os52/12d, 11 December 2013.
[85] Austrian Supreme Court, *Decision on request for renewal* Reference Number 15Os52/12d, 11 December 2013, cited in ECtHR, *E.S. v. Austria* (App. no. 38450/12), 25 October 2018, §14.
[86] See s. III.2.2. (Legitimacy) (Case Study: International Standards on Blasphemy Laws) See, e.g., M. Milanovic, 'Legitimizing Blasphemy Laws Through the Backdoor: The European Court's Judgment in E.S. v. Austria' (EJIL: Talk!, 29 October 2018); C. Yeginsu & J. Williams, 'Criminalizing Speech to Protect Religious Peace? The ECtHR Ruling in E.S. v. Austria' (Just Security, 28 November 2018).

2.2. Asia Pacific

2.2.1. Indonesia

In Indonesia, a number of prosecutions demonstrate how hate speech laws without robust harm and intent requirements can be used to stifle expression. One such law criminalizes speech 'aimed at inflicting hatred or dissension on individuals and/or certain groups' based on ethnicity, race or religion.[87] In 2012, civil servant Alexander Aan was convicted under the law and sentenced to two and a half years' imprisonment for posts in an atheist Facebook group that explained why he did not believe in God's existence. He was released on parole after serving 19 months in prison.[88]

More recently, Ahmad Dhani, an Indonesian musician and political figure, was sentenced to one year of imprisonment under the same provision.[89] The speech at issue was a series of tweets regarding the former Jakarta governor, then on trial, including a tweet stating that 'anyone who supports' the governor 'is scum and deserves to be spat [on] in the face'.[90] The decision has been criticized on the basis that 'none of the tweets in question mention the governor's ethnicity, religion or race—as specifically required' in the law and that the 'elasticity of these laws advantage whoever is in power'.[91] Although Indonesia's President has asked police officers to be 'selective' when using this law, it remains on the books in Indonesia.[92]

2.2.2. Myanmar

Myanmar has used hate speech laws to stifle expression on a very broad basis. This includes the conviction of three employees and managers of the 'V Gastro Bar' in Yangon for posting a Facebook advertisement that showed a Buddha wearing headphones, with accompanying text advertising 'bottomless frozen' cocktails.[93] Although the post was deleted and an apology was issued, it was reshared on social media and prompted an outcry from Buddhist nationalist groups. The bar owner and managers were subsequently charged with insulting 'religion' or 'religious beliefs' with 'deliberate and malicious intention'.[94]

The men were convicted and sentenced to over two years' imprisonment and hard labour.[95] The court reasoned that 'it is clear' that the speech 'offended the majority religion in this country' and that 'ignorance of the law is not an excuse', holding that the bar

---

[87] Indonesian Law Concerning Electronic Information and Transactions Arts 27(3), 28(2).
[88] J. Cochrane, 'Embrace of Atheism Put an Indonesian in Prison' (The New York Times, 3 May 2014).
[89] Indonesian Law Concerning Electronic Information and Transactions Arts 27(3), 28(2).
[90] 'Ahmad Dhani walks free after serving 11 months for hate speech' (The Jakarta Post, 30 December 2019).
[91] See T. Paterson, 'Indonesian Cyberspace Expansion: A Double-edged Sword' (2019) 4 *Journal of Cyber Policy* 216.
[92] 'Jokowi asks the police to use the ITE law wisely' (Netral.News, 16 February 2021); Office of Assistant to Deputy Cabinet Secretary of the Republic of Indonesia, 'President Jokowi: ITE Law Must Fulfill Public Sense of Justice' (15 February 2021).
[93] See, e.g., Columbia University Global Freedom of Expression Database, 'The Case of V Gastro Bar (Philip Blackwood, Htut Ko Ko Lwin and Tun Thurein)'; W. Moe & A. Ramzy, 'Myanmar Sentences 3 to Prison for Depicting Buddha Wearing Headphones' (The New York Times, 17 March 2015).
[94] Columbia University Global Freedom of Expression Database, 'The Case of V Gastro Bar' (n 93).
[95] See Myanmarese Penal Code Art. 295. An additional charge related to disobeying a civil servant under Art. 188 and their sentences reflected the conviction on both charges. A charge of destroying, damaging or defiling a place of worship or sacred object was dropped.

manager—a man from New Zealand—should have known better since he had 'stayed in Myanmar for more than three years'. And the bar's local owner 'failed to instruct his foreign staff about the culture and traditions of the country'.[96] The defendants' lawyer declined to comment on the verdict, stating 'if I make any comment on the court's decision I will end up in jail'.[97] The verdict was sharply criticized[98] and the bar manager was released following a presidential pardon after serving almost a year in prison, with his co-defendants reportedly released at the same time.[99]

2.2.3. Pakistan

In August 2021, an eight-year-old boy was charged under Pakistan's blasphemy laws, becoming the youngest person ever charged with blasphemy in that country, an offence which carries the death penalty.[100] He was accused of urinating in the library of a madrassa, and his release on bail prompted an attack on a Hindu temple. Police dropped the charges against him within days after media and government pressure.[101] Although no executions have taken place under the law since the death penalty was introduced for the crime in 1986, a number of defendants remain on death row or in solitary confinement,[102] and suspects are often attacked and in some instances killed by mobs.[103] Reports suggest at least 65 people have been killed over claims of blasphemy since 1990, and that blasphemy charges are often brought against religious minorities as a mechanism to settle personal disputes.[104] And in January 2023, lawmakers expanded Pakistan's blasphemy laws to include insult to the Prophet's wives, companions or close relatives, punishable by up to life imprisonment.[105] Blasphemy charges were also made a non-bailable offence.[106]

2.3. North and South America

2.3.1. Canada

The landmark decision of the Supreme Court of Canada in *R. v. Keegstra* upheld Canada's hate speech provisions as consistent with the free speech provisions enshrined in Canada's Charter of Rights and Freedoms.[107] Keegstra was a high school teacher who

---

[96] Columbia University Global Freedom of Expression Database, 'The Case of V Gastro Bar' (n 93).
[97] J. Callil, 'A Prison Sentence for a Facebook Image Shows How Restrictive Burma's Anti-Free-Speech Laws Have Become' (Vice, 24 March 2015) citing the Myanmar Times.
[98] Amnesty International, 'Myanmar: "Buddha bar" guilty verdict another blow to freedom of expression' (17 March 2015).
[99] 'Phil Blackwood en route to New Zealand after release' (Frontier Myanmar, 28 January 2016).
[100] H. Janjua, 'Eight-year-old becomes youngest person charged with blasphemy in Pakistan' (The Guardian, 9 August 2021).
[101] H. Janjua, 'Pakistan police drop blasphemy charges against eight-year-old' (The Guardian, 12 August 2021).
[102] Human Rights Watch, 'Pakistan: End Ordeal for 'Blasphemy' Defendants' (6 October 2019). Defendants continue to receive death penalty sentences: see, e.g., A. Hashim, 'Pakistan court sentences woman to death for WhatsApp "blasphemy"' (Al Jazeera, 20 January 2022).
[103] United States Commission on International Religious Freedom, *Violating Rights: Enforcing the World's Blasphemy Laws* (2020).
[104] Human Rights Watch, 'Pakistan: End Ordeal for 'Blasphemy' Defendants' (6 October 2019).
[105] S. Masood, 'Pakistan Strengthens Already Harsh Laws Against Blasphemy' (The New York Times, 21 January 2023).
[106] Ibid.
[107] Canadian Supreme Court, *R v. Keegstra* [1990] 3 S.C.R. 697, 13 December 1990 is the leading case in a trilogy of landmark Supreme Court decisions affirming the constitutional validity of hate speech limitations, including *R*

expressed anti-Semitic statements to his students, including describing Jewish people as 'subversive' and suggesting that they 'created the Holocaust to gain sympathy'. He requested that students reproduce his teachings and would mark them down in class if they did not.[108] Keegstra was convicted under article 319(2) of Canada's Criminal Code, which prohibits publicly communicating a statement that 'willfully promotes hatred against an identifiable group'.[109]

Canadian Charter protections, including the right to free speech, can be subject to any 'reasonable limits prescribed by law as can be demonstrably justified in a free and democratic society'.[110] For a restriction on the right to free speech to be permissible under the Canadian Charter, it must meet a two-pronged test: the objective of the restriction must be 'pressing and substantial' and it must be proportionate to this objective.[111] In *Keegstra*, Chief Justice Dickson, writing on behalf of the majority, found article 319(2) to have 'easily satisfied' this test, referencing the substantial harm caused by hate, the requirements of Canada's international treaty obligations, and values recognized in the Charter.

In its judgment, the majority defined hatred as a 'most extreme emotion that belies reason; an emotion that, if exercised against members of an identifiable group, implies that those individuals are to be despised, scorned, denied respect and made subject to ill-treatment on the basis of group affiliation'.[112] It also concluded that the word 'wilfully' denoted a 'stringent standard of *mens rea*' which 'is an invaluable means of limiting the incursion of s. 319(2) into the realm of acceptable (though perhaps offensive and controversial) expression'.[113] And the majority disagreed with the submission that section 319(2) was unacceptably broad because it failed to require 'proof of actual hatred resulting from a communication', holding that a causal link would be 'clearly difficult to prove' and 'gives insufficient attention to the severe psychological trauma suffered' by targeted groups.[114] The majority also found that the defences allowed under the legislation meant that the danger of overbreadth was 'significantly reduced',[115] and

---

v. Andrews [1990] 3 S.C.R. 870, 13 December 1990 which also concerned section 319(2) of the Canadian Criminal Code, and *Canada (Human Rights Commission) v. Taylor* [1990] 3 S.C.R. 892, 13 December 1990 on the civil liability provision, s. 13 of the Canadian Human Rights Act.

[108] Canadian Supreme Court, *R v. Keegstra* [1990] 3 S.C.R. 697, 13 December 1990, 714 (Dickson CJ).
[109] Canadian Criminal Code Art. 319(2). See s. II.1.4. (Exclusions, exceptions and defences).
[110] Canadian Constitution Act 1982 Part 1 Canadian Charter of Rights and Freedoms.
[111] Canadian Supreme Court, *R v. Keegstra* [1990] 3 S.C.R. 697, 13 December 1990, 734–735 (Dickson CJ) citing Canadian Supreme Court, *R v. Oakes* [1986] 1 S.C.R. 103.
[112] Canadian Supreme Court, *R v. Keegstra* [1990] 3 S.C.R. 697, 13 December 1990, 777 (Dickson CJ). See also T. Mendel, 'Does International Law Provide for Consistent Rules on Hate Speech?', in M. Herz & P. Molnar (eds), *The Content and Context of Hate Speech: Rethinking Regulation and Responses* (CUP 2012), 427–428.
[113] Canadian Supreme Court, *R v. Keegstra* [1990] 3 S.C.R. 697, 13 December 1990, 775.
[114] Ibid., 776 (Dickson CJ).
[115] Ibid., 779 (Dickson CJ): Defences are set out in s. 319(3) and include 'elements of good faith or honest belief' and therefore 'negate directly the mens rea in the offence', namely if '(a) [the defendant] establishes that the statements communicated were true; (b) if, in good faith, he expressed or attempted to establish by argument an opinion on a religious subject; (c) if the statements were relevant to any subject of public interest, the discussion of which was for the public benefit, and if on reasonable grounds he believed them to be true; or (d) if, in good faith, he intended to point out, for the purpose of removal, matters producing or tending to produce feelings of hatred toward an identifiable group in Canada'.

that the impugned provision was a constitutionally valid infringement on the right to free expression.

Accordingly, the majority found article 319(2) was a constitutionally valid infringement on the right to free expression, reasonably justified in a free and democratic society. It had both an important and necessary objective, and was a proportionate means to achieve this objective, in light of Canada's commitment to uphold its foundational values of dignity, equality, and multiculturalism, while combatting the harms of hate, in a narrowly tailored manner offering due process protections.

Three judges of the Supreme Court provided a forceful dissent, arguing that '[t]he breadth of the category of speech [section 319(2)] catches, the absolute nature of the prohibition it applies to such speech, the draconian criminal consequences it imposes coupled with the availability of preferable remedies, and finally, the counterproductive nature of its actual effects ... combine to make it an inappropriate means of protecting our society against the evil of hate propaganda'.[116] Justice McLachlin suggested that Canadian courts should 'follow the American approach' and require 'clear and present danger before free speech can be overridden'.[117]

2.3.2. United States

The US Supreme Court's interpretation of the First Amendment, which guarantees that 'Congress shall make no law ... abridging the freedom of speech, or of the press', has resulted in the United States being one of the most speech-protective jurisdictions across the world.[118] First Amendment jurisprudence 'require[s] a concrete link to violence or a breach of the peace' if speech is to be criminalized.[119] Criminal penalties for three categories of speech have been found permissible on this basis: speech inciting 'imminent lawless action', 'fighting words' and 'true threats'.[120]

The most significant category of permissible restrictions to speech is the first one.[121] This was developed in the seminal case of *Brandenburg v. Ohio*, when the Supreme Court ruled that a racist speech by a Ku Klux Klan leader was protected by the First Amendment because the state cannot proscribe advocacy of the use of force 'except where such advocacy is directed to inciting or producing imminent lawless action and is likely to incite or produce such action'.[122] The Court

---

[116] Ibid., 868. McLachlin J delivered a dissenting judgment, with Sopinka J agreeing and La Forest J agreeing on the issues respecting freedom of expression.

[117] Ibid., 807, 822. The dissenting judges criticized the majority's definition of hatred, arguing that 'it is not only the breadth of the term 'hatred' which presents dangers; it is its subjectivity'.

[118] Cf., ch. 5 (Espionage and Official Secrets Laws), s. I.3.4.1. (United States: Pentagon Papers); ch. 6 (Terrorism Laws), s. I.2.4.1. (United States). A number of sources chart the US Supreme Court's historical path towards this more speech protective position: see, e.g., M. Rosenfeld, 'Hate Speech in Constitutional Jurisprudence: A Comparative Analysis', in M. Herz & P. Molnar (eds), *The Content and Context of Hate Speech: Rethinking Regulation and Responses* (CUP 2012); E. Bleich, 'Freedom of Expression versus Racist Hate Speech: Explaining Differences Between High Court Regulation in the USA and Europe' (2014) 40 *Journal of Ethnic and Migration Studies* 283.

[119] A. Clooney & P. Webb, 'The Right to Insult in International Law' (2017) 48(2) *Columbia Human Rights Law Review* 1, 50.

[120] Ibid., 48.

[121] US Supreme Court, *Brandenburg v. Ohio* 395 U.S. 444, 9 June 1969.

[122] Ibid.

concluded that in that case 'the Klan may have *advocated* violence but had not *incited* it'.[123]

Subsequent US hate speech jurisprudence has solidified the requirement that speech must have a clear call to violence or lawless action if it is to be criminalized.[124] For example, when an anti-war protester said 'we'll take the fucking street later' in the context of a 100–150 person demonstration that had moved onto the public street and blocked traffic, the Supreme Court held that 'at worst, it amounted to nothing more than advocacy of illegal action at some indefinite future time' and that the words 'could not be punished by the State on the ground that they had a "tendency to lead to violence"'.[125] And in considering whether a speech made at a civil rights meeting in Mississippi that advocated for a boycott of white merchants was protected by *Brandenburg v. Ohio*, the Supreme Court held that 'an advocate must be free to stimulate his audience with spontaneous and emotional appeals for unity and action', and there was no evidence that the speaker 'authorized, ratified or directly threatened acts of violence'.[126] So in both cases the Court found that the First Amendment protected the impugned speech.

The second category of permissible restrictions to speech pertains to 'true threats', meaning statements through which 'the speaker means to communicate a serious expression of an intent to commit an act of unlawful violence to a particular individual or group of individuals'.[127] The statement at a public rally that '[i]f they ever make me carry a rifle the first man I want to get in my sights is L.B.J.' was found to be 'political hyperbole', rather than such a true threat.[128] Although scholars have questioned the parameters of this category of unprotected speech,[129] the Supreme Court recently confirmed that a defendant can be convicted under federal statutes criminalizing threats of violence.[130] In his partial concurrence, Justice Alito stated that 'it is settled that the Constitution does not protect true threats', because such statements 'inflict great harm and have little if any social value. A threat may cause serious emotional stress for the person threatened and those who care about that person, and a threat may lead to violent confrontation'.[131]

The final category of speech not protected by the First Amendment is that of 'fighting words', which encompasses 'those which, by their very utterance, inflict injury or tend to incite an immediate breach of the peace'.[132] This doctrine was enunciated in *Chaplinsky v. New Hampshire*, some 27 years before the Court decided *Brandenburg*. A conviction

---

[123] Rosenfeld (n 118) 254.
[124] See, e.g., US Supreme Court, *NAACP v. Claiborne Hardware Co.* 458 U.S. 886, 2 July 1982, 928.
[125] US Supreme Court, *Hess v. Indiana* 414 U.S. 105, 19 November 1973, 108–109.
[126] US Supreme Court, *NAACP v. Claiborne Hardware Co.* 458 U.S. 886, 2 July 1982, 928–930. Cf. ch. 6 (Terrorism Laws), s. I.2.4.1. (United States).
[127] US Supreme Court, *Virginia v. Black* 538 U.S. 343, 7 April 2003, 359. See also US Supreme Court, *Counterman v. Colorado* 600 U.S. 66, 27 June 2023.
[128] US Supreme Court, *Watts v. United States* 394 U.S. 705, 21 April 1969, 708.
[129] See, e.g., P. Crane, "'True Threats' and the Issue of Intent' (2006) 92 *Virginia Law Review* 1225; S. Gay, 'A Few Questions About Cross Burning, Intimidation and Free Speech' (2005) 80 *Notre Dame Law Review* 1287; 'Elonis v. United States' (2015) 129 *Harvard Law Review* 331.
[130] US Supreme Court, *Elonis v. United States* 575 U.S. 723, 1 June 2015.
[131] Ibid., Alito J, concurring in part and dissenting in part.
[132] US Supreme Court, *Chaplinsky v. New Hampshire* 315 U.S. 568, 9 March 1942, 571–572.

for saying the words 'You are a God damned racketeer' and a 'damned Fascist' to a public official was upheld on the basis that such words were 'likely to provoke the average person to retaliation, and thereby cause a breach of the peace'.[133] However, this doctrine has been described by the Third Circuit as an 'extremely narrow one', and by commentators as having emerged to be 'strikingly similar to the clear and present danger test' (later replaced by the 'imminent lawless action' test in *Brandenburg*).[134] For example, the Supreme Court considered that wearing a jacket that said 'Fuck the Draft' did not amount to 'fighting words', stating that the doctrine only covered 'personally abusive epithets which, when addressed to the ordinary citizen, are, as a matter of common knowledge, inherently likely to provoke violent reaction'.[135] And in *Gooding v. Wilson*, where the impugned speech included the phrases 'You son of a bitch, I'll choke you to death', the Court found that a statute criminalizing the use of 'opprobrious words or abusive language, tending to cause a breach of the peace' to be overbroad because it was not limited to words that 'have a direct tendency to cause acts of violence by the person to whom, individually, the remark was addressed'.[136]

Beyond these three categories and their requisite requirements for a clear link between speech and violent or illegal acts, US First Amendment jurisprudence also clearly rejects content-based restrictions to speech. For example, when a defendant was convicted for burning a cross pursuant to an ordinance that prohibited displaying symbols which knowingly 'arouse[] anger, alarm or resentment in others on the basis of race, color, creed, religion or gender', the Supreme Court held that the relevant statute was unconstitutional 'in that it prohibits otherwise permitted speech solely on the basis of the subjects the speech addresses'.[137] And in a more recent case, the Court confirmed that speech that demeans 'on the basis of race, ethnicity, gender, religion, age, disability, or any other similar ground is hateful; but the proudest boast of our free speech jurisprudence is that we protect the freedom to express "the thought that we hate"'.[138]

A recent example of a case in which the high bar provided by the First Amendment was met was the criminal conviction and sentence of Ryder Winegar. He had left six

---

[133] Ibid., 574.
[134] See US Court of Appeals, *Johnson v. Campbell* 332 F.3d 199, 5 June 2003, 212; M. Mannheimer, 'The Fighting Words Doctrine' (1993) 3 *Columbia Law Review* 1527; Clooney & Webb, 'The Right to Insult in International Law' (n 119) 48 (noting that the category 'has not been heavily relied on in practice and its contours are very narrow'); 'The Demise of the "Chaplinsky" Fighting Words Doctrine: An Argument for Its Interment' (1993) 106 *Harvard Law Review* 1129.
[135] US Supreme Court, *Cohen v. California* 403 U.S. 15, 7 June 1971, 20.
[136] US Supreme Court, *Gooding v. Wilson* 405 U.S. 518, 23 March 1972, 523 ('Our decisions since *Chaplinsky* have continued to recognize state power constitutionally to punish "fighting" words under carefully drawn statutes not also susceptible of application to protected expression').
[137] US Supreme Court, *R.A.V. v. City of St Paul, Minnesota* 505 U.S. 377, 22 June 1992, 381. See also US Supreme Court, *Matal v. Tam,* 137 S. Ct. 1744, 19 June 2017, 1751, Opinion of Alito J, joined by Roberts CJ, and Thomas and Breyer JJ (finding that an act prohibiting the registration of trademarks that may 'disparage ... or bring ... into contempt or disrepute' any living persons to be unconstitutional, on the basis that speech 'may not be banned on the ground that it expresses ideas that offend'). ('From 1791 to the present ... our society, like other free but civilized societies, has permitted restrictions upon the content of speech in a few limited areas, which are 'of such slight social value as a step to truth that any benefit that may be derived from them is clearly outweighed by the social interest in order and morality': US Supreme Court, *R.A.V. v. City of St Paul, Minnesota* 505 U.S. 377, 22 June 1992, 382–383).
[138] US Supreme Court, *Matal v. Tam* 137 S. Ct. 1744, 19 June 2017, 1764, Opinion of Alito J, joined by Roberts CJ, and Thomas and Breyer JJ.

members of Congress threatening voicemails two days after President Biden's election was confirmed by the electoral college in December 2020. One message described the 'massive fraud' that had taken place in the United States, and threatened 'if you don't support it, we're going to drag you out and we're going to hang you by your neck to die'. Winegar was sentenced to 33 months in federal prison after pleading guilty to six counts of threatening members of Congress and one count of transmitting interstate threatening communications.[139]

2.4. Middle East and Africa
2.4.1. Tunisia
An example of the misuse of hate speech laws in a religious context is the conviction of Emna Chargui, a 27-year-old Tunisian blogger, for 'inciting hatred between religions through hostile means or violence' and 'infringing an authorized religion' pursuant Tunisia's 'Law on Freedom of the Press'.[140] In 2020, Chargui shared text that imitated the format of a Quranic paragraph ('sura'), titled 'Sura Corona', encouraging readers to follow science and wash their hands, stating 'there's no difference between kings and slaves, follow science and ignore traditions'.[141] The verse made no comment on religion, beyond using the style of a sura. Chargui did not even write the text but reposted it because she 'thought it was a good way to make people be … careful with the coronavirus, with a style that everyone knows'.[142] At trial, prosecutors failed to present any evidence showing that Chargui had an intention to incite hostility or violence against Muslims, or that such violence was likely to occur as a result of her post. Instead, the prosecution argued that posting 'text similar to the Qu'ran' constituted an offence under articles 52 and 53 of Tunisia's press law. Article 52 sanctions the act of calling directly to hatred between races, religions or the population by inciting discrimination and using hostile means, violence or dissemination of ideas based on racial discrimination. Article 53 provides for the sentence of imprisonment and a fine for the act of intentionally infringing on a recognized religious rite.[143] She was convicted and sentenced to six months' imprisonment and a fine.[144] The decision has been condemned by human rights groups, which have described it as a 'bitter blow to freedom of expression in Tunisia'.[145] Although reports had suggested that Chargui's lawyers intended to appeal the decision, there is no record of the appeal and Chargui has since left the country.[146]

---

[139] G. Harkins, 'A man said he'd hang 6 members of Congress who didn't "get behind" Trump, feds say. He got 33 months in prison' (The Washington Post, 2 December 2021).
[140] See CFJ, 'Statement on the Conviction of Emna Chargui in Tunisia' (15 July 2020); A. Benchemsi & N. Slama, 'Humor Comes at a Price in Morocco and Tunisia' (Human Rights Watch, 13 May 2020).
[141] 'Tunisia: Woman gets six-month jail sentence for coronavirus post mimicking Quran' (Middle East Eye, 15 July 2020).
[142] L. Blaise & E. Peltier, 'Tunisian Woman Sentenced to Prison Over Joke Alluding to the Quran' (The New York Times, 17 July 2020).
[143] Tunisian Decree No. 115 on Freedom of the Press, Printing, and Publishing of 2 November 2011 Arts 52–53.
[144] Blaise & Peltier (n 142).
[145] Amnesty International, 'Tunisia: Blogger Emna Chargui sentenced to six months in prison for social media post' (15 July 2020).
[146] Human Rights Watch, 'Tunisia, Events of 2020'.

2.4.2. Saudi Arabia

In Saudi Arabia, prosecutions for anti-religious speech are routine and often accompanied by harsh penalties. Such was the case of Raif Badawi, who was sentenced to 10 years' imprisonment and one thousand lashes for insulting Islam.[147] In 2006, Badawi launched an 'online forum for political and social debate' called 'Saudi Arabian Liberals' and was subsequently arrested. He was detained for almost 10 years and remains subject to a travel ban.[148]

The criminal proceedings against Badawi have been described by the UN as a 'flagrant misadministration' of justice 'manifested in the repetition of … trials and convictions at different levels of the courts'.[149] He was ultimately sentenced to five years' imprisonment for contempt of religion, insulting Islam and disseminating 'electronic materials that may undermine public order or mock public morality or national figures' on the basis of pro-secular speech on his blog. This included posts which, according to the prosecutor, questioned the 'validity of prayer; wondered why Valentine's day is not celebrated in Saudi Arabia; and mocked … religious and political figures'.[150] However, it has been said that through his blog posts Badawi 'unmasked a culture of corruption and criminality, as well as the impunity that underpinned them. He challenged religious intolerance and extremism, and sparked a discussion on modernization' in Saudi Arabia.[151] The judge added two years to his sentence for 'insulting Islam and Saudi's religious police' during televised interviews and three months for 'parental disobedience', resulting in a total sentence of seven years and 600 lashes.[152] On appeal, the sentence was increased to 10 years' imprisonment, a fine amounting to approximately $250,000 US dollars and a 10-year ban on travel and journalistic activity. The appellate court rejected Badawi's submission that he should not be held responsible for speech by third parties posted on the blog on the basis that he was in control of it and 'disregarded the blasphemy being spread through it'.[153]

III. International Legal Standards

Freedom of expression is enshrined in article 19 of the Universal Declaration of Human Rights, article 19 of the ICCPR and regional human rights instruments including the European Convention, American Convention, African Charter on Human and Peoples' Rights, Arab Charter on Human Rights and the ASEAN Human Rights Declaration.[154]

---

[147] See, e.g., WGAD, *Sheikh Suliaman al-Rashudi and others v. Saudi Arabia* (Opinion no. 38/2015), 4 September 2015, §§24–27 and Raoul Wallenberg Centre for Human Rights, 'Appeal for Clemency for Raif Badawi'.
[148] WGAD, *Sheikh Suliaman al-Rashudi and others v. Saudi Arabia* (Opinion no. 38/2015), 26 October 2015, §24; 'Raif Badawi: Saudi blogger freed after decade in prison' (BBC, 11 March 2022).
[149] WGAD, *Sheikh Suliaman al-Rashudi and others v. Saudi Arabia* (Opinion no. 38/2015), 26 October 2015, §80.
[150] Columbia Global Freedom of Expression Database, 'Saudi Public Prosecutor v. Raif Badawi'. He was initially charged with the capital crime of apostasy but this was later dropped.
[151] B. Silver & E. Abitbol, 'One Way Crown Prince Mohamed bin Salman Can Prove He Is Sincere About His Reforms: Free Raif Badawi' (TIME, 5 April 2018).
[152] Human Rights Watch, 'Saudi Arabia: 600 Lashes, 7 Years for Activist' (30 July 2013).
[153] Jeddah District Appeal Court decision dated 27 May 2014 (unofficial translation).
[154] See ECHR Art. 10; ACHR Art. 13; ACHPR Art. 9; Arab Charter Art. 32; ASEAN Human Rights Declaration Art. 23; and Cairo Declaration on Human Rights in Islam Art. 22. Article 32 of the Arab Charter provides the same

Each defines the right to freedom of expression broadly. But international law also provides that states may—and in certain circumstances *must*—punish hate speech. This *requirement* that certain speech should be penalized, and even in some instances criminalized, is a key difference between international standards governing hate speech laws and standards relating to other types of speech. For instance, although speech that is defamatory in nature may be penalized, there is no international law *obligation* to do so.[155]

In the case of hate speech, three UN treaties mandate the imposition of penalties. First, article 20 of the ICCPR requires that 'propaganda for war' and 'advocacy of national, racial or religious hatred that constitutes incitement to discrimination, hostility or violence ... *shall be* prohibited by law'. Second, article 4 of CERD requires penalties for racist speech. And, third, the Genocide Convention requires penalties for speech that incites genocide. The ICCPR provision allows for civil and administrative penalties, as well as potentially criminal ones,[156] while the other two provisions mandate penalties that are criminal in nature.

In addition to mandatory restrictions on speech, international human rights law provides guidance on when such restrictions are permissible. Under article 19(3) of the ICCPR, a state is permitted to penalize speech if the state can prove that the restriction is (1) 'provided by law' and (2) necessary to (3) protect one of the following legitimate objectives: 'the rights or reputations of others', 'national security', 'public order' or 'public health or morals'. Mandatory restrictions on speech must also comply with this three-part test.[157]

1. Mandatory Restrictions on Hate Speech

Article 20 of the ICCPR mandates that 'propaganda for war' and 'advocacy of national, racial or religious hatred that constitutes incitement to discrimination, hostility or

---

legitimate aims by which expression can be restricted as article 19(3) of the ICCPR, but adds a caveat that rights must be 'exercised in conformity with the fundamental values of society', and the Charter currently lacks an enforcement mechanism. The ASEAN Human Rights Declaration is a non-binding instrument which, although providing a broad right to freedom of opinion and expression in article 23, has a number of general limitation clauses, for example article 7, which stated that 'realisation of human rights must be considered in the regional and national context bearing in mind different political, economic, legal, social, cultural and religious backgrounds'. The Cairo Declaration, a non-binding instrument, provides more extensive limits to speech than article 19 of the ICCPR, but the Organization of Islamic Cooperation has been revising the instrument, with finalization of an amended Declaration on Human Rights postponed due to the COVID-19 pandemic: see T. Kayaoglu, 'The Organization of Islamic Cooperation's declaration on human rights: Promises and pitfalls' (Brookings, 28 September 2020).

[155] Although an important component of the practical reality of litigating hate speech cases, due process issues such as the burden and standard of proof and limitation periods are not within the scope of this chapter. See A. Clooney & P. Webb, *The Right to a Fair Trial in International Law* (OUP 2020).

[156] The Human Rights Committee has not, to date, stated that any particular speech requires criminalization under Art. 20 of the ICCPR. Cf. HRC, *Faurisson v. France* (Comm. no. 550/1993), 8 November 1996 (overruled) (where the Committee found the French Gayssot Act which required criminalization of speech to be compliant with the ICCPR).

[157] HRC, General Comment No. 34 (2011), §50, citing HRC, *Ross v. Canada* (Comm. no. 736/1997), 18 October 2000. See also HRC, *Rabbae v. The Netherlands* (Comm. no. 2124/2011), 14 July 2016, §10.4.

violence ... *shall be* prohibited by law'. Speech falling within article 20 *must* be legally prohibited, but criminal sanctions are not required.

CERD and the Genocide Convention, on the other hand, mandate *criminal* penalties for certain forms of hate speech. CERD requires in article 4 that states '[s]hall declare [as] an offence ... all dissemination of ideas based on racial superiority or hatred, incitement to racial discrimination, as well as all ... incitement to ... acts [of violence] against any race or group of persons of another colour or ethnic origin'. This must, however, be done 'with due regard' to other human rights principles and obligations, including freedom of expression.[158] In its General Recommendation 35, the UN Committee on the Elimination of all Forms of Racial Discrimination, which is established by the Convention to monitor implementation of the treaty, clarified that 'states parties should take into account ... the intention of the speaker' and 'the imminent risk or likelihood that the conduct desired or intended by the speaker will result from the speech in question' when sanctioning racist hate speech that falls within the scope of article 4.[159] This authoritative guidance, as well as the 'due regard' clause, therefore significantly narrow the scope of the mandate to criminalize speech.

Article 3 of the Genocide Convention requires that 'direct and public incitement to commit genocide' *shall be* punishable. This has been interpreted by the International Criminal Tribunal for Rwanda as meaning punishment through criminal law.[160] The elements of this crime include the need to prove that: (1) the speaker specifically intended to cause genocide through their speech; (2) the incitement was 'direct', based on an assessment of the local context to determine how the speech would be understood by the intended audience; (3) the intended harm was genocide, which means a specific intent to eradicate particular groups in whole or in part through certain acts; and (4) the statements were made in public.[161]

The American Convention on Human Rights is the only regional human rights treaty that mandates the criminal prohibition of hate speech. This mandatory prohibition, contained in article 13 of the Convention, provides that '[a]ny propaganda for war and any advocacy of national, racial, or religious hatred that constitute incitements to lawless violence or to any other similar action against any person or group of persons on any grounds including those of race, color, religion, language, or national origin shall be considered as offenses punishable by law'. It is therefore narrower than article 20 of the ICCPR and is limited to situations of (1) 'propaganda', (2) that incites (3) an objective and imminent risk of 'lawless violence' or 'similar' harm (4) against any person

---

[158] Article 4 provides that states must have 'due regard to the principles embodied in the Universal Declaration of Human Rights and the rights expressly set forth in article 5 of this Convention'. Article 19 of the UDHR and sub-paragraph (d)(viii) of CERD article 5 protect freedom of expression.

[159] CERD Committee, General Recommendation No. 35 (2013), §16.

[160] See ICTR, *Prosecutor v. Akayesu* (ICTR-96-4-T), Judgement, 2 September 1998, §551 ('At the time the Convention on Genocide was adopted, the delegates agreed to expressly spell out direct and public incitement to commit genocide as a specific crime'). See also ICTR, *Prosecutor v. Nahimana et. al.* (ICTR-99-52-A), Judgement, 28 November 2007, §678; UN Special Rapporteur F. La Rue, *Promotion and protection of the right to freedom of opinion and expression* (2012) UN Doc. A/67/357, §40.

[161] ICTR, *Prosecutor v. Nahimana et. al.* (ICTR-99-52-A), Judgement, 28 November 2007, §§698–701, 709.

or group of persons on any grounds including those of race, colour, religion, language or national origin.

1.1. ICCPR Article 20

Article 20 of the ICCPR was first proposed by a Soviet diplomat who considered that such a provision would be a 'powerful weapon ... to restrict the dissemination of Nazi-Fascist propaganda'.[162] However, a number of delegations drafting the treaty opposed the proposal, with the US delegation warning that 'any criticism of public or religious authorities might all too easily be described as incitement to hatred and consequently prohibited', and the UK delegates arguing that hatred was 'not easy to define as a penal offence'.[163]

The UN Human Rights Committee has made clear that restrictions imposed under article 20 of the ICCPR must also meet article 19's tripartite test of legality, legitimacy and necessity.[164] The Human Rights Committee has not provided a detailed interpretation of article 20[165] but in the *Rabbae v. the Netherlands* case it closely reviewed the application of hate speech provisions enacted to give effect to article 20 in Dutch law and in doing so provided important guidance.[166]

The *Rabbae* case was brought by Dutch-Moroccan nationals who claimed that the Netherlands had violated article 20 by failing to convict Geert Wilders, a right-wing Dutch politician, for speech that was discriminatory on the grounds of race and religion.[167] The Committee found that the Netherlands had not violated the ICCPR since the treaty 'does not provide individuals with a right to have [specific] individuals prosecuted' let alone 'ensure that a person who is charged with incitement to discrimination, hostility and violence will invariably be convicted'.[168]

Although the Committee has not provided definitions of the terms 'advocacy', 'hatred' or 'incitement', members of the Committee were satisfied that the definition of incitement under Dutch law—'inflammatory behaviour that incites the commission of criminal offences or acts of violence'—was a proper implementation of article 20(2).[169] The Committee also confirmed that the prohibition provided by article 20 does not mandate criminalization of speech, but can be fulfilled by civil and administrative penalties.[170] A concurring opinion in *Rabbae* also noted that article 20 sets 'a high bar' and

---

[162] See Clooney & Webb, 'The Right to Insult in International Law' (n 119) 17.
[163] Ibid.; see ch. 1 (Introduction), s. II.1.2.1.2. (ICCPR Article 20).
[164] HRC, General Comment No. 34 (2011), §§50–52. See s. III.2. (Discretionary Restrictions on Hate Speech).
[165] In 1983, the Human Rights Committee issued a General Comment that focused primarily on improved reporting in states parties' periodic reports. HRC, General Comment No. 10 (1983), §1.
[166] HRC, *Rabbae v. The Netherlands* (Comm. no. 2124/2011), 14 July 2016; see s. II.2.1.1. (The Netherlands). Prior to *Rabbae,* the Committee had referenced and in one instance found a violation of article 20, but without opining on its parameters. See HRC, *J. R. T. and the W. G. Party v. Canada* (Comm. no. 104/1981), 6 April 1983, §8(b); HRC, *Faurisson v. France* (Comm. no. 550/1993), 8 November 1996, Individual Opinion of Committee members Elizabeth Evatt and David Kretzmer, co-signed by Eckart Klein, §4; HRC, *Ross v. Canada* (Comm. no. 736/1997), 18 October 2000, §11.5.
[167] HRC, *Rabbae v. The Netherlands* (Comm. no. 2124/2011), 14 July 2016, §3.1.
[168] Ibid., §§10.3, 10.7, 11.
[169] Ibid., §10.7, Individual Concurring Opinion of Committee members Sarah Cleveland and Mauro Politi, §6.
[170] Ibid., §10.4. This conclusion has also been reached by the UN Special Rapporteur: UN Special Rapporteur F. La Rue, *Promotion and protection of the right to freedom of opinion and expression* (2012) UN Doc. A/67/357, §47.

does not require legal prohibition of all advocacy of national, racial or religious hatred, 'but only of such advocacy that also "constitutes *incitement* to discrimination, hostility or violence"'.[171]

Further guidance about the parameters of article 20 is provided by 'soft law' instruments such as the Rabat Plan of Action, a codification of international standards endorsed by the UN High Commissioner for Human Rights.[172] These standards conclude that 'a high threshold' should apply to 'the application of article 20'.[173] They also recognize that '[c]riminal sanctions related to unlawful forms of expression' should only apply in the most serious cases.[174]

The Rabat Plan of Action identifies six factors relevant to determining whether hateful speech can reach this high threshold and be criminalized. These are: (1) the context in which the statement was made; (2) the position or status of the speaker; (3) the intent of the speaker (noting that negligence and recklessness would not suffice); (4) the content and form of the speech; (5) the 'reach' of the speech including the nature and size of the audience; and (6) the likelihood of imminent harm arising from the speech.[175] These principles have been endorsed by the UN High Commissioner for Human Rights and the UN Special Rapporteur on Freedom of Opinion and Expression and they remain relevant to assessing the validity of hate speech laws that seek to give effect to article 20.[176]

In addition, the UN Special Rapporteur stated that the plain language of article 20 establishes three threshold elements that a state must demonstrate for speech to qualify for prohibition under this provision:[177] (1) 'advocacy' of national, racial or religious hatred should mean the 'explicit, intentional, public and active support and promotion of hatred towards the target group';[178] (2) hatred must refer to the 'intense and irrational emotions of opprobrium, enmity and detestation'; and (3) there must be 'incitement' to the harms listed in article 20, meaning that the speech should 'create an *imminent risk*' of such harm.[179] He also noted that 'hostility' should be interpreted to mean 'a manifestation of hatred beyond a mere state of mind'.[180]

---

[171] HRC, *Rabbae v. The Netherlands* (Comm. no. 2124/2011), 14 July 2016, Individual Concurring Opinion of Committee members Sarah Cleveland and Mauro Politi, §4.
[172] Rabat Plan of Action on the prohibition of advocacy of nation, racial or religious hatred that constitutes incitement to discrimination, hostility or violence.
[173] Ibid., §29.
[174] Ibid., §34. This conclusion has also been reached by the UN Special Rapporteur: UN Special Rapporteur F. La Rue, *Promotion and protection of the right to freedom of opinion and expression* (2012) UN Doc. A/67/357, §47.
[175] Rabat Plan of Action, §29.
[176] UN Special Rapporteur D. Kaye, *Promotion and protection of the right to freedom of opinion and expression* (2019) UN Doc. A/74/486, §57(a). See s. V. (Approach of Private Companies to Online Hate Speech).
[177] UN Special Rapporteur F. La Rue, *Promotion and protection of the right to freedom of opinion and expression* (2012) UN Doc. A/67/357, §43.
[178] Ibid., §44(b) citing principle 12.1 of the Camden Principles (advocacy 'is to be understood as requiring an intention to promote hatred publicly towards the target group'); Rabat Plan of Action, n 5, §29(c).
[179] UN Special Rapporteur F. La Rue, *Promotion and protection of the right to freedom of opinion and expression* (2012) UN Doc. A/67/357, §44(a), (c) citing principle 12.1 of the Camden Principles (emphasis added). See also Rabat Plan of Action, §29.
[180] UN Special Rapporteur F. La Rue, *Promotion and protection of the right to freedom of opinion and expression* (2012) UN Doc. A/67/357, §44(e).

1.2. CERD Article 4

The CERD treaty also requires criminal penalties for certain hate speech. More specifically article 4 provides that states '[s]hall declare [as] an offence ... all dissemination of ideas based on racial superiority or hatred, incitement to racial discrimination, as well as all ... incitement to ... acts [of violence] against any race or group of persons of another colour or ethnic origin'. This must, however, be done 'with due regard' to other human rights principles and obligations, including freedom of expression.[181] Article 4 refers to 'offense[s] punishable by law', and thus explicitly mandates criminal sanctions.

As a result of the breadth of the wording of article 4(a), a number of states entered reservations and declarations that seek to limit its scope and provide more protection for speech. The United States, for example, entered a reservation that it 'does not accept any obligation under this Convention', in particular under article 4, to restrict protections of freedom of speech, expression and association 'to the extent that they are protected by the Constitution and laws of the United States'.[182] Similar reservations were made by some European states as well as Japan, Guyana and Jamaica.[183]

However, in 2013 the CERD Committee—the expert body charged with monitoring implementation of the Racial Discrimination Convention—issued 'General Recommendation 35', which adopted a narrower interpretation of the scope of article 4 than the Committee had previously espoused.[184] First, the Committee noted the five contextual factors 'adapted from' the Rabat Plan of Action that 'should be taken into account' when determining if speech should be punishable under article 4. These are: the 'content and form of speech'; the 'economic, social and political climate' at the time speech was disseminated; the 'position or status of the speaker' and the audience to which the speech was directed; 'the reach of the speech' and its 'objectives'.[185] Secondly, the Committee clarified that in interpreting and applying the term 'incitement', states parties should consider 'the intention of the speaker, and the imminent risk or likelihood that the conduct desired or intended by the speaker will result from the speech in question'.[186]

Indeed the Committee went further and clarified that the issue of intent and imminence should be relevant not only to incitement but to *all* speech criminalized by article 4, including 'all dissemination of ideas based on racial superiority or hatred', thereby interpreting this provision more closely in line with article 20 of the ICCPR.[187] As a result, the lead drafter of General Recommendation 35 considered that the Recommendation 'decisively rejects any suggestion of a "strict liability" approach to

---

[181] CERD Art. 4(a). Article 4 provides that states must have 'due regard to the principles embodied in the Universal Declaration of Human Rights and the rights expressly set forth in article 5 of this Convention'. Article 19 of the UDHR and sub-paragraph (d)(viii) of CERD article 5 protect freedom of expression.

[182] UNTC Depositary, Status of Treaties, ch. IV.2 CERD, Declarations and Reservations, United States of America.

[183] See ch. 1 (Introduction), s. II.1.3.1.3. (CERD Article 4) setting out reservations by Guyana, Jamaica and Japan as well as Austria, Belgium, France, Ireland, Italy and Monaco.

[184] CERD Committee, General Recommendation No. 35 (2013).

[185] Ibid., §15, n 17.

[186] Ibid., §16.

[187] Ibid., §§13, 16.

dissemination and incitement ... [by linking] them with principles of criminal law on mental elements in crime'.[188]

The Committee also clarified that the 'due regard' language of article 4 requires 'strict compliance with freedom of expression guarantees',[189] and that any criminal restrictions on speech 'should be reserved for serious cases, to be proven beyond reasonable doubt', and 'governed by principles of legality, proportionality and necessity'.[190] Finally, the Committee emphasized that 'the expression of ideas and opinions made in the context of academic debates, political engagement or similar activity, and without incitement to hatred contempt, violence or discrimination, should be regarded as legitimate exercises of the right to freedom of expression'.[191]

This clarification of the scope of article 4 brings the CERD Committee's pronouncements closer to the approach adopted by the Human Rights Committee.[192] And prior practice that did not consistently require specific intent and incitement, or address the applicability of ICCPR article 19(3)'s legality, necessity and proportionality principles in hate speech cases, is likely to be considered overturned.[193]

The Committee did, however, also take a step in the opposite direction by approving an expansion of potential liability in the definition of harms. First, it found that incitement to 'contempt' can be a harm justifying criminalization under article 4,[194] despite the fact that the text refers only to 'hatred' 'discrimination' and 'violence'.[195] The Committee also found that although the title of the Convention suggests that it is limited to 'racial' hatred, the harms that are recognized also extend to 'colour, descent or national or ethnic origin'.[196]

1.3. Genocide Convention Article 3

The most extreme form of hate speech addressed by international human rights law is 'direct and public incitement to commit genocide'. States are required, under the Genocide Convention, to punish such speech through the criminal law.[197]

---

[188] P. Thornberry, 'International Convention on the Elimination of All Forms of Racial Discrimination: The Prohibition of "Racist Hate Speech"', in T. McGonagle & Y. Donders (eds), *The United Nations and Freedom of Expression and Information: Critical Perspectives* (CUP 2015), 121, 131. Thornberry was a member of the Committee from 2001–2014.

[189] CERD Committee, General Recommendation No. 35 (2013), §19. See also UN Special Rapporteur D. Kaye, *Promotion and protection of the right to freedom of opinion and expression* (2019) UN Doc. A/74/486, §15.

[190] CERD Committee, General Recommendation No. 35 (2013), §12 (citing to HRC, General Comment No. 34 (2011)).

[191] CERD Committee, General Recommendation No. 35 (2013), §25.

[192] See P. Thornberry, *The International Convention on the Elimination of All Forms of Racial Discrimination* (OUP 2016), 297–298, 301–302 ('[T]he fresh reading of Article 4 takes the Convention closer to the ICCPR'); UN Special Rapporteur D. Kaye, *Promotion and protection of the right to freedom of opinion and expression* (2019) UN Doc. A/74/486, §15 (noting the CERD Committee's 'converging interpretations' with the HRC).

[193] See, e.g., CERD, *Adan v. Denmark* (Comm. no. 43/2008), 13 August 2010, §§7.2, 7.7; CERD, *The Jewish Community of Oslo v. Norway* (Comm. no. 30/2003), 15 August 2005, §§2.5, 10.5.

[194] CERD Committee, General Recommendation No. 35 (2013), §§13, 25.

[195] CERD Art. 4(a), CERD Committee, General Recommendation No. 35 (2013), §13(b), (d).

[196] CERD Committee, General Recommendation No. 35 (2013), §§6, 13. See also CERD Art. 1 which explicitly states: 'In this Convention, the term "racial discrimination" shall mean any distinction, exclusion, restriction or preference based on race, colour, descent, or national or ethnic origin.'

[197] Genocide Convention Art. 3(c). The Rome Statute of the ICC criminalizes incitement to genocide in a different format: 'the crime of genocide' is listed as one of the crimes within the jurisdiction of the Court under Art. 5 and is defined under Art. 6 without reference to direct and public incitement to commit genocide. However, Art.

Genocide offences have a high bar: the International Court of Justice has held that any crime under article 3 of the Convention, including incitement to commit genocide, must be proven by evidence that is 'fully conclusive'.[198] The key elements of the crime are set out in the *Nahimana* decision of the ICTR[199] in which three Rwandan media workers were convicted of direct and public incitement to genocide for disseminating extremist Hutu propaganda through radio broadcasts and newspapers during the Rwandan genocide.[200]

In this case—known as the Media Trial—the ICTR Appeals Chamber held that in order for speech to incite genocide, the speech must be public,[201] the speaker must have 'the intent to directly and publicly incite others' to commit this crime,[202] and the speech must be 'direct', based on 'the meaning of the words used in the specific context'. This means that if the relevant words do not amount to an explicit appeal to commit genocide, it must be shown that the intended audience 'immediately grasped' their implication.[203]

The *Nahimana* decision distinguished 'mere' hate speech from incitement to commit genocide, recognizing that more stringent requirements applied to the latter.[204] Judge Meron also emphasized in his dissent that 'there is no settled norm of customary

---

25 provides for modes of individual criminal responsibility across the Statute and specifically notes 'in respect of the crime of genocide, directly and publicly incites others to commit genocide': Art. 25(3)(e). Commentators have described this as having 'downgraded' incitement 'from a standalone crime in itself to a mode of participation in genocide' and that as 'proof of causation is required for modes of liability for completed crimes and furnishing such proof is an arduous undertaking, the ICC's unusual formulation of incitement to genocide means that prosecutions at the ICC for the crime are less likely to succeed': R.A. Wilson, *Incitement on Trial: Prosecuting International Speech Crimes* (CUP 2017), 34.

[198] ICJ, *Application of the Convention on the Prevention and Punishment of the Crime of Genocide (Croatia v. Serbia)*, Judgment of 3 February 2015, §178; see also §407 (when direct evidence of specific intent is absent, the Court requires that 'the only reasonable conclusion to be drawn [from conduct] is an intent' to 'destroy that substantial part of the group').

[199] ICTR, *Prosecutor v. Nahimana et. al.* (ICTR-99-52-A), Judgement, 28 November 2007, §677.

[200] The defendants were convicted under article 2(3)(c) of the Statute of the International Tribunal for Rwanda, which prohibits incitement to genocide in the same terms as the Genocide Convention. Two of them were political figures and the founders of an independent radio station Radio Télévision Libre des Milles Collines (RTLM) and the third was the owner and editor of a newspaper.

[201] In subsequent cases the ICTR elaborated on the requirement that the speech be 'public' to constitute 'incitement'. In one case the tribunal noted that 'all convictions before the Tribunal for direct and public incitement to commit genocide involve speeches made to large, fully public assemblies, messages disseminated by the media, and communications made through a public address system over a broad public area'. Crowds of between 20–30 people have satisfied this requirement and convictions may be based on 'communications to smaller audiences when the incriminating message is given in a public space to an unselected audience'. However, a meeting limited to only a group of public officials, even though it was in the 'presence of a journalist', did not fulfil the 'public' element of incitement. See ICTR, *Prosecutor v. Nzabonimana* (ICTR-98-44D-T), Judgement and Sentence, 31 May 2012, §§1754, 1772; ICTR, *Nzabonimana v. Prosecutor* (ICTR-98-44D-A), Judgement, 29 September 2014, §§126, 231, 385. See s. II.2.1.1. (The Netherlands).

[202] ICTR, *Prosecutor v. Nahimana et. al.* (ICTR-99-52-A), Judgement, 28 November 2007, §677; see also §709 (When determining intent, 'the fact that a speech leads to acts of genocide could be an indication that in that particular context the speech was understood to be an incitement to commit genocide', but this is not the only way to prove intent). The Tribunal also confirmed that as incitement to genocide is an 'inchoate crime', genocide need not actually occur since the inciting utterance itself constitutes the criminal conduct.

[203] Ibid., §§698, 701. See also the Partly Dissenting Opinion of Judge Shahabuddeen, which provides that the 'incitement must call for immediate action, but it certainly is not the case that the prosecution has to show that genocide in fact followed immediately after the message or at all': §65.

[204] Ibid., §692 (defining such speech as 'inciting discrimination or violence'). See also §693 (noting that as a result 'the jurisprudence on incitement to hatred, discrimination and violence is not directly applicable in determining what constitutes direct incitement to commit genocide').

international law that criminalizes hate speech', as the 'number and extent of the reservations' to article 4 of CERD and article 20 of the ICCPR reveal 'that profound disagreement persists in the international community as to whether mere hate speech [as opposed to incitement to genocide] is or should be prohibited'.[205]

In *Nahimana* and subsequent decisions, the ICTR confirmed that the crime of incitement to genocide does not incorporate a requirement of imminent or likely harm and instead focuses on the intent of the speaker, thereby diverging from the mandatory restrictions in article 20(2) of the ICCPR and article 4 of CERD on this point. The *travaux préparatories* illustrate that this was a point of tension in the drafting history of the Convention, with the United States putting forward alternative text which criminalized incitement to genocide only when 'such incitement takes place under circumstances which may reasonably result in the commission of acts of genocide'.[206] In *Nahimana*, the Appeals Chamber noted that although stringent *mens rea* requirements applied, 'direct and public incitement to commit genocide ... is itself a crime, and it is not necessary to demonstrate that it in fact substantially contributed to the commission of acts of genocide'.[207] This was reiterated in *Nzambonimana*, which concluded that 'the *actus reus* of direct and public incitement to genocide is satisfied when a person directly and publicly incites the commission of genocide, *irrespective of whether his or her acts were likely to cause the crime of genocide*'.[208]

However, some scholars have observed that 'a number of ICTR judgments felt it necessary to establish a direct causal link between speeches or broadcasts and actual genocide or other material crimes in the "findings of fact" sections', such as the *Nahimana* case, where the ruling 'asserts no less than sixteen times that speech acts directly caused genocidal killings'.[209] They argue that the ICTR seems to have thereby introduced 'a new criterion of contemporaneousness, in which genocidal speech acts had to be uttered very near or simultaneous with the onset of actual genocide' and made causation a requirement in its incitement jurisprudence after all.[210]

1.4. Mandatory restrictions at the regional level

The American Convention is the only regional human rights instrument containing a mandatory requirement to penalize specific speech. Article 13(5) of the American Convention provides that '[a]ny propaganda for war and any advocacy of national,

---

[205] Ibid., Partly Dissenting Opinion of Judge Meron, §§5–8. Judge Meron held that the Appeals Chamber impermissibly predicated convictions for crimes against humanity by persecution on the basis of hate speech, rather than the incitement to commit genocide convictions.

[206] Prevention and Punishment in the draft convention prepared by the Segretariat, Lake Success, N.Y. (1948) UN Doc. E/623 and Ad Hoc Committee on Genocide, Basic Principles of a Convention on Genocide Proposed by the Delegation of the Union of Societ Socialist Republics on 5 April 1948 (1948) UN Doc. E/AC.25/7, cited in W. Schabas, *Genocide in International Law: The Crime of Crimes* (1st edn, CUP 2000), 267. The USSR argued for broader versions of the provision that criminalized 'inciting racial, national or religious enmity or hatred': 271.

[207] ICTR, *Prosecutor v. Nahimana et. al.* (ICTR-99-52-A), Judgement, 28 November 2007, §678.

[208] ICTR, *Nzabonimana v. Prosecutor* (ICTR-98-44D-A), Judgement, 29 September 2014, §234 (emphasis added).

[209] See Wilson (n 197) 34–37.

[210] Ibid. See also S. Benesch, 'Vile Crime in Inalienable Right: Defining Incitement to Genocide' (2008) 48(3) *Virginia Journal of International Law* 485, 497 ('courts have indirectly relied on causation, in the absence of such a test, even where such reliance may have stretched the evidence thin').

racial, or religious hatred that constitute incitements to lawless violence or to any other similar action against any person or group of persons on any grounds including those of race, color, religion, language, or national origin shall be considered as offenses punishable by law'.[211]

The mandatory hate speech restriction in the Inter-American system is in some ways similar to the one contained in the ICCPR and CERD. It is subject to the three-part test set forth in the jurisprudence of the Inter-American Court of Human Rights which, like the ICCPR article 19(3) test, requires an assessment of legality, legitimacy and necessity.[212] And article 13(5) appears to incorporate similar intent and imminence standards as the ICCPR and CERD provisions, requiring that states must demonstrate 'actual, truthful, objective and strong proof that the person was not simply issuing an opinion (even if that opinion was hard, unfair or disturbing), but that the person had the clear intention of committing a crime and the actual, real and effective possibility of achieving this objective' before their speech can be criminalized.[213]

In one sense the Inter-American provision can capture more speech than the other treaties, because the list of target groups is wider: according to the Inter-American Commission, article 13(5) covers characteristics other than nationality, race and religion and extends to speech that is hateful on the basis of 'sexual orientation, gender identity, and bodily diversity'.[214]

But the harm threshold provided by article 13(5)—'lawless violence or other similar action' is much higher—and therefore more speech-protective—than the equivalent treaties.[215] Though 'similar action' is not defined, the drafting history of the treaty suggests that the harm should be comparable in severity to violence.[216] And in relation to

---

[211] ACHR Art. 13(5). However, as the OAS Special Rapporteur for Freedom of Expression has previously noted, there is a 'discrepancy' between the English and Spanish language versions of the text of article 13. The Spanish language version of article 13(5) – *'estará prohibida por la ley'* – suggests that speech must be 'prohibited' rather than 'punishable'. But the Inter-American Court is yet to comprehensively address the impact of this discrepancy – and whether it calls into question the mandatory nature of criminal restrictions under article 13(5) – in its jurisprudence: OAS Special Rapporteur for Freedom of Expression, *Hate Speech and the American Convention* (2004), §§37–38.

[212] See, e.g., IACtHR, *Herrera-Ulloa v. Costa Rica* (Series C, no. 107), 2 July 2004, §123. See also IACmHR, *Annual Report of the Inter-American Commission on Human Rights* (2009) OEA/Ser.L/V/II., Doc. 51, 247, 252 (stating that '"necessary" is not synonymous with "useful", "reasonable" or "convenient"' but requires states to use the least intrusive means to achieve their legitimate public interest purpose and that 'proportionate' means assessing 'whether the sacrifice of freedom of expression ... is excessive in relation to the advantages obtained through such measure'). Like the HRC, the IACmHR has clarified that the burden is on 'the authority imposing limitations to prove that these conditions have been met': 247.

[213] IACmHR, *Inter-American Legal Framework Regarding the Right to Freedom of Expression* (2009) OEA/Ser.L/V/II, CIDH/RELE/INF. 2/09, §59.

[214] IACmHR, *Violence against Lesbian, Gay, Bisexual, Trans and Intersex Persons in the Americas* (2015) OAS/Ser.L/V/II. Doc.36/15 Rev.2, §13, referring to 'the [IACmHR] and its Special Rapporteurship affirm that article 13(5) includes hate speech that incites lawless violence against a group' on those additional grounds. See s. VI. (Recommendations).

[215] See, e.g., OAS Special Rapporteur for Freedom of Expression, *Hate Speech and the American Convention* (2004), §46 (observing that article 13(5) 'suggest[s] that violence is a requirement for any restrictions' but that the ICCPR and European Convention 'do not have such a narrowly drawn requirement').

[216] Inter-American specialized conference on human rights, San José, Costa Rica, Minutes of the second plenary session (22 November 1969) Doc. 86, US Statement, 444. The original provision provided for violence as well as 'discrimination' and 'hostility', but the US delegate recommended that this wording be replaced with 'similar action' to ensure consistency with First Amendment jurisprudence. In addition the Spanish version of article 13(5) provides for 'similar *illegal action*' ('acción ilegal similar').

the causal link between speech and harm under article 13(5), it is not permissible to 'invoke as a reason to limit freedom of expression mere conjectures about eventual effects on the public order, or hypothetical circumstances derived from subjective interpretations by authorities of facts that do not clearly present a present, certain, objective and imminent risk of violence'.[217] Instead, a speaker must have a 'real, present and effective possibility of achieving his or her objectives'.[218]

1.5. Summary

In summary, the requirements in international and regional treaties that states impose mandatory penalties for hate speech, although not identical, share key common elements. Every mandatory penalty must comply with the permissible limitations to freedom of expression. Each infers an intent requirement, with article 3 of the Genocide Convention requiring the highest intent standard linked to the act of genocide. And each treaty requires speech to rise to the level of 'incitement', thereby incorporating an element of imminent risk of harm, despite article 4 of CERD on its face allowing a lower threshold of 'dissemination of ideas' only.[219]

The principal variation is in the harms that are recognized as legitimate bases for criminal penalties for speech. The recognized harms include discrimination, hostility or violence in the case of article 20 ICCPR; hatred, discrimination, violence and contempt under article 4 CERD; and 'lawless violence' or 'other similar action' in the Inter-American provision. The American Convention sets the highest bar, though there has been minimal authoritative guidance defining the contours of these terms in the jurisprudence of the Inter-American Court to date.

The targeted group each harm relates to also diverges, with the CERD only applying to 'racial' origin,[220] the ICCPR also including 'religious' groups and the American Convention—as interpreted by the Inter-American Commission—extending further to groups defined by gender and sexual orientation.[221] Finally, the penalties differ, with article 4 of CERD, article 3 of the Genocide Convention and article 13(5) of the American Convention[222] requiring criminalization, not just civil sanctions, for speech.

---

[217] IACmHR, *Democracy and Human Rights in Venezuela* (2009) OEA/Ser.L/V/II., Doc. 54, §379; IACmHR, *Annual Report of the Inter-American Commission on Human Rights* (2009) OEA/Ser.L/V/II., Doc. 51, 169.

[218] IACmHR, *Democracy and Human Rights in Venezuela* (2009) OEA/Ser.L/V/II., Doc. 54, §360; IACmHR, *Annual Report of the Inter-American Commission on Human Rights* (2009) OEA/Ser.L/V/II., Doc. 51, 174.

[219] See s. III.1.2. (CERD Article 4). Although article 3 of the Genocide Convention requires an element of 'incites', this has been held not to equate to a requirement of imminent risk of harm: See s. III.1.3. (Genocide Convention Article 3).

[220] The CERD Committee has, however, interpreted this to extend to 'colour, descent or national or ethnic origin'. CERD Committee, General Recommendation No. 35 (2013), §§6, 13. See also CERD Art. 1.

[221] See s. III.1.2. (CERD Article 4); see also CERD Committee, General Recommendation No. 35 (2013), §13; ICCPR Art. 20; IACmHR, *Violence against Lesbian, Gay, Bisexual, Trans and Intersex Persons in the Americas* (2015) OAS/Ser.L/V/II. Doc.36/15 Rev.2, §13.

[222] The IACtHR has rejected the use of criminal law to punish expressions in cases involving the public interest, and has favoured the use of the right of reply and civil damages to deal with abuses of freedom of expression. But the IACtHR has not ruled on cases of hate speech specifically. See IACtHR, *Álvarez Ramos v. Venezuela* (Series C, no. 380), 30 August 2019, §§120–122; see s. III.2.5. (Penalties).

2. Discretionary Restrictions on Hate Speech

In addition to treaty provisions governing when states *must* punish hate speech,[223] international and regional human rights law provides the legal framework for when states *may* do so. Under article 19(3) of the ICCPR, hate speech can be 'subject to certain restrictions' only as 'provided by law' and as 'necessary' for the protection of certain legitimate aims including the right to reputation, national security and public health. This tripartite test is often referred to as one of legality, legitimacy and necessity.[224] An element of the requirement of necessity is proportionality: any restrictive measure 'must be the least intrusive instrument amongst those which might achieve their protective function' and must be 'proportionate to the interest to be protected'.[225]

Article 10 of the European Convention sets out a tripartite test similar to article 19(3) of the ICCPR, but also provides a number of legitimate aims not explicitly recognized in article 19(3) of the ICCPR. These are: 'territorial integrity or public safety', the 'prevention of disorder or crime', 'preventing the disclosure of information received in confidence' and 'maintaining the authority and impartiality of the judiciary'. However, the Human Rights Committee has generally construed the limitations outlined in article 19(3) as encompassing the aims set out in article 10(2), for instance by way of a broad reading of the 'public order' limitation.[226]

The list of legitimate aims articulated in article 13(2) of the American Convention mirrors article 19(3) of the ICCPR and the Inter-American Court applies the three-part test of legality, legitimacy and necessity consistently with other regional bodies.[227] The American Convention is, however, more protective of speech than its equivalents in its explicit prohibition of prior restraints to speech in almost all circumstances,[228] as well as indirect government restrictions and 'private controls'.[229] The Inter-American Court has indeed explicitly stated that a textual comparison of article 13 with article 10 of the European Convention and article 19 of the ICCPR 'indicates clearly that the guarantees contained in the American Convention regarding freedom of expression were

---

[223] See s. III.1. (Mandatory Restrictions on Hate Speech).
[224] UN Special Rapporteur D. Kaye, *Promotion and protection of the right to freedom of opinion and expression* (2016) UN Doc. A/71/373, §57(a).
[225] HRC, General Comment No. 34 (2011), §34.
[226] See ch. 1 (Introduction), s. II.1.1.1. (Abuses by the state). See also HRC, *Lovell v. Australia* (Comm. no. 920/2000), 24 March 2004, §9.4; HRC, General Comment No. 34 (2011), §31; HRC, *Agazade and Jafarov v. Azerbaijan* (Comm. no. 2205/2012), 27 October 2016, §7.4; HRC, *Aleksandrov v. Belarus* (Comm. no. 1933/2010), 24 July 2014, §7.4.
[227] See, e.g., IACtHR, *Herrera-Ulloa v. Costa Rica* (Series C, no. 107), 2 July 2004, §120.
[228] ACHR Art. 13(2) ('The exercise of the right [to freedom of thought and expression] shall not be subject to prior censorship'), Art. 13(4) ('Notwithstanding the provisions of paragraph 2 above, public entertainments may be subject by law to prior censorship for the sole purpose of regulating access to them for the moral protection of childhood and adolescence'). See also IACtHR, *Compulsory Membership in an Association Prescribed by Law for the Practice of Journalism (Arts. 13 and 29 American Convention on Human Rights)*, Advisory Opinion OC-5/85 (Series A, no. 5), 13 November 1985, §38 ('Article 13 (2) ... stipulates, in the first place, that prior censorship is always incompatible with the full enjoyment of the rights listed in Article 13, but for the exception provided for in subparagraph 4 dealing with public entertainments, even if the alleged purpose of such prior censorship is to prevent abuses of freedom of expression').
[229] ACHR Art. 13(3).

designed to be more generous and to reduce to a bare minimum restrictions impeding the free circulation of ideas'.[230] While this speech-protective approach has not yet been applied to hate speech, it is indicative of the approach likely to be taken by the Inter-American Court.

Article 9(2) of the African Charter is unique in its lack of detail: the provision states only that '[e]very individual shall have the right to express and disseminate his opinions within the law'. However, the African Court has held that the term 'within the law' means that restrictions on speech must be 'prescribed by law, serve a legitimate purpose and [be] necessary and proportional as may be expected in a democratic society'.[231] The Court has also held that article 9(2) 'must be interpreted in the light of international human rights standards',[232] and its decisions related to the right to free speech draw on article 19 of the ICCPR to determine whether restrictions to speech violate the African Charter.[233]

The European Court of Human Rights has, for its part, emerged as an outlier in the extent to which it allows the penalization and even criminalization of hate speech, including Holocaust denial, religious insults and speech that does not incite violence. This is somewhat ironic given that other systems require mandatory prohibitions on such speech under certain circumstances, while the European Convention does not.[234]

There are two key divergences between the European Court and its counterparts that result in the Court being a less speech-protective human rights body. First, unlike the Human Rights Committee,[235] the European Court considers that states 'have a certain margin of appreciation' in assessing whether a 'pressing social need' makes a speech restriction 'necessary' to protect the objectives articulated in article 10(2) of the European Convention.[236] Although the European Court applies a narrow margin where speech relates to a matter of public concern,[237] it has also stated it affords governments a particularly wide margin of appreciation when expression is 'liable to offend intimate personal convictions within the sphere of morals or, especially, religion',[238] and 'where such remarks incite violence against an individual, a public official or a sector

---

[230] IACtHR, *Compulsory Membership in an Association Prescribed by Law for the Practice of Journalism (Arts. 13 and 29 American Convention on Human Rights)*, Advisory Opinion OC-5/85 (Series A, no. 5), 13 November 1985, §50.

[231] ACtHPR, *Umuhoza v. Rwanda* (App. no. 003/2014), 24 November 2017, §133.

[232] Ibid., §136. Article 60 of the ACHR provides that the African Commission 'must draw inspiration from international law on human and peoples' rights'. Although article 60 refers to the African Commission only, as the ACtHPR was established in 1998 after the Charter was adopted, the ACtHPR has since interpreted article 60 to grant the Court the same powers: see, e.g., ACtHPR, *Omary and others v. Tanzania* (App. no. 001/2012), 28 March 2014, §73 ('Article 60 of the Charter empowers the Court to "draw inspiration from international law on human and peoples' rights"').

[233] See, e.g., ACtHPR, *Umuhoza v. Rwanda* (App. no. 003/2014), 24 November 2017, §163; ACtHPR, *Konaté v. Burkina Faso* (App. no. 004/2013), 5 December 2014, §164.

[234] See s. III.1. (Mandatory Restrictions on Hate Speech).

[235] HRC, General Comment No. 34 (2011), §36.

[236] See, e.g., ECtHR (GC), *Zana v. Turkey* (App. no. 18954/91), 25 November 1997, §51. However, this margin is more 'limited' when freedom of the press is at stake: see s. III.2.4.4. ('Responsible journalism').

[237] ECtHR, *Otegi Mondragon v. Spain* (App. no. 2034/07), 15 March 2011, §51; ECtHR, *Tagiyev v. Azerbaijan* (App. no. 13274/08), 5 December 2019, §36.

[238] ECtHR, *Murphy v. Ireland* (App. no. 44179/98), 10 July 2003, §67. See also ECtHR, *Wingrove v. United Kingdom* (App. no. 17419/90), 25 November 1996, §58.

of the population'.[239] By contrast, the Human Rights Committee has explicitly rejected such an approach, observing that the scope of freedom of expression 'is not to be assessed by reference to a "margin of appreciation"'.[240]

The second critical difference between the European Court and its counterparts is the use of article 17 of the European Convention in cases involving speech. Article 17 provides that '[n]othing in th[e] Convention may be interpreted as implying ... any right to engage in any activity ... aimed at the destruction of any of the rights and freedoms' set out in the treaty, and the Court regularly dismisses claims related to hate speech as being non-admissible on this basis. This means that in some cases speech is not analysed using the balancing exercise provided by article 10(2).[241] The Court has construed article 17 as preventing 'individuals or groups with totalitarian aims from exploiting ... the principles enunciated in the Convention'.[242] And the Court has, on this basis, refused to consider claims involving 'speech [that] is incompatible with the values' of the Convention or 'contrary to' its 'text and spirit'.[243] Although the Court has stated that article 17 sets a 'high threshold'[244] and should only be applied 'on an exceptional basis and in extreme cases',[245] it has in effect operated as a form of guillotine provision which overrides the balancing exercise applicable to other types of speech.[246] And, ultimately, the 46 member states of the European Convention are also signatories to the ICCPR, and to the extent that their restrictions to speech are incompatible with article 19(3), they will be in breach of their international legal obligations.[247]

2.1. Legality

According to the Human Rights Committee, the requirement in article 19(3) of the ICCPR that a restriction on speech be 'provided by law' means that it must be public and 'formulated with sufficient precision to enable an individual to regulate his or her conduct'.[248]

---

[239] ECtHR, *Savva Terentyev v. Russia* (App. no. 10692/09), 28 August 2018, §65.
[240] HRC, General Comment No. 34 (2011), §36. The IACtHR and IACmHR have previously referred to states having a margin of appreciation, but have generally 'applied this doctrine with great caution and in many fewer instances than their European counterparts', and in relation to freedom of expression have 'been very hesitant to grant deference to States, preferring to examine closely the scope and effect of restrictive domestic measures': see B. Duhaime, 'Subsidiarity in the Americas: What Room Is There for Deference in the Inter-American System?', in L. Gruszczynski & W. Werner (eds), *Deference in International Courts and Tribunals: Standard of Review and Margin of Appreciation* (OUP 2014), 301, 307.
[241] See ECtHR, 'Factsheet—Hate Speech' (September 2023).
[242] ECtHR, *Hizb Ut-Tahrir v. Germany* (App. no. 31098/08), 12 June 2012, §72, citing ECtHR (GC), *Paksas v. Lithuania* (App. no. 34932/04), 6 January 2011, §§87–88.
[243] ECtHR, *Ivanov v. Russia* (App. no. 35222/04), 20 February 2007, §1; ECtHR, *Roj TV A/S v. Denmark* (App. no. 24683/14), 24 May 2018, §30.
[244] ECtHR, *Lilliendahl v. Iceland* (App. no. 29297/18), 12 May 2020, §§25–26.
[245] Ibid., §25. See also ECtHR (GC), *Perinçek v. Switzerland* (App. no. 27510/08), 15 October 2015, §114.
[246] ECtHR, *Pastörs v. Germany* (App. no. 55225/14), 3 October 2019, §36; UN Special Rapporteur D. Kaye, *Promotion and protection of the right to freedom of opinion and expression* (2019) UN Doc. A/74/486, §26.
[247] Russia having ceased to be a party to the European Convention on Human Rights on 16 September 2022. Council of Europe, 'Russia ceases to be party to the European Convention on Human Rights' (16 September 2022). UN Special Rapporteur D. Kaye, *Promotion and protection of the right to freedom of opinion and expression* (2019) UN Doc. A/74/486, §26. See ch 1 (Introduction), s. II.3. (Jurisprudence).
[248] HRC, General Comment No. 34 (2011), §25. Norms enshrined in traditional, religious or other customary laws are not sufficient: HRC, General Comment No. 34 (2011), §24.

The Committee has urged legislators to 'avoid' the 'vague terminology and overly broad restrictions' that exist in many states.[249] It has, for instance, concluded that Russia should 'clarify the vague, broad and open-ended definition of key terms' in laws criminalizing 'blasphemy'.[250] And it found that the offence of 'promoting propaganda of homosexuality' was 'highly ambiguous as to the actions being prohibited and therefore [did] not satisfy the requirement of lawfulness under article 19(3)'.[251] It has also requested that Kazakhstan '[c]larify the vague and broad definition of key terms' in its laws restricting speech, including the offence of incitement to 'social, national, clan, class or religious discord' to comply with article 19 of the ICCPR.[252]

Like the Human Rights Committee, the UN's Working Group on Arbitrary Detention has insisted on the need for precise laws—including in a case where a woman in Iran was convicted of 'spreading propaganda' and 'insulting the sanctity of Islam' for posts supporting Iranian dissidents and an entry in her private journal about a woman who burned a copy of the Qur'an.[253] The Working Group considered that the charges were 'so vague and overly broad' that she could not have foreseen a criminal penalty on this basis and that, as a result, her deprivation of liberty violated 'the principle of legality'.[254]

Similarly, the European Court has interpreted the legality (or 'prescribed by law') test in article 10(2) of the European Convention as requiring a law 'formulated with sufficient precision to enable the person concerned to regulate his or her conduct' and to 'foresee, to a degree that was reasonable in the circumstances, the consequences that a given action could entail'.[255] However, the Court has applied the legality test loosely, in some instances finding vague incitement laws that punish individuals for 'express[ing] contempt' or 'mock[ing]' persons for certain characteristics as having satisfied the legality test.[256] The European Court has also at times bypassed the legality test entirely by finding that vagueness concerns would be dealt with as part of its analysis of whether the interference with speech was necessary and proportionate.[257]

The Inter-American Court applies a stricter standard of legality than the European Court—more akin to the Human Rights Committee's jurisprudence—particularly when a state is seeking to limit speech through criminal sanctions. In these circumstances, 'it is necessary to use strict and unequivocal terms' to describe speech that can

---

[249] HRC, *Concluding Observations, Cambodia* (2015) UN Doc. CCPR/C/KHM/CO/2, §21. See s. II.1.1. (Type of speech).

[250] HRC, *Concluding Observations, Russian Federation* (2015) UN Doc. CCPR/C/RUS/CO/7, §§19–20 (Terrorism and public order offences are most commonly criticized by the Committee as impermissibly vague). See also ch. 6 (Terrorism Laws), s. III.4.2. (Truth and opinion).

[251] HRC, *Nepomnyashchiy v. Russian Federation* (Comm. no. 2318/2013), 17 July 2018, §7.7.

[252] HRC, *Concluding Observations, Kazakhstan* (2016) UN Doc. CCPR/C/KAZ/CO/2, §§49–50.

[253] WGAD, *Iraee v. Islamic Republic of Iran* (Opinion no. 33/2019), 12 August 2019, §51.

[254] Ibid., §§51–53 (also finding a violation under article 19 of the UDHR).

[255] ECtHR (GC), *Perinçek v. Switzerland* (App. no. 27510/08), 15 October 2015, §131 (citing ECtHR, *Sunday Times v. United Kingdom* (App. no. 6538/74), §§48–49).

[256] See, e.g., ECtHR, *Vejdeland v. Sweden* (App. no. 1813/07), 9 February 2012, §§24, 49; ECtHR, *Lilliendahl v. Iceland* (App. no. 29297/18), 12 May 2020, §§20, 42.

[257] See, e.g., ECtHR, *Otegi Mondragon v. Spain* (App. no. 2034/07), 15 March 2011, §§35, 45–46. See also ECtHR, *Savva Terentyev v. Russia* (App. No. 10692/09), 28 August 2018, §§42, 58.

be incriminated, 'setting its elements, and defining the behaviors that are not punishable or the illicit behaviors that can be punishable with non-criminal measures'.[258]

Unlike the other treaties, article 9 of the African Charter does not set out specific exceptions to the right to 'express and disseminate his opinions'. However, article 9(2) requires that this right be exercised 'within the law', and the African Court and Commission have held that this phrase 'must be interpreted in reference to international norms which can provide grounds of limitation on freedom of expression', thereby incorporating the principles of legality, legitimacy and necessity into the African Charter.[259] Adopting the Human Rights Committee's reasoning as to 'legality', the African Court has held that laws must be drafted with 'sufficient clarity' to enable an individual to adapt his or her conduct.[260] But in a decision regarding Rwandan laws criminalizing the 'minimization' or 'downplaying' of genocide,[261] the African Court recognized that although these laws were 'couched in broad and general terms', 'the nature of the offences ... is admittedly difficult to specify with precision' and that, 'considering the margin of appreciation that [the state] enjoys in defining and prohibiting some criminal acts in its domestic legislation, the Court is of the view that the impugned laws provide adequate notice for individuals to foresee and adapt their behaviour to the rules'.[262]

2.2. Legitimacy

Under UN human rights standards, any restriction on expression must fall into one of 'two limitative areas of restrictions': it must be aimed at (i) respecting the rights or reputation of others, or (ii) protecting national security, public order, public health or morality.[263] The European and Inter-American regional human rights instruments include similar requirements, and the African Charter has been construed as encompassing these legitimate aims as well.[264]

2.2.1. Human Rights Committee

The Human Rights Committee has emphasized that the legitimate aims enumerated in article 19(3) of the ICCPR are exhaustive and cannot be used as a pretext for other objectives.[265] And the burden of proof lies on the government to demonstrate that any

---

[258] IACtHR, *Usón Ramírez v. Venezuela* (Series C, no. 207), 20 November 2009, §55: see ch. 5 (Espionage and Official Secrets Laws), s. III.2. (Legality).

[259] ACtHPR, *Konaté v. Burkina Faso* (App. No. 004/2013), 5 December 2014, §129, citing ACmHPR, *Malawi African Association and Others v. Mauritania* (Comm. No. 54/91 and others), 11 May 2000, §102. See also ACtHPR, *Umuhoza v. Rwanda* (App. No. 003/2014), 24 November 2017, §133. See ch. 1 (Introduction), s. II.1.1.1. (Abuses by the state).

[260] ACtHPR, *Konaté v. Burkina Faso* (App. No. 004/2013), 5 December 2014, §131.

[261] ACtHPR, *Umuhoza v. Rwanda* (App. No. 003/2014), 24 November 2017, §137, 155.

[262] Ibid., §§137–138. The Court ultimately held that a 15-year term of imprisonment under these laws for a political speech at a Genocide Memorial was not necessary in a democratic society, as the speech was offensive but could not reasonably be considered capable of 'inciting strife', creating 'divisions among people' or 'threatening the security of the State': ibid., §§161–162. See ss II.1.1. (Type of speech) (Case study: Denial laws) and III.2.4.2. (Opinion).

[263] HRC, General Comment No. 34 (2011), §21.

[264] See s. III.1. (Mandatory Restrictions on Hate Speech).

[265] HRC, General Comment No. 34 (2011), §§22–30.

restriction to speech, including hate speech, satisfies the tests of legality, legitimacy and necessity.[266]

Respondent states in the small number of hate speech cases that have come before the Human Rights Committee have argued that restrictions on speech were justified to show respect for the rights of others.[267] The Committee has held in these cases that the term 'rights' 'includes human rights as recognized in the Covenant and ... international human rights law', and that 'others' relates to 'other persons individually or as members of the community'.[268] In a case in which a school teacher was transferred to a non-teaching position due to publications calling on Christians to 'question the validity of Jewish beliefs and teachings' and 'hold those of the Jewish faith and ancestry in contempt', the Committee held that the penalty was justified for the purpose of 'protecting the "rights or reputations" of persons of Jewish faith'. This included the right to have 'an education in the public school system free from bias, prejudice and intolerance'.[269]

2.2.2. European Court of Human Rights

Consistently with the Human Rights Committee's jurisprudence, hate speech is generally justified before the European Court under article 10(2) on the basis of 'protection of the rights or reputation of others'.[270] This notion has been construed broadly. For example, when a Russian author wrote a demeaning article about non-Russians but did not identify a particular ethnic group, the Court accepted that his conviction for inciting hatred and enmity was aimed at protecting the '"rights of others", specifically the dignity of people of a non-Russian ethnicity'.[271] When hate speech is 'capable of inciting to further violence', restrictions will more commonly be justified by reference to the maintenance of national security, territorial integrity or public safety, or for the prevention of disorder or crime.[272]

---

[266] Ibid., §27.
[267] See HRC, *Ross v. Canada* (Comm. No. 736/1997), 18 October 2000, §§6.11–6.12. Cf. HRC, *A.K. and A.R. v. Uzbekistan* (Comm. No. 1233/2003), 31 March 2009, §7.2 (where a conviction for incitement of ethnic, racial, or religious hatred was held to be justified on the basis of a 'perceived threat to national security (violent overthrow of the constitutional order) and to the rights of others'). See ch. 1 (Introduction), s. II.3.1.1. (Justifications for penalizing speech).
[268] HRC, General Comment No. 34 (2011), §28. See also HRC, *Ross v. Canada* (Comm. No. 736/1997), 18 October 2000, §11.5; HRC, *Faurisson v. France* (Comm. No. 550/1993), 8 November 1996, §9.6.
[269] HRC, *Ross v. Canada* (Comm. No. 736/1997), 18 October 2000, §§11.5–11.6. The Committee ultimately held that the restriction 'did not go any further than that which was necessary to achieve its protective functions', and therefore that there had been no violation of article 19. See also HRC, *Faurisson v. France* (Comm. No. 550/1993), 8 November 1996) (although this ruling was essentially overturned in HRC, General Comment No. 34 (2011): see ss II.1.1. (Type of speech) (Case Study: Denial laws) and III.2.4.2. (Opinion).
[270] See, e.g., ECtHR, *Lilliendahl v. Iceland* (App. No. 29297/18) 12 May 2020, §43; ECtHR, *Balsytė-Lideikienė v. Lithuania* (App. No. 72596/01), 4 November 2008, §73; ECtHR (GC), *Jersild v. Denmark* (App. No. 15890/89), 23 September 1994, §27 (where this legitimate aim was 'uncontested'). There are also a number of cases where the European Court has found a restriction justified on the basis of the rights of others as well as additional legitimate aims: see, e.g., ECtHR, *Féret v. Belgium* (App. No. 15615/07), 16 July 2009, §59 (holding that a criminal conviction for leaflets presenting non-European immigrants as criminally-minded protected the rights of others *and* the prevention of disorder).
[271] ECtHR, *Atamanchuk v. Russia* (App. No. 4493/11), 11 February 2020, §42.
[272] See e.g., ECtHR (GC), *Sürek v. Turkey (No. 1)* (App. No. 26682/95), 8 July 1999, §§51–52, 62. See also ch. 6 (Terrorism Laws), s. III.2. (Legitimacy).

In cases where the European Court has assessed Holocaust-denial laws, it has held that such laws pursue the legitimate aim of protecting the rights and reputation of others, as well as in some instances the 'prevention of disorder'.[273] For example, when a bishop denied the existence of the Holocaust in a TV interview and was charged under Germany's incitement-to-hatred law, the Court considered that this law 'pursued the legitimate aim of preventing a disturbance of the public peace in Germany and thus the prevention of disorder and crime'.[274] But the Court reached a different conclusion in a case in which a politician declared at a public event that the Armenian genocide was a 'lie'. Although the Court accepted that his criminal conviction for stirring up racial discrimination was justified on the basis of the rights of others—namely the 'dignity of present-day Armenians' who have constructed an 'identity around the perception that their community has been the victim of a genocide'—the Court did not accept that such speech should be restricted on the basis of preventing disorder.[275] Instead, it construed 'the prevention of disorder' as an objective that narrowly encompasses 'riots or other forms of public disturbance' and held that there was no evidence 'this kind of statement could risk unleashing serious tensions and giving rise to clashes' given the timing and location of the speech.[276]

Certain types of hate speech have also been found to fall within article 17—meaning that they are by definition unable to meet the 'legitimate aim' test and the case is deemed inadmissible. Speech has been considered ineligible for protection by the Court under this article on the basis that it contravenes values guaranteed by the Convention such as 'justice and peace'.[277] For example, the Court held that anti-Jewish speech constituted a 'general and vehement attack on one ethnic group' in a manner that violates the Convention's 'underlying values' of 'tolerance, social peace and non-discrimination'.[278] Displaying a poster showing the Twin Towers in flames and stating 'Islam out of Britain–Protect British People' in the speaker's home was considered contrary to the same values and therefore ineligible for protection as it constituted an attack 'against a religious group, linking the group as a whole with a grave act of terrorism'.[279] And calls for violence such as speech on television that 'included incitement to violence and support for terrorist activity' and YouTube videos 'call[ing] on viewers to overpower and fight non-Muslims' have been considered contrary to the 'values' of the Convention including tolerance, social peace and non-discrimination.[280]

---

[273] See, e.g., ECtHR, *Pastörs v. Germany* (App. No. 55225/14), 3 October 2019, §41; ECtHR, *Williamson v. Germany* (App. No. 64496/17), 8 January 2019, §24. See s. III.2.4.2. (Opinion).
[274] ECtHR, *Williamson v. Germany* (App. No. 64496/17), 8 January 2019, §24.
[275] ECtHR (GC), *Perinçek v. Switzerland* (App. No. 27510/08), 15 October 2015, §§154, 156.
[276] Ibid., §§146–154. The Court ultimately held that a violation of article 10 had taken place: see s. III.2.4.2. (Opinion).
[277] See s. III.2.4.2. (Opinion). ECtHR, *Garaudy v. France* (App. No. 65831/01), 24 June 2003, §1. Cf. ECtHR (GC), *Perinçek v. Switzerland* (App. No. 27510/08), 15 October 2015.
[278] ECtHR, *Ivanov v. Russia* (App. No. 35222/04), 20 February 2007, §1.
[279] ECtHR, *Norwood v. United Kingdom* (App. no. 23131/03), 16 November 2004.
[280] ECtHR, *Belkacem v. Belgium* (App. No. 34367/14), 27 June 2017, §§5–7; ECtHR, *Roj TV A/S v. Denmark* (App. No. 24683/14), 17 April 2018, §§47–48. See also ECtHR, *Hizb Ut-Tahrir v. Germany* (App. No. 31098/08), 12 June 2012, §72. Cf. ECtHR, *Ifandiev v. Bulgaria* (App. No. 14904/11), 18 April 2019, §24 (declining to apply article 17 unless 'it is immediately clear' that the impugned speech sought to 'deflect [article 10] from its real purpose by employing the right to freedom of expression for ends clearly contrary to the values of the Convention'); ECtHR, *Church of Scientology Moscow and Others v. Russia* (App. No. 37508/1 & 2 others), 14 December 2021, §§35, 59,

2.2.3. Inter-American Court and Commission

The Inter-American Court has not directly opined on restrictions to hate speech, but the Court has considered that 'respect for the rights or reputations of others' is a legitimate aim that justified certain restrictions to speech.[281] And the Court has recognized that 'the protection of a person's honor and reputation is a legitimate end',[282] and that 'it is necessary that the State weigh up the right to freedom of expression of the communicator and the right to honor of the person affected'.[283]

2.2.4. African Charter

The African Court has limited jurisprudence on restrictions to hate speech[284] but the phrase 'within the law' in article 9 of the African Charter has been interpreted to require that 'restrictions are prescribed by law, serve a legitimate purpose and are necessary and proportional as may be expected in a democratic society', thereby bringing the provision into line with international and regional equivalents.[285]

The African Court and Commission and the Economic Community of West African States Community Court of Justice have indeed specifically held that the aims listed in article 19(3) of the ICCPR are 'legitimate' grounds to restrict speech and these aims are stated to be exhaustive.[286] But it is not clear whether additional aims are also recognized. Article 27(2) of the African Charter provides that Charter rights generally 'shall be exercised with due regard to the rights of others, *collective security, morality and common interest*' and it is unclear whether the aims in article 19(3) of the ICCPR and article 27(2) of the Charter are considered cumulative or not. This uncertainty is

---

61 (declining to apply article 17 in a case involving a ban on speech promoting Scientology because there was no evidence 'that the impugned texts... used abusive terms' about persons who didn't believe in Scientology); ECtHR, *Ibragimov v. Russia* (App. nos. 1413/08 & 28621/11), 28 August 2018, §123 (declining to apply article 17 to a Muslim theologian's texts as the Court was 'unable to...conclude that the book in question incited violence, religious hatred or intolerance'); ECtHR, *Zemmour v. France* (App. no. 63539/19), 20 December 2022, §§28, 61, 64–67 (declining to apply article 17 to comments by a guest on a prime time television program describing Muslims in France as 'invaders' and 'colonisers' trying to 'Islamize' France despite the fact that they were 'shocking', 'controversial', 'discriminatory' and 'likely to stir up a rift between the French and Muslim community', but approving his conviction and 3,000 Euro fine under article 10 read 'in the light of Article 17').

[281] IACtHR, *Kimel v. Argentina* (Series C, no. 177), 2 May 2008, §71.
[282] Ibid.
[283] IACtHR, *Álvarez Ramos v. Venezuela* (Series C, no. 380), 30 August 2019, §107.
[284] With the exception its decision regarding Rwanda's denial and minimization of genocide laws: ACtHPR, *Umuhoza v. Rwanda* (App. no. 003/2014), 24 November 2017 and its decision regarding Benin's Digital Code which criminalizes 'racially motivated and xenophobic insults using a computer system' and 'incitement to hate and violence': ACtHPR, *Ajavon v. Republic of Benin* (App. no. 062/2019), 4 December 2020.
[285] ACtHPR, *Umuhoza v. Rwanda* (App. no. 003/2014), 24 November 2017, §133. See also ACtHPR, *Konaté v. Burkina Faso* (App. no. 004/2013), 5 December 2014, §129; ACmHPR, *Good v. Botswana* (Comm. no. 313/05), 26 May 2010, §188.
[286] ACtHPR, *Konaté v. Burkina Faso* (App. no. 004/2013), 5 December 2014, §§134–135; ACtHPR, *Umuhoza v. Rwanda* (App. no. 003/2014), 24 November 2017, §140; ECOWAS CCJ, *Federation of African Journalists v. The Gambia* (Suit no. ECW/CCJ/APP/36/15), 13 February 2018, 32–33; ECOWAS CCJ, *The Incorporated Trustees of Laws and Rights Awareness Initiatives v. Nigeria* (Suit no. ECW/CCJ/APP/53/2018), 10 July 2020, §§139–140. Similarly, the ECOWAS Community Court of Justice, which has jurisdiction over a number of western African states, has considered article 19(3) as providing the list of legitimate aims for restricting speech, either on its own or in addition to those recognized under article 27(2) of the African Charter: ECOWAS CCJ, *Federation of African Journalists v. The Gambia* (Suit no. ECW/CCJ/APP/36/15), 13 February 2018, 32–33; ECOWAS CCJ, *The Incorporated Trustees of Laws and Rights Awareness Initiatives v. Nigeria* (Suit no. ECW/CCJ/APP/53/2018), 10 July 2020, §§139–140.

compounded by the fact that the African Commission has cited article 27(2) as the 'only legitimate reasons' for limiting rights,[287] and that the Commission's 2019 Declaration of Principles on Freedom of Expression instead adopts the grounds enumerated in article 19(3), but excludes 'morals'.[288] The Commission has also said that 'public interest' can be recognized as a justifiable ground to limit expression under article 27(2), even though this is not listed in article 19(3).[289]

In one of the few cases in which the African Court has considered hate speech laws the Court cites a number of legitimate aims.[290] The Court assessed whether Benin's provisions which punish 'the offences of racially motivated and xenophobic insults using a computer system' and 'incitement to hatred and violence on such grounds as race, colour, national or ethnic origin, or religion' violated article 9(2) of the African Charter.[291] When considering whether this pursued a legitimate aim, the Court cited both article 27(2) and the fact that it had also 'previously concluded that national security, public order and public morals are legitimate restrictions'.[292] It then held that the law 'pursues a legitimate aim since it seeks to combat any form of incitement to hatred or discrimination'.[293]

Case Study: International Standards on Blasphemy Laws

The Human Rights Committee has found that certain aims are *not* legitimate bases for restricting speech, including laws that prohibit speech that is rude about religion or denies historic atrocities.[294] In the context of blasphemy, for instance, the Committee has made clear that '[p]rohibitions of displays of lack of respect for a religion or other belief system, including blasphemy laws, *are incompatible with the Covenant*, except in the specific circumstances envisaged in article 20, paragraph 2'.[295] The Committee has consequently recommended that states repeal their blasphemy laws.[296] And in the case of *Rabbae v. The Netherlands,* it was noted that

---

[287] ACmHPR, *Constitutional Rights Project v. Nigeria* (Comm. no. 140/1994), 15 November 1999, §41; ACtHPR, *Konaté v. Burkina Faso* (App. no. 004/2013), 5 December 2014, §§134–135 (stating that 'the only legitimate reasons' for limiting rights are stipulated in article 27(2) while also 'noti[ng] that the legitimate purpose of a restriction is stated in Article 19 (3) (a) and (b) of the Covenant').

[288] ACmHPR, Declaration of Principles of Freedom of Expression and Access to Information in Africa (2019), Principle 9.

[289] ACmHPR, *Good v. Botswana* (Comm. no. 313/05), 26 May 2010, §189.

[290] ACtHPR, *Ajavon v. Republic of Benin* (App. no. 062/2019), 4 December 2020. This case considered a number of other provisions of the Charter in addition to article 9.

[291] Ibid., §121. The case was brought by a Beninese businessman and political refugee who had not been charged under Benin's Digital Code, but could bring proceedings based on 'a peculiarity of the African regional human rights system characterized by the objective nature of human rights litigation' that meant he did not need to be a 'victim': ACtHPR, *Ajavon v. Republic of Benin* (App. no. 062/2019), 4 December 2020, §§58–59.

[292] ACtHPR, *Ajavon v. Republic of Benin* (App. no. 062/2019), 4 December 2020, §123 (citing ACtHPR, *Umuhoza v. Rwanda* (App. no. 003/2014), 24 November 2017).

[293] ACtHPR, *Ajavon v. Republic of Benin* (App. no. 062/2019), 4 December 2020, §123, §125.

[294] See s. III.2.4.2. (Opinion).

[295] HRC, General Comment No. 34 (2011), §48 (emphasis added).

[296] See HRC, *Concluding Observations, Kuwait* (2016) UN Doc. CCPR/C/KWT/CO/3, §§39, 41 ('The State party should eliminate all discriminatory legislation and practices that violate the right to freedom of thought, conscience and religion, including blasphemy laws that are incompatible with the Covenant'.); HRC, *Concluding Observation, Russian Federation* (2015) UN Doc. CCPR/C/RUS/CO/7, §19 (expressing concern about Russia's

'criticism of even the most deeply-held convictions of the adherents of a religion is protected by freedom of expression'.[297] The Working Group on Arbitrary Detention has upheld this position as well.[298] And the UN Special Rapporteur considers that blasphemy laws fail to pursue a legitimate aim under article 19(3) 'given that Article 19 protects *individuals* and their rights to freedom of expression and opinion ... [It does not] protect *ideas or beliefs* from ridicule, abuse, criticism or other "attacks" seen as offensive'.[299] In addition, under the Rabat Plan of Action, a codification of international standards supported by the UN, blasphemy laws are considered 'counterproductive' as 'the right to freedom of religion or belief, as enshrined in relevant international legal standards, does not include the right to have a religion or a belief that is free from criticism or ridicule'.[300]

Similarly, the Inter-American Court has not tolerated censorship of speech simply on the basis that it offends religious sensibilities.[301] And some European bodies, including the Venice Commission—an expert body that forms part of the Council of Europe—the European Union and the Organization for Security and Co-operation in Europe, have followed this approach and advocated for the decriminalization of blasphemy laws.[302]

The European Court has, however, taken a different view and does not accept that blasphemy laws cannot constitute legitimate restrictions on speech. The Court has recognized a 'wider margin of appreciation ... when regulating freedom of expression in relation to matters liable to offend intimate personal convictions within the sphere of ... religion', and has held that, because what 'is likely to cause substantial offence to persons of a particular religious persuasion will vary significantly from

---

'blasphemy law' and recommending Russia 'repeal or revise' its laws 'with a view to bringing them into conformity with its obligations under the Covenant'). See also HRC, *Concluding Observations, Ireland* (2014) UN Doc. CCPR/C/IRL/CO/4, §22; HRC, *Concluding Observations, Indonesia* (2013) UN Doc. CCPR/C/IDN/CO/1, §25.

[297] HRC, *Rabbae v. The Netherlands* (Comm. no. 2124/2011), 14 July 2016, §10.5.
[298] See, e.g., WGAD, *Mejri v. Tunisia* (Opinion no. 29/2013), 30 August 2013, §18; WGAD, *Amer v. Egypt* (Opinion no. 35/2008), 20 November 2008, §38. See also WGAD, *Ahmad v. Pakistan* (Opinion no. 7/2023), 3 May 2023, §74 (expressing 'serious concern about blasphemy laws in Pakistan'). See s. II.2.2.3. (Pakistan).
[299] UN Special Rapporteur D. Kaye, *Promotion and protection of the right to freedom of opinion and expression* (2019) UN Doc. A/74/486, §21 (emphasis added).
[300] See Rabat Plan of Action, §19. For over a decade beginning in the late 1990s, the Organization of Islamic Cooperation (OIC) pushed for the adoption of a number of contentious resolutions in the UN Human Rights Council and at the UN General Assembly that recognized the concept of 'defamation of religions' and sought to either prohibit or criminalize speech disrespectful of religion, while Western nations consistently rejected the concept and the resolutions that sought to entrench it. In 2011, a consensus was reached by way of the Human Rights Council's Resolution 16/18, which moved away from a legal prohibition regarding the defamation of religions and instead 'presents an action-oriented approach to combat religious intolerance through practical steps that states should take, such as enforcing anti-discrimination laws and speaking out against intolerance, while also protecting freedoms of speech and religion': see E. Aswad, R. Hussain, & A.M. Suleman, 'Why the United States Cannot Agree to Disagree on Blasphemy Laws' (2014) 32 *Boston University International Law Journal* 123, 144–145.
[301] See IACtHR, *'The Last Temptation of Christ' (Olmedo-Bustos et al.) v. Chile* (Series C, no. 73), 5 February 2001, §§71–73, 76–80 (holding that Chile's prohibition of the exhibition of the film 'The Last Temptation of Christ' on the basis that it 'deformed and diminished' the image of Christ constituted prior censorship in violation of article 13, and did not violate article 12 (freedom of religion)).
[302] Venice Commission, *Report on the Relationship between Freedom of Expression and Freedom of Religion: The Issue of Regulation and Prosecution of Blasphemy, Religious Insult and Incitement to Religious Hatred* (2008) CDL-AD(2008)026, §92; EU Guidelines on the promotion and protection of freedom of religion or belief; OSCE, 'OSCE Representative on Freedom of the Media welcomes Irish referendum on blasphemy' (2 October 2017).

time to time and place to place ... State authorities are in principle in a better position than an international judge to give an opinion' on the need for such a restriction.[303] According to the Court, although a 'religious group must tolerate the denial by others of their religious beliefs and even the propagation by others of doctrines hostile to their faith', this does not extend to statements that 'incite to hatred or religious intolerance'.[304]

The European Court has indeed gone as far as approving a criminal conviction for 'disparaging religious doctrines' in Austria after a woman referred to the 56-year-old Prophet Muhammad's marriage to a child as 'paedophilia'.[305] The Court upheld the conviction on the basis that 'expressions that seek to spread, incite or justify hatred based on intolerance, including religious intolerance, do not enjoy the protection afforded by Article 10 of the Convention', and that the 'paedophile' comment was a 'value judgment without sufficient factual basis'[306] and 'an abusive attack ... capable of stirring up prejudice and putting at risk religious peace'[307] even though it was accepted that the Prophet married the girl when she was six years of age.

2.3. Necessity

The third arm of the tripartite test under article 19(3) of the ICCPR and regional free speech treaties governing when restrictions on speech are permissible is whether a penalty for speech is 'necessary'.[308] The European Court has acknowledged that 'in the majority of cases, this is the question which determines the Court's conclusion in a given case', and the same applies to other international and regional bodies.[309] The potential harm arising from hate speech, the causal link between speech and harm and the intent of the speaker are all relevant to an assessment of necessity. The requirement of 'necessity' also encompasses proportionality, as any restrictive measure 'must be the least intrusive instrument amongst those which might achieve their protective function' and must be 'proportionate to the interest to be protected'.[310]

---

[303] ECtHR, *Murphy v. Ireland* (App. no. 44179/98), 10 July 2003, §67. See also ECtHR, *Wingrove v. United Kingdom* (App. no. 17419/90), 25 November 1996, §53.
[304] ECtHR, *Tagiyev v. Azerbaijan* (App. no. 13274/08), 5 December 2019, §44; ECtHR, *E.S. v. Austria* (App. no. 38450/12), 25 October 2018, §52. ECtHR, *Rabczewska v. Poland* (App. no. 8257/13), 15 September 2022, §57. See also ECtHR, *Yefimov and Youth Human Rights Group v. Russia* (App. nos. 12385/15 & 51619/15), 7 December 2021, §45 (finding no violation of article 10 when a speaker's 'criticism focused on the religious organization rather than on individual believers' and 'did not call for anyone's exclusion or discrimination, let alone incite to acts of violence or intimidation').
[305] ECtHR, *E.S. v. Austria* (App. no. 38450/12), 25 October 2018, §§43, 54. E.S. was charged under article 283 of the Austrian Criminal Code for inciting hatred. See s. II.2.1.2. (Austria).
[306] ECtHR, *E.S. v. Austria* (App. no. 38450/12), 25 October 2018, §§43–57. One expert has argued that the impact of this case will be that, '[g]iven the uncertainties that often surround historico-religious events, it may be impossible—or at least extremely challenging—to provide the factual basis the European Court now seems to require': S. Smet, 'Introductory Note to E.S. v. Austria' (2019) 58 *International Legal Materials* 628. The penalty of 480 Euros was also considered 'moderate' and therefore not disproportionate ECtHR, *E.S. v. Austria* (App. no. 38450/12), 25 October 2018, §56. See s. II.2.1.2. (Austria).
[307] ECtHR, *E.S. v. Austria* (App. no. 38450/12), 25 October 2018, §57.
[308] See s. III. (International Legal Standards).
[309] ECtHR, Guide on Article 10 of the European Convention on Human Rights—Freedom of Expression, 31 August 2022, §61.
[310] HRC, General Comment No. 34 (2011), §34.

2.3.1. Harm

In the leading case before a UN body related to hate speech, two members of the Human Rights Committee concluded that criminal penalties for hate speech should be limited to 'speech that incites the commission of *criminal offences or acts of violence*'.[311] And the Committee has found that '[w]hen a State ... invokes a legitimate ground for restrict[ing] freedom of expression, it must demonstrate in specific and individualized fashion the precise nature of the threat' caused by speech and establish a 'direct and immediate connection between the expression and the threat'.[312] In addition, UN-approved international instruments such as the Rabat Plan of Action require 'a *reasonable probability* that the speech would succeed in *inciting actual action* against the target group, recognizing that such causation should be rather direct'.[313] The 'likelihood, including imminence' of harm, is also one of the six threshold considerations identified as relevant to determining whether it is permissible to criminalize hate speech.[314]

The European Court has taken a different approach. The potential harm that hate speech may cause is not the determinative factor in the European Court's assessment of the necessity of restricting such speech, but one of a number of factors that are 'taken into account'.[315] The Court has adopted a broad conception of what harm hate speech laws may lawfully seek to prevent. This includes civil or criminal penalties for statements that 'could', when read in context, 'be seen as a call' for 'hatred or intolerance'.[316] In addition, in some of the hate speech cases that the European Court considers inadmissible under article 17, no assessment of harm is undertaken.[317] For instance, where the supporter of a far right political group possessed posters containing hateful messages such as 'Romania needs children, not homosexuals', his conviction was considered sound on the basis the posters 'were intended to instigate hatred' and 'were

---

[311] HRC, *Rabbae v. The Netherlands* (Comm. no. 2124/2011), 14 July 2016, Individual Concurring Opinion of Committee members Sarah Cleveland and Mauro Politi, §7 (emphasis added). This contrasts with an earlier decision by the Committee: HRC, *Faurisson v. France* (Comm. no. 550/1993), 8 November 1996 which has since essentially been overruled. See also HRC, *Ross v. Canada* (Comm. no. 736/1997), 18 October 2000, §11.6 (regarding non-criminal penalties); HRC, General Comment No. 34 (2011), §49; M. O'Flaherty, 'Freedom of Expression: Article 19 of the International Covenant on Civil and Political Rights and the Human Rights Committee's General Comment No 34' (2012) 12 *Human Rights Law Review* 627, 653 (describing General Comment No. 34 as 'overruling *Faurisson*'); HRC, *Faurisson v. France* (Comm. no. 550/1993), 8 November 1996, Individual Opinion of Committee members Elizabeth Evatt and David Kretzmer, co-signed by Eckart Klein, §9 (observing that the law used to convict the speaker did 'not link liability to ... the tendency of the publication to incite to anti-semitism').

[312] HRC, General Comment No. 34 (2011), §35, citing HRC, *Shin v. Republic of Korea* (Comm. no. 926/2000), 16 March 2004. See also HRC, *Ross v. Canada* (Comm. no. 736/1997), 18 October 2000, §11.5.

[313] Rabat Plan of Action, §29(f) (emphasis added).

[314] Ibid. See also UN Special Rapporteur F. La Rue, *Promotion and Protection of the Right to Freedom of Opinion and Expression* (2013) UN Doc. A/68/362, §§52, 53.

[315] These factors include 'the context in which the impugned statements were made, their nature and wording, their potential to lead to harmful consequences', whether 'the statements were made against a tense political or social background' and whether they 'could be seen as a direct or indirect call for violence or as a justification of violence, hatred or intolerance'. ECtHR, *Atamanchuk v. Russia* (App. no. 4493/11), 11 February 2020, §50. See also ECtHR, *Ibragimov v. Russia* (App. nos. 1413/08 & 28621/11), 28 August 2018, §99; ECtHR, *Alekhina v. Russia* (App. no. 38004/12), 17 July 2018, §221.

[316] ECtHR, *Ibragimov v. Russia* (App. nos. 1413/08 & 28621/11), 28 August 2018, §98; citing ECtHR (GC), *Perinçek v. Switzerland* (App. no. 27510/08), 15 October 2015, §206.

[317] See, e.g., ECtHR, *Ivanov v. Russia* (App. no. 35222/04), 20 February 2007. See also ECtHR, *Norwood v. United Kingdom* (App. no. 23131/03), 16 November 2004. See ss III.2.4.2. (Opinion) and III.2. (Discretionary Restrictions on Hate Speech).

likely to seriously disturb public order', even though the posters were never publicly displayed and these harms were merely hypothetical.[318]

The European Court considers that it may be necessary 'to sanction or even prevent all forms of expression which spread, incite, promote or justify hatred based on intolerance (including religious intolerance)', provided that restrictions are proportionate.[319] Speech does not need to 'involve an explicit call for an act of violence, or other criminal acts' for a penalty to be considered 'necessary', as states may choose to validly restrict speech 'insulting, holding up to ridicule or slandering specific groups of the population'.[320] The Court has applied this reasoning to speech targeting a range of different groups, including racist speech, religious intolerance, 'extreme nationalism' and discrimination on the basis of sexual orientation.[321]

The European Court has found that hate speech could be penalized even when the words used could be 'interpreted in several ways' and were contradictory.[322] For instance, France was held to have legitimately convicted and fined a cartoonist for publishing satirical drawings of the September 11, 2001 attacks with the caption 'We have all dreamt of it... Hamas did it'.[323] Since it was printed two days after the attacks, 'when the whole world was in a state of shock from the news' and 'in a politically sensitive [Basque] region' of France, the Court held that the cartoon 'elicited reactions which *could* have stirred up violence and which demonstrated its plausible impact on public order in the region'.[324] Commentators have, however, pointed to the small circulation of the local newspaper and the differences between terrorism in the United States and the Basque region and concluded that 'it is hard to maintain that the drawing in question created a 'credible' danger of violence, and that the case demonstrates that the 'capable of' causing harm test 'is a vague one that allows judges considerable scope to prohibit speech merely because they consider it to be highly offensive'.[325]

Despite states' wide 'margin of appreciation',[326] and the reliance on article 17, the European Court has sometimes found that a penalty for hate speech was not necessary

---

[318] ECtHR, *Molnar v. Romania* (App. no. 16637/06), 23 October 2012, §23 (some speech was also anti-Roma, and there was evidence before domestic courts that the applicant had previously displayed far-right posters publicly). See also ECtHR, *Lilliendahl v. Iceland* (App. no. 29297/18) 12 May 2020, §36.
[319] ECtHR, *Ibragimov v. Russia* (App. nos. 1413/08 and 28621/11), 28 August 2018, §94.
[320] Ibid. See also ECtHR, *Vejdeland v. Sweden* (App. no. 1813/07), 9 February 2012, §55.
[321] See ECtHR, *Ibragimov v. Russia* (App. nos. 1413/08 & 28621/11), 28 August 2018, §94 (observing that the Court 'has been particularly sensitive towards sweeping statements attacking or casting in a negative light entire ethnic, religious or other groups'); ECtHR, *Balsytė-Lideikienė v. Lithuania* (App. no. 72596/01), 4 November 2008, §80 (finding no violation of article 10 where statements 'promoted national hatred, xenophobia and territorial claims'); ECtHR, *Vejdeland v. Sweden* (App. no. 1813/07), 9 February 2012, §55 (holding that 'discrimination based on sexual orientation is as serious' as discrimination based on 'race, origin or colour').
[322] ECtHR (GC), *Zana v. Turkey* (App. no. 18954/91), 25 November 1997, §§58–62. See also ECtHR, *Atamanchuk v. Russia* (App. no. 4493/11), 11 February 2020, §64.
[323] ECtHR, *Leroy v. France* (App. no. 36109/03), 2 October 2008, §§6, 48.
[324] Ibid., §45 (emphasis added).
[325] S. Sottiaux, 'Leroy v. France: Apology of Terrorism and the Malaise of the European Court of Human Rights' Free Speech Jurisprudence' (2009) 3 *European Human Rights Law Review* 415, 424. See ch. 6 (Terrorism Laws), s. III.3.2. (Causal link between speech and harm). The Court will often consider the manner or medium in which a hateful statement is made to determine whether its capacity to lead to harmful consequences. See ECtHR (GC), *Perinçek v. Switzerland* (App. no. 27510/08), 15 October 2015, §207; ECtHR, *Vejdeland v. Sweden* (App. no. 1813/07), 9 February 2012, §56.
[326] See s. III.2. (Discretionary Restrictions on Hate Speech).

or proportionate because domestic courts failed to provide 'relevant and sufficient' reasons to justify the necessity of a penalty for speech. For example, when a writer and editor were convicted of incitement to religious hatred and hostility for publishing an article that criticized Islam by describing the Prophet as 'a frightful creature', the European Court found that the Azerbaijan courts had not explained 'why the remarks...constituted incitement to religious hatred and hostility' and that the speaker's rights had been violated on this basis.[327]

The approach of the Inter-American system is closer to that of the Human Rights Committee than the European Court. Its Rapporteur has held that states must demonstrate 'both the existence of an impending threat that [the speech] could cause real harm and that it is crucial to impose the restriction in order to prevent the harm'.[328] In order to justify restrictions on freedom of expression to protect the rights of others, those rights must 'be clearly harmed or threatened'.[329] A speaker must have had both intent to 'promot[e] lawless violence or similar action' and 'the capacity to achieve this objective and create an *actual* risk of harm'.[330]

Similarly, guidance from the African Commission provides that penalties for hate speech must be based on a 'real likelihood and imminence of harm' and 'a close causal link between the risk of harm and the expression'.[331] And in a short decision considering Benin's hate speech laws, the African Court held that in 'view of the harmful consequences such rhetoric can engender' a criminal penalty in such laws was not necessarily 'disproportionate given their deterrent function'.[332]

2.3.2. Intent

Unlike the clear intent requirements in the context of mandatory penalties for speech,[333] international and regional bodies have not been explicit when addressing intention in relation to discretionary restrictions of hate speech.

In the context of defamation laws, the Human Rights Committee has stated that 'consideration should be given to avoiding penalizing or otherwise rendering unlawful untrue statements that have been published in error but *without malice*'.[334] This endorses a very high standard of intent, codified at the domestic level in US federal law in the

---

[327] ECtHR, *Tagiyev v. Azerbaijan* (App. no. 13274/08), 5 December 2019, §47. The Court also found that the writer and editor's terms of imprisonment, being three and four years respectively, were disproportionate sanctions. See also ECtHR, *Ibragimov v. Russia* (App. nos. 1413/08 & 28621/11), 28 August 2018, §106; ECtHR, *Stomakhin v. Russia* (App. no. 52273/07), 9 May 2018, §129–132.

[328] IACmHR, *Annual Report of the Inter-American Commission on Human Rights: Report of the Special Rapporteur for Freedom of Expression* (2009) OEA/Ser.L/V/II., Doc. 51, 397.

[329] Ibid., 250.

[330] IACmHR, *Violence against Lesbian, Gay, Bisexual, Trans and Intersex Persons in the Americas* (2015) OAS/Ser.L/V/II. Doc.36/15 Rev.2, §235 (in the context of mandatory restrictions on speech).

[331] See ACmHPR, Declaration of Principles of Freedom of Expression and Access to Information in Africa (2019), Principle 22(5) (related to restrictions on grounds of public order or national security), Principle 23(2)(f).

[332] ACtHPR, *Ajavon v. Republic of Benin* (App. no. 062/2019), 4 December 2020, §127. See s. III.2.2. (Legitimacy).

[333] See s. III.1. (Mandatory Restrictions on Hate Speech).

[334] HRC, General Comment No. 34 (2011) (emphasis added). Cf., in the context of denial laws; HRC, *Faurisson v. France* (Comm. no. 550/1993), 8 November 1996, Individual Concurring Opinion of Committee members Elizabeth Evatt and David Kretzmer, co-signed by Eckart Klein, §9 stating that the restrictions in that case 'do not meet the proportionality test. They do not link liability to the intent of the author, nor to the tendency of the publication to incite anti-Semitism'.

seminal Supreme Court case of *New York Times v. Sullivan*.[335] In addition, in the context of hate speech laws, the UN Special Rapporteur has taken the position that '[n]o one should be penalized for the dissemination of hate speech unless it has been shown that they did so with the *intention of inciting* discrimination, hostility or violence'.[336]

Although the European Court considers intent a relevant factor in determining the necessity of restricting hate speech,[337] in a number of cases the Court has, even in the criminal context, allowed convictions without a clear showing of intent or simply implied intent on the basis of the content of the speech. For example, a cartoonist convicted for his cartoon of the September 11, 2001 attacks argued that he did not intend to encourage terrorism but to express his anti-American sentiment.[338] The Court, however, found no violation of article 10, noting that the drawing could 'in itself demonstrate the intention of the author', but that even when taken together with the accompany caption, 'the work does not criticize American imperialism, but supports and glorifies its destruction by violence'. The Court further adopted the domestic court's finding that 'the applicant's intentions are unrelated to the prosecution', given that his intentions had only been expressed retroactively and 'were not of such a nature, in view of the context, to erase [his] positive assessment of the consequences of a criminal act'.[339] In other decisions, speech restrictions have been justified even though the Court accepted that the speaker *did not* have intent to create a specific harm. For example, when homophobic leaflets were distributed at a school, the Court found that the conviction and fine against those who distributed the leaflets did not violate article 10, even though they 'had not intended to express contempt for homosexuals as a group' but to 'start a debate about the lack of objectivity in the education dispensed in Swedish schools'.[340]

The Inter-American Commission on Human Rights, adopting a position similar to US domestic law,[341] has held that hate speech sanctions can only be justified when a speaker was 'not simply issuing an opinion' but also had 'intent' to 'promot[e] lawless violence or similar action'.[342] And in the African context, the Declaration of Principles on Freedom of Expression in Africa provides that when determining if speech falls into

---

[335] US Supreme Court, *New York Times v. Sullivan* 376 U.S. 254, 9 March 1964.

[336] UN Special Rapporteur F. La Rue, *Promotion and protection of the right to freedom of opinion and expression* (2012) UN Doc. A/67/357, §50 (emphasis added).

[337] See, e.g., ECtHR (GC), *Jersild v. Denmark* (App. no. 15890/89), 23 September 1994, §33 ('the object of the programme was to address aspects of the problem, by identifying certain racist individuals and by portraying their mentality and social background. There is no reason to doubt that the ensuing interviews fulfilled that aim. Taken as a whole, the feature could not objectively have appeared to have as its purpose the propagation of racist views and ideas').

[338] ECtHR, *Leroy v. France* (App. no. 36109/03), 2 October 2008, §42. See s. III.2.3.1. (Harm).

[339] Ibid., §43. See also ECtHR (GC), *Sürek v. Turkey (No. 1)* (App. no. 26682/95), 8 July 1999, §62.

[340] ECtHR, *Vejdeland v. Sweden* (App. no. 1813/07), 9 February 2012, §10. See also ECtHR, *Nix v. Germany* (App. no. 35285/16), 13 March 2018, §51 (finding a criminal conviction and fine inadmissible even where '[t]he Court accepts that the applicant, by displaying the picture of Himmler in SS uniform with a swastika armband in his blog post, did not intend to spread totalitarian propaganda, to incite violence, or to utter hate speech, and that his expression had not resulted in intimidation').

[341] See s. II.2.3.2. (United States). See ch. 2 (Insulting Speech), s. II.1.2. (Intent) (regarding the adoption of the 'actual malice' standard in the Inter-American context).

[342] IACmHR, *Violence against Lesbian, Gay, Bisexual, Trans and Intersex Persons in the Americas* (2015) OAS/Ser.L/V/II. Doc.36/15 Rev.2, §235.

the exceptional category of warranting criminal sanctions, states should take into account the 'existence of a clear intent to incite'.[343]

2.4. Exclusions, exceptions and defences

2.4.1. Truth

The Human Rights Committee has made clear that, at least in the context of criminal laws that penalize defamatory speech, courts should recognize a 'defence of truth' and that such criminal laws 'should not be applied with regard to those forms of expression that are not, of their nature, subject to verification'.[344] In addition, the UN Special Rapporteur has recommended a number of limits on hate speech laws, including that 'no one should be penalized for statements that are true'.[345] Similarly, the Declaration of Principles on Freedom of Expression in Africa 2019 provides that, at least in relation to defamation laws, '[n]o one shall be found liable for true statements'.

The European Court, on the other hand, has not recognized a defence of truth in hate speech cases.[346] In some instances, the Court has simply asserted the falsity of a statement and considered this relevant to finding its penalization valid.[347] For instance, in a case in which a woman argued that her statement that the Prophet Muhammad was a 'paedophile' was true since the Prophet married a six-year-old girl,[348] the European Court disagreed and instead accepted the Austrian court's assessment that these statements were 'value judgments without sufficient factual basis'.[349] And it found that even if the speech was factual, the speaker had 'failed to adduce any evidence' of its truth and 'must have been aware that her statements were partly based on untrue facts'.[350]

2.4.2. Opinion

The Human Rights Committee recognizes a defence of opinion in the context of defamation law.[351] And in relation to denial laws, the Human Rights Committee has concluded that laws 'that penalize *the expression of opinions* about historical facts are incompatible' with 'respect for freedom of ... expression', and that the ICCPR 'does not permit general prohibition of expressions of an erroneous *opinion* or an incorrect interpretation of past events'.[352] This position represents a significant reversal of the

---

[343] ACmHPR, Declaration of Principles of Freedom of Expression and Access to Information in Africa (2019), Principle 23(2)(c).
[344] HRC, General Comment No. 34 (2011), §47.
[345] UN Special Rapporteur F. La Rue, *Promotion and protection of the right to freedom of opinion and expression* (2012) UN Doc. A/67/357, §50 (citing the UN Special Rapporteur on Freedom of Opinion and Expression, the OSCE Representative on Freedom of the Media and the OAS Special Rapporteur on Freedom of Expression, Joint Statement on Racism and the Media (2001)).
[346] The position is different when it comes to defamatory speech. See ch. 2 (Insulting Speech), s. III.4.1. (Truth).
[347] ECtHR, *Pastörs v. Germany* (App. no. 55225/14), 3 October 2019, §48. Cf. ECtHR (GC), *Perinçek v. Switzerland* (App. no. 27510/08), 15 October 2015, §243.
[348] ECtHR, *E.S. v. Austria* (App. no. 38450/12), 25 October 2018, §34.
[349] Ibid., §54. See s. III.2.2. (Legitimacy) (Case Study: International Standards on Blasphemy Laws).
[350] ECtHR, *E.S. v. Austria* (App. no. 38450/12), 25 October 2018, §§53–55. See also S. Smet, 'Case note: Free Speech versus Religious Feelings, the Sequel: Defamation of the Prophet Muhammad in *E.S. v Austria*' (2019) 15 *European Constitutional Law Review* 158, 166–167. See ss II.2.1.2. (Austria) and VI. (Recommendations).
[351] See ch. 2 (Insulting Speech), s. II.4.5. (Opinion).
[352] HRC, General Comment No. 34 (2011), §49.

Committee's earlier approach to this issue,[353] and the Committee has since criticized so-called 'denial laws' in a number of countries.[354] The Human Rights Committee has, however, suggested that some restrictions to freedom of expression regarding historical facts could be permitted if they constitute speech that *must be* penalized under article 20 of the ICCPR.[355]

The CERD Committee has taken a similar position, recommending that 'the expression of opinions about historical facts' should not be prohibited but acknowledging that 'public denials or attempts to justify crimes of genocide and crimes against humanity ... should be declared as offences punishable by law' if 'they clearly constitute incitement to racial violence or hatred'.[356] And the Inter-American Commission has suggested more broadly that states seeking to prohibit hate speech inciting violence 'must have as a prerequisite strong, objective evidence that the person was not simply expressing an opinion, but also had the clear intention to commit an unlawful act'.[357]

The European Court has taken a different approach and consistently held that stating certain opinions—such as a belief that the Holocaust did not take place—*cannot be* protected speech, and the Court frequently strikes out claims relating to such speech on the basis that they run counter to the 'fundamental values' under article 17 of the Convention.[358]

For instance, when a French philosopher published a book that disputed the commission of crimes against humanity during the Holocaust and was sentenced to a three-year suspended prison sentence and a fine, the Court held the case inadmissible because his work was not 'historical research akin to a quest for truth', with its 'real purpose being to rehabilitate the National-Socialist regime', thereby running counter to

---

[353] M. O'Flaherty (n 311) 627, 653 (referring to HRC, *Faurisson v. France* (Comm. no. 550/1993), 8 November 1996). The professor was convicted and fined under France's Gayssot Act. The Committee held that the law sought to ensure the Jewish community could 'live free from fear of an atmosphere of anti-semitism' and that the restriction to the professor's speech was necessary since 'the denial of the existence of the Holocaust' was a 'principle vehicle for anti-semitism': HRC, *Faurisson v. France* (Comm. no. 550/1993), 8 November 1996, §§9.6–9.7. See alsoIndividual Opinion of Committee members Elizabeth Evatt and David Kretzmer, co-signed by Eckart Klein, §10 (stating that while there is 'every reason to maintain protection of bona fide historical research against restriction, even when it challenges accepted historical truths and by so doing offends people, anti-semitic allegations of the sort made by the author ... do not have the same claim to protection'). Cf. HRC, *Zündel v. Canada* (Comm. no. 953/2000), 27 July 2003, §8.5.

[354] See s. III.1.1. (ICCPR Article 20). See, e.g., HRC, *Concluding Observations, Lithuania* (2018) UN Doc. CCPR/C/LTU/CO/4, §§27–28 (expressing concern 'at reports of recently proposed legislative amendments that would ban the sale of material that "distorts historical facts" about the nation'); HRC, *Concluding Observations, Russia* (2015) UN Doc. CCPR/C/RUS/CO/7, §19 (expressing concern at a law criminalizing 'distortion of the Soviet Union's role in the Second World War' and suggesting Russia 'repeal or revise' this and other laws to bring them into conformity with the ICCPR). See also HRC, *Concluding Observations, Poland* (2016) UN Doc. CCPR/C/POL/CO/7, §38.

[355] HRC, General Comment No. 34 (2011), §49.

[356] CERD Committee, General Recommendation No. 35 (2013), §14 (citing to HRC, General Comment No. 34 (2011), §49).

[357] IACmHR, *Annual Report of the Inter-American Commission on Human Rights: Report of the Special Rapporteur for Freedom of Expression* (2009) OEA/Ser.L/V/II., Doc. 51, §544. See also IACtHR, *Kimel v. Argentina* (Series C, no. 177), 2 May 2008, §93 (stating that 'an opinion cannot be subjected to sanctions' and that the 'truthfulness or falseness' of a statement 'may only be established in respect of facts'); IACtHR *Palacio Urrutia et al. v. Ecuador* (Series C, no. 446), 24 November 2021, §115.

[358] ECtHR, *Pastörs v. Germany* (App. no. 55225/14), 3 October 2019, §§36–37. See also ECtHR (GC), *Perinçek v. Switzerland* (App. no, 27510/08), 15 October 2015, §115.

the Convention's values of 'justice and peace'.³⁵⁹ The Court also held that—even though any restriction to statements made 'by elected representatives in Parliament' requires the 'closest scrutiny'—a parliamentarian who denied the Holocaust in a speech in Germany legitimately received an eight-month suspended sentence.³⁶⁰ And the Court considered that a comedian who brought a Holocaust-denying academic on stage to receive an 'award' from an actor dressed as a Jewish deportee in a concentration camp could be convicted of racial insults without any review by the Court.³⁶¹

The Court's approach to Holocaust denial may be something of an aberration that results from the fact that its membership is made up of states that were implicated in the events of the Second World War.³⁶² Although this historical significance is understandable, such a viewpoint-based approach to regulating speech, particularly through the criminal law, is an unwelcome legal precedent. It has also led to unprincipled line-drawing, for instance in a case in which the Court reviewed a conviction in Switzerland for the statement that 'there was no genocide of the Armenians in 1915'. The Court found that the Swiss law used to convict the speaker stood 'at one end of the comparative spectrum' by criminalizing the denial of any genocide, 'without the requirement that it be carried out in a manner likely to incite to violence or hatred' and that its application to the speaker violated his rights.³⁶³ It therefore made the question of whether genocide denial is protected dependent on which genocide was involved.

Although the African Court has generally interpreted the right to free expression in line with the approach of the Human Rights Committee, it considers—like the European Court but unlike the Committee—that opinions about historical facts can be appropriately penalized.³⁶⁴ The Court reached this conclusion in a case in which a Rwandan politician was sentenced to 15 years' imprisonment for a number of offences, including 'minimization' of genocide, after she expressed concern that a memorial 'only refers to the people who died during the genocide against the Tutsis' and not the 'untold story with regard to the crimes against humanity committed against the Hutus'.³⁶⁵ The Court observed that although her statement did not 'deny or belittle' the genocide,³⁶⁶ 'it [was] entirely legitimate for the State to have introduced laws on the "minimisation", "propagation" and "negation" of genocide' and that statements which 'deny or minimize the magnitude or effects of the genocide or that unequivocally insinuate the same

---

³⁵⁹ ECtHR, *Garaudy v. France* (App. no. 65831/01), 24 June 2003. Five separate criminal proceedings were brought against the author as a result of the book, with a number of suspended sentences being handed down, to be served concurrently with the longest in time being three years.
³⁶⁰ ECtHR, *Pastörs v. Germany* (App. no. 55225/14), 3 October 2019, §§46–49.
³⁶¹ ECtHR, *M'Bala M'Bala v. France* (App. no. 25239/13), 20 October 2015 (inadmissible under Art. 17) (noting that although article 17 has 'always been applied to explicit and direct remarks not requiring any interpretation', in this case that 'the blatant display of a hateful and anti-Semitic position disguised as an artistic production [was] as dangerous as a fully-fledged and sharp attack').
³⁶² See s. III.2.2. (Legitimacy).
³⁶³ ECtHR (GC), *Perinçek v. Switzerland* (App. no. 27510/08), 15 October 2015, §§255–257. See s. III.2.2. (Legitimacy).
³⁶⁴ See s. III.2.2. (Legitimacy).
³⁶⁵ ACtHPR, *Umuhoza v. Rwanda* (App. no. 003/2014), 24 November 2017, §§151, 158. The applicant was also convicted of other offences such as 'conspiracy to undermine established authority and violate constitutional principles by resorting to terrorism and armed force': §23. Some alleged offences were not based on speech.
³⁶⁶ Ibid., §158.

fall outside the domain of the legitimate exercise of the right to freedom of expression and should be prohibited by law'.[367]

2.4.3. Public interest

The Human Rights Committee has made clear that, in the context of defamation laws, a 'public interest in the subject matter of a criticism' should be recognized as a defence.[368] The Inter-American and African Courts have similarly expressed a high threshold for restricting speech that deals with matters of public interest or relates to public officials.[369]

Similarly, the European Court has recognized that there is 'little scope' under article 10(2) 'for restrictions to political speech or debates on questions of public interest', and it 'has been the Court's consistent approach to require very strong reasons for justifying restrictions on political debate', establishing a 'particularly narrow margin of appreciation' in such cases.[370] At the other end of the spectrum, when it comes to speech that 'incite[s] to violence', the state authorities 'enjoy a wider margin of appreciation when examining the need for an interference with freedom of expression', and the same applies to speech 'liable to offend intimate personal convictions within the sphere of morals or, especially, religion'.[371] As the Court has put it: 'expression on matters of public interest is in principle entitled to strong protection, whereas expression that promotes or justifies violence, hatred, xenophobia or another form of intolerance cannot normally claim protection' at all.[372] As a result, the Court has concluded that a state can impose criminal sanctions for speech 'on an issue of legitimate public interest ... only in exceptional circumstances, notably where other fundamental rights have been seriously impaired' but such circumstances include 'for example' both 'incitement to violence' *and* 'hate speech'.[373]

Speech determined to be in the public interest in this context includes a documentary describing the attitudes of members of a racist youth group in Denmark and the band Pussy Riot performing their song 'Punk Prayer—Virgin Mary, Drive Putin Away' in a church to highlight 'the political situation in Russia and the stance of [members of the Russian Orthodox Church] towards street protests in a number of Russian cities'.[374] And when two protesters set fire to a photograph of the Spanish royal couple during a rally, the Court considered that this act was 'part of a debate on issues of public interest,

---

[367] Ibid., §§147, 158. The Court found that the impugned speech did not amount to denying genocide, and that even 'if this Court were to accept that there was a need to put restrictions on such statements' a 15-year prison term 'was not proportionate to the legitimate purposes which the conviction and sentence seek to achieve': ACtHPR, *Umuhoza v. Rwanda* (App. no. 003/2014), 24 November 2017, §162.

[368] HRC, *Kozlov v. Belarus* (Comm. no. 1986/2010), 24 July 2014, §7.5–7.6.

[369] See ch. 2 (Insulting speech), s. II.4.2. (Public interest). See, e.g., IACtHR, *Herrera-Ulloa v. Costa Rica* (Series C, no. 107), 2 July 2004, §101(2)(c); ACtHPR, *Konaté v. Burkina Faso* (App. no. 004/2013), 5 December 2014, §155.

[370] ECtHR, *Alekhina v. Russia* (App. no. 38004/12), 17 July 2018, §212; ECtHR (GC), *Bédat v. Switzerland* (App. no. 56925/08), 29 March 2016, §49. Cf. ECtHR (GC), *Sanchez v. France* (App. no. 45581/15), 15 May 2023, §176.

[371] ECtHR, *Murphy v. Ireland* (App. no. 44179/98), 10 July 2003, §67; ECtHR (GC), *Sürek v. Turkey* (App. nos. 23927/94 and 24277/94), 8 July 1999, §34.

[372] ECtHR (GC), *Perinçek v. Switzerland* (App. no. 27510/08), 15 October 2015, §230.

[373] ECtHR, *Savva Terentyev v. Russia* (App. no. 10692/09), 28 August 2018, §83.

[374] ECtHR (GC), *Jersild v. Denmark* (App. no. 15890/89), 23 September 1994, §33; ECtHR, *Alekhina v. Russia* (App. no. 38004/12), 17 July 2018, §212.

namely Catalan independence, the monarchical form of the State and criticism of the King as a symbol of the Spanish nation'.[375]

The European Court has previously considered 'the role of religion in society and its role in the development of society' to be a matter of public interest, but overrides this principle when it considers that such speech 'incite[s] to hatred or religious intolerance'.[376] For instance, when a woman argued that her statement regarding the marriage of the Prophet Muhammad to a six-year-old had been 'an objective criticism of religion' and had 'contributed to a public debate', the Court endorsed the domestic court's view that these statements 'had not been made in an objective manner aiming at contributing to a debate of public interest, but could only be understood as having been aimed at demonstrating that Muhammad was not a worthy subject of worship'.[377] On the other hand, the Court held that the denial of the Armenian genocide by a politician was an issue of public interest, as 'part of a long-standing controversy' and a 'heated debate, not only within Turkey but also in the international arena' on the issue.[378] In that same decision, the Court also noted that 'statements on historical issues' are 'as a rule seen as touching upon matters of public interest', although the Court has never considered speech questioning the Holocaust to be in this category.[379]

2.4.4. 'Responsible journalism'

The European Court has held that when it comes to assessing the necessity of speech restrictions, special protections may apply to the press.[380] According to the Court, the doctrine of 'reasonable journalism' means that there should be 'increased protection' afforded to speech by the media and other 'public watchdogs' that have a duty to report on 'matters of public interest' as long as the reporting is objectively 'reasonable'.[381] Since the Court has held that 'public interest' may relate to the 'role of a religion in society and its role in the development of society'[382] and 'statements on historical issues',[383] this principle may apply in the context of hate speech.

---

[375] ECtHR, *Stern Taulats and Roura Capellera v. Spain* (Apps. no. 51168/15 & 51186/15), 13 March 2018, §36. The Court was not convinced that this could be regarded as 'incitement to hatred or violence' and found the protesters' convictions and 2,700 Euro fines to be a violation of article 10: §§40–42.

[376] ECtHR, *Tagiyev v. Azerbaijan* (App. no. 13274/08), 5 December 2019, §§44–45.

[377] ECtHR, *E.S. v. Austria* (App. no. 38450/12), 25 October 2018, §§34, 52. See ss II.2.1.2. (Austria) and III.2.2. (Legitimacy) (Case Study: International Standards on Blasphemy Laws).

[378] ECtHR (GC), *Perinçek v. Switzerland* (App. no. 27510/08), 15 October 2015, §231. See ss III.2.2. (Legitimacy) and III.2.4.2. (Opinion).

[379] ECtHR, *Perinçek v. Switzerland* (App. no. 27510/08), 15 October 2015, §230. See s. III.2.4.2. (Opinion).

[380] The IACtHR has quoted the approach of the ECtHR that journalists 'must, when exercising their duties, abide by the principles of responsible journalism, namely to act in good faith, provide accurate and reliable information, objectively reflect the opinions of those involved in a public debate, and refrain from pure sensationalism'. But the doctrine of '[r]esponsible journalism' appears to operate more as a general principle rather than a defence or a way of assessing whether a violation of the right to free expression has occurred: IACtHR, *Mémoli v. Argentina* (Series C, no. 265), 22 August 2013, §122; see ch. 2 (Insulting Speech), s. II.1.4.3. (Reasonable publication).

[381] ECtHR, Guide on Article 10 of the European Convention on Human Rights—Freedom of Expression, 31 August 2022, §305. See also ECtHR (GC), *Fressoz v. France* (App. no. 29183/95), 21 January 1999, §45(ii); ECtHR (GC), *Pedersen v. Denmark* (App. no. 49017/99), 17 December 2004, §71. The responsible journalism doctrine applies even where journalistic reporting does not concern matters in the public interest: ECtHR (GC), *Satakunnan Markkinapörssi Oy v. Finland* (App. no. 931/13), 27 June 2017, §§174–183. Cf. Dissenting Opinion of Judges Sajo and Karakas, §2.

[382] ECtHR, *Tagiyev v. Azerbaijan* (App. no. 13274/08), 5 December 2019, §45.

[383] ECtHR (GC), *Perinçek v. Switzerland* (App. no. 27510/08), 15 October 2015, §230. See s. III.2.4.2. (Opinion).

The Court has found that when freedom of the press is at stake, authorities have a limited margin of appreciation to decide that a 'pressing social need' for restrictions exists.[384] But the Court has also made clear that journalists do not have an unfettered right to claim immunity from criminal liability if an offence was committed during the performance of journalistic activities.[385] This protection is, according to the Court, therefore 'subject to the condition that they comply with the duties and responsibilities connected with the function of journalist, and the consequent obligation of "responsible journalism"'.[386] These duties and responsibilities 'assume an even greater importance in situations of conflict and tension'.[387] And this conditional protection has also been applied to other speakers, such as human rights activists, NGOs and whistleblowers who engage in public debate.[388] The European Court has held, in a case involving a journalist, that the Court 'will examine whether the journalist ... *acted in good faith in accordance with the tenets of responsible journalism*'.[389] Whether or not a journalist acted 'responsibly' is assessed on the basis of the content of the information which is collected and disseminated by journalistic means as well as the process of publication.[390]

For example, in a case concerning a documentary airing the views of a racist group of young people in Denmark known as the 'Greenjackets', the Court observed that 'methods of objective and balanced reporting may vary considerably' and that '[i]t is not for [the] Court, nor for the national courts for that matter, to substitute their own views for those of the press as to what technique of reporting should be adopted by journalists'.[391] However, the Court had regard to 'the manner in which the Greenjackets feature was prepared, its contents, the context in which it was broadcast and the purpose of the programme', and found that taken as a whole, the feature sought 'to expose, analyse and explain this particular group of youths' rather than propagate racist views.[392] As a result, even though the remarks made by the Greenjackets themselves were not protected, those of journalists were.[393]

---

[384] ECtHR, Guide on Article 10 of the European Convention on Human Rights—Freedom of Expression, 31 August 2022, §299. See ch. 1 (Introduction), s. II.3.1.5. (Importance of protecting the press).

[385] ECtHR, Guide on Article 10 of the European Convention on Human Rights—Freedom of Expression, 31 August 2022, §320; ECtHR (GC), *Stoll v. Switzerland* (App. no. 69698/01), 10 December 2007, §102. See also ECtHR, *De Haes v. Belgium* (App. no. 19983/92), 24 February 1997, §37; ECtHR (GC), *Bladet Tromsø v. Norway* (App. no. 21980/93), 20 May 1999, §62.

[386] ECtHR, Guide on Article 10 of the European Convention on Human Rights—Freedom of Expression, 31 August 2022, §380. See, e.g., ECtHR, *Kącki v. Poland* (App. no. 10947/11), 4 July 2017, §49.

[387] ECtHR, *Stomakhin v. Russia* (App. no. 52273/07), 9 May 2018, §102.

[388] ECtHR (GC), *Magyar Helsinki Bizottság v. Hungary* (App. no. 18030/11), 8 November 2016, §159; ECtHR, *Gawlik v. Liechtenstein* (App. no. 23922/19), 16 February 2021, §77.

[389] ECtHR, *Kącki v. Poland* (App. no. 10947/11), 4 July 2017, §49 (emphasis added). The Court has also asked whether the journalist 'act[ed] in good faith, respect[ed] the ethics of journalism and perform[ed] the due diligence expected in responsible journalism?' ECtHR, *Magyar Jeti Zrt v. Hungary* (App. no. 11257/16), 4 December 2018, §77.

[390] See ch. 1 (Introduction), s. II.3.1.5. (Importance of protecting the press).

[391] ECtHR (GC), *Jersild v. Denmark* (App. no. 15890/89), 23 September 1994, §31. See also ECtHR (GC), *Bladet Tromsø v. Norway* (App. no. 21980/93), 20 May 1999, §63.

[392] ECtHR (GC), *Jersild v. Denmark* (App. no. 15890/89), 23 September 1994, §§31, 33. This case also developed the Court's jurisprudence providing that 'the punishment of a journalist for assisting in the dissemination of statements made by another person in an interview would seriously hamper the contribution of the press to discussion of matters of public interest and should not be envisaged unless there are particularly strong reasons for doing so': §35.

[393] Ibid., §§35–37. See ch. 1 (Introduction), s. II.3.1.5. (Importance of protecting the press).

2.5. Penalties

An assessment of whether hate-speech restrictions are 'necessary' to protect a legitimate aim under international human rights law includes an analysis of the proportionality of the penalty imposed.[394] International courts and human rights bodies have made clear that criminal penalties are only justified in exceptional circumstances. However, the European Court defines such circumstances in broader terms than its counterparts and its jurisprudence is an outlier in finding that criminal convictions—including prison terms—for hate speech are compatible with the right to freedom of speech.[395]

In the small number of hate speech cases that have come before the Human Rights Committee, the Committee has recognized that even minor civil penalties can have a chilling effect on speech. And it has never approved of criminal penalties for speech except in one case involving a Korean election law (which did not involve a prison term) and a now-overturned decision on Holocaust-denial laws.[396] In a concurring opinion in *Rabbae v. The Netherlands*, the leading hate speech case, two Committee members urged 'great caution in the imposition of criminal penalties that punish speech', proposing that criminal penalties should be limited to speech 'that incites the commission of criminal offences or acts of violence', particularly in recognition of the fact that hate speech laws 'are often employed to suppress the very minorities they purportedly are designed to protect'.[397] The UN has also recommended a range of non-censorial means to combat intolerance without resorting to criminal penalties against speech, such as inter-faith dialogue, education and other policies to combat intolerance.[398]

The European Court, for its part, considers that it may be 'necessary in democratic societies to sanction or even prevent all forms of expression which spread, incite, promote or justify violence or hatred based on intolerance' provided that penalties imposed 'are proportionate'.[399] And the Court has defined 'hate speech' and 'incitement to violence' as falling within the 'exceptional circumstances' justifying a custodial sentence for speech.[400] Although the Court has found terms of imprisonment for hate

---

[394] See, e.g., HRC, General Comment No. 34 (2011), §§34–35; ECtHR, *Tagiyev v. Azerbaijan* (App. no. 13274/08), 5 December 2019, §38; IACtHR, *Palamara Iribarne v. Chile* (Series C, no. 135), 22 November 2005, §85; ACtHPR, *Konaté v. Burkina Faso* (App. no. 004/2013), 5 December 2014, §145.

[395] See, e.g., ECtHR (GC), *Zana v. Turkey* (App. no. 18954/91), 25 November 1997; ECtHR, *Molnar v. Romania* (App. no. 16637/06), 23 October 2012, §25; ECtHR, *Belkacem v. Belgium* (App. no. 34367/14), 27 June 2017, §§33–37 (finding the applicant's petition inadmissible under article 17 and forgoing review on the merits of a suspended prison sentence for incitement to discrimination, hatred and violence).

[396] HRC, *Kim v. Republic of Korea* (Comm. no. 968/2001), 27 July 2005; HRC, *Faurisson v. France* (Comm. no. 550/1993), 8 November 1996; see s. III.2.4.2. (Opinion). The Committee also found no violation of article 19(3) in the case of HRC, *A.K. and A.R. v. Uzbekistan* (Comm. no. 1233/2003), 31 March 2009 (where two individuals were initially convicted of speech-related offences but ultimately found guilty of association and overthrow of the constitutional order offences for recruiting and training others to undertake violent extremist activities).

[397] HRC, *Rabbae v. The Netherlands* (Comm. no. 2124/2011), 14 July 2016, Individual Concurring Opinion of Committee members Sarah Cleveland and Mauro Politi, §§7–8. Cf. HRC, *Ross v. Canada* (Comm. no. 736/1997), 18 October 2000, §§11.1–11.6. See s. III.1.1. (ICCPR Article 20).

[398] See, e.g., Human Rights Council Resolution 16/18, UN Doc. A/HRC/RES/16/18, 24 March 2011.

[399] ECtHR, *Tagiyev v. Azerbaijan* (App. no. 13274/08), 5 December 2019, §38. The Court has also held that where fundamental rights are seriously impaired by speech, the Court considers states are 'permitted, or even obliged, by their positive obligations under Article 8' to regulate such expression: ECtHR, *Atamanchuk v. Russia* (App. no. 4493/11), 11 February 2020, §70. Although this language could be read as imposing mandatory penalization for such speech the case law does not establish such an obligation.

[400] ECtHR, *Atamanchuk v. Russia* (App. no. 4493/11), 11 February 2020, §67. See ch. 1 (Introduction), s. II.3.1.6. (Criminal penalties for speech).

HATE SPEECH   205

speech to be necessary and proportionate under article 10 in a limited number of cases, many of these relate to denialism, hate speech or incitement to violence cases.[401]

For example, the Court held that a spokesperson for an extremist group could be sentenced to an 18-month suspended sentence in Belgium for uploading YouTube videos stoking 'hatred, discrimination and violence' against non-Muslims.[402] A six-month term of imprisonment given to a French-Romanian citizen for displaying posters containing anti-gay and anti-Roma propaganda was permissible on a threshold review.[403] An 18-month suspended sentence was held to be proportionate when a Russian social media user uploaded a 'mockumentary' which expressed xenophobic views about people of non-Russian ethnic origins.[404] The Court found a term of 2.5 months' imprisonment (most of which was served on parole) proportionate where a Turkish politician expressed support for the PKK in a manner 'likely to exacerbate an already explosive situation' in southeast Turkey.[405] And the Court upheld a suspended sentence and fines where homophobic leaflets were distributed to young people 'who were at an impressionable and sensitive age and who had no possibility to decline to accept them'.[406]

In other cases, the European Court has found non-custodial criminal penalties appropriate. For instance, when a member of the Belgian parliament distributed leaflets describing non-European immigrants as criminally minded was banned from running for office for 10 years—as well as given a 10-month suspended sentence and 250 hours of community service—the Court considered that his right to free expression had not been violated and that domestic courts had shown 'restraint' in his sentencing.[407] And when a local political commentator was fined and banned from journalistic activities for two years for authoring a demeaning article about non-Russians, the Court considered that his speech fell within the 'exceptional circumstances' that warranted such a punishment.[408] A criminal conviction and fine of 3,000 Euros was found permissible

---

[401] See, e.g., ECtHR, *Vejdeland v. Sweden* (App. no. 1813/07), 9 February 2012; ECtHR (GC), *Zana v. Turkey* (App. no. 18954/91), 25 November 1997; ECtHR, *Atamanchuk v. Russia* (App. no. 4493/11), 11 February 2020; ECtHR, *Soulas v. France* (App. no. 15948/03), 10 July 2008; ECtHR, *Féret v. Belgium* (App. no. 15615/07), 16 July 2009; ECtHR, *Balystė-Lideikienė v. Lithuania* (App. no. 72596/01), 4 November 2008; ECtHR, *İ.A. v. Turkey* (App. no. 42571/98), 13 September 2005 (blasphemy); ECtHR, *Kilin v. Russia* (App. no. 10271/12), 11 May 2021; ECtHR, *Otto-Preminger-Institut v. Austria* (App. no. 13470/87), 20 September 1994. There are also additional relevant cases at the ECtHR which relate to other forms of speech, including terror related speech, espionage and defamation laws. See ch. 1 (Introduction), s. II.3.1.6. (Criminal penalties for speech).

[402] ECtHR, *Belkacem v. Belgium* (App. no. 34367/14), 27 June 2017, §§33–37.

[403] ECtHR, *Molnar v. Romania* (App. no. 16637/06), 23 October 2012, §§23–26. The Court did reference proportionality, stating that 'given the content of the posters' the national courts' findings were 'relevant and sufficient': §25.

[404] ECtHR, *Kilin v. Russia* (App. no. 10271/12), 11 May 2021, §§84–95. The Court considered that domestic courts had 'convincingly demonstrated' a 'clear intention to bring about the commission of related acts of hatred or intolerance': §90.

[405] ECtHR (GC), *Zana v. Turkey* (App. no. 18954/91), 25 November 1997, §60. See s. III.2.3.1. (Harm).

[406] ECtHR, *Vejdeland v. Sweden* (App. no. 1813/07), 9 February 2012, §§56–58.

[407] ECtHR, *Féret v. Belgium* (App. no. 15615/07) 16 July 2009, §§34, 80. Cf. Dissenting Opinion of Judge Sajo, holding that 'it is surprising and contrary to well-established practice that the specific criminal measures and their severity are not addressed here, even though the possibility of ten months' imprisonment and ten years' ineligibility (in other words, a long-term preventive interference with political speech) represents a disproportionate penalty in view of the alleged offence and the Court's well-established jurisprudence on political speech by politicians'.

[408] ECtHR, *Atamanchuk v. Russia* (App. no. 4493/11), 11 February 2020, §72. The Court considered it relevant that the commentator's main professional activity was as an entrepreneur, and therefore that the prohibition would not have 'significant practical consequences'. It also held the impugned statements 'could be reasonably assessed

when a political candidate failed to delete Islamophobic comments posted by third parties on his publicly accessible Facebook 'wall', the Court considering that the 'degree of liability', 'notoriety' and 'representativeness' a local political candidate had in comparison to a private individual was relevant to its assessment of proportionality.[409]

The Inter-American Court of Human Rights has held that a state's penalty for speech 'must be proportionate to the right affected and to the responsibility of the perpetrator, so that it should be established based on the different nature and seriousness of the acts'.[410] It has not yet applied these principles in the context of hateful speech,[411] but, unlike the European Court, the Inter-American Court has only approved criminal sanctions for speech in one case, considered by many to be an outlier.[412]

The African Court has held that the principle of proportionality, implied by the term 'within the law' in article 9(2), 'seeks to determine whether, by state action, there has been a balance between protecting the rights and freedoms of the individual and the interests of society as a whole'.[413] In making this determination, the Court considers a number of questions: '[a]re there sufficient reasons to justify the action? Is there a less restrictive solution? Does the action destroy the essence of the rights guaranteed by the Charter?'[414] Custodial sentences for violations of the laws of freedom of speech will only be lawful in 'serious and very exceptional circumstances' such as 'incitement to international crimes, public incitement to hatred, discrimination or violence or threats against a person or group of people, because of specific criteria such as race, colour, religion and nationality'.[415] Although its practice in this area is limited, the Court has found that a 15-year prison sentence for minimizing and denying the Rwandan genocide was 'not proportionate to the legitimate purposes' which the sentence sought to achieve.[416] But in another case, the Court held that criminal offences of 'racially motivated and xenophobic insults using a computer system' and 'incitement to hatred and

---

as stirring up base emotions or embedded prejudices in relation to the local population of non-Russian ethnicity': ECtHR, *Atamanchuk v. Russia* (App. no. 4493/11), 11 February 2020, §64.

[409] ECtHR (GC), *Sanchez v. France* (App. no. 45581/15), 15 May 2023, §201. The Court also noted that his conviction and 3,000 EUR fine (along with 1,000 EUR payment for costs) did not prevent him from being elected mayor and that 'in an election context, the impact of racist and xenophobic discourse becomes greater and more harmful': §§176, 208. Four judges dissented against the finding there had been no violation of article 10: Dissenting Opinion of Judge Ravarani; Dissenting Opinion of Judge Bošnjak; Joint Dissenting Opinion of Judges Wojtyczek and Zünd.
[410] IACtHR, *Norín Catrimán et al. v. Chile* (Series C, no. 279), 29 May 2014, §374. See s. III.2.2. (Legitimacy).
[411] IACtHR, *Norín Catrimán et al. v. Chile* (Series C, no. 279), 29 May 2014, §374. See s. III.2.2. (Legitimacy).
[412] IACtHR, *Mémoli v. Argentina* (Series C, no. 265), 22 August 2013, §§141, 143. The judgment has been described as a 'regression' by Catalina Botero-Marino, Special Rapporteur for Freedom of Expression for the Commission from 2008 to 2014: see C. Botero-Marino, 'The Role of the Inter-American Human Rights System in the Emergence and Development of Global Norms on Freedom of Expression', in L.C. Bollinger & A. Callamard (eds), *Regardless of Frontiers: Global Freedom of Expression in a Troubled World* (Columbia University Press 2021) 193, 194. See also E. Bertoni, 'Setbacks and Tension in the Inter-American Court of Human Rights' (Media Defence, 1 December 2013) (deeming the decision a 'serious and notable setback').
[413] ACtHPR, *Konaté v. Burkina Faso* (App. no. 004/2013), 5 December 2014, §149, citing ACmHPR, *Zimbabwe Lawyers for Human Rights & Associated Newspapers of Zimbabwe v. Zimbabwe* (Comm. no. 284/03), 3 April 2009.
[414] ACtHPR, *Konaté v. Burkina Faso* (App. no. 004/2013), 5 December 2014, §149, citing ACmHPR, *Zimbabwe Lawyers for Human Rights & Associated Newspapers of Zimbabwe v. Zimbabwe* (Comm. no. 284/03), 3 April 2009.
[415] ACtHPR, *Konaté v. Burkina Faso* (App. no. 004/2013), 5 December 2014, §165.
[416] ACtHPR, *Umuhoza v. Rwanda* (App. no. 003/2014), 24 November 2017, §162.

violence' were 'not disproportionate given their deterrent function', without addressing the permissible maximum penalties under these laws.[417]

IV. Key Divergences in International and Regional Guidance

Although limited hate speech cases have come before the Human Rights Committee, African Court and Inter-American Commission, these bodies have demonstrated that stringent conditions must be met—when it comes to intent, harm and penalties—before they will consider any punishment for hate speech to be compatible with freedom of expression. In contrast, the European Court has upheld penalties for hate speech, including criminal penalties, on a broader basis.

International bodies converge in that most cases involve balancing the right to free expression against the legitimate aim of protecting 'the rights' or 'reputation' of 'others'.[418] But the European Court has departed from other bodies by finding that protecting religious sensibilities through blasphemy laws and protecting a version of history through denial laws can fall within this legitimate aim.[419] And where the Court considers speech to contravene an open-ended set of broad values guaranteed by the Convention it will not even inquire about whether there was a legitimate aim for the restriction.[420]

When it comes to harm, members of the Human Rights Committee have proposed that criminal penalties for hate speech offences should be limited to 'speech that incites the commission of criminal offences or acts of violence', the African Commission has required a 'real likelihood and imminence of harm' and the Inter-American Commission requires 'an impending threat that could cause real harm'.[421] The European Court's assessment of harm is broader, and encompasses speech that 'could' be 'seen as a call for ... hatred or intolerance'[422] and does not need to 'involve an explicit call for an act of violence, or other criminal acts'.[423]

The Human Rights Committee and other UN bodies have also placed a higher bar for the harm that is required for penalties on hate speech to be considered 'necessary'. The Committee has held that states must demonstrate the direct and imminent nature of the harm likely to be caused by the speech, a position that has been reiterated by the

---

[417] ACtHPR, *Ajavon v. Republic of Benin* (App. no. 062/2019), 4 December 2020, §127. See s. III.2.2. (Legitimacy).
[418] See, e.g., HRC, *Ross v. Canada* (Comm. no. 736/1997), 18 October 2000, §11.5; *v. Sweden* (App. no. 1813/07), 9 February 2012, §49; ECtHR, *Lilliendahl v. Iceland* (App. no. 29297/18), 12 May 2020, §43; ECtHR, *Balsytė-Lideikienė v. Lithuania* (App. no. 72596/01), 4 November 2008, §73.
[419] See, e.g., ECtHR, *Williamson v. Germany* (App. no. 64496/17), 31 January 2019, §§16, 24; ECtHR, *Otto-Preminger-Institut v. Austria* (App. no. 13470/87), 20 September 1994, §48; ECtHR, *E.S. v. Austria* (App. no. 38450/12), 25 October 2018, §41.
[420] See, e.g., ECtHR, *Norwood v. United Kingdom* (App. no. 23131/03), 16 November 2004.
[421] HRC, *Rabbae v. The Netherlands* (Comm. no. 2124/2011), 14 July 2016, Individual Concurring Opinion of Committee members Sarah Cleveland and Mauro Politi, §7; IACmHR, *Annual Report of the Inter-American Commission on Human Rights: Report of the Special Rapporteur for Freedom of Expression* (2009) OEA/Ser.L/V/II., Doc. 51, 397 (referring to regulation of broadcasting and not specifically to hate speech); ACmHPR, Declaration of Principles of Freedom of Expression and Access to Information in Africa (2019), Principle 23(2)(f).
[422] ECtHR, *Ibragimov v. Russia* (App. nos. 1413/08 and 28621/11), 28 August 2018, §§94–98.
[423] Ibid.; ECtHR, *Stomakhin v. Russia* (App. no. 52273/07), 9 May 2018, §§129–130, see s. III.2.3.1. (Harm).

Inter-American Commission and African human rights bodies.[424] And although the European Court will address whether speech is 'capable' of causing harm within its assessment of necessity, in practice, it has found restrictions to be valid without a clear demonstration of the likelihood or imminence of harm, and in its article 17 cases does not engage in this assessment at all.[425]

A final and key point of divergence has been the European Court's willingness to consider criminal convictions, including prison terms, for hate speech to be compatible with freedom of expression.[426] In contrast, the Human Rights Committee, Inter-American Court and African Court and Commission do not endorse criminal penalties for such speech.[427]

But ultimately, regional standards cannot be used to justify departures from international standards.[428] There are 46 state parties to the ICCPR that are also parties to the European Convention,[429] and where those countries provide fewer freedom of expression protections than are afforded in the ICCPR, they are in breach of their international human rights obligations even when they are complying with regional standards.[430] This means that the more protective international standard should prevail when states are applying these standards around the globe.

V. Approach of Private Companies to Online Hate Speech

Technology and social media companies are at the forefront of responding to hate speech online: in 2020, Facebook/Meta's removal of hate speech had risen tenfold in two years, and TikTok removed more than 100 million videos in the first half of the year.[431] A number of technology and social media companies have committed to ensuring that they address hateful speech in a manner consistent with international human rights standards.[432] For example, Twitter's Rules reference freedom of expression grounded

---

[424] HRC, General Comment No. 34 (2011), §35; Rabat Plan of Action, §29(f); IACmHR, *Violence against Lesbian, Gay, Bisexual, Trans and Intersex Persons in the Americas* (2015) OAS/Ser.L/V/II. Doc.36/15 Rev.2, §235; ACmHPR, Declaration of Principles of Freedom of Expression and Access to Information in Africa (2019), Principle 23(2)(f).

[425] See, e.g., ECtHR, *Ivanov v. Russia* (App. no. 35222/04) 20 February 2007; ECtHR, *Norwood v. UK* (App. no. 23131/03) 16 November 2004. See s. III.2.3.1. (Harm).

[426] See s. III.2.5. (Penalties). See, e.g., ECtHR, *Vejdeland v. Sweden* (App. no. 1813/07), 9 February 2012; ECtHR (GC), *Zana v. Turkey* (App. no. 18954/91), 25 November 1997; ECtHR, *Belkacem v. Belgium* (App. no. 34367/14), 27 June 2017; ECtHR, *Molnar v. Romania* (App. no. 16637/06), 23 October 2012; ECtHR, *Garaudy v. France* (App. no. 65831/01), 24 June 2003.

[427] With the exception of HRC, *Faurisson v. France* (Comm. no. 550/1993), 8 November 1996 (which has effectively been overruled): See s. III.2.5. (Penalties) and ACtHPR, *Ajavon v. Republic of Benin* (App. no. 062/2019), 4 December 2020.

[428] UN Special Rapporteur D. Kaye, *Promotion and protection of the right to freedom of opinion and expression* (2019) UN Doc. A/74/486, §26.

[429] See Council of Europe, 'Chart of signatures and ratifications of Treaty 005'.

[430] UN Special Rapporteur D. Kaye, *Promotion and protection of the right to freedom of opinion and expression* (2019) UN Doc. A/74/486, §26.

[431] 'Social media's struggle with self-censorship' (The Economist, 22 October 2020).

[432] UN Special Rapporteur D. Kaye, *Report of the Special Rapporteur on the promotion and protection of the right to freedom of opinion and expression* (2018) UN Doc. A/HRC/38/35, §70. See also E.M. Aswad, 'The Future of Freedom of Expression Online' (2018) 17 *Duke Law & Technology Review* 26, 34.

in 'the United States Bill of Rights and the European Convention on Human Rights', and informed by 'works such as United Nations Principles on Business and Human Rights'.[433] Meta's policy declares that it is 'committed to respecting human rights as set out in ... the International Covenant on Civil and Political Rights' and other treaties.[434] It also has Community Standards stating that it 'look[s] to international human rights standards to make ... judgments' about content moderation.[435] And the Global Network Initiative, an alliance of internet companies that includes Meta, Microsoft and other tech giants recognizes that such companies 'have the responsibility to respect and promote the freedom of expression', and 'should comply with ... internationally recognized human rights' including the rights set out in the ICCPR,[436] with the scope of article 19(3) to be 'read within the context of further interpretations issued by international human rights bodies, including the Human Rights Committee and the Special Rapporteur on the promotion and protection of the right to freedom of opinion and expression'.[437] The decisions of Meta's Oversight Board—a group of experts established in 2018 to determine 'what to take down, what to leave up and why'[438]—also assess whether Meta's conduct complies with 'international human rights standards'.[439]

For example, the Oversight Board considered a post by a Facebook user in Myanmar saying that there was something wrong with Muslim men psychologically and questioning the lack of response by Muslims to the treatment of Uyghurs. Facebook removed this on the basis that it was unprotected hate speech—defined as a 'direct attack against people' on the basis of 'protected characteristics'.[440] But the Oversight Board disagreed, holding that 'restoring the post is consistent with international human rights standards', including article 19 of the ICCPR, General Comment No. 34, the Rabat Plan of Action and the UN Special Rapporteur's report on Online Hate Speech.[441] Applying these principles, the Board found that the content did not constitute 'advocacy of

---

[433] Twitter (known as X since July 2023), 'Defending and respecting the rights of people using our service'; See also V. Türk, 'Open letter from Volker Türk, United Nations High Commissioner for Human Rights, to Mr. Elon Musk, Chief Executive Officer at Twitter' (5 November 2022).

[434] Meta, 'Corporate Human Rights Policy'.

[435] Meta, 'Facebook Community Standards'. See also TikTok, 'Upholding human rights' ('Our philosophy is informed by the International Bill of Human Rights ... and the United Nations Guiding Principles on Business and Human Rights'); Facebook Newsroom, 'Hard Questions: Where Do We Draw the Line on Free Expression?' (9 August 2018) ('We look for guidance in documents like Article 19 of the International Covenant on Civil and Political Rights (ICCPR), which set standards for when it's appropriate to place restrictions on freedom of expression').

[436] Global Network Initiative, 'GNI Principles on Freedom of Expression and Privacy'.

[437] Ibid., n 7. The GNI Principles have also 'been drafted with reference to' the Johannesburg Principles: Ibid., n 9. And Facebook, Google, Microsoft and Twitter also have policies in place to engage with human rights experts and civil society organizations to ensure they are correctly implementing these standards. See, e.g., Meta, 'Facebook Community Standards'.

[438] Oversight Board, 'Oversight Board'.

[439] Oversight Board, 'Case decision 2021-015-FB-UA Asking for Adderall'; Oversight Board, 'Case decisions and policy advisory opinions'. See also Oversight Board, 'Case decision 2020-003-FB-UA Armenians in Azerbaijan' (although 'companies do not have the obligations of Governments, their impact is of a sort that requires them to assess the same kind of questions about protecting their users' right to freedom of expression').

[440] Meta, 'Community Standards: Hate Speech'.

[441] Oversight Board, 'Case decision 2020-002-FB-UA Myanmar post about Muslims'. The decisions of the Oversight Board are 'binding', however, if a decision or policy advisory opinion includes recommendations, Meta is only required to analyse its operational procedures and consider such recommendations: see Oversight Board, 'Oversight Board Charter, 7–8.

religious hatred constituting incitement to discrimination, hostility or violence, which states are required to prohibit under ICCPR Article 20, para. 2'. The Board then considered 'whether this content could be restricted under ICCPR Article 19, para 3', and concluded that its removal was not necessary to protect the rights of others.[442]

Similarly, in a case approving Facebook's decision to remove a post which used a slur to insult Azerbaijanis, the Board noted that 'Facebook has ... indicated that it looks to authorities such as the ICCPR and the Rabat Plan of Action when making content decisions'. Applying these, it found that Facebook's removal of the post met 'the three-part test of legality, legitimacy and necessity and proportionality' required by article 19, particularly since the speech was posted during the fighting in Nagorno-Karabakh, and the dangers of dehumanizing slurs proliferating in a way that escalates into violence.[443]

The Oversight Board recently assessed Meta's balancing act between limiting the spread of violent hate speech and protecting valid forms of political expression in a case regarding a Facebook post calling for the end of Iranian leader Ayatollah Khamenei's regime.[444] In a public group describing itself as supporting freedom in Iran, a Facebook user posted in July 2022 a caricature of Iran's Supreme Leader with a text bubble saying that being a woman is forbidden, and a caption calling for death to the 'anti-women Islamic government' and its 'filthy leader Khamenei', as well as encouraging Iranian women not to collaborate with the oppression of women. This was posted just months before the death of Mahsa Amini in custody which sparked widespread protests in Iran.[445] Meta removed the post and restricted the user's Facebook access on the basis that it prohibits calls for death or high-severity violence, but when the Board selected the case for review, Meta reversed its decision on the basis that the post fell within its 'newsworthiness' exception, where keeping content online is 'in the public interest'.

The Oversight Board found that removing the post was inconsistent with Meta's 'human rights responsibilities as a business' because the post was a 'rhetorical, political slogan, not a credible threat' and 'posed very little risk of inciting violence'.[446] However, the Board did not consider all 'death to' statements to be the same: for example, 'death to' statements against Salman Rushdie would 'pose a much more significant risk' in light of the fatwa against him and ongoing concerns for his safety. And 'death to' statements

---

[442] Oversight Board, 'Case decision 2020-002-FB-UA Myanmar post about Muslims'.
[443] Oversight Board, 'Case decision 2020-003-FB-UA Armenians in Azerbaijan'.
[444] Oversight Board, 'Case decision 2022-013-FB-UA Iran protest slogan'.
[445] F. Fassihi & C. Engelbrecht, 'Tens of Thousands in Iran Mourn Mahsa Amini, Whose Death Set Off Protests' (The New York Times, 26 October 2022).
[446] Oversight Board, 'Case decision 2022-013-FB-UA Iran protest slogan'. Because the Board found that the post did not violate Meta's Violence and Incitement Community Standard, it considered that an assessment of the 'newsworthiness allowance was not required', which is the balancing test that Meta conducts comparing the public interest in the content against the risk of harm. Notwithstanding this finding, the Board held that when Meta applied the newsworthiness allowance to the post 'it should have been scaled to apply to all "marg bar Khamenei" slogans, regardless of the speaker'.

during the events of the January 6 riots in Washington, D.C., were not comparable, as 'politicians were clearly at risk and 'death to' statements are not generally used as political rhetoric in English'.[447] The Board also considered the political context in Iran, noting that in an environment where 'the Iranian government systematically represses freedom of expression ... it is vital that Meta supports users' voice'. The Board ultimately recommended that Meta amend its Violence and Incitement Community Standard to provide 'the criteria used to determine when rhetorical threats against heads of state are permitted', and that these criteria should 'protect clearly rhetorical political speech, used in protest contexts, that does not incite violence, and should take language and context into account'.[448]

Although some internet companies have committed themselves to the minimum international standards on speech, it is not clear how they will address divergences in the guidance. Twitter grounds its values in both the First Amendment *and* the European Convention, two very different bodies of law.[449] The Oversight Board, on the other hand, has stated that it would not 'apply the First Amendment of the US Constitution' as this 'does not govern the conduct of private companies', but also noted that 'in many relevant respects the principles of freedom of expression reflected in the First Amendment are similar or analogous to the principles of freedom of expression in ICCPR Article 19'.[450] And the Board has recognized that human rights standards designed for countries may need to be transposed or interpreted differently when applied to companies under some circumstances.[451]

VI. Recommendations

The following recommendations are based on international standards applicable to hate speech, or where there is a divergence or lacunae in such standards, a suggestion as to the best policy or approach. They are addressed to states because states have ratified the international treaties that underlie the standards. However, they are also intended to guide private companies seeking to apply international standards in line with the UN Guiding Principles on Business and Human Rights.[452]

---

[447] Oversight Board, 'Case decision 2022-013-FB-UA Iran protest slogan'.
[448] Ibid.
[449] See ss III.2. (Discretionary Restrictions on Hate Speech) and II.2.3.2. (United States).
[450] Oversight Board, 'Case decision 2021-001-FB-FBR Former President Trump's suspension', 28.
[451] The Board has noted with approval the fact that the UN Special Rapporteur sees greater leeway for speech restriction by a company than by a government. See Oversight Board, 'Case decision 2020-003-FB-UA Armenians in Azerbaijan'. See also Oversight Board, 'Case decision 2021-001-FB-FBR Former President Trump's suspension', 25.
[452] See Twitter (known as X since July 2023), 'Defending and respecting the rights of people using our service'; Meta, 'Corporate Human Rights Policy'; see s. V. (Approach of Private Companies to Online Hate Speech). As all restrictions to speech, discretionary or purportedly mandatory, must comply with article 19(3) of the ICCPR, our recommendations regarding the limits of discretionary restrictions to speech apply with equal force to mandatory restrictions.

1. Blasphemy laws are not compatible with freedom of expression under international human rights law and should be repealed.

Restrictions on speech cannot be vague or overly broad, as individuals must know how to regulate their conduct to avoid penalties imposed through the law.[453] And to be legitimate, hate speech laws must fall within the two exhaustive aims of article 19(3): respecting the rights or reputations of others, or the protection of national security, public order or public health or morals.[454]

Although at least 95 countries still punish blasphemy with criminal penalties,[455] blasphemy laws do not meet this test.[456]

The UN Human Rights Committee has made clear that '[p]rohibitions of displays of lack of respect for a religion or other belief system, including blasphemy laws, are incompatible with' article 19 of the Covenant, and that 'criticism of even the most deeply-held convictions of the adherents of a religion is protected by freedom of expression'.[457] Similarly, the Inter-American Court has not tolerated censorship of speech simply on the basis that it offends religious sensibilities.[458] And some European bodies, including the European Union and the Venice Commission (an expert body that forms part of the Council of Europe), have followed this approach and recommended the decriminalization of blasphemy laws.[459]

This approach is preferable to the one adopted by the European Court of Human Rights which has, in effect, allowed restrictions to speech on the basis of distasteful content—rather than based on the intent of the speaker and the harm caused by the speech—even in cases involving criminal penalties. Viewpoint-based restrictions set a worrying precedent whereby the state decides which content is or is not acceptable or even whether the

---

[453] HRC, General Comment No. 34 (2011), §25; UN Special Rapporteur D. Kaye, *Promotion and protection of the right to freedom of opinion and expression* (2019) UN Doc. A/74/486, §§6(a), 32, 46; ECtHR, *Dink v. Turkey* (App. nos. 2668/07 & others), 14 September 2020, §114 (although cf. s. III.2.1. (Legality), discussing the Court's more lenient application of this principle); IACtHR, *Usón Ramírez v. Venezuela* (Series C, no. 207), 20 November 2009, §55; ACtHPR, *Konaté v. Burkina Faso* (App. no. 004/2013), 5 December 2014, §131.

[454] ICCPR Art.19(3). See ss III.2.2. (Legitimacy) and III.2 (Discretionary Restrictions on Hate Speech).

[455] See United States Commission on International Religious Freedom, 'Legislation Factsheet: Blasphemy (September 2023)'; see ss II.1.1. (Type of speech) (Case Study: Blasphemy Laws) and II.1.1. (Type of speech) (Case Study: Denial laws).

[456] HRC, General Comment No. 34 (2011), §48. See also HRC, *Rabbae v. The Netherlands* (Comm. no. 2124/2011), 14 July 2016, §10.5; Venice Commission, *Report on the Relationship between Freedom of Expression and Freedom of Religion: The Issue of Regulation and Prosecution of Blasphemy, Religious Insult and Incitement to Religious Hatred* (2008) CDL-AD(2008)026, §92; EU Guidelines on the promotion and protection of freedom of religion or belief, §32; OSCE, 'OSCE Representative on Freedom of the Media welcomes Irish referendum on blasphemy' (2 October 2017). See s. III.2.2. (Legitimacy) (Case Study: International Standards on Blasphemy Laws).

[457] HRC, General Comment No. 34 (2011), §48; HRC, *Rabbae v. The Netherlands* (Comm. no. 2124/2011), 14 July 2016, §10.5. See also HRC, *Concluding Observations, Kuwait* (2016) UN Doc. CCPR/C/KWT/CO/3, §§39, 41; HRC, *Concluding Observations, Russian Federation* (2015) UN Doc. CCPR/C/RUS/CO/7, §19. See also e.g., WGAD, *Mejri v. Tunisia* (Opinion no. 29/2013), 30 August 2013 §18; WGAD, *Amer v. Egypt* (Opinion no. 35/2008), 20 November 2008, §38.

[458] See IACtHR, '*The Last Temptation of Christ*' (*Olmedo-Bustos et al.) v. Chile* (Series C, no. 73), 5 February 2001, §§71–73, 76–80 (holding that Chile's prohibition of the exhibition of the film 'The Last Temptation of Christ' on the basis that it 'deformed and diminished' the image of Christ constituted prior censorship in violation of article 13, and did not violate article 12 (freedom of religion)).

[459] Venice Commission, *Report on the Relationship between Freedom of Expression and Freedom of Religion: The Issue of Regulation and Prosecution of Blasphemy, Religious Insult and Incitement to Religious Hatred* (2008) CDL-AD(2008)026, §92; EU Guidelines on the promotion and protection of freedom of religion or belief; OSCE, 'OSCE Representative on Freedom of the Media welcomes Irish referendum on blasphemy' (2 October 2017).

content has been expressed in an acceptable way. The decision in *E.S. v. Austria*, upholding a conviction under Austria's blasphemy law for referring to Prophet Muhammad's marriage to a six-year-old girl as paedophilia epitomizes the low bar for allowing a conviction for blasphemous speech in Europe.[460] Although such speech may be offensive or even reprehensible, the European Court's approval of criminal penalties in such instances runs counter to the minimum international standards that bind all states.

As the UN Special Rapporteur has said, 'article 19 protects *individuals* ... [it does not] protect *ideas or beliefs* from ridicule, abuse, criticism or other "attacks" seen as offensive'.[461] And as the UN-approved Rabat Plan of Action puts it, blasphemy laws are 'counterproductive, since they may result in de facto censure of all inter-religious or belief and intra-religious or belief dialogue, debate and criticism, most of which could be constructive, healthy and needed'.[462] We therefore urge states to repeal such provisions and in doing so ensure compliance with international law.

Repealing blasphemy provisions does not of course mean that any attack against religious groups or on the grounds of religion should go unaddressed. There are other ways to combat such speech without resorting to the blunt instrument of the criminal law. As recognized by the Human Rights Council, the 'open public debate of ideas, as well as interfaith and intercultural dialogue ... can be among the best protections against religious intolerance'.[463] The fact that blasphemous speech may lead to a violent response from those who are incensed by the speech does not change this analysis: international human rights law does not allow for a 'heckler's veto', 'which would mandate the stifling of speakers when those who are offended choose to show their displeasure through harmful acts'.[464] If the speech constitutes not just blasphemy but incitement to discrimination, hostility or violence, international law provides that it should be sanctioned.[465]

2. 'Denial laws' are not compatible with international human rights law and should be repealed.

The UN Human Rights Committee has held that opinions denying or calling into question genocide[466] or historical narratives cannot be penalized.[467] We endorse the Committee's position that '[l]aws that penalize the expression of opinions about historical facts are incompatible with the obligations that the [ICCPR] imposes on state parties in relation to the respect for freedom of opinion and expression'.[468] And we agree

---

[460] ECtHR, *E.S. v. Austria* (App. no. 38450/12), 25 October 2018, §§43–57.
[461] UN Special Rapporteur D. Kaye, *Promotion and protection of the right to freedom of opinion and expression* (2019) UN Doc. A/74/486, §21 (emphasis added).
[462] Rabat Plan of Action, §19.
[463] Human Rights Council Resolution 16/18, UN Doc. A/HRC/RES/16/18, 24 March 2011, §4.
[464] UN Special Rapporteur D. Kaye, *Promotion and protection of the right to freedom of opinion and expression* (2019) UN Doc. A/74/486, §10; E. Aswad, 'To Ban or Not to Ban Blasphemous Videos' (2013) 44 *Georgetown Journal of International Law* 1313, 1322.
[465] See ICCPR Art. 20; CERD Art. 4.
[466] Professor Irwin Cotler endorses all recommendations in this book except for this one.
[467] HRC, General Comment No. 34 (2011), §49; CERD Committee, General Recommendation No. 35 (2013), §14.
[468] HRC, General Comment No. 34 (2011), §49.

with the Committee that international law 'does not permit general prohibition of expressions of an erroneous opinion or an incorrect interpretation of past events'.[469]

Yet the European Court and a number of European nations have adopted the opposite position,[470] with the European Court finding that denial of the Holocaust is unprotected under any circumstances and that a claim that such speech is protected cannot even be considered by the Court.[471] In such decisions the European Court has allowed criminal penalties to be meted out against speech on the basis of its content, rather than the intent of the speaker and likely harm caused by the speech, a notion that sets a worrying precedent whereby a state or court decides which viewpoint is or is not acceptable or even whether a viewpoint has been expressed in an acceptable way.[472] But ultimately the intent of the speaker, the harm that is caused by the speech, and any extenuating or aggravating circumstances are best assessed on a case-by-case basis.[473]

The European Court's position that denial of the Holocaust is criminal but denial of the Armenian genocide is acceptable is also problematic as it creates a 'speculative hierarchy between the Holocaust and other twentieth-century mass atrocities'.[474] It also begs many questions: is it only historic events that cannot be denied? Does it have to be a past genocide or can it be an ongoing one? Does there need to be a court judgment confirming such a genocide—if so, which court counts? Does this mean that denial of crimes against humanity, or torture, or rape can also be criminalized? Why these and not other viewpoints? Instead of opening floodgates or engaging in unprincipled line-drawing, statements of opinion should be protected unless they violate article 20 of the ICCPR[475] and denial laws should be abolished.

3. States should only criminalize hate speech if it is intended to incite the commission of serious criminal offences, acts of violence or similar action and there is at least a likelihood, if not probability, that such offences or acts will imminently occur as a direct result of the speech.

States can only impose penalties on hate speech to the extent that the penalty is necessary and proportionate to advancing a legitimate aim.[476] Although the vast majority

---

[469] Ibid.

[470] In 2020, Facebook also announced that it would prohibit 'any content that denies or distorts the Holocaust': Meta, 'Removing Holocaust Denial Content' (12 October 2020).

[471] See s. III.2. (Discretionary Restrictions on Hate Speech). The ACtHPR has also expressed openness to laws which penalize negation or minimization of genocide in the context of the Rwandan genocide, presenting a rare instance in which the ACtHPR has veered away from HRC jurisprudence. See ACtHPR, *Umuhoza v. Rwanda* (App. no. 003/2014), 24 November 2017, §158; see s. III.2.4.2. (Opinion). See also H. Cannie & D. Voorhoof, 'The Abuse Clause and Freedom of Expression in the European Human Rights Convention: An Added Value for Democracy and Human Rights Protection?' (2011) 29 *Netherlands Quarterly of Human Rights* 54, 67–68.

[472] See ECtHR, *Garaudy v. France* (App. no. 65831/01), 24 June 2003, §1.

[473] See s. III.2.2. (Legitimacy).

[474] A. Cherviatsova, 'Memory as a Battlefield: European Memorial Laws and Freedom of Speech' (2021) 25 *The International Journal of Human Rights* 675, 684.

[475] But see s. VI.3.2 (Recommendations).

[476] See s. III.2.3. (Necessity).

of state hate speech laws are criminal in nature,[477] international standards dictate that criminal penalties for speech should only be resorted to in exceptional circumstances.[478] The lack of cases condoning criminal penalties for hate speech by international and regional human rights bodies is a clear marker that hate speech will rarely be considered sufficiently exceptional to warrant criminal sanctions, especially if these include imprisonment.[479] Even when it comes to mandatory penalties for speech imposed by treaty, international guidance provides that states should use criminal sanctions 'only [in] serious and extreme instances'.[480] And such standards cannot be read to require that a prosecution—let alone a conviction—must eventuate.[481]

3.1. The speaker must have 'intended' to incite harm.
The Genocide Convention has an explicit and high intent requirement: the intent to directly and publicly incite others to commit genocide.[482] Although article 20 of the ICCPR does not contain an express intent requirement, persuasive soft law guidance construes 'advocacy' as 'the explicit, *intentional*, public and active support and promotion of hatred towards the target group'.[483] General Comment No. 35 holds that states should take into account 'the intention of the speaker' when applying article 4 of CERD, and must demonstrate that the speaker 'seeks to influence others to engage in certain forms of conduct ... through advocacy or threats'.[484] Finally, the UN-approved Rabat Plan of Action includes intent as one of the six factors that states should consider when criminalizing hateful speech and holds that '[n]egligence and recklessness are not sufficient for [a speech] act to be an offence'.[485] Strict liability offences or laws that do

---

[477] See Alkiviadou, Mchangama & Mendiratta (n 19); see s. III.2.5. (Penalties).
[478] See, e.g., IACtHR, *Álvarez Ramos v. Venezuela* (Series C, no. 380), 30 August 2019, §§119, 120; ACtHPR, *Konaté v. Burkina Faso* (App. no. 004/2013), 5 December 2014, §165; HRC, General Comment No. 34 (2011), §47 (in the context of defamation); CERD Committee, General Recommendation No. 35 (2013), §12.
[479] Even the European Court has only upheld criminal sanctions for hate speech in a small fraction of its decisions, even less so where the speaker was sentenced to a term of imprisonment. See, e.g., ECtHR, *Atamanchuk v. Russia* (App. no. 4493/11), 11 February 2020; ECtHR, *Soulas v. France* (App. no. 15948/03), 10 July 2008; ECtHR, *Ivanov v. Russia* (App. no. 35222/04), 20 February 2007; ECtHR, *Nix v. Germany* (App. no. 35285/16), 13 March 2018; ECtHR, *Vejdeland v. Sweden* (App. no. 1813/07), 9 February 2012; ECtHR, *Belkacem v. Belgium* (App. no. 34367/14), 27 June 2017; ECtHR, *Féret v. Belgium* (App. no. 15615/07), 16 July 2009; ECtHR, *Le Pen v. France* (App. no. 18788/09), 7 May 2010; ECtHR, *Molnar v. Romania* (App no. 16637/06), 23 October 2012; ECtHR, *Norwood v. United Kingdom* (App no. 23131/03), 16 November 2004.
[480] UN Special Rapporteur F. La Rue, *Promotion and protection of the right to freedom of opinion and expression* (2012) UN Doc. A/67/357, §47. See IACmHR, *Violence against Lesbian, Gay, Bisexual, Trans and Intersex Persons in the Americas* (2015) OAS/Ser.L/V/II. Doc.36/15 Rev.2, ch. IV, s. F. (proposing non-legal measures to counter hate speech, including preventive and educational mechanisms).
[481] HRC, *Rabbae v. The Netherlands* (Comm. no. 2141/2011), 14 July 2016, §10.7 ('The obligation under article 20 (2), however, does not extend to an obligation for the State party to ensure that a person who is charged with incitement to discrimination, hostility or violence will invariably be convicted by an independent and impartial court of law'). The CERD Committee has, however, also held that 'effective implementation' of article 4 is 'characteristically achieved through investigations of offences set out in the Convention and, *where appropriate, the prosecution of offenders*'. See CERD Committee, General Recommendation No. 35 (2013), §17 (emphasis added); see also §12.
[482] See s. III.1.3. (Genocide Convention Article 3).
[483] UN Special Rapporteur F. La Rue, *Promotion and protection of the right to freedom of opinion and expression* (2012) UN Doc. A/67/357, §§43–44 (emphasis added); Rabat Plan of Action, §21, n 5.
[484] CERD Committee, General Recommendation No. 35 (2013), §16.
[485] Rabat Plan of Action, §29(c). See also UN Special Rapporteur F. La Rue, *Promotion and protection of the right to freedom of opinion and expression* (2012) UN Doc. A/67/357, §50. See also IACmHR, *Violence against Lesbian, Gay, Bisexual, Trans and Intersex Persons in the Americas* (2015) OAS/Ser.L/V/II. Doc.36/15 Rev.2, §235; ACmHPR, Declaration of Principles of Freedom of Expression and Access to Information in Africa (2019), Principle 23(2)(c).

not set out a sufficiently stringent intent requirement are therefore at odds with minimum international standards. Recklessness could, however, be sufficient to render the speaker civilly liable where speech is restricted on a discretionary basis under article 19 of the ICCPR.[486]

3.2. The harm that the speaker intended to incite should be 'the commission of criminal offences, acts of violence or similar action'.

A discrepancy exists between international instruments as to what harm justifies the penalization or criminalization of hate speech. States' obligation to restrict speech under article 20 of the ICCPR and article 4 of CERD only applies to speech that amounts to 'incitement'[487] but the incited harms that can justify penalization are broad: including 'hostility' under the ICCPR, 'contempt' and 'hatred' under CERD as well as the common harms of 'discrimination' and 'violence'.[488] A higher harm standard is required by the American Convention: 'lawless violence' or 'similar action', similar to US First Amendment principles.[489] And a similar standard was articulated by members of the Human Rights Committee who held that speech should incite to 'criminal offences or acts of violence'—at least before mandatory penalties or criminal sanctions can be justified.[490]

This higher standard is preferable as it avoids overbroad criminalization. As noted by members of the Human Rights Committee, international law 'urges great caution in the imposition of criminal penalties that punish speech'.[491] And terms such as 'hostility', 'hatred' and 'contempt' are subjective states of mind rather than objective hate-fuelled acts that result from the speech.[492] Authoritarian regimes can easily manipulate such terms to silence criticism and would no doubt be glad to say that they were just following international agreed standards in doing so.[493] Such vague concepts, if used in criminal laws, may well also violate the principle of legality (also known as *nullum crimen sine lege*) as it would be difficult for an individual to predict

---

[486] See ch. 2 (Insulting Speech), s. IV. (Recommendations) and ch. 4 (False Speech), s. IV. (Recommendations).

[487] With incitement incorporating an 'imminent risk' of harm: see HRC, *Rabbae v. The Netherlands* (Comm. no. 2124/2011), 14 July 2016, Individual Concurring Opinion of Committee members Sarah Cleveland and Mauro Politi, §4; UN Special Rapporteur F. La Rue, *Promotion and protection of the right to freedom of opinion and expression* (2012) UN Doc. A/67/357, §43; Rabat Plan of Action, §21, n 5; CERD Committee, General Recommendation No. 35 (2013), §13(b), (d).

[488] CERD Committee, General Recommendation No. 35 (2013), §13(b), (d).

[489] See s. III.1.4. (Mandatory restrictions at the regional level).

[490] HRC, *Rabbae v. The Netherlands* (Comm. no. 2124/2011), 14 July 2016, Individual Concurring Opinion of Committee members Sarah Cleveland and Mauro Politi, §7. See s. III.1.1. (ICCPR Article 20).

[491] HRC, *Rabbae v. The Netherlands* (Comm. no. 2124/2011), 14 July 2016, Individual Concurring Opinion of Committee members Sarah Cleveland and Mauro Politi, §7.

[492] Some UN documents have suggested that terms such as 'hostility' be interpreted to mean 'a manifestation of hatred beyond a mere state of mind' but this has not been adopted by international courts and still leaves terms such as 'hatred' and 'contempt' undefined: See, e.g., UN Special Rapporteur F. La Rue, *Promotion and protection of the right to freedom of opinion and expression* (2012) UN Doc. A/67/357, §44(e).

[493] See s. III.2.5. (Penalties).

what speech may lead to a criminal penalty.[494] And they are overbroad: as polarized political views are evident in much of today's news media, much of the content of our newspapers or news programs might easily pass the test of inspiring 'hostility' or 'contempt' in audiences.

States should therefore consider entering a reservation to article 20 of the ICCPR and article 4 of CERD in a manner that would allow them to apply these provisions as imposing permission but not a requirement to penalize speech, and to apply a high intent and harm requirement to any penalization—such as an intent to cause violence or illegal acts that may cause serious physical injury or death through speech—rather than the more vague ills such as hostility, contempt and discrimination that are mentioned in these treaty provisions.

3.3. There should be a 'probability' that the harm the speaker intended to invite would 'imminently occur as a direct result of the speech'.

The Human Rights Committee has held that states must 'demonstrate in specific and individualized fashion the precise nature of the threat' posed by speech and establish a 'direct and immediate connection between the expression and the threat' if it is to be penalized.[495] Under the UN-approved Rabat Plan of Action, this means that there should be 'a *reasonable probability* that the speech would succeed in *inciting actual action* against the target group, recognizing that such causation should be rather direct'.[496] The CERD Committee has provided a similar threshold, being that (at least in criminal cases) states must demonstrate the 'imminent risk of likelihood that the conduct ... intended by the speaker will result from the speech'.[497]

Yet currently, in practice, speech is often sanctioned without any demonstrated connection between speech and harm, let alone an objective probability (meaning that it is more probable than not) of harm that is imminent.[498] Weak causation tests such as the European Court's standard of whether speech 'could' be 'seen as a call for violence, hatred or intolerance',[499] or total disregard of causation by virtue of article 17,[500] leave too much speech unprotected or subject to viewpoint-based restrictions.[501]

---

[494] See ch. 4 (False Speech), s. III.1. (Legality).
[495] HRC, General Comment No. 34 (2011); Rabat Plan of Action, §29(f); UN Special Rapporteur on the right to freedom of opinion and expression, Frank LaRue, *Report of the Special Rapporteur on the Promotion and Protection of the Right to Freedom of Opinion and Expression (4 September 2013)*, UN Doc. A/68/362, §§52, 53.
[496] Rabat Plan of Action, §29(f) (emphasis added).
[497] CERD Committee, General Recommendation No. 35 (2013), §16.
[498] See s. III.2.3.1. (Harm). See, e.g., ECtHR (GC), *Zana v. Turkey* (App. no. 18954/91, 25 November 1997, §60; ECtHR, *Molnar v. Romania* (App. no. 16637/06), 23 October 2012, §23.
[499] ECtHR, *Ibragimov v. Russia* (App. nos. 1413/08 & 28621/11), 28 August 2018, §98; ECtHR (GC), *Perinçek v. Switzerland* (App. no. 27510/08), 15 October 2015, §207.
[500] See, e.g., ECtHR, *Lilliendahl v. Iceland* (App. no. 29297/18), 12 May 2020, §36.
[501] For example, blasphemy or denialism laws which prohibit speech on the basis of content rather than harm or intent: See s. VI. (Recommendations).

4. When it is legitimate to penalize hate speech, this can be on the ground of prohibited harm to individuals on the basis of sexual orientation, gender, political affiliation, or other protected characteristics, not just discrimination based on race, ethnicity or religion.

States' obligations to limit hate speech vary based on the target of the speech: article 20 of the ICCPR applies to 'national, racial or religious' hatred. Article 4 of CERD only applies to 'racial' hatred, though the CERD Committee has construed this to extend to 'colour, descent or national or ethnic origin'.[502]

The Inter-American approach covers characteristics other than nationality, race and religion and extends to speech that is hateful on the basis of 'sexual orientation, gender identity, and bodily diversity'.[503] Similarly, the European Court has held that 'discrimination based on sexual orientation is as serious' as discrimination based on 'race, origin or colour'.[504]

International human rights treaties were drafted in the wake of World War II with a specific threat of totalitarianism in mind. But it is time to recognize that the protection in international treaties for the 'rights of others' includes other characteristics such as those outlined in article 26 of the ICCPR, which prohibits 'discrimination on any ground such as race, colour, sex, language, religion, political or other opinion, national or social origin, property, birth or other status'. But balancing the protection from discrimination against the right to free speech would need to remain in line with the other recommendations related to strict requirements of intent, causation, harm and guidance of proportionality of penalties as set out above.

5. Tech companies should recognize international human rights standards as a floor, not a ceiling, of free speech protection.

Social media and technology companies should uphold the commitment to regulating speech in line with the GNI principles, which recognize that international human

---

[502] See CERD Committee, General Recommendation No. 35 (2013), §13 ('States parties are required ... [to] sanction as offences punishable by law: ... All dissemination of ideas based on racial or ethnic superiority or hatred ... Incitement to hatred, contempt or discrimination against members of a group on grounds of their *race, colour, descent, or national or ethnic origin*') (emphasis added); §6 ('article 4 ... *forbids discrimination on grounds of race, colour, descent, or national or ethnic origin*—such as indigenous peoples, descent-based groups, and immigrants or non-citizens, including migrant domestic workers, refugees and asylum seekers, as well as speech directed against women members of these and other vulnerable groups') (emphasis added).
[503] IACmHR, *Violence against Lesbian, Gay, Bisexual, Trans and Intersex Persons in the Americas* (2015) OAS/Ser.L/V/II. Doc.36/15 Rev.2, §13; see s. III.1.4. (Mandatory restrictions at the regional level).
[504] ECtHR, *Vejdeland v. Sweden* (App. no. 1813/07, 9 February 2012, §55.

rights law including article 19 of the ICCPR should be respected and 'read within the context of further interpretations issued by international human rights bodies'.[505] International human rights standards are, however, a floor rather than a ceiling of protection for speech—and should be treated as such by private companies that have a role in regulating speech.

---

[505] Global Network Initiative, 'GNI Principles on Freedom of Expression and Privacy', n 7. See also Forum of Information & Democracy, 'Principles on Information & Democracy' (endorsed by 51 states from across the world that comprise the International Partnership for Information and Democracy).

4
False Speech

Marko Milanovic and Philippa Webb

I.	Introduction	220	2. Legitimacy	240
II.	State Practice	223	2.1. States must not restrict false speech for ulterior purposes	241
	1. Overview of Laws Regulating False Speech Around the World	224	2.2. What objectives can justify the penalization of false speech?	242
	1.1. Vagueness and overbreadth	224	3. Necessity	244
	1.2. Harm	225	3.1. Harm	245
	1.3. Intent	229	3.2. Intent	249
	1.4. Exclusions, exceptions and defences	231	4. Exclusions, Exceptions and Defences	253
	1.5. Penalties	231	4.1. Truth	253
	2. Application of False Speech Laws Around the World	234	4.2. Opinion	254
	2.1. Europe	234	4.3. Public interest and 'responsible journalism'	255
	2.2. Asia Pacific	235	5. Penalties	257
	2.3. Middle East and Africa	236	5.1. Criminal	257
III.	International Legal Standards	237	5.2. Civil	259
	1. Legality	238	IV. Recommendations	260

I. Introduction

In the early 2020s the world witnessed not only a global pandemic but also the grave harm that can result from misinformation about it.[1] As the coronavirus spread across the world, so did false information about the virus, causing what the UN has deemed an 'infodemic'.[2] False information about vaccines also led to 'an urgent threat to public health' due to vaccine hesitancy.[3] Following Donald Trump's assertion, while President of the United States, that injecting disinfectant could cure Covid-19, more than 16,000 cases of chlorine dioxide poisoning occurred in the United States alone.[4] And in Iran,

---

[1] 'Countries urged to act against COVID-19 "infodemic"' (UN News, 23 September 2020).

[2] Ibid.

[3] US Department of Health & Human Services, 'US Surgeon General Issues Advisory During COVID-19 Vaccination Push Warning American Public About Threat of Health Misinformation' (15 July 2021). A study analysing almost one million Covid-19 anti-vaccine misinformation posts on social media found that the majority were attributable to just 12 individuals, known as the 'disinformation dozen', with a combined following of nearly 60 million people: see E. Salam, 'Majority of Covid misinformation came from 12 people, report finds' (The Guardian, 17 July 2021).

[4] E. Pilkington, 'Bleach touted as "miracle cure" for Covid being sold on Amazon' (The Guardian, 19 September 2020).

over 700 people died from alcohol poisoning following false claims that ingesting methanol could cure coronavirus.[5] This illustrates how truthful information, such as health warnings issued by official bodies, can be disregarded and misinformation spread globally at the cost of people's lives—a phenomenon that has been called 'truth decay'.[6]

Although prohibitions on false speech have existed for at least 140 years, many laws criminalizing it have been introduced much more recently.[7] The Covid-19 pandemic has accelerated the introduction and use of such laws, including 'as a pretext to restrict information and stifle criticism'.[8] This began at the pandemic's very inception: Dr Li Wenliang, the Wuhan doctor who issued an early warning to his colleagues about the new virus on a messaging platform, was detained by police for 'spreading false rumours' and forced to sign a confession that he had 'severely disturbed the social order'.[9] He later died of the virus.[10] By the end of 2020, hundreds of journalists had been arrested or detained over pandemic-related reporting.[11]

In parallel, laws have been introduced or are contemplated in response to the rise of social media and its use in spreading harmful speech of all kinds, including false information on elections.[12]

The theoretical justification for prohibiting false speech is contested. In classical liberal thought, more truthful speech has always been considered to be the best remedy for falsehoods, with truth to be established through a process of debate and contestation in what has been termed the 'marketplace of ideas'.[13] And there are fears of a slippery slope, that opening the doors to the regulation of speech on the basis of truthfulness provides a pretext for authoritarians clamping down on critics to argue that they are simply trying to prevent social harms caused by falsehoods, just as democracies do.

But fear of a slippery slope need not mean the state's hands are tied when it is faced with substantial harms caused by falsehoods. Lies should not, alone, be the basis for legal sanction.[14] But there are circumstances under which false speech can, and indeed

---

[5] ' Iran: Over 700 dead after drinking alcohol to cure coronavirus' (Al Jazeera, 27 April 2020).
[6] 'Barack Obama: One election won't stop US "truth decay" ' (BBC, 15 November 2020).
[7] See, e.g., French Law on the Freedom of the Press of 29 July 1881; cf. Turkish Capital Market Law No. 6362 2012 Art. 107(2); United Arab Emirates Federal Decree Law No. 34 of 2021 on Combatting Rumors and Cybercrimes Arts 25, 52.
[8] ' "No time to blame the messenger" warns UN rights chief, amidst media clampdowns surrounding COVID-19' (UN News, 24 April 2020); International Press Institute, 'Rush to pass "fake news" laws during Covid-19 intensifying global media freedom challenges' (3 October 2020).
[9] ' "Hero who told the truth": Chinese rage over coronavirus death of whistleblower doctor' (The Guardian, 7 February 2020).
[10] Ibid.
[11] See A. Berry & M. Fürstenau, 'Press freedom: Journalists jailed for COVID reporting' (DW, 14 December 2020).
[12] Access Now, Civil Liberties Union for Europe and European Digital Rights (EDRi), *Informing the 'Disinformation' Debate* (2018), 18.
[13] See US Supreme Court, *Abrams v. United States* 250 U.S. 616, 10 November 1919, 630 (Holmes J): 'the best test of truth is the power of the thought to get itself accepted in the competition of the market'. The marketplace of ideas has become a constant theme in US First Amendment jurisprudence. See, e.g., US Supreme Court, *United States v. Alvarez* 567 U.S. 709, 28 June 2012, where the metaphor is invoked expressly or impliedly by all three opinions in the case (Kennedy J (opinion) at 2545, quoting US Supreme Court, *Hustler Magazine Inc. v. Falwell*, 485 U.S. 46, 24 February 1988, 52; Breyer J (concurring opinion), at 2552; Alito J (dissenting) at 2560 also quoting US Supreme Court, *Hustler Magazine Inc. v. Falwell*, 485 U.S. 46, 24 February 1988).
[14] See s. III.2. (Legitimacy).

should, be penalized.[15] Historically, democratic societies have been comfortable with the state deciding matters of truth in some settings, such as defamation or fraud (where the truth is established by a court) or advertising standards and consumer protection (where the truth may be established by an executive agency or an independent regulator).[16] Punishing false speech that intentionally causes harm to public health or to the integrity of democratic elections is also largely uncontroversial.[17] But criminalization should be reserved for serious harm that a prosecutor can prove was directly and intentionally caused by speech.[18] And the politicization of certain factual issues (like climate change or accounts of historical events), even ostensibly technical ones (such as the utility of wearing masks during the Covid-19 pandemic) raises complicated questions about when the state can be an arbiter of truth and where lines should be drawn.

Under international law, state regulation of false speech (misinformation)[19] must comply with individuals' freedom of expression, and this chapter explores where these lines are drawn in international treaties and human rights jurisprudence.[20] Because this is a developing area of law, much of the jurisprudence of international courts and human rights bodies is drawn from other contexts, in particular standards relating to false speech that is defamatory, causing reputational harm. The chapter outlines international standards relating to when false speech can be penalized and makes recommendations as to how the law should be applied and reformed to meet the challenges of 'truth decay'.[21]

---

[15] M. Milanovic, 'Viral Misinformation and the Freedom of Expression: Part I' (EJIL: Talk!, 13 April 2020).
[16] Ibid.
[17] See s. III.3.1. (Harm).
[18] See s. III.5. (Penalties). See, e.g., HRC, General Comment No. 34 (2011), §47 noting (in the context of defamation) that the application of 'criminal law should only be countenanced in the most serious of cases and imprisonment is never an appropriate penalty'.
[19] This chapter uses the term misinformation in a broad sense, denoting information on any topic that is objectively factually untrue, regardless of the speaker's mental state (unless otherwise specified). We will also use false speech as a synonym. Scholars have often distinguished between misinformation and disinformation, with the former connoting the innocent dissemination of false information and the latter implying an intention to deceive. Malinformation and 'fake news' are also widely used. These terminological distinctions are, in our view, not helpful in the criminal context, where there may be many gradations of culpability—in particular, one can be culpable without having intent, for example by recklessly or negligently failing to verify the truthfulness of a statement. The use of the term misinformation in this chapter is thus meant to be neutral on the question of the speaker's mental state, so that it can capture situations in which the speaker is acting entirely innocently, but also those in which they are acting unintentionally but with a lesser form of fault. However, to ensure clarity, when used in this chapter the term disinformation refers specifically to knowingly false speech. For an overview of the terminological issue, see K. Jones, *Online Disinformation and Political Discourse: Applying a Human Rights Framework* (2019) Chatham House Research Paper, Royal Institute of International Affairs, 7.
[20] States also have a positive duty to protect and fulfil the right to free speech, which may include a duty to actively promote access to accurate information. See UN Special Rapporteur D. Kaye, *Disease pandemics and the freedom of opinion and expression* (2020) UN Doc. A/HRC/44/49, §§7–8, 11–12, 18.
[21] Our focus in this chapter is on *criminal* laws used by states to penalize false speech rather than the (equally important) issue of how false speech can be penalized under regulatory regimes such as those that impose accuracy standards on journalists or 'community standards' for social media users.

II. State Practice

False speech laws[22] are not new: states such as China and Iran have had laws prohibiting 'information ... providers' from disseminating 'rumours' on their books for decades.[23] But in the last 10 years a raft of new misinformation laws have been enacted globally, especially related to speech on the internet.[24]

With the onset of a pandemic in 2020, at least 18 states passed some form of legislation against 'online misinformation' or 'fake information'.[25] For example, the UK[26] Government enacted new laws which criminalized individuals who knowingly provide false or misleading information to police and certain medical professionals dealing with the coronavirus pandemic.[27] Thailand enacted a new emergency decree prohibiting the 'reporting or spreading of information regarding Covid-19 which is untrue and may cause public fear', and 'distort[ing] information which causes misunderstanding and hence affects peace and order or good morals of people'.[28] And in Hungary, criminal penalties apply to individuals who are 'spread[ing] a distorted truth in relation to the emergency' in a way that could be 'alarming or agitating for a large group'.[29]

Many laws regulating misinformation make it a criminal offence[30] and have extraterritorial reach.[31] In addition, the practice of states using these laws has very frequently involved cases in which institutions of the state—the judiciary, the military or the government—have been insulted: an application of the laws that clearly violates international legal standards.[32]

---

[22] The review of state laws and practice on false speech contained in this chapter does not aim to be comprehensive but rather to identify significant examples and trends. Therefore, where the language of a statute is set out, this does not necessarily include an analysis of all case law interpreting that language in the jurisdiction under review.

[23] Chinese Provisions for the Administration of Internet News Information Service Art. 16. See also Iranian Computer Crimes Law 2010 Art. 18. See also Article 19, 'Islamic Republic of Iran: Computer Crimes Law' (2012) 37–40.

[24] See, e.g., 'Censorious governments are abusing "fake news" laws' (The Economist, 13 February 2021).

[25] International Press Institute, 'IPI's Press Freedom Tracker'; International Press Institute, 'Rush to pass 'fake news' laws during COVID-19 intensifying global media freedom challenges' (3 October 2020).

[26] Unless otherwise indicated, references to the United Kingdom and the UK refer to England and Wales, Scotland and Northern Ireland. Although many of the same laws apply across these jurisdictions, these laws can vary and Scotland has a separate legal system.

[27] UK Coronavirus Act 2020, Sch. 21, Parts 2–5, §§23(1)(d), 45(1)(d), 67(1)(d), 88(1)(d). These offences were repealed with respect to England in December 2021: see UK Coronavirus Act 2020 (Early Expiry) (No. 2) Regulations 2021/1399, reg. 5(7). See also South African Disaster Management Act: Regulations relating to COVID-19, reg. 14(2) (addressing statements made with the intention to deceive another about COVID-19, a person's COVID-19 '*infection status*' or '*any measure taken by the Government to address COVID-19*' (emphasis added)).

[28] Thai Regulation Issued under Section 9 of the Royal Decree on Public Administration in Emergency Situation 2005 (No. 27), s. 9(3). See also CPJ, 'Thailand declares state of emergency, imposes press restrictions' (26 March 2020).

[29] Hungarian Act C of 2012 on the Penal Code, s. 337(1). See CPJ, 'Proposed Hungarian laws could imprison journalists covering coronavirus response' (24 March 2020).

[30] All 45 countries that were analysed in this chapter have at least one law on their books that *criminalizes* false speech.

[31] See, e.g., Iranian Computer Crimes Law 2010 Art. 28; Omani Penal Law, Promulgated by Royal Decree 7/2018 Arts 17–18; Rwandan Law Determining Offences and Penalties in General No. 68 2018 Arts 11–13. See s.II.1.1. (Vagueness and overbreadth).

[32] Compare s. II.2. (Application of False Speech Laws Around the World) and s. III (International Legal Standards).

1. Overview of Laws Regulating False Speech Around the World

1.1. Vagueness and overbreadth

A trend among states that criminalize the spreading of misinformation is the use of vague wording. For instance, some states criminalize the spreading of 'fake news', without more, even though the term is not defined[33] or is defined in a circular way.[34] Many states also use vague and overbroad terminology to define the harm that false speech must cause, such as speech that may 'weaken the country's financial credibility, dignity and prestige',[35] cause 'needless anxiety'[36] or 'is likely to be prejudicial to the friendly relations of [the state] with other countries'.[37]

Qatar recently introduced a false speech law that is permeated by vagueness. Article 136(bis), introduced in the 2020 amendments to Qatar's Penal Code, criminalizes the broadcasting, publishing or re-publishing of 'rumours, statements, false or malicious news or propaganda, at home or abroad, with the intention of harming national interests, provoking public opinion or violating the social system or public order of the state'.[38] The penalties are imprisonment of up to five years and/or a fine of up to approximately $27,500 US dollars.[39]

It is unclear whether this Qatari law extends to expressions of opinion rather than only of fact; the harmful proscribed consequences are so open-ended ('national interests' or 'violating the social system') that they are entirely at the discretion of the interpreter; and there is no specification of any causal connection between the speech and the harm. With regard to *mens rea*, while the required harm needs to be intentional, there is no specification of the mental state of the speaker with regard to the statement itself, for example, whether the information has to be knowingly false.

Some domestic courts have construed misinformation laws narrowly to mitigate the impact of vague language. For example, the French Constitutional Court construed a French law prohibiting misinformation that cast doubt on the reliability of elections as requiring that misinformation be confined to information that is *manifestly inexact or misleading* and *manifestly* poses a risk to the integrity of the elections.[40] Similarly, the High Court of England and Wales refused to allow the common law offence of 'misfeasance in public office' to capture false statements of fact during a referendum campaign,

---

[33] See, e.g., Kazakhstani Criminal Code 2014 (amended 2018) Art. 274; Philippine Revised Penal Code Art. 154(1) ('false news').

[34] See, e.g., Singaporean Protection from Online Falsehoods and Manipulation Act 2019 s. 2(2)(b) ('a statement is false if it is false or misleading, whether wholly or in part, and whether on its own or in the context in which it appears').

[35] Egyptian Penal Code Law No. 58 1937 Art. 80D.

[36] Nigerian Cybercrimes (Prohibition, Prevention, Etc) Act 2015 s. 24(1)(b); Rwandan Law Governing Information and Communication Technologies No. 24 2016 Art. 60.

[37] Singaporean Protection from Online Falsehoods and Manipulation Act 2019 s. 7(1)(b)(iii). See also United Arab Emirates Federal Decree Law No. 34 of 2021 on Combatting Rumors and Cybercrimes Arts 25, 52.

[38] Qatari Penal Code (Amended 2020) Art. 136(bis).

[39] Ibid.

[40] French Constitutional Court, *Décision no. 2018-773 DC*, 20 December 2018, §§23, 26.

such as Boris Johnson's untruthful claim—painted on the side of his campaign bus—that the United Kingdom would be able to divert 350 million pounds weekly to its National Health Service upon leaving the European Union.[41] The court reasoned that the statement was not made by a public officer 'acting as such', as the offence required, since Mr. Johnson 'simply held the office and while holding it expressed a view' that was 'contentious and widely challenged', rather than stating the view while acting in the discharge of the duties of the office.[42]

In addition to being vague, a number of misinformation laws are universal, meaning that they apply to speech in any location.[43] Other laws apply to speech abroad if the victim of the offence is a citizen of the state,[44] if the offence harms the interests of the state,[45] if the speech has some connection to information-technology infrastructure in the state[46] or if one of the constituent elements of the crime was committed within the territory of the state that has passed the law.[47] Jurisdictions such as Egypt make it an offence to 'deliberate[ly] ... disseminat[e] false news abroad'.[48] For some laws, the broadened scope is applicable only if the offence is also recognized in the territory in which it was committed,[49] or if no prosecution has occurred abroad.[50]

1.2. Harm

Misinformation laws vary considerably between states as to the nature of the harms caused by false speech that warrant penalization. Some laws make any false speech criminal without requiring any harm to be intended or caused (or even the speech to be public).[51] For example, Nigerian law prohibits a person 'knowingly or intentionally send[ing] a message or other matter by means of computer systems or network that ... he knows to be false'.[52]

---

[41] UK High Court of England and Wales, Queen's Bench Division, *Johnson v. Westminster Magistrates' Court* [2019] EWHC 1709 (Admin), 3 July 2019.

[42] Ibid., §§29–35 (noting that there was no precedent for prosecuting as misconduct in public office misleading statements made 'for the purposes of political campaigning'). The High Court also noted that the 'problem of false statements in the course of political campaigning is not new and has not been overlooked by Parliament', but that legislation sanctioning such conduct relates to false statements as to the personal character or conduct of a candidate during an election only, and 'in enacting the prohibition Parliament must have deliberately excluded any other form of false statement of fact, including those relating to publicly available statistics': §36.

[43] See, e.g., Iranian Computer Crimes Law 2010 Art. 28; Omani Penal Law, Promulgated by Royal Decree 7/2018 Arts 17–18; Rwandan Law Determining Offences and Penalties in General No. 68 2018 Arts 11–13 (providing that any offences committed 'against the interests of Rwanda' outside of the territory can be tried as if committed within that country).

[44] See, e.g., Nigerian Cybercrimes (Prohibition, Prevention, Etc) Act 2015 s. 50(1)(d)(i); Thai Computer Crime Act (2016 Amendment) s. 17(2).

[45] See, e.g., Chinese Criminal Law (amended through 2021) Art. 8; Kazakhstani Criminal Code 2014 Art. 8(4); Qatari Penal Code (Amended 2020) Art. 16(3).

[46] See, e.g., United Arab Emirates Federal Decree Law No. 34 of 2021 on Combatting Rumors and Cybercrimes Art. 69; Iranian Computer Crimes Law 2010 Art. 28.

[47] See, e.g., Qatari Penal Code (Amended 2020) Art. 13 (which applies if the consequence of the act is realized within the State).

[48] Egyptian Penal Code Law No. 58 1937 Art. 80D. See also Cambodian Criminal Code Art. 425; Nigerian Cybercrimes (Prohibition, Prevention, Etc) Act 2015 s. 50; Omani Penal Law, Promulgated by Royal Decree 7/2018 Art. 115.

[49] See, e.g., Thai Computer Crime Act (2016 Amendment) s. 17(1).

[50] Cambodian Criminal Code Arts 19, 23; Kazakhstani Criminal Code 2014 Art. 8(1).

[51] See, e.g., Qatari Penal Code (Amended 2020) Art. 136(bis).

[52] Nigerian Cybercrimes (Prohibition, Prevention, Etc) Act 2015 s. 24(1)(b).

Where misinformation laws do identify harms linked to the speech, these differ considerably. First, some laws prohibit the dissemination of false 'information' or 'news' in the interests of protecting the 'public order' or 'public safety'.[53] In some states, this relates to ensuring the physical safety of persons and property.[54] Others extend beyond physical injury and protect against false statements that 'disturb the public peace',[55] 'weaken the nation's endurance',[56] 'disturb the social or public order',[57] are likely to cause 'fear or alarm to the public',[58] or spread 'horror among the people'.[59] Laws in Kazakhstan,[60] China,[61] and the Philippines[62] refer to harm to 'public order' or 'public safety' but leave these terms undefined. And following the Russian invasion of Ukraine in February 2022, the Russian Criminal Code was amended to make it a crime to state 'false information' about the activities of Russian armed forces and state organs abroad', punishable by up to 15 years' imprisonment if this leads to 'grave consequences'.[63]

Second, misinformation laws may claim to protect a state's interests in upholding 'national security' and 'defence'.[64] These stated interests can extend beyond internal security to address a state's international relationships and 'foreign security',[65] such as by creating a 'hostile international environment against the Government'.[66]

Third, some misinformation laws seek to protect the reputation of the state or its institutions, matters that are left unaddressed by defamation laws that protect individuals. Misinformation laws in this category are often broadly worded, referring to 'endanger[ment of] … national honor',[67] or preventing 'false or malicious' news that 'undermine[s] the stature of the state'.[68] States have also sought to protect against misinformation that 'humiliates or contempts national institutions'[69] or that has 'brought

---

[53] See, e.g., Taiwanese Social Order Maintenance Act (2021 amendment) Art. 63(1)(5); Mauritian Criminal Code Act 1838 Art. 299; Kazakhstani Code of Administrative Offences No. 235-V 2014 Art. 456-1; Maltese Criminal Code 2003 s. 82.

[54] See, e.g., Cambodian Criminal Code Art. 425; South Sudanese Penal Code 2008, s. 75(a)(i); Russian Penal Code Art. 207.1 (prohibiting the 'dissemination of knowingly false information under the guise of truthful statement, concerning circumstances involving danger to life and safety of citizens').

[55] Ghanaian Criminal Code Act 29 1960 s. 208(2). See also Yemeni Law Concerning Crimes and Penalties No. 12 1994 Art. 198(1).

[56] Egyptian Penal Code Law No. 58 1937 Art. 80C.

[57] Qatari Penal Code (Amended 2020) Art. 136(bis).

[58] Malaysian Penal Code s. 505(b).

[59] Egyptian Penal Code Law No. 58 1937 Art. 102bis. See also Egyptian Penal Code Law No. 58 1937 Art. 188; Bahraini Penal Code 1976 Arts 133, 168 (amended by Legislative Decree No. 9 1982); Moroccan Penal Code 2018 Art. 72.

[60] Kazakhstani Criminal Code 2014 Art. 274.

[61] Chinese Criminal Law (amended through 2021) Art. 293.

[62] Philippine Revised Penal Code Art. 154(1).

[63] Russian Penal Code Art. 207.3; 'New Russian Law on "False Information" About Army being Used Against Activists' (Radio Free Europe, 17 March 2022); Human Rights Watch, 'Russia Criminalizes Independent War Reporting, Anti-War Protests' (7 March 2022).

[64] Thai Computer Crime Act (2016 Amendment) s. 14. Zimbabwean Criminal Law (Codification and Reform) Act [Chapter 09:23] 2004 s. 31(a)(ii); South Sudanese Penal Code 2008 Art. 75(a)(ii).

[65] See, e.g., Qatari Cybercrime Prevention Law No. 14 2014 Art. 6.

[66] Rwandan Law Determining Offences and Penalties in General No. 68 2018 Art. 194.

[67] Chinese Cybersecurity Law 2017 Art. 12. See also Bahraini Penal Code 1976 Art. 174.

[68] Omani Penal Law, Promulgated by Royal Degree 7/2018 Art. 115(a). See also Egyptian Penal Code Law No. 58 1937 Art. 178bis third; Iraqi Penal Code Law No. 111 1969 §180. Zimbabwean Criminal Law (Codification and Reform) Act [Chapter 09:23] 2004 s. 31(a)(iii).

[69] Cambodian Law on the Press 1995 Art. 13.

discredit to public institutions or their functioning'.[70] These laws supplement insult laws and *lèse-majesté* laws that penalize speech that is insulting to rulers without requiring the speech to be false.[71]

Fourth, the laws of certain states refer to a state's economic interests and financial credibility as being the harm that misinformation laws seek to address. Many states define these interests broadly,[72] referring to 'public finances',[73] 'national economic security',[74] information that weakens the 'country's financial credibility'[75] or 'confidence in its financial markets or its economic and financial standing'.[76] And EU law covers the dissemination of information, including rumours, which give or are likely to give, 'false or misleading signals' as to 'the supply of, demand for, or price of, a financial instrument'.[77]

Fifth, an increasing number of misinformation laws focus on harm to elections. According to the OECD, the proportion of elections targeted by cyber threats, including misinformation campaigns, has risen more than 75 per cent from 2015 to 2018, and the number of laws addressing election-related misinformation has grown along with it.[78] In 2018, following disinformation campaigns during a presidential election, France enacted a law allowing judges to order the removal of online articles that constitute misinformation and granting the French national broadcasting agency the power to suspend television channels controlled by other states if they 'deliberately disseminate false information likely to affect the sincerity of the ballot'.[79] Other laws are framed more broadly as prohibiting the transmission of false information that is likely to 'influence the outcome of an election',[80] or personal opinions that lead to 'confusion or loss of confidence' during an election.[81]

---

[70] Senegalese Penal Code 1965 Art. 255. See also South Sudanese Penal Code 2008 s. 75(a)(iii) ('undermining public confidence in a law enforcement agency, or the Defence Forces of Southern Sudan').

[71] See, e.g., United Arab Emirates Federal Decree Law No. 34 of 2021 on Combatting Rumors and Cybercrimes Art. 25 (prohibiting the dissemination of rumours or information—regardless of the statement's veracity—intended to 'damage the reputation, prestige or stature of the State or any of its institutions or its president, vice-president, any of the rulers of the Emirates, their crown princes, or the deputy rulers of the Emirates, the State flag, the national peace, its logo, national anthem or any of its symbols').

[72] See, e.g., Lebanese Penal Code 1943 Art. 297 (amended according to Act No. 239 of 27 May 1993) prohibiting the broadcast of 'false or exaggerated news' that 'would undermine the prestige of the state and its financial position'; Bahraini Penal Code 1976 Art. 169 ('cause damage to ... the State's creditworthiness').

[73] Nigerian Protection from Internet Falsehoods and Manipulation and other related matters Bill 2019 s. 3(1)(b)(ii).

[74] Thai Computer Crime Act (2016 Amendment) s. 14(2).

[75] Egyptian Penal Code No. 58 1937 Art. 80D.

[76] Omani Penal Law, Promulgated by Royal Decree 7/2018 Art. 115(a).

[77] Regulation (EU) No. 596/2014 of the European Parliament and of the Council of 16 April 2014 on market abuse (market abuse regulation) and repealing Directive 2003/6/EC of the European Parliament and of the Council and Commission Directives 2003/124/EC, 2003/125/EC and 2004/72/EC Art. 12(1)(c).

[78] T. Nagasako, 'Global Disinformation Campaigns and Legal Challenges' (2020) 1 *International Cybersecurity Law Review* 125, 129.

[79] French Law No. 2018-1202 of 22 December 2018 on the fight against the manipulation of information; M. Fiorentino, 'France passes controversial "fake news" law' (Euronews, 22 November 2018); UK House of Commons Digital, Culture, Media and Sport Committee, *Disinformation and 'fake news': Final Report* (2019) HC 1791, 13.

[80] See, e.g., Nigerian Protection from Internet Falsehoods and Manipulation and other related matters Bill 2019 (SB 132) s. 3(1)(b)(iv).

[81] See International Federation of Journalists, 'Cambodia: Controlling election reporting guidelines released' (5 June 2018). Misinformation and disinformation laws that do not address elections expressly may still be enforced against journalists who report during elections: see, e.g., 'Nine arrested in Thailand for posting election "fake news"' (France 24, 28 March 2019).

Some election-related false speech laws predate recent technological threats. In the United Kingdom and India, it has long been a crime to make or publish 'any false statement of fact' about a candidate's 'personal character or conduct' for the purpose of 'affecting the return of any candidate at the election', unless the speaker can show 'he had reasonable grounds for believing, and did believe, the statement to be true'.[82] When a politician in the United Kingdom said a candidate from another party had 'reneged on his promise to live in his constituency', this was found not to qualify as relating to his 'personal character or conduct', but a statement that he had 'attempted to woo' Muslims 'who advocate violence' was found to fall within the scope of the law.[83] Canada has a similar offence which prohibits anyone who, 'with the intention of affecting the results of an election', makes (1) false statements that a candidate has committed an offence or is being investigated for an offence; (2) false statements about a candidate's listed personal characteristics, including their education or place of birth; or (3) false statements that a candidate has withdrawn from the election.[84]

Finally, the protection of 'public health' has been included as a protected interest under misinformation laws, especially since the pandemic in 2020.[85] Before that time, laws in countries such as Tanzania,[86] Russia,[87] and Singapore[88] included undefined references to 'life', 'human health' and 'public health' alongside other interests like public order, public safety and national security in their misinformation laws.[89] Other laws referenced the spread of communicable diseases, such as China's Criminal Law, which prohibits the fabrication of 'false reports of danger, epidemic, security alerts or disasters'.[90]

---

[82] UK Representation of the People Act 1983 s. 106(1). See also Indian Penal Code 1860 Chapter IXA s. 171G; Indian Supreme Court, *N.S. Vardachari v. G. Vasantha Pai* (1972) 2 S.C.C. 594, 21 August 1972: Breach of s. 171G was not established because the speaker did not attack the character of the candidate by saying that he was not qualified by not being a graduate.

[83] The penalty for this conduct was that the election was declared void, it was reported to the Speaker of the House that the politician was guilty of an illegal practice, and he was compelled to vacate his seat and was barred from being elected to the House of Commons for three years: see, e.g., UK High Court of England and Wales, Queen's Bench Division, *R (Woolas) v. Parliamentary Election Court* [2010] EWHC 3169 (Admin), 3 December 2010, §§5, 13.

[84] Canadian Elections Act 2000 ss 91–92. See also Canadian Elections Act 2000 ss 486(3)(c), (3)(d) and 486(4) (criminalizing the relevant prohibitions). In 2021, Ontario's Superior Court found s. 91(1) to infringe on a Charter protection or fundamental rights in a manner that could not be considered a reasonable limit demonstrably justified in a free and democratic society and was therefore invalidated: Ontario Superior Court of Justice, *Canadian Constitutional Foundation v. Attorney General of Canada* 2021 ONSC 1224, 19 February 2021. Canadian law also criminally punishes the publication of false material that purports to have been produced by election officers, political parties, or candidates, if such publication is done with the intent of misleading the public: Canadian Elections Act 2000 s. 481.

[85] See, e.g., International Press Institute, 'Rush to pass 'fake news' laws during Covid-19 intensifying global media freedom challenges' (3 October 2020).

[86] Tanzanian Media Services Act 2016 s. 50.

[87] Russian Federal Law No. 149-FZ on Information, Informational Technologies and the Protection of Information 2006 (amended 2019) Art. 15.1. See also the Russian Code of Administrative Offences No. 195-FZ 2001 Art. 13.15.(1). Since 1996, Russian Penal Code article 237(1) has also criminalized '[c]oncealment or distortion of information about events, facts or phenomena that create a danger to life or health of people or to the environment, committed by a person obligated to provide the population and bodies authorized to take measures to eliminate such a danger with the information indicated'.

[88] Singaporean Protection from Online Falsehoods and Manipulation Act 2019 s. 7(1)(b)(ii).

[89] See also Nigerian Protection from Internet Falsehoods and Manipulation and other related matters Bill 2019 (SB 132) s. 3(1)(b)(ii).

[90] Chinese Criminal Law (amended through 2021) Art. 291(1).

Since the pandemic, the enactment of false speech laws related to public health has accelerated. Some nations such as South Africa,[91] Jordan[92] and Thailand[93] have specifically limited new provisions to false speech relating to the coronavirus. Thailand's laws apply more broadly to speech about the pandemic that 'may cause public fear'.[94] Other countries' laws have been justified by the pandemic but passed in even broader terms such as criminalization of speech that may 'misinform or cause uncertainty' in Bolivia,[95] false speech that 'compromises general security or public order' in Algeria[96] and false or 'twisted' speech that hinders a 'successful defence' against a 'state of emergency' in Hungary.[97]

1.3. Intent

Misinformation laws can encompass two distinct culpability requirements: a mental state (*mens rea*) related to the *falsity* of the speech and to its *consequences*.

Some misinformation laws have high *mens rea* standards requiring that the person actually knew the information was false, intentionally disseminated it and in some instances had the intention that others would be misled or deceived.[98] For example, South Africa made it an offence to publish a statement through any medium with the intention to deceive others about Covid-19 generally, an individual's infection status or government measures to address the pandemic.[99] And in the case of a US statute criminalizing the conduct of any person who 'falsely represents himself ... to have been awarded any decoration or medal authorized ... for the Armed Forces of the United States', the Supreme Court read into the provision that the offender must have acted *knowingly*, even though on its face the relevant statute imposed no *mens rea* requirement.[100]

Some misinformation laws have lower thresholds of 'negligence',[101] recklessness[102] or 'wilful blindness' regarding whether the statement is false.[103] Others are strict liability offences, prohibiting speech even when the person is unaware of the falsity of the

---

[91] South African Disaster Management Act: Regulations relating to COVID-19, s. 14(2). Article 19, 'South Africa: Prohibitions of false COVID-19 information must be amended' (23 April 2021).
[92] Human Rights Watch, 'Jordan: Free Speech Threats Under Covid-19 Response' (5 May 2020).
[93] Thai Emergency Decree on Public Administration in Emergency Situation 2005 s. 9(3); Human Rights Watch, 'Thailand: Immediately Repeal Emergency Regulation that Threatens Online Freedoms' (3 August 2021).
[94] Ibid.
[95] Bolivian Decree 4200 Art. 13.2; Human Rights Watch, 'Bolivia: COVID-19 Decree Threatens Free Expression' (7 April 2020).
[96] Algerian Law No. 20-06 amending and supplementing Decree No. 66-156 of June 8, 1966 on the Penal Code Art. 196 bis.
[97] Hungarian Act C of 2012 on the Penal Code s. 337(2), introduced by Act XII of 2020 on the containment of Coronavirus 31 March 2020 s. 10(2).
[98] See, e.g., Chinese Criminal Law (amended through 2021) Art. 291(1); Omani Penal Law 2018, Promulgated by Royal Decree 7/2018 Art. 115(a); and Turkish Capital Market Law No. 6362 2012 Art. 107(2).
[99] South African Disaster Management Act: Regulations relating to COVID-19 §14(2). See D. Milo, 'Criminalising fake news about COVID-19' (Musings on Media, 25 March 2020).
[100] US Supreme Court, *United States v. Alvarez* 567 U.S. 709, 28 June 2012 (although the majority of justices concluded that the statute at issue was unconstitutional, all of the justices agreed that the statute should be interpreted to capture only knowing falsehoods).
[101] UK Representation of the People Act 1983; UK High Court of England and Wales, Queen's Bench Division, *R (Woolas) v. Parliamentary Election Court* [2010] EWHC 3169 (Admin), 3 December 2010, §84.
[102] Gambian Criminal Code No. 25 1933 s. 181A(1). Provision available in the Gambian Supreme Court, *Gambia Press Union v. The Attorney General* Civil Suit No.1/2014, 9 May 2018.
[103] Nigerian Criminal Code Act (1916) Cap (C.38) s. 59(1) Laws of the Federation of Nigeria 2004.

information or the potential risks their speech poses.[104] For example, Cambodia prohibits 'communicating or disclosing false information', with no reference to knowledge of falsity of the information.[105]

For *mens rea* as to *consequence*, some laws require that the person intended to cause resulting harm.[106] For example, Tanzania's Cybercrimes Act applies to those who disseminate false information 'with intent to ... deceive or mislead the public'.[107] Others rely on actual or constructive knowledge of consequences, such as Singapore, which prohibits speech while 'knowing or having reason to believe' not only that '(a) it is a false statement of fact' but also that '(b) the communication of the statement in Singapore is likely to' be 'prejudicial to public health, public safety, public tranquility or public finances' or the security of Singapore, prejudicial to Singapore's friendly relations with other countries, influence the outcome of an election, incite feelings of enmity, hatred or ill-will between different groups or 'diminish public confidence in the performance of any duty or function of ... the Government'.[108] A number of laws are based on objective, rather than subjective, foreseeability,[109] and others contain no *mens rea* requirement as to the consequence of the speech at all.[110]

Causation is also addressed in diverse ways in national misinformation laws. Some laws make no reference to the relationship between the speech and consequences flowing from it.[111] Others require proof that the speaker intended to cause a harmful effect, but do not require any actual consequences to occur.[112] For instance, Rwandan law states that 'no person may send ... false messages ... for purposes of causing annoyance, inconvenience, or needless anxiety'.[113] In a number of laws, the speech need only be 'capable of' causing or 'likely to' cause the given consequence.[114] In the United Arab Emirates, it is an offence to provide an organization with 'any incorrect or misleading information which may damage the interests of the State or injures its reputation, prestige or stature'.[115] Another option is to specify a more stringent direct causation of proscribed consequences, which has been done by the United States in a non-legislative

---

[104] See, e.g., Iranian Press Law 2002 Art. 6; United Arab Emirates Federal Decree Law No. 34 of 2021 on Combatting Rumors and Cybercrimes Art. 52.

[105] Cambodian Criminal Code Art. 425.

[106] Cambodian Criminal Code Art. 425; French Law on the Freedom of the Press of 29 July 1881 Art. 27; Rwandan Law Governing Information and Communication Technologies No. 24 2016 Art. 60.

[107] Tanzanian Cybercrimes Act 2015 s. 16.

[108] Singaporean Protection from Online Falsehoods and Manipulation Act 2019 s. 7(1).

[109] See, e.g., Egyptian Penal Code No. 58 1937 Art. 80D; French Code Électoral Art. L163-2-1.

[110] Belarusian Penal Code 1999 Art. 340(2); Chinese Criminal Law (amended through 2021) Art. 291(1); Kazakhstani Criminal Code 2014 (amended 2018) Art. 274-1. See also offences that do not contain prohibited consequences (no corresponding mental element): Chinese Criminal Law (amended through 2021) Art. 291(1); Chinese Cybersecurity Law 2017 Art. 12; Gambian Information and Communication (Amendment) Act 2013 s. 173; Gambian Criminal Code No. 25 1933 s. 181.

[111] Canadian Elections Act 2000 ss 91(1), 92; Chinese Criminal Law (amended through 2021) Art. 291(1); Iranian Press Law 2002 Art. 6; Iranian Computer Crimes Law 2010 Art. 18; Tanzanian Media Services Act 2016 s. 50(1).

[112] See, e.g., United Arab Emirates Federal Decree Law No. 34 of 2021 on Combatting Rumors and Cybercrimes Art. 25; Malaysian Communications and Multimedia Act 1998 s. 211.

[113] Rwandan Law Governing Information and Communication Technologies No. 24 2016 Art. 60.

[114] Egyptian Penal Code No. 58 1937 Art. 80D; French Law on the Freedom of the Press of 29 July 1881 Art. 27; Rwandan Law Determining Offences and Penalties in General No. 68 2018 Art. 194; Rwandan Law on Prevention and Punishment of Cyber Crimes No. 24 2016 Art. 39.

[115] United Arab Emirates Federal Decree Law No. 34 of 2021 on Combatting Rumors and Cybercrimes Art. 52.

setting to address hoaxes.[116] Similarly, a 2020 amendment to the Russian Criminal Code criminalizes the 'public dissemination of knowingly false information of public importance' that *has caused* severe consequences such as harm to human health or death.[117]

1.4. Exclusions, exceptions and defences

Many misinformation laws do not contain an affirmative defence.[118] Some do include affirmative defences relating to the actions taken by the person to verify the information before disseminating it.[119] And certain misinformation laws prevent or reduce penalties in the case of disclaimers or information obtained from or reported to the state. In Tanzania, false content cannot be published 'unless it is clearly pre-stated that the content is—(i) satire and parody; (ii) fiction; and (iii) where it is preceded by a statement that the content is not factual'.[120] There is no liability for disseminating false information in Belarus if that information was disseminated by members of the media and was received from state entities, news agencies or official messages from political parties or legal entities.[121] And in Qatar, a person shall be exempt from penalties if they intend to 'inform the competent authorities of any information about [a] crime and its participants before their knowledge thereof'.[122]

1.5. Penalties

Misinformation laws provide for a variety of penalties, ranging from fines to life imprisonment.[123] Some states also provide for corporal punishment, the loss of civil liberties, censorship or removal of the speech, and increased penalties under certain conditions, such as when the misinformation is disseminated during wartime or anonymously.

1.5.1. Criminal

Custodial sentences are a regular feature of misinformation laws, although the length of such penalties varies widely. Rwanda's misinformation offence has a maximum penalty of life imprisonment when committed during

---

[116] See the US Federal Communication Commission's rules against hoaxes, which prohibit 'broadcasting false information concerning a crime or catastrophe if' the broadcaster (1) 'knows this information is false'; (2) 'it is foreseeable that broadcast of the information will cause substantial public harm' and (3) 'broadcast of the information does in fact directly cause substantial public harm'. FCC, 'Hoaxes'. See also US Supreme Court, *Brown v. Entertainment Merchants Association* 564 U.S. 786, 27 June 2011, 799 (asserting there must be 'a direct causal link' between the speech and alleged harm in order for a statute to pass strict scrutiny review).

[117] Russian Criminal Code Art. 207.2.

[118] However, some states' laws contain general defences applicable to all crimes or to a category of offences.

[119] See, e.g., Gambian Criminal Code No. 25 1933 s. 181A(2); Nigerian Criminal Code Act (1916) Cap (C.38) s. 59(2) Laws of the Federation of Nigeria 2004.

[120] Tanzanian Electronic and Postal Communications (Online Content) Regulations 2018 reg. 12(l).

[121] Belarusian Law on Mass Media 2008 Art. 52.1 (the media law applying to persons such as a 'journalist, founder (founders) of a mass media outlet, editor-in-chief of a mass media outlet').

[122] Qatari Cybercrime Prevention Law No. 14 2014 Art. 54.

[123] Rwandan Law Determining Offences and Penalties in General No. 68 2018 Art. 194 (where spreading false information or harmful propaganda 'with intent to cause public disaffection against the Government of Rwanda, or where such information ... is likely or calculated to cause public disaffection or a hostile international environment' against Rwanda and the offence occurs in wartime).

wartime.[124] In other states, prison terms may extend to 20 years,[125] five years,[126] one year,[127] or three months.[128] In the United Arab Emirates, for example, an Emirati man was sentenced to 10 years in prison for publishing 'false information' that was 'detrimental to the country and its foreign policies'.[129]

Certain criminal misinformation laws provide for increased penalties in particular circumstances. Cameroonian law doubles the sentence for the dissemination of false news from a maximum of five years to 10 years if done anonymously.[130] Singaporean law provides for increased penalties of up to 10 years in prison when 'an inauthentic online account or bot is used' to spread misinformation.[131] Speech may also attract a harsher penalty if it inflicts 'heavy' or 'large scale' damage,[132] is for the benefit of 'a foreign country or any terrorist group',[133] occurs in 'time of war',[134] or when it is 'likely to shake the discipline or the morale of the armies or to hinder the nation's war effort'.[135] Other laws increase the penalty if the misinformation offence is committed or facilitated by a public employee 'taking advantage of his ... authority'[136] or by a repeat offender.[137]

1.5.2. Civil

Financial penalties are a common feature of civil legislation on misinformation.[138] Civil penalties may also be imposed in combination with prison sentences.[139] In France, the publication of false news in bad faith and likely to disturb public peace is punishable by fines of up to 45,000 Euros (or 135,000 Euros in aggravating circumstances).[140] Saudi law allows for fines of up to approximately $800,000 US dollars alongside prison sentences.[141] In Singapore, a fine of over $35,000 US dollars can be imposed if an individual

---

[124] Rwandan Law Determining Offences and Penalties in General No. 68 2018 Art. 194.
[125] South Sudanese Penal Code 2008 Act 9 ss. 12 and 75.
[126] Belarusian Penal Code 1999 Art. 340(1). See also Canadian Elections Act 2000 s. 500(5)(b): summary conviction (the penalty is a fine of up to $20,000 (approximately 15,000 USD) and/or imprisonment for up to a year) and conviction on indictment (fine of up to $50,000 (approximately 37,000 USD) and/or imprisonment for up to five years).
[127] Kazakhstani Criminal Code 2014 (amended 2018) Art. 274-1.
[128] Omani Penal Law, Promulgated by Royal Decree 7/2018 Art. 115(a)–(c), potentially going up to three years' imprisonment.
[129] M. Al Zarooni, 'Emirati fined Dh1 million, jailed for publishing fake news' (Khaleej Times, 1 January 2019).
[130] Cameroonian Penal Code 2016 s. 240.
[131] Singaporean Protection from Online Falsehoods and Manipulation Act 2019 s. 7(3).
[132] Belarusian Penal Code 1999 Art. 340(2); Kazakhstani Criminal Code 2014 (amended 2018) Art. 274-3.
[133] United Arab Emirates Federal Decree Law No. 34 of 2021 on Combatting Rumors and Cybercrimes Art. 60 (on aggravating circumstances).
[134] Egyptian Penal Code Law No. 58 1937 Art. 80D; Qatari Penal Code (Amended 2020) Art. 136(bis); Rwandan Law Determining Offences and Penalties in General No. 68 2018 Art. 194.
[135] French Law on the Freedom of the Press of 29 July 1881 Art. 27.
[136] Qatari Cybercrime Prevention Law No. 14 2014 Arts 6, 51. See also Iranian Computer Crimes Law 2010 Art. 26(A)—it is an aggravating circumstance if a state employee commits a computer crime in performance of their duties, 'punished by more than two thirds of the maximum extent of one or both the punishments'.
[137] See, e.g., Belarusian Penal Code 1999 Art. 340(2); Cambodian Criminal Code Arts 83–92.
[138] See, e.g., Belarusian Law on Mass Media 2008 Art. 48; Cambodian Law on the Press 1995 Art. 13; Kazakhstani Code of Administrative Offences No. 235-V 2014 Art. 456(1).
[139] For combined fine and imprisonment, see, e.g., United Arab Emirates Federal Decree Law No. 34 of 2021 on Combatting Rumors and Cybercrimes Art. 25.
[140] French Law on the Freedom of the Press of 29 July 1881 Art. 27.
[141] SR 3,000,000. D. Al-Khudair, 'Saudi residents spreading "fake news" face five years' jail' (Arab News, 3 May 2020).

shares false information, increasing to double that amount and up to 10 years' imprisonment if it is published by an 'inauthentic online account or a bot'.[142] Rwanda fines business entities that commit an offence under Rwanda's 'cybercrime' law up to 30–70 per cent of the company's annual profits.[143] In China, a journalist was fined $990,000 US dollars alongside a 15-year prison sentence for 'picking quarrels and provoking trouble', after he alleged fraud and corruption by regional party officials.[144]

A number of misinformation laws also make provision for the loss of civil liberties and confiscation of property in addition to fines or imprisonment.[145] These include loss of the right to vote,[146] deportation,[147] restrictions on residency,[148] ongoing monitoring or surveillance,[149] confiscation of devices and funds and the forced closure of a website.[150]

Other types of media regulation of false speech exist in parallel with criminal laws.[151] For example, Belarus' law allows the government to suspend mass media without a court decision for up to three months if, for example, two or more written requests have been issued to the owner of the publication within two years alleging dissemination of either 'untrue information that may harm state or public interests' or 'data not corresponding to reality and disgracing the honour, dignity or business' of individuals.[152] This law has been used to block hundreds of information resources and websites.[153] In Russia, 'immediately upon receipt' of a notice from the relevant federal executive body that information is 'socially significant false information', the 'online publication must delete the information'.[154] And in Singapore, any Minister may make orders requiring publication of a correction and block future communication in the event of non-compliance.[155] In other jurisdictions,

---

[142] Singaporean Protection from Online Falsehoods and Manipulation Act 2019 s. 7 (50,000 or 100,000 Singapore dollars (approximately 37,000 or 75,000 USD)).
[143] Rwanda Law on Prevention and Punishment of Cyber Crimes No. 24 2016 Art. 51.
[144] CPJ, 'Chinese police arrest critical blogger Chen Jieren' (11 July 2018); A. France-Presse, 'Chinese journalist jailed for 15 years for attacking Communist Party' (South China Morning Post, 1 May 2020).
[145] See, e.g., Rwandan Law on Prevention and Punishment of Cyber Crimes No. 60 2018 Art. 9, Rwandan Law Determining Offences and Penalties in General No. 68 2018 Arts 42–45 (however, civil rights may only be deprived for those who have been sentenced to life imprisonment under Rwanda's criminal misinformation laws); United Arab Federal Decree Law No. 34 of 2021 on Combatting Rumors and Cybercrimes Arts 41–43.
[146] Cambodian Criminal Code Arts 55, 426; Rwandan Law Determining Offences and Penalties in General No. 68 2018 Art. 43.
[147] Qatari Cybercrime Prevention Law No. 14 2014 Art. 52.
[148] Cambodian Criminal Code Art. 426.
[149] United Arab Emirates Federal Decree Law No. 34 of 2021 on Combatting Rumors and Cybercrimes Art. 59.
[150] Qatari Cybercrime Prevention Law No. 14 2014 Art. 53; Rwandan Law on Prevention and Punishment of Cyber Crimes No. 60 2018 Art. 52 (allowing the confiscation of a computer system or software used to commit an offence, as well as the closure of a premise or corporate body); United Arab Emirates Federal Decree Law No. 34 of 2021 on Combatting Rumors and Cybercrimes Art. 59.
[151] Regulatory regimes that pertain to traditional or social media are not the focus of this chapter. See s. I. (Introduction).
[152] Belarusian Law on Mass Media 2008 Arts 49–50.
[153] Freedom House, 'Freedom on the Net 2019: Belarus' (2019).
[154] Russian Federal Law No. 149-FZ on Information, Informational Technologies and the Protection of Information 2006 (amended 2019) Art. 15.3(1). Socially significant false information is defined to include information distributed under the guise of truthful messages if they create a threat that endangers people's lives, health, or property; create possibilities for mass violations of public order or public security; or possibly hinder the work of transportation and social infrastructure, credit institutions, lines of communications, industry and energy enterprises.
[155] Singaporean Protection from Online Falsehoods and Manipulation Act 2019 ss 4, 10–13, 16. Part 4 of the Act contains similar provisions, but directed towards 'internet intermediaries and providers of mass media

convictions for misinformation may result in the suspension of a publication or broadcast license.[156]

2. Application of False Speech Laws Around the World

There have been some striking cases of prosecutions under false speech laws, both against journalists and other speakers such as lawyers and human rights activists.[157] The examples provided below are illustrative of this practice and demonstrate how misinformation laws can be abused for ulterior purposes: to suppress critical journalism, quash dissent or silence speech that embarrasses the government of the day.

2.1. Europe
2.1.1. Serbia

Free speech can be suppressed not only through vaguely worded misinformation laws, but also through the *application* of otherwise reasonably precise laws. Serbia has false speech laws with stringent legal protections on paper, but its response to the Covid-19 pandemic included misuse of these laws to chill journalistic speech critical of the government. Article 343 of Serbia's Criminal Code, which makes it an offence to cause panic and disorder by disseminating false information, requires the offender to actually *cause* panic or disorder by spreading misinformation and to do so with *intent*.[158] In other words, the offence has very high *mens rea* and causality requirements, even if the prohibited consequences (causing panic and disorder or frustrating the enforcement of the decisions of governmental authorities) are somewhat ill-defined.

The law had previously been used in relatively uncontroversial circumstances, such as bomb hoaxes. For example, in one case an individual who was due to face trial falsely reported that there was a bomb in the building, forcing the building to be evacuated and his trial to be delayed. He was convicted for impeding the work of Serbian judicial authorities through his false report.[159] But during the pandemic it was used against Ana Lalić, a Serbian journalist working for an online media outlet, who reported that a hospital in a Serbian city had run out of personal protective equipment, citing testimony from doctors and nurses.[160] Her reporting was immediately denounced as 'fake news' by Serbian political leadership and hospital management, and police conducted a late-night raid, search, and arrest at her apartment on the same day the article was

services', rather than the communicators of the statement. These orders may be made against persons outside of Singapore: see s. II.1.1. (Vagueness and overbreadth).

[156] See, e.g., French Law on the Freedom of the Press of 29 July 1881 Art. 62.
[157] See UN Special Rapporteur D. Kaye, *Disease pandemics and the freedom of opinion and expression* (2020) UN Doc. A/HRC/44/49, §§34–39.
[158] See Serbian Criminal Code Art. 343.
[159] See Appeals Court of Belgrade, *Judgment Kž-po1 8/11*, 25 May 2011.
[160] Council of Europe, 'Safety of Journalists Platform: Journalist Ana Lalic Detained Overnight after Reporting on Conditions in Hospital' (1 April 2020).

published.[161] By doing so, the police sent a clear message to other members of the press and even anyone online who might consider making similar allegations, even though the charges against her were ultimately dropped.[162]

2.2. Asia Pacific
2.2.1. China
China is one of the 'world's most restrictive media environments'[163] and the 'world's biggest captor of journalists'.[164] An important tool of suppression is the broadly worded law criminalizing 'picking quarrels and provoking trouble', which has been used by Chinese authorities since 2013 to prosecute people for allegedly false speech, especially online speech about human rights and politics.[165] In 2020, a former Chinese state media journalist turned anti-corruption blogger, Chen Jieren, was sentenced under this law to 15 years in prison and fined approximately $990,000 US dollars after publishing two articles on his blog about corruption by political officials.[166] The court stated that he had 'attacked and vilified the Communist Party and government' by publishing 'false or negative information' and through 'malicious speculation'.[167] Another journalist, Zhang Zhan, was sentenced under the same law to four years in prison for covering the beginning of the pandemic on social media; she had been reporting from Wuhan in February 2020.[168] The law has been condemned by the UN Working Group on Arbitrary Detention as 'so vague and broad that it could be used to deprive individuals of their liberty without a specific legal basis'.[169]

2.2.2. Myanmar
Following the military coup in February 2021, Myanmar authorities enacted a new provision of Myanmar's Penal Code that has been a key tool to stifle dissent.[170] The new broadly-worded section 505A criminalizes comments that 'cause fear' or spread 'false news', punishable by up to three years' imprisonment.[171] The Committee to Protect Journalists reports that at least 17 journalists were imprisoned on false news charges

---

[161] M. Stojanovic, 'Serbian Reporter's Arrest Over Pandemic Article Draws PM's Apology' (Balkan Insight, 2 April 2020).
[162] See also Article 19, 'Serbia: Journalist Ana Lalic arrested for reporting on inadequate hospital facilities for coronavirus' (2 April 2020).
[163] Freedom House, 'Freedom in the World: China' (2022).
[164] Reporters Without Borders, 'An unprecedented RSF investigation: The Great Leap Backwards of Journalism in China' (7 December 2021).
[165] Chinese Criminal Law (amended through 2021) Art. 293; G. Rui, "Picking quarrels and provoking trouble': how China's catch-all crime muzzles dissent' (South China Morning Post, 25 August 2021).
[166] CPJ, 'Chen Jieren: Imprisoned in China' (4 July 2018).
[167] J. Griffiths, 'Chinese journalist jailed for 15 years for "vilifying the Communist Party and government"' (CNN, 1 May 2020).
[168] Reporters Without Borders, 'The Great Leap Backwards of Journalism in China' (7 December 2021), 50. See also WGAD, *Zhang v. China* (Opinion no. 25/2021), 6 September 2021, §42.
[169] WGAD, *Zhang v. China* (Opinion no. 25/2021), 6 September 2021, §52.
[170] Human Rights Watch, 'Myanmar: Post-Coup Legal Changes Erode Human Rights' (2 March 2021).
[171] Ibid. Myanmar State Administration Council Law No. 5/2021 Law Amending the Penal Code 1861, s. 505A (this offence is also punishable by fine). It is also an offence in Myanmar to incite disaffection towards the defence services or defence services personnel, or for individuals holding peaceful assembly and procession to circulate false information, rumours and/or false data: Myanmar Penal Code 1861, s. 124A; Myanmar Law relating to the Right of Peaceful Assembly and Peaceful Procession 2011, s. 12(f).

in Myanmar in 2021.[172] Among them was American journalist Danny Fenster, former managing editor of independent news outlet Frontier Myanmar, who was sentenced to 11 years' imprisonment for a slew of offences including spreading false information.[173]

2.3. Middle East and Africa

2.3.1. Egypt

Egypt also frequently misuses false speech laws against journalists reporting on truthful political issues or criticisms of government.[174] One of the best known examples is the use of false speech and terrorism charges against Mohamed Fahmy, a Canadian-Egyptian citizen and head of the Al Jazeera bureau in Cairo, and his colleagues Australian correspondent Peter Greste and Egyptian producer Baher Mohamed.[175] The men were convicted of a string of offences, including broadcasting 'false news to give the outside world an impression that [Egypt] is undergoing a state of internal strife', thereby damaging public security and spreading fear.[176] The Court argued that the journalists had been brought together 'by the devil' to destabilize Egypt, and sentenced Fahmy and Greste to seven years' imprisonment and Mohamed to 10 years.[177] The sentence was later reduced to three years and the men were eventually pardoned and released.[178]

Similar tactics have been adopted against journalists and activists speaking out about the pandemic in Egypt. Just hours after journalist Mohamed Monir appeared in an Al Jazeera interview (and published a corresponding article) criticizing the Egyptian government's pandemic response, Monir's apartment was raided by Egyptian security officers.[179] The raid was captured and uploaded on Facebook.[180] Two days later, Monir's family reported that he was kidnapped and placed in pre-trial detention for 15 days.[181] While no specific examples of his journalistic work were cited, Monir was charged with 'joining a terrorist group, spreading fake news, and misusing social media'.[182] After 17 days in detention, Monir was released after contracting Covid-19 while in custody.[183] A week later, Monir died while in medical isolation.[184]

---

[172] CPJ, '30 Journalists Imprisoned in Myanmar' (1 December 2021).
[173] Fenster was sentenced to 'three years for incitement for spreading false or inflammatory information, three years for contacting illegal organisations and five years for violating visa rules', but has since been released: M. Moe & R. Ratcliffe, 'Myanmar junta jails US journalist Danny Fenster for 11 years' (The Guardian, 12 November 2021).
[174] See, e.g., CPJ, 'Egypt's top prosecutor orders authorities to monitor media for "fake news."' (28 February 2018).
[175] Al Jazeera has been banned by the Egyptian government following the 2013 military coup on the rationale that it was a platform for the Muslim Brotherhood political movement. See ch. 6 (Terrorism Laws) ss. II.2.3.1 (Egypt). See also Amnesty International UK, 'Egypt frees Al Jazeera staff jailed for journalism' (18 May 2020).
[176] Giza Criminal Court Fifth Circuit, Criminal Case No. 1145 of 2014, 23 June 2014 (unofficial translation). The Court also sentenced a number of other individuals at the same trial.
[177] 'Timeline: The two trials of Mohamed Fahmy' (CTV News, 29 August 2015).
[178] K. Fahim, 'Egypt Pardons Al Jazeera Journalists Mohamed Fahmy and Baher Mohamed' (The New York Times, 23 September 2015).
[179] CPJ, 'Egyptian journalist Mohamed Monir detained, charged with spreading false news' (15 June 2020).
[180] Ibid.
[181] 'Lawyer: Egyptian journalist detained on fake news charges' (AP News, 15 June 2020).
[182] CPJ, 'Egyptian journalist Mohamed Monir detained, charged with spreading false news' (15 June 2020).
[183] Monir was arrested on 15 June 2020 and released on 2 July 2020. CPJ, 'Egyptian journalist Mohamed Monir dies after contracting COVID-19 in pretrial detention' (13 July 2020).
[184] Ibid.

Similarly, Sanaa Seif, a prominent human rights activist, was sentenced to 18 months' imprisonment in March 2021 for 'disseminating false news', 'misuse of social media' and insulting a police officer on duty, after she took to social media to speak out about an altercation she had with a police officer, and to criticize the lack of response to Covid-19 in Egypt's overcrowded prison system.[185] This followed a separate case against her brother, activist Alaa Abd El Fattah, a significant figure in the 2011 uprising in Egypt[186] who was also sentenced to five years' imprisonment for spreading fake news after a trial that allegedly lacked basic due process guarantees.[187] Human rights groups described Seif's conviction and sentence as 'yet another crushing blow for the right to freedom of expression in Egypt'.[188]

III. International Legal Standards

Under international law, states may not impose penalties on speech on the basis of its falsity alone. The list of legitimate grounds for restricting speech set out in human rights treaties is exhaustive. While some of the grounds set out are broad, none can be interpreted as permitting restrictions on speech simply on grounds of its falsity.[189] Lying alone cannot be a crime, nor the basis for civil sanctions if there is no demonstrable harm. But when false speech is likely to cause or has caused prohibited harms, the speaker intends to cause such harms, and the penalty is proportionate, penalties for false speech may be permissible in line with international standards.

There are few cases litigated before international human rights bodies that specifically address the question of how misinformation can be regulated by a state.[190] But as this issue has gained prominence in recent years, soft law guidance has started to fill this gap.[191] Many soft law standards correspond closely to those in the defamation context, which also, of course, applies to false speech but only the subset of such speech that harms reputation.[192] The question that arises, therefore, is which harms other than reputation warrant the penalization of false speech? And where should the lines be drawn? If the lines are to be drawn differently from those in the defamation context, this should be justified by a difference in the nature of the harm caused by the speech.[193]

---

[185] Amnesty International, 'Egypt: Sanaa Seif's conviction on bogus charges a travesty of justice' (17 March 2021).
[186] 'Alaa Abdel Fattah: Leading Egyptian activist jailed for five years' (BBC, 20 December 2021).
[187] Human Rights Watch, 'Egypt: Wave of Unjust "Emergency" Trials' (19 December 2021). Two other defendants, Mohamed al-Baqer and Mohamed Ibrahim, were both sentenced to four years' imprisonment at the same trial.
[188] Amnesty International, 'Egypt: Sanaa Seif's conviction on bogus charges a travesty of justice' (17 March 2021).
[189] See HRC, General Comment No. 34 (2011), §22: 'Restrictions are not allowed on grounds not specified in paragraph 3, even if such grounds would justify restrictions to other rights protected in the Covenant.' See also §§28–32 (discussing the scope of legitimate aims enumerated in Art. 19(3)).
[190] See s. III.3.1. (Harm).
[191] See, e.g., UN Special Rapporteur on Freedom of Opinion and Expression, OSCE Representative on Freedom of the Media, OAS Special Rapporteur on Freedom of Expression and ACmHPR Special Rapporteur on Freedom of Expression and Access to Information, *Joint Declaration on Freedom of Expression and 'Fake News', Disinformation and Propaganda* (2017) FOM.GAL/3/17.
[192] Ibid., §2.
[193] See e.g., M. Milanovic, 'Viral Misinformation and the Freedom of Expression: Part I' (EJIL:Talk!, 13 April 2020).

International standards relevant to misinformation derive from the basic framework of limitations on the freedom of expression, and the three-part test for justifying the imposition of penalties for speech under international law.[194] This provides that any restriction on expression (1) must be provided for by law (legality requirement); (2) must pursue a legitimate aim (legitimacy requirement); and (3) must be necessary to achieve that aim (necessity requirement).[195] An analysis of necessity includes an assessment of proportionality measured against the specific legitimate aim that the state is pursuing.[196] This requires examining whether the restriction on speech is a suitable measure for achieving the legitimate aim, whether there are less restrictive measures that could have achieved it, and whether a fair balance has been struck between the aim pursued and the interests of the individual whose speech is being restricted.[197]

1. Legality

International human rights law requires restrictions on freedom of expression to be set out in domestic law, which must meet qualitative criteria of accessibility, precision and clarity.[198] Vagueness in misinformation laws is therefore fatal from a human rights standpoint—not only because overly vague laws offend against rule of law values, but also because they tend to chill far too much truthful, protected speech.[199]

Vague definitions vest state authorities that interpret and apply a misinformation law with excessive discretion that can be used subjectively, inconsistently or arbitrarily.[200] As noted by the UN Special Rapporteur on freedom of opinion and expression, '[v]ague prohibitions of disinformation effectively empower government officials with the ability to determine the truthfulness or falsity of content in the public and political domain, in conflict with the requirements of ... article 19(3)' of the ICCPR.[201] And as both UN and regional experts have confirmed, '[g]eneral prohibitions on the dissemination of information based on vague and ambiguous ideas, including "false news"

---

[194] Human Rights Council Resolution 44/12 Freedom of opinion and expression (A/HRC/RES/44/12) 16 July 2020 ('responses to the spread of disinformation and misinformation must be grounded in international human rights law, including the principles of lawfulness, legitimacy, necessity and proportionality').

[195] See ICCPR Art. 19(3); ECHR Art. 10(2); ACHR Art. 13(2); ACHPR Art. 9(2). See s. I. (Introduction).

[196] See HRC, General Comment No. 34 (2011), §34; IACmHR, *The Inter-American Legal Framework Regarding the Right to Freedom of Expression* (2009) OEA/Ser.L/V/II CIDH/RELE/INF. 2/09, §88.

[197] See HRC, General Comment No. 34 (2011), §34; IACmHR, *The Inter-American Legal Framework Regarding the Right to Freedom of Expression* (2009) OEA/Ser.L/V/II CIDH/RELE/INF. 2/09, §§85–87; Human Rights Council Resolution 44/12 Freedom of opinion and expression (A/HRC/RES/44/12) 16 July 2020, §8(e).

[198] See ICCPR Art. 19(3); ECHR Art. 10(2); ACHR Art. 13(2); ACHPR Art. 9(2); HRC, General Comment No. 34 (2011), §25. See also ECtHR (GC), *Rotaru v. Romania* (App. no. 28341/95), 4 May 2000, §52; ECtHR (GC), *Maestri v. Italy* (App. no. 39748/98), 17 February 2004, §30.

[199] See IACmHR, *The Inter-American Legal Framework Regarding the Right to Freedom of Expression* (2009) OEA/Ser.L/V/II CIDH/RELE/INF. 2/09, §§70–71.

[200] In that regard, the European Court has consistently held that the law must 'afford adequate legal protection against arbitrariness and accordingly indicate with sufficient clarity the scope of discretion conferred on the competent authorities and the manner of its exercise': ECtHR (GC), *S. and Marper v. United Kingdom* (App. Nos. 30562/04 & 30566/04), 4 December 2008, §95.

[201] See UN Special Rapporteur D. Kaye, *Disease Pandemics and the freedom of opinion and expression* (2020) UN Doc. A/HRC/44/49, §49.

or "non-objective information" are incompatible with international standards for restrictions on freedom of expression'.[202] For example, UN Special Rapporteurs have expressed concern that 'the vague language' of Qatar's misinformation law[203] 'may result in disproportionate restrictions on freedom of expression'.[204] This has been borne out in practice, with individuals arrested under the law for protesting a voting ban for certain families.[205]

Vague misinformation laws that are criminal in nature are of the gravest concern. Not only do they exacerbate the chilling effects of criminal punishment, they also go against the bedrock *nullum crimen sine lege* principle of criminal law and may violate human rights on that basis as well.[206] As the Community Court of Justice of the Economic Community of West African States has stated, '[n]arrowly drawing offences has been treated as particularly important in the case of free speech because of what is known as the "chilling effect" which occurs when a wide or vague speech-restricting provision forces self-censorship on speakers ... because they do not wish to risk being caught on the wrong side of it'.[207]

International and regional human rights bodies have consistently criticized vague wording in criminal misinformation offences. The UN's Human Rights Committee has expressed concern about the prosecution of journalists using laws that criminalize spreading or disseminating 'false news'.[208] The Working Group on Arbitrary Detention has similarly critiqued misinformation laws, describing Bahrain's offences of 'spreading false news abroad which damages the national interest' and 'spreading false rumours in wartime' as 'so vague and overly broad that they could ... result in penalties being imposed on individuals who had merely exercised their rights under international law'.[209] The Working Group also described the offence of 'harming the image of the State by disseminating false information to foreign groups' as one of many laws in Saudi Arabia that 'fall short of international standards and can easily be used to criminalize the peaceful exercise of the rights to freedom of expression'.[210]

---

[202] UN Special Rapporteur, OSCE Representative on Freedom of the Media, OAS Special Rapporteur and ACmHPR Special Rapporteur on Freedom of Expression and Access to Information, *Joint Declaration on Freedom of Expression and 'Fake News', Disinformation and Propaganda* (2017) FOM.GAL/3/17, §2(a).

[203] See s. II.1.1. (Vagueness and overbreadth).

[204] UN Special Rapporteurs D. Kaye and M. Forst, *Letter to the Government of Qatar dated 14 April 2020*, Ref OL QAT 1/2020, 3.

[205] Qatari Penal Code (Amended 2020) Art. 136 (criminalizing 'false or malicious news' disseminated with the intention of 'harming national interests, provoking public opinion, or violating the social system or public order of the state'); T. M. Issa, 'Qatar arrests seven people for racial speech, 88 others for breaking COVID measures' (Al Arabiya, 10 August 2021); "Qatar's new electoral law stirs up tribal sensitivities' (Reuters, 12 August 2021).

[206] See IACmHR, *The Inter-American Legal Framework Regarding the Right to Freedom of Expression* (2009) OEA/Ser.L/V/II CIDH/RELE/INF. 2/09, §72. See, generally, ICCPR Art. 15; ECHR Art. 7; ACHPR Art. 7(2); ACHR Art. 9.

[207] ECOWAS CCJ, *Federation of African Journalists v. The Gambia* (Suit no. ECW/CCJ/APP/36/15), 13 February 2018, §41.

[208] HRC, *Concluding Observations: Cameroon* (2010) UN Doc CCPR/C/CMR/CO/4, §25; HRC, *Concluding Observations: Sudan* (2014) UN Doc. CCPR/C/SDN/CO/4, §21. See also HRC, *Concluding Observations: Macao* (2013) UN Doc. CCPR/C/CHN-MAC/CO/1, §16.

[209] WGAD, *Rajab v. Bahrain* (Opinion no. 13/2018), 19 April 2018, §§7, 29.

[210] WGAD, *Sheikh Suliaman al-Rashudi and others v. Saudi Arabia* (Opinion no. 38/2015), 4 September 2015, §73.

Regional courts have reached similar conclusions. For instance, the East African Court of Justice found the offence of publishing a false statement 'likely to cause fear and alarm to the public or to disturb the public peace' in Tanzania was 'too vague' since it 'does not enable individuals to regulate their conduct'.[211] Similarly, the ECOWAS Court has determined that the Gambian offence of publishing any statement 'likely to cause fear and alarm to the public or to disturb the public peace, knowing or having reason to believe that the statement, rumour or report is false' is impermissibly vague, as it is difficult to discern with any certainty what constitutes an offence and it consequently has 'a chilling effect that may unduly restrict the exercise of freedom of expression of journalists'.[212]

2. Legitimacy

International law provides a list of objectives that permit the restriction of speech.[213] This list of 'legitimate aims' in article 19(3) of the ICCPR does not include the prevention of falsehoods, without more.[214] Instead, article 19(3) provides that speech can only be legitimately restricted when this is necessary for the 'respect of the rights or reputations of others' or for 'the protection of national security or of public order ... or of public health or morals'. This list is exhaustive.[215] Human rights law simply 'does not permit general prohibition of expressions of an erroneous opinion'.[216] As noted by the UN Special Rapporteur, 'the right to freedom of expression applies to all kinds of information and ideas ... irrespective of the truth or falsehood of the content'.[217]

Regional human rights treaties contain similar lists.[218] And even though article 10 of the European Convention on Human Rights enumerates some 'aims' that are not listed in the ICCPR and other treaties, the Human Rights Committee has considered 'public order' to encompass the additional aims expressly listed in article 10 of the European Convention.[219] Like UN bodies, the European Court of Human Rights has been clear

---

[211] EACJ, *Media Council of Tanzania and others v. Attorney General of the United Republic of Tanzania* (Ref no. 2/2017), 28 March 2019, §§92–95. However, the Court accepted that more precisely worded offences passed the test of legality, including criminalizing the use of mass media to publish information 'maliciously or fraudulently fabricated' or 'intentionally or recklessly falsified' that threatens the 'interests of defence, public safety, public order, the economic interests of the United Republic, public morality or public health or is injurious to others' rights and reputation'.

[212] ECOWAS CCJ, *Federation of African Journalists v. The Gambia* (Suit no. ECW/CCJ/APP/36/15), 13 February 2018, 47.

[213] See ch. 1 (Introduction), s II.3.1. (Key convergences).

[214] ICCPR Art. 19(3).

[215] Ibid.

[216] HRC, General Comment No. 34 (2011), §49.

[217] UN Special Rapporteur I. Khan, *Disinformation and freedom of opinion and expression* (2021) UN Doc. A/HRC/47/25, §38, citing HRC, General Comment No. 34 (2011), §§47, 49; ECtHR, *Salov v. Ukraine* (App. no. 65518/01), 6 September 2005, §113.

[218] See ch. 1 (Introduction), s. II.1.1. (Treaty language).

[219] See HRC, *Lovell v. Australia* (Comm. no. 920/2000), 29 March 2004, §9.4; HRC, General Comment No. 34 (2011), §31 ('Contempt of court proceedings relating to forms of expression may be tested against the public order (*ordre public*) ground'); HRC, *Aleksandrov v. Belarus* (Comm no. 1933/2010), 24 July 2014, §7.4 (holding that Belarus had not explained how the actions of a protester 'would have violated the rights and freedoms of others or would have posed a threat to public safety or public order (ordre public)'); COE, *Report of the Committee of Experts on Human Rights to the Committee of Ministers* (1970) H(70)7, 2, 175–77. See ch. 1 (Introduction).

that '[a]rticle 10 of the Convention as such does not prohibit discussion or dissemination of information ... even if it is strongly suspected that this information might not be truthful'.[220] Similarly, in the words of the Inter-American Court of Human Rights, '[a] system that controls the right of expression in the name of a supposed guarantee of the correctness and truthfulness of the information that society receives can be the source of great abuse and, ultimately, violates the right to information that this same society has'.[221]

Since international law requires a specific legitimate aim to restrict speech, a legal regime that seeks to enable the state to police the truthfulness of free expression for the sake of the truth alone would be categorically incompatible with international human rights standards. For example, the state has no business restricting the online speech of flat-Earthers or moon-landing conspirators if that speech, however false, does not endanger 'the rights of others', 'national security' or other prohibited harms enumerated in article 19(3). But the state might be justified in limiting the speech of anti-vaccination activists that foreseeably caused harms to public health.

2.1. States must not restrict false speech for ulterior purposes

When assessing whether a law is pursuing a legitimate aim, '[r]estrictions must be applied only for those purposes for which they were prescribed and must be directly related to the specific need on which they are predicated'.[222] If state authorities articulate a rationale for restricting speech that is legitimate on paper but in practice is merely a pretext for clamping down on critical speech, this will not pass muster under international law.[223] The Human Rights Committee has held, as a result, that the 'penalization of a media outlet, publisher or journalist solely for being critical of the government or the political social system espoused by the government can never be considered to be a necessary restriction of freedom of expression'.[224] And even if a legitimate aim for a restriction of false speech exists at the legislative stage, investigative or prosecutorial authorities may well be acting with an improper purpose when executing the law. For example, a state that enacts a misinformation law with the nominal purpose of protecting public health during a pandemic, but uses it to suppress criticism and exercise more control over the media will be judged by its practice—it is the real use and not the pretextual aim that counts.[225]

---

[220] ECtHR, *Salov v. Ukraine* (App. no. 65518/01), 6 September 2005, §113. Cf. partly Concurring Opinion of Judge Mularoni, stating ('I am not ready to consider that freedom of expression entails the right to disseminate false information').

[221] IACtHR, *Compulsory Membership in an Association Prescribed by Law for the Practice of Journalism (Arts. 13 and 29 American Convention On Human Rights)*, Advisory Opinion OC-5/85 (Series A, no. 5), 13 November 1985, §77.

[222] HRC, General Comment No. 34 (2011), §22; ECHR Art. 18; ICCPR Art. 5(1).

[223] See ACmHPR Special Rapporteur P. Tlakula, *Activity Report of the Special Rapporteur on Freedom of Expression and Access to Information in Africa presented on the 51st Ordinary Session of the African Commission on Human and Peoples' Rights* (2012), §66.

[224] HRC, General Comment No. 34 (2011), §42. See also HRC, General Comment No. 34 (2011), §23; IACmHR, *The Inter-American Legal Framework Regarding the Right to Freedom of Expression* (2009) OEA/Ser.L/V/II CIDH/RELE/INF. 2/09, §38.

[225] See UN Special Rapporteur, OSCE Representative on Freedom of the Media, OAS Special Rapporteur and ACmHPR Special Rapporteur on Freedom of Expression and Access to Information, *Joint Declaration on Freedom*

Whether state authorities are acting with an ulterior purpose may not be easy to prove, but international human rights bodies have repeatedly highlighted the importance of the inquiry, both in the context of assessing the legitimacy of restrictions of a particular human right and in the context of treaty provisions that prohibit the restriction of human rights for ulterior purposes, such as article 18 of the European Convention.[226] International human rights bodies do not necessarily require direct forms of proof of improper purposes, which could be exceptionally difficult to come by.[227] Rather, they accept indirect and circumstantial evidence, drawing inferences where necessary from contextual factors and patterns of behaviour by state authorities.[228] In that regard, the gross disproportionality of the penalty being imposed may be a telling indicator that the restriction on speech was motivated by an improper purpose.[229]

2.2. What objectives can justify the penalization of false speech?

The European Court has been asked to rule on the validity of misinformation laws more frequently than other bodies at the international level.[230] But in assessing laws that penalize speech, the European Court has not always been clear about which objectives are a legitimate basis for restricting false speech. For example, the European Court found that the conviction of a political candidate who disseminated false information about the alleged death of another candidate was for the 'legitimate purpose' of 'providing the voters with true information in the course of [a] presidential campaign', without specifying which of the aims listed in article 10(2) of the Convention this related to.[231] But in a similar case the Human Rights Committee allowed restrictions to expression for the purpose of 'maintain[ing] the integrity of the electoral process' specifically on the basis that such restrictions are 'justified' both 'in terms of the protection of public order' and on the basis that they are 'necessary for the respect of the rights of others'.[232]

---

of Expression and 'Fake News', Disinformation and Propaganda (2017) FOM.GAL/3/17, Preamble §12; OHCHR, 'COVID-19: States should not abuse emergency measures to suppress human rights—UN experts' (16 March 2020): 'Restrictions taken to respond to the virus must be motivated by legitimate public health goals and should not be used simply to quash dissent'.

[226] See, e.g., ECtHR, *OOO Flavus v. Russia* (App. nos. 12468/15 & others), 23 June 2020, §§37–38 (the European Court finding that Russian authorities blocked websites 'on spurious grounds or outright arbitrarily' for the purpose of suppressing dissent). For an overview of cases on ECHR Art. 18, see J. Gavron & R. Remezaite, 'Has the ECtHR in Mammadov 46(4) opened the door to findings of "bad faith" in trials?' (EJIL:Talk!, 4 July 2019).

[227] See ECtHR (GC), *Merabishvili v. Georgia* (App. no. 72508/13), 28 November 2017, §316: 'no reason for the Court to restrict itself to direct proof in relation [allegations of ulterior purpose] or to apply a special standard of proof to such allegations'.

[228] See, e.g., ECtHR, *Navalnyy v. Russia (No. 2)* (App. no. 43734/14), 9 April 2019, §§96–98 (the Court relying on 'converging contextual evidence' to establish that the restrictions on the applicant's liberty were implemented with the ulterior purpose of 'suppress[ing] political pluralism'); ECtHR (GC), *Merabishvili v. Georgia* (App. no. 72508/13), 28 November 2017, §317; ECtHR, *Aliyev v. Azerbaijan* (App. nos. 68762/14 & 71200/14), 20 September 2018, §215.

[229] See, e.g., ECtHR, *Navalnyy v. Russia (No. 2)* (App. no. 43734/14), 9 April 2019, §§96–98.

[230] See, e.g., ECtHR, *Hertel v. Switzerland* (App. no. 25181/94), 25 August 1998, §42.

[231] ECtHR, *Salov v. Ukraine* (App. no. 65518/01), 6 September 2005, §110. The candidate was charged with having interfered with citizens' right to vote for the purpose of influencing election results by means of fraudulent behaviour, and the European Court ultimately held that his sentence of five years' imprisonment, which was suspended for two years, and fine, as well as annulment by the Bar Association to practice law constituted a 'very severe penalty' and a violation of article 10 had arisen. See s. III.2. (Legitimacy).

[232] HRC, *Kim v. Republic of Korea* (Comm. No. 968/2001), 27 July 2005, §8.3 (relating to speech that did not necessarily have to be false); HRC, General Comment No. 34 (2011), 37. See s. II.1.2. (Harm). For an example of a

FALSE SPEECH   243

A challenging area for international human rights bodies has been the assessment of speech denying the occurrence of specific historical events, in particular the existence of and details about the Holocaust.[233] The Human Rights Committee has stated unequivocally that '[l]aws that penalize the expression of opinions about historical facts are incompatible with the obligations that the Covenant imposes on States parties in relation to the respect for freedom of opinion and expression'.[234] But this goes against the jurisprudence of the European Court, which has held that there is a 'category of clearly established historical facts—such as the Holocaust—whose negation or revision would be removed from the protection of article 10 by article 17'.[235] Article 17 provides that the European Convention may not be interpreted as implying the right to engage in any act 'aimed at the destruction of the rights and freedoms' contained in the treaty.[236] Statements about the Holocaust that are not true have been deemed 'one of the most serious forms of racial defamation of Jews and of incitement to hatred of them' and ineligible for protection under any circumstances under the terms of article 17 for this reason.[237]

The European Court was, however, unwilling to extend this reasoning to the case of a politician who denied the Armenian genocide, even though the Court accepted the 'rights of Armenians to respect for their and their ancestors' dignity, including their right to respect for their identity constructed around the understanding that their community has suffered genocide'.[238] This was because the Court reasoned that the justification for making the denial of the Holocaust a criminal offence lies 'not so much in that it is a clearly established historical fact but in that, in view of the historical context in the States concerned [being Austria, Belgium, Germany and France] ... its denial, even if dressed up as impartial historical research must invariably be seen as connoting an antidemocratic ideology and anti-Semitism'.[239]

In this way false speech about the Holocaust has been given a unique status by the European Court. While this is perhaps understandable given the historical context, it is nevertheless inconsistent with international human rights standards related to freedom of expression and inconsistent with the Court's own related case law.[240] But even the

---

law prohibiting certain types of speech to maintain the integrity of elections: see, e.g., Canadian Elections Act 2000 s. 91(1).

[233] See generally U. Belavusau & A. Gliszczyńska-Grabias (eds), *Law and Memory: Towards Legal Governance of History* (CUP 2017). See ch. 3 (Hate Speech), s. III.2.4.2. (Opinion).
[234] HRC, General Comment No. 34 (2011), §49 (reversing a previous decision of the Committee allowing a conviction under denial laws). See ch. 3 (Hate Speech), s. III.2.4.2. (Opinion).
[235] ECtHR, *Garaudy v. France* (App. no, 65831/01), 24 June 2003, 28, citing ECtHR, *Lehideux and Isorni v. France* (App. no. 24662/94), 23 September 1998, §47.
[236] See ch. 3 (Hate Speech), s. III.2.4.2. (Opinion); see, e.g., ECtHR, *Williamson v. Germany* (App. no. 64496/17), 8 January 2019; ECtHR, *Pastörs v. Germany* (App. no. 55225/14), 3 October 2019; ECtHR, *M'Bala M'Bala v. France* (App. no. 25239/13), 20 October 2015.
[237] ECtHR, *Garaudy v. France* (App. no. 65831/01), 24 June 2003, 29; ECtHR, *M'Bala M'Bala v. France* (App. no. 25239/13), 20 October 2015, §40 ('the blatant display of a hateful and anti-Semitic position disguised as an artistic production is as dangerous as a head-on and abrupt attack').
[238] ECtHR (GC), *Perinçek v. Switzerland* (App. no. 27510/08), 15 October 2015, §227.
[239] Ibid., §243.
[240] Ibid.; HRC, General Comment No. 34 (2011), §49. See ch. 3 (Hate Speech), s. III.2.4.2. (Opinion). Cf. ACtHPR, *Umuhoza v. Rwanda* (App. no. 003/2014), 24 November 2017, §158.

European Court's approach to Holocaust denial can be regarded as supporting the basic proposition that false speech cannot be criminalized simply on the basis of its falsity.[241] Rather, such speech can be punished only because of the specific and serious harms that it causes, with the required degree of causal connection. Our survey of international jurisprudence indicates that the following harms might, under the right conditions, reasonably justify criminalization of false speech: if it incites violence, causes other serious harms to human life and health, or directly and immediately harms the integrity of elections and other democratic processes, thereby undermining 'public order' and the 'rights of others' whose protection is a 'legitimate aim' under international law.

3. Necessity

Any restriction on speech needs to be necessary and proportionate to the harm it is seeking to guard against.[242] A necessary restriction on speech is more than one that is merely useful, reasonable or desirable; it can only be justified if other, less restrictive forms of limitations of free expression are incapable of remedying the harm.[243] And in a free society, the default remedy for falsehoods is more truthful speech, not penalties imposed by the state.[244]

But harms caused by misinformation cannot always be remedied—at least not fully—through more truthful speech, particularly when the target of misinformation cannot easily and speedily reach the same audience, or where any correction would be too late to address the damage, as is often the case in the online context.[245] For instance, misinformation that causes direct harms to human health—such as the peddling of cures for an infectious disease that are not only false, but lethal—can lead to many deaths before it is successfully countered by truthful speech.[246]

A state should be expected to provide a full accounting of proactive measures that it took, or at least considered, to mitigate harms before resorting to restrictions on free expression.[247] The state must also demonstrate that the necessity for speech regulation is continuing: that there is an *ongoing* need for a restriction on speech due to continuing harms caused by misinformation that cannot be remedied through less restrictive means. It is perfectly possible for certain speech-restrictive measures to be necessary

---

[241] See, e.g., ECtHR, *Pastörs v. Germany* (App. no. 55225/14), 3 October 2019, §§40–42.

[242] ECtHR, *Lingens v. Austria* (App. no. 9815/82), 8 July 1986, §39: 'The adjective "necessary"... implies the existence of a "pressing social need"'. See also IACtHR, *Compulsory Membership in an Association Prescribed by Law for the Practice of Journalism (Arts. 13 and 29 American Convention On Human Rights)*, Advisory Opinion OC-5/85 (Series A, no. 5), 13 November 1985, §46 (endorsing this approach).

[243] See HRC, General Comment No. 34 (2011), §§33, 35; IACtHR, *Compulsory Membership in an Association Prescribed by Law for the Practice of Journalism (Arts. 13 and 29 American Convention On Human Rights)*, Advisory Opinion OC-5/85 (Series A, no. 5), 13 November 1985, §46. See also ECtHR, *The Sunday Times v. United Kingdom* (App. no. 6538/74), 26 April 1979, §59.

[244] See UN Special Rapporteur F. La Rue, *Promotion and protection of the right to freedom of opinion and expression* (2011) UN Doc. A/66/290, §41.

[245] See Z. Tufekci, 'It's the (Democracy-Poisoning) Golden Age of Free Speech' (Wired, 16 January 2018).

[246] UN Special Rapporteur D. Kaye, *Disease pandemics and the freedom of opinion and expression* (2020) UN Doc. A/HRC/44/49, §45.

[247] Ibid., §47.

only for a limited time (such as for the duration of a pandemic), but then no longer because the circumstances that once generated the necessity have changed.[248]

Most cases analysing the permissibility of state regulation of misinformation turn on the question of necessity and proportionality of the law as applied.[249] And international standards dictate that the necessity and proportionality of the penalization of misinformation depend on a number of factors: (1) the severity and imminence of the harm caused by the untruthful speech and the causal link between the untruthful speech and the harm; (2) the intent of the speaker; and (3) the penalty that is imposed.[250]

3.1. Harm
3.1.1. Severity and imminence of harm

States seeking to penalize speech must demonstrate that some degree of a prohibited harm is likely to result from it.[251] The Human Rights Committee has found that '[w]hen a State ... invokes a legitimate ground for restriction of freedom of expression, it must demonstrate in specific and individualized fashion the precise nature of the threat' posed by the speech.[252] But the required severity and imminence of the harm that is sufficient to justify penalties for misinformation has not yet been clearly articulated by international bodies.

Although there is no clear case law from the Human Rights Committee on requirements for harm in the context of misinformation laws, the Committee has found a violation of freedom of expression in the context of defamation where the damage to a public servant's reputation was 'only of a limited nature'.[253] And the Committee has stated that criminal defamation laws should only be countenanced in the 'most serious of cases'.[254] In addition, some members of the Human Rights Committee have suggested, in the context of mandatory restrictions on hate speech, that the application of criminal penalties should be limited to 'speech that incites the commission of criminal offences or acts of violence'.[255]

---

[248] Ibid., §15 ('the ensuing interference with third parties' rights must be limited and justified in the light of the interest supported by the intrusion').

[249] See ch. 1 (Introduction), s. II.3.1.1. (Justifications for penalizing speech).

[250] See HRC, General Comment No. 34 (2011), §35; ECtHR, *Mariya Alekhina and Others v. Russia* (App. no. 38004/12), 17 July 2018, §220 (the Court noting the importance of whether the speech had the 'capacity—direct or indirect—to lead to harmful consequences').

[251] HRC, General Comment No. 34 (2011), §35. See s.III.2.2 (What objectives can justify the penalization of false speech?).

[252] Ibid., §35, citing HRC, *Shin v. Republic of Korea* (Comm. no. 926/2000), 16 March 2004 (where a professional painter of a political artwork titled 'Rice Planting' who was convicted under Korean law for 'enemy-benefiting expression', the Committee held that Korea must demonstrate 'in specific fashion the precise nature of the threat' caused by the author's conduct 'as well as why seizure of the painting and the author's conviction were necessary'. The Committee found a violation of article 19(2) in the absence of an 'individualized justification'). Cf. HRC, *Ross v. Canada* (Comm. no. 736/1997), 18 October 2000, §11.5 (noting that 'the [Canadian] Supreme Court found that it was reasonable to anticipate that there was a causal link between the expressions of the author and the "poisoned school environment" experienced by Jewish children').

[253] HRC, *Kozlov v. Belarus* (Comm. no. 1986/2010), 24 July 2014, §7.6 (in circumstances where the defamatory remarks were sent in a letter rather than made public).

[254] HRC, General Comment No. 34 (2011), §47. See s.III.5. (Penalties) (noting the Human Rights Committee's position that imprisonment is 'never an appropriate penalty' for defamatory speech).

[255] See, e.g., HRC, *Rabbae v. The Netherlands* (Comm no. 2124/2011) 14 July 2016, Individual Concurring Opinion of Committee members Sarah Cleveland and Mauro Politi, §7. See also the standard for mandatory

The harm threshold applied by the European Court depends on the speech at issue. In the context of hate speech, the Court will consider whether speech 'could be seen as a direct or indirect call for violence or as a justification of violence, hatred or intolerance' as a factor relevant to the assessment of whether a penalty was necessary.[256] In order to trigger the protection of the Convention for defamatory speech, the Court requires that an attack on reputation must 'attain a certain level of seriousness and be in a manner causing prejudice to personal enjoyment of the right to respect for private life'.[257] When false speech falls into either of these categories these standards will therefore likely apply.

In the handful of cases in which the European Court has addressed misinformation laws, it has considered the impact of the impugned speech in its assessment of necessity, but it has not articulated a specific harm threshold. For example, the Court considered misinformation when a political candidate in a presidential election disseminated forged copies of a newspaper which suggested—incorrectly—that his opponent had died.[258] The candidate was convicted of interfering with the exercise of citizens' electoral rights and sentenced to five years' imprisonment.[259] In assessing this penalty to be disproportionate, the Court took into account the potential harm of the information, noting 'the impact of the information contained in the newspaper was minor as he only had eight copies of the forged ... newspaper and spoke to a limited number of persons about it, a fact that should have been taken into account by the domestic courts'.[260] And the Court invoked similar reasoning in a case involving speech that was published in a specialized scientific journal 'distributed almost entirely by subscription' with 'in all likelihood, a specific readership such that the impact of the ideas it contains should be limited'.[261]

The Inter-American Court has traditionally been a speech-protective jurisdiction,[262] and emphasized the importance of 'promoting information pluralism' rather than a system that controls speech 'in the name of a supposed guarantee of the correctness and truthfulness' of certain information.[263] This position has translated to stringent harm requirements before false speech can be penalized. For instance, the Court has criticized slander laws that do not 'specify the injury required' and made clear that

---

non-criminal penalties set out in ICCPR Art. 20. See ch. 1 (Introduction), s. II.1.2.1.2. (ICCPR Article 20) and ch. 3 (Hate Speech), s. III.1.1. (ICCPR Article 20).

[256] ECtHR (GC), *Perinçek v. Switzerland* (App. no. 27510/08), 15 October 2015, §§206, 208. See ch. 3 (Hate Speech), s. II.1.2. (Harm). See ch. 6 (Terrorism Laws) ss. II.1.3 (Harm).
[257] ECtHR (GC), *Axel Springer AG v. Germany* (App. no. 39954/08), 7 February 2012, §83; ECtHR, *A v. Norway* (App. no. 28070/06), 9 April 2009, §64 (both in the context of Art. 8, not 10).
[258] ECtHR, *Salov v. Ukraine* (App. no. 65518/01), 6 September 2005.
[259] Ibid., §28. See s. III.2. (Legitimacy).
[260] ECtHR, *Salov v. Ukraine* (App. no. 65518/01), 6 September 2005, §114.
[261] ECtHR, *Hertel v. Switzerland* (App. no. 25181/94), 25 August 1998, §49.
[262] See, e.g., IACtHR, *Compulsory Membership in an Association Prescribed by Law for the Practice of Journalism (Arts. 13 and 29 American Convention On Human Rights)*, Advisory Opinion OC-5/85 (Series A, no. 5), 13 November 1985, §50.
[263] IACtHR, *Tristán Donoso v. Panamá* (Series C, no. 193), 27 January 2009, §113; IACtHR, *Compulsory Membership in an Association Prescribed by Law for the Practice of Journalism (Arts. 13 and 29 American Convention On Human Rights)*, Advisory Opinion OC-5/85 (Series A, no. 5), 13 November 1985, §77.

defamatory speech must constitute a 'serious attack' or do 'serious damage'.[264] Article 13(5) of the American Convention on Human Rights requires that speech rises to the level of incitement to 'lawless violence' or 'similar action' when it comes to mandatory penalties for hateful speech.[265] And the Rapporteur of the Organization of American States (OAS Rapporteur) has indicated that any restriction to speech 'must be based on real and objectively verifiable causes that present the certain and credible threat of a potentially serious disturbance of the basic conditions for the functioning of democratic institutions'.[266] This jurisdiction is therefore likely to find that misinformation laws require that serious potential harm would likely flow or did flow from the speech.

Although African courts have reviewed a number of misinformation laws, they have generally done so with respect to the 'legality' requirement, without analysing necessity and the requisite harm thresholds.[267] But the African Court on Human and Peoples' Rights has noted that custodial sentences for speech are contrary to freedom of expression '[a]part from [in] serious and very exceptional circumstances, for example incitement to international crimes, public incitement to hatred [or] discrimination or violence or threats against a person or a group of people, because of a specific criteria'.[268] Criminal misinformation laws are therefore not likely to be compatible with article 9 of the African Charter on Human and Peoples' Rights unless they meet these conditions.[269]

In sum, international jurisprudence supports the position that criminalizing false speech can only be done if it causes serious proscribed harms. The necessity of speech restriction, especially through criminal means, will depend on the nature, degree and imminence of the harm produced by the false speech. For example, it might be necessary for the state to restrict the speech of an individual who is promoting a false cure for Covid-19, which may directly lead to harms to the lives or health of the audience.[270] But it would arguably not be necessary for the state to restrict the speech of climate change deniers.[271] Even if that speech is equally untruthful, and although in aggregate

---

[264] IACtHR, *Usón Ramírez v. Venezuela* (Series C, no. 207), 20 November 2009, §§56, 73–75.
[265] ACHR Art. 13(5). Though the scope of 'similar action' is not defined, the drafting of the text suggests that the harm should be comparable in severity to violence: see ch. 3 (Hate Speech), s. III.1.4. (Mandatory restrictions at the regional level).
[266] IACmHR, *Freedom of Expression Standards for Free and Inclusive Broadcasting* (2009) OEA/Ser.L/V/II CIDH/RELE/INF. 3/09, §22, citing IACmHR, *Annual Report of the Office of the Special Rapporteur for Freedom of Expression* (2008) OEA/Ser.L/V/II. 134, Chapter 3, §75.
[267] See s. II.1.1. (Vagueness and overbreadth). See, e.g., EACJ, *Media Council of Tanzania and others v. Attorney General of the United Republic of Tanzania* (Ref no. 2/2017), 28 March 2019; ECOWAS CCJ, *Federation of African Journalists v. The Gambia* (Suit no. ECW/CCJ/APP/36/15), 13 February 2018.
[268] ACtHPR, *Konaté v. Burkina Faso* (App. no. 004/2013), 5 December 2014, §165.
[269] Ibid., §§165–166.
[270] Cf. The Meta Oversight Board, 'Case Decision 2020-006-FB-FBR Claimed COVID-19 cure' (finding Facebook's decision to remove a post criticizing French authorities for refusing to authorize hydroxychloroquine combined with azithromycin as a cure for Covid-19 was inconsistent with article 19(3) of the ICCPR. The Board found that Facebook had failed to demonstrate how removing the post was the least intrusive method of protecting public health despite having a range of enforcement options that deal with misinformation through less extreme means, and considered that Facebook's rules on misinformation also failed the legality test).
[271] Cf. Private corporations banning climate misinformation content and ads on their platforms: C. Duffy, 'Pinterest bans misinformation about climate change' (CNN, 6 April 2022); R. Maruf, 'Twitter bans "misleading" climate change ads' (CNN, 23 April 2022); K. Chan, 'Google cracks down on climate change denial by targeting ads' (AP News, 8 October 2021).

the denials of climate change undoubtedly adversely affect efforts to curb and mitigate it, these harms are on a longer timescale and the causal link between the untruthful speech of any given individual and a concrete harmful consequence is more tenuous. International bodies would therefore likely find that it is more appropriate for this type of misinformation to be addressed through public education and debate, rather than through state-imposed penalties.[272]

3.1.2. *Causal relationship between the speech and the harm*

International human rights law requires that the state establish a causal link between false speech and concrete harms that are likely to result from it.[273] But international bodies have not yet articulated a clear and consistent standard for this.

According to the Human Rights Committee, a state seeking to restrict expression must establish 'a direct and immediate connection between the expression and the threat'.[274] And in the context of incitement to violence, UN-approved standards set out in the 'Rabat Plan of Action' provide that in restricting speech 'the courts will have to determine that there was a reasonable probability that the speech would succeed in inciting actual action against the target group, *recognizing that such causation should be rather direct*'.[275] But there are no detailed requirements about the foreseeability of the harm, whether this test should be objective or subjective, whether the harm should possibly, likely, probably, almost certainly or actually result from the speech, or whether the harm must be imminent.[276]

The European Court has considered in some cases whether speech had the 'capacity—*direct or indirect*—to lead to harmful consequences'; but its jurisprudence does not examine the objective likelihood of a certain result or data on what, in fact, happened following the speech.[277] And in some cases involving racist or homophobic speech, the Court has sidestepped an assessment of causation of harm entirely, basing its decision 'on an assessment of the content of the expression and the manner of its delivery' alone.[278] The 2019 Declaration of Principles of Freedom of Expression and Access to Information in Africa only speak of 'a close causal link between the risk of harm and the expression' in the context of restricting speech on public order or national security grounds, without providing further detail.[279] And multiple

---

[272] See UN Special Rapporteur J. Knox, *Report of the Special Rapporteur on the issue of human rights obligations relating to the enjoyment of a safe, clean, healthy and sustainable environment* (2016) UN Doc. A/HRC/31/52, §60 ('[t]o enable informed public participation, the rights of freedom of expression and association must be safeguarded for all people in relation to all climate-related actions, including for individuals who oppose projects designed to mitigate or adapt to climate change').

[273] UN Special Rapporteur I. Khan, *Disinformation and freedom of opinion and expression* (2021) UN Doc. A/HRC/47/25, §41.

[274] HRC, General Comment No. 34 (2011), §35.

[275] Rabat Plan of Action, §29(f) (emphasis added).

[276] Ibid.

[277] ECtHR, *Alekhina v. Russia* (App. no. 38004/12), 17 July 2018, §220 (emphasis added). See also ECtHR (GC), *Perinçek v. Switzerland* (App. no. 27510/08), 15 October 2015, §207. See ch. 3 (Hate Speech).

[278] See, e.g. ECtHR, *Lilliendahl v. Iceland* (App. no. 29297/18), 12 May 2020, §36. See ch. 3 (Hate Speech), s. II.1.2. (Harm).

[279] ACmHPR, Declaration of Principles of Freedom of Expression and Access to Information in Africa (2019), Principle 22(5).

international bodies assume that harm exists in the context of speech that is found to be defamatory.[280]

3.2. Intent

International bodies assessing the appropriateness of criminalizing false statements must address a number of questions about the state of mind of the speaker. What level of fault is required for restrictions on speech to be compatible with freedom of expression? Are statements that are false but made in good faith always protected? And do knowing falsehoods enjoy *any* level of protection under international law? At the highest end of the culpability spectrum, a criminal statute would punish a speaker who knew that the information they were disseminating was false (or intended to deceive their audience), and who knew or intended for the false speech to cause a prohibited harm. These would be cases of lies or *dis*information. At the lowest end of the spectrum, false speech would be a strict liability offence, or one that required only objective negligence.

International standards in relation to defamation law require a high level of culpability to penalize defamatory speech, at least when it concerns public officials.[281] The Inter-American bodies have adopted the 'actual malice' test articulated by the US Supreme Court in *New York Times v. Sullivan,* holding that 'erroneous statement is inevitable in free debate' and 'must be protected if the freedoms of expression are to have the "breathing space" that they "need ... to survive"' and that defamatory statements about a *public official* are only actionable in a civil defamation claim if made with 'actual malice', i.e. 'with knowledge that it was false or with reckless disregard of whether it was false or not'.[282] The Human Rights Committee has similarly recommended that '[a]t least with regard to comments about public figures, consideration should be given to avoiding penalizing or otherwise rendering unlawful untrue statements that have been published in error *but without malice*'.[283] And although African courts have not formally adopted the 'actual malice' standard,[284] the East African Court of Justice

---

[280] For a discussion on the treatment of defamation in international human rights law, see A. Clooney & P. Webb, 'The Right to Insult in International Law' (2017) 48(2) *Columbia Human Rights Law Review* 1, 44–46. But, e.g., the Inter-American Court considers causation in determining damages and reparations: see IACtHR, *Tristán Donoso v. Panamá* (Series C, no. 193), 27 January 2009, §120. For speech alleged to have incited violence, the Court requires that the imposition of sanctions 'must be backed up by actual, truthful, objective and strong proof that the person was not simply issuing an opinion (even if that opinion was hard, unfair or disturbing), but that the person had the clear intention of committing a crime and the actual, real and effective possibility of achieving this objective': IACmHR, *The Inter-American Legal Framework Regarding the Right to Freedom of Expression* (2009) OEA/Ser.L/V/II CIDH/RELE/INF. 2/09, §58. See ch. 3 (Hate Speech).

[281] See ch. 2 (Insulting Speech), s. III.3.1. (Intent of the speaker).

[282] US Supreme Court, *New York Times v. Sullivan* 376 U.S. 254, 9 March 1964, 271–272, 279–280; IACmHR, Declaration of Principles on Freedom of Expression (2000), Principle 10; IACtHR, *Tristán Donoso v. Panamá* (Series C, no. 193), 27 January 2009, §§119–120, 125, 134. See also IACtHR, *Usón Ramírez v. Venezuela* (Series C, no. 207), 20 November 2009, §56; IACtHR, *Mémoli v. Argentina* (Series C, no. 265), 22 August 2013, §§139, 141.

[283] HRC, General Comment No. 34 (2011), §47 (emphasis added). See also HRC, *Akhmedyarov v. Kazakhstan* (Comm. no. 2535/2015), 23 July 2020, §9.8; HRC, *Adonis v. The Philippines* (Comm no. 1815/2008) 26 October 2011, §7.9; HRC, *Concluding observations: The United Kingdom of Great Britain and Northern Ireland* (2008) UN Doc. CCPR/C/GBR/CO/6, §25 (recommending that the United Kingdom 'consider the utility of a so-called "public figure" exception, requiring proof by the plaintiff of actual malice in order to go forward on actions concerning reporting on public officials and prominent public figures').

[284] See ch. 2 (Insulting Speech), s. III.3.1. (Intent of the speaker).

considered misinformation offences in Tanzania that imposed high *mens rea* requirements, such as malice and actual knowledge, to be 'largely unobjectionable'.[285]

The European Court's assessment of the requisite *mens rea* is different. In defamation cases, the Court has declined to adopt the 'actual malice' standard.[286] And in hate speech cases it has considered intent to be a relevant factor, but has allowed even criminal penalties without a clear showing of intent.[287]

Outside the context of defamation, a difficult question is whether knowing falsehoods (*dis*information) should enjoy *any* level of protection. Normatively, the question is whether lies possess any intrinsic value of their own that would make them worthy of protection, or whether they should be protected only incidentally or instrumentally, in order to prevent chilling effects on speech that is either truthful or is untruthful but uttered in good faith.[288] As a matter of principle the question is also whether the value of outright lies should be measured against their motives, against their consequences, or in another way.

International human rights bodies have not yet directly addressed the level of protection to be given to knowing falsehoods.[289] British courts have commented that '[t]here is no human right to disseminate information that is not true' since 'the working of a democratic society depends on the members of that society being informed not misinformed', and suggested that such speech could not be protected under article 10 of the European Convention.[290] But they also confirm that '[s]ome degree of tolerance for factual inaccuracy has to be accepted', including in the context of defamation laws.[291]

In the United States, the degree of protection to be afforded to false speech has been at issue in the defamation context.[292] However, decades after *Sullivan*, the Supreme

---

[285] EACJ, *Media Council of Tanzania and others v. Attorney General of the United Republic of Tanzania* (Ref no. 2/2017), 28 March 2019, §94.

[286] ECtHR, *McVicar v. United Kingdom* (App. no. 46311/99), 7 May 2002, §§27, 65, 73; ECtHR, *Kasabova v. Bulgaria* (App. no. 22385/03), 19 April 2011, §§48, 63–68; see ch. 2 (Insulting Speech), s. III.3.1. (Intent).

[287] ECtHR, *Leroy v. France* (App. no. 36109/03), 2 October 2008, §42; ECtHR, *Nix v. Germany* (App. no. 35285/16), 13 March 2018, §54; see ch. 3 (Hate Speech), s. III.2.3.2. (Intent).

[288] See in particular the different opinions of the justices of the US Supreme Court, *United States v. Alvarez* 567 U.S. 709, 28 June 2012, discussed later in this subsection.

[289] See ACmHPR, Declaration of Principles on Freedom of Expression and Access to Information in Africa (2019), Principle 21(1) (holding that 'no one shall be liable for true statements, opinions or statements' regarding public figures 'which are reasonable to make in the circumstances', without expressing a view on knowingly false statements). Cf. HRC, *Concluding Observations: Cameroon* (1999) UN Doc. CCPR/C/79/Add.116, §24 (expressing deep concern at 'the prosecution and punishment of journalists for the crime of publication of false news merely on the ground, without more, that the news was false, in clear violation of article 19 of the Covenant').

[290] See UK House of Lords, *Reynolds v. Times Newspapers Ltd* [2001] 2 AC 127, 28 October 1999, 238 (Lord Hobhouse): 'The liberty to communicate (and receive) information has a similar place in a free society but it is important always to remember that it is the communication of information not misinformation which is the subject of this liberty. There is no human right to disseminate information that is not true. No public interest is served by publishing or communicating misinformation ... These are general propositions going far beyond the mere protection of reputations'. See also UK High Court of England and Wales, Queen's Bench Division, *R (Woolas) v. Parliamentary Election Court* [2010] EWHC 3169 (Admin), 3 December 2010, §§105–106 (per Thomas LJ): 'Article 10 was not engaged in relation to the statements in *The Examiner* and *Labour Rose* which the Election Court found were made dishonestly. Dishonest statements are aimed at the destruction of the rights of the public to free elections ... and the right of each candidate to his reputation ... Article 10 does not protect a right to publish statements which the publisher knows to be false ... or does not believe it to be true ... The right to freedom of expression under Article 10 does not extend to a right to be dishonest and tell lies'.

[291] See UK House of Lords, *Reynolds v. Times Newspapers Ltd* [2001] 2 AC 127, 28 October 1999, 238 (Lord Hobhouse).

[292] See ch. 2 (Insulting Speech), s. III.3.1. (Intent).

Court split rather fundamentally on the level of protection to be given to knowing falsehoods in the case of *Alvarez*, concerning the constitutionality of the Stolen Valor Act, which made it a crime to falsely claim receipt of military decorations or medals.[293] This was, in other words, a criminal law prohibiting a very specific type of disinformation. *Alvarez* is particularly instructive regarding the question of whether *lies*, i.e. 'disinformation' or knowingly false speech, should enjoy *any* protection.

By six votes to three the Supreme Court declared the statute unconstitutional, but was divided in doing so. Writing for a plurality of the Court, Justice Kennedy ruled that the First Amendment recognized no category of knowing falsehood that was completely excluded from protection.[294] Subjecting the statute to strict scrutiny, he held further that a criminal prohibition on uttering falsehoods in this particular context lacked a sufficient causal link to the government's interest in protecting the integrity of military honours, and that the government's purpose could have been achieved through less restrictive means, specifically through more truthful speech.[295] In his concurrence, Justice Breyer employed an intermediate level of scrutiny[296] and similarly thought that lies were not categorically excluded from protection.[297] In particular, he thought that the statute was overly broad and that it lacked limiting features that would confine it to a 'subset of lies where specific harm is more likely to occur'.[298]

In his dissent, Justice Alito endorsed a categorical exception from First Amendment protection for knowing falsehoods, which in his view had no intrinsic value.[299] Such falsehoods could, however, still be protected incidentally if the relevant statute created significant chilling effects on speech otherwise entitled to protection.[300] In his view that was not the case with the Stolen Valor Act, which was precise and dealt with a specific issue.[301] However, Justice Alito concluded that the danger of chilling effects on debate on matters of public interest warranted a categorical rule. In his words:

> there are broad areas in which any attempt by the state to penalize purportedly false speech would present a grave and unacceptable danger of suppressing truthful speech. Laws restricting false statements about philosophy, religion, history, the social sciences, the arts, and other matters of public concern would present such a threat. The point is not that there is no such thing as truth or falsity in these areas or that the truth is always impossible to ascertain, but

---

[293] US Supreme Court, *United States v. Alvarez* 567 U.S. 709, 28 June 2012.
[294] Ibid., 718–722 (Kennedy J, whom Roberts CJ and Ginsburg and Sotomayor JJ joined).
[295] Ibid., 724–730.
[296] Ibid., 730–732 (Breyer J, whom Kagan J joined).
[297] Ibid., 733: 'False factual statements can serve useful human objectives, for example: in social contexts, where they may prevent embarrassment, protect privacy, shield a person from prejudice, provide the sick with comfort, or preserve a child's innocence; in public contexts, where they may stop a panic or otherwise preserve calm in the face of danger; and even in technical, philosophical and scientific contexts, where (as Socrates' methods suggest) examination of a false statement (even if made deliberately to mislead) can promote a form of thought that ultimately helps realize the truth.'
[298] Ibid., 736.
[299] Ibid., 746–750 (Alito J, whom Scalia and Thomas JJ joined).
[300] Ibid., 751.
[301] Ibid., 752: 'In stark contrast to hypothetical laws prohibiting false statements about history, science, and similar matters, the Stolen Valor Act presents no risk at all that valuable speech will be suppressed. The speech punished by the Act is not only verifiably false and entirely lacking in intrinsic value, but it also fails to serve any instrumental purpose that the First Amendment might protect.'

rather that it is perilous to permit the state to be the arbiter of truth ... the potential for abuse of power in these areas is simply too great.[302]

In sum, four justices thought that knowing falsehoods were not substantially different from truthful speech in terms of the level of protection that should be afforded. Two justices thought they were still protected, but less valuable and therefore subject to a less searching scrutiny in assessing justifications for restricting it. Three justices thought that knowing falsehoods should not enjoy any protection except to the extent necessary to prevent chilling effects on truthful speech in certain topics of public concern.

The European Court is yet to authoritatively rule on the degree of protection to be afforded to knowingly false speech.[303] But it is unlikely that the Court or other international human rights bodies will find lies to be categorically excluded from protection; such an approach has so far been reserved for very extreme types of expression, such as child pornography[304] and, in some European Court cases, for Holocaust denial.[305] In particular it seems difficult to make such an exclusion regardless of the nature of the harmful consequences of knowingly false expression, and regardless of whether these consequences were intended or not. At least theoretically, misinformation, whether through the withholding of accurate information or through outright lies, could in some cases be motivated by a desire to *prevent* socially harmful consequences, such as panic or disorder.[306] And disinformation may not do any harm. But deliberate or knowing falsehoods would presumably enjoy a lesser degree of protection than an innocent, negligent or reckless falsehood.[307]

This prediction is supported by the limited existing jurisprudence. For example, in a case against Ukraine in which an individual was convicted for spreading misinformation that a presidential candidate in an election had died and was being impersonated, the European Court found the conviction disproportionate in part because:

[t]he domestic courts failed to prove that he was *intentionally trying to deceive* other voters and to impede their ability to vote during the 1999 presidential elections. Furthermore, Article 10 of the Convention as such does not prohibit discussion or dissemination of information received

---

[302] Ibid., 751–752.
[303] See European Parliament, The fight against disinformation and the right to freedom of expression (2021), 24–26. Cf. ch. 6 (Terrorism), s. III.3.3 (Intent) (regarding the European Union's decision to sanction Russia state media on the basis that Russian media outlets were broadcasting 'massive propaganda and disinformation').
[304] See IACmHR, *The Inter-American Legal Framework Regarding the Right to Freedom of Expression* (2009) OEA/Ser.L/V/II CIDH/RELE/INF. 2/09, §60. For an extensive analysis of whether pornography generally should be protected by the freedom of expression, see E. Barendt, *Freedom of Speech* (2nd edn, OUP 2007), 352–391.
[305] See s. III.2.2. (What objectives can justify the penalization of false speech?) and ch. 3 (Hate Speech), s. III.2.2. (Legitimacy).
[306] See, e.g., US Supreme Court, *United States v. Alvarez* 567 U.S. 709, 28 June 2012, 733: 'False factual statements can serve useful human objectives, for example ... in public contexts, where they may stop a panic or otherwise preserve calm in the face of danger'.
[307] See IACmHR, *The Inter-American Legal Framework Regarding the Right to Freedom of Expression* (2009) OEA/Ser.L/V/II CIDH/RELE/INF. 2/09, §113: 'even if the stated facts (for example, the commission of a crime) cannot be proven in a trial, the individual who made the statements in question will be protected as long as he or she had no prior knowledge of the falsity of the statement or did not act with grave negligence (total disregard for the truth)'. See also J. Rowbottom, 'Lies, Manipulation and Elections—Controlling False Campaign Statements' (2012) 32 *Oxford Journal of Legal Studies* 507, 521.

even if it is strongly suspected that this information might not be truthful. To suggest otherwise would deprive persons of the right to express their views and opinions about statements made in the mass media and would thus place an unreasonable restriction on the freedom of expression set forth in Article 10 of the Convention.[308]

To conclude, the culpability element of a misinformation offence is one of the most important factors in assessing its proportionality and by extension its compliance with 'necessity' requirements in international law. Offences that do not incorporate demanding *mens rea* standards, such as a requirement of knowing falsehood or intention to deceive, are less likely to satisfy this test.

4. Exclusions, Exceptions and Defences

Many legal systems consider defences as simply a negation of one of the constituent elements of a crime.[309] Others may provide some additional, affirmative grounds which a defendant may raise in response to particular claim or charge.[310] Possible defences to misinformation offences, in addition to lack of proof of a necessary element, include: (1) truth, since the factual predicate for any such offence is that the information at issue was false;[311] (2) opinion, on the basis that at least some such statements cannot be true or false. In addition: (3) the political or 'public interest' subject-matter of the speech; and, according to the European Court, (4) 'responsible journalism' by a 'public watchdog' may mean that speech either cannot be sanctioned or will enjoy a higher degree of protection.

4.1. Truth

International law provides that truth should be an absolute defence in the context of defamation laws.[312] But truth and falsity may be a matter of degree. The European Court in particular has recognized that 'substantial truth', as opposed to 'exact truth' should be a sufficient basis to avoid liability in civil defamation cases.[313] For example, in a case involving a newspaper that published accounts of patients who were dissatisfied with their cosmetic surgery, the Court found a violation of article 10 by placing 'considerable weight' on the fact that the accounts were 'essentially correct'.[314] The Court has

---

[308] ECtHR, *Salov v. Ukraine* (App. no. 65518/01), 6 September 2005, §113 (emphasis added).
[309] See s.II.1.4 (Exclusions; exceptions and defences). See, e.g., W. R. LaFave, *Criminal Law* (5th edn, West Academic Publishing 2010), 469, §9.1.
[310] Ibid.
[311] See Colombian Constitutional Court, *Tutela judgment T-293/2018* 8 May 2017, §§5.1–5.3 (extensively discussing the *exceptio veritatis* as a general defence in criminal law).
[312] See ch. 2 (Insulting Speech), s. III.4.1. (Truth). See, e.g., HRC, General Comment No. 34 (2011), §47; HRC, *Adonis v. The Philippines* (Comm. no. 1815/2008), 26 October 2011, §7.9; ECtHR, *Castells v. Spain* (App. no. 11798/85), 23 April 1992, §48; ECtHR, *Colombani v. France* (App. No. 51279/99), 25 June 2002, §66; IACmHR, Declaration of Principles on Freedom of Expression (2000), Principle 7; ACmHPR, Declaration of Principles on Freedom of Expression and Access to Information in Africa (2019), Principles 21.
[313] See, e.g., ECtHR, *Bergens Tidende v. Norway* (App. no. 26132/95), 2 May 2000, §56.
[314] Ibid.

generally required that there is a 'sufficiently accurate and reliable factual basis proportionate to the nature and degree of the ... statements and allegations'.[315]

International bodies have also found that an honest or reasonable belief in the truth of a statement should be a defence in contexts beyond defamatory speech. For example the authenticity of leaked official secrets was a key aspect of the leading European Court case of *Bucur and Toma v. Romania,* which considered disclosure of an unlawful wiretapping operation by a whistleblower in Romania.[316] The Court ultimately found a violation of the right to freedom of expression, noting the whistleblower 'had reasonable grounds to believe that the information disclosed was true'.[317] Soft law instruments regarding unauthorized disclosures also recommend a defence of truth.[318] And the UN Special Rapporteur has recommended that no one should be penalized under hate speech laws 'for statements that are true'.[319] In the context of misinformation laws, establishing that a statement is not true should be proved by a prosecutor as an element of any criminal offence.

4.2. Opinion

Since the *Lingens* judgment of the European Court,[320] international human rights bodies have repeatedly affirmed the distinction between statements of opinion and fact, holding that only the latter can be restricted on the basis of their falsity.[321]

That case law was principally developed in the defamation context,[322] but it can be applied to the regulation of false statements more broadly. And it is undoubtedly correct as a matter of principle. There *is* a fundamental difference between a statement claiming that Barack Obama was a bad president and one claiming that he was born in Kenya, and therefore ineligible to be president. There is a difference between a claim that Christianity is the best of all religions and an assertion that the Earth is flat. There is a difference between a claim that the state should not impose lockdowns and one that the novel coronavirus has not led to any deaths. Only the latter are statements of fact that are capable of objective proof.

---

[315] ECtHR, *Monica Macovei v. Romania* (App. no. 53028/14), 28 July 2020, §89; ECtHR, *Reznik v. Russia* (App. no. 4977/05), 4 April 2013, §46; ECtHR, *Rungainis v. Latvia* (App. no. 40597/08), 14 June 2018, §63.
[316] ECtHR, *Bucur v. Romania* (App. no. 40238/02), 8 January 2013.
[317] Ibid., §§107–113, 117–118.
[318] See ch. 5 (Espionage and Official Secrets Laws), s. III.5.3. (Truth); ACmHPR, Declaration of Principles of Freedom of Expression and Access to Information in Africa (2019), Principle 35; Tshwane Principles, Principle 38.
[319] UN Special Rapporteur F. La Rue, *Promotion and protection of the right to freedom of opinion and expression* (2012) UN Doc. A/67/357, §50 (citing the 2001 Joint Statement on Racism and the Media).
[320] ECtHR, *Lingens v. Austria* (App. no. 9815/82), 8 July 1986, §46: 'a careful distinction needs to be made between facts and value-judgments. The existence of facts can be demonstrated, whereas the truth of value-judgments is not susceptible of proof... As regards value-judgments this requirement is impossible of fulfilment, and it infringes freedom of opinion itself.'
[321] See HRC, General Comment No. 34 (2011), §47; ACmHPR, Declaration of Principles on Freedom of Expression and Access to Information in Africa (2019), Principle 21(1); OAS Special Rapporteur, *The Inter-American Legal Framework Regarding the Right to Freedom of Expression* (2009) OEA/Ser.L/V/II CIDH/RELE/INF. 2/09, §109. See also IACtHR, *Usón Ramírez v. Venezuela* (Series C, no. 207), 20 November 2009, §86; IACtHR, *Tristán Donoso v. Panamá* (Series C, no. 193), 27 January 2009, §124.
[322] See, e.g., ECtHR (GC), *Morice v. France* (App. no. 29369/10), 23 April 2015; ECtHR (GC), *Bladet Tromsø v. Norway* (App. no. 21980/93), 20 May 1999.

Whether a statement is qualified as an assertion of fact or of opinion will depend not simply on the words used, but also on the overall context in which the statement was made.[323] In defamation cases the European Court has held that mixed statements of fact and opinion enjoy a greater degree of protection than plain assertions of fact[324] and in some cases it has required the showing of a sufficient factual basis or link between the facts and their evaluation.[325] Similarly, mixed statements of opinion and fact can be used as *satire*, 'a form of artistic expression and social commentary which, by its inherent features of exaggeration and distortion of reality, naturally aims to provoke and agitate. Accordingly, any interference with the right to use this means of expression should be examined with particular care'.[326] The type of statement at issue (opinion or mixed statement of fact/opinion) as well as its tone (satirical or humorous) may therefore either make speech inappropriate for regulation or grant it a higher degree of protection under international law.

4.3. Public interest and 'responsible journalism'

Speech that is 'political' or deals with a matter that is in the 'public interest' is entitled to greater protection than speech that is not.[327] In assessing false speech in the context of defamation laws, the Human Rights Committee has made clear that public interest in the subject matter of a criticism 'should be recognized as a defense'.[328] Similarly, the European Court has emphasized that state restrictions on speech that are 'capable of discouraging the participation of the press in debates over matters of legitimate public concern' call for the 'most careful scrutiny'.[329] The Inter-American Court also provides heightened protection to speech regarding public officials or individuals who perform public services.[330] Conversely, the European Court is also clear that commercial speech enjoys a lower degree of protection, such as in the context of state regulation of advertising, which often relates to the accuracy of the information being conveyed.[331]

The situation is more complex when it comes to speech that is simultaneously commercial and deals with matters of public interest, for example paid political advertising. The European Court has given these mixed kinds of speech an intermediate level of

---

[323] ECtHR (GC), *Morice v. France* (App. no. 29369/10), 23 April 2015, §126.
[324] For a particularly good example, see ECtHR, *Monica Macovei v. Romania* (App. no. 53028/14), 28 July 2020, §89.
[325] See, e.g., ECtHR, *Jerusalem v. Austria* (App. no. 26958/95), 27 February 2001, §43; ECtHR, *Feldek v. Slovakia* (App. no. 29032/95), 12 July 2001, §86. See ch. 2 (Insulting Speech) on this issue.
[326] ECtHR, *Ziembiński v. Poland (No. 2)* (App. no. 1799/07), 5 July 2016, §§44–45.
[327] See also HRC, General Comment No. 34 (2011), §§2–3; UN Special Rapporteur A. Ligabo, *Civil and Political Rights, Including the Question of Freedom of Expression* (2006) UN Doc. E/CN.4/2006/55, §47; ECtHR, *Lingens v. Austria* (App. no. 9815/82), 8 July 1986, §§41–42; ECtHR, *Ärztekammer für Wien and Dorner v. Austria* (App. no. 8895/10), 16 February 2016, §§65–66; IACmHR, *The Inter-American Legal Framework Regarding the Right to Freedom of Expression* (2009) OEA/Ser.L/V/II CIDH/RELE/INF. 2/09, §§8, 32, 99–101.
[328] HRC, General Comment No. 34 (2011), §47. See also HRC, *Kozlov v. Belarus* (Comm. no. 1986/2010), 24 July 2014, §§7.5–7.6 ('public interest in the subject matter of a criticism is a factor to be taken into account when considering allegations of defamation').
[329] ECtHR, *Tønsbergs Blad A.S. v. Norway* (App. no. 510/04), 1 March 2007, §88.
[330] IACtHR, *Ricardo Canese v. Paraguay* (Series C, no. 111), 31 August 2004, §§96–98; IACtHR, *Álvarez Ramos v. Venezuela* (Series C, no. 380), 30 August 2019, §§121, 124.
[331] See ECtHR, *Ärztekammer für Wien and Dorner v. Austria* (App. no. 8895/10), 16 February 2016, §§65–66. For an extensive discussion, see Barendt (n 304) 392–416.

protection, and has accepted, for example, the proportionality of comprehensive, viewpoint-neutral bans on political advertising in the broadcast media.[332]

Some legal systems may employ dedicated defences for journalists, which exclude liability for false speech if the statement was made in the course of certain journalistic activities.[333] This is also reflected in the concept of 'responsible journalism' in the case law of the European Court, which affords 'increased protection' to speech by 'public watchdogs' and particularly the press because these speakers have a duty to impart information and ideas 'on all matters of public interest'.[334] The Court has indeed found that when freedom of the press is at stake, authorities have a limited margin of appreciation to decide that a 'pressing social need' for restrictions exists.[335] But the Court has also made clear that the press must not 'overstep certain bounds': they do not have an unfettered right to claim immunity from criminal liability because an offence was committed during the performance of journalistic activities.[336] The additional protection offered to the press is, according to the Court, therefore '*subject to the proviso* that they act in good faith to provide accurate and reliable information in accordance with the tenets of responsible journalism'.[337] And this conditional protection has also been applied to other speakers, such as human rights activists, NGOs and whistleblowers who engage in public debate.[338] Under this doctrine, whether or not a journalist acted 'responsibly' is assessed on the basis of the content of the information which is collected and disseminated by journalistic means as well as the process of publication.[339]

This doctrine has, however, not been relied upon by UN human rights bodies to decide cases involving freedom of expression, nor has it been adopted by other regional human rights courts, which have addressed misinformation by journalists based on the same considerations as other speakers: harm, culpability, whether the speech was political or related to a matter of public interest.[340]

In the context of misinformation laws, the nature of the speech and the existence of dedicated affirmative defences are tightly interwoven with how a misinformation offence defines the culpability of the speaker. If the mental elements of a misinformation offence are appropriately exacting (such as knowledge of the falsity of the speech plus intent to bring about the prohibited harm), then there appears to be little room for

---

[332] But not without controversy—see especially the judgment of a divided European Court in ECtHR (GC), *Animal Defenders International v. United Kingdom* (App. no. 48876/08), 22 April 2013, §123 ('allowing a somewhat wider margin of appreciation than that normally afforded to restrictions on expressions on matters of public interest'). See also Barendt (n 304) 444–445.
[333] See ch. 2 (Insulting Speech), s. II.1.4.3. (Reasonable publication).
[334] See, e.g., ECtHR (GC), *Fressoz v. France* (App. no. 29183/95), 21 January 1999, §45(ii); ECtHR (GC), *Pedersen v. Denmark* (App. no. 49017/99), 17 December 2004, §71.
[335] ECtHR, Guide on Article 10 of the European Convention on Human Rights—Freedom of Expression, 31 August 2022, §299.
[336] ECtHR, *De Haes v. Belgium* (App. no. 19983/92), 24 February 1997, §37; ECtHR (GC), *Bladet Tromsø v. Norway* (App. no. 21980/93), 20 May 1999, §62; ECtHR, *Thoma v. Luxembourg* (App. no. 38432/97), 29 March 2001, §45.
[337] See, e.g., ECtHR, *Kącki v. Poland* (App. no. 10947/11), 4 July 2017, §§48–49.
[338] ECtHR (GC), *Magyar Helsinki Bizottság v. Hungary* (App. no. 18030/11), 8 November 2016, §159; ECtHR, *Gawlik v. Liechtenstein* (App. no. 23922/19), 16 February 2021, §77.
[339] See ch. 1 (Introduction), s. II.3.2.5. (Relevance of whether the speaker is a journalist); see ch. 2 (Insulting Speech), s. III.4.3. (Reasonable publication).
[340] See ch. 1 (Introduction), s. II.3.2.5. (Relevance of whether the speaker is a journalist).

a 'public interest' defence. If a speaker knows that their speech is false, and intends or foresees that the false speech will cause a specific harm, it will be difficult for the speaker to convincingly argue that the speech was nonetheless in the public interest or that they were acting as a 'responsible journalist'. If, however, the *mens rea* requirement is at the lower end of the spectrum, such as negligence, then such exceptions or defences may have a role to play, by analogy to the defamation context.[341]

5. Penalties

5.1. Criminal

The severity of a criminal penalty is crucial, and in some cases dispositive,[342] in determining whether a penalty on false speech complies with international human rights standards.[343]

International courts and human rights bodies have made clear that criminal penalties for speech are proportionate only exceptionally. The Human Rights Committee has approved of criminal penalties for speech in only a handful of cases.[344] And in a concurring opinion in *Rabbae v. The Netherlands,* two Committee members urged 'great caution in the imposition of criminal penalties that punish speech', proposing that criminal penalties should be limited to speech 'that incites the commission of criminal offences or acts of violence'.[345]

The Inter-American Court has found criminal penalties compatible with article 13 of the American Convention in a single case, considered by many to be an outlier.[346] Similarly, the African Court has held that custodial sentences for speech will only be lawful in 'serious and very exceptional circumstances' such as 'incitement to international crimes, public incitement to hatred, discrimination or violence or threats

---

[341] See ch. 2 (Insulting Speech), s. II.1.4. (Exclusions, exceptions and defences).

[342] See ECtHR, *Kasabova v. Bulgaria* (App. no. 22385/03), 19 April 2011, §§69–71 (violation solely because of the excessive penalty (fine plus damages in criminal defamation)).

[343] See ECtHR, *Salov v. Ukraine* (App. no. 65518/01), 6 September 2005, §115 (five years of imprisonment for spreading electoral misinformation a 'very severe penalty'); ECtHR, *Alekhina v. Russia* (App. no. 38004/12), 17 July 2018, §215 ('very severe' punishment of imprisonment imposed due to a protest in a church); §221 (noting that it was 'the interplay between the various factors involved rather than any one of them taken in isolation that determined the outcome' of the proportionality analysis); §229 (concluding that criminal punishment was disproportionate, particularly 'bearing in mind the exceptional seriousness of the sanctions involved').

[344] HRC, *Kim v. Republic of Korea* (Comm. no. 968/2001), 27 July 2005, §8.3; HRC, *Faurisson v. France* (Comm. no. 550/1993), 8 November 1996, §9.7; HRC, *A.K. and A.R. v. Uzbekistan* (Comm. no. 1233/2003), 31 March 2009, §7.2; see ch. 1 (Introduction), s. II.3.1.6. (Criminal penalties for speech).

[345] HRC, *Rabbae v. The Netherlands* (Comm. no. 2124/2011), 14 July 2016, Individual concurring opinion of Committee members Sarah Cleveland and Mauro Politi, §§7–8. Cf. HRC, *Ross v. Canada* (Comm. no. 736/1997), 18 October 2000, §§11.1–11.6.

[346] IACtHR, *Mémoli v. Argentina* (Series C, no. 265), 22 August 2013, §§141, 143, 148–149. The judgment has been described as a 'regression' by Catalina Botero-Marino, Special Rapporteur for Freedom of Expression for the Commission from 2008 to 2014: see, C. Botero-Marino, 'The Role of the Inter-American Human Rights System in the Emergence and Development of Global Norms on Freedom of Expression', in L. Bollinger & A. Callamard (eds), *Regardless of Frontiers* (Columbia University Press 2021), 193. See also E. Bertoni, 'Setbacks and Tension in the Inter-American Court of Human Rights' (Media Defence, 1 December 2013) (deeming the decision a 'serious and notable setback').

against a person or a group of people, because of specific criteria such as race, colour, religion and nationality'.[347]

Although the European Court has sometimes allowed criminal penalties in broader circumstances, the Court has nonetheless held that in any given case it 'must be satisfied that the penalty does not amount to a form of censorship intended to discourage the press from expressing criticism' or is 'likely to deter journalists from contributing to public discussion of issues affecting the life of the community'.[348] And it has noted that even when imprisonment is not imposed, 'the fact of a person's [criminal] conviction may in some cases be more important than the minor nature of the penalty imposed'.[349]

In the defamation context, UN Special Rapporteurs, the Working Group on Arbitrary Detention, the ECOWAS Court, the African Commission on Human and Peoples' Rights and the OSCE have all taken the position that any criminal penalty for defamation violates the right to freedom of expression.[350] Similarly the Human Rights Committee, the Council of Europe, Inter-American bodies and the African Court have each held that *imprisonment* is 'never an appropriate penalty' for defamatory speech, which is by definition false.[351]

The European Court has however been willing to accept criminal sanctions, though never imprisonment, for defamation at least, partly as a result of the margin of appreciation doctrine.[352] The Court has repeatedly found that in view of this doctrine, 'a criminal measure as a response to defamation cannot, as such, be considered disproportionate to the aim pursued'.[353] But it has applied 'strict scrutiny', the 'most careful scrutiny' and 'utmost caution' when assessing criminal sanctions imposed for defamation,[354] and noted that the authorities [must] show 'restraint in resorting to criminal proceedings' when dealing with speech.[355]

---

[347] ACtHPR, *Konaté v. Burkina Faso* (App. no. 004/2013), 5 December 2014, §165.
[348] ECtHR (GC), *Bédat v. Switzerland* (App. no. 56925/08), 29 March 2016, §79. See also ECtHR, *Toranzo Gomez v. Spain* (App. no. 26922/14), 20 November 2018, §64; ECtHR, *Lewandowska-Malec v. Poland* (App. no. 39660/07), 18 September 2012, §70.
[349] ECtHR (GC), *Bédat v. Switzerland* (App. no. 56925/08), 29 March 2016, §79. See also ECtHR (GC), *Stoll v. Switzerland* (App. no. 69698/01), 10 December 2007, §154; ECtHR, *Haldimann v. Switzerland* (App. no. 21830/09), 24 February 2015, §67.
[350] See ch. 2 (Insulting Speech), s. III.6.1. (Criminal penalties). See, e.g., UN Special Rapporteur D. Kaye, *Disease pandemics and the freedom of opinion and expression* (2020) UN Doc. A/HRC/44/49, §40; WGAD, *Maseko v. Swaziland* (Opinion no. 6/2015), 22 April 2015, §27; WGAD, *Amer v. Egypt* (Opinion no. 35/2008), 20 November 2008, §§33, 36; ECOWAS CCJ, *Federation of African Journalists v. The Gambia* (Suit no. ECW/CCJ/APP/36/15), 13 February 2018, 40, 47–48; OSCE Parliamentary Assembly Warsaw Declaration, 8 July 1997, §140; ACmHPR, Resolution on Repealing Criminal Defamation Laws in Africa (Res.169 (XLVIII) 10), 24 November 2010.
[351] HRC, General Comment No. 34 (2011), §47; Parliamentary Assembly of the Council of Europe, Towards decriminalisation of defamation (Resolution 1577) 04 October 2007, §17.1; IACtHR, *Álvarez Ramos v. Venezuela* (Series C, no. 380), 30 August 2019, §§120–121; ACtHPR, *Konaté v. Burkina Faso* (App. no. 004/2013), 5 December 2014, §165.
[352] See ch. 2 (Insulting speech), s. III.6.1. (Criminal penalties). See ch. 1 (Introduction), s. II.3. (Jurisprudence).
[353] See, e.g., ECtHR (GC), *Lindon, Otchakovsky-Laurens and July v. France* (App. nos. 21279/02 & 36448/02), 22 October 2007, §59; ECtHR, *Radio France v. France* (App. no. 53984/00), 30 March 2004, §40; T. McGonagle, *Freedom of Expression and Defamation: A study of the case law of the European Court of Human Rights* (COE 2016), 18.
[354] McGonagle (ibid.) 57.
[355] See, e.g., ECtHR, *Castells v. Spain* (App. no. 11798/85), 23 April 1992, §46; ECtHR (GC), *Incal v. Turkey* (App. no. 22678/93), 9 June 1998, §54; ECtHR (GC), *Öztürk v. Turkey* (App. no. 22479/93), 28 September 1999, §66.

In one of its key decisions on misinformation, the European Court assessed speech by a presidential candidate who published false information suggesting that the incumbent had died.[356] The Court considered that a five-year sentence, suspended for two years, as well as a fine and disbarment as a lawyer 'constituted a very severe penalty', and that the conviction and penalties were 'manifestly disproportionate' to the legitimate aim pursued.[357]

In the context of misinformation offences, the proportionality of a penalty should always be measured against the specific harm that the misinformation caused, or was objectively likely to cause, and the culpability of the offender.[358] Although international standards relating to penalties for defamation may apply to misinformation laws in some circumstances, it would be difficult to adopt the same categorical approach to misinformation offences in all contexts. This is because misinformation offences could be designed to remedy other, more pressing harms than reputation, such as the protection of human life or health. There could, in other words, be cases in which imprisonment is a proportionate sentence for a misinformation offence that deals with certain serious harms, but only if it complies with international human rights standards on culpability, causation, and the type, severity, foreseeability and imminence of harms that can justify restrictions on speech.[359] This will inevitably be a very narrow category of cases.

5.2. Civil

Defamation is essentially a sub-species of misinformation; civil defamation is also the only private tort that is of systemic relevance to how misinformation should be regulated by a state. It is certainly possible for tort law to apply to harms caused by misinformation—for example, a person seriously injured as a result of a false statement during the Covid-19 pandemic, say that drinking bleach would cure the virus, could conceivably sue the utterer of that statement for damages.[360] So could a person defrauded out of their money by misinformation peddling false cures for the virus.[361] But tort law or private law is not generally used in comparative practice to systemically regulate misinformation.

Far more consequential are the various administrative mechanisms that the state has at its disposal to regulate speech, offline or online, which are often buttressed by the ability to impose fines, mandate the removal or correction of published content or close down media outlets.[362] This type of regulation of false speech is not the focus

---

[356] ECtHR, *Salov v. Ukraine* (App. no. 65518/01), 6 September 2005.
[357] Ibid., §§115–116. See s. III.2. (Legitimacy).
[358] See, e.g., Human Rights Council Resolution 44/12 on freedom of opinion and expression, 16 July 2020, 2.
[359] See further, s. III.3. (Necessity).
[360] See D. Reiss & J. Diamond, 'Tort Law: Liability for Anti-Vaccine Misinformation' (2020) 4 *The Judges' Book* 107–108 (discussing the use of tort law to provide remedy 'to people harmed by disease outbreaks when the outbreak generally, or the specific harm can be fairly traced to misinformation').
[361] UN Special Rapporteur D. Kaye, *Disease pandemics and the freedom of opinion and expression* (2020) UN Doc. A/HRC/44/49, §46 (citing the use of consumer protection laws against false information regarding cures for Covid-19). Other relevant examples could be torts or delicts such as invasion of privacy or the intentional infliction of emotional distress, all of which could involve false statements of some kind.
[362] See HRC, General Comment No. 34 (2011), §39 (on the various State regulatory measures on media).

of our analysis, but we note that any administrative penalties need to comply with the essence of the principles articulated in this chapter. In particular, severe fines or the shutting down of media outlets should require higher degrees of culpability and causality, in order to limit impacts on speakers and the chilling effects of such serious penalties.[363] This is because, as rightly explained by the Venice Commission, 'excessively high fines pose a threat with almost as much chilling effect as imprisonment, albeit more insidious'.[364]

The Human Rights Committee has also held that the proportionality of civil penalties for speech may differ depending on how it is disseminated, including by 'tak[ing] into account the differences between the print and broadcast sectors and the internet'.[365] Recent research has indicated, for instance, that falsehoods spread faster than the truth online, at least partly due to the novelty of misinformation and the emotional reactions that it provokes in its recipients,[366] and online falsehoods may be more difficult to correct.

IV. Recommendations

The following recommendations are based on minimum international human rights standards applicable to misinformation and—where there is a divergence or lacuna in such standards—a suggestion as to best practice drawn from national systems or emerging international standards. Our recommendations apply cumulatively: in other words, they should all be implemented for misinformation laws to meet international legal or best practice standards. As an example, it would not be sufficient for a law to comply with minimum international standards when it comes to defining the intent or fault of the speaker if the required type and severity and imminence of harm created by the speech is not established.

The recommendations are addressed to states because states have ratified the international treaties that underlie international standards. They can, however, also guide private companies, especially digital platforms, seeking to apply international standards in line with the UN Guiding Principles on Business and Human Rights, although their ability to regulate false speech is broader and not confined only to the most severe types of misinformation that may warrant criminalization by states.[367]

---

[363] IACmHR Special Rapporteur E. Lanza, *Childhood, freedom of expression, and the media in the Americas* (2019) OEA/Ser. L/V/II CIDH/RELE/INF.13/19, §145: 'economic penalties should be proportionate to their potential harm to freedom of expression and should not be arbitrary or disproportionate or have a general chilling effect'. See also UN Special Rapporteur D. Kaye, *Letter dated 1 May 2019*, Ref OL RUS 4/2019, 5 (noting the disproportionate effects of 'crippling monetary penalties').
[364] Venice Commission, *Opinion on the Legislation on Defamation of Italy* (2013) CDL-AD(2013)038, §62.
[365] HRC, General Comment No. 34 (2011), §39.
[366] See S. Vosoughi & others, 'The Spread of True and False News Online' (2018) 359 *Science* 1146; A. Acerbi, 'Cognitive Attraction and Online Misinformation' (2019) 5 *Palgrave Communications* 1.
[367] See ch. 3 (Hate Speech), s. V. (Approach of Private Companies to Online Hate Speech).

1. Criminal penalties for false speech should be a last resort. Where possible, state authorities should employ alternative means to prevent or mitigate harm caused by such speech.

Under international law, laws that penalize speech must be 'the least intrusive instrument amongst those which might achieve their protective function'.[368] This means that states cannot restrict harmful false speech through force of law if there are less restrictive means that could achieve the same goals, such as by providing more accurate information.[369] Indeed, the primary remedy for untruthful speech should be more truthful speech.[370]

States should take all feasible steps 'to ensure that they disseminate reliable and trustworthy information, including about matters of public interest, such as the economy, public health, security and the environment'.[371] This should include long-term measures such as promoting media and digital literacy, covering these topics as part of the regular school curriculum and taking other steps to raise awareness about these issues and help people identify what is false and where to access reliable data.[372]

An example of a successful campaign to combat misinformation without the use of legal penalties comes from South Korea, where health officials successfully combated misinformation around a 2020 national flu vaccination campaign by providing transparent information that created trust in a vaccine.[373] Similarly, following a drop in HPV vaccinations due to misinformation, Danish authorities collaborated with newspapers, magazines and social media to increase confidence in that vaccine.[374]

Of course, misinformation can affect states, or segments of societies within states, in different ways. Some states may have a prevalence of health-related misinformation, whereas others are dealing with election-related misinformation or a flood of false speech related to a minority group. In some states the traditional media might still be dominant, whereas in others its importance may have been eclipsed by social media.

---

[368] HRC, General Comment No. 34 (2011), §34.
[369] Human Rights Council Resolution 44/12 on freedom of opinion and expression, 16 July 2020, 2: '[R]esponses to the spread of disinformation and misinformation must be grounded in international human rights law, including the principles of lawfulness, legitimacy, necessity and proportionality [with the Council underlining] the importance of free, independent, plural and diverse media and of providing and promoting access to independent, fact-based and science-based information to counter disinformation and misinformation'.
[370] US Supreme Court, *United States v. Alvarez* 567 U.S. 709, 28 June 2012, 727: 'The remedy for speech that is false is speech that is true. This is the ordinary course in a free society'. See also OAS Special Rapporteur, 'Guide to guarantee freedom of expression regarding deliberate disinformation in electoral contexts' (October 2019), 25 ('there is no better response to an opinion formed on the wrong basis or false information than an opposing or correct opinion or true information').
[371] UN Special Rapporteur, OSCE Representative on Freedom of the Media, OAS Special Rapporteur and ACmHPR Special Rapporteur on Freedom of Expression and Access to Information, *Joint Declaration on Freedom of Expression and 'Fake News', Disinformation and Propaganda* (2017) FOM.GAL/3/17, §2(d).
[372] Ibid., §3(e).
[373] C. Sang-Hun & D. Grady, 'How South Korea's Flu Vaccine Scare Offers Lessons for Other Nations' (The New York Times, 24 November 2020).
[374] World Health Organization, 'Denmark campaign rebuilds confidence in HPV vaccination' (27 February 2018).

Instead of seeking legislative one-size-fits-all solutions, states should pursue measures that are most effective to address harmful misinformation in each given context.

State authorities should also conduct regular evidence-based assessments to ensure that their regulation of misinformation is effective and is not serving to amplify misinformation rather than correct it.[375] Such reviews are needed as harms caused by a misinformation law can outweigh any benefits gained, or even stifle the media and public debate more generally.[376] Indeed, misinformation is most likely to proliferate in environments in which people have lost trust in governmental and other institutions due to censorship and the suppression of dissent.[377]

It is also possible for restrictions on misinformation by means of criminal law to be necessary and proportionate only temporarily.[378] For example, the proliferation of health-related misinformation during a pandemic may justify criminal punishment in certain circumstances while the pandemic lasts.[379] When the emergency subsides, such laws would no longer be necessary, and their existence could produce chilling effects on speech even if they are not used in practice.[380] Lawmakers should therefore consider using mechanisms such as sunset clauses in order to ensure that legislative responses to misinformation are limited to situations of genuine necessity.

2. Misinformation laws should not be vague or overbroad and should not grant excessive discretion to state authorities.

Misinformation laws that use ambiguous, vague or undefined terms may not be compatible with the 'legality' requirement imposed by international human rights law.[381] Criminal legislation should be drafted precisely, and at a minimum define four key elements to ensure compliance with legality requirements. First, they should define the nature of the false speech that may attract penalties.[382] Second, they should specify the prohibited consequence of the misinformation, such as harm to health or to the

---

[375] See, e.g., K. Clayton & others, 'Real Solutions for Fake News? Measuring the Effectiveness of General Warnings and Fact-Check Tags in Reducing Belief in False Stories on Social Media' (2020) 42 *Political Behavior* 1073; H. Larson, 'Blocking Information on COVID-19 Can Fuel the Spread of Misinformation' (2020) 580 *Nature* 306.

[376] UN Special Rapporteur D. Kaye, *Disease pandemics and the freedom of opinion and expression* (2020) UN Doc. A/HRC/44/49, §48: 'Measures to combat disinformation must never prevent journalists and media actors from carrying out their work or lead to content being unduly blocked on the Internet.'

[377] Larson (n 375) 306.

[378] UN Special Rapporteur I. Khan, *Disinformation and freedom of opinion and expression* (2021) UN Doc. A/HRC/47/25, §42 (noting that there may be instances where speech may be restricted to forbid propagation of falsehoods, but the restriction must be 'narrowly construed, *time-limited*, and tailored so as to avoid limiting' discourse (emphasis added)).

[379] See, e.g., 'COVID-19: States should not abuse emergency measures to suppress human rights—UN experts' (UN News, 16 March 2020). Cf. 'COVID-19: Governments must promote and protect access to and free flow of information during pandemic—International experts' (UN News, 19 March 2020) (noting that 'Any attempts to criminalise information relating to the pandemic may create distrust in institutional information, delay access to reliable information and have a chilling effect on freedom of expression').

[380] See 'Censorious governments are abusing "fake news" laws' (The Economist, 13 February 2021).

[381] See UN Special Rapporteur D. Kaye, *Disease pandemics and the freedom of opinion and expression* (2020) UN Doc. A/HRC/44/49, §44.

[382] HRC, General Comment No. 34 (2011), §34.

integrity of elections, as well as how serious and imminent such harm should be and the required causal link between the misinformation and the harm.[383] Third, the required level of the speaker's fault (*mens rea*) should be set out—for example, a requirement that the speaker knew that their speech was false and that they intended to cause specified harms through the false speech.[384] Finally, misinformation laws must also specify exclusions, protections or defences that apply—for instance the fact that truthful speech as well as opinions are always protected and that political or 'public interest' speech deserves extra protection.[385]

Existing misinformation offences that are incompatible with international standards should be amended or repealed, even if they are not applied, or are only rarely applied, in practice.[386] Even laws that are never or rarely applied can produce chilling effects on speech, and it is problematic as a matter of principle to retain laws that are never used.[387] This is especially the case with vague laws since the size of the net they cast on speech is unclear. Legislative authorities must have regard to potential chilling effects when drafting misinformation laws, and existing laws that fail to pass muster should be abolished or revised to ensure compatibility with international law.[388]

State authorities are often granted broad discretion by law, for example with regard to the time, place and manner of an arrest. Prosecutors, the police and other investigative authorities should be mindful that the manner in which these powers are exercised may create a climate of fear and stifle free debate, especially if the target of the investigation is a journalist or a media outlet, and regardless of whether the prosecution ultimately results in a conviction. The suppression of misinformation through heavy-handed action may also amplify any harm that the misinformation causes. State authorities should be instructed and trained to avoid such effects, for example with regard to the manner of arrests, interrogations, searches, other investigative steps and pre-trial detention. They should exercise any discretion granted to them by law so as to minimize such chilling effects. And independent and impartial courts should provide oversight over the exercise of such powers. In doing so, courts should interpret misinformation offences strictly in order to mitigate the negative impact of vague or overbroad provisions in these laws on freedom of speech, and if necessary and appropriate read into them limiting conditions, such as more rigorous requirements for *mens rea* or the causal nexus between the speech and the harm.

---

[383] See s. III.3. (Necessity).
[384] See s. III.3.2. (Intent).
[385] See s. III.4. (Exclusions, Exceptions and Defences).
[386] UN Special Rapporteur, OSCE Representative on Freedom of the Media, OAS Special Rapporteur and ACmHPR Special Rapporteur on Freedom of Expression and Access to Information, *Joint Declaration on Freedom of Expression and 'Fake News', Disinformation and Propaganda* (2017) FOM.GAL/3/17, §2(a); UN Special Rapporteur D. Kaye, *Disease pandemics and the freedom of opinion and expression* (2020) UN Doc. A/HRC/44/49, §49. See also HRC, General Comment No. 34 (2011), §25.
[387] See, e.g., T. Mendel, 'The Case against Criminal Defamation Laws', in A. Karlsreiter & H. Vuokko (eds), *Ending the Chilling Effect—Working to Repeal Criminal Libel and Insult Laws* (OSCE 2004), 25.
[388] UN Special Rapporteur, OSCE Representative on Freedom of the Media, OAS Special Rapporteur and ACmHPR Special Rapporteur on Freedom of Expression and Access to Information, *Joint Declaration on Freedom of Expression and 'Fake News', Disinformation and Propaganda* (2017) FOM.GAL/3/17, §2(a). See also HRC, General Comment No. 34 (2011), §25.

3. **States should not penalize speech simply on the basis that it is false. They may only impose restrictions on false speech when doing so advances an aim that is recognized as legitimate under international human rights law.**

Laws prohibiting the dissemination of false information on the basis of its falsity alone violate international human rights law.[389] Misinformation laws must advance a specific purpose recognized under international standards, namely: (a) respect for the rights or reputations of others; or (b) national security, public order or public health.[390] The Human Rights Committee has made clear that the purpose of 'maintain[ing] the integrity of the electoral process' falls within the subset of the 'protection of public order' or 'respect of the rights of others'.[391] Although 'public morals' are also a justification recognized under international human rights law, this basis is vague, anachronistic and unlikely to justify a restriction on speech today.[392]

A number of states use misinformation laws that prohibit disseminating false information without a link to any concrete harm caused by false speech, and consequently without a link to a legitimate aim that can justify restricting speech.[393] Such general misinformation laws do not comply with minimum international standards and should be repealed. The same conclusion applies to laws that criminalize misinformation to promote non-legitimate aims focused on quelling dissent or penalizing reputational 'injury' to the state, such as Oman's prohibition on 'false or malicious' news that 'undermine[s] the stature of the state'.[394] A law narrowly tailored to advancing a specific legitimate aim, such as in the electoral or public health context, is more likely to be necessary and proportionate.

Under international law, restrictions on speech 'must be applied only for those purposes for which they were prescribed and must be directly related to the specific need on which they are predicated'.[395] Even if misinformation laws comply with international standards on paper, they would violate such standards if used for ulterior purposes to suppress political debate or criticism. A review of state practice demonstrates that this

---

[389] See s. III.2. (Legitimacy); UN Special Rapporteur, OSCE Representative on Freedom of the Media, OAS Special Rapporteur and ACmHPR Special Rapporteur on Freedom of Expression and Access to Information, *Joint Declaration on Freedom of Expression and 'Fake News', Disinformation and Propaganda* (2017) FOM.GAL/3/17, §2(a): 'General prohibitions on the dissemination of information based on vague and ambiguous ideas, including "false news" or "non-objective information", are incompatible with international standards for restrictions on freedom of expression, as set out in paragraph 1(a), and should be abolished.'
[390] ICCPR Art. 19. Harms to other interests provided by article 10(2) of the European Convention, such as protecting the authority of the judiciary, fall within the scope of harms to public order: See s. III.2. (Legitimacy) and ch.1. (Introduction).
[391] HRC, General Comment No. 34 (2011), §37 citing HRC, *Kim v. Republic of Korea* (Comm. no. 968/2001), 27 July 2005, §8.3. See s. III.2. (Legitimacy).
[392] See A. Clooney & P. Webb, *The Right to a Fair Trial in International Law* (OUP 2020), Chapter 2: Right to a Public Trial, 197.
[393] See s. II.1.2. (Harm).
[394] See further s. III.2. (Legitimacy); WGAD, *Rajab v. Bahrain* (Opinion no. 13/2018), 19 April 2018, §29; WGAD, *Sheikh Suliaman al-Rashudi and others v. Saudi Arabia* (Opinion no. 38/2015), 4 September 2015, §73.
[395] HRC, General Comment No. 34 (2011), §22.

happens all too often.[396] For instance, dozens of governments used misinformation laws to clamp down on legitimate criticism of their response to the Covid-19 pandemic rather than to address the real and dangerous spread of misinformation about the pandemic.[397] Domestic courts can play an important role in ensuring that state authorities are not acting with an ulterior purpose. And best practice would not require direct proof of an ulterior purpose: indirect and circumstantial evidence, drawing inferences where necessary from contextual factors and patterns of behaviour by state authorities, should suffice and indeed is often the only available evidence.[398]

4. States should not penalize misinformation unless it is objectively likely to cause serious and direct or imminent harm; in the context of criminal laws such harm should be objectively probable and limited to incitement to violence or a serious criminal offence, endangerment of human life, or serious harm to health or the integrity of democratic elections.

States must demonstrate a link between the speech they seek to penalize and 'in specific and individualized fashion the precise nature of the threat' likely to result from such speech.[399] Drawing on existing international standards, we recommend that states may impose criminal penalties for disseminating false information if doing so (a) incites violence or a serious criminal offence,[400] (b) endangers human life or seriously harms health, or (c) seriously harms the integrity of democratic elections.[401] The protection of the reputation of the state or its organs—including the head of state, military or judiciary—is not a legitimate basis for restricting false speech.[402] Laws that criminalize 'picking quarrels and provoking trouble'[403] do not meet the international standard. And when criminalizing misinformation is justified on the basis that the speech is likely to incite a serious criminal offence, that offence must itself comply with international standards.[404] For example, offences such as sodomy laws—themselves incompatible

---

[396] See s. II.2. (Application of False Speech Laws Around the World).
[397] See s. II. (State Practice).
[398] See s. III.2.2. (What objectives can justify the penalization of false speech?).
[399] See HRC, General Comment No. 34 (2011), §35. See also UN Special Rapporteur D. Kaye, *Disease pandemics and the freedom of opinion and expression* (2020) UN Doc. A/HRC/44/49, §15.
[400] See s. III.3.1.1. (Severity and imminence of harm); HRC, *Rabbae v. The Netherlands* (Comm. no. 2124/2011), 14 July 2016, Individual Concurring Opinion of Committee members Sarah Cleveland and Mauro Politi, §4.
[401] This standard also accounts for historical bases for penalizing false speech, such as commercial fraud or medical and legal professionals misrepresenting their qualifications, on the basis that such acts would constitute serious criminal offences in many states: See ch. 1 (Introduction), s. II. (International Standards on Freedom of Speech and of the Press).
[402] HRC, General Comment No. 34 (2011), §38 ('States parties should not prohibit criticism of institutions, such as the army or the administration').
[403] G. Rui, "Picking quarrels and provoking trouble': how China's catch-all crime muzzles dissent' (South China Morning Post, 25 August 2021).
[404] See, e.g., UN Special Rapporteur I. Khan, *Disinformation and freedom of opinion and expression during armed conflicts* (2022) UN Doc. A/77/288, §38: 'Disinformation cannot be prohibited under international human rights law unless it amounts to advocacy of hatred that constitutes incitement to hostility, violence and discrimination. It may be restricted only if it meets the requirements of legality, necessity, and legitimate objectives' set out in the ICCPR.

with international human rights law—cannot be used as a legitimate basis to penalize speech likely to incite the 'crime' of being gay.[405]

5. To penalize misinformation, states should require that it is at least objectively likely that the false speech will cause serious harm that is direct or imminent. A higher standard should apply in any criminal law.

In addition to precisely defining the harm that a misinformation law seeks to remedy, a misinformation law must also specify the degree of the causal connection between the false speech and the relevant harm. This is particularly important for criminal statutes. According to the Human Rights Committee, the state must establish 'a direct and immediate connection between the expression and the threat' of harm.[406] However, the European Court has, in some cases, found that criminal penalties could be appropriate even for speech that was 'capable of' causing or 'could have' caused prohibited harms, and in some instances it has sidestepped consideration of a causal requirement entirely.[407]

A criminal statute can establish this connection between the misinformation and the harm in several different ways. The more intense the connection, the easier it is to justify the offence as a necessary and proportionate restriction on speech.

First, a statute can limit the offence to situations in which the harm *has actually occurred*, with the misinformation either being a 'but for' cause of the harm, or having causally contributed to it at some lower standard.

Second, the statute could expand the consequence element of the offence to include harms that did *not* occur, but *could have* occurred as a result of the false speech. Again, the key issue here would be in defining the degree of causal connection between the speech and the harm. A more intense requirement would be for the harm to be a *likely* consequence of the speech. A less intense requirement would impose liability for speech that was *capable* of causing or *could or may* have caused the harm. Such a low intensity requirement would be difficult to justify under international human rights law in terms of its necessity and proportionality in the absence of any such harm materializing.[408]

Third, the connection between the false speech and the harm could be described solely in terms of intention rather than causality. Thus, Qatari law punishes

---

[405] UN High Commissioner for Human Rights, *Discriminatory laws and practices and acts of violence against individuals based on their sexual orientation and gender identity* (2011) UN Doc. A/HRC/19/41, §41 ('The criminalization of private consensual homosexual acts violates an individual's rights to privacy and to non-discrimination and constitutes a breach of international human rights law').

[406] HRC, General Comment No. 34 (2011), §35. See also UN Special Rapporteur D. Kaye, *Disease pandemics and the freedom of opinion and expression* (2020) UN Doc. A/HRC/44/49, §15; ACmHPR, Declaration of Principles on Freedom of Expression in Africa (2019), Principle 9(4), Principle 22(2) requiring 'a close causal link between the risk of harm and the expression'.

[407] See s. III.3.1.2. (Causal relationship between the speech and the harm); see ch. 3 (Hate Speech), s. III.2.3.1. (Harm).

[408] See s. III.3.1.2. (Causal relationship between the speech and the harm).

misinformation uttered 'with the intention' of harming certain interests.[409] An offence that does not require *any* causal connection would be difficult to justify, since a person could be punished regardless of the fact that their speech actually caused no serious social harm and regardless of the fact that it could have been extremely unlikely for the speech to cause such harms.

Finally, a criminal misinformation law could have no stipulated connection whatsoever between expression and a specific harm, either in terms of causality or in terms of culpability. Such laws will, again, be difficult to justify, since their (implicit) goals, say that of protecting public health, could have been achieved through a more narrowly tailored law, i.e. through less restrictive means that would have had a lower chilling effect. A good example is the misinformation offence in article 207.1 of the Russian Criminal Code, which punishes the 'public dissemination, under the guise of a truthful message, of knowingly false information about circumstances that pose a threat to the life and safety of citizens, and (or) about measures taken to ensure the safety of the population and territories… from these circumstances'.[410] This offence requires no concrete harm to have occurred as the result of the misinformation, nor even for such harm to have been a likely or possible consequence thereof.[411] The crime is completed simply by the speech act, unlike the offence in article 207.2 examined above, which does require the causation of specific harm.[412]

To conclude, there is no doubt that higher-intensity causal requirements are much more likely to satisfy a necessity and proportionality analysis and to avoid having excessive chilling effects on protected speech. The dangers of the chilling effects of overbroad criminal laws punishing false speech, and of their abuse, are such that we recommend the use of high causal requirements in defining misinformation offences. At a minimum such offences should require an objective likelihood that the speech would cause direct or imminent harm. A criminal misinformation law would be easier to justify with an even higher threshold, that of false speech actually causing harm which did occur (for example, if an individual died or their health was harmed as a result of the promotion of false remedies for a disease). High causal requirements should apply alongside a sufficiently high *mens rea* standard.[413]

---

[409] See s. II.1.1. (Vagueness and overbreadth).
[410] Amnesty International, 'Russian Federation: "Fake news" bill prompted by COVID-19 threatens freedom of expression' (3 April 2020).
[411] See CFJ, 'Statement in the Conviction of Journalist Alexander Pichugin on 'Fake News' Charges in Russia' (11 November 2020) (noting that the prosecution 'made no effort to show how [the speech] posed any kind of danger to public health or public order').
[412] The offence in Art. 207.2 imposes more severe penalties on the offender: see Amnesty International, 'Russian Federation: "Fake news" bill prompted by COVID-19 threatens freedom of expression' (3 April 2020).
[413] See s. IV. (Recommendations): 'Our recommendations apply cumulatively: in other words, they should all be implemented for misinformation laws to meet international legal or best practice standards'.

6. Misinformation offences should have high culpability (*mens rea*) requirements.

The fault element of a misinformation offence is one of the most important factors in assessing its necessity and proportionality under international human rights law.[414] False speech offences that do not incorporate a *mens rea* standard—for instance a requirement of knowing falsehood or intention to deceive—would create 'strict liability' and in doing so violate not only the right to freedom of expression but also potentially the presumption of innocence as part of the right to a fair trial.[415]

Deliberate falsehoods enjoy a lesser degree of protection than innocent, negligent or reckless falsehoods, although recklessness could be sufficient to render a speaker civilly liable in certain circumstances.[416] It is particularly important that criminal laws have sufficiently stringent *mens rea* requirements if they are to be considered necessary and proportionate, and for such culpability requirements to be prescribed with regard to all constituent elements of the offence (including the falsity of the statement and the harm caused by it).[417]

A law that falls closer to the line is the offence introduced into South African law during the Covid-19 pandemic, which punishes any person 'who publishes any statement ... *with the intention to deceive* any other person about— (a) COVID-19; (b) [the] COVID-19 infection status of any person; or (c) any measure taken by the Government to address COVID-19'.[418] The *mens rea* requirement as to conduct is high—the intention to deceive—but there is no specified harm or required fault as to that harm. In other words, a person could be punished for this offence even if no concrete harm arises—or could have arisen—from the false utterance, and even if the speaker lacked any intent to bring about that harm. The fact that the incrimination extends to false statements about Covid-19 *generally* or as to any remedial measures taken by the government means that it could be applied very broadly indeed, and is unlikely to be considered proportionate by an international human rights body on that basis.[419]

It should be borne in mind that while misinformation frequently *originates* from persons acting knowingly or with an intent to cause harm (i.e. engaging in disinformation), it is most often *spread* by people who subjectively believe it to be true and intend to cause no harm. 'Many people have shared misleading or false information with well-meaning intentions.'[420] Imposing criminal liability on such individuals solely on the basis of an objectivized, negligent failure to verify facts, especially if the offence is otherwise defined quite broadly, is likely to produce substantial chilling effects on free

---

[414] See s. III.3.2. (Intent).
[415] See Clooney & Webb (n 392) Chapter 4 (The Right to be Presumed Innocent), 210.
[416] See further s. III.3.2. (Intent).; see ch. 3 (Hate Speech), s. II.1.3. (Intent).
[417] See further s. III.3.2. (Intent).
[418] South African Disaster Management Act 2020 s. 14(2).
[419] Ibid.
[420] UK Parliament, Misinformation in the COVID-19 Infodemic (2020), §6.

speech and should fail the least restrictive means limb of the justifiability test under international law.[421]

7. Decisions on arrests and criminal charges related to political speech or involving a journalist should be approved by a high-ranking official such as the Minister of Justice, Attorney-General or a senior police official or prosecutor.

Although international standards do not expressly require this, requiring an extra layer of consent from an official or at higher levels of police and prosecutorial authorities can be an important best-practice safeguard against abuse of misinformation laws that can produce chilling effects even if any charges are eventually dismissed.[422] It can also assist in ensuring consistency of approach by officials. This is particularly important given the scope for abuse when it comes to political speech, including by members of the media.

8. Misinformation laws must never penalize substantially truthful speech, or opinions, and should provide additional protection to speech that is political or in the public interest.

When *mens rea* or harm requirements—or both—are at the lower end of the permissible scale,[423] affirmative defences will be particularly important to mitigate the chilling effects of misinformation offences and render them permissible under international law.[424] Such defences should include the defences recognized in international law in the defamation context, which already apply to false speech, and adjusted where necessary.[425] All elements of a misinformation offence must be proved in court, and a defendant must have a meaningful opportunity to negate them.[426]

---

[421] An instructive example in that regard is the misinformation offence in the UK Representation of the People Act 1983 s. 106, which prohibits, before or during an election, making false statements about the 'personal character' of a candidate, and essentially does so on the basis of a negligent failure to verify facts. The main redeeming feature of the offence is that it is applied with exceptional rarity. But it is nonetheless both vague and has a very low *mens rea* requirement. For an extended discussion, see Rowbottom (n 307) 507. Contrast with far more rigorous Canadian misinformation offences discussed in s. II.1.2. (Harm).

[422] Reporters Without Borders (RSF) considers express consent must be given by an independent judicial authority, i.e., a court or an investigating judge in civil law countries. See Foreword.

[423] See s. IV.6. (Recommendations).

[424] See further s. III.4. (Exclusions, Exceptions and Defences).

[425] See ch. 2 (Insulting Speech), s. III.4. (Exclusions, Exceptions and Defences).

[426] See UN Special Rapporteur, OSCE Representative on Freedom of the Media, OAS Special Rapporteur and ACmHPR Special Rapporteur on Freedom of Expression and Access to Information, *Joint Declaration on Freedom of Expression and 'Fake News', Disinformation and Propaganda* (2017) FOM.GAL/3/17, §1(d), (h); ACmHPR, Declaration of Principles on Freedom of Expression and Access to Information in Africa (2019), Principle 9(2). See also Clooney & Webb (n 392) Chapter 4 (The Right to Prepare a Defence).

8.1. Truth

Falsity must be an element of a misinformation crime; truth should consequently always exempt a statement from liability.[427] And a defendant should always have a meaningful opportunity to negate any of the constituent elements of the offence.[428] The determination of the existence of all elements of a misinformation offence must be in the hands of an independent and impartial court.[429] This includes the determination of whether the defendant's statement was true or false.[430] The role of assessing whether speech is false should never be delegated to officials in the executive branch, as doing so creates enormous potential for abuse, and insufficient protection for speech.[431] To the extent that the court's establishment of the truth requires reliance on experts, the court must provide a reasoned explanation as to why it found the views of particular experts credible.[432] Independent criminal courts must retain control of the fact-finding process.

Substantial truth should be sufficient to exempt a statement from liability.[433] For instance, consider a scenario in which a journalist claims that a hospital ran out of personal protective equipment (PPE) during the Covid-19 pandemic. It later turns out that there was shortage of only one type of PPE, say masks, but not gloves and gowns. The original report is not true in its totality, but it is true *substantially* or *in essence*—there was in fact a shortage of a key piece of equipment, and the purpose of the report was to criticize the authorities for this shortage to hold them accountable. Or, similarly, consider a report in which a journalist claims that a politician corruptly appropriated 10 million dollars, when he in fact stole five million. The key message was to expose the corrupt behaviour of the official, not the exact amount of money that he stole. As these examples demonstrate, imposing criminal liability on individuals for speech that is not wholly true, even if it was substantially true, would not satisfy the necessity and proportionality requirements of human rights law, notwithstanding the fact that the required

---

[427] See HRC, General Comment No. 34 (2011), §47 (noting, with regard to penal defamation laws, that these 'should include such defences as the defence of truth and they should not be applied with regard to those forms of expression that are not, of their nature, subject to verification'). See s. III.4.2. (Opinion). See also UN Special Rapporteur, OSCE Representative on Freedom of the Media, OAS Special Rapporteur and ACmHPR Special Rapporteur on Freedom of Expression and Access to Information, *Joint Declaration on Freedom of Expression and Responses to Conflict Situations* (2015), §4(a).
[428] See Clooney & Webb (n 392) Chapter 4 (The Right to Prepare a Defence).
[429] See, e.g., ACmHPR, Declaration of Principles on Freedom of Expression and Access to Information in Africa (2019), Principle 9(2).
[430] See UN Special Rapporteur, OSCE Representative on Freedom of the Media, OAS Special Rapporteur and ACmHPR Special Rapporteur on Freedom of Expression and Access to Information, *Joint Declaration on Freedom of Expression and 'Fake News', Disinformation and Propaganda* (2017) FOM.GAL/3/17, §2(d).
[431] UN Special Rapporteur, OSCE Representative on Freedom of the Media, OAS Special Rapporteur and ACmHPR Special Rapporteur on Freedom of Expression and Access to Information, *Joint Declaration on Freedom of Expression and 'Fake News', Disinformation and Propaganda* (2017) FOM.GAL/3/17, §1(d), (h). See also EACJ, *Media Council of Tanzania and others v. Attorney General of the United Republic of Tanzania* (Ref no. 2/2017), 28 March 2019, §§108–110.
[432] See Clooney & Webb (n 392) Introduction, 52 (noting that the HRC refused to defer to domestic courts' findings 'when the courts failed to provide reasons and justifications for their assessment of the evidence') and Chapter 1 (The Right to a Competent, Independent and Impartial Tribunal Established by Law), 125–126.
[433] See further s. III.4.1. (Truth); ECtHR, *Bergens Tidende v. Norway* (App. no. 26132/95), 2 May 2000, §56.

elevated culpability and harm elements of the offence could not be met in such cases in any event.[434]

8.2. Opinion

Misinformation laws must exclude opinions from their ambit. This is in line with international standards related to defamation laws, which also provide that opinion must not be captured by such laws.[435] A court must therefore also carefully distinguish between statements of fact and statements of opinion (including humour and satire), since only the former are capable of proof and can constitute misinformation.[436]

8.3. Public interest

Misinformation laws should, like defamation laws, provide additional protection for political or 'public interest' speech. The Human Rights Committee has held, in the context of defamation, that the public interest in the subject matter of a criticism 'should be recognized as a defence'.[437] Political speech, such as criticism of the work of the government or the positions of a political party, should enjoy a high level of protection. So should speech on any matter broadly of public interest, such as state policy regarding climate change, and the like.[438] Given the value of such speech, it is appropriate to apply a higher standard of protection, including when such speech involves the media.[439] It is in principle difficult for the state to justify restrictions on this type of expression, even if it pursues a legitimate aim in doing so. An affirmative public interest defence would be of particular importance if the *mens rea* of the misinformation did not, contrary to our recommendation, require the knowing or intentional dissemination of falsehoods, but employed lesser forms of culpability.

A degree of falsity and exaggeration is inevitable in political debate and must be tolerated by the state, in order to avoid chilling effects on socially beneficial speech.[440] If the target of the speech is a politician, public official or potentially another public figure in a position of power they must expect greater exposure to public scrutiny and criticism.[441] The European Court also considers that if the speaker is a journalist or

---

[434] See also Colombian Constitutional Court, *Accion de Tutela contra Particulares (Procedencia excepcional)*, Tutela judgment T-293/2018, 24 July 2018, §7.3.1 (requiring proof of a *reasonable degree* of truth only).
[435] See further s. III.4.2. (Opinion). ECtHR, *Lingens v. Austria* (App. no. 9815/82), 8 July 1986, §46: 'a careful distinction needs to be made between facts and value-judgments. The existence of facts can be demonstrated, whereas the truth of value-judgments is not susceptible of proof... As regards value-judgments this requirement is impossible of fulfilment, and it infringes freedom of opinion itself'; ECtHR, *Hertel v. Switzerland* (App. no. 25181/94), 25 August 1998, §50.
[436] See further s. III.4.2. (Opinion).
[437] HRC, General Comment No. 34 (2011), §47; HRC, *Kozlov v. Belarus* (Comm. no. 1986/2010), 24 July 2014, §§7.5–7.6.
[438] See HRC, General Comment No. 34 (2011), §§2–3, 30. See further s. III.4.3. (Public interest and 'responsible journalism').
[439] See ch. 2 (Insulting Speech), s. IV. (Recommendations); ch. 3 (Hate Speech), s. VI. (Recommendations).
[440] See, e.g., ECtHR, *Steel v. United Kingdom* (App. no. 68416/01), 15 February 2005, §90.
[441] See ACmHPR, Declaration of Principles on Freedom of Expression and Access to Information in Africa (2019), Principle 21(1); IACmHR, *The Inter-American Legal Framework Regarding the Right to Freedom of Expression* (2009) OEA/Ser.L/V/II CIDH/RELE/INF. 2/09, §§39–52; ECtHR, *Lingens v. Austria* (App. no. 9815/82), 8 July 1986, §42; HRC, General Comment No. 34 (2011), §§34, 38.

other 'public watchdog', increased protection may be appropriate if certain conditions are met.[442]

9. Penalties must be proportionate to the harm caused by false speech and the speaker's level of fault. Custodial sanctions will be justified only exceptionally.

Criminal misinformation laws generally pose particularly grave restrictions on freedom of expression and are necessary and proportionate only in response to specific and sufficiently serious social harms caused by the speech.[443] Heavy penalties can be one of many factors that render a misinformation offence, as prescribed or applied, to be unnecessary and disproportionate. A severe sentence may even on its own render a criminal conviction disproportionate.[444] Sentences should depend primarily on the culpability of the offender and the gravity of the harm that the misinformation caused.[445] Custodial sentences will be proportionate only exceptionally and require a weighty justification, for example causing death or serious harms to health.[446]

Criminal misinformation laws that can be or are applied to reporting or debate on matters of public interest are particularly concerning.[447] Imposing criminal liability on such speech is the most restrictive measure possible, with the greatest potential for chilling effects and greatest possible detriment to democracy. Indeed, even when a restriction on speech pursues a clearly legitimate aim, like the protection of public health, criminalization should be reserved only for specific and sufficiently serious harms and be subject to rigorous causality and culpability requirements.[448] That said, there are historically uncontroversial examples of criminal responsibility and custodial sentences being imposed for false statements of fact, including offences such as perjury, where the harm is to public order and integrity of the judicial process,[449] and fraud, where the

---

[442] See ch. 2 (Insulting Speech), s. III.4.3. (Reasonable publication); But see ch.1 (Introduction), s. II.3.2.5. (Relevance of whether the speaker is a journalist). See also ECtHR, *Prager and Oberschlick v. Austria* (App. no. 15974/90), 26 April 1995, §38; IACmHR, *The Inter-American Legal Framework Regarding the Right to Freedom of Expression* (2009) OEA/Ser.L/V/II CIDH/RELE/INF. 2/09, §38.

[443] See s. IV.4. (Recommendations); OAS Guide to Guarantee Freedom of Expression Regarding Deliberate Disinformation in Electoral Contexts, 30.

[444] See ECtHR (GC), *Bédat v. Switzerland* (App. no. 56925/08), 29 March 2016, §79; see s. III.5. (Penalties).

[445] See s. IV.4. (Recommendations).

[446] See s. III.2.2. (What objectives can justify the penalization of false speech?).

[447] See, e.g., Cameroonian Penal Code 2016 s. 240 (which punishes the dissemination of *any* false news, on whatever topic and regardless of the harm it causes, but punishes such dissemination with imprisonment up to five years, *doubling* that penalty if the dissemination is done anonymously).

[448] See ss IV.4. (Recommendations) and IV.6. (Recommendations). See HRC, General Comment No. 34 (2011), §47 (discussing criminalization of defamation).

[449] It is possible for other offences against the administration of justice to include false statements of fact as an element of the offence. In English law, for example, a strict liability contempt of court rule exists for any publication relating to active judicial proceedings which creates a substantial risk that the course of justice in the proceedings in question will be seriously impeded or prejudiced. Liability is excluded, however, 'in respect of a *fair and accurate report* of legal proceedings held in public, published contemporaneously and in good faith': UK Contempt of Court Act 1981 s. 4(1) (emphasis added).

primary harm is to individual property rights. Generally speaking, with the exception of criminal defamation, such offences are tailored relatively narrowly to these harms, can be committed only in specific contexts or with regard to a particular subject-matter, and are therefore not likely to stifle debate on matters of public interest.[450]

Fines and other penalties that can adversely affect the operation of a media outlet require substantial justification.[451] This also applies to any administrative measures that may be ancillary to a criminal conviction, such as the blocking of websites or applications. As explained by UN and regional mandate-holders on freedom of expression, '[s]tate mandated blocking of entire websites, IP addresses, ports or network protocols is an extreme measure which can only be justified where it is provided by law and is necessary to protect a human right or other legitimate public interest, including in the sense of that it is proportionate, there are no less intrusive alternative measures which would protect the interest and it respects minimum due process guarantees'.[452]

Other severe civil and administrative measures that may be ancillary to the commission of misinformation offences, such as the revocation of broadcast licences, are likely to be considered proportionate only exceptionally, for instance as a response to deliberate, repeated and systematic spreading of misinformation that causes or can cause serious prohibited harms, on the basis of clear and foreseeable rules as to when such sanctions can be imposed and an impartial application of these standards by an independent entity such as a court.[453] Severe sanctions should not be imposed without recourse to judicial review by an independent and impartial court, and generally should not be enforced while such review is pending.[454]

---

[450] See, e.g., United States Congressional Research Service, *False Speech and the First Amendment: Constitutional Limits on Regulating Misinformation* (2022), 'Fraud and False Commercial Speech', 1–2. See also UK Contempt of Court Act 1981 s. 4(1).

[451] See, e.g., UN Special Rapporteur D. Kaye, *Letter dated 1 May 2019*, Ref OL RUS 4/2019, 5 (noting the disproportionate effects of 'crippling monetary penalties').

[452] UN Special Rapporteur, OSCE Representative on Freedom of the Media, OAS Special Rapporteur and ACmHPR Special Rapporteur on Freedom of Expression and Access to Information, *Joint Declaration on Freedom of Expression and 'Fake News', Disinformation and Propaganda* (2017) FOM.GAL/3/17, §1(f).

[453] E.g., when commenting on Hungary's Media Act the Venice Commission noted that the 'Media Council may use its powers to impose heavy sanctions (such as high fines or interruption of broadcasting, blocking of access etc.) only as a measure of last resort, where all other reasonable attempts to steer the media outlet on the right path have failed, and where its publications repeatedly... endangered public peace and order (for example, where the media outlet has repeatedly made calls for unlawful violence in respect of minority groups or advocated a violent overthrow of a democratic public order). In addition, there is a need to develop policy guidelines on administrative sanctions which would explain how the Media Council exercises its discretion in this sphere': Venice Commission, *Opinion on Media Legislation (Act CLXXXV on Media Services and on the Mass Media, Act CIV on the Freedom of the Press, and the Legislation on Taxation of Advertisement Revenues of Mass Media) of Hungary* (2015) CDL-AD(2015)015, §41.

[454] See Venice Commission, *Opinion on Media Legislation (Act CLXXXV on Media Services and on the Mass Media, Act CIV on the Freedom of the Press, and the Legislation on Taxation of Advertisement Revenues of Mass Media) of Hungary* (2015) CDL-AD(2015)015, §§42–46.

10. State officials should refrain from disseminating or amplifying harmful misinformation.

Misinformation that emanates from state actors is often more harmful than misinformation disseminated by non-state actors.[455] Depending on the nature of the misinformation and the harm that it causes, the dissemination of misinformation by the state may violate the state's obligation to respect a number of human rights, including freedom of expression.[456] A state's involvement in spreading misinformation also hinders its ability to credibly restrict misinformation by private actors.

11. States must protect the public from human rights violations by private actors, including companies.

Minimum international standards require that the state protects individuals from human rights violations by private actors, including media companies,[457] by 'taking appropriate steps to prevent, investigate, punish and redress such abuse through effective policies, legislation, regulations and adjudication'.[458] In particular, states need to provide 'effective guidance to business enterprises on how to respect human rights throughout their operations'.[459] Companies that become dominant in a particular area and produce outsized impacts on speech, such as Facebook/Meta, require particular scrutiny.[460] This includes scrutiny of both whether digital platforms and other companies cause systematic social harms by enabling the spread of misinformation, and whether, conversely, these companies are suppressing too much speech when taking measures to combat misinformation. Any regulatory systems used by states in this regard should depend primarily on the work of independent regulatory bodies free from political control or influence,[461] which must act according to fair and transparent procedures, providing reasons for their decisions and with appropriate remedies available to challenge them.[462] As explained above, regulatory interventions by means of criminal law will be justified only rarely.

---

[455] UN Special Rapporteur, OSCE Representative on Freedom of the Media, OAS Special Rapporteur and ACmHPR Special Rapporteur on Freedom of Expression and Access to Information, *Joint Declaration on Freedom of Expression and 'Fake News', Disinformation and Propaganda* (2017) FOM.GAL/3/17, §§2(c), 2(d).

[456] See, e.g., ibid.

[457] See HRC, General Comment No. 34 (2011), §7. See ch. 1 (Introduction), s. II.1.1.2. (Obligation to prevent abuses by others).

[458] UN Guiding Principles on Business and Human Rights, Principle 1.

[459] Ibid., Principle 3(c).

[460] See ch. 3 (Hate Speech), s. V. (Approach of Private Companies to Online Hate Speech).

[461] See ACmHPR, Declaration of Principles on Freedom of Expression and Access to Information in Africa (2019), Principles 9(2), 17, 34, 39(4).

[462] See ACmHPR, Declaration of Principles on Freedom of Expression and Access to Information in Africa (2019), Principles 9(2), 17, 34, 39(4); UN Special Rapporteur, OSCE Representative on Freedom of the Media, OAS Special Rapporteur and ACmHPR Special Rapporteur on Freedom of Expression and Access to Information, *Joint Declaration on Freedom of Expression and Responses to Conflict Situations* (2015), §4(a). See also UN Special Rapporteur, OSCE Representative on Freedom of the Media, OAS Special Rapporteur and ACmHPR Special

12. In designing and applying their policies on misinformation, digital platforms and other media companies should be guided by international human rights standards related to freedom of expression, in line with their own undertakings and the UN Guiding Principles on Business and Human Rights.

While media companies are not directly bound by international human rights treaties, they have a responsibility to respect human rights.[463] As set out in the UN Guiding Principles on Business and Human Rights, which all major technology companies claim to subscribe to, '[b]usiness enterprises should respect human rights. This means that they should avoid infringing on the human rights of others and should address adverse human rights impacts with which they are involved'.[464] While international human rights standards have been developed to regulate the relationship between individuals and states, as sovereign, public actors, they should be applied with any necessary and appropriate adjustments by private companies to guide their own decision-making.[465] It is encouraging that an increasing number of digital platforms that play a dominant role in regulating speech have accepted international human rights as part of their internal regulatory frameworks.[466]

Digital platforms have long resisted attempts to become 'arbiters of truth'[467] but their very dominance and assumption of the role of the public square online, coupled with often serious harms caused by the spread of misinformation via these platforms and the need to respond in real-time, make it inevitable that these platforms will have to make at least some judgements on truth and falsity and what to do about speech that is clearly false. Criminal misinformation laws adopted by the state will inevitably play only a limited role in that regard; the justifiability bar for self-regulatory measures by digital platforms, such as content moderation or the suspension of user accounts, is lower than that required for the imposition of criminal or civil legal liability on the relevant individual by the state. In other words, digital platforms may in appropriate circumstances restrict false speech even when that speech is not illegal.[468]

Rapporteur on Freedom of Expression and Access to Information, *Joint Declaration on Freedom of Expression and 'Fake News', Disinformation and Propaganda* (2017) FOM.GAL/3/17, §3(b).

[463] See ch. 3 (Hate Speech), s. V. (Approach of Private Companies to Online Hate Speech); UN Guiding Principles on Business and Human Rights, General Principles.
[464] UN Guiding Principles on Business and Human Rights, Principle 11. See also Forum of Information & Democracy, 'Principles on Information & Democracy' (endorsed by 51 states from across the world that comprise the International Partnership for Information and Democracy).
[465] For an instructive example, see the decision of the Oversight Board, 'Case Decision 2020-006-FB-FBR Claimed COVID-19 cure'.
[466] See ch. 3 (Hate Speech), s. V. (Approach of Private Companies to Online Hate Speech). See also E. M. Aswad, 'The Future of Freedom of Expression Online' (2018) 17 *Duke Law & Technology Review* 26, 34.
[467] T. McCarthy, 'Zuckerberg says Facebook won't be "arbiters of truth" after Trump threat' (The Guardian, 28 May 2020). See also M. Adler, 'Twitter Says it Stopped Policing COVID Misinformation Under Musk' (TIME, 29 November 2022) noting Musk's 'mission to remake the social network as a place for unmoderated speech'.
[468] The Oversight Board has noted with approval the fact that the UN Special Rapporteur sees greater leeway for speech restriction by a company than by a government. See Oversight Board, 'Case Decision 2020-003-FB-UA

It is recommended that in making decisions about the necessity and proportionality of the measures they take to combat harmful misinformation, digital platforms should make clear how they reconcile divergences in international standards or transpose them to the context of non-state actors. And they should also ensure that they comply with the principles of legality and due process,[469] including by being transparent in defining what type of misinformation is subject to removal or other types of penalties.[470]

Armenians in Azerbaijan'. See also Oversight Board, 'Case Decision 2021-001-FB-FBR Former President Trump's suspension'.

[469] UN Special Rapporteur, OSCE Representative on Freedom of the Media, OAS Special Rapporteur and ACmHPR Special Rapporteur on Freedom of Expression and Access to Information, *Joint Declaration on Freedom of Expression and 'Fake News', Disinformation and Propaganda* (2017) FOM.GAL/3/17, §4(c); OAS Guide to Guarantee Freedom of Expression Regarding Deliberate Disinformation in Electoral Contexts (2019), 39.

[470] UN Special Rapporteur D. Kaye, *Letter to Mark Zuckerberg dated 1 May 2019*, Ref OL OTH 24/2019, 3.

5

Speech Related to National Security: Espionage and Official Secrets Laws

Amal Clooney and Alice Gardoll

I. Introduction	277	III. International Legal Standards	306
II. State Practice	280	1. International Standards Related to Speech Affecting National Security	307
1. Overview of Laws Regulating Disclosure of 'Secret' Material	280	2. Legality	313
1.1. Type of speech	280	3. Legitimacy	315
1.2. Harm	283	4. Necessity	316
1.3. Intent	284	4.1. Secrecy	318
1.4. Exclusions, exceptions and defences	285	4.2. Harm	320
1.5. Penalties	287	4.3. Intent	325
2. Application of Espionage and Official Secrets Laws Around the World	288	5. Exclusions, Exceptions and Defences	325
2.1. Europe and United Kingdom	288	5.1. Public interest defence	325
2.2. Asia Pacific	293	5.2. Reasonableness of the publication	329
2.3. Middle East and Africa	298	5.3. Truth	333
2.4. North and South America	300	5.4. Opinion	334
		6. Penalties	334
		IV. Recommendations	337

I. Introduction

The principle that certain speech can be penalized if it jeopardizes national security, defence, military operations or diplomatic relations is not controversial.[1] Laws providing for the secrecy of some government information are ubiquitous across democracies and authoritarian regimes alike. But legal responses to the disclosure of material deemed secret by the state vary widely. Some states classify limited information as secret and accept a culture of leaking, either through prosecutorial discretion or laws that allow such conduct. Others, including democratic states, clamp down heavily on the disclosure of any government-derived information whether it is classified or not.

A striking feature of this area of the law is that leading democracies that are generally considered protective of speech are among the governments with particularly

---

[1] The authors and editors are grateful for the excellent research and work done by Professor Vincent Wong of the University of Windsor Faculty of Law and his clinical students in relation to this chapter. Professor Wong served as the lead project manager at the University of Toronto Law School on the media freedom initiative led by the High-Level Panel of Legal Experts on Media Freedom, an expert group established at the behest of the governments of Canada and the United Kingdom.

harsh laws and practices. One example is the United Kingdom. The UK Official Secrets Act, originally enacted in 1889, has been widely criticized as one of the most illiberal iterations of official secrets laws.[2] Prior to its 1989 amendments, any unauthorized disclosure of official information entrusted to a Crown servant by a state official was prohibited, regardless of the level of secrecy of a document, the harm it may have caused or the individual's intention.[3] And although this law has only been used in a small number of high-profile cases in the United Kingdom,[4] due to Britain's colonial reach, iterations of this law were adopted in British colonies across the globe. Many former colonies maintain these laws, with the result that legislation that significantly curtails speech related to 'secret' material applies to millions of people across the world from Uganda and Zimbabwe to India, Pakistan, Sri Lanka, Myanmar, Singapore and Malaysia.[5]

Similarly, the United States, one of the most speech-friendly states in the world thanks to its First Amendment jurisprudence,[6] has in recent years made significant recourse to espionage laws to clamp down on speech. Prior to 2009, only a handful of prosecutions for disclosing confidential information to the press had ever taken place under the US Espionage Act, even though the United States has a 'longstanding culture of leaking', with press breaking a number of high-profile stories on the basis of leaks.[7] This included revealing the CIA's use of secret prisons and the human rights abuses at the Abu Ghraib detention facility in Iraq.[8] But both the Obama and Trump administrations increased prosecutions of government sources under the Espionage Act in an unprecedented manner. And the indictment of Wikileaks' Julian Assange represents the first time an individual who *published* classified information has been successfully indicted, raising the spectre that traditional journalists are no longer off limits for prosecution under a law intended to catch spies.[9] Recent US prosecutorial practice has therefore applied the US

---

[2] See, e.g., C. W. Cheong, 'Section 5 of the Official Secrets Act, Bridges and Beyond' (1998) 2 *Singapore Journal of Legal Studies* 260, 261. Unless otherwise indicated, references to the United Kingdom and the UK refer to England and Wales, Scotland, and Northern Ireland. Although many of the same laws apply across these jurisdictions, these laws can vary and Scotland has a separate legal system.

[3] See UK Official Secrets Act, s. 2. See UK Law Commission, *Protection of Official Data Report* (2020), §§4.4–4.6; G. Bartlett & M. Everett, 'Briefing Paper: The Official Secrets Act and Official Secrecy' (House of Commons Library, 2 May 2017), 18–21.

[4] Bartlett & Everett (n 3) (listing 12 '[n]otable cases involving the Official Secrets Act or leaks of Government information'). See s. II.2.1.1. (United Kingdom).

[5] Indian Official Secrets Act 1923; Pakistani Official Secrets Act 1923; Malaysian Official Secrets Act 1972; Myanmar Official Secrets Act 1923; Singaporean Official Secrets Act 1935; Sri Lankan Official Secrets Act, No. 32 of 1955; Ugandan Official Secrets Act 1964, ch. 302; Zimbabwean Official Secrets Act 1970.

[6] A number of sources chart the US Supreme Court's historical path towards this more speech protective position: see, e.g., M. Rosenfeld, 'Hate Speech in Constitutional Jurisprudence: A Comparative Analysis', in M. Herz & P. Molnar (eds), *The Content and Context of Hate Speech: Rethinking Regulation and Responses* (CUP 2012); E. Bleich, 'Freedom of Expression versus Racist Hate Speech: Explaining Differences Between High Court Regulation in the USA and Europe' (2013) 40(2) *Journal of Ethnic and Migration Studies* 283. See ch. 1 (Introduction), ss II.1.2.1.2. (ICCPR: Article 20) and II.2.1.3. (CERD: Article 4) discussing US reservations.

[7] See, e.g., Knight First Amendment Institute at Columbia University, 'Press-related prosecutions under the Espionage Act'; K. Feuer, 'Protecting Government Secrets: A Comparison of the Espionage Act and the Official Secrets Act' (2015) 38(1) *Boston College International and Comparative Law Review* 91, 95.

[8] Ibid., 98.

[9] See s. II.2.4.3. (United States: Julian Assange). See also G. Rottman, 'Special Analysis of the May 2019 Superseding Indictment of Julian Assange' (Reporters Committee, 30 May 2019).

Espionage Act in a way that creates a glaring exception to the United States' proud history of free speech protection and 'potentially opens the door for journalists anywhere in the world to be extradited to the US for exposing information deemed classified by Washington'.[10]

A central tension within this area of the law is the relevance of the 'public interest' in assessing whether speech should be unlawful. International standards dictate, at a minimum, that both the public interest in the speech and the potential harm to national security arising from speech are relevant to determining whether it is legally 'necessary' to penalize it using civil or criminal sanctions.[11] However, many national laws do not reflect this standard, either on paper or in practice, and many autocratic governments brand journalists as 'spies' and use 'national security' as a pretext to stifle the press as well as ordinary citizens.[12]

This disconnect has led to increasing calls for reform. The Global Principles on National Security and the Right to Information (known as the Tshwane Principles), drafted in 2013 in consultation with over 500 legal experts, including civil society actors and government officials, support an affirmative public interest defence, and have been endorsed by five UN and regional Special Rapporteurs and the Parliamentary Assembly for the Council of Europe.[13] The Law Commission of England and Wales also recently recommended an amendment of the UK Official Secrets Act to allow a public interest defence to prosecutions of speech that reveals government secrets.[14]

This chapter considers state practice in this area,[15] international standards governing the language and use of such laws[16] and recommendations as to how such laws should be drafted, interpreted and applied to comply with international law and best practices.[17]

---

[10] 'The Guardian view on Julian Assange's extradition: a bad day for journalism' (The Guardian, 17 June 2022).
[11] See s. II.1.2. (Harm) and s. III.5.1. (Public interest defence).
[12] See, e.g., CPJ, 'Database of attacks on the press—Journalists imprisoned between 1992 and 2020' (concerning data on journalists imprisoned between 1992 and 2020 for 'anti-state' charges). See also ss II.2.1.2. (Slovenia); II.2.2.2. (Australia); II.2.2.3. (Cambodia).
[13] Tshwane Principles. See s. III.1. (International Standards Related to Speech Affecting National Security).
[14] See UK Law Commission, *Protection of Official Data Report* (2020).
[15] The definition of 'official secret' or 'espionage' varies by jurisdiction, and neither has a consistent interpretation under international law. For the purposes of this chapter, 'official secrets' or 'state secrets' refer to confidential or classified information held by a public authority, and protected against unauthorized disclosure on grounds such as national security and intelligence, or international relations. 'Espionage' is understood as referring to unlawfully obtaining information held in confidence by the government, usually (but not always) for the benefit of another state or foreign power. Although espionage laws generally encompass a range of offences related to 'spying' that extend beyond speech-related conduct, such as theft, this chapter focuses on espionage laws which capture 'pure speech' behaviour, and takes no position on the need or appropriateness of more traditional 'spying' provisions under international law.
[16] This chapter does not examine the corollary right to *receive* information that is relevant to official secrets laws. Protection of sources and materials, as well as whistle-blowing regimes that protect public officials or contractors from civil and administrative repercussions are also not within the scope of this chapter.
[17] See s. IV. (Recommendations).

II. State Practice

1. Overview of Laws Regulating Disclosure of 'Secret' Material

Laws regulating disclosure of 'secret' material—usually espionage or 'official secrets' legislation—exist in states across the globe.[18] All of the laws surveyed in this chapter include criminal penalties for unauthorized disclosures.[19]

But the requirements for penalization set out in these laws—including the scope of the speech that is covered, the required intent of the speaker, harm caused by the speech, defences and penalties—differ considerably. Some states prohibit the disclosure of *any* governmental information while others require that information to be 'secret' or 'classified', and also define these terms differently. States define harm differently and a large number of states do not set out any harm requirement at all, perhaps on the assumption that some harm always results from the disclosure of 'secret' information. Penalties also significantly vary, although many states' laws provide for heavy maximum penalties of between 10–15 years' imprisonment for spilling secrets through speech. Only a small number of countries have an affirmative public interest defence, and even those that do can be narrowly worded. These include Canada, Australia, Denmark and Slovenia, while countries such as the United Kingdom and the United States are yet to adopt such a defence despite strong calls for them to do so.[20]

In certain nations, special approvals are needed before a prosecution under espionage or official secrets laws can be triggered. This is the case, for instance, in the United Kingdom, Ghana, Singapore and Australia, although a number of earlier steps such as arrest and charges can take place in Australia without such consent.[21] And prosecutorial guidance in Canada and the United States establishes approval procedures for certain prosecutions, including official secrets charges.[22]

1.1. Type of speech

Many state laws use vague wording or fail to define key terms in official secrets laws such as 'secret', 'confidential' or 'national security'. Examples include Cambodia, where 'facilitating easy access' by foreign agents to information which 'undermines the national security' is criminalized with up to 15 years' imprisonment, and Myanmar, which criminalizes obtaining, collecting, recording, publishing or communicating

---

[18] The review of state official secrets and espionage laws and practice contained in this chapter does not aim to be comprehensive but rather to identify significant examples and trends. In addition, references to the language of a statute are not necessarily accompanied by an analysis of all case law interpreting that language in the jurisdiction under review.
[19] This chapter reviews 46 countries' laws related to espionage and official secrets.
[20] See s. II.1.4.1. (Public interest).
[21] See UK Official Secrets Act 1989 s. 9 (requiring consent for the prosecution of offences based on unauthorized disclosure of official information); Australian Criminal Code s. 93.1; Singaporean Official Secrets Act s. 14; Ghanian State Secrets Act 1962 (Act 101) s. 11.
[22] Public Prosecution Service of Canada, *Public Prosecution Service of Canada Deskbook, Guideline of the Director Issued under Section 3(3)(c) of the Director of Public Prosecutions Act* (2021); US Department of Justice, *Justice Manual: Title 9-90.020, National Security Matters*.

information which might be 'directly or indirectly, useful to an enemy' if this is done 'for any purpose prejudicial to the safety and interests' of the state.[23] A number of laws have not been amended since their enactment many decades ago and use language such as 'enemy' which may be poorly suited to modern day national security concerns.[24]

1.1.1. Secrecy

The 'secrecy' element of official secrets laws has several components: whether governmental information must be classified as 'secret' to be unlawfully disclosed, how secrecy is defined, and whether all persons are captured by the law or only those who owe a duty of secrecy.

Certain official secrets and espionage laws prohibit the possession or communication of certain governmental information with no additional 'secrecy' requirement. For example, the US Espionage Act applies to 'information respecting the national defense'.[25] US courts have interpreted this section as not requiring that information is classified, although the government must, as a preliminary matter, show that steps were taken to maintain its secrecy. Similarly, US courts have found that the classification of a document alone may be sufficient to prove its link to national defence.[26]

A number of countries prohibit the disclosure of any 'secret' or 'secret official' information, consistent with early versions of the UK Official Secrets Act that were imported into Commonwealth countries' laws across the world.[27] For example, Singapore's Official Secrets Ordinance provides criminal penalties for communicating directly or indirectly 'any secret official code word, countersign or password, or any photograph, drawing, plan, model, article, note, document or information' obtained in contravention of the Act.[28] But Singaporean courts have interpreted this provision as capturing two types of expression: any 'word, countersign or password', which must be 'secret official', and the other listed types of expression, which do not have to be 'secret official'.[29]

Similarly the United Kingdom's official secrets laws criminalize the disclosure of six categories of information: information relating to 'security and intelligence';[30] 'defence';[31] 'international relations';[32] information the disclosure of which 'results in the commission of an offence' or impacts law enforcement efforts;[33] information acquired

---

[23] Cambodian Criminal Code 2009 Art. 445; Myanmar Official Secrets Act s. 3(1)(c).
[24] See, e.g., 18 U.S.C. § 794(b) (this chapter uses the shorthand term the US Espionage Act to describe the current provisions in the Unites States Code that were originally enacted as the US Espionage Act).
[25] Ibid., s. 793.
[26] Feuer (n 7) 91, 117, citing US District Court, District of Columbia, *United States v. Kim* 808 F. Supp. 2d 44, 24 August 2011, 55 and US Court of Appeals, Fourth Circuit, *United States v. Morison* 844 F.2d 1057, 1 April 1988, 1074.
[27] See Bangladeshi Official Secrets Act 1923 s. 5(1) (except to a person to whom one is 'authorized to communicate' the information, or to a 'Court of Justice or a person to whom it is, in the interests of the State, one's duty to communicate' the information); Ugandan Official Secrets Act 1964 ch. 302 s. 4.
[28] Singaporean Official Secrets Act s. 5(1).
[29] Cheong (n 2), 263–264, citing Singapore High Court, *Public Prosecutor v Bridges Christopher* [1998] 3 SLR 467 (CA).
[30] UK Official Secrets Act 1989 s. 1(1).
[31] Ibid., s. 2.
[32] Ibid., s. 3.
[33] Ibid., s. 4.

by a civil servant;[34] and information related to security, intelligence, defence or international relations 'communicated in confidence by or on behalf of the United Kingdom to another State or to an international organisation'.[35] These categories, with the exception of the final one, do not require information to be secret or classified.

Other states have more precise definitions of secrecy. For instance, Germany defines state secrets as 'facts, objects or knowledge' accessible to a limited category of persons and which must be kept secret 'from foreign powers in order to avert a danger of serious prejudice to the external security' of Germany.[36] Other nations, such as Slovenia, Peru and El Salvador link secrecy to the classification of information by certain government bodies.[37]

1.1.2. Who does the duty of secrecy apply to?
Although many espionage and official secrets laws apply to all persons,[38] some states have legislation that limits penalties for publishing state secrets to government officials, employees or those with a specific duty of secrecy. For example, in Georgia a person can only be responsible for the disclosure of a secret if they had an official duty or civil agreement to protect its confidentiality and the disclosure 'creates obvious, direct and essential danger, to the interests protected under the law'.[39] Some countries limit criminal responsibility for disclosure of official secrets to public officials.[40] Germany's criminal law was amended in 2012 to ensure that journalists cannot be charged with aiding the 'violation of official secrets' for disclosing classified information.[41] And a number of states provide lesser penalties for unauthorized disclosures of secret information by private persons rather than public officials.[42]

1.1.3. Type of disclosure
Laws vary as to what conduct relating to official secrets is prohibited. States such as Albania do not punish the possession of secret information, only its disclosure or use.[43] But states such as the United States and Canada prohibit mere receipt and retention of secret information.[44] Similarly, a number of countries whose laws are modelled on early versions of the UK Official Secrets Act continue to penalize a wide range of acts,

---

[34] Ibid., s. 5.
[35] Ibid., s. 6.
[36] German Criminal Code s. 93.
[37] Slovenian Criminal Code Art. 260(1); Peruvian Legislative Decree 1141 Art. 4; El Salvador State Intelligence Body Law Decree No. 554 Art. 8.
[38] See, e.g., 18 U.S.C. §793; UK Official Secrets Act 1989 ss 5–6; Canadian Security of Information Act s. 4; Indonesian Law No. 17 of 2011 Art. 26; Japan's Act on the Protection of Specially Designated Secrets No. 108 of 2013 Art. 24.
[39] Georgian Law on Freedom of Speech and Expression, as amended in 2012, Art. 12.
[40] See, e.g., Moldovan Criminal Code Art. 344 (although this provision also covers individuals who are not necessarily public officials but to whom information 'was entrusted' or 'became known in connection with his/her official position or professional duties'); Colombian Criminal Code Art. 418.
[41] German Criminal Code s. 353(b)(3a).
[42] See, e.g., Belgian Penal Code Art. 118; Bolivian Penal Code Art. 116; German Criminal Code ss 94–96; Panamanian Criminal Code Art. 428; Ugandan Official Secrets Act of 1964 ch. 302 s. 15; Ugandan Security Organisations Act (1987) ch. 305 s. 10.
[43] Albanian Criminal Code Arts 213, 214, 294, 295. Cf. Albanian Criminal Code Art. 296 (criminalizing 'loss' of secret documents).
[44] 18 U.S.C. §793(e). See s. II.2.4.3. (United States: Julian Assange); Canadian Security of Information Act s. 4.

such as retaining information 'when he has no right to retain it'.[45] Australia's espionage and state secrets laws capture any manner of 'dealing' with such information, which encompasses receiving, collecting, reviewing, possessing, making a record of, copying, altering, concealing or making available information in addition to disclosing it.[46] And some nations criminalize both disclosure and lesser forms of conduct such as possession but provide differing criminal penalties depending on the conduct in question.[47]

1.2. Harm

Official secrets laws are grounded in the idea that speech disclosing confidential official material harms the government. And yet the requirement that the disclosure in question in fact does cause harm, or is reasonably likely to do so, is not always present in official secrets laws. And in the case of laws that do incorporate such a requirement, the definition of damage or harm can be expansive, or presumed to be met without proof if certain conditions are satisfied.

Nations such as Indonesia provide no explicit harm requirement in their laws.[48] The US Espionage Act also does not include a harm requirement. Although courts have interpreted 'respecting the national defense' to mean information that 'would be *potentially damaging* to the United States or *might be* useful to the enemy of the United States',[49] US courts have interpreted the classified status of a document as being sufficient evidence of its potentially damaging nature.[50] Australia's official secrets legislation considers certain information 'inherently harmful', namely classified information or information held, or relating to, any intelligence agency, and a public servant who discloses such information may be convicted of an offence which has no further harm element.[51]

By contrast, other countries, including Cambodia, Serbia and the Philippines include as a necessary condition for criminal liability a showing of damage, or likely damage, resulting from the speech.[52] Article 445 of Cambodia's Criminal Code criminalizes giving or 'facilitating easy access by foreign agents' to information which 'undermines

---

[45] Singaporean Official Secrets Act. See also Pakistani Official Secrets Act s. 5(c); Ugandan Official Secrets Act of 1964 ch. 302 s. 4. Uganda also criminalizes by separate provision employees of Ugandan 'security organizations' who release or disclose 'any information relating to his or her duties': Ugandan Security Organisations Act of 1987 ch. 305 s. 10.

[46] Australian Criminal Code Act s. 90.1, which defines 'deal'. When a Bill inserting this definition was brought to a parliamentary inquiry, 14 Australian media organizations expressed concern that journalists, editorial, and support staff, would be at significant 'risk of jail time as a result of merely having certain information in their possession in the course of news reporting', including the receipt of unsolicited information and making a record of such information: Joint Media Organisations, 'Submission to the Inquiry into the National Security Legislation Amendment (Espionage and Foreign Interference) Bill 2017' (22 January 2018).

[47] See, e.g., Turkish Penal Code Arts 327, 329, 330.

[48] Indonesian State Intelligence Act 2011 Arts 44 and 45.

[49] US Court of Appeals, Fourth Circuit, *United States v. Morison* 844 F.2d, 1 April 1988, 1057, 1071 (emphasis added). See also D. McCraw & S. Gikow, 'The End to an Unspoken Bargain? National Security and Leaks in a Post-Pentagon Papers World' (2013) 48 *Harvard Civil Rights-Civil Liberties Law Review* 473, 497.

[50] See, e.g., Feuer (n 7) 126, citing US District Court for the Eastern District of Virginia, *United States v. Kiriakou* No. 1:12cr127 (LMB) 8 August 2012, 1, 15–16.

[51] Australian Criminal Code Act s. 121.1, which defines 'inherently harmful information'. Australia's espionage offences are complex and Australian law also includes other piecemeal disclosure provisions that could be applied to journalists: see S. Kendall, 'Espionage and Press Freedom In Australia' (The University of Queensland, 2020).

[52] Cambodian Criminal Code 2009 Art. 445; Serbian Criminal Code 2005 Art. 316; Philippine Revised Penal Code Act No. 3815 Art. 229.

the national security'.[53] And in some jurisdictions, the existence or degree of harm influences the level of punishment for the disclosure.[54]

The United Kingdom's official secrets laws are mixed as to whether criminal liability requires proof of damage, depending on which category of information is disclosed and who discloses it. No showing of damage is required for disclosures of information 'relating to security or intelligence' by members of the security services, whereas all other individuals (civil servants and members of the public alike) will be liable only when disclosing information that 'causes damage' or 'would be likely to cause' damage, and the definition of damage depends on the nature of the information disclosed.[55]

1.3. Intent

States impose varying standards for mental culpability in laws that penalize disclosures of government material, often addressing two distinct forms of criminal intent: the intent to disseminate the protected information, and the intent to cause harm through the disclosure. As to the first prong, many states such as Norway, Turkey and Indonesia criminalize even the negligent disclosure of state secrets, often as a lower-level offence with reduced penalties.[56] Nations including Denmark and Bolivia provide less severe penalties if disclosure is a result of negligence.[57]

When it comes to the intent to cause harm through the disclosure, some states have expressly provided for a criminal penalty *without* any such intent, effectively creating a strict liability offence for disclosure. For example, Spain's Penal Code criminalizes '[a]nyone who, without intending to benefit a foreign power' discloses legally classified or secret information 'related to national security or national defence or to technical methods or systems used by the Armed Forces or by industries of military interest'.[58] In contrast, a number of states provide explicit intent to harm standards but set a fairly low bar. For instance, the US Espionage Act requires that a defendant who possesses and 'willfully transmits' or 'willfully retains' information relating to the national defence 'has reason to believe' that the information 'could be used to the injury of the United States or to the advantage of any foreign nation'.[59]

Other states require intent to harm, but put in place broad presumptions for the defendant to rebut. For example, section 3(1) of Myanmar's Official Secrets Act criminalizes any person who 'for any purpose prejudicial to the safety and interests' of that state

---

[53] Cambodian Criminal Code 2009 Art. 445.
[54] See, e.g., Norwegian Penal Code s. 124 (providing a term of imprisonment not exceeding 15 years for the aggravated disclosure of a state secret: 'In determining whether the disclosure is aggravated, particular weight shall be given to whether ... (d) considerable harm has resulted'); Georgian Criminal Code Art. 313(2).
[55] UK Official Secrets Act ss 1–6. These offences (with the exception of section 6) also have a corresponding defence of 'not knowing and having no reasonable cause to believe' that the disclosure would be damaging: UK Official Secrets Act ss 1(5), 2(3), 3(4), 4(4), 5(2). See s. II.2.1.1. (United Kingdom).
[56] Indonesian Draft Law Number 17 of 2011 Arts 44–45; Norwegian Penal Code s. 125; Turkish Penal Code Arts 329(3), 338.
[57] See Danish Criminal Code Art. 152; Bolivian Penal Code Art. 115.
[58] Spanish Penal Code Art. 598. The penalty under this provision is one to four years, but Art. 599 provides that the penalty should be applied 'in the upper half' in circumstances where the speaker had knowledge of the information due to his office or post, or the disclosure consists of publicizing the information on social media or 'in a way that ensures its diffusion'.
[59] 18 U.S.C. §793(e).

'obtains ... or communicates' 'any secret ... information which is calculated to be or might be or is intended to be, directly or indirectly, useful to an enemy'.[60] Section 3(2) of the legislation then provides that:

> it shall not be necessary to show that the accused person was guilty of any particular act tending to show a purpose prejudicial to the safety and interests of the State, and, notwithstanding that no such act is proved against him, he may be convicted if, *from the circumstances of the case of his conduct or his known character as proved*, it appears that his purpose was a purpose prejudicial to the safety or interests of the State.[61]

Bangladesh and Uganda's Official Secrets Acts incorporate the same presumption.[62]

1.4. Exclusions, exceptions and defences
1.4.1. Public interest

Many countries with a reputation for vigorous protection of freedom of the press—notably the United Kingdom and the United States—do not consider the public interest in disclosure of official secrets to be an exception to criminal liability. There are, however, states that do enshrine such a defence in their espionage and official secrets laws to varying degrees.

For example, Denmark's Criminal Code provides an absolute public interest defence for disclosure of confidential information obtained while in public service, holding that state secrets laws 'do not apply in cases where the person in question ... acted in order to lawfully safeguard obvious public interests or the interest of himself or other persons'.[63] Slovenia, Canada and Australia incorporate conditional public interest defences in certain circumstances or consider the issue of public interest as a factor in a balancing test. In Slovenia's case, an individual disclosing classified information no longer incurs criminal liability provided that 'the public interest in the disclosure of classified information prevails over the public interest in maintaining its secrecy' and if the disclosure 'does not directly endanger the life of one or more persons'.[64] This legislation was passed following backlash surrounding the prosecution of a journalist who disclosed links between Slovenian political and military officials and neo-Nazi groups.[65]

Canadian law creates a stringent public interest balancing exercise that only applies to a small subset of Canada's official secrets provisions relating to those 'bound to secrecy', making it of limited utility to journalists or other non-state actors.[66] A speaker seeking to argue public interest in disclosure must meet a two-part test: showing that they acted 'for the purpose of disclosing an offence ... that he or she reasonably believes has been, is being or is about to be committed by another person in the purported performance

---

[60] Myanmar Official Secrets Act s. 3(1)(c).
[61] Ibid., s. 3(2) (emphasis added).
[62] Ugandan Official Secrets Act 1964 ch. 302 s. 2(2); Bangladesh Official Secrets Act s. 3(2).
[63] Danish Criminal Code Art. 152 (e). Journalists who obtain or use this confidential information are also protected under Art 152 (d). Not all Danish official secrets laws incorporate a public interest defence: see Danish Criminal Code, Arts 107 (disclosure of secret information to a foreign power or organization), 109 (disclosure of secret information regarding 'secret negotiations, consultations or resolutions of the state in matters affecting the security or rights of the state relative to foreign states or involving substantial economic interests').
[64] Slovenian Criminal Code Art. 260(4).
[65] See s. II.2.1.2. (Slovenia).
[66] Canadian Security of Information Act RSC 1985 c. O-5 s. 15.

of that person's duties and functions for, or on behalf of, the Government of Canada', and that the public interest in the disclosure of this offence outweighs the public interest in non-disclosure.[67] But a strict pre-condition of the latter prong requires showing that the speaker made a prior disclosure to certain government officials or agencies, unless a 'direct' disclosure was necessary to avoid grievous bodily harm or death.[68]

Australia's official secrets laws, on the other hand, include a public interest reporting defence available to 'persons engaged in the business of reporting news, presenting current affairs or expressing editorial or other content in news media' as well as administrative staff acting under direction at news media entities.[69] This law provides for a defence to the prosecution under official secrecy laws if such a person communicated or dealt with information in their capacity as a person engaged in reporting news and 'at that time, the person reasonably believed that engaging in that conduct was in the public interest'.[70] This provision includes a number of exceptions: a person may not reasonably believe that disclosing or dealing with information is in the public interest if that conduct would involve publication of the identity of an Australian intelligence employee or affiliate, would involve an offence under witness protection legislation or if that conduct was in engaged in 'for the purpose of directly or indirectly assisting a foreign intelligence agency or foreign military organisation'.[71] And media organizations and civil society groups have argued that the defence does not go far enough as it may not cover individual bloggers, and 'does not extend to a journalist's sources, or to civil society groups or advocates, an obvious impediment to political debate and to reporting these kinds of stories'.[72]

Other states provide public interest defences for state officials—and in some circumstances, the wider population—under their laws. For instance, Rwanda and Nigeria include carve-outs in their laws for public interest disclosures related to official wrongdoing, abuse of authority or acts of negligence.[73] Thailand's legislation provides an exemption from liability for disclosures by state officials who act in good faith and disclose information for the purpose of 'securing a benefit of greater importance which relates to public interest, life, body, health or other benefit of a person and such an order is reasonable'.[74]

---

[67] Ibid., s. 15(2). The provision also provides a number of relevant considerations that must be addressed, including whether the person resorted to reasonable alternatives and the 'nature of the harm or risk of harm created by the disclosure': s. 15(4).

[68] Canadian Security of Information Act RSC 1985 c O-5 s. 15(5). Cf. Canadian Superior Court of Justice of Ontario, *O'Neill v. Canada (Attorney General)* (2006) 82 O.R. (3d) 241, 19 October 2006.

[69] Australian Criminal Code Act s. 122.5(6). However, Australia's public interest offence does not apply to all espionage and official secrets laws that might capture journalistic speech, and a recent Parliamentary Committee has recommended that the 'Government give consideration to whether defences for public interest journalism should be applied to other secrecy provisions': Parliament of the Commonwealth of Australia Parliamentary Joint Committee on Intelligence and Security, *Inquiry into the impact of the exercise of law enforcement and intelligence powers on the freedom of the press* (2020), §3.198.

[70] Australian Criminal Code Act s. 122.5(6). The defendant bears the evidential onus of proof in relation to this defence.

[71] Australian Criminal Code Act s. 122.5(7). See Kendall (n 51) 9.

[72] L. Taylor, 'We need to talk about press freedom before it's too late' (The Guardian Australia, 22 June 2018).

[73] Rwandan Law Relating to Access to Information Arts 4, 16, providing a defence 'if the person believes on reasonable grounds that the information is accurate and the disclosure is in the public interest'. Cf. Rwandan Law Determining Offences and Penalties in General Art. 192; Nigerian Freedom of Information Act s. 27(2) (which provides that nothing in the Criminal Code or Official Secrets Act shall prejudice a public officer who 'without authorisation, discloses to any person' information which he reasonably believes to show mismanagement, fraud, abuse of authority or 'a substantial and specific danger to public health or safety').

[74] Thai Official Information Act 1997 ss 15, 20.

1.5. Penalties

Penalties for violations of espionage and official secrets laws cover a very wide range.[75] Table A shows the spread of *maximum* penalties for official secrets and espionage laws for a range of countries analysed for or mentioned in this chapter.

Table A: Range of Penalties in National Laws[76]

Maximum sentence	Countries
0–4 years	Slovenia
5–9 years	Bolivia, France, Poland
10–15 years	Argentina, Austria, Canada, Germany, Ghana, India, Indonesia, Iran, Japan, Myanmar, Nigeria, Norway, Panama, Peru, Qatar, Serbia, Singapore, Spain, Sri Lanka, United Kingdom
16–25 years	Albania, Belgium, Georgia, Moldova, Rwanda, Zimbabwe
26 years–life	Australia, Cambodia, Czech Republic, Denmark, El Salvador, Hong Kong, Philippines, The Gambia, Malaysia, Turkey
Capital punishment	Bangladesh, Republic of Korea, Pakistan, Thailand, Uganda, United States

---

[75] The use of injunctive relief to prevent the disclosure of unauthorized information is beyond the scope of this report. The penalties described in this section relate to pure speech offences rather than other, more traditional, spying laws. See s. I. Introduction.

[76] This table is non-exhaustive: Albanian Criminal Code 2017 Art. 213; Argentine Penal Code Art. 222 (lesser penalties apply if the offender is not a member of the military); Austrian Criminal Code Arts. 252, 253, 254; Australian Criminal Code Act s. 91(6) (s. 91(6) penalizes aggravated espionage, however lesser terms of imprisonment apply to other Australian official secrets laws: see Australian Criminal Code Act ss 122.4; 122.4A(1)); Belgian Penal Code Arts. 118, 119 (up to 20 years' imprisonment if committed by a public official or 15 years' imprisonment if committed by a private person); Bangladesh Official Secrets Act 1923 s. 3; Bolivian Penal Code Art. 115; Cambodian Criminal Code 2009 Art. 443; Canadian Security of Information Act s. 27 (although a range of penalties apply under this Act); Czech Criminal Code (2009) ss 316(4), 54 (1); Danish Criminal Code Art. 109 (if information is passed on to a foreign power or if espionage is committed in war time); El Salvador Criminal Code Art. 356 (penalizing espionage, cf. Art. 355 (penalizing disclosure of state secrets by up to 8 years' imprisonment)); French Penal Code Art. 413-10 and Official Secrets Act s. 17; Georgian Criminal Code Art. 314; The Gambia Official Secrets (Amendment) Act 2008 s. 17(1)(a); German Criminal Code ss 95, 96; Ghanaian State Secrets Act 1962 (Act 101) s. 14; Hong Kong National Security Law Arts 20, 22 (penalizing secession or subversion 'of a grave nature', cf. Hong Kong Official Secrets Ordinance s. 25, providing lesser penalties for other violations of official secrets offences); Indian Official Secrets Act s. 3; Indonesian Draft Law No. 17 of 2011 Art. 46; Iranian Islamic Penal Code Art. 501; Japanese Act on Protection of Specially Designated Secrets Arts 23, 24; Korean Criminal Code Art. 98 and National Security Act Art. 4(1), item 2; Malaysian Penal Code s. 124M and Official Secrets Act 1972 s. 3; Moldovan Criminal Code Art. 338; Myanmar Official Secrets Act s. 3 and Myanmar Electronic Transactions Law s. 33; Nigerian Official Secrets Act s. 7; Norwegian Penal Code ss 123, 124; Pakistani Official Secrets Act s. 3 (added by the Official Secrets (Amdt.) Act 1966 (8 of 1966)); Panama Criminal Code Art. 428; Peruvian Criminal Code Arts 330–331; Philippine Act to Punish Espionage and Other Offenses Against the National Security s. 2 (if committed during war time, cf. Philippine Revised Penal Code Art. 117); Polish Penal Code Art. 265(1) (if acting in the name of or on behalf of a foreign entity); Qatari Penal Code Art. 110; Rwandan Law Determining Offences And Penalties In General Art. 192 (applicable in war time); Serbian Criminal Code Art. 316; Singaporean Official Secrets Act s. 17(1); Slovenian Criminal Code s. 260(1); Spanish Criminal Code Art. 584; Sri Lankan Official Secrets Act s. 26(1); Thai Criminal Code s. 124; Turkish Penal Code Arts. 328, 329, 330 (the maximum penalty of life imprisonment applying if the disclosure is 'military espionage'); Ugandan Security Organisations Act (1987) ch. 305 s. 10(1) (applying to employees of security organizations releasing information relating to their duties, cf. Ugandan Official Secrets Act ch. 302 Art. 15 (applying to all persons, punishable by 14 years' imprisonment)); UK Official Secrets Act 1989 s. 10 and Official Secrets Act 1920 s. 8 (providing for up to 14 years' imprisonment for offences under the Official Secrets Act 1911); 18 U.S.C. §794 (gathering or delivering defence information to aid a foreign government); cf. 18 U.S.C. §793 (gathering, transmitting or losing information 'relating to the national defense', punishable by up to 10 years' imprisonment); Zimbabwean Official Secrets Act s. 3.

This range of criminal penalties can equate to very expansive sentences, especially when other offences are said to be involved. For instance, the indictment of Edward Snowden covered three counts, for theft of government property, unauthorized communication of national defence information and wilful communication of classified intelligence information to an unauthorized person, and on this basis could expose him to up to 30 years in prison.[77] In many states, a defendant may also be subject to heavy fines.[78]

Some states set out factors which may aggravate or mitigate penalties when it comes to sentencing. For example, Norway provides for a list of factors to determine whether a disclosure is 'aggravated', such as whether:

> a) the perpetrator is a member of the Government, the Parliament or the Supreme Court, or a member of the country's highest civilian or military leadership, b) the secret was entrusted to the perpetrator in the course of service or work, c) the secret has been disclosed to a foreign state or a terrorist organization, d) considerable harm has resulted.[79]

Australia's Criminal Code includes aggravated offences that increase prescribed penalties for underlying offences. Aggravating circumstances include where the underlying offence was committed in circumstances including dealing with information from a foreign military agency, dealing with five or more security classified records, altering a record to remove or conceal its security classification and holding an Australian government security clearance allowing access to at least 'secret' security classified information at the time the person dealt with the information.[80]

2. Application of Espionage and Official Secrets Laws Around the World

Espionage laws of every stripe have been used across the globe to punish state officials, ordinary citizens and journalists and to deter others from reporting on legitimate stories of public interest at odds with the government's perspective. Cases that showcase key trends, set important precedents, or have prompted significant reforms are outlined below.

2.1. Europe and United Kingdom
2.1.1. United Kingdom
The British case of Clive Ponting, although dated, reflects the challenges of official secrets laws that are devoid of a public interest defence.[81] Ponting, an employee at the

---

[77] S. Shane, 'Ex-Contractor Is Charged in Leaks on N.S.A. Surveillance' (The New York Times, 21 June 2013).
[78] See, e.g., UK Official Secrets Act 1989 s. 10; French Penal Code Art. 413-10; French Official Secrets Act s. 17 (100,000 EUR).
[79] Norwegian Penal Code ch. 17 s. 124.
[80] Australian Criminal Code Act ss 91.6, 122.3.
[81] UK Central Criminal Court, *R. v. Ponting* 1985 Crim L.R. 318, 11 February 1985.

UK Ministry of Defence, admitted to disclosing classified documents to a Member of Parliament about the sinking of an Argentine warship during the Falklands conflict in 1985.[82] Prior to the disclosure, Prime Minister Margaret Thatcher had told Parliament that the warship had been steaming towards, and therefore threatening, the British Royal Navy, and on that basis she had accepted a naval commander's request to sink the ship despite over 1,000 sailors being onboard.[83] However, Ponting uncovered information that suggested that the ship was in fact steaming *away* from the British, and after being told by his superiors to keep quiet, Ponting reported this to one of Thatcher's opponents, Labour MP Tam Dalyell.[84]

Ponting was charged under section 2(1) of the Official Secrets Act 1911, which provided that it was an offence to communicate any official information to a person other than 'a person to whom it is in the interest of the State his duty to communicate it'.[85] The law did not include an explicit public interest defence.[86] At his trial, Ponting argued that the phrase 'in the interests of the State' amounted to an implicit public interest defence and submitted that, in communicating the impugned information to Dalyell, he had acted in the public interest—which, he made clear, need not be the same as the interests of the government of the day.[87] The judge disagreed with this construction, summing up to the jury as follows:

> What, then of the words, 'the interests of the state'? Members of the jury I direct you that those words mean the policies of the state as they were in July 1984 when Mr Pointing communicated the information to Mr Dalyell, and not the policies of the state as Mr Ponting, Mr Dalyell, you or I might think they ought to have been ... I direct you in law that it is no defence that he honestly believed that it was his duty to leak the documents in the interests of the state if, in fact, it was not his duty to do so in the interests of the state.[88]

Despite this direction, the jury acquitted Ponting.[89] The case led to a debate as to whether, and if so how, the Official Secrets Act should be reformed. A private members Bill which included an explicit public interest defence was introduced, and defeated, in 1988. The British Government ultimately passed the Official Secrets Act 1989, which amended the 1911 Act but did not incorporate a public interest defence. The government of the day argued at the time that 'it cannot be acceptable that a person can lawfully disclose information which he knows may, for example, lead to

---

[82] M. Rosenbaum, 'Clive Ponting case: Where is the investigators' report?' (BBC News, 18 May 2011).
[83] P. Davison, 'Clive Ponting, British defense official who turned whistleblower, dies at 74' (The Washington Post, 11 August 2020).
[84] Ibid.
[85] UK Official Secrets Act 1911 s. 2: see Bartlett & Everett (n 3) 12–13, 42.
[86] However, an earlier version of the same offence, section 2 of the UK Official Secrets Act 1889, did explicitly reference the public interest, prohibiting breaches of official trust, but only those contrary to the 'interests of the State' or 'the public interest'. The 1911 Act was passed after successive attempts to tighten the 1889 law, which British governments considered weak and difficult to prosecute as it only applied to Crown Servants and government contractors and when a communication was *not* in the public interest.
[87] Rosenbaum (n 82).
[88] Bartlett & Everett (n 3) 5.6.
[89] D. Hewitt, ' "Not only a right, but a duty": A history of perverse verdicts' (The Justice Gap, 1 May 2018).

loss of life simply because he conceives that he has a general reason of a public character for doing so'.[90]

However, the Law Commission of England and Wales has since called for the introduction of such a defence in English law[91] on the basis that it was 'unable to state with confidence' that the current law on unauthorized disclosures 'afford[ed] adequate protection to Article 10 rights' protecting freedom of expression.[92] The Commission considered that a reasonable belief that the disclosure was in the public interest was insufficient and that to benefit from this defence the speaker must prove,[93] on the balance of probabilities, that the subject matter of the disclosure, and the manner in which it was disclosed, were in the public interest.[94] The Commission considered making a public interest defence available for journalists or those engaged in 'journalistic activity', similar to Australia's legislation and the UK Data Protection Act. Although it did not reach a clear conclusion on this point,[95] it considered it 'important to note' that European case law 'does not depend on the definition of "journalist" '.[96]

The Law Commission report also recommended expanding the territorial ambit of the United Kingdom's espionage provisions,[97] removing the requirement to prove

---

[90] L. Maer & O. Gay, 'Official Secrecy' (UK House of Commons Library, 30 December 2008), 2, 3, 6; A. Bailin, 'Let's free the Official Secrets Act from its cold war freeze' (The Guardian, 22 September 2011).

[91] The public interest defence recommended by the Commission has two components. For public servants, the Commission recommended that a statutory commissioner be established, and that there should be a 'strong presumption' of disclosure to the commissioner, although a public interest defence would nonetheless be available. For non-public servants, the Commission considered that the defence should be available to anyone charged under the Official Secrets Act 1989. UK Law Commission, *Protection of Official Data Report* (2020), §§9.153, 10.71. The Commission recommended some minimum requirements for such a statutory commissioner: independence, the ability to meaningfully investigate allegations, compel cooperation with investigation and act expeditiously and incorporate a right to appeal against its decisions: §§10.108–10.110.

[92] Ibid., §§9.6, 11.13–14 (citing the ECHR's *Bucur and Toma v. Romania* case and noting that such a defence would 'increase the likelihood' of compliance with article 10 'in all situations', as it 'provides a backstop in the event that the mechanisms for investigation and redress are rendered ineffective'); UK Law Commission, '*Protection of Official Data: Summary*' (2020), 9. See s. III.4 (Necessity).

[93] UK Law Commission, *Protection of Official Data Report* (2020), §11.79. Although it considered whether only an evidential burden should lie with the defence (whereby 'the defence must raise an issue of public interest sufficient for the prosecution to disprove it as part of the burden of proof resting on the prosecution'), the Commission ultimately favoured a more stringent 'persuasive burden', whereby the defendant must show on the balance of probabilities that the disclosure was in the public interest: §§11.28–11.34. The Commission considered the former formulation might place 'impossible demands on the prosecution', require extensive disclosure of information and was not unduly challenging for the defence as it was only a balance of probabilities burden: §§11.31, 11.34.

[94] UK Law Commission, *Protection of Official Data Report* (2020), §11.28. The Commission considered whether the public interest should be a 'subject matter' approach, in which a disclosure would only be considered in the public interest if it fell within certain categories of information: §§11.54–11.59. However, the Commission preferred a broader approach consistent with Canadian law, whereby legislation provides types of disclosures that are *not* in the public interest as well as a list of factors which are relevant to whether the disclosure *is* in the public interest: §§11.60–11.66, 11.76–11.81.

[95] Ibid., §§11.67–11.75.

[96] Ibid., §§11.70. The Commission's recommendation to implement a public interest defence only extends to offences under the Official Secrets Act 1989 and not to espionage offences. The Commission argued that 'to be guilty of espionage, an individual would have to act with a purpose they knew or had reasonable cause to believe was prejudicial to the interests of the state' and as such 'is not commensurate with a public interest defence': UK Law Commission, '*Protection of Official Data: Summary*' (2020), 10.

[97] UK Law Commission, *Protection of Official Data Report* (2020), §§3.150–3.152. The Commission also recommended that the territorial ambit of ss 1–4 of the Official Secrets Act 1989 should be amended so that offences of disclosure by government contractors apply irrespective of whether he or she is a British citizen, in effect expanding the territorial application of that Act: §5.222.

damage from certain unauthorized disclosure provisions[98] and increasing maximum[99] penalties.[100] These recommendations were strongly opposed by a number of media organizations and civil rights groups. But the Commission considered that such concerns 'will have been addressed by fortifying and balancing this recommendation' with its most significant proposed amendment: the inclusion of a public interest defence for those charged under the Official Secrets Act 1989.[101]

In a consultation paper published in 2021 following the Law Commission's report, the UK Home Office stated that it disagreed with the proposal for a public interest defence, observing that it 'believes that existing offences are compatible with Article 10 and that these proposals could in fact undermine our efforts to prevent damaging unauthorized disclosures, which would not be in the public interest'.[102] The government also argued that a whistleblower will 'rarely (if ever) be able to accurately judge whether the public interest in disclosing the information outweighs the risks against disclosure'.[103] The Home Office sought consultation on its own set of recommendations, focused on adopting some of the Law Commission's stricter provisions[104] while disregarding the balancing it recommended through a public interest defence.[105] The National Security Act, sponsored by the Home Office and enacted into law in July 2023, includes a reform

---

[98] The current Act requires proof that the disclosure caused, or was likely to cause, damage to a specific state interest before primary disclosures (by public officials) and secondary disclosures (by members of the public, including journalists) will be unlawful (except for certain information disclosed by a member of the security and intelligence services). However, the Commission recommended that damage only need be proved for secondary disclosures, rather than primary disclosures by public officials. The rationale behind this recommendation was that the 'damage requirement presented a practical hurdle for prosecutors who would be required to disclose further sensitive information at trial'. See UK Law Commission, *Protection of Official Data Report* (2020), §§4.80–4.83, 4.14–4.15.

[99] Ibid., §§5.47, 5.55, 5.70–5.72. The Commission described the existing two-year maximum sentence under the Official Secrets Act 1989 as 'low when compared to the maximum available sentence in similar jurisdictions', for example Canada's Security and Information Act 2001, which provides a 14-year maximum. Guardian News and Media questioned the validity of this assertion, noting that many countries limit the maximum sentence to five years' imprisonment absent proof of delivery of information to a foreign state or intent to prejudice security or defence. The Commission did not specify what the maximum sentences should be, but noted that a distinction should be made between offences committed by civil servants versus others. The UK Government has supported all but the final component of the Commission's recommendation on penalties, and asked consultees whether there should be such a distinction. UK Home Office, *Legislation to Counter State Threats (Hostile State Activity) Government Consultation* (2021), 19–20.

[100] It also proposed updating some 'archaic' language in the Official Secrets Act 1911 and 1920. See UK Law Commission, *Protection of Official Data Report* (2020), §§3.32, 3.110 (such as replacing references to 'sketch, plan, model, note ...' with 'document, information or other article', and replacing 'enemy' with 'foreign power').

[101] Ibid., §4.80. The United Kingdom has previously had some form of a public interest defence in that a criminal sanction for a breach of official trust was limited to breaches which could be shown to be contrary to the public interest. Section 2(1) of the Official Secrets Act 1889 prohibited communication of information to any person to whom it 'ought not, in the interest of the State, or otherwise in the public interest' to be communicated. This was repealed and replaced by a more narrow provision in section 2 of the Official Secrets Act 1911, which again was repealed with the passage of the Official Secrets Act 1989: see Bartlett & Everett (n 3) 12–13, 19–21.

[102] UK Home Office, *Legislation to Counter State Threats (Hostile State Activity) Government Consultation* (2021), 24. See s. IV. (Recommendations).

[103] Ibid.

[104] The UK Government welcomed the proposal to remove the harm requirement, noting 'that both primary and onward disclosures have the potential to cause equal amounts of harm' and has requested consultation as to whether this proposal should be extended even further, to secondary disclosures: UK Home Office, *Legislation to Counter State Threats (Hostile State Activity) Government Consultation* (2021) 18. This sits in contrast to the Law Commission, which was at pains to distinguish primary and secondary disclosures on the basis that 'concerns about over-criminalising conduct that is not causing damage are quite different' in each case: UK Law Commission, *Protection of Official Data Report* (2020), §§4.13, 4.34; 4.43.

[105] UK Home Office, *Legislation to Counter State Threats (Hostile State Activity) Government Consultation* (2021), 24.

of espionage offences under the Official Secrets Acts 1911–1939.[106] While the Home Office maintains that the Act 'does not replace' the offences of unauthorized disclosure under the Official Secrets Act 1989,[107] journalists have expressed concern that the new offences 'risks lumping in investigative journalists, whistleblowers and civil-society groups with spies' and lamented the absence of a statutory public interest defence.[108]

2.1.2. Slovenia

In Slovenia, recent amendments to official secrets laws to incorporate a public interest defence were introduced into law following backlash against the attempted prosecution of investigative journalist Anuška Delić. Delić, a reporter for Slovenian newspaper Delo, published a series of articles ahead of Slovenia's 2011 elections revealing connections between a neo-Nazi group 'Blood & Honour' and members of the major political party which ultimately succeeded in forming government.[109]

The Slovenian Intelligence and Security Agency (SOVA) charged Delić under article 260 of Slovenia's Criminal Code with dissemination of classified information, punishable by up to three years' imprisonment. The indictment alleged that Delić's articles contained classified information acquired from an unidentified SOVA official and that she had compromised SOVA's methods by publishing the information.[110]

At trial, Delić gave evidence that the articles contained information already in the public domain and that, in any event, it did not harm SOVA or Slovenia's interests. For example, Delić argued that her sources included Facebook posts which identified the leader of the Blood and Honour group, as well as publicly available registers.[111] And the materials at trial included an internal SOVA report conceding that the agency had not suffered negative consequences as a result of the articles in question.[112] On 15 April 2015, moments before judgment was set to be handed down, state prosecutors withdrew all charges against Delić, but maintained her guilt in a statement before the judge and media.[113]

The case became a catalyst for reform: in October 2014, Slovenia's then Prime Minister said that the case demonstrated 'the need to consider legislation on media freedom', and that '[j]ournalists must be protected from criminal liability for publishing information that is in the public interest'.[114] And in July 2015, Slovenia's parliament

---

[106] See UK National Security Bill 2022. See also UK Home Office, 'Policy paper—New espionage offences: fact sheet' (13 July 2023) (noting that '[e]spionage is now addressed by 3 offences in the Bill: obtaining or disclosing protected information; obtaining or disclosing trade secrets; and assisting a foreign intelligence service' and that '[t]he Bill repeals the Official Secrets Acts 1911, 1920 and 1939, which contain the existing provisions').
[107] UK Home Office, 'Policy paper—Journalistic freedoms: National Security Bill factsheet' (13 July 2023).
[108] See, e.g., The Editorial Board, 'Another threat to media freedom' (Financial Times, 29 January 2023).
[109] M. Nazar, 'Slovenia: How a neo-Nazi exposé almost landed a journalist in jail' (Index on Censorship, 17 February 2016).
[110] See also R. Greenslade, 'Slovenian journalist facing jail for revealing party's neo-Nazi links' (The Guardian, 15 September 2014).
[111] European Federation of Journalists, 'EFJ demands Slovenian authorities to drop charges against journalist' (4 August 2015).
[112] M. Nazar, 'Slovenia: How a neo-Nazi exposé almost landed a journalist in jail' (Index on Censorship, 17 February 2016). But the report also included a handwritten note from a high-ranking senior official requesting a further report be drafted with a different result, which the prosecution did not produce.
[113] Ibid.
[114] M. Cerar, Tweet 1/2 of 14 October 2014; M. Cerar, Tweet 2/2 of 14 October 2014.

voted 86–1 to introduce a public interest defence for all persons charged under article 260.[115] Although this defence remains in place, Slovenia has experienced a 'swift downturn in press and media freedom' by other means after the Slovenian Democratic Party, the subject of Delić's investigations, returned to power in March 2020, with the International Press Institute reporting extensive social media attacks on journalists and attempts to defund and discredit the state's public broadcaster.[116]

2.2. Asia Pacific
2.2.1. Myanmar

In Myanmar, colonial-era secrecy laws have been used to crack down on journalists and human rights defenders critical of the government. A striking example is the case of Reuters journalists Wa Lone and Kyaw Soe Oo, who were arrested and charged in 2017 under the Official Secrets Act for possessing classified documents containing information about police personnel, arms and ammunition, and attacks in the Rakhine area of Myanmar.

The journalists were convicted despite evidence that the information in the documents was already public, that neither journalist had shared or published the information and that the documents had been planted on them by the police. One police officer, who testified for the prosecution, shocked observers by telling the court that he was present at the meeting at which a police brigadier instructed subordinates to plant the documents on Wa Lone and arrest him.[117] Evidence at trial showed that the true motive for the arrest was the journalists' investigation into the executions of Rohingya Muslims in a village called Inn Dinn in Rakhine State.[118]

The defence centred on evidence that Wa Lone and Kyaw Soe Oo had been lured into a restaurant and had documents planted on them, and that the prosecution had failed to prove the key elements of the charge. First, the prosecution had failed to prove that the documents had been published or shared. Second, there was no evidence the documents were in fact secret, since they were either non-substantive or already in the public domain. Finally, the prosecution had not shown that the documents were intended to be useful to any 'enemy', or that Wa Lone and Kyaw Soe Oo had acted for 'any purpose prejudicial to the safety and interests of the state'.

---

[115] Slovenia Criminal Code, Art. 260(4). See II.1.4.1. (Public interest); International Press Institute, 'Slovenia introduces public interest defence for those who publish classified information' (IFEX, 21 July 2015). However, Slovenia has retained other misdemeanour offences for disclosure of classified information by persons entrusted with such information which do not incorporate a public interest defence: Slovenian Classified Information Act Arts 44, 44a and 45.

[116] J. Wiseman, 'New Administration, Old Agenda: Press Freedom Strained Again in Slovenia Under Veteran PM Janša' (International Press Institute, 1 September 2020). According to Reporters Without Borders, '[a] climate of hostility toward journalists has defused since Prime Minister Janez Janša's departure in 2022 and the legal framework protecting press freedom remains strong. But the media continues to face political pressure': Reporters Without Borders, 'Slovenia'.

[117] R. Paddock & others, 'Who Was Most Opposed to Freeing 2 Reporters in Myanmar? Aung San Suu Kyi' (The New York Times, 10 May 2019).

[118] Section 3 of Myanmar's Official Secrets Act prohibits the conduct of a person who 'obtains, collects, records or publishes or communicates to any other person any secret official … document or information' that may be 'useful to an enemy'.

Nevertheless, in September 2018, both men were found guilty and sentenced to seven years' imprisonment. The Court held that it was the defendants' responsibility to prove their innocence, refused to accept any exculpatory evidence and considered the documents found on the defendants' phones to contain 'security sensitive matters' which could 'serve as useful information to' armed 'insurgent groups' if it got into their hands.[119] A few months later, the High Court of Yangon Region dismissed the journalists' appeal, focusing on section 3(2) of the Official Secrets Act which provides that it is not necessary to prove a prejudicial purpose if 'from the circumstances of the case' or a defendant's 'conduct or his known character as proved, it appears' that he had such a purpose. The High Court considered that since Wa Lone had tried to meet victims of the Inn Dinn attack, had a notebook allegedly containing phone numbers of members of the Arakan Army, had contacted the officer in question and been in possession of the impugned documents, the prosecution had proved a prejudicial purpose. Myanmar's highest court, the Supreme Court, rejected a further appeal in April 2019.[120]

International outcry followed these decisions. The UN High Commissioner for Human Rights at the time, Michelle Bachelet, stated that the verdict 'sends a message to all journalists in Myanmar that they cannot operate fearlessly, but must rather make a choice to either self-censor or risk prosecution'.[121] Both men were awarded the Pulitzer Prize for their journalism and were ultimately released and relocated abroad.[122]

Since the February 2021 *coup d'etat* in the country, the military junta has charged the country's de facto head of government, Aung San Suu Kyi, and her advisors under the same official secrets laws that were used to convict the 'Reuters two'.[123] In September 2022, Aung San Suu Kyi was convicted and sentenced to three years' imprisonment for this crime.[124]

2.2.2. Australia

In two recent cases, the Australian Federal Police (AFP) conducted raids as part of its investigations into the unauthorized disclosure of classified information.[125] In June 2019,

---

[119] Yangon Northern District Court, *Police Lieutenant Colonel Yu Naing v. Thet Oo Maung (Wa Lone) and Kyaw Soe Oo (Moe Aung)*, 3 September 2018 (unofficial translation).

[120] S. Naing & S. Lewis, 'Myanmar's top court rejects final appeal by jailed Reuters journalists' (Reuters, 23 April 2019).

[121] OHCHR, 'Comment by UN High Commissioner for Human Rights Michelle Bachelet on the conviction of two Reuters journalists in Myanmar' (3 September 2018).

[122] The Pulitzer Prizes, 'Staff of Reuters, with notable contributions from Wa Lone and Kyaw Soe Oo' (8 February 2018); J. van Leuven, 'Wa Lone and Kyaw Soe Oo honored with the Pulitzer Prize' (Deutsche Welle, 17 April 2019). Following pressure from civil rights groups and diplomatic channels, and after almost a year and a half behind bars, Wa Lone and Kyaw Soe Oo were released in May 2019 as part of a presidential amnesty for 6,520 prisoners. S. Lewis & S. Naing, 'Two Reuters reporters freed in Myanmar after more than 500 days in jail' (Reuters, 7 May 2019).

[123] 'Myanmar: Aung San Suu Kyi charged with violating secrets law' (BBC, 2 April 2021).

[124] This is one of many cases against Suu Kyi, who was sentenced to a total of 33 years in prison: 'Court rulings against Myanmar's Aung San Suu Kyi' (Reuters, 30 December 2022). In August 2023, the military junta announced a partial pardon of Suu Kyi, reducing her 33-year sentence by six years: C. Hall, 'Myanmar Supreme Court dismisses appeals of Aung San Suu Kyi corruption convictions' (JURIST, 6 October 2023).

[125] Australia does not have a right to freedom of speech that is generally understood as a 'personal' or 'individual' right like freedoms conferred by a Bill of Rights in the American model. Rather, Australian courts have held that provisions of the Australian Constitution that created a system of representative government gave rise to an 'implied' freedom to discuss political and governmental affairs. See High Court of Australia, *Lange v Australian*

the AFP conducted a search at the home of News Corp journalist Annika Smethurst, after Smethurst published allegations that the Australian Government had considered a proposal to expand programs to spy on Australian citizens without warrants.[126]

Within a day of the Smethurst raid, the AFP conducted a second raid, this time at the Sydney headquarters of Australia's public broadcaster, the Australian Broadcasting Commission (ABC). The raid concerned reports known as the 'Afghan Files', published nearly two years earlier by journalists Dan Oakes and Sam Clark. The reports alleged the unlawful killing of Afghan civilians by Australian special forces soldiers, revealed by way of 'hundreds of pages of secret defence force documents leaked to the ABC'.[127] The search warrant was issued under section 3E of the Crimes Act 1914, and named Mr. Oakes and whistleblower and former military lawyer David McBride. The raids prompted significant public outcry from journalists and human rights advocates,[128] with The New York Times' Editorial Board describing the raids as 'straight from the playbook of authoritarian thugs'.[129]

Both warrants were challenged in court. Smethurst was successful on narrow grounds in what was described as a 'pyrrhic victory' for press freedom,[130] and the ABC's challenge failed.[131] In rejecting the ABC's grounds for challenging the warrant, Justice Abraham dismissed the argument the AFP's conduct may have a chilling effect on prospective whistleblowers, noting 'that the US doctrine of "chilling effect" has no place in the Australian constitutional context'.[132] The ABC's Managing Director announced that the broadcaster would not appeal the decision, stating 'we don't believe we can litigate our way to reforming fundamentally bad laws'.[133]

Despite the raids, Australian prosecutors ultimately declined to follow the AFP recommendation to charge Mr. Oakes, stating that they had 'determined the public interest does not require a prosecution in the particular circumstances of the case'.[134]

Broadcasting Corporation [1997] HCA 25; (1997) 189 CLR 520, 8 July 1997; High Court of Australia, *McCloy v New South Wales* [2015] HCA 34; (2015) 257 CLR 178, 07 October 2015.

[126] Smethurst published details of a proposal to allow the Australian Signals Directorate (ASD) to secretly access the communications, bank records and other materials of Australian citizens with ministerial authorization.

[127] D. Oakes & S. Clark, 'The Afghan Files: Defence leak exposes deadly secrets of Australia's special forces' (ABC News, 10 July 2017).

[128] See, e.g., M. Ketchell, 'Australia doesn't protect free speech but it could' (The Conversation, 6 June 2019); A. Galloway, 'A chilling effect': Human Rights Watch slams Australia's raids on the media' (Sydney Morning Herald, 15 January 2020); Amnesty International, 'Response to AFP raids on Australian Press' (5 June 2019).

[129] 'Why Are the Australian Police Rummaging Through Journalists' Files?' (The New York Times, 6 June 2019).

[130] Due to errors on the face of the warrant, none of the seven High Court judges that ruled on the matter thought it necessary to answer a much anticipated question on infringement of the implied freedom of political communication: D. Levitan & D. Hurley, 'Memo from our lawyers to journos everywhere: Smethurst's win is a pyrrhic victory for freedom' (Crikey, 17 April 2020); High Court of Australia, *Smethurst v. Commissioner of Police* [2020] HCA 14; (2020) 376 ALR 575, 15 April 2020.

[131] Federal Court of Australia, *Australian Broadcasting Corporation v. Kane (No. 2)* [2020] FCA 133, 17 February 2020.

[132] Ibid., §231, citing High Court of Australia, *Brown v. Tasmania* [2017] HCA 43; (2017) 261 CLR 328, 18 October 2017, at [262] per Nettle J.

[133] 'ABC statement on Federal Court ruling' (ABC, 28 February 2020).

[134] As quoted by the AFP, 'AFP statement on investigation into ABC journalist' (15 October 2020). Sam Clark, the producer of the program, was cleared by the AFP of any potential charges in July 2020: see 'Journalists express concerns as AFP recommends charges against ABC Reporter' (SBS News, 3 July 2020). In November 2020, the Inspector-General of the Australian Defence Force released the results of an inquiry into the Australian special

The investigation against Smethurst was also dropped.[135] Journalists and human rights advocates have argued that nevertheless the chilling impact of the AFP's actions has fundamentally impacted Australia's media environment, and the episode led to two parliamentary inquiries reviewing the relevant laws.[136]

2.2.3. Cambodia

The arrest and trial of Cambodian journalists Yeang Sothearin and Uon Chhin is an example of a vague state secret law being used to harass journalists and criminalize speech that is neither secret nor harmful. In 2017, Yeang Sothearin and Uon Chhin, two journalists who had worked for Radio Free Asia, were charged with committing an 'act of giving or facilitating easy access by a foreign state or its agents, to information ... which undermine[s] the national defence'.[137] The Cambodian government claimed that one of the journalists took broadcasting equipment from the Radio Free Asia bureau, installed it in a private residence and the journalists then used this equipment to continue to transmit reports to Radio Free Asia's Washington D.C. Headquarters.[138] These charges came one month after Cambodian authorities ordered the closure of 32 radio frequencies, particularly stations that relayed independent Khmer language news broadcasts.[139] After the closure of the Radio Free Asia bureau, senior officials from the government threatened that any journalists still filing media reports would be labelled as spies.[140]

Uon Chhin and Yeang Sothearin admitted to sharing publicly available information about local events with Radio Free Asia but denied having undermined national security in any manner.[141] At trial, the prosecution was not able to identify any information disclosed by the defendants that was not publicly available at the time of the alleged disclosure and failed to explain the impact of any alleged transmissions on Cambodia's national security.[142] Instead, they simply alleged that the defendants were making the

---

forces' conduct in Afghanistan, which found credible information of 23 incidents of war crimes committed by Australian personnel: Inspector-General of the Australian Defence Force, *Afghanistan Inquiry Report* (2020), 28–29. However, charges against whistleblower David McBride, a former military lawyer who was named in the search warrant against the ABC as the source of the leaked information regarding war crimes in Afghanistan, have not been dropped. See C. Knaus, 'Defence whistleblower David McBride to stand trial four years and eight months after being charged' (The Guardian, 13 April 2023).

[135] J. Hayne, 'AFP will not lay charges against Annika Smethurst over publishing of classified intelligence documents' (ABC News, 26 May 2020).
[136] See, e.g., S. Ludlam & D. Paris, 'Breaking: A report on the erosion of press freedom in Australia' (Digital Rights Watch, 2019); 'ABC raid: Outcry as Australian police search public broadcaster' (BBC, 5 June 2019); Parliament of Australia, 'Inquiry into the impact of the exercise of law enforcement and intelligence powers on the freedom of the press: Terms of Reference'; Parliament of Australia, *Inquiry into the impact of the exercise of law enforcement and intelligence powers on the freedom of the press* (2020).
[137] Cambodian General Provisions for Implementation of Criminal Code, Art. 445.
[138] P. Cobus, 'Cambodian Appeals Court Rejects RFA Reporters' Motion for Dismissal' (Voice of America, 29 January 2020).
[139] Ibid.
[140] Editorial Board, 'In Cambodia, journalism has become a crime' (The Washington Post, 23 August 2019).
[141] See G. Sluiter, 'Cambodia vs. Uon Chhin and Yeang Sothearin' (American Bar Association, CFJ, January 2020).
[142] Ibid.

information known abroad, rather than just available in Cambodia.[143] The trial was also tainted by a number of abuses of process.[144]

In October 2019, the Phnom Penh Municipal Court of First Instance ultimately ruled that there was insufficient evidence to convict Uon Chhin and Yeang Sothearin.[145] But instead of dismissing the case, the court sent it for reinvestigation without stipulating a timeline for completion.[146] In 2020, the journalists' appeal to reverse the court's decision to re-investigate their case was rejected by the Court of Appeal and the Supreme Court respectively.[147] Both journalists continue to be on bail and face constraints on their freedom of movement while under judicial supervision.[148]

2.2.4. Hong Kong and China

On 30 June 2020, Chinese authorities passed a draconian 'National Security Law' described as 'Beijing's most aggressive assault on Hong Kong people's freedoms since the transfer of sovereignty in 1997'.[149] The National Security Law criminalizes secession, subversion, terrorist activity and 'collusion with a foreign country' in a manner that is so broad and imprecise that it appears to be capable of capturing any speech critical of the government, wherever uttered at any time in perpetuity.[150] The penalty for secession or subversion 'of a grave nature' is a minimum 10 year prison sentence or a maximum of life imprisonment.[151] And the Law provides that trials 'involving State secrets or public order' can be partially or entirely closed to the public.[152]

The chilling impact of the National Security Law was quickly felt by Hong Kong's press and population. The day after it was passed, over 370 protesters were arrested by police in Hong Kong under its provisions, including for waving independence flags.[153] The following month, over 200 police officers raided the offices of a major pro-democracy newspaper in Hong Kong and arrested and charged its owner Jimmy Lai with 'incitement' and 'colluding with foreign elements'.[154]

---

[143] Ibid., 26.
[144] Ibid. In 2018, WGAD held that both journalists' right to freedom of expression had been violated and that the 'appropriate remedy' would be to release both men unconditionally and accord them an enforceable right to compensation and reparations: WGAD, *Chhin v. Cambodia* (Opinion no. 3/2019), 24 April 2019, §§64–66.
[145] Human Rights Watch, 'Cambodia: Drop Charges Against Journalists' (19 January 2020).
[146] G. Sluiter, 'Cambodia vs. Uon Chhin and Yeang Sothearin' (American Bar Association, CFJ, January 2020).
[147] UN Secretary-General, *Report of the Secretary General on the Role and achievements of the Office of the United Nations High Commissioner for Human Rights in assisting the Government and people of Cambodia in the promotion and protection of human rights* (2021) UN Doc. A/HRC/48/49, §20.
[148] Human Rights Watch, 'Cambodia: Drop Charges Against Journalists' (19 January 2020).
[149] Human Rights Watch, 'China: New Hong Kong Law a Roadmap for Repression' (29 July 2020).
[150] The Law of the People's Republic of China on Safeguarding National Security in the Hong Kong Special Administrative Region (Hong Kong National Security Law) Arts 20–30. See Amnesty International, 'Hong Kong's national security law: 10 things you need to know' (17 July 2020).
[151] Hong Kong National Security Law Arts 20, 22.
[152] Ibid., Art. 41.
[153] H. Davidson & L. Kuo, 'Hong Kong: hundreds arrested as Security law comes into effect' (The Guardian, 1 July 2020).
[154] Human Rights Watch, 'China/Hong Kong: Mass Arrests Under Security Laws' (11 August 2020); 'Jimmy Lai appears in Hong Kong court in metal chain' (Al Jazeera, 12 December 2020); 'United Nations experts raise concerns with China that proceedings against Jimmy Lai violating his fundamental rights' (Doughty Street Chambers, 31 May 2023); Lai remains in prison awaiting trial, scheduled to begin in December 2023: D. De Luce & J. M. Frayer, 'Jimmy Lai's son says the jailed Hong Kong media tycoon "refuses to be cowed"' (NBC News, 26 September 2023).

The ramifications of the National Security Law in Hong Kong are indicative of a broader crackdown on speech in China ostensibly on the basis of national security concerns. China has been the one of the most prolific jailers of reporters in the world for several years, according to the Committee to Protect Journalists,[155] and prominent journalists have recently been detained under security laws.[156] For example, in August 2020, at a time of increasing tensions between China and Australia, Cheng Lei, an Australian journalist and the face of China's state-run English news service, suddenly disappeared and was charged with 'illegally supplying state secrets overseas'.[157] Chinese authorities also detained a popular Chinese-Australian human rights blogger and charged him with espionage,[158] even though the then Australian Prime Minister decried the allegations as 'absolutely untrue'.[159]

2.3. Middle East and Africa

2.3.1. Iran

A case that illustrates Iranian authorities' pretextual use of espionage offences, alongside fair trial violations and inhumane conditions of detention, is that of Jason Rezaian, a journalist for The Washington Post. Rezaian is a dual American-Iranian national who worked as The Washington Post's Tehran bureau chief from 2012. In 2014, Rezaian and his wife Yeganeh Salehi, also a journalist, were apprehended at their apartment by agents of the Iranian Revolutionary Guard Corps who produced an arrest warrant issued by the Revolutionary Court, which hears alleged crimes relating to national security.[160] The agents forced entry into their apartment, confiscated their passports and electronic equipment and demanded passwords for their social media and email accounts. Both journalists were blindfolded and sent to Evin Prison in Tehran. Salehi was released on bail after approximately 60 days in prison. But Rezaian was ultimately detained for 544 days, and was subjected to long periods of solitary confinement, death threats, sleep deprivation and lack of medical care.[161]

---

[155] CPJ, 'Number of journalists behind bars reaches global high' (9 December 2021).

[156] J. Griffiths, 'Detention of CGTN anchor shows that in Xi Jinping's China, not even the propagandists are safe' (CNN Business, 1 September 2020).

[157] Ibid.; D. Mendoza, 'Australian Journalist Arrested By Chinese Authorities On Espionage Charge' (OWP, 1 March 2021). See also F. Mao, 'Cheng Lei: Why has an Australian TV anchor been detained by China?' (BBC, 9 September 2020). Cheng Lei was released in October 2023 after serving three years in prison: B. Doherty, H. Davidson & D. Hurst, '"Tight hugs, teary screams": Cheng Lei releases first statement after release from detention in China' (The Guardian, 11 October 2023).

[158] B. Doherty, 'Yang Hengjun: Australian writer held in China for almost two years officially charged with espionage' (The Guardian, 9 October 2020). Hengjun's trial was held in May 2021 but as of August 2023, he had still not received a verdict or sentence: B. Doherty & R. Touma, 'Detained Australian writer fears he may die of kidney condition in China jail' (The Guardian, 27 August 2023).

[159] Ibid. In a September 2020 consular meeting, the first time anyone outside China's justice system had seen Yang in months, Yang maintained his innocence and stated he had endured more than 300 interrogations and was totally isolated without calls or correspondence in an attempt to 'break him'.

[160] WGAD, *Rezaian v. Iran* (Opinion no. 44/2015), 3 December 2015, §7.

[161] WGAD, UN Special Rapporteur on the promotion and protection of the right to freedom of opinion and expression, UN Special Rapporteur on the situation of human rights defenders, UN Special Rapporteur on the situation of human rights in the Islamic Republic of Iran, UN Special Rapporteur on torture and other cruel, inhuman or degrading treatment or punishment, *Letter to the Representative of the Islamic Republic of Iran*, Reference No. IRN 13/2015, 12 August 2015; US District Court for the District of Columbia, *Rezaian v. Iran* Civil Case No. 16-1960, Memorandum Opinion, 21 November 2019 and Complaint, §50.

Although the Revolutionary Court did not publicly disclose the charges against Rezaian, his lawyer—who 'is believed to be the only person outside the judiciary to have read the indictment'—has stated that Iranian authorities laid four charges, including espionage, collaborating with hostile governments, collecting and distributing information about foreign policies with malicious intent and propaganda against the establishment of Iran.[162] The Iranian Government purportedly relied on two pieces of evidence to sustain these charges: an unsolicited and unsuccessful job application to join the Obama-Biden 'transition team' in 2008, and correspondence between Rezaian and US officials in Dubai, where Rezaian requested his wife's visa process to be expedited as 'sometimes [Iran is] not the best place to be a journalist'.[163]

Following a trial marred with due process violations,[164] the Iranian authorities announced that Rezaian had been found guilty of espionage and sentenced to an unspecified prison term.[165] Rezaian was ultimately released as part of a prisoner swap in January 2016, following extensive public outcry about the case[166] and a decision by the UN Working Group on Arbitrary Detention finding that his detention was arbitrary and a violation of his right to freedom of expression.[167] Rezaian and his family members have since succeeded in a claim in a US federal court under the US Foreign Sovereign Immunities Act in which the Rezaian family was awarded almost $180 million US dollars in damages.[168]

Iran continues to use espionage offences to detain journalists on political grounds. In 2022, two reporters were charged with conspiring with the intelligence agencies of foreign powers to undermine Iran's national security when they reported the brutal police beating of a 22-year-old protester arrested for failing to cover her hair properly.[169] The death of the protester sparked nationwide unrest.[170] The journalists remain in prison.[171]

---

[162] WGAD, UN Special Rapporteur on the promotion and protection of the right to freedom of opinion and expression, UN Special Rapporteur on the situation of human rights defenders, UN Special Rapporteur on the situation of human rights in the Islamic Republic of Iran, UN Special Rapporteur on torture and other cruel, inhuman or degrading treatment or punishment, *Letter to the Representative of the Islamic Republic of Iran*, Reference No. IRN 13/2015, 12 August 2015; WGAD, *Rezaian v. Iran* (Opinion no. 44/2015), 3 December 2015, §16; C. Morello, 'Post reporter jailed in Iran faces 4 charges including espionage' (The Washington Post, 20 April 2015). See R. Gladstone & T. Erdbrink, 'Charges Against Jason Rezaian, Washington Post Reporter Held in Iran, Include Espionage' (The New York Times, 20 April 2015).

[163] N. Karimi, 'Closed-door Trial in Iran of Washington Post reporter begins' (The Press Democrat, 26 May 2015); WGAD, *Rezaian v. Iran* Urgent Petition submitted by the Washington Post (21 July 2015), 23–24.

[164] WGAD, *Rezaian v. Iran* (Opinion no. 44/2015), 3 December 2015, §14; US District Court for the District of Columbia, *Rezaian et al v. Iran* Civil Case No. 16-1960, Complaint, 3 October 2016, §88.

[165] US District Court for the District of Columbia, *Rezaian et al v. Iran*, Civil Case No. 16-1960, Complaint, 3 October 2016, §§82, 92.

[166] Ibid.

[167] OHCHR, 'UN human rights experts call on Iran to release journalist Jason Rezaian as he awaits verdict' (14 August 2015); WGAD, *Rezaian v. Iran* (Opinion no. 44/2015), 3 December 2015.

[168] US District Court for the District of Columbia, *Rezaian v. Iran*, Civil Case No. 16-1960, Memorandum Opinion, 21 November 2019. Iran failed to respond to the lawsuit, and Rezaian's US lawyers have noted that Iran is unlikely to pay the judgment voluntarily: 'WilmerHale Wins $180 Million Judgment Against Iran for Jason Rezaian and Family' (WilmerHale, 12 December 2019).

[169] See J. Rezaian, 'Niloofar Hamedi and Elaheh Mohammadi' (Time, 13 April 2023).

[170] A. Kohli, 'What to Know About the Iranian Protests Over Mahsa Amini's Death' (Time, 24 September 2022).

[171] See A. Pourahmadi, 'Hundreds of Iranian journalists call for the release of two colleagues jailed in Evin prison' (CNN, 31 October 2022). CPJ, 'Iranian journalists Niloofar Hamedi and Elahe Mohammadi sentenced' (22 October 2023).

2.4. North and South America

2.4.1. United States: Pentagon Papers

Prior to 2009, only a handful of cases had been brought by the US government against public servants for disclosing confidential information to the media in violation of the Espionage Act.[172] The first, and most famous, concerned The New York Times' publication of portions of the Pentagon Papers, a 7,000-page top secret report commissioned by the Nixon Administration detailing the United States' involvement in Vietnam.[173] Daniel Ellsberg, one of the government contractors involved in the Papers' preparation, transferred the report to New York Times reporter Neil Sheehan. Ellsberg and a colleague who had helped photocopy the Papers were charged with conspiracy, misappropriation of government property and violations of the Espionage Act.[174] The case was ultimately dismissed on the basis of government misconduct after the court found that Ellsberg's phone had been unlawfully tapped and his psychiatrist's office had been broken into by government agents.[175] And the US Supreme Court rejected a parallel application by the US Government to enjoin The New York Times as well as The Washington Post from publishing the full report's contents and findings in the case of *New York Times v. United States*, a decision that has long been heralded as a victory for the free press.[176] While the government argued that publication would 'result in irreparable injury to the national defense',[177] this argument 'fared poorly in court because the most recent of the documents was three years old and because much of the information about which the Government was upset either had no military significance or was already in the public domain, having been revealed at Congressional hearings or published in newspapers'.[178]

Although Justice Blackmun warned in his dissent that if publication results in 'the death of soldiers, the destruction of alliances, the greatly increased difficulty of negotiation with our enemies, the inability of our diplomats to negotiate… prolongation of the war and … further delay in the freeing of United States prisoners, then the Nation's people will know where the responsibility for these sad consequences rests',[179] it appears

---

[172] See s. I. (Introduction).
[173] US Supreme Court, *New York Times Co. v. United States* 403 U.S. 713, 30 June 1971, Dissenting Opinion of Burger J., 749 n. 6.
[174] N. Chokshi, 'Behind the Race to Publish the Top-Secret Pentagon Papers' (The New York Times, 20 December 2017); S. V. Roberts, 'Ellsberg Indicted Again in Pentagon Case' (The New York Times, 31 December 1971).
[175] M. Arnold, 'Pentagon Papers Charges Are Dismissed; Judge Byrne Frees Ellsberg and Russo, Assails "Improper Government Conduct"' (The New York Times, 11 May 1971). Ellsberg leaked a still-classified study about the Taiwan Strait crisis which he had copied at the same time as the Pentagon Papers but chose not to disclose, which shows that the United States was considering the use of atomic weapons against mainland China if the crisis escalated. Ellsberg, who passed away in 2023, released the study in 2017 and highlighted it amid new tensions between the United States and China regarding Taiwan. Ellsberg also suggested that he could have become a test case to challenge the use of the Espionage Act to 'criminalize classified truth-telling in the public interest': see C. Savage, 'Risk of Nuclear War Over Taiwan in 1958 Said to Be Greater Than Publicly Known' (The New York Times, 22 May 2021).
[176] See US Supreme Court, *New York Times Co. v. United States* 403 U.S. 713, 30 June 1971, Dissenting Opinion of Burger J., 749 n. 6.
[177] F. Abrams, 'The Pentagon Papers a Decade Later' (The New York Times, 7 June 1981).
[178] Ibid.
[179] US Supreme Court, *New York Times v. United States* 403 U.S. 713, 30 June 1971, Dissenting Opinion of Blackmun J., 763.

that '[n]one of the dire consequences of publication foreseen by the Government came to pass'.[180]

Although *New York Times v. United States* represents a victory for press freedom, several Justices of the Supreme Court accepted the premise that journalists could be subjected to criminal charges for publishing government information in violation of the Espionage Act.[181] Justice Black and Justice Douglas, in one of the concurring judgments, disagreed, holding that 'there is... no statute barring the publication by the press of the material which the Times and Post seek to use', because Congress used the word 'communicates' in the relevant law, as opposed to 'publish'.[182] Additionally, the Supreme Court did not definitively resolve that issue of the requisite intent, but two concurring Justices stated that the 'Government need not prove an intent to injure the United States or to benefit a foreign nation, but only willful and knowing conduct'.[183] Nor was the Act declared unconstitutional or reformed since then.

2.4.2. United States: Edward Snowden

In 2013, while working as a consultant for the NSA in Hawaii, whistleblower Edward Snowden downloaded a large but 'still-unknown amount of information' which revealed that the NSA was acquiring, storing and searching the telephone call, text and email data of millions of Americans and individuals around the globe.[184] Snowden travelled to Hong Kong and provided journalists with hundreds of classified documents, leading to the publication of a series of articles in The Guardian and The Washington Post exposing this mass surveillance program. Snowden's leaks also led to revelations about similar programs in nations across the world.[185]

In June 2013 the Obama administration charged Snowden with three counts, for theft of government property, unauthorized communication of national defence information and wilful communication of classified intelligence information to an unauthorized person, the latter two charges falling under the Espionage Act.[186] After the United States revoked Snowden's passport and filed a request for Hong Kong to arrest him, Snowden left Hong Kong and flew to Moscow.[187] He then spent 40 days in the

---

[180] F. Abrams, 'The Pentagon Papers a Decade Later' (The New York Times, 7 June 1981).
[181] See US Supreme Court, *New York Times v. United States* 403 U.S. 713, 30 June 1971, Concurring Opinion of White J., Stewart J., 733–737. See also Concurring Opinion of Marshall J., 745.
[182] Ibid. Section 793(e) of the US Espionage Act provides that 'whoever having unauthorized possession of, access to, or control over ... information relating to the national defense ... wilfully communicates, delivers [or] transmits ... the same to any person not entitled to receive it'. Although the government argued that 'communicates' is 'broad enough to encompass publication', the Justices noted the eight other sections of the law specifically mention 'publish', and held that 'Congress was capable of and did distinguish between publishing and communication in various sections of the Espionage Act'. Ibid. Concurring Opinion of Douglas J., Black J., 721.
[183] Ibid., Concurring Opinion of White J., Stewart J., 738, n 9.
[184] L. Downie & S. Rafsky, 'The Obama Administration and the Press: Leak investigations and surveillance in post-9/11 America' (CPJ, 10 October 2013).
[185] Amnesty International UK, 'Why Edward Snowden should be pardoned' (5 May 2023).
[186] S. Shane, 'Ex-Contractor Is Charged in Leaks on N.S.A. Surveillance' (The New York Times, 21 June 2013). These charges are punishable by up to 10 years' imprisonment each, exposing Snowden to up to 30 years' imprisonment if convicted. See E. MacAskill, 'Edward Snowden: what would happen if He went home—pardon or prison?' (The Guardian, 4 March 2015).
[187] P. Walker & J. Newell, 'Edward Snowden asks for asylum in Ecuador—as it happened' (The Guardian, 23 June 2013).

Moscow airport, seeking (and being rejected for) asylum from 27 countries, before he was granted temporary asylum in Russia, where he remains today.[188]

Snowden stated that he considered his disclosures different from other whistleblowers, arguing that he 'carefully evaluated every single document I disclosed to ensure that each was legitimately in the public interest', and that he chose to allow reputable journalists to determine which documents should be disclosed to the public.[189] He has indicated that he would return to the United States to face trial if given the opportunity to argue a public interest defence.[190] In 2015 the European Parliament narrowly voted in favour of granting protection to Snowden 'in recognition of his status as whistleblower and international human rights defender' and in 2016 a campaign to push for Snowden's pardon amassed support from key human rights organizations such as Human Rights Watch, Amnesty International and the ACLU.[191] And in September 2020, a US federal court found the 'the government may have violated the Fourth Amendment and did violate the Foreign Intelligence Surveillance Act ("FISA") when it collected the telephony metadata of millions of Americans'.[192]

2.4.3. United States: Julian Assange

The case against Ellsberg represents one of the few prosecutions for unauthorized disclosures prior to 2009.[193] From that point the Obama administration commenced an unprecedented number of prosecutions for whistleblowing, including against 10 government employees and contractors prosecuted for leaking classified information, eight of these under the Espionage Act.[194] This trend was continued by the Trump administration, which instigated nine prosecutions, six under the Espionage Act,[195] including the indictment against Julian Assange, the first non-government employee or contractor to be charged under the Act for the act of publishing confidential material.[196]

---

[188] See, e.g., D. Davies, 'Edward Snowden Speaks Out: "I Haven't and I Won't" Cooperate with Russia' (NPR, 19 September 2019); In October 2020, Snowden was granted permanent residency in Russia: A. Troianovski, 'Edward Snowden, in Russia Since 2013, Is Granted Permanent Residency' (The New York Times, 23 October 2020).

[189] G. Greenwald & others, 'Edward Snowden: the whistleblower behind the NSA surveillance revelations' (The Guardian, 11 June 2013).

[190] J. Grierson, 'Edward Snowden would be willing to return to US for fair trial' (The Guardian, 21 February 2016).

[191] T. McCarthy, 'Edward Snowden praises EU parliament vote against US extradition' (The Guardian, 29 October 2015); American Civil Liberties Union (ACLU), 'High-Profile Campaign Calls on Obama to Pardon Edward Snowden' (14 September 2016). See also S. Coliver, 'Why Snowden Won't Get the Public Interest Defense He Deserves' (Open Society Justice, 24 June 2015); D. Ellsberg, 'Daniel Ellsberg: Snowden would not get a fair trial—and Kerry is wrong' (The Guardian, 30 May 2014).

[192] US Court of Appeals, Ninth Circuit, *United States v. Moalin* 973 F.3d 977, 2 September 2020, 7.

[193] See, e.g., US Supreme Court, *New York Times Company v. United States* 403 U.S. 713, 30 June 1971. See also US Court of Appeals, Fourth Circuit, *United States v. Morison* 844 F.2d 1057, 1 April 1988, affirming the 1985 District Court conviction of naval intelligence officer Samuel Morison, for allegedly selling secret photos of a Soviet naval base to the British publication *Jane's Defence Weekly*. He was sentenced under Sections 793(d) and (e) of the US Espionage Act and for theft of government property, and sentenced to two years' imprisonment.

[194] G. Rottman, 'On Leak Prosecutions, Obama Takes it to 11. (Or Should We Say 526?)' (ACLU, 14 October 2014). The two other cases were treated as misdemeanours: see S. Ackerman & E. Pilkington, 'Obama's war on whistleblowers leaves administration insiders unscathed' (The Guardian, 16 March 2015).

[195] US Press Freedom Tracker, 'Incident Database: Leak Cases' reporting on cases between 1/20/2017 to 01/20/2021.

[196] See E. Tucker, 'US Charges WikiLeaks founder with publishing classified info' (Associated Press, 24 May 2019).

Despite the tradition of non-enforcement against journalists, section 793(e) of the Espionage Act prohibits the unauthorized *receipt* of national security secrets which on its face might create criminal liability for reporters, either as co-conspirators or for aiding and abetting the individuals who provided the information.[197] Some legal scholars argue, however, consistently with Justice Douglas and Black's concurrence in *New York Times Co v. United States*, that by omitting 'publishing' from section 793(e), Congress intentionally and purposefully excluded section 793(e)'s applicability to the press.[198]

But in 2019 the US Department of Justice indicted WikiLeaks founder Julian Assange for crimes committed under the Espionage Act, including under section 793(e), and sought to have him returned to the United States from the United Kingdom. The indictment related both to Assange allegedly conspiring with Army Intelligence Analyst Chelsea Manning to hack a US Department of Defense computer,[199] as well as WikiLeaks' publishing secret information. Wikileaks published thousands of documents obtained through Manning, including footage of US personnel killing civilians from a helicopter in Iraq, war logs from Afghanistan and Iraq, diplomatic cables and files from Guantánamo Bay which revealed abuses against inmates such as waterboarding and sleep deprivation.[200] However, the indictment alleges that Assange also published materials 'containing the names of individuals, who risked their safety and freedom by providing information to the United States and our allies' and that he 'communicated the documents containing names of those sources to all the world by publishing them on the Internet'.[201]

Before the UK court determining whether Assange should be extradited, counsel for the US Government emphasized that the publishing charges were 'expressly limited to documents which contained the names of human sources',[202] and alleged that hundreds of sources had been put 'at risk', with some relocated and others having 'disappeared', although 'the US cannot prove at this point that their disappearance was the result of being outed by WikiLeaks'.[203] Assange's defence counsel claimed that the prosecution had misrepresented the facts, and that WikiLeaks had worked for months in partnership with professional media organizations to redact the leaked documents but that one of the media partners had published a book containing the leaked password to the unredacted dataset, leading to its access and publication by other parties. The defence also argued that Assange had attempted to mitigate

---

[197] S. Vladeck, 'The Espionage Act and National Security Whistleblowing after *Garcetti*' (2007–2008) 57 *American University Law Review* 1531, 1536. See also US Espionage Act 1917, 18 U.S.C. §§793–799.

[198] See K. Wimmer & S. Kiehl, 'Prosecution of Journalists under the Espionage Act: Not so Fast' (2017) 33 *Communications Lawyer* 24, 25.

[199] US Department of Justice, 'WikiLeaks Founder Julian Assange Charged in 18-Count Superseding Indictment' (23 May 2019). See also US Department of Justice, 'WikiLeaks Founder Charged in Superseding Indictment' (24 June 2020), broadening 'the scope of the conspiracy surrounding alleged computer intrusions with which Assange was previously charged'.

[200] See C. Savage, 'Soldier Admits Providing Files to WikiLeaks' (The New York Times, 28 February 2013).

[201] US District Court for the Eastern District of Virgina, *United States v. Julian Assange* Crim. Case 1:18-cr-11, Superseding Indictment, 23 May 2019, Counts 15–17.

[202] UK Westminster Magistrates' Court, *The Government of the United States of America v. Julian Paul Assange*, 11 January 2021, §123.

[203] Ibid., §20.

any risk to sensitive sources by notifying the White House and State Department that publication outside WikiLeaks' control was potentially forthcoming.[204]

However, the defence did not dispute that after the initial disclosure by third parties unrelated to Wikileaks, Wikileaks did publish a full unredacted version of the 250,000 diplomatic cables, including the names of human sources, which the United States argued was to prevent Wikileaks from being 'scooped' by others.[205] Assange's defence counsel submitted that Wikileaks' disclosure of the names of human sources was protected by article 10 of the European Convention on Human Rights, on the basis that the risk of harm to a small number of sources was 'unintentional, small and unsubstantiated'[206] and should be weighed against the US Government's involvement in 'serious criminal activity' that the disclosures revealed.[207]

Judge Baraitser, sitting in the English magistrates court, found that the US charges against Assange did not violate the right to freedom of expression under English law and the European Convention on Human Rights.[208] She acknowledged the 'inevitable tension' between the 'vital importance of the press in exposing abuses and miscarriages of justice by reporting information they have received' and the 'strong public interest in keeping the security or intelligence service secure', but noted that no public interest defence is available to charges under the UK Official Secrets Act.[209] The court ultimately held that prosecution of the disclosure of informants' names is necessary in a democratic society in the interests of national security.[210] In response to defence submissions that Wikileaks went to 'extraordinary lengths' to publish the material in a responsible manner, and that the harm to informants alleged by the US Government may not have occurred, the court held that these issues were matters to be determined at Assange's trial, rather than extradition proceedings, but did make a number of comments reflecting disapproval of this argument.[211]

Judge Baraitser opined that 'in the modern era, where "dumps" of vast amounts of data onto the internet can be carried out by almost anyone, it is difficult to see how the concept of 'responsible journalism' can sensibly be applied'.[212] The concept could not, according to the Judge, vest in Assange the right to make the decision to sacrifice the safety of individuals in the name of free speech while 'knowing nothing of their

---

[204] Reporters without Borders, 'UK: Legal arguments during the first week of Julian Assange's extradition hearing highlight lack of US evidence' (28 February 2020).
[205] UK Westminster Magistrates' Court, *The Government of the United States of America v. Julian Paul Assange*, 11 January 2021, §391–392.
[206] Ibid., §122.
[207] Ibid., §122.
[208] Ibid., §122, 137.
[209] Ibid., §147. The decision of *R v. Shayler* [2002] UKHL 11 relates to sections 1 and 4 of the UK Official Secrets Act 1989, both sections that apply to Crown servants: UK House of Lords, *R v. Shayler* [2002] UKHL 11, 21 March 2002. However, the Court in *The Government of the United States of America v Julian Paul Assange* appears to have accepted that both these sections and those which apply to all persons do not incorporate a public interest defence: see, e.g., UK Westminster Magistrates' Court, *The Government of the United States of America v. Julian Paul Assange*, 11 January 2021, §147: 'Nor is a "public interest" defence available under the OSA 1989; this was made clear by the House of Lords in *Shayler*.'
[210] UK Westminster Magistrates' Court, *The Government of the United States of America v. Julian Paul Assange*, 11 January 2021, §137.
[211] Ibid., §§390, 402.
[212] Ibid., §131.

circumstances or the dangers they faced'.[213] The Court also contrasted Assange's conduct to the 'traditional press' since he was a person who chose to disclose information on the internet without being 'bound by a professional code or ethical journalistic duty or practice', and provided examples of the 'careful editorial decisions' made by news outlets in 'stark contrast' to Assange's 'final, indiscriminate disclosure' on 2 September 2011.[214] Ultimately, however, the Judge found that extradition would be oppressive in light of the 'substantial' risk Assange might commit suicide if extradited.[215] Assange's legal counsel later commented that 'while we were successful ... in that we achieved the right outcome' before the Court, it was 'unfortunately for all the wrong reasons' because the Judge 'rejected all of the free speech arguments ... all of the arguments about the public interest of these disclosures'.[216]

In December 2021 this decision was overturned by the High Court on the basis of assurances made by the United States as to the prison conditions Assange would face during pretrial or post-conviction detention, and assurances that Assange would be eligible for—and the United States would consent to—a transfer to an Australian prison to serve any custodial sentence imposed on him.[217] Assange continues to appeal his decision in British courts and before the European Court of Human Rights.[218]

Journalists and human rights groups have expressed alarm that the indictment against Assange sets a precedent that allows for criminalization of journalistic activities. Marty Baron, then editor of The Washington Post, decried the indictment as 'criminalizing common practices in journalism that have long served the public interest'.[219] First Amendment experts also opined that 'the U.S. indictment of Assange will continue to cast a dark shadow over investigative journalism'.[220] It is understood that the Obama administration did not go after Assange because of the so-called 'New York Times problem': if prosecutors could charge Wikileaks they could also charge the New York Times for the same conduct, an outcome that many would consider an anathema in the United States.[221] Following the indictment, The New York Times in fact confirmed that it 'obtained precisely the same archives of documents from WikiLeaks, without authorization from the government—the act that most of the charges addressed'. The

---

[213] Ibid., §131.
[214] Ibid., §§131–132.
[215] Ibid., §§337, 363.
[216] J. Robinson, 'Julian Assange: Repression, Isolation & Lockdown' (Disruption Network Lab, 6 May 2021), at 7:10 mark.
[217] UK High Court of Justice Queen's Bench Division Administrative Court, *The Government of the United States of America v. Julian Paul Assange* [2021] EWHC 3313 (Admin), 10 December 2021. In January 2022, the High Court ruled that Assange could bring a further appeal to the UK Supreme Court on the narrow issue of the timing of the US' assurances regarding Assange's treatment in prison. But in March 2022 the UK Supreme Court refused to hear the appeal on the basis that Assange's application did not 'raise an arguable point of law'. The case went back for determination by Judge Baraister, before the UK Home Secretary signed the extradition order in June 2022. In June 2023, Assange's appeal was rejected by the High Court and a further appeal was signaled: B. Doherty, 'Julian Assange "dangerously close" to US extradition after losing latest legal appeal' (The Guardian, 8 June 2023).
[218] M. Holden, 'Julian assange appeals to European court over U.S. extradition' (Reuters, 2 December 2022).
[219] L. Grove, 'America's Top Newspaper Editors Alarmed by Assange Indictment' (The Daily Beast, 25 May 2019).
[220] Knight First Amendment Institute at Columbia University, 'Knight Institute Comments on Decision to Reject U.S. Request for Extradition of Julian Assange' (4 January 2021).
[221] S. Horwitz, 'Julian Assange unlikely to face U.S. charges over publishing classified documents' (The Washington Post, 25 November 2013).

New York Times also noted that although it 'did take steps to withhold the names of informants in the subset of the files it published', 'it is not clear how that is legally different from publishing other classified information'.[222] An example of a common journalistic practice that the Assange indictment has the potential to criminalize is the use by journalists of secure cloud drop boxes, which allow sources to submit unsolicited material. The use of a SecureDrop box was allegedly pioneered by Wikileaks and is referenced a number of times in the Assange indictment,[223] a process that is now 'a feature' of '21st century journalism'.[224]

One of the reasons that a prosecution against Assange would be so significant is that it would establish a new precedent involving the publication of unlawfully acquired information. The leading First Amendment cases which protect journalists and publishers involve individuals who have obtained information lawfully, whereas even receipt or possession of defence information is criminalized by the Espionage Act.[225] One such case is *Smith v. Daily Mail*,[226] in which the Supreme Court invalidated a West Virginian statute criminalizing the publication of the name of any youth charged as a juvenile offender without approval from the juvenile court. There, the Court held that '[i]f the information is lawfully obtained, as it was here, the state may not punish its publication except when necessary to further an interest' of substantial import.[227] The Supreme Court came to the same conclusion in *Bartnicki v. Vopper*,[228] observing that *New York Times v. United States*, 'raised, but did not resolve, the question 'whether, in cases where information has been acquired *unlawfully* by a newspaper or by a source, government may ever punish not only the unlawful acquisition, but the ensuing publication as well'.[229] This remains an open question that the Assange prosecution—if it takes place—may decide, with far-reaching consequences.

III. International Legal Standards

As there has been an uptick in espionage and official secrets laws being used against journalists and whistleblowers across the globe, international and regional standards on the free speech implications of this behaviour have developed considerably in recent years. The European Court of Human Rights has amassed a significant body of jurisprudence, including the seminal case of *Bucur and Toma v. Romania*, involving a whistleblower who uncovered unlawful wiretapping by authorities in Romania a few

---

[222] C. Savage, 'Assange Indicted Under Espionage Act, Raising First Amendment Issues' (The New York Times, 23 May 2019); 'Piecing Together the Reports, and Deciding What to Publish' (The New York Times, 25 July 2010).
[223] US District Court for the Eastern District of Virgina, *United States v. Julian Assange* Crim. No. 1:18-cr-111 (CMH), Second Superseding Indictment, 24 June 2020, §§17, 25.
[224] See UK Westminster Magistrates' Court, *The Government of the United States of America v. Julian Paul Assange*, 11 January 2021, Consolidated Annex, §63 (summarizing witness testimony of Professor Michael Tigar).
[225] 18 U.S.C. §§793(c) and (e).
[226] US Supreme Court, *Smith v. Daily Mail Pub. Co.* 443 U.S. 97, 26 June 1979.
[227] Ibid., 104.
[228] US Supreme Court, *Bartnicki v. Vopper*, 532 U.S. 516, 21 May 2001.
[229] Ibid., 528.

months before Edward Snowden's revelations came to light in 2013. Although other bodies have more limited jurisprudence, soft law instruments such as the Tshwane Principles also provide 'highly persuasive' guidance on the international standards that are applicable to secrecy laws.[230] In addition, the wider body of jurisprudence governing the interplay between speech and national security can be applied to the use of espionage and official secrets laws to stifle speech.

1. International Standards Related to Speech Affecting National Security

The 'protection of national security' is one of the legitimate purposes for which speech can be restricted under article 19(3) of the ICCPR,[231] as well as the European Convention and American Convention.[232] Although article 9 of the African Charter on Human and Peoples' Rights does not specify legitimate aims for curtailing 'the right to express and disseminate ... opinions within the law', this provision has been consistently interpreted as incorporating the aim of protecting national security, in line with other international treaty standards.[233] 'Security' or 'national security' considerations may also limit the scope of other human rights.[234]

But as the Human Rights Committee has made clear, the restrictions a state imposes on freedom of expression cannot 'put in jeopardy the right itself' and 'the relation between right and restriction and between norm and exception must not be reversed'.[235] As with all restrictions under article 19 of the ICCPR, restrictions for the legitimate purpose of national security must be 'provided by law', pursue a legitimate aim and conform to the strict tests of necessity and proportionality.[236] The burden lies with the state to demonstrate the legal basis for any restrictions to speech.[237] And restrictions must not only comply with the requirements of article 19(3), but must themselves be 'compatible with the provisions, aims and objectives of the Covenant'.[238]

---

[230] Open Society Justice Initiative, 'Understanding the Tshwane Principles' (12 June 2013). Sometimes the abuses of freedom of expression are so flagrant that courts are not required to examine the nuances and limits of this jurisprudence. See, e.g., WGAD, *Piskorski v. Poland* (Opinion no. 18/2018), 20 April 2018; WGAD, *61 individuals v. United Arab Emirates* (Opinion no. 60/2013), 22 November 2013.

[231] ICCPR Art. 19(3). See ch. 1 (Introduction), s. II.1.2.1.1. (ICCPR: Article 19).

[232] ECHR Art. 10(2); ACHR Art. 13(2)(b).

[233] See ch. 1 (Introduction), s. II.1.2.2.3. (African Charter). ACmHPR, *Good v. Botswana* (Comm. no. 313/2005), 26 May 2010, §§188–189. The ASEAN Human Rights Declaration provides as a general principle that human rights shall be subject to limitations determined by law 'to meet the just requirements of national security' among other purposes: ASEAN Human Rights Declaration Art. 8.

[234] The protection of national security is a legitimate purpose by which six rights under the ICCPR can be limited: Art. 12 (free movement), Art. 13 (procedures applicable to aliens' expulsion), Art. 14 (fair trial), Art. 19 (speech), Art. 21 (assembly) and Art. 22 (association). See also ACHR Arts. 27(1), 32(2); American Declaration Art. XXVIII.

[235] HRC, General Comment No. 34 (2011), §21.

[236] Ibid., §22; see, e.g., ECtHR (GC), *Stoll v. Switzerland* (App. no. 69698/01), 10 December 2007, §101; IACtHR, *Usón Ramírez v. Venezuela* (Series C, no. 207), 20 November 2009, §49.

[237] See HRC, General Comment No. 34 (2011), §27; WGAD, *Chhin v. Cambodia* (Opinion no. 3/2019), 24 April 2019, §48.

[238] HRC, General Comment No. 34 (2011), §26.

308   FREEDOM OF SPEECH IN INTERNATIONAL LAW

The Human Rights Committee has cautioned that 'extreme care must be taken' by states to ensure that treason laws, and 'similar provisions relating to national security, whether described as official secrets or sedition laws or otherwise' are crafted and applied in conformity with the 'strict requirements' of article 19(3).[239] For example, the Committee has held that it is not permissible to 'invoke such laws to suppress or withhold from the public information in the legitimate public interest that does not harm national security or to prosecute journalists, researchers, environmental activists, human rights defenders or others, for having disseminated such information'.[240] Although this statement is somewhat circular since it relates only to information that 'does not harm national security', the prohibition on criminal prosecution for publishing such information is clear.

A state's assertion that national security interests are at stake will be given considerable deference by international bodies.[241] The European Court has noted that 'the judgment by the national authorities in a case involving national security is one which [the Court] is not well equipped to challenge'.[242] The Court considered that 'significant weight must' therefore 'attach to the judgment of the domestic authorities, and especially of the national courts, who are better placed to assess the evidence relating to the existence of a national security threat'.[243] The Court found that it 'seldom challenges the legitimate national security aim adduced by the state'.[244]

However, international bodies will not simply accept a state's bald assertion that national security is implicated without reaching their own view.[245] According to the Human Rights Committee, a state must 'demonstrate in a specific and individualized fashion the precise nature of the threat' and 'a direct and immediate connection between the expression and the threat'.[246] For example in a case before the Human Rights Committee, a newspaper editor was convicted for publishing classified reports by security services revealing misconduct within the service.[247] The editor argued that the files did not contain 'any information disclosing forces, means and methods of investigation of criminal cases affecting security interests' of Kazakhstan, but 'merely disclosed possible misconduct by members of the security services ... and such information by no

---

[239] Ibid., §30.
[240] Ibid. General Comment No. 34 also notes that it is generally not appropriate to restrict information relating to the commercial sector, banking, or scientific progress under national security laws.
[241] See, e.g., ECtHR (GC), *Janowiec v. Russia* (App. nos. 55508/07 & 29520/09), 21 October 2013, §213.
[242] Ibid. See also ECtHR, *Yam v. United Kingdom* (App. no. 31295/11), 16 January 2020, §§56, 58 (noting that in cases where there are legitimate reasons for the European Court not to 'have sight of the national security material on which decisions restricting' public trials are based, it will 'scrutinise the national decision-making procedure to ensure that it incorporated adequate safeguards to protect the interests' of defendants).
[243] ECtHR, *Liu v. Russia (No. 2)* (App. no. 29157/09), 26 July 2011, §85.
[244] ECtHR Research Division, National security and European case-law (2013), §46.
[245] See, e.g., WGAD, *Xiyue Wang v. Iran* (Opinion no. 52/2018), 23 August 2018, §75 (holding that the government 'did not establish a clear connection between this activity and contemporary national security interests protected under article 19(3)'); ACmHPR, *Media Rights Agenda v. Nigeria* (Comm. no. 224/98), 23 October–6 November 2000, §53 (stating that there must be more than an 'omnibus statement' from the state authorities claiming a security threat).
[246] HRC, General Comment No. 34 (2011), §35 (citing HRC, *Shin v. Republic of Korea* (Comm. no. 926/2000), 16 March 2004, §35).
[247] HRC, *Esergepov v. Kazakhstan* (Comm. no. 2129/2012), 29 March 2016.

means implicates the national security of the State'.[248] The Committee also considered the case of a professional artist who painted and distributed a political artwork entitled 'Rice Planting', and was convicted under the Republic of Korea's National Security Law for 'enemy-benefiting expression'.[249] The Committee held that Korea must demonstrate 'in specific fashion the precise nature of the threat' caused by the author's conduct 'as well as why seizure of the painting and the author's conviction were necessary'.[250] In the absence of this 'individualized justification', the Committee found a violation of article 19(2) and ordered compensation, an annulment of the artist's conviction, legal costs and the painting to be returned in original condition.[251] And where a member of a US youth organization which discussed peace issues between North and South Korea was convicted under the same National Security Law as being a member of an 'enemy-benefiting organization', the Committee held that, even though South Korea had invoked national security concerns by reference to the 'general situation in the country and the threat posed by "North Korean communists" ', it had failed to specify the 'precise nature of the threat' the expression posed.[252] As a result, the Committee found the author's conviction was not necessary for the protection of a legitimate aim under article 19(3) and that South Korea should provide compensation and ensure that similar violations do not take place.[253]

The UN Working Group on Arbitrary Detention has required a similar clear and causal link between the restricted expression and the alleged endangerment of national security. In a case in which two Rwandan journalists were charged with crimes against national security for publishing articles that alleged government corruption and criticized the Rwandan authorities, the Working Group held that restrictions under article 19(3) 'must not be overbroad' and that the expression in question did not pose 'any actual, imminent or hypothetical threat to national security'.[254] The Working Group noted that statements such as 'Rwandans have spent 15 years in a coma', 'the war between Kagame's regime and the population' and 'Kagame in difficult times' could not be regarded as 'establishing a sufficient causal link to endangering national security'.[255]

The Working Group has, in some instances, also required states to show a nexus between the expression that has been restricted on the basis of national security and a call for violence.[256] For example, the Working Group found that a women's rights activist in Kurdistan had her freedom of expression violated under the ICCPR when she was

---

[248] Ibid., §3.8.
[249] HRC, *Shin v. Republic of Korea* (Comm. no. 926/2000), 16 March 2004, §§2.1, 2.2.
[250] Ibid., see also §7.3.
[251] Ibid., §§7.3–7.8. Korean authorities did not return the artwork to the artist and kept it in storage for 29 years, where it suffered some damage. In 2018, the Ministry of Justice decided to transfer the painting to the National Museum of Contemporary Art: see H. Hwang, 'Controversy over anti-state propaganda painting' (The Dong-a-Ilbo, 30 December 2017); 'Controversial painting "Rice Planting" unveiled to public for first time since 1989' (Hankyoreh, 30 January 2018).
[252] HRC, *Park v. Republic of Korea* (Comm. no. 628/1995), 20 October 1998, §§2.2, 2.3, 10.3.
[253] Ibid., §10.3, §12.
[254] WGAD, *Agnès Uwimana Nkusi & Saïdati Mukakibibi v. Rwanda* (Opinion No. 25/2012), 29 August 2012, §57.
[255] Ibid.
[256] See J. Genser, *The Working Group on Arbitrary Detention: Commentary and Guide to Practice* (CUP 2019), 208. See ch. 6 (Terrorism Laws), s. III.3.1 (Harm).

convicted of crimes against the Iranian state for allegedly being a member of a political opposition group, even though she was working within the non-militant wing of that group. The Working Group held that 'the Government did not provide any information ... that Ms. Jalalian [was] involved in violent activities ... and there were no legitimate grounds to restrict the exercise of her freedoms'.[257] In contrast, the Working Group considered the conviction and detention of a political figure in Bhutan to be lawful in circumstances where he had 'sowed communal discord' between ethnic communities within Bhutan and had 'conspired with others to achieve his ends by violent [as well as] non-violent means'.[258]

Similarly, the European Court has emphasized that the concepts of 'national security' and 'public order' need to be applied with restraint and when 'necessary to suppress release of the information for the purposes of protecting national security and public safety'.[259] And 'even where national security is at stake', the European Court has held that 'measures affecting fundamental human rights must be subject to some form of adversarial proceedings before an independent body competent to review the reasons for the decision'.[260] This requires domestic courts to have access to the classified information needed to effectively assess whether national security interests are enlivened.[261]

In one of the few cases decided by the Inter-American Court of Human Rights touching on speech and national security, *Palamara-Iribarne v. Chile,* the Court ultimately relied on witness testimony that the expression in question did not contain either secret material or information relevant to national security.[262] In this case, Mr. Palamara-Iribarne was convicted for breach of military duties after he attempted to publish a book titled '*Ética y Servicios de Inteligencia*' ('Ethics and Intelligence Services') in which he addressed issues related to military intelligence and the need to ensure compliance with ethical standards. When the author sought the necessary authorization to publish this book, it was denied on the basis that the book threatened 'national security and defence'. However, the Court accepted expert evidence that the book did 'not breach the secrecy and security of the Chilean Navy', but rather contained information obtained from open sources and was written on the basis of Mr. Palamara-Iribarne's training as an intelligence specialist. The Court considered that it was 'logical' that Mr. Palamara-Iribarne's training and military experience helped him to write the book, and to interpret this as entailing an abuse of his freedom of expression 'would prevent individuals from using their education or professional training to enrich the expression of their ideas and opinions'.[263]

---

[257] WGAD, *Zeinab Jalalian v. Iran* (Opinion no. 1/2016), 18 April 2016, §35. See also WGAD, *Moti Biyya v. Ethiopia* (Opinion no. 18/1999), 15 September 1999, §10.
[258] WGAD, *Tek Nath Rizal v. Bhutan* (Opinion no. 48/1994), 1 December 1994, §18.
[259] ECtHR (GC), *Stoll v. Switzerland* (App. no. 69698/01), 10 December 2007, §54. See also ECtHR, *Görmüş and Others v. Turkey* (App. no. 49085/07), 19 January 2016, §37 (where the Court was 'not convinced' that a search and seizure of a magazine's officers were for the purposes of national security in circumstances where the authorities had not 'instituted criminal proceedings ... for activities threatening national security).
[260] ECtHR (GC), *Janowiec v. Russia* (App. nos 55508/07 & 29520/09), 21 October 2013, §213.
[261] Ibid. (in the case of an alleged violation of fair trial rights).
[262] IACtHR, *Palamara-Iribarne v. Chile* (Series C, No. 135), 22 November 2005, §75.
[263] Ibid., §§75–76.

The African Commission addressed an ostensible reliance on national security to restrict expression in a case concerning an Australian academic who was deported by Botswana for an article titled 'Presidential Succession in Botswana: No Model for Africa', in which he criticized the government. The Commission found that such expression was 'purely academic work which criticizes the political system' and that 'there is nothing in the article that has the potential to cause instability, unrest or any kind of violence in the country'.[264] Consequently, the Commission held 'the article posed no national security threat' and Botswana's actions were unnecessary and disproportionate.[265]

Despite this growing body of national security-related jurisprudence, advocates in this area have argued that international treaties and case law provide insufficient guidance on what constitutes national security for the purpose of restricting information, or on how the competing interests should be weighed.[266] Soft law guidance has sought to bolster existing jurisprudence on these issues.

A helpful starting point is the Siracusa Principles on the Limitation and Derogation of Provisions in the International Covenant on Civil and Political Rights,[267] which relate to exceptions to human rights obligations in general and provide that national security may be invoked only when measures are being taken 'to protect the existence of the nation or its territorial integrity or political independence against force or threat of force', as opposed to 'merely local or relatively isolated threats to law and order'.[268] The Principles provide that national security concerns cannot be used as a pretext for imposing 'vague or arbitrary limitations', and may only be invoked 'when there exist adequate safeguards and effective remedies against abuse'.[269] Finally, countries must not invoke national security to justify measures 'aimed at suppressing opposition' to human rights violations, or to perpetuate repressive practices.[270]

The Johannesburg Principles on National Security, Freedom of Expression and Access to Information[271] were developed in the mid-1990s by a group of experts, and have since been cited as authoritative by a number of international and regional human

---

[264] ACmHPR, *Good v. Botswana* (Comm. no. 313/2005), 26 May 2010, §199.
[265] Ibid., §199–200.
[266] S. Coliver, 'The Tshwane Principles on National Security and the Right to Information: Their Origins, Contribution to Norm Development, and Impact' (Open Society Justice Initiative, February 2017); see also M. O'Flaherty, 'Freedom of Expression: Article 19 of the International Covenant on Civil and Political Rights and the Human Rights Committee's General Comment No 34' (2012) 12(4) *Human Rights Law Review* 627, 652: 'With regard to the other grounds for the restriction of freedom of expression (respect for the rights and reputation of others, protection of national security, public order and public health), the Committee declined to elaborate definitions [in General Comment No. 34] ... Committee members were understandably reluctant to erect strict definitions that might hamper legitimate future application of Article 19, paragraph 3. Nevertheless, in the view of the present writer the Committee may thus have missed an opportunity to impede abusive invocation by States of the various grounds'.
[267] International Commission of Jurists, 'Siracusa Principles' (1 July 1984).
[268] Siracusa Principles, §§29–30.
[269] Ibid., §31.
[270] Ibid., §32.
[271] Johannesburg Principles. See also UN Special Rapporteur, the OSCE Representative on Freedom of the Media and the OAS Special Rapporteur, Joint Declaration on Access to Information and Secrecy Legislation (2004).

rights bodies.[272] The Principles are more specific in addressing the interplay between speech and national security concerns.[273] They clarify the requisite harm and requirement of secrecy, providing that speech may be sanctioned as a threat to national security only if a government can demonstrate that the expression is intended, and likely to, incite immediate violence and there is a 'direct and immediate connection between the expression and the likelihood or occurrence of such violence'.[274] Further, punishment for disclosure of information on national security grounds is not permissible where 'the disclosure does not actually harm and is not likely to harm a legitimate national security interest'.[275]

Most recently, the Global Principles on National Security and the Right to Information, commonly known as the Tshwane Principles, were issued by 22 civil society organizations and academic centres in June 2013.[276] The Tshwane Principles were drafted over a period of two years and involved consultation with over 500 civil society actors, government officials and security experts, as well as five UN and regional 'Special Rapporteurs' whose mandates address freedom of expression and human rights.[277] The Tshwane Principles are 'based on international (including regional) and national law, standards and good practice, and the writing of experts' and provide guidance to those drafting or implementing laws related to state's withholding information on national security grounds, or punishing the publication of such information.[278] They have been endorsed by a broad range of actors, including the UN Special Rapporteur of Freedom of Opinion and Expression, the Parliamentary Assembly of the Council of Europe (PACE) and the Organization for Security and Co-operation in Europe (OSCE).[279]

The Principles recommend that 'national security' is precisely defined in national law.[280] They set out what is *not* a legitimate national security interest, namely if the 'real purpose or primary impact is to protect an interest unrelated to national security'

---

[272] See WGAD, *Karma v. Indonesia* (Opinion no. 48/2011), 2 September 2011, §21; ACmHPR, *Good v. Botswana* (Comm. no. 313/2005), 26 May 2010, §194; UN Special Rapporteur F. La Rue, *Report on the promotion and protection of the right to freedom of opinion and expression* (2011) UN Doc. A/HRC/17/27, §36.

[273] Johannesburg Principles, Preamble.

[274] Johannesburg Principles, Principle 6. See s. III.4.2.2. (Causation). The Principles also provide a non-exhaustive list of expression which 'shall not constitute a threat to national security': Principle 7.

[275] Johannesburg Principles, Principle 15. See s. III.4.2.1. (Type and severity of harm).

[276] Tshwane Principles (12 June 2013).

[277] Coliver (n 266). The five Special Rapporteurs were: Frank LaRue, the UN Special Rapporteur; Ben Emmerson, the UN Special Rapporteur on Counter-Terrorism and Human Rights; Pansy Tlakula, the ACmHPR Special Rapporteur on Freedom of Expression and Access to Information; Catalina Botero, the OAS Special Rapporteur on Freedom of Expression; and Dunja Mijatovic, the OSCE Representative on Freedom of the Media. The Tshwane Principles are said to build on the Johannesburg Principles as the 'international right of access to information was in the early stages of its development' when the earlier Principles were drafted, and therefore only eight of the principles addressed this right in broad terms.

[278] Tshwane Principles, Introduction and Preamble.

[279] See, e.g., UN Special Rapporteur Frank La Rue: 'The Principles are a major contribution to the right of access to information and the right to truth concerning human rights violations, and I believe they should be adopted by the Human Rights Council. All states should reflect these Principles in their interpretations of national security law' (cited in the Tshwane Principles); 'The Assembly supports the Tshwane Principles and calls on the competent authorities of all member States of the Council of Europe to take them into account in modernising their legislation and practice concerning access to information': Parliamentary Assembly of the COE Resolution 1954 (2013) on national security and access to information, 2 October 2013. See also Open Society Justice Initative, 'New Principles Address the Balance between National Security and the Public's Right to Know' (12 June 2013).

[280] Tshwane Principles, Definitions.

such as the 'protection of government or officials from embarrassment or exposure of wrongdoing; concealment of information about human rights violations, any other violation of law or the functioning of public institutions; strengthening or perpetuating a particular political interest, party or ideology; or suppression of lawful protests'.[281] They also provide that governments can only restrict information where the disclosure of the information poses 'a real and identifiable risk of significant harm to a national security interest' and the risk of harm 'must outweigh the overall public interest in disclosure'.[282] It is not enough that a public authority simply asserts a risk of harm—they must provide 'specific, substantive reasons to support its assertion'.[283] And the Principles make clear that journalists and non-public officials 'may not be sanctioned for the receipt, possession or disclosure to the public of classified information' in any circumstances, and for public personnel, the 'law should provide a public interest defence if the public interest in disclosure of the information ... outweighs the public interest in non-disclosure'.[284]

2. Legality

International human rights treaties that restrict speech require that such restrictions are 'provided by law'.[285] This means that, at a minimum, state laws must be precisely drafted and not unduly vague.

International bodies have frequently criticized espionage and official secrets laws on the basis that they are impermissibly vague. For example, the Human Rights Committee expressed concern that Japan's legislation contains 'a vague and broad definition of the matters that can be classified as secret and general preconditions for classification'. The Committee insisted that Japan should ensure that categories of classified information are 'narrowly defined' and that any restriction to the right to receive information 'complies with the principles of legality, proportionality and necessity to prevent a specific and identifiable threat to national security'.[286] Similarly, the Working Group has 'consistently found that vague and overly broad provisions that could result in penalties being imposed on individuals who have merely exercised their rights cannot be regarded as being consistent' with the ICCPR or UDHR.[287] For example, the Working Group condemned Cambodia's espionage provision criminalizing the 'act of giving or facilitating easy access by a foreign States or its agents to information ... which undermine[s] the national defence'.[288] In finding a contravention of article 19 of the ICCPR, the Working Group observed that the law is 'so vague as to be inconsistent with international human

---

[281] Ibid., Definitions.
[282] Ibid., Principle 3.
[283] Ibid., Principle 4.
[284] Ibid., Principles 43, 47. See s. III.5.1. (Public interest defence).
[285] See ch. 1 (Introduction), s. II.1.1.1. (Abuses by the state).
[286] HRC, *Concluding Observations: Japan* (2014) UN Doc. CCPR/C/JPN/CO/6. The Committee also noted, with regard to the same Japanese law, that no individual should be punished 'for disseminating information of legitimate public interest that does not harm national security'. See also s. III.5.1. (Public interest defence).
[287] WGAD, *Chhin v. Cambodia* (Opinion no. 3/2019), 24 April 2019, §49.
[288] Ibid., §19.

rights law', because the 'determination of what constitutes an offence under this provision appears to be left entirely to the discretion of the authorities'.[289]

The European Court of Human Rights also requires laws to be precise. A norm cannot be regarded as a 'law' unless it is 'formulated with sufficient precision to enable the person concerned to regulate his or her conduct: he or she needed to be able—if need be with appropriate advice—to foresee, to a degree that was reasonable in the circumstances, the consequences that a given action could entail'.[290] However, 'consequences need not be foreseeable with absolute certainty'.[291] This approach is reflected in a 2007 resolution by the Parliamentary Assembly for the Council of Europe which proposes that 'legislation on official secrecy, including lists of secret items serving as a basis for criminal prosecution must be clear and, above all, public', with any 'secret decrees establishing criminal liability' considered incompatible with the Council of Europe's legal standards.[292]

Similarly, the Inter-American Court has insisted that if states choose to restrict or limit speech under the criminal law, 'it is necessary to use strict and unequivocal terms, clearly restricting any punishable behaviors, giving meaning to the principle of criminal legality'.[293] For example, in the case of military slander, the Court required the law to describe 'clearly and without ambiguities' the damage that illicit behaviour will cause, or how that behaviour might jeopardize military benefits 'so that the exercise of a military punitive power is justified'.[294] Where such a provision did not delimit the elements of criminal behaviour or 'consider the existence of injury', the Inter-American Court found the law 'too vague and ambiguous' to comply with the legality requirements under article 9 of the Convention or the free-speech protections of article 13.[295]

And the African Court on Human and Peoples' Rights has held, consistent with other regional human right bodies, that domestic laws which restrict freedom of expression must be 'sufficiently clear, foreseeable and compatible with the purpose of the Charter and international human rights conventions'.[296]

Soft law instruments provide further detail as to what is entailed by the requirement that restrictions are 'prescribed by law'. Principle 3(a) of the Tshwane Principles states that laws restricting the right to information on national security grounds must

---

[289] Ibid., §44. The Working Group has similarly criticized article 443 of Cambodia's Criminal Code, which criminalizes 'the act of having a secret agreement with a foreign State or its agents, with a view to fomenting hostilities or acts of aggression against Cambodia' as impermissibly 'vague and imprecise': WGAD, *Sokha v. Cambodia* (Opinion no. 9/2018), 19 April 2018, §44.

[290] ECtHR (GC), *Perinçek v. Switzerland* (App. no. 27510/08), 15 October 2015, §131.

[291] ECtHR (GC), *Satakunnan Markkinapörssi Oy v. Finland* (App. no. 931/13), 27 June 2017, §143.

[292] Parliamentary Assembly of the COE Resolution 1551 on the Fair trial issues in criminal cases concerning espionage or divulging state secrets, 19 April 2007, §10.2.

[293] IACtHR, *Usón Ramírez v. Venezuela* (Series C, No. 207), 20 November 2009, §55.

[294] Ibid. See s. III.4.2. (Harm). Although *Usón Ramírez v. Venezuela* relates to military slander laws, this case may be indicative of the Court's expected reasoning in future state secrets cases.

[295] IACtHR, *Usón Ramírez v. Venezuela* (Series C, No. 207), 20 November 2009, §57. Article 9 of the American Convention provides that '[n]o one shall be convicted of any act or omission that did not constitute a criminal offense, under the applicable law, at the time it was committed'.

[296] ACtHPR, *Umuhoza v. Rwanda* (App. no. 3/2014), 24 November 2017, §136.

be 'accessible, unambiguous, drawn narrowly and with precision so as to enable individuals to understand what information may be withheld, what should be disclosed, and what actions concerning the information are subject to sanction'.[297] The Tshwane Principles also require 'adequate safeguards against abuse, including prompt, full and effective judicial scrutiny' of the validity of any restrictions.[298]

3. Legitimacy

The legitimate aim generally cited by states as justification for espionage and official secrets laws is the protection of national security. A state's claim that speech is being restricted for this purpose will warrant some deference from human rights bodies, albeit not by any means of an unlimited nature. States are still required to point to a 'specific and individualized ... threat' rather than a general situation of uncertainty.[299]

Another 'legitimate aim' is however articulated in article 10(2) of the European Convention—one that is not replicated in other international or regional human rights treaties—'preventing the disclosure of information received in confidence'.[300] This limitation 'encompasses confidential information disclosed either by a person subject to a duty of confidence or by a third party, and in particular ... by a journalist'.[301] The Court applied this exception in a case in which a journalist was convicted and fined for publishing extracts from a 'confidential' diplomatic paper regarding compensation for Holocaust victims out of assets deposited in Swiss bank accounts.[302] The Court concluded that the journalist could not have obtained the documents without a breach of official secrecy by another individual.[303] And it considered that the relevant 'legitimate aim' that the government was advancing was prevention of the 'disclosure of information received in confidence', not the protection of national security.[304] However, the analysis of proportionality proceeded in largely the same manner as in cases in which the protection of 'national security' was the legitimate aim being pursued.[305]

---

[297] Tshwane Principles, Principle 3(a). This builds on Johannesburg Principles Principle 1.1. See also UN Special Rapporteur, the OSCE Representative on Freedom of the Media and the OAS Special Rapporteur, Joint Declaration on Access to Information and Secrecy Legislation (2004). See s. III.4.1. (Secrecy).

[298] Tshwane Principles, Principle 3.

[299] HRC, General Comment No. 34 (2011), §35 (citing HRC, *Shin v. Republic of Korea* (Comm. no. 926/2000), 16 March 2004, §35). See s. III.1. (International Standards Related to Speech Affecting National Security).

[300] ECHR Art. 10(2).

[301] ECtHR (GC), *Stoll v. Switzerland* (App. no. 69698/01), 10 December 2007, §61. Although these principles apply to both members of the public and civil servants, the Court considers that the 'very nature of civil service requires that a civil servant is bound by a duty of loyalty and discretion', and therefore that the 'duty of discretion owed by civil servants will also generally be a strong one' (ECtHR (GC), *Guja v. Moldova* (App. no. 14277/04), 12 February 2008, §§70, 71).

[302] ECtHR (GC), *Stoll v. Switzerland* (App. no. 69698/01), 10 December 2007, §§14–19.

[303] Ibid., §17.

[304] Ibid., §§54, 62.

[305] Ibid., §108–162. See also s. III.4. (Necessity).

4. Necessity

The leading cases at the international level setting out the necessity of interference with speech related to disclosures affecting national security come from the European Court. An early case, *Guja v. Moldova,* involved an employee at the prosecutor's office who sent letters to a newspaper alleging corruption by the prosecutor's office, President and members of parliament in Moldova.[306] The employee was dismissed on the basis that the letters contained information that was secret.[307]

Holding that the employee had a 'duty of discretion', the Court considered that the 'disclosure should be made in the first place to the person's superior', and only where 'this is clearly impractical … the information could, as a last resort, be disclosed to the public'.[308] The Court then articulated five factors that must be considered when assessing the proportionality of restrictions to a whistleblower's speech.[309] First, 'particular attention shall be paid to the public interest involved in the disclosed information'.[310] Second, the authenticity of the information disclosed is relevant and persons who choose to disclose information should 'carefully verify, to the extent permitted by the circumstances, that it is accurate and reliable', consistently with the duties and responsibilities attached to the right to freedom of expression.[311] Third, the Court will consider the damage suffered by the public authority as a result of the disclosure, and whether such damage 'outweighed the interest of the public in having the information revealed'.[312] Fourth, the 'motive behind the actions of a reporting employee is another determinant factor', particularly whether the speaker 'acted in good faith and in the belief the information was true, that it was in the public interest to disclose it and that no other, more discreet, means of remedying the wrongdoing' were available.[313] Finally, an analysis of the penalty and its impact on the speaker is required.[314]

In applying these factors, the Court found a violation of article 10, as the employee had acted in good faith, there were no available procedures for him to report irregularities and the disclosed letters dealt with issues of improper conduct by politicians and the government's attitude to police brutality, matters 'so important in a democratic society' that they outweighed the interest in maintaining public confidence in the prosecutor's office.[315]

These principles were later extended to the national security context in *Bucur and Toma v. Romania,* where an employee of Romania's intelligence service noticed

---

[306] ECtHR (GC), *Guja v. Moldova* (App no. 14277/04), 12 February 2008.
[307] Ibid., §21.
[308] Ibid., §73. The Court held that it 'must take into account whether there was available to the applicant any other effective means of remedying the wrongdoing which he intended to uncover'.
[309] Ibid., §§74–78. See also ECtHR, Guide on Article 10 of the Convention, 31 August 2022, §§411–415.
[310] ECtHR (GC), *Guja v. Moldova* (App no. 14277/04), 12 February 2008 §74.
[311] Ibid., §75.
[312] Ibid., §76.
[313] Ibid., §77.
[314] Ibid., §78.
[315] Ibid., §§90–97.

irregularities suggestive of unlawful telephone tapping and, after being reprimanded by his superiors for raising this, on an MP's advice he announced his findings at a press conference.[316] The employee was convicted of gathering and imparting secret information and given a two-year suspended sentence.[317]

Although the Court considered the legitimate aim of Romania's interference with the employee's speech was to protect national security, rather than the protection of information disclosed in confidence as in *Guja v. Moldova*, it applied the same five factors articulated in *Guja*.[318] The result was that the Court considered the information divulged was 'clearly of public interest', in light of Romanian society experiencing close surveillance as a former communist regime, the 'extensive media coverage' that followed the press conference, and the fact that interest in publishing the information was 'so important in a democratic society that it outweighs the interest in maintaining public confidence' in the security services.[319] The Court also accepted the good faith of the employee, the fact that he had 'reasonable grounds to believe that the information disclosed was true' and that the penalty was severe and likely to have a 'deterrent effect' on other intelligence officers.[320]

In a 2023 decision concerning disclosure of confidential tax returns by an employee of PricewaterhouseCoopers (PwC) to a journalist, the European Court noted that it was 'fully conscious of the developments which have occurred since the *Guja* judgment was adopted in 2008', particular the 'leading role' that whistleblowers play in democratic societies 'by bringing to light information that is in the public interest'.[321] In this context, the Court decided to 'confirm and consolidate' the *Guja* principles.[322] The Court identified the 'criteria' in the Guja decision as follows:

- 'whether or not alternative channels for the disclosure were available';
- 'the public interest in the disclosed information';
- 'the authenticity of the disclosed information';
- 'the detriment to the employer';
- 'whether the whistle-blower acted in good faith'; and
- 'the severity in of the sanction'.[323]

It then elaborated on each factor. As to the alternative channels for disclosure, the Court recognized that 'certain circumstances may justify the direct use of "external reporting"', such as where the internal reporting channel is 'unreliable or ineffective', the whistle-blower is 'likely to be exposed to retaliation' or the disclosure 'pertains to the

---

[316] ECtHR, *Bucur and Toma v. Romania* (App. no. 40238/02), 8 January 2013.
[317] Ibid., §41.
[318] Ibid., §§84, 93.
[319] Ibid., §101.
[320] Ibid., §§111–113, 115–119.
[321] ECtHR (GC), *Halet v. Luxembourg* (App. no. 21884/18), 14 February 2023, §120. See s. III.5.1 (Public interest defence).
[322] Ibid.
[323] Ibid., §114.

very essence of the activity of the employer'.[324] Regarding the authenticity of the disclosed information, the Court held that a whistle-blower cannot be refused the protection of article 10 'on the sole ground that the information was subsequently shown to be inaccurate' if they have 'diligently taken steps to verify, as far as possible the authenticity' of such information.[325] The Court described the criterion of good faith as a 'determinant factor' in deciding whether a disclosure should be protected, and the Court should accordingly consider whether a whistle-blower was 'motivated by a desire for personal advantage, a 'personal grievance' or 'any other ulterior motive'.[326] On the question of the public interest in disclosures, the Court observed that 'information concerning unlawful acts and practices is undeniably of particularly strong public interest', but that lawful but 'nonetheless reprehensible or controversial' practices may also constitute public interest issues.[327] Similarly, 'a matter that sparks a debate giving rise to controversy' might be in the public interest.[328] Applying these principles, the Court held that the public interest in the information, which 'opened the door to public debate in Europe and Luxembourg on corporate taxation' and 'tax fairness in general',[329] outweighed the detrimental effects to PwC, and accordingly there was no violation of article 10.[330]

4.1. Secrecy

International bodies require that states have an objective basis for designating information as 'secret' or as damaging to national security. The Working Group has found violations of article 19(3) in circumstances where states have failed to provide such reasons.[331] For example, where two individuals were convicted under South Korea's National Security Law, one for allegedly passing information about South Korea's defence budget to a North Korean agent and another for belonging to a pro-reunification group considered to be an 'anti-State organization',[332] the Working Group found that South Korea had not 'specified the secret material in question or the reason for which it was considered to constitute a State secret'.[333] As a result, their convictions violated articles 19 of the ICCPR and UDHR.

Publishing evidence of human rights violations cannot be characterized as a state secret.[334] The Working Group considered China characterizing the names of victims of

---

[324] Ibid., §122.
[325] Ibid., §126.
[326] Ibid., §128.
[327] Ibid., §141.
[328] Ibid. Four judges in a dissenting opinion held that while they agreed on the need to 'revisit' the *Guja* criteria, the majority's concept of 'public interest', in particular the categories of 'reprehensible while remaining legal' and 'sparking public debate' were 'excessively vague', and that 'anything can fall' into the latter criterion of sparking debate. The dissenting judges also took the view that the domestic courts had remained within the margin of appreciation when balancing the *Guja* criteria: Joint Dissenting Opinion of Judges Ravarani, Mourou-Vikström, Chanturia and Sabato.
[329] Ibid., §185.
[330] Ibid., §202. The Court noted that no long term damage was established by PwC §194.
[331] See, e.g., WGAD, *Abdolfattah Soltani v. Iran* (Opinion no. 26/2006), 1 September 2006, §14; WGAD, *Shi Tao v. China* (Opinion no. 27/2006), 1 September 2006, §19.
[332] WGAD, *Lee Kun-hee v. South Korea* (Opinion no. 29/1994), 29 September 1994, §5.
[333] Ibid., §§5–6. See also WGAD, *Zhao Yan v. China* (Opinion no. 33/2005), 2 September 2005.
[334] WGAD, *Li Hai v. China* (Opinion no. 19/1999) 16 September 1999, §12.

human rights violations as a state secret to be 'contrary to the international procedural standards prescribed in the field of human rights'.[335] Similarly, when a journalist was charged for publishing articles decrying Russia's failure to process radioactive waste material from old nuclear submarines,[336] the Working Group held that 'in no case may information on environmental conditions, emergencies and disasters posing a risk to human life and health be considered a State secret'.[337]

The European Court will find a violation of article 10 if a domestic court accepts that information is classified without examining it on its merits. For example, the Court found a violation of article 10 where a magazine published 'confidential' documents revealing a system of excluding journalists from invitations based on their political leanings, and a military court ordered a search and seizure at the magazine's officers.[338] In circumstances where national courts 'had not verified if the "confidential" classification of the documents in question was justified', the Court held that the interference with expression was not 'necessary'.[339]

Similarly, the European Court has held that information that has become public has lost its confidentiality.[340] In a case concerning the memoirs of a former member of MI5 which included an account of alleged unlawful activities by British security services, the Court considered it 'incontrovertible' that the interference was for the legitimate purpose of the protection of national security; 'likely' that the material was detrimental; and 'improbable' that public interest concerns would outweigh national security implications.[341] However, as the book had already been published in the United States the 'the contents of the book ceased to be a matter of speculation and their confidentiality was destroyed', and in those circumstances restrictions on publication were not necessary in a democratic society.[342]

The Tshwane Principles also provide that if a state wishes to classify a document, classification levels must correspond to the level and likelihood of the harm of disclosure, and that states must provide reasons for classification which 'describe the harm that could result from disclosure, including its level of seriousness and degree of likelihood'.[343] And both the Tshwane and Johannesburg Principles note that once information has been made 'generally available to the public', whether or not by lawful means, a

---

[335] Ibid., §§9–12.
[336] WGAD, *Grigorii Pasko v. Russian Federation* (Opinion No. 9/1999), 20 May 1999, §§5, 7.
[337] Ibid.
[338] ECtHR, *Görmüş v. Turkey* (App. no. 49085/07), 19 January 2016, §§76–77.
[339] Ibid., §§66, 76–77.
[340] ECtHR, *Observer and Guardian v. United Kingdom* (App. no. 13585/88), 26 November 1991; ECtHR, *Sunday Times v. United Kingdom (No. 2)* (App. no. 13166/87), 26 November 1991.
[341] ECtHR, *Observer and Guardian v. United Kingdom* (App. no. 13585/88), 26 November 1991, §56. See also ECtHR, *Vereniging Weekblad Bluf! v. the Netherlands* (App. no. 16616/90), 9 February 1995, §§40–46 (where a report of the Dutch internal secret service was published and had been widely disseminated and commented on by the media, and therefore 'the protection of the information as a State secret was no longer justified' or necessary in a democratic society).
[342] ECtHR, *Observer and Guardian v. United Kingdom* (App. no. 13585/88), 26 November 1991, §§66, 69–70. Australia's High Court also declined to enforce the UK Attorney General's attempts to seek an injunction to restrain the publication of the memoirs in Australia, on the basis that Australian domestic courts will not enforce the governmental interests of a foreign state: High Court of Australia, *Attorney-General (UK) v. Heinemann Publishers Australia Pty Ltd* ('Spycatcher case') [1988] HCA 25; 165 CLR 30, 2 June 1988.
[343] Tshwane Principles, Principle 11(a)–(c).

state presumptively loses the ability to penalize its publication. The Tshwane Principles state that any effort to stop further publication is presumptively invalid,[344] and the Johannesburg Principles go even further, stating that 'any justification for trying to stop further publication will be overridden by the public's right to know'.[345]

In 2007, the Parliamentary Assembly of the Council of Europe adopted a resolution stating that 'information that is already in the public domain cannot be considered as a state secret, and divulging such information cannot be punished as espionage, even if the person concerned collects, sums up, analyses or comments on such information'.[346] Further, the question of whether the information disclosed is already in the public domain 'should always be a question of fact to be decided by' a judge or jury and 'upon an affirmative answer' the judge 'must in all cases direct an acquittal'.[347]

Similarly, the 2004 Joint Declaration on Access to Information and Secrecy Legislation, an instrument drafted and adopted by a number of UN and regional Special Rapporteurs on free speech, recommends that 'secrecy laws should define national security precisely and indicate clearly the criteria which should be used in determining whether or not information can be declared secret, so as to prevent abuse of the label "secret" for purposes of preventing disclosure of information which is in the public interest'.[348]

4.2. Harm

4.2.1. Type and severity of harm

Under international standards, speech cannot be penalized on national security grounds without establishing harm. The Human Rights Committee requires a state to show the 'specific and individualized ... threat' that a restriction to speech is addressing if penalties are to be considered necessary.[349] The Working Group has also found that certain harm must flow from the speech, at least before any criminal penalty can be imposed. In a case where a writer and history teacher was sentenced to 10 years' imprisonment for allegedly seeking to publish separatist content regarding Tibet, including the number and location of Chinese military installations, the Working Group found a violation of article 19 of the ICCPR.[350] The Working Group held that 'even though the

---

[344] Ibid., Principle 49(b).
[345] Johannesburg Principles, Principle 17.
[346] Parliamentary Assembly of the COE Resolution 1551 on Fair trial issues in criminal cases concerning espionage or divulging state secrets (2007), §10.1. The Resolution was spurred by a number of high-profile espionage cases against journalists, lawyers and scientists in Russia, as well as US, German, Italian and Swiss authorities threatening to prosecute journalists in relation to the CIA's extraordinary rendition program. This Resolution was cited by the European Court in ECtHR, *Gîrleanu v. Romania* (App. no. 50376/09), 26 June 2018, §88.
[347] Parliamentary Assembly of the COE Resolution 1551 on Fair trial issues in criminal cases concerning espionage or divulging state secrets (2007), §10.9.
[348] UN Special Rapporteur, the OSCE Representative on Freedom of the Media and the OAS Special Rapporteur, Joint Declaration on Access to Information and Secrecy Legislation (2004).
[349] See, e.g., HRC, General Comment No. 34 (2011), §35; HRC, *Esergepov v. Kazakhstan* (Comm. no. 2129/2012), 29 March 2016, §11.9 (finding a violation of article 19 'in the absence of sufficient justification ... as to the way publishing the documents in question jeopardized the public order', beyond 'a general reference to the permissible grounds for restrictions under art. 19(3)'). See s. III.1. (International Standards Related to Speech Affecting National Security).
[350] See WGAD, *Dolma Kyab v China* (Opinion no. 36/2007), 30 November 2007, §15.

ideas of the group may be contradicting the official policy of the government, the exercise of the right to freedom of expression and association cannot be punished as such, if there are no violent acts committed on behalf of the group and there is no factual proof of resort to or advocacy of violence'.[351]

The European Court of Human Rights has required a demonstration that the speech is 'capable of causing considerable damage' to national security or a state institution before it can be penalized under national security laws.[352] The Court considered this in a case where an engineer in the air force was sentenced by a Greek military court to a suspended sentence of five months' imprisonment for disclosing military secrets to a private company. The prosecution arose after he prepared a study for that company about a different missile to the one he was designing for the air force, but experts suggested this nonetheless involved 'some transfer of technical knowledge'.[353] The Court took the view that 'disclosure of the State's interest in a given weapon and that of the corresponding technical knowledge, which may give some indication of the state of progress of its manufacture, are capable of causing considerable damage to national security', and consequently that the Greek courts had not overstepped the 'margin of appreciation' left to domestic authorities on national security matters in convicting and sentencing the speaker.[354]

The Court however reached the opposite conclusion—and found that there was no 'considerable damage to national security'—in a case where a journalist was convicted and fined for 'sharing secret information' with colleagues about Romanian military operations in Afghanistan.[355] The Court weighed whether 'the applicant's actions were, at the relevant time, capable of causing "considerable damage" to national security'[356] and concluded that the government had not demonstrated this harm, even though 'secret information concerning military operations in a conflict zone is *a priori* information that must be protected'.[357] This was because the information was outdated and declassified and a Romanian prosecutor had considered that it 'was not likely to endanger national security but would only harm the interests of the Romanian State and its armed forces'.[358] As a result, the measures taken against the journalist 'were not reasonably proportionate to the legitimate aim pursued, in view of the interests of a democratic society in ensuring and maintaining freedom of the press'.[359]

---

[351] Ibid. See also WGAD, *Chhin v. Cambodia* (Opinion no. 3/2019), 24 April 2019, §46. Cf. WGAD, *Shi Tao v. China* (Opinion no. 27/2006), 1 September 2006, §7 (where the Working Group found a violation of article 19 in circumstances where it was 'not convinced' that a journalist providing overseas publications with the Chinese government's warnings regarding the anniversary of Tianamen Square could 'result in a situation of extreme gravity').
[352] See, e.g., ECtHR, *Hadjianastassiou v. Greece* (App. no. 12945/87), 16 December 1992, §§45–47.
[353] Ibid.
[354] Ibid.
[355] ECtHR, *Gîrleanu v. Romania* (App. no. 50376/09), 26 June 2018, §89.
[356] Ibid., §89, citing ECtHR, *Hadjianastassiou v. Greece* (App. no. 12945/87), 16 December 1992. The other factors considered by the Court, citing ECtHR (GC) *Stoll v. Switzerland*, were 'the interests at stake, the conduct of the applicant, the review of the measure by the domestic courts and whether the penalty imposed was proportionate': ECtHR, *Gîrleanu v. Romania* (App. no. 50376/09), 26 June 2018, §86.
[357] ECtHR, *Gîrleanu v. Romania* (App. no. 50376/09), 26 June 2018, §89.
[358] Ibid., §§28, 89.
[359] Ibid., §99.

According to the European Court, the question of whether speech causes 'considerable damage' is one of many factors to be balanced in an assessment of necessity. And on a number of occasions the Court has found that the public interest in speech which reveals illegal or questionable activities within state institutions outweighs the damage such speech causes to 'public confidence' in that institution.[360] For example, in the *Bucur* case, the Court found that 'the general interest in the disclosure of information revealing illegal activities within the [Romanian Intelligence Services] was so important in a democratic society that it prevailed over the interest in maintaining public confidence in that institution'.[361]

The European Court adopted similar reasoning in finding a violation of article 10(2) where a military court ordered a search of a magazine's offices after it published 'confidential' documents revealing that the armed forces were excluding certain journalists from invitations based on their political leanings.[362] The Court held that neither the authorities nor the national courts had demonstrated why the article could be the source of 'difficulties of such a nature as to cause "considerable damage" to the interests of the state', and that the public interest in disclosing the armed forces' questionable practices outweighed 'the interest in maintaining public confidence in this institution'.[363]

The European Court's assessment of harm also takes into account how widely the information was disseminated through the speech.[364] When a journalist had only disclosed to his colleagues, and not yet published, copies of secret documents belonging to a Romanian military unit, the European Court considered this limited disclosure as a relevant—but not determinative—factor to be weighed in the overall assessment of necessity.[365] The European Court did not explicitly reject the Romanian courts' finding that the journalist 'had committed an offence by virtue of having shared secret military information with other people'.[366] This was despite third party interveners such as the Open Society Justice Initiative and the International Commission of Jurists pressing the Court to do so, arguing that there was 'growing support in international and national law and practice against sanctions for unauthorized possession, including in the area of national security', citing European countries such as Albania, Moldova and Poland which do not publish unauthorized possession alone, as well as other states which apply sanctions only to public servants.[367] The organizations submitted that 'journalists and

---

[360] ECtHR, *Bucur and Toma v. Romania* (App. no. 40238/02), 8 January 2013, §115. See ss III.4. (Necessity) and III.5.1. (Public interest defence); ECtHR, *Görmüş v. Turkey* (App. no. 49085/07), 19 January 2016, §63.

[361] ECtHR, *Bucur and Toma v. Romania* (App. no. 40238/02), 8 January 2013, §115.

[362] ECtHR, *Görmüş and others v. Turkey* (App. no. 49085/07), 19 January 2016.

[363] Ibid., §§62–63.

[364] Most cases that come before international human rights bodies relating to espionage and official secrets laws address the publication of secret material. Cases addressing receipt and possession of information do not impact speech directly and are therefore outside the scope of this chapter. There is however international guidance suggesting that espionage or official secrets laws with criminal penalties should only cover public disclosures, as opposed to non-communicative behaviour such as the possession or gathering of information. See, e.g., ECtHR, *Gîrleanu v. Romania* (App. no. 50376/09), 26 June 2018, §§68–72.

[365] ECtHR, *Gîrleanu v. Romania* (App. no. 50376/09), 26 June 2018, §98.

[366] Ibid., §85.

[367] Ibid., §§66–67; ECtHR, *Gîrleanu v. Romania* (App. No. 50376/09), 26 June 2018, Open Society Justice Initiative et. al, Joint Third Party Submission (8 October 2013). See s. II.1.1.3. (Type of disclosure).

other similarly protected persons may be subject to sanctions for possession or disclosure [of information of] public interest ... only in exceptional circumstances'.[368] The Court noted that the sanctions were imposed before publication, and therefore 'had the purpose of preventing him from publishing and sharing the secret documents he had in his possession'.[369] And it ultimately found a violation of article 10, holding that the sanctions against the journalist—fees totalling 870 Euros—were disproportionate.[370]

The Inter-American Court has not articulated a detailed harm test for restrictions to speech by way of official secrets laws, but has held that, at a minimum, laws penalizing speech must 'specify the injury required' for conduct to fall within their ambit.[371] The Court considered this requirement in a case in which a former member of the military was sentenced to five years and six months' imprisonment in military criminal court for slandering the armed forces of Venezuela by making comments in a television program regarding the alleged use of a 'flamethrower' as punishment against soldiers.[372] The Court criticized the slander provision as 'limited to foreseeing the sanction, without taking into account the specific injury of causing discredit, damaging the good reputation or prestige, or causing damage to the detriment of the passive subject'.[373] Without the inclusion of a damage requirement, the Court reasoned, this law 'allows that the subjectivity of the offended party determine the existence of crime, even when the active subject did not have the intent to injure, offend, or disparage the passive subject', and it was therefore in violation of the right to freedom of expression in the American Convention.[374]

The Tshwane Principles also specify the need for a state to show harm before penalizing speech on national security grounds. Specifically, there should be a requirement to show 'a real and identifiable risk of causing significant harm' to a legitimate national security interest before prosecuting public officials for leaks of national security information.[375] A public authority must provide 'specific, substantive reasons' to support its assertion that a risk of harm exists, and that risk 'must outweigh the overall public interest in disclosure'.[376] And the 2019 Declaration of Principles of Freedom of Expression and Access to Information in Africa considers that speech cannot be restricted on national security grounds unless 'there is a real risk of harm to a legitimate interest'.[377]

---

[368] ECtHR, *Gîrleanu v. Romania* (App. no. 50376/09), 26 June 2018, §67.
[369] Ibid., §98.
[370] Ibid., §99. The Court also considered the journalist's 'conduct', observing that his 'first step after coming into possession of the information in question was to discuss it with the institution concerned by the leak, the Romanian Armed Forces'. And it found that in circumstances where the documents had been declassified, the decision to impose sanctions 'should have been more thoroughly weighed'. See ss III.5.2. (Reasonableness of the publication) and III.6. (Penalties). ECtHR, *Gîrleanu v. Romania* (App. no. 50376/09), 26 June 2018, §92–98.
[371] IACtHR, *Usón Ramírez v. Venezuela* (Series C, No. 207), 20 November 2009, §56. Although *Usón Ramírez v. Venezuela* relates to military slander laws, this case may be indicative of the Court's expected reasoning in future state secrets cases.
[372] Ibid., §37.
[373] Ibid., §56.
[374] Ibid., §56 (finding violations of both Arts 9 and 13).
[375] Tshwane Principles, Principle 46(b)(ii).
[376] Tshwane Principles, Principles 3–4. See also Johannesburg Principles, Principles 1.3, 2, 6.
[377] ACmHPR, Declaration on Principles of Freedom of Expression and Access to Information in Africa (2019), Principle 22(5). See s. III.4.2.2. (Causation).

4.2.2. Causation

Limited jurisprudence from international bodies has grappled with the question of whether a state is required to demonstrate a causal link between the speech and the harm to national security, and if so to what standard. The Human Rights Committee stated in General Comment No. 34 that 'when a State party invokes a legitimate ground for restriction of freedom of expression, it must demonstrate ... the necessity and proportionality of the specific action taken, in particular by establishing a direct and immediate connection between the expression and the threat'.[378] However, there is only limited case law that examines how the 'direct and immediate connection' standard should be applied in practice.[379] The Working Group on Arbitrary Detention has also referenced, but not explained, this standard on a number of occasions.[380] Similarly, although the European and Inter-American Courts have articulated harm requirements[381] they have not set out detailed guidance on how to apply them.[382]

Aside from the requirement that disclosures by public personnel of national security information which do not 'pose a real and identifiable risk of significant harm' are not sanctioned, the Tshwane Principles do not impose a specific causation standard.[383] But the Johannesburg Principles adopt the Human Right Committee's 'direct and immediate' standard, and state that expression may be punished as a threat to national security only if a government can demonstrate that (a) the expression is intended to incite immediate violence; (b) is likely to incite such violence; and (c) there is a *direct and immediate* connection between the expression and the likelihood or occurrence of violence.[384] And the 2019 Declaration of Principles of Freedom of Expression and Access to Information in Africa states that there should be 'a close causal link between the risk of harm and the expression' for states to restrict such expression on national security grounds.[385]

---

[378] HRC, General Comment No. 34 (2011), §35, citing *Shin v. Republic of Korea* (Comm. no. 926/2000), 16 March 2004.

[379] See ch. 3 (Hate Speech), s. II.1.2. (Harm); Michael O'Flaherty, who served as the Human Rights Committee's rapporteur for the development of General Comment No. 34, has noted that this nexus was not in the original draft of the General Comment and 'sets a high bar for restrictions—it will be of interest to see whether it will be accepted by commentators': O'Flaherty (n 266) 627, 649.

[380] WGAD, *Gulmira Imin v. China* (Opinion no. 29/2012), 29 August 2012, §28; WGAD, *Ziyuan Ren v. China* (Opinion no. 55/2014), 21 November 2014, §28; WGAD, *Zhen Jianghua v. China* (Opinion no. 20/2019), 1 May 2019, §71.

[381] See s. III.4.2. (Harm).

[382] See s. III.4.2.1. (Type and severity of harm). In the context of defamation laws, the European Court has considered whether speech had the 'capacity—direct or indirect—to lead to harmful consequences'. ECtHR, *Alekhina v. Russia* (App. no. 38004/12), 17 July 2018, §220 (emphasis added). See also ECtHR (GC), *Perinçek v. Switzerland* (App. no. 27510/08), 15 October 2015, §207. See ch. 2 (Insulting Speech), s. III.3.2. (Causal link between the speech and the harm). See further IACtHR, *Usón Ramírez v. Venezuela* (Series C, no. 207), 20 November 2009, §55.

[383] Tshwane Principles, Principle 3. However, the Tshwane Principles suggest that when classifying documents, public authorities should provide reasons for classification which describe the harm that could result from disclosure, 'including its level of seriousness and degree of likelihood': Principle 11.

[384] Johannesburg Principles, Principle 6 (emphasis added).

[385] ACmHPR, Declaration of Principles of Freedom of Expression and Access to Information in Africa (2019), Principle 22.

4.3. Intent

The minimum intent that should be required for prosecution or other penalization of the publication of secret government material is not generally addressed in detail by international human rights bodies.[386] But international bodies take motive and intent into account in the context of assessing the *conduct* of a speaker to determine whether there is an applicable 'reasonable publication' or 'responsible journalism' defence for a speaker who was acting in good faith.[387] And the European Court considers the motive of a whistleblowing employee to be a 'determinant factor in deciding whether a particular disclosure should be protected or not'.[388] The Court has held that 'it is important to establish that, in making the disclosure, the individual acted in good faith and in the belief that the information was true, that it was in the public interest to disclose it and that no other, more discreet, means of remedying the wrongdoing was available to him or her'.[389]

5. Exclusions, Exceptions and Defences

5.1. Public interest defence

Although state practice is very mixed, and many leading democracies fail to recognize a 'public interest defence' in their laws,[390] there is consensus among international and regional human rights bodies that the 'public interest' in the content of information is a relevant factor in the determination of whether it is 'necessary' to penalize its publication, and must be weighed against the harm speech may cause.

The Human Rights Committee has stated that it is not permissible to use national security laws 'to suppress or withhold from the public information of legitimate public interest that does not harm national security or to prosecute journalists, researchers, environmental activists, human rights defenders, or others, for having disseminated such information'.[391]

Similarly the European Court of Human Rights has held that that there is 'little scope' for restrictions on free speech 'in two fields, namely political speech and matters of public interest'.[392] Accordingly, 'a particularly narrow margin of appreciation' will be accorded to states attempting to penalize speech concerning a 'matter of the public interest'.[393] The European Court has held that 'the public interest involved in

---

[386] Cf. ch. 2 (Insulting Speech), s. III.3.1. (Intent) and ch. 3 (Hate Speech), s. III.2.3.2. (Intent).
[387] See s. III.5.2.3. ('Responsible journalism').
[388] ECtHR (GC), *Guja v. Moldova* (App. no. 14277/04), 12 February 2008, §77.
[389] Ibid., §77.
[390] See s. II.1.4.1. (Public interest).
[391] HRC, General Comment No. 34 (2011), §30. General Comment No. 34 also notes that it is generally not appropriate to restrict information relating to the commercial sector, banking, or scientific progress under national security laws.
[392] ECtHR (GC), *Bédat v. Switzerland* (App. no. 56925/08), 29 March 2016, §49. See, similarly, ECtHR (GC), *Sürek v. Turkey (No. 2)* (App. no. 24122/94), 8 July 1999, §60, citing *Wingrove v. United Kingdom* (App. No. 17419/90), 25 November 1996, §58.
[393] ECtHR (GC), *Bédat v. Switzerland* (App. no. 56925/08), 29 March 2016, §49. For discussion on the 'margin of appreciation' doctrine generally, see ch. 1 (Introduction), s. II. 3 (Jurisprudence). See also ECtHR, Guide on Article 10 of the Convention, 31 August 2022, §488.

the disclosed information' constitutes a factor to be balanced in its proportionality assessment where whistleblowers disclosed information received in confidence.[394] The Court has recognized that public officials may become 'aware of in-house information, including secret information, whose divulgation or publication corresponds to a strong public interest', and therefore the signalling of this illegal conduct or wrongdoing should, 'in certain circumstances, enjoy protection', as 'the interest the public may have in particular information can sometimes be so strong as to override even a legally imposed duty of confidence'.[395] And the Court has held that this may be particularly relevant when analysing speech by a journalist since the press has a 'duty ... to impart ... information and ideas on all matters of public interest'[396] and 'press freedom assumes even greater importance in circumstances in which State activities and decisions escape democratic or judicial scrutiny on account of their confidential or secret nature'.[397]

The European Court applied these factors in *Stoll v. Switzerland*, finding that the publishing of extracts from a confidential diplomatic paper regarding compensation for Holocaust victims out of assets deposited in Swiss bank accounts was in the public interest as it addressed issues of a 'significant moral dimension which meant that it was of interest even to the wider international community', and considering the impassioned debate in Switzerland about this issue at the time.[398] However, the Court found that the publication was liable to 'cause considerable damage' in Swiss negotiations, that the truncated and reductive article was liable to mislead readers, which detracted from its public interest and finally that the fine imposed was not disproportionate. Consequently, the Court found no violation of article 10.

And in *Bucur and Toma v. Romania*, these principles were applied in a national security context. The Court held that the information—which revealed state-sponsored surveillance of journalists, politicians and businessmen—was 'clearly in the public interest'. The 'extensive media coverage' of the press conference at which the information was revealed was held to 'demonstrate' this public interest.[399] And the Court observed that although the information disclosed related to 'abuses committed by high-ranking officials' and therefore 'affected the democratic foundations' of Romania, the domestic

---

[394] ECtHR (GC), *Guja v. Moldova* (App no. 14277/04), 12 February 2008, §74. See also §76: A further factor was the damage 'suffered by the public authority as a result of the disclosure in question and ... whether such damage outweighed the interest of the public in having the information revealed'. See s. III.4.2. (Harm). The other factors considered by the court where 'the authenticity of the information'; 'the motive behind the actions of the reporting employee'; whether the employee took steps to report the matter internally or whether this was 'impracticable'; and 'the penalty imposed ... and its consequences': ECtHR (GC), *Guja v. Moldova* (App no. 14277/04), 12 February 2008, §§74–79, 112, 137. See s. III.4 (Necessity).

[395] ECtHR (GC), *Guja v. Moldova* (App no. 14277/04), 12 February 2008, §§72–74.

[396] ECtHR (GC), *Pentikäinen v. Finland* (App. no. 11882/10), 20 October 2015, §88. See ch. 1 (Introduction), s. II.3.2.5. (Relevance of whether the speaker is a journalist). See also ECtHR (GC), *Von Hannover v. Germany (No. 2)* (App. nos. 40660/08 & 60641/08), 7 February 2012, §102; ECtHR (GC), *Bédat v. Switzerland* (App. no. 56925/08), 29 March 2016, §50.

[397] ECtHR (GC), *Stoll v. Switzerland* (App. no. 69698/01), 10 December 2007, §110.

[398] Ibid., §§115–120.

[399] ECtHR, *Bucur and Toma v. Romania* (App. no. 40238/02), 8 January 2013, §101. See also ECtHR (GC), *Stoll v. Switzerland* (App. no. 69698/01), 10 December 2007, §120 ('there can be no doubting the public interest in the issue ... which was the subject of impassionate debate in Switzerland').

courts had not taken the public interest in the information into account.[400] Taking the other factors articulated in *Guja* into account—namely the authenticity of the information disclosed, the good faith of the official and the severity of the sanction—the Court held that the two-year suspended sentence for imparting secret information was disproportionate.

International bodies have not clearly defined the term 'public interest': in particular whether this is an objective test or a description of what the public is *interested in* regardless of its objective worth.[401] However, the European Court has held that 'the definition of what might constitute a subject of public interest will depend on the circumstances of each case' and that 'the public interest relates to matters which affect the public to such an extent that it may legitimately take an interest in them, which attract its attention or which concern it to a significant degree ... especially in that they affect the well-being of citizens or the life of the community'.[402] The Court has therefore made clear that 'the press's contribution to a debate of public interest cannot be limited merely to current events or pre-existing debates', as the press can also have the role of bringing issues to light.[403]

The European Court has recently provided a more detailed definition of the 'public interest' in a case concerning the disclosure of confidential tax returns to a journalist by an employee of the accounting firm PwC who was later dismissed.[404] The European Court held that that 'information concerning unlawful acts and practices is undeniably of particularly strong public interest', but that lawful but 'nonetheless reprehensible or controversial' tax evasion practices may also constitute public interest issues, as can 'a matter that sparks a debate giving rise to controversy'.[405]

---

[400] ECtHR, *Bucur and Toma v. Romania* (App. no. 40238/02), 8 January 2013, §103. Although the Court did not address this directly in finding that domestic courts had not considered the public interest, the applicant argued that the documents disclosed could not be classified pursuant to article 24(5) of Romania's law on the protection of classified information, which forbids the classification of any information for the purpose of concealing violations of law: §88.

[401] Cf. UK Law Commission, *Protection of Official Data Report* (2020), §§11.76–11.81, which provides that there should be a public interest defence under the UK Official Secrets Act if a person 'proves, on the balance of probabilities, that: (a) it was in the public interest for the information disclosed to be known by the recipient; and (b) the manner of the disclosure was in the public interest'. However, the Law Commission decided to 'make no further recommendation beyond this in respect of the form of the defence', acknowledging that 'there are various ways such a defence could be drafted'.

[402] ECtHR (GC), *Satakunnan Markkinapörssi Oy v. Finland* (App. no. 931/13), 27 June 2017, §171; ECtHR (GC), *Magyar Helsinki Bizottság v. Hungary* (App. no. 18030/11), 8 November 2016, §162. See ch. 2. (Insulting Speech), s. III.4.2. (Public interest).

[403] ECtHR, *Couderc and Hachette Filipacchi Associés v. France* (App. no. 40454/07), 10 November 2015, §114. See also Baroness Hale of Richmond in UK House of Lords, *Jameel & others v. Wall Street Journal Europe* [2006] UKHL 44, 57: 'there must be a real public interest in communicating and receiving the information. This is, as we all know, very different from saying that it is information which interests the public—the most vapid tittle-tattle about the activities of footballers' wives and girlfriends interests large sections of the public but no-one could claim any real public interest in our being told all about it. It is also different from ... whether the information is "newsworthy". That is too subjective a test, based on the target audience, inclinations and interests of the particular publication. There must be some real public interest in having this information in the public domain'. See ch. 2 (Insulting Speech), ss IV.3, 9, 12, 14 (Recommendations).

[404] ECtHR (GC), *Halet v. Luxembourg* (App. no. 21884/18), 14 February 2023, §120. See s. III.4 (Necessity) (discussing *Halet v. Luxembourg*).

[405] Ibid., §141. However, four judges of the Court argued that the latter two categories were 'excessively vague', and in particular that 'anything can fall' within the category of a matter which 'sparks a debate giving rise to a controversy': see Ibid., Joint Dissenting Opinion of Judges Ravarani, Mourou-Vikström, Chanturia and Sabato.

The Inter-American Court of Human Rights similarly considers the public interest to be a relevant factor in determining the necessity of any restriction on speech. The Court considers it 'logical and appropriate that statements concerning public officials and other individuals who perform public services are afforded ... greater protection, thus allowing some latitude for broad debate, which is essential for the functioning of a truly democratic system'.[406] The Court applied this reasoning to speech regarding the conduct of a Naval prosecutor in military proceedings in Chile, holding that using criminal contempt laws was a disproportionate response to 'criticism leveled at government institutions and their members, thus suppressing debate' and restricting freedom of expression.[407] More recently, the OAS Special Rapporteur confirmed that 'under no circumstances journalists, members of the media, or members of civil society who have access to and distribute classified information they consider to be in the public interest may be subjected to subsequent punishment'.[408]

International experts have called for public interest to be clearly defined as a defence to any charge under espionage and official secrets laws.[409] According to the Tshwane Principles, non-public officials should receive a total exemption from liability, and cannot be sanctioned for the receipt, possession or disclosure to the public of classified information that is in the public interest in any circumstances.[410] When a disclosure is made by a state official, the Tshwane Principles advocate for a three-part test.

First, certain categories of wrongdoing should be considered a 'protected disclosure', regardless of the classification of the information, namely: criminal offences; human rights or humanitarian law violations; corruption; damage to public health and safety; danger to the environment; abuse of public office; miscarriages of justice; mismanagement or waste of resources and retaliation for disclosure or deliberate concealment of any of the categories.[411] Secondly, public personnel who make disclosures should be protected if the person had reasonable grounds to believe the disclosure tended to show one of the protected categories of wrongdoing.[412] Thirdly, the Principles outline the manner in which public personnel must first disclose internally or to an independent oversight body, and when it is reasonable not to have done so.[413] The Tshwane Principles also include a proportionality component, requiring that the person making the disclosure only disclosed the information that was reasonably necessary to bring to light

---

[406] IACtHR, *Palamara-Iribarne v. Chile* (Series C, No. 135), 22 November 2005, §82.
[407] Ibid., §88.
[408] OAS Special Rapporteur, *Derecho a la información y seguridad national* (2020), § 185 (citing UN Special Rapporteur and OAS Special Rapporteur, Joint declaration on surveillance programs and their impact on the freedom of expression (2013)).
[409] See also, e.g., UK Law Commission, *Protection of Official Data Report* (2020).
[410] Tshwane Principles, Principle 47. Principle 47(b) also provides that persons cannot be charged with conspiracy or other crimes for having 'sought and obtained' classified information. However, the Principles are 'not intended to preclude the prosecution of a person for other crimes, such as burglary or blackmail, committed in the course of seeking or obtaining the information'. Principle 48 provides for the protection of the confidential sources of non-public personnel.
[411] Ibid., Principle 37.
[412] Ibid., Principle 38. Motivation for disclosure is irrelevant except where a disclosure is proven to be knowingly untrue.
[413] See s. III.5.2. (Reasonableness of the publication).

the wrongdoing.[414] If these conditions are fulfilled, the Tshwane Principles hold that a whistleblower should not be subjected to criminal or civil liability or other forms of retaliation.[415] The Tshwane Principles also provide a 'catchall' provision recommending that even if a disclosure does not fall within a specifically protected category, public personnel should nonetheless be protected from prosecution for disclosures where the public interest in the disclosure of the information outweighs the public interest in its non-disclosure.[416]

The Johannesburg Principles provide for a similar, albeit less detailed, balancing framework centred on the idea that no person should be punished for disclosure of information if the disclosure does not or is not likely to harm a legitimate national security interest, or the public interest in knowing the information outweighs the harm in disclosure, and establishing a category of 'protected information' including 'information communicating alleged violations of human rights and humanitarian law'.[417] The 2004 Joint Declaration on Access to Information and on Secrecy Legislation issued by UN and regional Special Rapporteurs on freedom of expression, Parliamentary Assembly of the Council of Europe and the OSCR also advocate for states to amend secrecy legislation to accommodate a public interest defence.[418]

5.2. Reasonableness of the publication

The European Court and the Tshwane Principles suggest that the conduct of the speaker may be relevant to a determination of whether their speech can be penalized.[419] This relates to the manner in which the material was obtained, steps taken to verify the material, and efforts to report the wrongdoing it exposes using internal channels.

5.2.1. Manner of obtaining the information and steps to verify it

According to the European Court, 'freedom of expression carries with it duties and responsibilities and any person who chooses to disclose information must carefully verify, to the extent permitted by the circumstances, that it is accurate and reliable'.[420]

---

[414] Tshwane Principles, Principle 40(b).
[415] Ibid., Principle 41. And these rights and remedies cannot be waived or limited by an agreement or condition of employment: Principle 41(e).
[416] Ibid., Principle 43. A list of factors is provided as relevant considerations in this balancing exercise: whether the extent of the disclosure was reasonably necessary; the extent and risk of harm to the public interest caused by the disclosure; whether the whistleblower had reasonable grounds to believe the disclosure was in the public interest; whether they attempted to make the disclosure through the internal or independent procedures and the existence of exigent circumstances justifying the disclosure.
[417] Johannesburg Principles, Principle 7. The category of 'protected expression', the 'peaceful exercise of which shall not be considered a threat to national security' includes but 'is not limited to': advocacy of non-violent change of government, criticism or insult to the nation, government and its agents, objection on the grounds of religion, belief or conscience and information communicating alleged violations of human rights and humanitarian law.
[418] UN Special Rapporteur, the OSCE Representative on Freedom of the Media and the OAS Special Rapporteur, Joint Declaration on Access to Information and Secrecy Legislation (2004). See also Parliamentary Assembly of the COE Resolution 1729(2010) on Protection of 'whistle-blowers', 29 April 2010; CoM Recommendation CM/Res (2014)7 of the Committee of Ministers to member States on the protection of whistleblowers, 30 April 2014; OSCE, 'Access to information by the media in the OSCE region: trends and recommendations' (2 May 2007); ACmHR, Declaration of Principles on Freedom of Expression and Access to Information in Africa (2019), Principle 35.
[419] See ss III.4.3. (Intent) and III.5.1. (Public interest defence).
[420] ECtHR (GC), *Guja v. Moldova* (App. no. 14277/04), 12 February 2008, §75.

The Court also considers whether the speaker has 'acted in good faith and in the belief that the information was true',[421] and whether 'the manner in which a person obtains information considered to be confidential or secret may be of some relevance for the balancing of interests to be carried out in the context of article 10 §2'.[422]

The Court applied these principles in a case in which a journalist was convicted and fined for 'sharing secret information' with colleagues concerning Romanian military operations in Afghanistan.[423] The Court noted that the journalist 'did not obtain the information in question by unlawful means and the investigation failed to prove that he had actively sought to obtain such information'.[424] The Court also observed that although journalists have duties and responsibilities, it is for states to 'organise their services and to train their personnel ... to ensure that no confidential information is disclosed', ultimately finding that the journalist's conviction constituted a violation of article 10.[425]

Similar reasoning was applied when a court reporter asked an administrative assistant at a prosecutor's office to provide him with confidential documents connected to a high-profile robbery, and was prosecuted for inciting another to disclose official secrets and fined approximately 325 euros.[426] Although it was argued that the court reporter, an 'experienced columnist', should have known the information was confidential, the Court considered it relevant that the reporter had not resorted to trickery or pressure to obtain the information, and that the prosecutor's office played 'an important part of the responsibility for the indiscretion'.[427] The Court ultimately found the reporter's conviction to be disproportionate in light of this conduct.

In contrast, the Court held there was no violation of article 10 when a case file of a controversial murder trial was left in a shopping centre and an unknown person provided a copy to a journalist who was later convicted and fined for publishing the file in a magazine. The Court noted that the fact the journalist had not obtained the material by unlawful means 'is not necessarily a determining factor in assessing whether or not he complied with his duties and responsibilities when publishing the information'.[428] Rather, 'as a professional journalist', he 'could not have been unaware of the confidential nature of the information he was planning to publish'.[429] Considering this alongside the proportionality of the penalty and the impact on the accused's private life and criminal proceedings, the Court held that no violation of article 10 had taken place.

5.2.2. Publication as a last resort?

Another aspect of a whistleblower's conduct that the European Court will closely consider—and that the Tshwane Principles also prioritize—is whether the

---

[421] Ibid., §77.
[422] ECtHR (GC), *Bédat v. Switzerland* (App. no. 56925/08), 29 March 2016, §56.
[423] ECtHR, *Gîrleanu v. Romania* (App. no. 50376/09), 26 June 2018. See s. III.4.2.1. (Type and severity of harm).
[424] Ibid., §§91–92.
[425] Ibid., §92.
[426] ECtHR, *Dammann v. Switzerland* (App. no. 77551/01), 25 April 2006.
[427] Ibid., §55.
[428] ECtHR (GC), *Bédat v. Switzerland* (App. no. 56925/08), 29 March 2016, §57.
[429] Ibid., §57.

whistleblower used alternative channels of reporting before publishing secret information. The Court will consider 'whether there was available ... any other effective means of remedying the wrongdoing' and have held that 'disclosure should be made in the first place to the person's superior or other competent authority or body' and only where this is 'clearly impracticable ... as a last resort, be disclosed to the public'.[430] For example, when the Court found that a journalist's conviction for sharing secret information concerning Romania's military operations in Afghanistan violated his right to free speech, the Court noted that the journalist's first step 'after coming into possession of the information in question was to discuss it with the institution concerned by the leak', and that the institution then made no attempts to recover the documents.[431] And similarly in the *Bucur* case, the Court took into account that there appeared to be no procedure for expressing concerns with Romania's intelligence services other than raising these with superiors, which the employee in question had done.[432] And as the leaks directly concerned superiors, the Court also expressed doubt as to the 'effectiveness of any reports that the applicant may have made'.[433]

Similarly, the Tshwane Principles provide that the law should protect from penalties for disclosures if:

a) the person made the disclosure to an internal or independent oversight body which either refused or failed to investigate, or the person did not receive a reasonable and appropriate outcome within a reasonable and legally defined time period; or
b) the person reasonably believed there was a significant risk that making the disclosure internally or to an independent oversight body would have resulted in the destruction or concealment of evidence, interference with a witness or retaliation against the person or a third party; or
c) there were no established bodies to which the disclosure could have been made; or
d) the disclosure related to an act or omission that constituted a serious and imminent risk of danger to the life, health and safety of persons, or to the environment.

The Principles also provide for residual protection even where these conditions have not been met, protecting speakers from retaliation unless the harm of the speech outweighs the public interest in it being disclosed.[434]

5.2.3. *'Responsible journalism'*

According to the European Court of Human Rights, the 'protection' afforded to the press as a 'watchdog' in democratic society is 'subject to the proviso that they act in

---

[430] ECtHR (GC), *Guja v. Moldova* (App. no. 14277/04), 12 February 2008, §73.
[431] ECtHR, *Gîrleanu v. Romania* (App. no. 50376/09), 26 June 2018, §§91–92.
[432] ECtHR, *Bucur and Toma v. Romania* (App. no. 40238/02), 8 January 2013, §§96–98. See s. III.4. (Necessity).
[433] Ibid., §97. See s. III.4. (Necessity). The Court also considered a second route suggested by the government for disclosure, namely the referral to a parliamentary committee, but noted that the MP that was contacted about the leaks was in fact a member of that Committee. Ibid., §§98–99.
[434] Tshwane Principles, Principle 43.

good faith in order to provide accurate and reliable information in accordance with the tenets of responsible journalism'.[435] And although the Inter-American Court has referenced the 'responsible journalism' doctrine, no other international body has used it to determine the outcome of cases involving speech by the press.[436]

The European Court applies the doctrine by addressing three questions. First, it considers whether a journalist has acted unlawfully in the manner in which the information was obtained since journalists are not above the law.[437] The fact that a journalist has breached the law in his or her public interaction with authorities when exercising journalist functions is considered 'a most relevant, albeit not decisive, consideration when determining whether he or she has acted responsibly'.[438] Secondly, 'responsible journalism requires that the journalists check the information provided to the public to a reasonable extent'. In particular, 'special grounds' are required before the media can be dispensed from their 'ordinary obligation to verify' the content they disseminate.[439] And finally, the Court considers the manner of presentation of the speech, recognizing that although a court should not seek to determine 'what technique of reporting should be adopted by journalists', and journalistic freedom allows 'recourse to a degree of exaggeration, or even provocation', this deference is not 'unlimited'.[440]

The Court has applied this doctrine even in circumstances where it does not consider that an impugned publication could be regarded as 'contributing to a debate of public interest' or as constituting 'political speech' so in these cases at least it seems to be establishing a separate standard based on the speaker, and not the subject matter of the

---

[435] ECtHR, *Gîrleanu v. Romania* (App. no. 50376/09), 26 June 2018, §84.

[436] See ch. 1 (Introduction), s. II.3.2.5. (Relevance of whether the speaker is a journalist). See IACtHR, *Mémoli v. Argentina* (Series C, no. 265), 22 August 2013, §122 (where 'responsible journalism' is referenced but does not appear to be dispositive of the case).

[437] ECtHR (GC), *Pentikäinen v. Finland* (App. no. 11882/10), 20 October 2015, §90. See also ECtHR, *Brambilla v. Italy* (App. no. 22567/09) 23 June 2016, §64 ('The Court reiterates that the concept of responsible journalism requires that whenever a journalist's conduct flouts the duty to abide by ordinary criminal law, the journalist has to be aware that he or she is liable to face legal sanctions, including of a criminal character'); ECtHR, *Salihu v. Sweden* (App. no. 33628/15), 10 May 2016, §59 (where journalists purchased a firearm to demonstrate the ease of doing so, and the Court held this 'could have been illustrated by other means').

[438] ECtHR (GC), *Pentikäinen v. Finland* (App. no. 11882/10), 20 October 2015, §90. The UK courts in Julian Assange's case also considered the lawfulness of the manner in which the information was acquired as being relevant and potentially dispositive. In the extradition proceedings, experts gave evidence that Assange was 'doing no more than what many investigative reporters in the US already do', as the reporter–source relationship is 'a constant back-and-forth between parties, and good newsgatherers actively solicit their sources for information'. But in finding that these charges were compatible with UK law and article 10 of the European Court, Judge Baraister held that Assange's 'activities went beyond the mere encouragement of a whistle-blower', and that his assistance to Manning in seeking to decipher a code 'most obviously demonstrates' his complicity with her theft and 'separates his activity from that of the ordinary investigative journalist'. She concluded that '[h]ad Mr. Assange decided not to assist Ms. Manning to take the information in [this manner], *and merely received it from her*, then the Article 10 considerations would be different'. See, e.g., UK Westminster Magistrates' Court, *The Government of the United States of America v. Julian Paul Assange*, Consolidated Annex, 11 January 2021(evidence of Professor Feldstein, §40); UK Westminster Magistrates' Court, *The Government of the United States of America v. Julian Paul Assange*, 11 January 2021, §§96, 99, 118.

[439] ECtHR, *Kącki v. Poland* (App. no. 10947/11), 4 July 2017, §52; ECtHR (GC), *Pedersen and Baadsgaard v. Denmark* (App. no. 49017/99), 17 December 2004, §78; ECtHR, *Flux v. Moldova (No. 6)* (App. no. 22824/04), 29 July 2008, §26.

[440] ECtHR (GC), *Jersild v. Denmark* (App. no. 15890/89), 23 September 1994, §31; ECtHR (GC), *Bladet Tromsø and Stensaas v. Norway* (App. no. 21980/93), 20 May 1999, §§59, 63; ECtHR (GC), *Couderc and Hachette Filipacchi Associés v. France* (App. no. 40454/07), 10 November 2015, §144.

speech.⁴⁴¹ But the doctrine has also been applied to non-journalists, such as human rights activists, NGOs and whistleblowers who engage in public debate and are also considered 'watchdogs'.⁴⁴² And the questions that the Court asks—essentially relating to whether the speaker was negligent or reckless as to the falsity of the speech—overlap with the questions the Court deems relevant to any speaker who discloses confidential official data.⁴⁴³ This means that the responsible journalism doctrine, although in many cases applied in a manner that is protective of journalists, adds unnecessary doctrinal confusion.

5.3. Truth

The truthfulness of a statement will generally be of less significance in the area of official secrets and espionage than, for example, defamatory speech.⁴⁴⁴ But truthfulness remains relevant to the analysis of the mental culpability and reasonableness of the conduct of the speaker and is also relevant in assessing whether speech is in the public interest. The European Court has held that the 'authenticity' of information disclosed, and whether it had been 'carefully verified' is one of a number of factors to be balanced when determining the necessity of a restriction to the disclosure of information receiving in confidence.⁴⁴⁵ Another 'determinant factor' is the motive behind the actions of the reporting employee, with the Court holding that it is 'important to establish that, in making the disclosure, the individual acted in good faith and in the belief that the information was true'.⁴⁴⁶

The authenticity of leaked information was a key aspect of the leading case of *Bucur*, as the Romanian government argued that the whistleblower in that case had provided false information to the public.⁴⁴⁷ The Court 'bore in mind' Resolution 1729 (2010) of the Parliamentary Assembly of the Council of Europe, which provides that any 'whistle-blower shall be considered as having acted in good faith provided he or she had *reasonable grounds to believe* that the information disclosed was true, even if it later turns out that this was not the case, and provided he or she did not pursue any unlawful or unethical objectives'.⁴⁴⁸ The Court noted that several factors, uncontested by the Romanian Government, supported the whistleblower's belief that unlawful telephone tapping had taken place but had not been considered by domestic courts.⁴⁴⁹ And the judges ultimately held that Mr. Bucur 'had reasonable grounds to believe that the

---

⁴⁴¹ ECtHR, *Satakunnan Markkinapörssi Oy v. Finland* (App. no. 931/13), 27 June 2017, §§174–178. Cf. Dissenting Opinion of Judges Sajo and Karakas.
⁴⁴² ECtHR (GC), *Magyar Helsinki Bizottság v. Hungary* (App. no. 18030/11), 8 November 2016, §159; ECtHR, *Gawlik v. Liechtenstein* (App. no. 23922/19), 16 February 2021, §77.
⁴⁴³ In addition, the issue of intent or mental fault is relevant to an analysis of all speech under international standards. See ss III.4. (Necessity) and III.5.1. (Public interest defence).
⁴⁴⁴ See ch. 2 (Insulting Speech), s. III.4.1. (Truth); HRC, General Comment No. 34 (2011), §47.
⁴⁴⁵ ECtHR (GC), *Guja v. Moldova* (App. No. 14277/04), 12 February 2008, §75.
⁴⁴⁶ Ibid., §77. As part of its 'responsible journalism' analysis the Court also considers that heightened protection is 'subject to the proviso' that a speaker is 'acting in good faith in order to provide *accurate and reliable* information'. See, e.g., ECtHR (GC), *Bédat v. Switzerland* (App. no. 56925/08), 29 March 2016, §58 (emphasis added). See s. III.5.2.3. ('Responsible journalism').
⁴⁴⁷ ECtHR, *Bucur and Toma v. Romania* (App. no. 40238/02), 8 January 2013, §107.
⁴⁴⁸ Ibid., §107 citing Parliamentary Assembly of the COE Resolution 1729(2010) on Protection of 'whistleblowers', 29 April 2010, 6.2.4 (emphasis added).
⁴⁴⁹ Ibid., §108.

information disclosed was true', and that he was acting in good faith motivated by respect for Romanian laws and the Constitution.[450]

Certain soft law instruments also incorporate a reasonable belief in the truth of the impugned speech as a condition of, or relevant factor in the assessment of whether penalties are appropriate for leaks of confidential information. The African Commission's 2019 Declaration of Principles on Freedom of Expression provides that all persons should be protected from penalties for disclosures 'in the public interest, in the honest belief that such information is substantially true'.[451] The Tshwane Principles framework protects public officials who have 'reasonable grounds to believe' that information discloses wrongdoing. The Principles also provide that the 'motivation for a protected disclosure [by public officials] is irrelevant except where the disclose is proven to be *knowingly* untrue'.[452]

5.4. Opinion

International standards related to espionage and official secrets laws rarely refer to whether speech disclosing confidential information can be considered an 'opinion', though this is a basis for the exclusion of liability for defamatory speech.[453] The Inter-American Court of Human Rights has however extended the principle that opinion cannot be the object of sanction to the national security context in *Usón Ramírez v. Venezuela*. In that case, the Court found a violation of free speech rights where Mr. Usón Ramírez was not stating that a premeditated crime had been committed, but that *in his opinion* such a crime seemed to have been committed, and therefore could not be convicted under military slander laws.[454]

6. Penalties

All international human rights bodies consider penalties to be relevant to the assessment of whether a restriction to speech is 'necessary' and can therefore comply with international standards.[455] A number of international human rights bodies have

---

[450] Ibid., §§107–113, 117–118.
[451] Tshwane Principles, Principle 35.
[452] Tshwane Principles, Principle 38. Although the 'right to truth' concerning human rights violations is an area of jurisprudence beyond the scope of this report, the Tshwane Principles provide that the extent to which a disclosure may 'shed light on the truth' about alleged human rights violations is a relevant factor when determining if information may be disclosed: Principle 10(A)(4). However, the Tshwane Principles' position is that persons who are *not* public personnel should *never* be sanctioned for the dissemination of classified information (Tshwane Principles, Principle 47).
[453] See ch. 2 (Insulting Speech), s. III.4.5. (Opinion).
[454] Cf. IACtHR, *Usón Ramírez v. Venezuela* (Series C, no. 207), 20 November 2009, §86 (emphasis added). See also IACtHR, *Palamara-Iribarne v. Chile* (Series C, no. 135), 22 November 2005, §§87–88 (finding that, by way of contempt charges, 'Mr. Palamara-Iribarne suffered serious consequences for having voiced his opinion on the manner in which officers of the military justice were conducting the proceedings against him and the manner in which military authorities were treating him and his family').
[455] See, e.g., HRC, General Comment No. 34 (2011), §§34–35; ECtHR (GC), *Guja v. Moldova* (App. no. 14277/04), 12 February 2008, §69; IACtHR, *Palamara-Iribarne v. Chile* (Series C, no. 135), 22 November 2005, §85; ACtHPR, *Konaté v Burkina Faso* (App. no. 4/2013), 5 December 2014, §145.

expressed disapproval of criminal sanctions on the basis that it is a disproportionate response to speech, including in the national security context.

The Human Rights Committee has observed that states should exercise 'great caution in the imposition of criminal penalties that punish speech',[456] to the point that a term of imprisonment has *never* been found an appropriate restriction on speech in the Committee's decisions.[457] The Human Rights Committee has also criticized certain spying offences that carry the death penalty under Bangladesh's Official Secrets Act.[458] And the Working Group has asserted that 'a vague and general reference to the interests of national security or public order, without being properly explained and documented, is insufficient to convince the Working Group that ... restrictions ... by way of deprivation of liberty are necessary'.[459]

The European Court of Human Rights has held that authorities must generally 'show restraint in resorting to criminal proceedings in matters of freedom of expression'.[460] The Court has also warned that a penalty imposed on speech should not 'amount to a form of censorship intended to discourage the press from expressing criticism', particularly when a sanction could deter journalists from 'contributing to public discussion of issues affecting the life of the community'.[461] Consequently, 'the fact of a person's conviction may in some cases be more important than the minor nature of the penalty imposed'.[462]

However, the European Court provides some leeway to states when it comes to criminal penalties for hate speech[463] and has similarly held that 'in cases concerning criminal sanctions for the disclosure of classified military information ... the margin of appreciation is to be left to the domestic authorities in matters of national security'.[464]

On this basis, the European Court has in a small number of cases allowed terms of imprisonment for the disclosure of official secrets, particularly where conduct constituted traditional spying offences by public officials, rather than simply speech by journalists or others. For example, where a Russian naval officer allegedly transferred information to Japanese journalists about the Russian navy's military exercises and financial situation, the European Court considered that domestic courts had not 'overstepped the limits of the margin of appreciation ... in matters of national security' by convicting the officer of treason, through espionage, and sentencing him to four years' imprisonment.[465] The Court held that the officer had been convicted 'as a serving military officer, and not as a journalist, of treason through espionage for having collected

---

[456] HRC, *Rabbae v. Netherlands* (Comm. no. 2124/2011), 14 July 2016, Individual Opinion (Concurring) of Committee members Sarah Cleveland and Mauro Politi, §7.
[457] See ch. 1 (Introduction), s. II.3.1.6. (Criminal penalties for speech).
[458] HRC, *Concluding Observations: Bangladesh* (2017) UN Doc. CCPR/C/BGD/CO/1, §§23–24.
[459] WGAD, *Gulmira Imin v. China* (Opinion no. 29/2012), 29 August 2012, §29.
[460] ECtHR (GC), *Bédat v. Switzerland* (App. no. 56925/08), 29 March 2016, §81.
[461] Ibid., §79.
[462] Ibid., §79.
[463] See ch. 1 (Introduction), s. III.3.1.1. (Justification for penalizing speech).
[464] ECtHR, *Gîrleanu v. Romania* (App. no. 50376/09), 26 June 2018, §96, citing ECtHR, *Hadjianastassiou v. Greece* (App. no. 12945/87), 16 December 1992, §47.
[465] ECtHR, *Pasko v. Russia* (App. no. 69519/01), 22 October 2009.

and kept, with the intention of transferring it to a foreign national, information of a military nature that was classified as a State secret', and considered the sentence to be 'very lenient'.[466]

And where an air force engineer was sentenced by a Greek military court to a suspended sentence of five months' imprisonment for disclosing his technical knowledge about a missile for commercial gain, the Court considered it necessary to account for the 'specific "duties" and "responsibilities" incumbent on the members of the armed forces' and held that the Greek courts had not overstepped the 'margin of appreciation' left to domestic authorities on national security matters.[467]

But the European Court has also been clear that the discretion left to states in such cases is not unlimited. As a result, the Court found a violation of article 10 where a journalist had been ordered to pay a fine of 870 Euros after sharing 'secret' information concerning Romanian military operations with colleagues.[468] While noting that a margin of appreciation applies to penalties in matters of national security, the Court held that 'the applicant in the current case is a journalist claiming to have made the disclosure in the context of a journalistic investigation and not a member of the military who collected and transmitted secret military information to foreign nationals' and that the penalty was, accordingly, 'not reasonably proportionate to the legitimate aim pursued'.[469]

The Inter-American Court of Human Rights has also voiced a strong rebuke to criminal sanctions even in a national security context in *Palamara-Iribarne v. Chile*.[470] In that case, Mr. Palamara-Iribane, a naval mechanic engineer, was sentenced to a 61-day prison term, a fine and suspension from public office for contempt, after he criticized the way military authorities responded to him publishing a book regarding ethical standards within military intelligence. The Court noted that criminal law is 'the most restrictive and severe means of imposing liability for illegal conduct', and that Mr. Palarmara-Iribarne had suffered 'serious consequences', including four days in pre-trial custody. And it ultimately held that the 'sanctions were disproportionate to the criticism levelled at government institutions and their members, thus suppressing debate, which is essential to the functioning of a truly democratic system, and unnecessarily restricting the right to freedom of thought and expression'.[471]

Similarly, the African Court on Human and Peoples' Rights has held that custodial sentences for violations of the laws of freedom of speech are generally inappropriate, and will only be lawful in 'serious and very exceptional circumstances' such as 'incitement to international crimes, public incitement to hatred, discrimination or violence

---

[466] Ibid., §§86–87.
[467] ECtHR, *Hadjianastassiou v. Greece* (App. no. 12945/87), 16 December 1992, §44–47.
[468] This amount was a combination of a fine and judicial costs. ECtHR, *Gîrleanu v. Romania* (App. no. 50376/09), 26 June 2018, §§96–99.
[469] Ibid.
[470] IACtHR, *Palamara-Iribarne v. Chile* (Series C, No. 135), 22 November 2005. See s. III.1. (International standards related to speech affecting national security).
[471] Ibid., §88.

or threats against a person or group of people, because of specific criteria such as race, colour, religion and nationality'.[472]

The Tshwane Principles provide that, even if public personnel are not protected by the public interest framework the Principles advocate, they should not be subjected to criminal penalties.[473] If criminal penalties are used, they should only apply to 'narrow categories of information that are clearly set forth in law'.[474] Penalties for disclosures which 'pose a real and identifiable risk of causing significant harm' should be 'proportional to the harm caused' and the catch-all public interest defence provided by the Principles must be available.[475] And according to the 2013 Joint Declaration by the UN and OAS Special Rapporteurs on freedom of expression, the imposition of criminal sanctions for the disclosure of confidential information 'must be exceptional and strictly limited according to necessity and proportionality'.[476]

IV. Recommendations

The following recommendations are based on minimum international human rights standards applicable to espionage and official secrets laws. Where there is a divergence or lacuna in such standards, we advocate for a best practice based on national systems or emerging international standards. A common theme articulated in these recommendations is the significant disconnect between international minimum standards and state laws on espionage and official secrets. Despite increasingly crystallized international standards which, at a minimum, necessitate clear harm thresholds and consideration of the public interest in disclosure, many state laws fall short, even in leading democracies.

A further theme of these recommendations is the primacy given to the Tshwane Principles. Drafted by 17 organizations and five academic centres, in consultation with 500 experts across the globe, including government officials and military officers, and endorsed by UN and regional Special Rapporteurs in the space, we consider these Principles to be highly persuasive.[477] The Principles' requirement that states recognize a public interest defence is a particularly compelling extension of existing international standards that we endorse. But it cannot provide sufficient protection for speech in the

---

[472] ACtHPR, *Konaté v Burkina Faso* (App. no. 4/2013), 5 December 2014, §165. Although this case grapples with criminal defamation laws, it reflects the Court's reluctance to consider criminal penalties for expression proportionate in any circumstances. Cf. *Federation of African Journalists v. Gambia*, where the Community Court of Justice of ECOWAS held that the practice of imposing criminal sanctions for sedition, defamation and false news publication has a chilling effect that may unduly restrict journalists' freedom of expression: ECOWAS CCJ, *Federation of African Journalists v. Gambia* (Suit no. ECW/CCJ/APP/36/15), 13 February 2018.
[473] Tshwane Principles, Principle 46.
[474] Tshwane Principles, Principle 46(b).
[475] Tshwane Principles, Principle 46(b). See s. III.5.1. (Public interest defence).
[476] UN Special Rapporteur & OAS Special Rapporteur, Joint declaration on surveillance programs and their Impact on freedom of expression (2013) ('Any attempt to impose subsequent punishment on those who reveal classified information must be based on previously established laws applied by impartial and independent bodies with full due process guarantees, including the right to appeal the ruling'). See also, e.g., Johannesburg Principles, Principle 22.
[477] Open Society Justice Initiative, 'Understanding the Tshwane Principles' (12 June 2013).

absence of laws that are holistically fair: for instance, by also requiring proof of harm and proportionate penalties. The recommendations below should therefore be considered in their entirety.

1. Espionage and official secrets laws must not be vague or overbroad.

Espionage and official secrets laws must be 'accessible, unambiguous, drawn narrowly and with precision so as to enable individuals to understand what information may be withheld, what should be disclosed, and what actions concerning the information are subject to sanction'.[478] Laws must be 'formulated with sufficient precision to enable the person concerned to regulate his or her conduct'.[479] Anachronistic terms whose meaning is unclear in the modern day, such as 'enemy'—which is used in dozens of colonial-era laws that are still on the books—and 'subversion', are unlikely to satisfy this legality requirement.[480] Neither will laws that effectively leave what constitutes an offence 'to the discretion of the authorities', like Cambodia's use of the phrasing 'undermin[ing] the national defence'.[481]

2. States must provide adequate reasons to justify penalties for speech on the grounds of 'national security'. Classification of information as 'secret' is not in itself a sufficient basis for penalizing the disclosure of information. Protecting the reputation of governments, government organs or state officials is not a legitimate 'national security' interest that can serve as a basis to penalize speech.

States should clearly define national security in their espionage and official secrets laws.[482] The fact that information has been 'classified' does not in itself demonstrate that secrecy is justified.[483] Information in the public domain, even in circumstances

---

[478] Tshwane Principles, Principle 3(a). See also Johannesburg Principles, Principle 1.1(a).
[479] ECtHR (GC), *Perinçek v. Switzerland* (App. no. 27510/08), 15 October 2015, §131.
[480] See UK Law Commission, *Protection of Official Data Report* (2020), §§3.88–3.110. See also UK Law Commission, *Protection of Official Data: A Consultation Paper* (2017), §2.164.
[481] WGAD, *Chhin v. Cambodia* (Opinion no. 3/2019), 24 April 2019, §49. Some laws misuse presumptions to impose guilt in an overbroad manner. Because this concerns general criminal law principles this issue is beyond the scope of the book, but relevant guidance can be found in A. Clooney & P. Webb, *The Right to a Fair Trial in International Law* (OUP 2021), ch. 4. See s. II.2.2.3. (Cambodia).
[482] Tshwane Principles, definition of 'legitimate national security interest'. This recommendation is intended to cover not only criminal sanctions but also potentially civil penalties, even though the review of state practice has shown that these laws are usually criminal in nature. Other recommendations, in particular Recommendations 3–5, all explicitly relate only to criminal laws.
[483] WGAD, *Lee Kun-hee v. South Korea* (Opinion no. 29/1994), 29 September 1994, §6. See also ECtHR (C), *Vereniging Weekblad Bluf! v. Netherlands* (App. no. 16616/90), 9 February 1995, §41, ECtHR, *Görmüş v. Turkey* (App. no. 49085/07), 19 January 2016, §62.

where it was previously afforded a high degree of protection, is not 'sufficiently sensitive' to warrant restrictions under official secrets laws.[484] And states must interpret the concept of national security 'with restraint'.[485] They must also allow domestic courts to have access to sufficient information to effectively assess whether national security interests are at stake.[486]

A restriction on speech on national security grounds is not legitimate 'unless its genuine purpose and demonstrable effect is to protect a country's existence or its territorial integrity against the use or threat of force, or its capacity to respond to the use or threat of force, whether from an external source, such as a military threat, or an internal source, such as incitement to violent overthrow of the government'.[487] States cannot restrict speech on the basis of the 'general situation in the country: they must demonstrate a 'specific and individualized' threat to national security.[488] And definitions of national security such as Australia's, which encompass 'the country's political, military or economic relations with another country or other countries' are overbroad.[489]

If states adopt a list of categories of information that must be kept secret to protect a legitimate national security interest, these should be narrowly defined.[490] States may also incorporate a list of information which is not—or is presumed not to be—secret.[491]

Protecting the reputation of governments, government organs or state officials is not a legitimate 'national security' interest that can serve as a basis to penalize speech. International bodies have also made clear that the following do *not* constitute national security interests:

- Protecting a government or its officials from embarrassment or exposure of wrongdoing;
- Preventing disclosure of information about the functioning of public institutions;
- Preventing disclosure of information about human rights violations or other serious violations of law;[492]
- Preventing disclosure of evidence pertaining to 'environmental conditions, emergencies and disasters posing a risk to human life and health';[493]

---

[484] See, e.g., ECtHR (C), *Vereniging Weekblad Bluf! v. Netherlands* (App. no. 16616/90), 9 February 1995, §§41–46; ECtHR, *Observer and Guardian v. United Kingdom* (App. no. 13585/88), 26 November 1991, §§69–70; Tshwane Principles, Principle 49(b); Johannesburg Principles, Principle 17; IACtHR, *Palamara-Iribarne v. Chile* (Series C, no. 135), 22 November 2005, §77; Parliamentary Assembly of the COE, Resolution 1551 on Fair trial issues in criminal cases concerning espionage or divulging state secrets, 19 April 2007, §10.1. Some dated or historical information may also fall into this category. See, e.g., WGAD, *Xiyue Wang v. Iran* (Opinion no. 52/2018), 23 August 2018, §§32–33; ECtHR (Plenary Court), *The Observer and The Guardian v. United Kingdom* (App. no. 13585/88), 26 November 1991, §§69–70; ECtHR (C), *Vereniging Weekblad Bluf! v. Netherlands* (App. no. 16616/90), 9 February 1995, §§41–46.

[485] See ECtHR, Guide on Article 10 of the Convention, 31 August 2022, §543, citing ECtHR (GC), *Stoll v. Switzerland* (App. no. 69698/01), 10 December 2007, §54.

[486] ECtHR (GC), *Janowiec v. Russia* (App. nos 55508/07 & 29520/09), 21 October 2013, §213.

[487] Johannesburg Principles, Principle 2(a).

[488] HRC, General Comment No. 34 (2011), §35.

[489] See Australian Criminal Code Act s. 90.4(1).

[490] See, e.g., Tshwane Principles, Principle 9. See s. III.4.1. (Secrecy). These categories are provided by the Tshwane Principles as 'information that legitimately may be withheld'.

[491] Tshwane Principles, Principle 10. See s. III.4.1. (Secrecy).

[492] Tshwane Principles, Principle 10; WGAD, *Li Hai v. China* (Opinion No. 19/1999) 16 September 1999, §12.

[493] Tshwane Principles, Principle 10; WGAD, *Grigorii Pasko v. Russian Federation* (Opinion No. 9/1999), 20 May 1999, §7.

- Entrenching or strengthening a particular ideology, political interest or party;
- Suppressing industrial unrest;
- Suppressing lawful protests.[494]

3. Criminal liability under official secrets and espionage laws should be conditional on the demonstration of a sufficiently high mental culpability by the speaker, a showing of an objective probability of serious harm caused by the speech and be subject to a 'public interest' defence.

3.1. *Mens rea requirement:* Criminal liability under official secrets and espionage laws should be conditional on the demonstration of a sufficiently high mental culpability by the speaker.

Speech should only be prosecuted under espionage or official secrets laws if a prosecutor can prove that the speaker intended to disclose the secret material and intended to harm national security interests.[495] States should expressly provide for a high *mens rea* standard in official secrets laws, particularly those of a criminal nature, to justify restricting speech and any criminal penalties.[496] This intent requirement should be accompanied by a high harm and causation threshold, rather than be a replacement for such requirements, as has been suggested by the Law Commission.[497]

Although international human rights bodies have rarely opined on the precise intent requirements for official secrets and espionage laws, international standards are clear that the intent of a speaker is a relevant factor in determining the necessity of any restriction of the right to free expression under international law. International bodies have found that to ensure compliance with the principle of legality, states should explicitly provide a precise and sufficiently high intent element within their secrecy and espionage laws.[498] And the European Court makes clear that a determining 'factor in deciding whether a particular disclosure should be protected or not' is the motive of the whistleblower, considering it 'important to establish that, in making the disclosure, the individual acted in good faith and in the belief that the information was true that it was in the public interest to disclose it and that no other, more discreet, means of remedying the wrongdoing was available to him or her'.[499] In addition, the Tshwane Principles

---

[494] Johannesburg Principles, Principle 2(b); Tshwane Principles, definition of 'legitimate national security interest'.
[495] In some legal systems this may include recklessness as to such harm being created. See ch. 3 (Hate Speech), s. VI.3.1 (Recommendations) and ch. 4 (False Speech), s. IV.6 (Recommendations).
[496] This can include an assessment of whether publication was a last resort, whether the person disclosing the information tried to report the issue being disclosed internally before publishing, and so on.
[497] See s. II.2.1.1. (United Kingdom). See UK Law Commission, *Protection of Official Data Report* (2020) §4.15.
[498] See, e.g., IACtHR, *Usón Ramírez v. Venezuela* (Series C, no. 207), 20 November 2009, §56; ECOWAS CCJ, *Federation of African Journalists v. Gambia* (Suit No. ECW/CCJ/APP/36/15), 13 February 2018.
[499] ECtHR (GC), *Guja v. Moldova* (App. no. 14277/04), 12 February 2008, §77. See s. III.5.1. (Public interest defence), s. III.5.2. (Reasonableness of the publication), s. III.5.3. (Truth).

also provide that a public interest defence should be available to those who 'reasonably believed' both that they were disclosing wrongdoing and that the public interest in the information being revealed outweighed any harm that would be caused by its publication.[500]

The 'intent' formulation put forward by the Law Commission presents some challenges. The Commission has suggested the following test: 'that the defendant (i) knew; (ii) believed; or (iii) was reckless as to whether the disclosure (a) would cause damage; (b) was likely to cause damage; (c) risked causing damage; or (d) was *capable of* causing damage'.[501] Media organizations have criticized this test, arguing that 'if you have been told by an official that a disclosure would be damaging, but have good reason not to believe it, you might still commit an offence—because having been told you may now have reasonable cause to believe that it is "capable" of being so'.[502] The BBC stated that 'the use of the words "capable of" would significantly lower the threshold of criminal liability as it could encompass disclosure which has only a remote possibility of causing damage'.[503] And the Guardian News and Media complained that this 'means that a disclosure which is *unlikely* to cause damage may nevertheless be an offence because in circumstances that are highly unlikely to ever arise, it *might* cause damage'.[504] They point out that in practice, editors ask 'is this information damaging or is it embarrassing', and that the proposed amendment is 'a much less certain and much more subjective test'.[505] We agree with these concerns and urge states to adopt clear and sufficiently rigorous intent requirements.

3.2. **Harm requirement: States should only criminalize speech when they can prove that there was an objective probability that the speech would cause serious harm such as violence, a serious criminal offence or endangerment to human life.**

International standards make clear that espionage and official secrets laws must establish a 'direct and immediate connection between the expression and the threat' of

---

[500] Tshwane Principles, Principles 38, 40. The Principles also note that it is 'ultimately for an independent court or tribunal to determine whether this test has been satisfied so as to qualify the disclosure for protection': Principle 40. The Principles distinguish intent from motive, noting that the motive for disclosing information should be irrelevant 'except where the disclosure is proven to be knowingly untrue': Principle 38.

[501] UK Law Commission, *Protection of Official Data Report* (2020), Recommendation 11 (emphasis supplied). The ECtHR has previously applied a similar test of whether speech would be 'capable of' causing harm in relation to hateful and terror-related speech: see ch. 3 (Hate Speech), s. III.2.3.1 (Harm). See also ch. 6 (Speech related to National Security: Terrorism Laws), s. III.3.1 (Harm).

[502] Guardian News & Media, *Response to Law Commission Consultation Paper no 230 on protection of Official Data* (2017), 55.

[503] UK Law Commission, *Protection of Official Data Report* (2020), §4.67. The UK Law Commission recognized 'the weight of consultees' strong opposition to this recommendation', but considered these concerns would be addressed by 'fortifying and balancing this recommendation with the public interest disclosure recommendations': §4.80. The British Government strongly agreed with the UK Law Commission's proposal to create an explicit fault element 'on the assumption that the fault element will remain as construed in *Keogh*', as any higher test 'would compound the difficulties of prosecuting the offence': §4.71.

[504] Guardian News & Media, *Response to Law Commission Consultation Paper no 230 on protection of Official Data* (2017), 55; UK Law Commission, *Protection of Official Data Report* (2020), Recommendation §4.55.

[505] Guardian News & Media, *Response to Law Commission Consultation Paper no 230 on protection of Official Data* (2017), 53-4.

harm[506] and states must demonstrate a link between the speech they seek to penalize and 'in specific and individualized fashion the precise nature of the threat' that may result from such speech.[507] International bodies have also made clear that the harm must be serious. For example, the European Court has found a violation of article 10 when a state has argued that the harm justifying official secrets laws is 'the interest in maintaining public confidence in [an] institution'.[508] The Tshwane Principles provide that harm must be 'significant' and the Johannesburg Principles suggest that speech can only be sanctioned on the grounds of national security if this is likely to 'incite imminent violence'.[509]

We recommend that speech only be restricted when there is an objective probability (meaning that it is more probable than not) of serious harm that is direct and imminent. This standard should be set out in national laws.[510] This high bar is preferable to lower standards such as in the United States, where criminal penalties may apply to the disclosure of information that 'would be *potentially damaging* to the United States or *might be* useful' to an enemy, or the UK standard of 'likelihood' of damage.[511] We also recommend that states limit the use of espionage and official secrets laws to harm that takes the form of violent or illegal acts[512] that may cause serious physical injury or death through speech. These causation and harm requirements should exist alongside high intent standards.[513]

This recommendation is at odds with the Law Commission of England and Wales proposal to remove the requirement to prove 'damage' or the likelihood of damage for unauthorized disclosure for offences committed by public servants in national law. The Law Commission and UK Government suggest that a whistleblower's culpability is the same whether or not the disclosure has been damaging.[514] And they argue that proving harm is too difficult: it 'can make it difficult to bring a prosecution'.[515] The UK Government has suggested that this is because of the requirement to place highly

---

[506] See s. III.4.2. (Harm); HRC, General Comment No. 34 (2011), §35. Cf. the ACmHPR, Declaration of Principles of Freedom of Expression and Access to Information (2019) (requiring 'a close causal link between the risk of harm and the expression').

[507] HRC, General Comment No. 34 (2011), §35. See also UN Special Rapporteur D. Kaye, *Report of the Special Rapporteur on the promotion and protection of the right to freedom of opinion and expression: Disease pandemics and the freedom of opinion and expression* (2020) UN Doc. A/HRC/44/49, §15.

[508] See s. III.4.2.1. (Type and severity of harm); ECtHR, *Bucur and Toma v. Romania* (App. no. 40238/02), 8 January 2013, §115; ECtHR, *Görmüş v. Turkey* (App. no. 49085/07), 19 January 2016, §63.

[509] Johannesburg Principles, Principle 6.

[510] See IACtHR, *Usón Ramirez v. Venezuela* (Series C, no. 207), 20 November 2009, §56 (where the Inter-American Court criticized a military slander provision on the basis that the article did 'not specify the injury required', and therefore 'such law allows that the subjectivity of the offended party determine the existence of the crime').

[511] See s. III.4.2. (Harm); Feuer (n 7) 117, citing D. McCraw & S. Gikow, 'The End to an Unspoken Bargain? National Security and Leaks in a Post-Pentagon Papers World' (2013) 48 *Harvard Civil Rights-Civil Liberties Law Review* 473, 492 (emphasis added); UK Official Secrets Act 1989 ss 1–6 (see, e.g., ss 1(4)(b), 3(2)(b)).

[512] Assuming these do not themselves violate international human rights law due to overbreadth or on other grounds.

[513] See s. IV.3.1. (Recommendations).

[514] See s. II.2.1.1. (United Kingdom).

[515] UK Law Commission, *Protection of Official Data Report* (2020), §§4.12–4.18.

sensitive information before juries so as to prove damage[516] and that, as a result, prosecutions under the Official Secrets Acts are 'challenging and rare'.[517]

The Law Commission also overstate the problem. In the United Kingdom—and across the world—domestic courts implement a range of safeguards to ensure that evidence on national security proceedings can be adduced. As argued by the Guardian News and Media, 'day in day out, FOI tribunals are dealing with the question of whether disclosures are 'likely' to harm defence, international relations, law enforcement—without causing the enormous harm [the Law Commission] see as inevitable'.[518] In addition, other elements—such as proving a fault element and assessing a 'public interest' defence[519]—'would *still* require the prosecution to show that a disclosure would cause damage', and would '*still* require an explanation of how that damage would be caused'.[520] Citing prosecutions such as that against journalist Duncan Campbell, 'simply for reporting the *existence*' of the United Kingdom's signals intelligence service, civil rights organization Liberty argued that 'the lesson of many of the trials under the Official Secrets Act is not that they have harmed national security, but that they have simply been embarrassing to Government'.[521] Prosecutions may also be rare under official secrets laws because of the infrequency with which these crimes are committed, rather than challenges with the laws themselves.

And such proposals to remove proof of harm requirements run contrary to international standards and provide insufficient safeguards to speech.[522] The damage caused by speech is one of the five factors articulated by the European Court of Human Rights in *Guja v. Moldova* as central to the question of proportionality.[523] Ignoring this central tenet of proportionality is particularly troubling given that the Law Commission has recommended a seven-fold increase in criminal penalties for such speech.

---

[516] Ibid., §4.14.
[517] UK Home Office, *Legislation to Counter State Threats (Hostile State Activity) Government Consultation* (May 2021), 14, 18.
[518] Guardian News & Media, *Response to Law Commission Consultation Paper no 230 on protection of Official Data* (2017), 5. See also Campaign for Freedom of Information and Article 19, 'Joint Response to Law Commission Consultation Paper' (4 May 2017), §§16–17. See further UK Law Commission, Protection of Official Data: A Consultation Paper (2017), §3.143, citing G. Robertson, 'Freedom, the Individual and the Law' (Law Commission, 1993), 167, where the Law Commission noted 'our research stands in contrast to those commentators who expressed the view that the damage requirement would be easy to satisfy'.
[519] The Commission suggests that an explicit fault (*mens rea*) requirement and the introduction of a public interest defence will act as sufficient safeguards against the removal of the requirement to prove damage. See UK Law Commission, *Protection of Official Data Report* (2020), §4.15. See s. II.2.1.1, (United Kingdom). But it concedes that '[d]amage and the public interest are not necessarily mutually exclusive concepts', with a public interest defence allowing a defendant to argue that the disclosure was in the public interest *despite* the fact it was damaging'. UK Law Commission, *Protection of Official Data Report* (2020), §4.45.
[520] Campaign for Freedom of Information and Article 19, 'Joint Response to Law Commission Consultation Paper' (4 May 2017), §18.
[521] Liberty Human Rights Organization, 'Liberty's Response to the Law Commission's Consultation on Official Secrecy' (May 2017), §11.
[522] See s. II.2.1.1. (United Kingdom).
[523] See s. III.5.1. (Public interest defence).

3.3. Prosecutions under espionage and official secrets laws should be subject to a 'public interest' defence.

At a minimum, under current international standards, states must balance the public interest in the disclosure of information implicating national security with the harm a disclosure may cause.[524] Laws like the US Espionage Act that do not allow a judge to consider the public interest in their assessment of whether criminal liability is appropriate for speech are not compatible with international minimums standards. States must ensure when applying espionage and official secrets laws that the public interest in the speech is considered in any assessment of the necessity and proportionality of criminalizing it.

In our view, public interest should be an affirmative defence to criminal liability, as set out in the Tshwane Principles.[525] Under these Principles, the speaker must have actually held the belief that the public interest in having the information revealed outweighed the harm in its disclosure, and it must have been reasonable for them to hold that belief. The objective arm of this test ensures that individuals will be held to an appropriately high standard. The Principles also take into account the fact that a disclosure should include only the amount of information 'reasonably necessary to bring to light the wrongdoing'. By balancing between harm and public interest, this public interest defence does not create a *carte blanche* rule where speech involving a matter of public interest is always lawful. Disclosures which intentionally and foreseeably cause very serious harm are likely to outweigh the public interest in disseminating such information and will continue to be sanctioned under official secrets laws, although public interest factors could still in such a case be relevant to mitigation.

This public interest formulation should be preferred to other more narrowly tailored defences which do not sufficiently protect speech. An example is the Australian public interest defence, which is restricted to those engaged in the business of reporting news.[526] This defence arguably leaves vulnerable non-traditional actors in the media space, such as bloggers, as well as sources and human rights groups. Similarly, Canada's public interest defence is unduly narrow as it is only available to individuals 'bound by secrecy', meaning it assists civil servants but provides no protection for journalists.[527]

On the other hand, the suggestion by the Law Commission that a public interest defence should be inserted into the UK Official Secrets Act 1989 is an encouraging development which we fully support. We disagree with the UK Government that the existing UK Official Secrets Act, which pays no regard to the public interest, is compatible with European Court jurisprudence.[528] At a minimum, the European Court considers

---

[524] See s. III.5.1. (Public interest defence); see, e.g., HRC, General Comment No. 34 (2011), §30. See also Tshwane Principles, Principle 38.
[525] Tshwane Principles, Principle 43.
[526] Australian Criminal Code Act s. 122.5(6).
[527] See s. II.1.4.1. (Public interest).
[528] UK Home Office, *Legislation to Counter State Threats (Hostile State Activity) Government Consultation* (May 2021), 24, 64.

the public interest a relevant criterion in determining the necessity and proportionality of restricting speech.[529] We consider that the defendant's reasonable belief that disclosure was in the public interest is the appropriate test for this defence, consistently with the Tshwane Principles. This formulation provides an appropriate balance by incorporating both subjective and objective considerations.[530]

4. Decisions on arrests and criminal charges under official secrets laws should be approved by a senior authority such as the Minister of Justice, Attorney-General, police chief or chief prosecutor and/or independent expert.

Although international standards do not expressly require this, mandating an extra layer of consent from an official or at higher levels of police and prosecutorial authorities can be an important safeguard against abuse of espionage laws that can produce chilling effects even if any charges are eventually dismissed.[531] This proposal is consistent with Australian, American, Canadian, Ghanaian and Singaporean laws or policies.[532] Alternatively, and ideally, states should adopt a policy whereby an independent expert's consent is required.[533]

5. Criminal sanctions for espionage and official secrets laws should only be used in exceptional circumstances.

The proportionality of penalties imposed on speech is a key element of international standards regulating freedom of speech.[534] The imposition of criminal sanctions, especially imprisonment, for the disclosure of confidential information must be exceptional, and should only apply to disclosures of narrow categories of information set forth in law, that would objectively probably cause serious damage, were committed with a high intent element and are not in the public interest.[535] And governments

---

[529] ECtHR (GC), *Bédat v. Switzerland* (App. no. 56925/08), 29 March 2016, §49. See, similarly, ECtHR (GC), *Sürek v. Turkey (No. 2)* (App. no. 24122/94), 8 July 1999, §34, citing *Wingrove v. United Kingdom* (App. No. 17419/90), 25 November 1996, §58.

[530] Cf. UK Law Commission, *Protection of Official Data Report* (2020). The UK Law Commission did not detail 'the factors that courts and juries must take into account when deciding whether the defence is made out', noting that it did not have the 'evidence necessary to draft with confidence on these matters': §11.8. However, the UK Law Commission concluded that 'it does not serve the public interest to excuse those who damage national security simply because they believed that the disclosure was in the public interest': §11.78.

[531] Reporters Without Borders (RSF) considers express consent must be given by an independent judicial authority, i.e., a court or an investigating judge in civil law countries.

[532] See s. II.1. (Overview of Laws Regulating Disclosure of 'Secret' Material).

[533] See ch. 4 (False Speech), s. IV.7. (Recommendations).

[534] See, e.g., HRC, General Comment No. 34, §§34–35; ECtHR, *Guja v. Moldova* (App. no. 14277/04), 12 February 2008, §78.

[535] See ss IV.1. and IV.3. (Recommendations).

should distinguish between state officials who have assumed a 'duty of confidence' and members of the public not bound by such a duty when determining appropriate penalties,[536] as states such as Norway, Bolivia and Belgium have already adopted this practice.[537]

---

[536] See, e.g., ECtHR (GC), *Guja v. Moldova* (App. no. 14277/04), 12 February 2008, §§70–73; ECtHR (C), *Gîrleanu v. Romania* (App. no. 50376/09), 26 June 2018, §§86, 90–93. A number of soft law instruments, including the Tshwane Principles and the OAS Joint Declaration on Access to Information and on Secrecy Legislation, go further and state that only state officials should be subject to such laws. See, e.g., Tshwane Principles, Principle 47; OAS, Joint Declaration on Access to Information and on Secrecy Legislation, 6 December 2004 ('Public authorities and their staff bear sole responsibility for protecting the confidentiality of legitimately secret information under their control. Other individuals, including journalists and civil society representatives, should never be subject to liability for publishing or further disseminating this information, regardless of whether or not it has been leaked to them, unless they committed fraud or another crime to obtain the information'). This requirement is 'not [however] intended to preclude the prosecution of a person for other crimes, such as burglary or blackmail, committed in the course of seeking or obtaining the information'. Tshwane Principles, Principle 47.

[537] See, e.g., Belgium Criminal Code Arts 118–120, Bolivia Decree Law 10426 Arts 111, 115; Bolivian Military Criminal Code 2002, Arts 56, 58; German Criminal Code ss 94–96, 353b; Norwegian Criminal Code s. 124(a) and (b).

6
Speech Related to National Security: Terrorism Laws

Alice Gardoll

I. Introduction	347	III. International Legal Standards	373
II. State Practice	350	1. Legality	374
1. Terrorism Laws and Associated Offences	350	2. Legitimacy	379
1.1. Type of speech	351	3. Necessity	382
1.2. Intent	356	3.1. Harm	382
1.3. Harm	357	3.2. Causal link between speech and harm	389
1.4. Exclusions, exceptions and defences	358	3.3. Intent	397
1.5. Penalties	359	4. Exclusions, Exceptions and Defences	403
2. Application of Terrorism Laws Around the World	360	4.1. Public interest	403
2.1. Europe	361	4.2. Truth and opinion	406
2.2. Asia Pacific region	365	5. Penalties	407
2.3. Middle East and Africa	367	6. Approach of Private Companies to Online Incitement to Terrorism	411
2.4. North and South America	369	IV. Recommendations	414

I. Introduction

Speech, particularly online speech, can play a role in inciting terror.[1] In the wake of the 2005 London bombings, the United Nations Security Council called on states to '[p]rohibit by law incitement to commit a terrorist act'.[2] And in the years since then, states enthusiastically embraced this request: at least 112 have criminalized incitement to commit a terrorist act in their national legislation.[3]

---

[1] The author and editors of this book would like to thank the Sciences Po Law School Clinic and in particular students who carried out extensive research of legislation and jurisprudence into media freedom and counter-terrorism.

[2] UNSC Res. 1624 (2005), 14 September 2005, §1(a). This provision requires 'prohibition', rather than criminalization, and was passed under Chapter VI (as opposed to Chapter VII, which permits coercive enforcement action).

[3] UN Security Council Counter-Terrorism Committee Executive Directorate (CTED), *Global survey of the implementation of Security Council resolution 1624 (2005) by Member States* (2021) UN Doc. S/2021/973 (Annex), §2. This number is, in practice, even higher, as in 2016, the CTED stated that 'at least 135 states have effectively prohibited by law incitement to commit terrorist acts', on the basis of general laws which 'prohibit incitement to commit any crime': CTED, *Global survey of the implementation of Security Council resolution 1624 (2005) by Member States* (2016) UN Doc. S/2016/50 (Annex), §15. The Counter-Terrorism Committee and the CTED assess states' implementation of UNSC Res. 1624: see UNSC Res. 1373 (2001), 28 September 2001, §6; UNSC Res. 1535 (2004) 16 March 2004, §2; UNSC Res. 1624 (2005), 14 September 2005, §6.

Legal regulation of terrorist-related speech pits democratic values against each other. Terrorist attacks can of course lead to huge loss of life, and limiting their occurrence is a key priority of governments and social media companies the world over. But fundamental disagreements exist about the definition of terrorism, the type of speech that may cause or contribute to it, and where the line should be drawn between protecting speech versus protecting communities against potential violence.[4] This is complicated by the fact that, as the UN Security Council's Counter-Terrorism Committee Executive Directorate has put it, some speech aimed at promoting radicalization may 'not rise to the level of criminal incitement under national laws and may be protected by the right to freedom of expression', but may still 'play a role in helping to convince susceptible persons to cross the line into territorist activity'.[5]

Today, many states criminalize a broad range of speech such as 'glorification', 'promotion', 'apology for' and 'justification of' terrorism, as well as 'extremist' speech.[6] This trend is apparent in democracies and autocracies alike, for instance in Australia, France, Spain, Russia and Egypt.[7] And the reach of these offences can be sweeping, since 'liability is based on the content of the speech, rather than the speaker's intention or the actual impact'.[8]

International human rights bodies such as the Human Rights Committee have criticized many such laws and set out requirements related to the speaker's intent and resulting harm if restrictions to speech are to pass muster under international law.[9] The European Court has taken a broader approach, considering whether speech 'could' be 'seen as a call for violence, hatred or intolerance' as one factor to consider in determining such laws' incompatibility with the European Convention on Human Rights.[10] And it has in certain cases permitted criminal penalties—including imprisonment—for glorification of or apology for terror.[11]

Such laws are also open to abuse: indeed, many states have a strategy of branding journalists as 'terrorists' or 'spies', limiting their ability to do work even before they are

---

[4] This chapter recommends that states adopt a clear and precise definition of terrorism, which has been the topic of decades of debate, without positing one specific definition. There is some consensus about the two fundamental elements of a legal definition of an act of terrorism: the perpetration of a serious criminal *act*, committed with the *intent* to 'provoke a state of terror in the general public or in a group of persons or particular persons, intimidate a population or compel a government or an international organization to do or to abstain from doing any act': see UNSC Res. 1566 (2004), 8 October 2004, §3. However, some argue that there should be exceptions to this definition, such as where an act is committed for a 'just cause', by state-sponsored violence, or is not transnational: see, e.g., B. Saul, 'Defining Terrorism: A Conceptual Minefield', in E. Chenoweth & others (eds), *The Oxford Handbook of Terrorism* (OUP 2019) 34.

[5] CTED, *Global survey of the implementation of Security Council resolution 1624 (2005) by Member States* (2016) UN Doc. S/2016/50 (Annex), §6.

[6] See s. II.1.1.2. (Glorification or justification of terrorism); s. II.2.1.3. (Russia).

[7] Australian Commonwealth Criminal Code s. 80.2C(3); Spanish Criminal Code Art. 578; French Penal Code Art. 421-2-5; Russian Criminal Code Arts 205.2, 280.1, 290; Egyptian Anti-Terrorism Law 2015 Art. 29.

[8] UN Special Rapporteur B. Emmerson, *Report on the promotion and protection of human rights and fundamental freedoms while countering terrorism* (2016) UN Doc. A/HRC/31/65, §39.

[9] See HRC, General Comment No. 34 (2011), §46; HRC, *Concluding Observations, Ethiopia* (2011) UN Doc. CCPR/C/ETH/CO/1, §15; s. III.3. (Necessity).

[10] See s. III.3.1. (Harm); see, e.g., ECtHR (GC), *Perinçek v. Switzerland* (App. no. 27510/08), 15 October 2015, §206.

[11] See s. III.5. (Penalties).

convicted.[12] Russia's arrest of Wall Street Journal reporter Evan Gershkovich for 'espionage' has accelerated 'an exodus' of foreign correspondents, resulting in fears that the country 'may become a black hole of information'.[13] Iran has adopted a similar strategy of accusing journalists of being spies after they report on the state's political affairs and repression of women.[14]

States around the world use these laws to chill political speech, a category of speech that should be given the highest protection, under the pretext of 'terrorism' or 'subversion'. Glaring examples include Al Jazeera's staff in Egypt being branded terrorists and paraded in a cage with members of the Muslim Brotherhood who they had never met after they reported the news in Cairo.[15] Or Belarusian authorities forcibly grounding a commercial airliner to arrest a journalist who was placed on a list of terrorists six months earlier after running a Telegram channel central to organizing protests against the Belarusian President.[16] And in 2020 in Turkey, more than 85 journalists and media workers were in pre-trial detention or serving sentences for terrorism offences as a result of charges targeting ordinary journalistic activity,[17] leading The Economist to observe that although 'few countries have suffered as many terrorist attacks as Turkey in the past five years', 'few governments have invented as many terrorists as Mr. Erdogan's'.[18] And in Spain, musicians and rappers have been sentenced to terms of imprisonment for lyrics supportive of terrorist groups that are no longer actively operating.[19]

This chapter explores terrorism laws that impact speech, as well as the broad array of 'public order' offences prohibiting speech that threatens national security.[20] It sets out

---

[12] See, e.g., UN Human Rights Special Rapporteur on the situation of human rights defenders, *Global Study on the Impact of Counter-Terrorism on Civil Society and Civil Space* (2023) 27.

[13] T. Law, 'Russia's Arrest of a Wall Street Journal Reporter Has More to Do with Geopolitics Than Espionage' (Time, 30 March 2023); J. Parkinson & D. Hinshaw, Evan Gershkovich Loved Russia, the Country That Turned on Him (The Wall Street Journal, 31 March 2023). See also US Department of State, 2021 Country Reports on Human Rights Practices: Turkey (2021), 30 ('The government frequently responded to expression critical of it by filing criminal charges alleging affiliation with terrorist groups, terrorism, or otherwise endangering the state').

[14] See ch. 5 (Speech Related to National Security: Espionage and Official Secrets Laws), s. II.2.3.1. (Iran). See, e.g., WGAD, *Rezaian v. Iran* (Opinion no. 44/2015), 3 December 2015, §35; J. Rezaian, 'Jailing journalists in Iran is a threat against all civil society' (The Washington Post, 1 November 2022) (describing 'ridiculous' allegations levelled against journalists Niloofar Hamedi and Elahe Mohammadi of being 'agents of the CIA, MI6 and Mossad'. Hamedi and Mohammadi reported on the story of Mahsa Amini, whose death in police custody led to an uprising in Iran).

[15] See A. Clooney, 'The Anatomy of an Unfair Trial' (HuffPost, 18 August 2014).

[16] A. Troianovski & I. Nechepurenko, 'Belarus Forces Down Plane to Seize Dissident; Europe Sees "State Hijacking"' (The New York Times, 23 May 2021). The journalist Roman Pratasevich was convicted in eight years' imprisonment for a number of offences including inciting social hatred, inciting '"terrorism", organising mass disturbances and slandering Belarusian President Alexander Lukashenko' but was subsequently pardoned: 'Belarusian Activist Roman Protasevich "pardoned by Minsk"' (Al Jazeera, 22 May 2023).

[17] Human Rights Watch, 'Turkey: Events of 2020' (2020).

[18] 'One man's terrorist: Covid-19 and repression in Turkey' (The Economist, 16 January 2021).

[19] See s. II.2.1.1. (Spain).

[20] Laws and jurisprudence on 'violent extremism' are also referenced to the extent they are illustrative of key principles applicable to terrorism and speech. By 'violent extremism' we refer to a 'wider category of manifestations' including 'forms of conduct that should not qualify as terrorist acts' and against which 'security-based counter-terrorism measures' have proved insufficient: UN Secretary-General, *Plan of Action to Prevent Violent Extremism* (2015) UN Doc. A/70/674, §4. Minor nuisance offences such as obscene language or drunkenness, even when defined as public order offences, fall outside the ambit of this chapter, as does the lawfulness of bans on wearing hijabs, niqabs and burqas in public places on the ostensible basis of protecting the public order: see, e.g., HRC, *Yaker v. France* (Comm. no. 2747/2016), 17 July 2018; ECtHR (GC), *S.A.S. v. France* (App. no. 43835/11), 1 July 2014. The use of certain civil penalties or measures such as injunctions and press restrictions and the issue of due process and fair trial guarantees are also beyond the scope of this chapter.

the international standards governing the permissibility of restricting speech on the basis of terrorism or public order.[21] And it offers recommendations—to both governments and social media companies—as to how such laws should be drafted, interpreted and applied to comply with international law and best practices.

II. State Practice

1. Terrorism Laws and Associated Offences

Numerous states employ vague or broad definitions of terrorism in their criminal codes, and this threatens freedom of speech.[22] Examples include Egypt, which defines terrorism as 'any use of force, violence' or 'threat or intimidation' for purposes including 'disturbing public order', harming 'national unity', 'social peace' or impeding public authorities from 'carrying out their work or exercising some or all of their activities'.[23]

Other countries link criminality to undermining the state's systems, reputation or stability. For example in Saudi Arabia, terrorism includes 'any act committed ... with the intention to disturb public order, destabilize the security of society and the stability of the state', 'endanger its national unity' or 'harm the reputation of the state or its standing'.[24] And Bangladesh's law criminalizes 'publish[ing] or circulat[ing] any statement, rumour or report, which is, or which is likely to be prejudicial to the interests of the security of Bangladesh or public order'.[25] To somewhat similar effect, India punishes whoever 'commits', 'advocates, advises or incites the commission of, any unlawful activity', being any 'action, whether by act or by speech' that 'disclaims, questions, disrupts or is intended to disrupt, the sovereignty and territorial integrity of India' or that 'is intended, or supports any claim, to bring about' the cession of any part of India.[26]

In Switzerland, recently passed legislation proposed a definition of terrorist activity as 'efforts intended to influence or modify state order, likely to be achieved or favoured

---

[21] International standards relating to terrorism intersect with more general standards applicable to national security restrictions to speech, as well as hate speech standards: see ch. 3 (Hate Speech), s. III (International Standards on Hate Speech) and ch. 5 (Speech Related to National Security: Espionage and Official Secrets Laws), s. III.1. (International Standards Related To Speech Affecting National Security).

[22] The review of state terrorism laws and practice contained in this chapter does not aim to be comprehensive but rather to identify significant examples and trends. In addition, references to the language of a statute are not necessarily accompanied by an analysis of all case law interpreting that language in the jurisdiction under review.

[23] Egyptian Anti-Terrorism Law Art. 2(2). See also Myanmar Counter Terrorism Law s. 3 (criminalizing acts causing 'fear among the public' or which 'severely damage the security or the life and property of the public or infrastructure which is fundamental to the public or an individual').

[24] Saudi Arabian Law of Combatting Terrorist Crimes and Its Financing Art. 1(3).

[25] Bangladeshi Penal Code s. 505A. Bangladesh also has a Special Powers Act 1974 which provides sweeping detention and deportation orders to prevent someone from committing a 'prejudicial act', which includes endangering the 'maintenance of public order': Bangladeshi Special Powers Act 1974 ss 2, 3. See also Cambodian Press Laws Arts 11, 12 (making it an offence, punishable by fine only, for the press to 'publish anything that may affect public order by directly inciting one or more persons to commit violence' or any information 'that may affect national security and political stability').

[26] Indian Unlawful Activities (Prevention) Act, ss 2(o), 3. Section 15 of the Act also includes an expansive definition of terrorism. See also s. II.2.2.3. (India).

by committing or threatening to commit serious criminal offenses, or by spreading fear and terror'.[27] In May 2020, five UN Special Rapporteurs sent a letter expressing alarm that the definition of 'terrorist activity' was wider than that set by international standards and included 'acts which seek to influence or modify the state order' that may encompass a 'range of behaviours which are not terrorist in nature'.[28] These experts also considered the offence of 'spreading fear' as 'ill-defined and open to a wide range of interpretations'.[29] As a result, 'journalistic reporting or the legitimate activities of civil society, including humanitarian and human rights organizations, may fall within its scope'.[30] The Swiss parliament passed the legislation in September 2020, and although opponents of the law triggered a referendum, almost 57 per cent of those voters approved the law, which came into force in June 2022.[31]

Similarly, many laws criminalize those who 'disturb' the 'public order' or 'public peace', without defining these terms.[32] For example, Singapore lists disturbing or damaging public order as an act falling within the definition of criminal terrorist conduct.[33]

1.1. Type of speech

Most states prohibit not just the actual commission of violent terrorist acts, or material or financial support for them, but also speech that is linked to terrorism. At one end of the spectrum, incitement offences prohibit speech that is intended to have, and has, a direct, causal connection to the commission of a violent terrorist act. At the other end of the spectrum are offences that criminalize 'apologizing for' terrorism without any intent that a violent terrorist act will result. Often states have multiple laws across this spectrum on their books.

A small number of states only criminalize violent terrorist acts, rather than speech, although speech may still be captured by inchoate criminal provisions such as conspiracy and attempt. For example, Sweden has indicated that incitement to terrorism can be punishable but only if it falls within Swedish aiding and abetting, complicity or conspiracy offences.[34] The same applies in Germany, which does not have any specific provisions for incitement to commit a terrorist act, but the German Criminal Code does

---

[27] Swiss Federal Law on Measures to Safeguard International Security Art. 23(3)I(2).
[28] See OHCHR, 'Switzerland's new 'terrorism' definition sets a dangerous precedent worldwide, UN human rights experts warn' (11 September 2020).
[29] Ibid.
[30] The letter requested changes to the draft law, which the Swiss government refused to implement. See OHCHR, 'Switzerland's new "terrorism" definition sets a dangerous precedent worldwide, UN human rights experts warn' (11 September 2020).
[31] S. Koltrowitz, 'Swiss government defends anti-terrorism law against criticism over child rights' (Reuters, 13 April 2021); U. Geiser, 'Controversial anti-terrorism law wins voter approval' (Swissinfo.ch, 13 June 2021).
[32] See, e.g., Romanian Criminal Code Art. 371 ('Any person who, in public, by violence committed against persons or property or by threats or serious threats to the dignity of persons, disturbs public order'); Mexican Federal Penal Code Art. 131 ('those who gather tumultuously and disturb the public order with violence against people or things').
[33] Singaporean Internal Security Act s. 2 (defining a terrorist as, among other things, a person who 'by use of any firearm, explosive or ammunition acts in a manner prejudicial to the public safety or to the maintenance of public order or incites to violence or counsels disobedience to the law or to any lawful order').
[34] Swedish Criminal Code chapter 23 s. 4; UNSC, *National Report of Sweden on Implementation of UNSCR 1624* (2006) UN Doc. S/2006/551 (Annex). Swedish law does, however, criminalize inciting rebellion and unlawful threats: Swedish Criminal Code chapter 16 s. 5.

include general criminal offences for abetting and attempted participation.[35] Consistent with its history as a speech-protective nation, US federal law does not provide for an incitement of terrorism offence. Related offences such as seditious conspiracy, advocating the overthrow or destruction of the United States and material support for terrorism as well as general 'inchoate crimes' provisions such as aiding, abetting or conspiring offences generally require acts other than speech to be triggered.[36]

1.1.1. Inciting or encouraging terrorism

Incitement of terrorism is widely criminalized under national laws, consistent with UN Security Council Resolution 1624 (2005) which called on states to adopt measures to '[p]rohibit by law incitement to commit a terrorist act or acts'.[37] In 2021, the Security Council's Counter-Terrorism Committee Executive Directorate reported that at least 112 states 'had expressly criminalized incitement to commit a terrorist act or acts in their national legislation', and in 2016 the Directorate noted that a higher figure—135 countries—had effectively criminalized the same offence by way of general provisions that prohibit 'incitement to commit any crime'.[38]

Many of these laws are imprecise, criminalizing incitement without (a) defining the term, (b) requiring intent by the speaker to bring about any harm or (c) a link to an act of terrorist violence.[39] An example is the recently enacted Anti-Terrorism Act in the Philippines, which exposes any person who 'without taking any direct part in the commission of terrorism, shall incite others to the execution' of terrorism 'by means of speeches, proclamations, writings, emblems, banners or other representations tending to the same end' to up to 12 years' imprisonment.[40] Some nations prohibit the incitement of a wider range of offences on a national security basis, such as China's Criminal Code, which criminalizes 'whoever incites others by spreading rumors or slander or any other means to subvert the State power or overthrow the socialist system' as well as incitement to 'split the State or undermine unity of the country'.[41]

---

[35] See UNSC, *Report of Germany pursuant to resolution 1624 (2005)* (2006) UN Doc. S/2006/527; German Criminal Code ss 26, 30.

[36] However, certain provisions may capture terrorist-related speech, such as the offence of seditious conspiracy, advocating the overthrow or destruction of the United States and material support for terrorism (see s. II.2.4.1. (United States)) as well as general 'inchoate crimes' provisions such as aiding, abetting or conspiring offences. And the United States considers incitement to commit a terrorist act as a basis of designating a group a 'foreign terrorist organisation'. See UNSC, *Report of the United States of America pursuant to resolution 1624 (2005)* (2006) UN Doc. S/2006/397.

[37] UNSC Res. 1624 (2005), 14 September 2005, §1(a).

[38] CTED, *Global survey of the implementation of Security Council resolution 1624 (2005) by Member States* (2021) UN Doc. S/2021/973 (Annex), §2; CTED, *Global survey of the implementation of Security Council resolution 1624 (2005) by Member States* (2016) UN Doc. S/2016/50 (Annex), §15.

[39] See, e.g., Norwegian Penal Code (2005) s. 136 ('A penalty of imprisonment for a term not exceeding 6 years shall be applied to any person who: a) publicly incites another person to commit a criminal act specified in sections 131, 134 or 135, or sections 137 to 144'); Estonian Penal Code Art. 237(2) ('preparation of and (public) incitement to acts of terrorism'); Saudi Arabia Penal Law for Crimes of Terrorism and its Financing Art. 35 ('Whoever incites another to join any terrorist entity, or participate in its activities, or recruits it, or contributes to financing').

[40] Philippine Anti-Terrorism Act s. 9; Amnesty International, 'Philippines: Dangerous anti-terror law yet another setback for human rights' (3 July 2020).

[41] Chinese Criminal Law Arts 103, 105.

In contrast, 42 states have ratified the Council of Europe Convention on the Prevention of Terrorism, which requires states to criminalize incitement in domestic law in a narrower form by way of an offence of 'public provocation': 'the distribution, or otherwise making available, of a message to the public, with the intent to incite the commission of a terrorist offence, where such conduct, whether or not directly advocating terrorist offences, causes a danger that one or more such offences may be committed'.[42] But only a small number of states, including Ireland, Luxembourg and Austria have since reformed their criminal laws on this basis.[43]

Canadian law makes it an offence to 'counsel another person to commit a terrorism offence', with 'counsel' defined as including speech to 'procure, solicit or incite' an act of terror.[44] This offence was adopted in 2019 after an earlier bill that criminalized advocating or promoting terrorism received heavy criticism for impinging on Canadian rights and freedoms.[45]

Other offences prohibit 'encouragement' of terrorism and define it by reference to how speech may be understood by others, rather than the speaker's intent. For example, Ethiopia criminalizes speech 'likely to be understood by some or all of the members of the public to whom it is published as a direct or indirect encouragement or other inducement to them to the commission or preparation or instigation of an act of terrorism'.[46]

The United Kingdom's encouragement offence is an example of a more narrowly worded provision, criminalizing the publication of a statement where a person intends that or is reckless as to whether members of the public will be 'directly or indirectly encouraged or otherwise induced by the statement to commit, prepare or instigate' a terrorist offence.[47] This offence also has an objective element, as it only applies to statements 'likely to be understood by a reasonable person as a direct or indirect encouragement or other inducement' to acts of terrorism, however this requirement is fulfilled where a statement 'glorifies the commission or preparation' of a terrorist offence.[48] But the provision's key terms, including 'encouragement', 'inducement' and 'glorifi[cation]' are broad and vague.[49]

---

[42] COE Convention on the Prevention of Terrorism Art. 5. This includes Russia, who ratified the Convention but as of 2022 is no longer a member of the Council of Europe.

[43] Irish Criminal Justice (Terrorist Offences) 2005 ss 4, 4A (as amended by the Irish Criminal Justice (Terrorist Offences) (Amendment) Act 2015 ss 3, 4); Luxembourg Criminal Code Art. 135(11); Austrian Criminal Code s. 282a.

[44] Canadian Criminal Code c. C-46 ss 22(3), 83.221. For intent requirements of this offence, see s. II.1.2(Intent).

[45] See, e.g., Government of Canada, 'Our Security, Our Rights'. Amnesty International, 'Insecurity and Human Rights: Concerns and Recommendations with Respect to Bill C-51, the *Anti-Terrorism Act, 2015*' (19 March 2015). Australian law also prohibits 'counsel[ing]' another to commit a terrorist offence: Australian Commonwealth Criminal Code s. 80.2C(3).

[46] Ethiopian Anti-Terrorism Proclamation (2009) Art. 6.

[47] UK Terrorism Act 2006 s. 1(2). Conviction for encouragement of terrorism can carry a sentence of up to 15 years' imprisonment. See UK Terrorism Act 2006 s. 1(7). It is also a defence if it was clear, in all the circumstances, that the impugned statement did not express the speaker's views and did not have his or her endorsement: UK Terrorism Act s. 1(6).

[48] UK Terrorism Act 2006 ss 1(1), 1(3). Section 1(3)(b) also provides that statements will be 'indirectly encouraging' terrorism if 'members of the public could reasonably be expected to infer that what is being glorified is being glorified as conduct that should be emulated'.

[49] See, e.g., Article 19, 'The Impact of UK Anti-Terror Laws on Freedom of Expression, Submission to ICJ Panel of Eminent Jurists on Terrorism, Counter-Terrorism and Human Rights' (April 2006).

1.1.2. Glorification or justification of terrorism

A number of nations, including Russia, the United Kingdom, Slovenia and Pakistan, criminalize 'glorification', 'justification' or 'apology' of terrorism.[50] Certain European countries broadened these provisions around the time of the 2015 'Charlie Hebdo' attack in France.[51] For example, in 2015 Spain broadened its existing glorification offence to make the commission of the offence online an aggravating factor and increased the maximum penalty from two to three years' imprisonment.[52] The provision also makes it an offence to engage in 'glorification' or 'justification' of terror crimes or 'the performance of acts that entail discredit, contempt or humiliation' of victims of terrorism or their relatives.[53] Prosecutions have rapidly increased since the amendment, but five UN Special Rapporteurs have expressed their concern that the provision is 'too broad and vague'.[54]

While the offence of 'public apology for acts of terrorism' has existed as a provision of French press law since 1881, its enforcement was 'limited to symbolic and/or very serious cases' until 2014, when amendments were introduced into the French Penal Code as a result of increased terrorist threats in Europe and the proclamation of the Islamic State.[55] This offence is now punishable by up to seven years' imprisonment or 100,000 Euro fines when committed online.[56]

Similarly, Australia prohibits advocating acts of terrorism, encompassing anyone who 'counsels, promotes, encourages or urges the doing of a terrorist act or the commission of a terrorism offence'.[57] Australian legal experts have expressed concern

---

[50] UK Terrorism Act 2006 ss 1(3). 2(4), 3(8); Slovenian Criminal Code Art. 110(2); Pakistani Prevention of Electronic Crimes Act 2016 s. 9; Punjab Maintenance of Public Order (Amendment) Ordinance 2015 s. 6-A; Russian Criminal Code Art. 205.2. See s. II.2.1.3. (Russia). A recent example is Ukraine's 2022 amendments to its Criminal Code, which criminalize 'justification, recognition as legitimate' or 'denial' of the 'armed aggression of the Russian Federation against Ukraine that started in 2014', or 'glorification' of persons who carried out this aggression: Ukrainian Criminal Code Art. 436. The offence is punishable by correctional labour for up to two years, arrest for a term of up to six months, or restriction of liberty for up to three years. However, increased penalties apply for the 'production' or 'dissemination' of 'materials' justifying or denying Russia's aggression (up to five years' imprisonment) or if the offence is committed through 'abuse of office', 'repeatedly' or 'through the media' (up to eight years' imprisonment).

[51] Over the course of three days in January 2015, multiple attacks took place in Paris and surrounds killing 17 people, including an attack on satirical magazine Charlie Hebdo. Police identified three attackers (all of whom died in shootouts), who were linked to both ISIS and Al Qaeda: 'Five years on, France to try suspects in Charlie Hebdo killings' (Reuters, 28 August 2020). Cf. the Netherlands, where the Christian Democratic Party proposed a bill in 2016 to prohibit 'glorification of terrorism', which was the subject of public criticism and was not supported by the Dutch Cabinet.

[52] Spanish Criminal Code Art. 578. See Amnesty International, 'Spain: Tweet ... if you dare: How counter-terrorism laws restrict freedom of expression in Spain' (13 March 2018), 2. The Spanish Criminal Code also includes the offence of provocation, conspiracy and solicitation of terrorist offences under Art. 579 and 'indoctrination or training' others to commit terrorist acts under Art. 575, which includes a presumption that such acts take place whenever an individual 'regularly accesses one or more online communication services ... whose content is directed or suitable for inciting incorporation into a terrorist organization or group'.

[53] Spanish Criminal Code Art. 578. See Amnesty International, 'Dangerously Disproportionate: The ever-expanding security state in Europe' (17 January 2017), 41–42. Art. 578 criminalizes 'enaltecimiento', which can be translated to either 'glorification' or 'exaltation'.

[54] OHCHR, '"Two legal reform projects undermine the rights of assembly and expression in Spain"—UN experts' (23 February 2015). See s. II.2.1.1. (Spain).

[55] A. Callamard, 'Religion, Terrorism and Speech in a Post Charlie Hebdo World' (2015) 10 *Religion & Human Rights* 207, 218; French Penal Code Art. 421-2-5: in its decision no.2020-845 QPC (19 June 2020), the French Constitutional Council held that the provision complied with the French Constitution. See also N. Houry, 'France's Creeping Terrorism Laws Restricting Free Speech' (Human Rights Watch, 30 May 2018).

[56] French Penal Code Art. 421-2-5 (2).

[57] Australian Commonwealth Criminal Code s. 80.2C(3).

that 'the idea of "promotion" could even plausibly extend to a "retweet" or Facebook "like" of another person's words, meaning that an individual could be prosecuted for words they did not say, but simply repeated or agreed with'.[58] In 2019, following the Christchurch terrorist attack in New Zealand, Australian lawmakers went further by passing an act to criminalize failures by technology companies to remove or report to police material showing 'abhorrent violent conduct' such as a person engaging in a 'terrorist act'.[59] Although in its first two years no one was fined or prosecuted under the law, tech companies such as Google Australia and Twitter Australia expressed concern that the law's heavy penalties (including imprisonment and/or fines of up to 10 per cent of global revenue) could result in 'providers erring on the side of caution' and removing lawful content.[60]

Countries including Kazakhstan,[61] Turkey[62] and Russia also criminalize spreading terrorist 'propaganda', often an undefined or broadly defined term which focuses on the content of speech rather than its impact. For example, Russia prohibits 'public calls for terrorist activity [and] public justification or propaganda of terrorism', with propaganda defined as 'information aimed at developing the ideology of terrorism, convincing a person of its attractiveness or creating the sense of permissibility with respect to terrorist activities'.[63]

1.1.3. Publishing terrorism-related information

A number of states include explicit reference to publishing or distributing terrorist materials as a central element of criminal liability. These provisions range in breadth, for example narrowly worded iterations such as the offence of disseminating terrorist publications in the United Kingdom, which includes a subjective intent requirement; an

---

[58] K. Hardy & G. Williams, 'Free Speech and Counter-Terrorism in Australia', in I. Cram (ed), *Extremism, Free Speech and Counter-Terrorism Law and Policy: International and Comparative Perspectives* (Routledge 2019) 172.

[59] Australian Criminal Code Amendment (Sharing of Abhorrent Violent Material) Act 2019.

[60] J. Taylor, 'Australian law preventing sharing video of terror attacks results in zero convictions or fines' (The Guardian, 18 November 2021); Communications Alliance, Digital Industry Group Inc., Digital Rights Watch, Tik Tok Australia and New Zealand, Google Australia and New Zealand, IBM Australia, Twitter Australia and New Zealand: 'Group Submission to the Parliamentary Joint Committee on Law Enforcement in relation to the AVM Act' (2021). See s. III.6. (Approach of Private Private Companies to Online Incitement to Terrorism).

[61] Kazakhstani Penal Code Art. 256 (the offence of 'propaganda of terrorism or public calls for commission of an act of terrorism', punishable for up to 12 years' imprisonment when committed 'with the use of mass media or information and communication networks') (unofficial translation).

[62] Turkish Law on the Fight Against Terrorism Art. 7(2) (2013) which criminalizes 'propaganda that legitimizes the methods of a terrorist organization which involves forces, violence or threats' or 'praises' or 'encourages resorting' to such methods. In response to criticism about the law's overbreadth, the Turkish legislature in 2019 inserted an amendment to the effect that 'statements made within the limits of providing information or made with the purpose of criticism cannot be criminalized': Joint International Press Freedom Mission to Turkey, 'Mission Report: Turkey's Journalists in the Dock: Judicial Silencing of the Fourth Estate' (September 2019), 15. See Turkish Prevention of Terrorism Act. However, Turkey continues to use these provisions to silence legitimate journalistic activity: see s. II.2.1.2. (Turkey).

[63] See CFJ, 'TrialWatch Fairness Report—Russian Federation v. Svetlana Prokopyeva' (January 2021), 7, n. 36 (citing the Note to the Russian Criminal Code Art. 205.2). Russia is an example of a state that employs a wide range of terrorism and anti-extremist offences. The Russian Criminal Code prohibits public calls for terrorist activity and public justification or propaganda of terrorism under article 205.2, public calls for the broadly defined notion of 'extremist activity' pursuant to article 290 as well as public calls for violating the territorial integrity of Russia, under article 280.1. The Code of Administrative Offences also contains the related provisions of distribution of extremist materials (Art. 20.29) and abuse of freedom of mass information (Art. 13.15). See Article 19, 'Rights in extremis: Russia's anti-extremism practices from an International perspective' (23 September 2019).

objective causation element where the publication must be 'understood by a reasonable person as a direct or indirect encouragement or other inducement' to acts of terrorism, or may be useful for such acts; and a defence if in all the circumstances the speaker did not endorse the publication.[64]

In contrast, Egypt criminalizes whoever 'establishes or uses a communications site, website, or other media for the purpose of promoting ideas or beliefs calling for the perpetration of terrorist acts'.[65] Russian law prohibits 'bloggers'—defined as owners of a website that has more than 3,000 visitors a day—from 'disseminating the materials containing public appeals for carrying out terrorist activities or publicly justifying terrorism'.[66]

There are also a number of states that fall in between these two extremes, for example Algeria, which criminalizes 'anyone who knowingly reproduces or distributes documents, printed material or information condoning' terrorist acts, and Austria, where the 'prompting' of terrorism in 'a printed work, on the radio or in another medium or in any other public way that makes it accessible to many people' is punishable by two years' imprisonment.[67] Finally, countries such as Ghana and Cambodia have enacted offences for publishing information that can impact—with varying degrees of causal link required—the public order.[68]

1.2. Intent

Incitement to terrorism offences in some states such as Tunisia and Saudi Arabia do not encompass any explicit intent requirement.[69] In contrast, the Council of Europe recommends that a state's 'public provocation' of terrorism offences should include two forms of criminal intent: the intent to communicate the impugned speech and the intent to encourage the commission of a terrorist act.[70] Ireland's public provocation offence, for example, criminalizes 'the intentional distribution, or otherwise making available, by whatever means of communication by a person of a message to the public, with the intent of encouraging, directly or indirectly, the commission by a person of a terrorist

---

[64] UK Terrorism Act 2006 ss 2(1), 2(3), 2(9).
[65] Egyptian Anti-Terrorism Act Art. 29.
[66] Russian Federal Law No. 149-FZ Art. 10.2.
[67] Algerian Penal Code Art. 87(5); Austrian Criminal Code s. 282a.
[68] Cambodian Press Law Arts 11 ('The press shall not publish anything that may affect public order by directly inciting one or more persons to commit violence'), 12 ('the press shall not publish or reproduce any information that may affect national security and political stability'); Ghanian Criminal Code s. 208 ('publishing information with the intention to cause fear or harm to the public or to disturb the public peace'); see also Ghanian Anti-Terrorism Act s. 2(1). Some states also criminalize the collection and possession of 'terrorist materials', although such laws are beyond the scope of this chapter: see, e.g., UK Terrorism Act 2000 s. 58(1)(a) (criminalizing the collection of information 'likely to be useful to a person committing or preparing an act of terrorism'); UK Terrorism Act 2006 ss 2(2)(f), 2(3)(b) (criminalizing the 'possession with a view to' dissemination of documents 'likely ... to be useful in the commission or preparation of' terrorist acts).
[69] Saudi Arabia Penal Law for Crimes of Terrorism and its Financing Art. 35 ('Whoever incites another to join any terrorist entity, or participate in its activities, or recruits it, or contributes to financing'); Tunisian Law on Fight Against Terrorism and Money Laundering Art. 5 ('whoever incites by whatever means, others to commit terrorist acts').
[70] 42 European states have ratified the 'public provocation' formulation articulated by the COE, although this does not mean that this has resulted in amendments to their domestic laws: see s. II.1.1.1. (Inciting or encouraging terrorism).

activity'.[71] US jurisprudence provides for a high intent threshold for any speech-related offence, namely the intent to incite unlawful action, and a requirement that the speech is objectively likely to incite imminent unlawful action.[72] And nations such as Algeria criminalize anyone who 'promotes, encourages or finances' terrorist acts, without requiring a showing of intent, but with an increased penalty of life imprisonment where acts 'are intended to harm the interests of Algeria'.[73]

Other countries include an explicit recklessness standard, such as Australia's advocacy of terrorism provision, which criminalizes a person who 'advocates' the doing of a terrorist act and is 'reckless as to whether another person will' engage in such an act.[74] The United Kingdom makes it an offence to speak with 'inten[t]' or 'reckless[ness] as to whether' others will be 'directly or indirectly encouraged or otherwise induced by the statement to commit, prepare or instigate' terrorist acts.[75] Similarly, Canadian jurisprudence has interpreted the *mens rea* standard for Canada's offence of 'counselling' another person to commit a terrorist offence as either intent or recklessness. This offence will be made out if a speaker has 'intent or conscious disregard of the substantial and unjustified risk inherent' in counselling a person to commit terrorism.[76]

1.3. Harm

Some terrorism laws do not require a showing of likely harm, or that an act of terrorism has, in fact, resulted from the impugned speech. Indeed, offences such as the 'apology', 'glorification' or 'justification' of terrorism typically criminalize speech irrespective of its link to the commission of a terrorist offence.[77] And certain countries, such as Australia and Canada, explicitly state that criminal liability can apply to incitement offences whether or not a terrorist act was actually committed.[78]

But some states do include a harm requirement in their laws. European states that have adopted the Council of Europe's recommended legislation, such as Slovenia, require that speech 'causes a danger' that a terrorist offence may be committed.[79] And the test of 'likely to incite unlawful action' articulated in the US Supreme Court case of *Brandenburg v. Ohio* also applies to terrorism offences.[80]

In 2016, the Belgian parliament rushed through a bill which removed the requirement that incitement entail a risk of a terrorist offence actually being committed,

---

[71] Irish Criminal Justice (Terrorist Offences) Act 2005 ss 4, 4A (as amended by the Irish Criminal Justice (Terrorist Offences) (Amendment) Act 2015 ss 3, 4).

[72] US Supreme Court, *Brandenburg v. Ohio* 395 U.S. 444, 9 June 1969, 447. See ch. 3 (Hate Speech), s. II.2.3.2. (United States). See E. J. Skyes, 'In Defense of Brandenburg: The ACLU and Incitement Doctrine in 1919, 1969 and 2019' (2019) 85 (1) *Brooklyn Law Review* 15, 24, n. 66, 25.

[73] Algerian Penal Code Art. 87(6).

[74] Australian Commonwealth Criminal Code s. 80.2C.

[75] UK Terrorism Act 2006 s. 1(2)(b).

[76] See Canada Supreme Court, *R v. Hamilton* [2005] 2 S.C.R. 432, 444, cited in A. Bayesfky & L. Blank, 'Canadian Legal Perspectives on Incitement to Terrorism' in A. Bayefsky & L. Blank (eds), *Incitement to Terrorism* (Nijhoff Law Specials 2018), 58. See also K. Roach, *Criminal Law* (8th edn, Irwin Law 2022), +.

[77] See s. II.1.1.2. (Glorification or justification of terrorism).

[78] Australian Commonwealth Criminal Code s. 80.2C (4); Canadian Criminal Code s. 83.221(2).

[79] See s. II.1.1.1. (Inciting or encouraging terrorism). See, e.g., Slovenian Criminal Code Art. 110(2) (which requires speech to 'cause a risk' that a terrorist offence may be committed).

[80] See s. II.2.4.1. (United States).

instead adding that a defendant had to have 'an intention to incite, directly or indirectly' the commission of an offence.[81] But in 2018, a Belgian human rights group successfully challenged the amendments before the Belgian Constitutional Court on the basis that they violated the Belgian Constitution and were contrary to European Parliament directives.[82]

A number of public order offences incorporate a causal link to possible harm, since these offences are generally focused on the impact of speech rather than its content. However, the harm is often very vaguely or broadly defined. For example, India's unlawful activity law criminalizes 'unlawful activity', being 'any action … whether by committing an act or by words' which among other things 'causes or is intended to cause disaffection against India'.[83] Chinese law includes the offences of 'disrupting social order', 'endangering national security', 'violating the unity and integrity of the State' and 'subverting public order'.[84] A recent addition to Myanmar's Penal Code is similarly broad, criminalizing whoever 'causes or intends to cause fear to a group of citizens or to the public' or 'causes or intends to commit or to agitate directly or indirectly [a] criminal offence against a Government employee'.[85] The UN Special Rapporteur on the situation of human rights in Myanmar has described these as 'illegitimately imposed new laws' which 'are now being used at an alarming rate to justify' the arbitrary 'detentions of individuals'.[86]

1.4. Exclusions, exceptions and defences

Some states' laws, including those of the United Kingdom and Australia, provide for 'good faith' or 'reasonable excuse' defences in their speech-related terrorism offences. In Australia, it is a defence to the charge of advocating the commission of a terrorist act if a defendant: 'publishes in good faith a report or commentary about a matter of public interest'; 'points out in good faith' matters that are producing feelings of ill-will between different groups 'in order to bring about the removal of those matters'; or 'urges in good faith another person to attempt to lawfully procure a change' to laws, policies or practices of Australia or any other country.[87] The evidential burden is on the defendant to prove this defence.[88] This provision also provides that, in considering this defence, a court may have regard to the fact that speech was part of an artistic work, said for a

---

[81] Amnesty International, 'Europe: Dangerously disproportionate: The ever expanding national security state in Europe' (17 January 2017). EDRi 'Belgium Constitutional Court decision on the concept of incitement to terrorism' (30 May 2018).
[82] EDRi, 'Belgium Constitutional Court decision on the concept of incitement to terrorism' (30 May 2018). The Court annulled the new article so that the previous offence was reinstated.
[83] Indian Unlawful Activities (Prevention) Act 1967 ss 2, 13.
[84] See WGAD, *Gulmira Imin v. China* (Opinion no. 29/2012), 29 August 2012, §30.
[85] Myanmar Penal Code 1861 s. 505A.
[86] UN Special Rapporteur T.H. Andrews, *Report on the situation of human rights in Myanmar* (2021) UN Doc. A/HRC/46/56, §63.
[87] Australian Commonwealth Criminal Code ss 80.3(c), 80.3(d), 80.3(f).
[88] Under Australian law, the evidential burden means 'the burden of adducing or pointing to evidence that suggests a reasonable possibility that the matter exists or does not exist', rather than the higher legal burden of proving its existence: see Australian Commonwealth Criminal Code s. 13.3(6).

'genuine academic, artistic or scientific purpose or any other genuine purpose in the public interest' or spoken 'in the dissemination of news or current affairs'.[89]

Similarly, in the United Kingdom, a person who collects or possesses information 'likely to be useful to a person committing or preparing an act of terrorism' has a defence if he or she has a 'reasonable excuse' for doing so, and this includes acting for the purposes of 'carrying out work as a journalist' or 'academic research'.[90] However, no such defence is provided for other terrorism-related offending, such as expressing an opinion supportive of a proscribed organization, encouraging terrorism and disseminating terrorist publications.[91] The US material support of terrorism provisions, which have previously been applied to speech,[92] state that they shall not 'be construed or applied so as to abridge the exercise of rights guaranteed under the First Amendment',[93] but do not incorporate any specific media-related defence or defence of reasonable excuse.[94] Nor does the Canadian offence of counselling another person to commit a terror offence,[95] or the Council of Europe's 'public provocation to commit a terrorist offence' contained in the Convention on the Prevention of Terrorism.[96]

1.5. Penalties

At least 112 states sanction incitement to terrorism by way of *criminal* provisions.[97] Many states have severe penalties for terror-related speech offences because these offences are incorporated in the same provisions that criminalize violent terrorist or anti-state conduct. Capital punishment is prescribed by states including Mali, Egypt, Algeria, Ethiopia and Thailand for a range of terrorist or public order offending that could capture speech.[98]

Sentences of up to life imprisonment can be meted out in India for advocating or inciting the commission of a terrorist act.[99] Life imprisonment is the penalty for Iraq's offence of committing 'an act with intent to violate the independence of the country or the security of its territory and that act, by its nature, leads to such violation', and any person who 'incites the commission' of this offence—or a range of other anti-state offences—'even though such incitement produces no effect' is punishable by up

---

[89] Australian Commonwealth Criminal Code s. 80.3(3).
[90] UK Terrorism Act 2000 s. 2, as amended by the UK Counter-Terrorism and Border Security Act 2019.
[91] Contrary to UK Terrorism Act 2000 s. 12 and UK Terrorism Act 2006 ss 1, 2.
[92] See s. I.2.4.1. (United States).
[93] 18 U.S. Code §2339B(i).
[94] 18 U.S. Code §2339B. However, this provision does include an exception 'if the provision of that material support or resources to a foreign terrorist organization was approved by the Secretary of State with the concurrence of the Attorney General': 18 U.S. Code §2339B(j).
[95] Canadian Criminal Code c. C-46 ss 22(3), 83.221; see s. II.1.1.1. (Inciting or encouraging terrorism).
[96] COE Convention on the Prevention of Terrorism Art. 5. However, article 12 of the Convention provides certain 'conditions and safeguards' including that states shall ensure that the 'establishment, implementation and application of the criminalization' of article 5 is 'carried out while respecting human rights obligations, in particular the right to freedom of expression'. See s. II.1.1.1. (Inciting or encouraging terrorism).
[97] CTED, *Global survey of the implementation of Security Council resolution 1624 (2005) by Member States* (2021) UN Doc. S/2021/973 (Annex), §2.
[98] See Cornell Law School Death Penalty Worldwide Database, 'Republic of Mali'; Algerian Penal Code Art. 87; Ethiopian Anti-Terrorism Proclamation 2009 Art. 3; Thai Criminal Code ss 135/1, 135.3; Egyptian Anti-Terrorism Law Arts 6, 12.
[99] Indian Unlawful Activities (Prevention) Act 1967 s. 18.

to 10 years' imprisonment.[100] Reports indicate that Iraqi authorities recently accused an Iraqi Kurdish photojournalist, Qaraman Shukri, of violating this provision through speech alone, sentencing Shukri to seven years' imprisonment in a closed door trial in June 2021.[101]

Lengthy maximum terms of imprisonment are also common across the world: up to 20 years' imprisonment pursuant to the United States' material support provision (although this offence can apply to both speech and conduct);[102] 12 years' imprisonment under the Philippines' incitement to terrorism provision;[103] 10 years' imprisonment under Norway's Penal Code for threatening terrorist acts;[104] and up to 30 years' imprisonment for threats of terrorism in Brazil.[105] Spain's glorification of terrorism offence has a maximum of three years' imprisonment and a comparable law in France exposes speakers to up to 7 years' imprisonment when committed online.[106] In addition, certain countries increase criminal penalties where offences are committed online or by way of mass media.[107]

2. Application of Terrorism Laws Around the World

Across the world, states employ legitimate laws to combat the scourge of violent terrorist activity which has had devastating effects across the globe. The Global Terrorism Index, which tracks terrorist attacks, recorded that deaths from terror attacks across the world have significantly increased since 2000, when more than 3,300 individuals died as a result of such attacks, to a peak in 2015 of over 10,000 deaths in a single year while ISIS controlled large swathes of Syria and Iraq.[108] ISIS and other transnational terrorist groups continue to engage in deadly attacks, including ISIS-affiliated attacks in 21 different countries in 2022.[109]

But a range of counterterrorism and public order laws have also been used to chill speech by journalists or critics. The UN identified as a 'major concern' states acting against alleged terrorist incitement in circumstances where 'the targeted behaviour may not be incitement at all, but rather another form of expression that a State may find objectionable, such as political dissent or advocacy of controversial beliefs or views that does not, in itself, create a danger of terrorist violence'.[110] Terrorism laws

---

[100] Iraqi Penal Code Arts 156, 170.
[101] CPJ, 'Iraqi Kurdish court sentences photojournalist Qaraman Shukri to 7 years in prison in secret trial' (28 June 2021).
[102] 18 U.S.C. §2339B; see s. I.2.4.1. (United States). See also, e.g., US Department of Justice, 'Lafarge Pleads Guilty to Conspiring to Provide Material Support to Foreign Terrorist Organizations' (18 October 2022).
[103] Philippine Anti-Terrorism Law s. 9.
[104] Norwegian Penal Code s. 134.
[105] Brazilian Anti-Terrorism Act Art. 2.
[106] French Penal Code Art. 421-2-5; OHCHR, '"Two legal reform projects undermine the rights of assembly and expression in Spain"—UN experts' (23 February 2015). Spanish Criminal Code Art. 578(1). See s. II.2.1.1. (Spain).
[107] See, e.g., French Penal Code Art. 421-2-5; Kazakhstani Penal Code (2014) Art. 256.
[108] Institute for Economics & Peace, 'Global Terrorism Index 2015' (November 2015).
[109] Vision of Humanity, 'Global Terrorism Index 2023: Key findings in 5 Charts' (2023).
[110] CTED, *Global survey of the implementation of Security Council resolution 1624 (2005) by Member States* (2016) UN Doc. S/2016/50 (Annex), §11.

which criminalize speech without imposing clear definitions of terrorism or stringent requirements related to the intent of the speaker and foreseeable harm caused by the speech are particularly effective tools to stifle legitimate dissent.[111] Similarly, association and membership provisions which allow states to deem certain groups or actors as 'terrorists', and then to criminalize the speech of anyone remotely linked to those groups, can be sweeping in their effect.[112]

The examples provided below are illustrative of these practices and demonstrate how overbroad terrorism laws, like many other broad national security provisions,[113] can be abused to suppress legitimate speech, often by journalists or political actors.

2.1. Europe
2.1.1. Spain

Spain's counterterrorism laws have frequently been used against a surprising category of defendants: rappers. The most prominent case relates to Spanish rapper José Miguel Arenas Beltrán, known as Valtonyc.[114] In 2012 and 2013, Valtonyc released music online which praised the actions of the Basque separatist group Euskadi Ta Askatasuna (ETA) and the First of October Anti-Fascist Resistance Group (GRAPO), both dissolved but classified as terrorist organizations in Europe.[115] His lyrics included: 'let them be as frightened as a police officer in the Basque country', 'the king has a rendezvous at the village square, with a noose around his neck', and a comment that a certain politician 'deserves a nuclear destruction bomb'.[116]

Valtonyc was convicted of 'exalting terrorism and humiliating its victims' and sentenced to two years' imprisonment.[117] In finding Valtonyc guilty, the Spanish first instance court distinguished between an expression of political opinion intended to stimulate debate and expression of personal hatred and intolerance, the latter being liable to restriction. This decision was affirmed in February 2018 by the Spanish Supreme Court, which held that hateful speech 'encouraging or promoting, even indirectly, a situation of risk for people or rights of third parties or of the system of freedoms itself' can be lawfully restricted.[118] The Court found that Valtonyc's lyrics met this threshold, as his songs 'praising terrorist organizations ... and their violent actions ... are an incitement to imitations of such acts'.[119]

---

[111] Ibid., §20.
[112] See, e.g., International Commission of Jurists, 'Danger in Dissent: Counterterrorism and Human Rights in the Philippines' (January 2022), 3–6 (on the 'red-tagging' of civil society organizations, human rights defenders and others as 'terrorists').
[113] See ch. 5 (Speech Related to National Security: Espionage and Official Secrets Laws), s. I.2. (Application of Espionage and Official Secrets Laws Around the World).
[114] See Spanish Supreme Court, Sentencia num. 79/2018 (15 February 2018). See also Columbia Global Freedom of Expression, Case of Jose Miguel Arenas (Valtonyc) (2018).
[115] Columbia Global Freedom of Expression, Case of Jose Miguel Arenas (Valtonyc) (2018).
[116] S. Jones, 'Spanish rapper due to begin jail term vows to 'disobey fascist state'' (The Guardian, 24 May 2018).
[117] Spanish Criminal Code Arts 578, 579. Art. 578 criminalizes 'enaltecimiento', which can be translated to either 'glorification' or 'exaltation'. See s. II.1.1.2. (Glorification or justification of terrorism). Valtonyc was also sentenced to six months for slander against the Crown (Art. 490.3); and six months for threats of harm to a politician (Art. 169.2).
[118] Spanish Supreme Court, Sentencia num. 79/2018 (15 February 2018).
[119] Ibid.

Valtonyc, who was on bail during the proceedings, has since absconded to Belgium and a legal battle has ensued regarding his extradition. In September 2018, a Ghent court rejected Spain's extradition request, holding that incitement to terrorism under Belgian law 'mainly refers to international terrorism and not—as in the current case— to historical national terrorism' involving organizations that are no longer active.[120] This decision was upheld on appeal in 2022.[121]

Valtonyc's case is one of a number of similar cases in Spain against musicians.[122] In June 2020, the Spanish Supreme Court affirmed six-month terms of imprisonment for 12 members of the rap group 'La Insurgencia'.[123] The group members were charged with 'glorifying terrorism' on the basis of their songs praising the far-left terrorist organization GRAPO, such as the lyric 'more dead Nazis are needed'.[124] Despite the musicians arguing that their art is provocative and should not be taken literally, the Court held that the expression did not 'imply a criticism, nor an opinion, nor a democratic use of social networks. It is about exalting violent behaviour and seeking to reinforce the ideology of those who carried out terrorist acts by praising them'.[125] The Court therefore found that a six-month sentence for each rapper was legitimate.

Spain's Supreme Court also confirmed a nine-month sentence against rapper 'Pablo Hasél' for 'glorifying' or 'exalting' terrorism.[126] Hasél was convicted in 2018 of insulting the monarchy and glorifying terrorism for tweets which praised armed groups ETA and GRAPO, stating among other things that 'demonstrations are necessary but not enough, we must support those who go further' and that he was 'proud of those who reacted to police aggression'.[127] He was initially sentenced to two years' imprisonment for this speech, reduced to nine months in part because GRAPO and ETA are not currently active.[128] Protests in support of Hasél took place in a number of Spanish cities in early 2021, and in February 2021 he was arrested and taken into custody after failing to

---

[120] S. Vazquez Maymir & P. de Hert, 'First Periodic Country Report: Belgium' (Stream, 2022). The Court also held that glorification of terrorism does not have an equivalent under Belgian law. A Belgian appellate court referred the matter to the European Court of Justice to advice on a technical point regarding an amendment to the offence in the intervening period and its retroactive application: CJEU (GC), *Proceedings relating to the execution of a European arrest warrant against X C-717/18*, 3 March 2020.
[121] 'Valtònyc: Belgian appeals court rules out extradition for Spanish rapper' (Euronews, 17 May 2022).
[122] The provision has also been applied against speakers other than musicians: see, e.g., Columbia Global Freedom of Expression, 'The State v. Cassandra Vera' (2018). And in a recent case the Spanish Constitutional Court overturned a one-year term of imprisonment handed down by the Spanish Supreme Court against another singer, César Strawberry, for a series of tweets supporting ETA and GRAPO. The Constitutional Court held that imprisonment was a disproportionate interference with the singer's free speech: Columbia Global Freedom of Expression, 'The Case of César Strawberry' (2020).
[123] Human Rights Watch, 'Spain: Events of 2020' (2020).
[124] Spanish Penal Code Art. 578.
[125] 'The Supreme Court confirms six-month prison sentence for rappers of La Insurgencia for lorifying terrorism' (El País, 24 June 2020).
[126] Spanish Penal Code Art. 578.
[127] See 'Explainer: The tweets that landed Spanish rapper Pablo Hasel in jail' (The Local, 20 February 2021). Hasél had also previously been sentenced to two years' imprisonment for glorifying terrorism in his YouTube songs: A. Taylor, 'A Spanish rapper was arrested for tweets praising terrorists and mocking royals. Then the protests began' (The Washington Post, 23 February 2021).
[128] Taylor (n 127). He was also fined 25,000 EUR for insulting the monarchy, libel and slander: 'Explainer: The Tweets that Landed Spanish Rapper Pablo Hasel in Jail' (The Local, 20 February 2021).

turn himself in to begin his prison term.[129] Amnesty International Spain's Director has argued that if 'these articles of the Criminal Code are not amended, freedom of expression will continue to be silenced and artistic expression will continue to be restricted.'[130]

2.1.2. Turkey

Since the 2016 coup attempt in Turkey,[131] President Erdogan's government has arrested or imprisoned more than 95,000 citizens, and closed over 1,500 NGOs on terrorism-related grounds, typically for alleged links to Fethullah Gülen, who Erdogan blamed for the coup, or links to the Kurdish Worker's Party (PKK).[132] As noted by Human Rights Watch in 2016, although 'Turkey has a long tradition of misusing terrorism laws against journalists', the political situation in 2016 saw 'journalists from mainstream media organs targeted'.[133] And this trend has continued: reports indicate that terrorism-related charges accounted for more than 42 per cent of charges brought against journalists in Turkey in 2022.[134]

For instance, in 2018 Alaaddin Akkaşoğlu, owner of a left-leaning local newspaper, was convicted of membership in a terrorist organization and sentenced to nearly nine years in prison.[135] Reports indicate that the only allegation against him was the use of an encrypted communication app which authorities alleged was proof of membership of what the Turkish government has categorized as Gülen's terrorist organization.[136]

Such prosecutions are possible due to Turkey's 'arsenal of counter-terrorism laws', which it routinely uses against journalists and human rights defenders,[137] including the offence of 'disseminating propaganda that legitimizes the methods of a terrorist organisation'.[138] And these laws were bolstered in 2020 by a new law on Preventing Financing of Proliferation of Weapons of Mass Destruction. Ostensibly introduced to ensure that Turkey was compliant with its international counter-terrorism financing obligations, UN experts have expressed concern that some provisions 'greatly exceed' this aim, and fear that this law 'may lead to targeting and suspending activities of associations which are critical of the Government, under the cover of investigation for

---

[129] C. King, 'Riots In Barcelona In Support Of Rapper Hasél' (Euroweekly News, 31 January 2021); A. Congostrina, 'Spanish rapper convicted over tweets arrested after ignoring prison deadline' (El País, 16 February 2021).

[130] Amnesty International, 'Spain: Jailing of rapper for song lyrics and tweets "unjust and disproportionate"' (21 February 2021).

[131] Turkey has been characterized in this chapter as a European nation because it is a member of the Council of Europe, a state party to the European Convention on Human Rights and is subject to the jurisdiction of the European Court of Human Rights.

[132] US Department of State, 2021 Country Report on Human Rights Practices: Turkey (2021).

[133] Human Rights Watch, 'Silencing Turkey's Media: The Government's Deepening Assault on Critical Journalism' (15 December 2016).

[134] International Press Institute, 'IPI monitoring: At least 227 journalists faced trial in Turkey in 2022' (31 January 2023).

[135] CPJ, 'People: Alaaddin Akkaşoğlu' (August 2018).

[136] It is called Fethullahist Terrorist Organization/Parallel State Structure, or FETÖ/PDY: ibid.

[137] Amnesty International, 'Turkey: Measures to prevent terrorism financing abusively target civil society and set dangerous international precedent' (18 June 2021).

[138] Turkish Law on the Fight Against Terrorism Art. 7(2) (2006). See s. II.1.1.2. (Glorification or justification of terrorism).

terrorism related offences'.[139] This new law establishes a permanent ban against holding executive office in civil organizations for those convicted of terrorist financing, and grants the Minister of the Interior power to suspend individuals, or the activities of an organization, where an individual is being prosecuted for terrorist-related offences.[140] UN experts have argued that 'under the guise of addressing terrorism', such measures send 'a clear signal ... that civil society actors are legitimate targets for attacks and then legitimizes the adoption of further restrictive measures' against them for what they say.[141]

2.1.3. Russia

Since Russia's invasion in Ukraine, terrorism charges have been one of the myriad ways in which Russian authorities have sought to stifle any criticism of the war, with reports indicating that over 100 defendants have been charged with extremism or for terrorism-related speech since the war began.[142]

Examples include Olesya Krivtsova, a 19-year-old student who was charged with offences including 'justifying terrorism' for an Instagram post to her private account which stated that she understood why Ukrainians were rejoicing after Ukrainian forces had successfully bombed a bridge connecting Russia with Crimea.[143] Her classmates, who provided the post to the authorities, were key witnesses in the prosecution's case against her.[144] She faced up to 10 years' imprisonment for the post but fled Russia.[145] Other cases include that of Andrey Boyarshinov, a former university employee and a civil society activist who was put under house arrest for 'public justification of terrorism' on the basis of an alleged anti-war speech made on a Telegram channel.[146] Boyarshinov was taken into pre-trial detention[147] and faces up to seven years in prison.[148]

---

[139] Mandates of the Special Rapporteur on the promotion and protection of human rights and fundamental freedoms while countering terrorism; the Special Rapporteur on the rights to freedom of peaceful assembly and of association; and the Special Rapporteur on the situation of human rights defenders, *Letter to the Government of Turkey* (2021)OL TUR 3/2021.

[140] Turkish Law on Preventing the Financing of Proliferation of Weapons of Mass Destruction (amending the Turkish Law of Associations, Arts 3a and 30/A) Arts 12, 15.

[141] Mandates of the Special Rapporteur on the promotion and protection of human rights and fundamental freedoms while countering terrorism; the Special Rapporteur on the rights to freedom of peaceful assembly and of association; and the Special Rapporteur on the situation of human rights defenders, *Letter to the Government of Turkey* (2021) OL TUR 3/2021.

[142] 'The Anti-War Case' (OVD-Info, 25 November 2022). Russia has been characterized in this chapter as a European nation because it is a former member of the Council of Europe, was a state party to the European Convention of Human Rights and is subject to the jurisdiction of the European Court of Human Rights prior to 16 September 2022.

[143] 'Inside Russia's Crackdown on Dissent' (The New York Times, 11 April 2023).

[144] Ibid.

[145] Ibid.

[146] Pursuant to Art. 205.2(2) of the Russian Criminal Code: Amnesty International, 'Russia: Authorities launch witch-hunt to catch anyone sharing anti-war views' (30 March 2022); M. Kuznetsova, 'How Russian anti-war protesters face persecution' (DW, 20 April 2022).

[147] 'Pretrial Detention Extended for Anti-War Activist in Russia's Tatarstan' (Radio Free Europe/Radio Liberty, 11 November 2022).

[148] 'The Anti-War Case' (OVD-Info, 25 November 2022). See also 'Detention of Russian director and playwright extended for two months' (AP, 30 June 2023).

Terrorism and extremism charges have also been part of the multi-pronged campaign against prominent opposition figure Aleksei Navalny and his supporters.[149] In June 2021, President Putin signed into law new legislation barring anyone who founded, led, worked for or otherwise participated in 'extremist' organizations from running for elected office for a period of three to five years.[150] Days later, three organizations founded by Navalny were banned as 'extremist'.[151] And in June 2023, Navalny appeared in court after Russian authorities filed new charges against him for allegedly promoting terrorism, calling for and financing extremism and rehabilitating Nazism.[152] Navalny was convicted of those charges and sentenced to 19 years imprisonment, added to the 11 and a half years he was already serving.[153] Several of Navalny's colleagues are detained or wanted on a range of similar charges such as 'participation in an extremist community', 'dissemination of purposely false information about the Russian Armed Forces' and 'justification of terrorism'.[154]

2.2. Asia Pacific region
2.2.1. Myanmar

Authorities in Myanmar have consistently used counterterrorism and public order laws to suppress free speech and critical reporting of the government's actions. In March 2020, the government declared the Arakan Army, the ethnic armed group in Rakhine State, a terrorist organization under Myanmar's Counter-Terrorism Law and an unlawful association pursuant to the Unlawful Associations Act.[155] This declaration spurred a series of arrests of journalists who had reported on the conflict in Rakhine.

For example on 30 March 2020, Nay Myo Lin, the editor-in-chief of the Voice of Myanmar, was charged under sections 50(a) and 52(a) of Myanmar's Counter-Terrorism Law for interviewing a spokesperson of the Arakan Army.[156] Nay Myo Lin's

---

[149] Navalny has been subjected to an assassination attempt, multiple criminal proceedings, and in 2022 was sentenced to nine years in a penal colony for fraud and contempt of court: Amnesty International, 'Russia: Opposition leader Aleksei Navalny sentenced to 9 years in prison in cynical deprivation of his human rights' (22 March 2022).
[150] Amnesty International, 'Russia: Aleksei Navalny's NGOs banned as "extremist", depriving thousands of their rights' (10 June 2021). According to Russian law on combating extremist activity, an organization may be banned as 'extremist', which can entail also administrative or criminal sanctions for participants of such organizations: see SOVA Center, 'The Structure of Russian Anti-Extremist Legislation' (November 2010).
[151] Amnesty International, 'Russia: Aleksei Navalny's NGOs banned as "extremist", depriving thousands of their rights' (10 June 2021).
[152] 'Russia's Navalny defends himself over "extremism charges"' (Al Jazeera, 19 June 2023).
[153] In September 2023, Navalny's appeal was rejected: 'Russia's Navalny loses appeal against 19-year jail term' (Al Jazeera, 26 September 2023).
[154] Amnesty International, 'Russia: Two years after Aleksei Navalny's arrest, Russian opposition figures suppressed, jailed or exiled' (23 January 2023). See s. II.1.1.2. (Glorification or justification of terrorism).
[155] A declaration of an 'unlawful association'—being one which 'encourages or aids persons to commit acts of violence or intimidation'—has serious criminal implications. For example, being a member of any unlawful organization or assisting the association 'in any way' is punishable by up to two years' imprisonment: Myanmar Unlawful Association Act 1908 ss 15–17. See also N. Nyein, 'Myanmar Govt Declares Arakan Army a Terrorist Group' (The Irrawaddy, 24 March 2020).
[156] International Federation for Human Rights, 'Myanmar: Arbitrary detention of Mr. Nay Myo Lin and judicial harassment of four other journalists' (3 April 2020); Human Rights Watch, 'Myanmar: Editor Wrongfully Charged Counter-Terrorism Law Threatens Press Freedom, Freedom of Information' (2 April 2020). These provisions criminalize 'acts of terrorism', broadly defined to include 'to cause fear among the public ... with the aim of forcing the government or a local or foreign organization to do an unlawful act or making them avoid acting lawfully, and other actions'; 'actions to form a terrorist group' or that 'knowingly involve in a terrorist group' or 'actions to allow a terrorist or a member of a terrorist group' to use, gather or hold a meeting: Pyidaungsu Hluttaw Law No. 23 (2014).

interview, titled 'Peace Process has Stopped', focused on the Arakan Army's reaction to their designation as a terrorist organization and the impact of this decision on the ongoing peace process.[157] The UN Special Rapporteur on the situation of human rights in Myanmar condemned these charges, and similar charges levelled against other journalists, arguing that '[t]hese journalists were reporting on the escalating armed conflict in Rakhine State, where the Government has imposed a mobile internet shutdown' and that 'their reporting was of the highest public interest value and should be protected'.[158] The Committee to Protect Journalists also called for Nay Myo Lin's immediate release, stating that 'reporting on armed conflict is not the same as being a terrorist'.[159] The charges against Nay Myo Lin were ultimately dropped, and although police and government spokespeople declined to comment on the case, Nay Myo Lin reported that police told him 'it was their mistake'.[160]

The use of public order and terrorism offences against journalists has intensified since Myanmar's coup d'état in February 2021 and the accompanying expansion of Myanmar's public order offences. In 2021 existing public order provisions in Myanmar's Penal Code were broadened including by criminalizing any attempt to 'hinder, disturb, damage the motivation, discipline, health and conduct' of military personnel or cause their hatred, disobedience or 'disloyalty'.[161] A new provision, section 505A, criminalizes anyone who 'causes or intends to cause fear to a group of citizens or to the public' or 'causes or intends to commit or to agitate directly or indirectly [a] criminal offence against a Government employee'.[162] Over 176 journalists have been detained since the coup began, many accused of violating section 505A.[163] The UN Special Rapporteur on the situation of human rights in Myanmar has described these as 'illegitimately imposed new laws' which 'are now being used at an alarming rate to justify detentions of individuals'.[164]

2.2.2. India

In India, widely drawn terrorism and public order laws give police and prosecutors extensive powers that can chill speech and send journalists and human rights defenders to prison for years even before a conviction. One example is the use of the Unlawful Activities (Prevention) Act as a mechanism to silence journalists reporting on the politically volatile region of Kashmir. Under the Act, 'unlawful activity' includes 'words ... which [are] intended, or suppor[t] any claim, to bring about ... the cession

---

[157] International Federation for Human Rights, 'Myanmar: Arbitrary detention of Mr. Nay Myo Lin and judicial harassment of four other journalists' (3 April 2020).

[158] OHCHR, 'Myanmar must allow free flow of information and aid to protect right to health in COVID-19 crisis—UN Special Rapporteur Yanghee Lee' (4 April 2020).

[159] 'Myanmar Journalist Arrested For Interview With Blacklisted Arakan Army' (Radio Free Asia, 31 March 2020).

[160] 'Myanmar frees journalist who was charged under terrorism law' (Reuters, 10 April 2020); K. Y. Lynn, 'Myanmar report released after charged over interview' (Anadolu Agency, 10 April 2020).

[161] Human Rights Watch, 'Myanmar: Post-Coup Legal Changes Erode Human Rights' (2 March 2021).

[162] Myanmar Penal Code 1861 s. 505A.

[163] A. Nachemson, 'In 2021, Myanmar journalists risked lives to tell world of coup' (Al Jazeera, 29 December 2021); 'More than 130 journalists arrested in Myanmar, media group says' (Radio Free Asia, 4 April 2022). IFJ, 'Myanmar: Five journalists freed as human rights abuses escalate' (8 May 2023).

[164] UN Special Rapporteur T.H. Andrews, *Report on the situation of human rights in Myanmar* (2021) UN Doc. A/HRC/46/56, §63.

of a part of a territory of India', 'which disclaims, questions, disrupts or is intended to disrupt the sovereignty or territorial integrity of India', or 'which causes or is intended to cause disaffection against India'.[165] The Act also allows the government to declare an association unlawful, and any individual who assists the operation of an unlawful association can be liable to up to five years' imprisonment.[166]

In 2019 this Act was amended to allow an individual to be deemed a 'terrorist' if that individual 'promotes or encourages terrorism' or is 'otherwise involved in terrorism'.[167] This provision has been criticized on the basis that Indian authorities can now designate individuals as 'terrorists' without charge or trial.[168] The same year as these amendments were passed saw Indian authorities arrest 1,948 people under the Act, an almost 37 per cent increase from the previous year.[169]

Journalists charged under the Act include Aasif Sultan, assistant editor of a Kashmir-based English magazine, who was accused of 'harbouring terrorists' and conspiracy against the state by giving assistance to rebels, after publishing an article about a Kashmiri rebel commander killed by Indian authorities.[170] Sultan has been in pre-trial detention and has spent more than five years in jail.[171] UN experts have also condemned the arrests of human rights defenders in the region, including cases involving the death penalty,[172] and noted India's 'misuse' of its 'anti-terrorism framework ... to smear and silence human rights defenders'.[173] Repeated calls have been made against the use of the Act 'as a means of coercion against civil society, the media, and human rights defenders in Indian-administered Jammu and Kashmir'.[174]

2.3. Middle East and Africa

2.3.1. *Egypt*

A high-profile example of Egypt's use of terrorism charges against journalists is the case of Mohamed Fahmy, head of the Al Jazeera bureau in Cairo, and his colleagues Peter Greste and Baher Mohamed.[175] In 2014 the men were convicted of a string of

---

[165] Indian Unlawful Activities (Prevention) Act 1967 s. 2.
[166] Ibid., ss 3, 10, 13.
[167] Ibid., 7 s. 35(3)(c).
[168] A. Vishwanath & K. Sheriff M., 'Amendments to anti-terror law: Onus will be on individual to prove he is not terrorist' (The Indian Express, 26 July 2019) ('The law does not require any other offences to be filed against the individual to declare him/her a terrorist. The law also does not specify any process for the designation').
[169] '"Misused, abused": India's harsh terror law under rare scrutiny' (Al Jazeera, 16 August 2021): 'only 2.2 percent of cases registered under the Act from 2016 to 2019 ended in a court conviction'.
[170] B. Kichay, 'Kashmiri journalist Aasif Sultan kept in jail for more than 1,000 days' (Al Jazeera, 31 May 2021). According to Al Jazeera, the police added Sultan's name 'to a first information report' about a gunfight with the rebels in 2018. The charges against Sultan included non-speech offences such as 'murder, attempt to murder and other crimes', even though Sultan's lawyer has denied his client being present at the fight and reported that this fact is 'admitted by the prosecution'. See also CPJ, 'Kashmiri journalist Aasif Sultan granted bail, then re-arrested under preventative detention law' (11 April 2022).
[171] 'India arrest Kashmir journalist Irfan Mehraj on "terror" charges' (Al Jazeera, 21 March 2023).
[172] OHCHR, 'One year in detention: UN experts demand immediate release of Kashmiri activist Khurram Parvez' (22 November 2022).
[173] OHCHR, 'India: UN expert demands immediate end to crackdown on Kashmiri human rights defenders' (24 March 2023). See also WGAD, *Parvez v. India* (Opinion no. 8/2023), 28 March 2023, §70.
[174] OHCHR, 'One year in detention: UN experts demand immediate release of Kashmiri activist Khurram Parvez' (22 November 2022).
[175] See ch. 4 (False Speech), s. II.2.3.1. (Egypt).

offences, including possession of publications and records promoting the aims of a terrorist group and spreading false news. The judgment convicted the three journalists on the basis that 'through their actions, [they] had compiled audiovisual film material and falsified untrue events to be broadcast by a satellite channel in order to stir conflict within the Egyptian State'. More specifically, the court condemned them for betraying 'the noble profession of journalism' by 'portraying the Country—untruthfully—to be in a state of chaos ... internal strife and disarray'. This sinister plot was apparently orchestrated 'upon the instructions of the ... terrorist Muslim Brotherhood Group' and the court even concluded that 'Satan joined [the journalists] in the exploitation of this media activity to direct it against this country. Fahmy and Greste were sentenced to 7 years' imprisonment and Mohamed to 10 years.[176]

This conviction was entered despite the fact that no substantive evidence was placed before the court to justify these charges.[177] The court's reasoning listed seized equipment, which comprised computers, cameras and other standard journalistic equipment, and none of the video footage shown in court established that the journalists were members of or even supportive of the Muslim Brotherhood. Indeed, the defendants stated that they had never seen the 14 alleged Brotherhood members who were co-defendants at their trial until they were placed alongside them in a cage in court on the first day of the trial.[178] International condemnation followed the decision,[179] but at a retrial they were re-convicted of the same offences, which resulted in three-year sentences for each journalist on the basis that 'it has been proven beyond reasonable doubt that the al-Jazeera media channel has dedicated its broadcasting to the service and support of the Muslim Brotherhood faction and that they have permanently sided with them at the expense of their media ethics'.[180] Although they were eventually released following a presidential pardon,[181] the journalists each spent more than a year in prison.[182]

2.3.2. Iran

In 2019, Iranian activist and human rights lawyer Nasrin Sotoudeh was convicted of a range of offences and sentenced to 33 years in prison and 148 lashes for her peaceful

---

[176] They were also sentenced for possessing communications and broadcasting equipment without a press permit. See A. Clooney, 'The Anatomy of an Unfair Trial' (HuffPost, 18 August 2014). See also Egypt Justice, 'Al Jazeera English Journalists Case—Unofficial English Translation of Court of Cassation Judgment' (1 January 2015), 6–9.

[177] See A. Clooney, 'The Anatomy of an Unfair Trial' (HuffPost, 18 August 2014).

[178] Ibid.

[179] 'Timeline: The two trials of Mohamed Fahmy' (CTV, 13 October 2015).

[180] Mohamed received an additional six months' imprisonment for possessing a single bullet. The court relied on the same evidence as that relied on in the first trial. Columbia Global Freedom of Expression, 'The Case of Al Jazeera Journalists' (2015).

[181] In February 2015, Greste was freed from prison and deported to Australia following presidential 'approval', and Fahmy and Mohamed were released on bail. See Egypt Justice, 'Al Jazeera English Journalists Case—Unofficial English Translation of Court of Cassation Judgment' (1 January 2015); 'Egypt Pardons Al Jazeera Journalists Mohamed Fahmy and Baher Mohamed' (The New York Times, 23 September 2015).

[182] Baher Mohamed and Mohamed Fahmy spent over 14 months in prison: see 'Baher Mohamed: My 1,124 hours of Solitary Confinement in Prison' (Al Jazeera, 17 August 2017).

advocacy for women's rights and against Iran's compulsory hijab requirements.[183] Following a trial which Sotoudeh refused to attend after being denied the right to choose her own lawyer, Sotoudeh was found guilty of seven different offences, including 'assembly and collusion with an intention to commit a crime against national security', 'propaganda against the state', membership of an illegal group, 'publishing falsehoods with the intention to disturb public opinion' and 'disturbing public order'.[184] Sotoudeh is required to serve at least 12 years in prison.

According to the court's verdict, Sotoudeh's illegal conduct was publishing a statement demanding a referendum; conducting 'interviews with foreign media outlets opposed to the Islamic Republic'; 'publish[ing] a video message without a hijab' on social media platforms to show her solidarity with women campaigning against the compulsory hijab; distributing button badges with the slogan 'I am against forced hijab' and participating in 'illegal' anti-death penalty demonstrations.[185] A number of UN human rights experts decried the sentence as 'deeply concerning' and urged her immediate release.[186] Sotoudeh was temporarily released in September 2020, after her health deteriorated due to a six-week hunger strike. But Iranian authorities ordered her return to prison in December 2020.[187]

2.4. North and South America
2.4.1. *United States*

Although the United States Supreme Court's first amendment jurisprudence makes the United States perhaps the world's most speech-protective nation, US law includes a crime of material support of terrorism that has been applied to speech.[188] In 1996, shortly after the infamous bombing in Oklahoma City, the US Government enacted

---

[183] Sotoudeh was arrested in June 2018 on the basis that she was yet to serve a five-year sentence handed down in 2016 *in absentia*, the existence of which Sotoudeh had been unaware. As a result, her total sentence is 38 years. See Amnesty International, 'Iran: Shocking 33-year prison term and 148 lashes for women's rights defender Nasrin Sotoudeh' (11 March 2019).

[184] Pursuant to Arts 610, 500, 499, 639, 638, 698 and 618 of the Iranian Penal Code. Center for Human Rights Iran, 'Defying Unjust Court Process, Nasrin Sotoudeh Refuses to Appeal Prison Sentence' (19 March 2019). Amnesty International, 'Iran: Shocking 33-year prison term and 148 lashes for women's rights defender Nasrin Sotoudeh' (11 March 2019). Sotoudeh was only permitted to take a note of the charges of which she was convicted, which her husband later published. Following her conviction, the Islamic Republic News Agency reported that Sotoudeh had been sentenced to seven years' imprisonment: five for 'gathering and concluding to commit crimes against national security' and two for 'insulting the Supreme Leader': see also 'Human rights lawyer Nasrin Sotoudeh jailed 'for 38 years' in Iran' (The Guardian, 11 March 2019).

[185] Center for Human Rights Iran, 'Defying Unjust Court Process, Nasrin Sotoudeh Refuses to Appeal Prison Sentence' (19 March 2019); T.S. Far, 'Why Nasrin Sotoudeh is on Hunger Strike to Protest Iran's Dire Prison Conditions' (Human Rights Watch, 10 September 2020).

[186] Special Rapporteur on the situation of human rights defenders; Special Rapporteur on the independence of judges and lawyers; Chair-Rapporteur of WGAD; Chair of the Working Group on the issue of discrimination against women in law and in practice; Special Rapporteur on the situation of human rights in the Islamic Republic of Iran: see OHCHR, 'Iran: UN experts "shocked" at lengthy prison sentence for human rights lawyer Nasrin Sotoudeh' (14 March 2019).

[187] See OHCHR, 'Iran: Nasrin Sotoudeh must be released, say UN experts' (9 December 2020); J. Hincks, '"It's Like We're Hanging in the Air". Iranian Activist Nasrin Sotoudeh's Husband on Her Temporary Release from Prison' (TIME, 20 November 2022). Sotoudeh was again released from prison on medical leave in July 2021 and remains on medical leave: IBAHRI, 'Iran: IBAHRI condemns prison sentence against Reza Khandan and calls for charges to be dropped' (21 February 2023).

[188] See, e.g., D. Barak-Erez & D. Scharia, 'Freedom of Speech, Support for Terrorism, and the Challenge of Global Constitutional Law' (2011) 2 *Harvard National Security Journal* 1, 3.

federal statute 18 U.S.C §2993B, making it a crime, punishable by up to 20 years' imprisonment, to 'knowingly provid[e] material support or resources to a foreign terrorist organization', with 'material support' defined to include 'expert advice or assistance', 'training' and 'personnel'.[189] This law has since emerged as 'the chief statute for charging terrorism suspects in federal courts'.[190]

In 2010, the Supreme Court decided a case, *Holder v. Humanitarian Law Project*, that was brought by US citizens and domestic human rights organizations who wished to provide support such as advocacy training, requesting aid and relief, and using humanitarian and international law to peacefully resolve disputes to two classified terrorist organizations: the Kurdistan Workers' Party (the PKK) and the Liberation Tigers of Tamil Eelam (LTTE).[191]

The US Government argued that the statute limited only *conduct* rather than speech, and that, in any event, its interest in 'combating terrorism is an urgent objective of the highest order'. The plaintiffs agreed that the Government had a strong interest in combating terrorism, but argued that 'the objective of combating terrorism does not justify prohibiting their speech ... because their support will advance only the legitimate activities of the designated terrorist organizations, not their terrorism'.[192]

Chief Justice Roberts, delivering the 6:3 majority judgment for the Court, held that the statute was 'constitutional as applied to the particular activities plaintiffs have told us they wish to pursue', including 'train[ing]' members of the designated terrorist group 'to use humanitarian and international law to peacefully resolve disputes'; 'teaching' members of the designated terrorist group 'how to petition various representative bodies such as the United Nations for relief'; and 'engag[ing] in political advocacy' on behalf of specific Kurdish communities.[193] This meant that it was permissible to impose up to 20 years' imprisonment—or life imprisonment if 'the death of any person results'—under US law if these activities were conducted by the plaintiffs.[194] According to the Chief Justice, section 2993B demonstrated Congress and the Executive's position that 'providing material support to a designated foreign terrorist organization—even seemingly benign support—bolsters the terrorist activities of that organization'.[195] The Chief Justice accepted that support of non-violent activities would free up other resources that may be put to violent ends, and that such support lends 'legitimacy' to terrorist groups.[196]

---

[189] 18 U.S.C. §§2339A, 2339B.
[190] See, e.g., W.E. Said, 'The Material Support Prosecution and Foreign Policy' (2011) 86 *Indiana Law Journal* 543, 544.
[191] US Supreme Court, *Holder v. Humanitarian Law Project* 561 U.S. 1, 21 June 2010.
[192] Ibid., 29.
[193] Ibid., 14. The Court also held that the statute was not unconstitutionally vague and did not violate the plaintiffs' freedom of association, the latter on the basis that the statute criminalized specific types of conduct instead of membership, and therefore was sufficiently protective of the right to association. See also FBI, 'Staten Island Man Sentenced to 69 Months in Prison for Providing Material Support and Resources to Hizballah' (23 April 2009) (sentencing the defendant to over five years in prison following a guilty plea under the same statute for helping to broadcast Hezbollah's TV station Al-Manar).
[194] 18 U.S.C. §2339B; US Supreme Court, *Holder v. Humanitarian Law Project* 561 U.S. 1, 21 June 2010, 39.
[195] US Supreme Court, *Holder v. Humanitarian Law Project* 561 U.S. 1, 21 June 2010, 36.
[196] Ibid., 30.

The majority judgment also drew a careful distinction between independent advocacy and coordinated speech. In response to the dissenting Justices' argument that 'there is "no natural stopping place" for the proposition that aiding a foreign terrorist organization's lawful activities promotes the organization as a whole', the Chief Justice considered the statute to delineate such a place, as 'the statute reaches only material support coordinated *with or under the direction* of a designated foreign terrorist organization'.[197] As a result, the Court held that it 'in no way suggest[ed] that a regulation of *independent speech* would pass constitutional muster, even if the Government were to show that such speech benefits foreign terrorist organizations'.[198]

In his dissenting judgment, Justice Breyer (with Justices Ginsburg and Sotomayor joining) argued that the Government had not made the 'strong showing necessary to justify under the First Amendment the criminal prosecution of those who engage in these activities', which all concern political speech.[199] The dissenters returned to the principles related to hate speech articulated in *Brandenburg v. Ohio*, arguing that the plaintiffs 'seek to advocate peaceful, *lawful* action to secure political ends' and therefore do not fall within the incitement test in *Brandenburg*.[200] The dissent described the government's arguments in support of combatting terrorism as 'general and speculative', and applicable to 'virtually all speech-related support for a dual-purpose group's peaceful activities'.[201] The dissent also expressed concern as to the distinction between coordinated and independent speech, describing the distinction as an 'arbitrary' one incapable of clear definition.[202] In light of this 'serious doubt' as to the statute's constitutionality, Justice Breyer proposed a construction consistent with the First Amendment, namely that the statute criminalizes speech 'only when the defendant knows or intends those activities will assist the organization's unlawful terrorist actions'.[203]

The decision has been strongly condemned, including by The New York Times Editorial Board, which called it a 'bruise on the First Amendment'.[204] An amicus brief filed by a diverse coalition of academic and advocacy groups expressed concern with section 2339B, arguing that effective peace-making, conflict resolution and human rights advocacy 'sometimes requires direct engagement with groups and individuals that resort to or support violence', and that such a broadly worded material-support provision punishes association with a group even where intended to *dissuade* that group from engaging in unlawful activities.[205]

Similarly, First Amendment academics have suggested that this precedent 'has the potential to limit freedom of speech far beyond content-based prohibitions of the sort

---

[197] Ibid. (emphasis added).
[198] Ibid., 39 (emphasis added).
[199] Ibid., Dissenting Opinion of Breyer J, 42.
[200] Ibid., Dissenting Opinion of Breyer J, 44. See ch. 3 (Hate Speech), s. II.2.3.2. (United States).
[201] Ibid., Dissenting Opinion of Breyer J, 55 .
[202] Ibid., Dissenting Opinion of Breyer J, 51–52.
[203] Ibid., Dissenting Opinion of Breyer J, 55–56. Justice Breyer recommended the case be remanded to lower courts to consider more specifically the precise activities in which the plaintiffs still wish to engage and determine whether and to what extent a grant of declaratory or injunctive relief was warranted: 60.
[204] 'A Bruise on the First Amendment' (The New York Times, 21 June 2010).
[205] Amicus Brief of the Carter Center and other humanitarian groups in support of Humanitarian Law Project, et al. in US Supreme Court, *Holder v. Humanitarian Law Project* 561 U.S. 1, 21 June 2010, 2, 6.

prevalent in Europe', such as glorification and propaganda offences.[206] This is because *Holder v. Humanitarian Law Project* 'opens the door for prohibiting any speech related to a terrorist organization, no matter how peaceful it is, as long as it is expressed *in co-ordination with or under the direction* of a terrorist organization'.[207] Further difficulties arise as the decision 'did not explicitly define what coordination entails', leaving 'considerable uncertainty as to what sort of relationship an individual must have with an organization to be convicted under §2339B'.[208] Others have recognized the challenge this presents for social media companies, as the Court's construction of the statute does not capture speech glorifying terrorism if unconnected to a terrorist group, but may prohibit the exact same speech when uttered 'in coordination with or at the behest of [a] terrorist group'.[209] In these circumstances, '[h]ow would a social media provider know whether such coordination has occurred?'[210]

In its 2006 report to the UN Counter-Terrorism Committee,[211] the US Government noted that the First Amendment 'limits the ability of the U.S. to prosecute incitement to commit acts of terrorism to the strict set of circumstances set forth in Brandenburg'.[212] However, the United States argued that it already had 'in place a number of legal measures that comport with these provisions',[213] including the material support provisions in section 2339B, the federal offences of solicitation to violence and advocacy of the overthrow of the government, as well as 'inchoate crimes' that prohibit preparatory acts to substantive criminal offences. And 'given the overlap between supporters of terrorism and those who incite terrorism', the United States noted that material support and inchoate provisions 'further the goals set forth in [UN Security Council resolution] 1624 of preventing and prohibiting incitement to terrorism'.[214] Nonetheless, the United States recognized that 'the majority of the terrorist propaganda found on the Internet today could not be prosecuted under U.S. criminal law', in light of First Amendment principles that place high limits on restrictions to speech.[215]

A case which demonstrates the use of US solicitation and 'inchoate crimes' provisions against speech inciting terrorist acts is the *al-Timimi* case. Al-Timimi, an Islamic scholar and American citizen, attended a dinner five days after the September 11 attacks with a small group of Muslim men to discuss the possibility of backlash against American Muslims, and suggested that the men should leave the United States, join the mujahideen and fight enemies of Islam.[216] He also read a fatwa issued by a Saudi scholar

---

[206] Barak-Erez & Scharia (n 188).
[207] Ibid.
[208] N. Abel, '*United States vs. Mehanna*, the First Amendment and Material Support in the War on Terror' (2013) 54 *Boston College Law Review* 2, 711, 730.
[209] R. VanLindingham, 'Jailing the Twitter Bird: Social Media, Material Support to Terrorism and Muzzling the Modern Press' (2017) 39 *Cardozo Law Review* 1, 35.
[210] Ibid. See s. III.6 (Approach of Private Companies to Online Incitement to Terrorism).
[211] This is the entity tasked with monitoring the implementation of the UN call for states to prohibit incitement to terrorism. See UNSC Res. 1624 (2005). See also s. III.5. (Penalties).
[212] UNSC, *Report of the United States of America pursuant to resolution 1624 (2005)* (2006) UN Doc. S/2006/397.
[213] Ibid.
[214] Ibid.
[215] Ibid. See, e.g., s. III.6. (Approach of Private Companies to Online Incitement to Terrorism).
[216] See, e.g., T. Healy, '*Brandenburg* in a Time of Terror' (2009) 84 *Notre Dame Law Review* 2.

declaring that Muslims were obliged to defend Afghanistan against the United States. Four of the men later flew to Pakistan to attend a training camp but ultimately returned to the United States after Pakistan had closed its border to Afghanistan. In 2005, al-Timimi was convicted of 10 separate offences including '[s]oliciting others to levy war against the United States', inducing others to 'attempt to aid the Taliban' and 'use firearms during and in relation to crimes of violence' and was sentenced to life in prison.[217] Scholars have argued that al-Timimi's speech was 'clearly protected' on a literal reading of *Brandenburg v. Ohio,* as there was no evidence of inciting imminent action since the dinner took place in the United States before hostilities had begun and the men arrived at the camp weeks after al-Timimi's speech.[218] The conviction in this case has therefore been held to sidestep the '*Brandenburg* framework', which requires a likelihood of imminent physical harm.[219] Al-Timimi's appeal continues, and after 15 years in prison in 2020, a US federal court judge ruled that al-Timimi could remain on home confinement until his appeal was finalized, holding that if his convictions under some counts were reversed he 'would have already served more time in prison than warranted'.[220]

III. International Legal Standards

Freedom of expression is enshrined in article 19 of the Universal Declaration of Human Rights, article 19 of the ICCPR and regional human rights instruments.[221] Under article 19(3) of the ICCPR, a state is permitted to restrict speech if the state can prove that the restriction is (1) 'provided by law' (legality requirement); (2) pursues one of the following legitimate objectives: (i) 'respect of the rights or reputations of others' or (ii) 'the protection of national security or of public order ... or of public health or morals' (legitimacy requirement); and (3) is 'necessary' to achieve that objective (necessity requirement).[222] An analysis of necessity includes an assessment of proportionality, namely that restrictions are 'appropriate to achieve their protective function', 'the least intrusive instrument amongst those which might achieve their protective function', and 'proportionate to the interest to be protected'.[223] Like the ICCPR, regional human rights treaties recognize the protection of 'national security' as a legitimate reason to punish speech.[224]

Although many national laws criminalize terrorism and public order offences, there are few cases litigated before international and regional human rights bodies that test

---

[217] US District Court, E.D., Virginia, Alexandria, *United States v. Al-Timimi* 1:04-cr-385 (LMB), 1-2 18 August 2020, affirmed by US Court of Appeals, Fourth Circuit, *United States v. Al-Timimi* No. 20-4442, 31 August 2020.
[218] T. Healy (n 216) 659.
[219] Ibid., 2.
[220] US District Court, E.D., Virginia, Alexandria, *United States v. Al-Timimi* 1:04-cr-385 (LMB), 1-2 18 August 2020, affirmed by US Court of Appeals, Fourth Circuit, *United States v. Al-Timimi* No. 20-4442, 31 August 2020.
[221] ECHR Art. 10; ACHR Art. 13; ACHPR Art. 9; Arab Charter Art. 32; ASEAN Human Rights Declaration Art. 23; Cairo Declaration on Human Rights in Islam Art. 22. See ch. 1 (Introduction), s. II.1.1. (Treaty language).
[222] See also HRC, General Comment No. 34 (2011), §22.
[223] Ibid., §34.
[224] See ch. 5 (Speech Related to National Security: Espionage and Official Secrets Laws), s. III.1. (International Standards Related to Speech Affecting National Security).

whether and to what extent they may extend to *speech* in support of terrorism.[225] An exception is the European Court of Human Rights, which has considered a number of cases involving terrorist-related speech. But there is a wider body of international standards governing the interplay between speech and national security—for instance in the context of espionage laws—that is relevant to terrorism and public order laws.[226] And standards relating to insulting speech and hate speech are also relevant to terrorism restrictions, as both require an assessment of whether speech extends beyond merely insulting or abhorrent expression to inciting violence or other criminal actions or prohibited outcomes.[227]

A key question is the degree to which speech supporting terrorism must be causally linked to the commission of a terrorist act. The Human Rights Committee, UN Special Rapporteur on terrorism, Council of Europe and UN Secretary-General have all criticized terror offences with a less stringent causal link than 'incitement', such as 'glorifying', 'apologizing' or 'justifying' terrorism, on the basis that they do not incorporate 'intent to incite the commission of a terrorist offence' or 'increas[e] the actual likelihood of a terrorist act occurring'.[228] But the European Court of Human Rights has become an outlier, applying a looser causal standard than its counterparts, with the result that it has found offences such as 'apology' for terrorist acts and engaging in separatist 'propaganda' compatible with article 10.[229]

Although the international human rights framework was developed to apply to states, a number of technology and social media companies have committed to ensuring they regulate speech—including terrorist and violent extremist content—in a manner consistent with international human rights standards.[230] These international standards represent a floor, not a ceiling, for free speech protection.[231]

1. Legality

1.1. Definition of terrorism

Since there is no agreed definition of 'terrorism' under international law, international and regional human rights bodies do not specify a particular definition for states to adopt. But the requirement that a restriction on human rights be 'provided by law'—also known as the 'principle of legality'—requires that a law must be public

---

[225] See ch. 1 (Introduction), s. II.1.1. (Treaty Language).
[226] See ch. 5 (Speech Related to National Security: Espionage and Official Secrets Laws), s. III.1. (International Standards Related to Speech Affecting National Security).
[227] See ch. 2 (Insulting Speech) and ch. 3 (Hate Speech).
[228] See UN Secretary-General, *Report on the protection of human rights and fundamental freedoms while countering terrorism* (2008) UN Doc. A/63/337, §61. See s. III.3.2. (Causal link between speech and harm).
[229] See s. III.3.2. (Causal link between speech and harm); s. III.3.2.1. ('Glorification', 'justification' and 'apology' offences).
[230] See ch. 3 (Hate Speech), s. V (Approach of Private Companies to Online Hate Speech); The Christchurch Call to Action to Eliminate Terrorist and Violent Extremist Content Online (2019).
[231] See ch. 3 (Hate Speech), s. VI.5. (Recommendations).

and 'formulated with sufficient precision to enable an individual to regulate his or her conduct'.[232] It means that a speaker should be able 'to foresee, to a degree that was reasonable in the circumstances, the consequences that a given action could entail'.[233] As the UN Security Council's Counter-Terrorism Committee has put it: if an 'underlying definition [of terrorism] includes overly broad terms, then the incitement to commit terrorist acts offence will likely also be problematic' under international law.[234]

The Human Rights Committee has criticized certain laws for being overly vague since this 'can lend itself to arbitrary and abusive implementation'.[235] For instance, it expressed concern about Vietnam's offence of 'terrorism to oppose the people's Government' on this basis.[236] And it found that Niger's definition, by referring to an 'act' committed 'with the intention of disrupting the normal functioning of public services' could 'by its vague and ambiguous nature, result in the penalization of peaceful activities linked to the right to freedom of expression'.[237] It also critiqued Jordan's definition of terrorism, which includes 'such acts as disturbing the public order, acts that sow discord and online activity that supports or spreads ideas of terrorist groups', on the basis that it allows authorities to prosecute 'individuals who exercise their right to freedom of expression'.[238]

Like the Human Rights Committee, the Working Group on Arbitrary Detention and the UN Special Rapporteur on terrorism[239] have criticized Saudi Arabia's definition of terrorism—which criminalizes acts or omissions endangering 'national unity' or undermining 'the reputation or position of the State'—on the basis it enables the 'criminalisation of a wide spectrum of acts of peaceful expression'.[240] Although the Working Group accepted that 'any definition of terrorism' could cover 'threats' as well as 'acts' of 'violence', it found that the offence 'should be confined to [those] that are committed for religious, political or ideological motives, and that are aimed at putting the public or

---

[232] HRC, General Comment No. 34 (2011), §25. See ch. 2 (Insulting Speech), s. III.1. (Legality); ch. 4 (False Speech), s. III.2.1. (Legality); ch. 3 (Hate Speech), s. III.2.1. (Legality); ch. 5 (Speech Related to National Security: Espionage and Official Secrets Laws), s. III.2. (Legality).

[233] ECtHR (GC), *Perinçek v. Switzerland* (App. no. 27510/08), 15 October 2015, §131 (citing ECtHR, *The Sunday Times v. United Kingdom (No. 1)* (App. no. 6538/74), 26 April 1979, §§48–49). But 'consequences need not be foreseeable with absolute certainty': ECtHR (GC), *Satakunnan Markkinapörssi Oy v. Finland* (App. no. 931/13), 27 June 2017, §143.

[234] CTED, *Global survey of the implementation of Security Council resolution 1624 (2005) by Member States* (2021) UN Doc. S/2021/973 (Annex), §10.

[235] HRC, *Concluding Observations, Vietnam* (2019) UN Doc. CCPR/C/VNM/CO/3, §§11–12. Article 113(1) of Vietnam's Criminal Code criminalizes any person 'who, for the purpose of opposing the people's government, infringes upon life or officials or other people'. Article 113(2) also includes the offence of 'forcing, persuading other people to participate in terrorism', punishable by 10–15 years' imprisonment: Vietnamese Criminal Code Art. 113.

[236] HRC, *Concluding Observations, Vietnam* (2019) UN Doc. CCPR/C/VNM/CO/3, §§11–12.

[237] HRC, *Concluding Observations, Niger* (2019) UN Doc. CCPR/C/NER/CO/2, §14.

[238] HRC, *Concluding Observations, Jordan* (2017) UN Doc. CCPR/C/JOR/CO/5, §12. See also HRC, *Concluding Observations, Bahrain* (2018) UN Doc. CCPR/C/BHR/CO/1, §§29–30; HRC, *Concluding Observations, Pakistan* (2017) UN Doc. CCPR/C/PAK/CO/1, §§21–22; HRC, *Concluding Observations, Bangladesh* (2017) UN Doc. CCPR/C/BGD/CO/1, §§9–10; HRC, *Concluding Observations, Morocco* (2016) UN Doc. CCPR/C/MAR/CO/6, §§17–18.

[239] The full title is: the 'UN Special Rapporteur on the promotion and protection of human rights and fundamental freedoms while countering terrorism' but the abbreviated title will be used throughout the chapter.

[240] WGAD, *Waleed Abulkhair v. Saudi Arabia* (Opinion no. 10/2018), 19 April 2018, §§26, 67 (citing OHCHR, 'UN Special Rapporteur on the promotion and protection of human rights and fundamental freedoms while countering terrorism concludes visit to Saudi Arabia' (4 May 2017)).

section of the public in fear or to coerce a Government or international organization to take or refrain from taking a particular action'.[241]

The European Court also requires that restrictions on speech should be 'provided by law', which means that laws penalizing speech should be 'formulated with sufficient precision to enable people to regulate their conduct' and to 'foresee, to a degree that is reasonable in the circumstances, the consequences which a given action may entail'.[242] The European Court is 'mindful of the difficulties linked to preventing terrorism and formulating anti-terrorism criminal laws', and therefore has recognized that states 'inevitably have recourse to somewhat general wording' for these laws, 'the application of which depends on the practical interpretation by the judicial authorities'.[243] The Court has noted that 'it is not for it to rule on the constituent elements of the offences under domestic law of terrorism and threat of terrorism' and found instead that the 'Court's task is merely to review under Article 10' decisions by domestic courts 'delivered pursuant to their power of appreciation. In so doing, it must satisfy itself that the national authorities based their decisions on an acceptable assessment of the relevant facts'.[244]

In practice, in the 'majority of cases' the European Court's analysis will turn on whether a restriction is 'necessary' and proportionate,[245] and the Court is often reluctant to find a violation of article 10 on the basis of the threshold question of legality.[246] For example, when the feminist punk band Pussy Riot's music videos were banned under Russia's Suppression of Extremism Act, members of the band argued that the Act 'was vague to the point of making the legal rule in question unforeseeable'.[247] The Court decided to 'leave the question open' as to whether the provisions were prescribed by law, on the basis the applicants' grievances fell to be examined 'from the point of view of the proportionality of the interference'.[248]

The Inter-American Court of Human Rights has imposed similar standards for terrorism offences. According to the Court, 'offenses of a terrorist nature' must be formulated precisely, as 'the principle of legality requires that a necessary distinction be made between such offenses and ordinary offenses, so that every individual and also the criminal judge have sufficient legal elements to know whether an action is penalized under one or the other offense'.[249] The Inter-American Court considers this distinction

---

[241] WGAD, *Waleed Abulkhair v. Saudi Arabia* (Opinion no. 10/2018), 19 April 2018, §67.
[242] ECtHR, *Alekhina v. Russia* (App. no. 38004/12), 17 July 2018, §254.
[243] ECtHR (GC), *Demirtaş v. Turkey (No. 2)* (App. no. 14305/17), 22 December 2020, §275.
[244] ECtHR, *Fatullayev v. Azerbaijan* (App. no. 40984/07), 22 April 2010, §112.
[245] See s. III.5. (Penalties).
[246] ECtHR, Guide on Article 10 of the Convention, 31 August 2022, §61 ('The Court ... analyses whether the interference was "prescribed by law" and whether it "pursued one of the legitimate aims" within the meaning of Article 10 § 2, and lastly whether the interference was "necessary in a democratic society"; in the majority of cases, this is the question which determines the Court's conclusion in a given case'). See ch. 1 (Introduction), s. III.3.1.1. (Justifications for penalizing speech).
[247] ECtHR, *Alekhina v. Russia* (App. no. 38004/12), 17 July 2018, §256. Criminal proceedings for hooliganism were also instituted against the band members for the performance and considered by the ECtHR.
[248] Ibid., §§209, 258. See also ECtHR, *Şahin Alpay v. Turkey* (App. no. 16538/17), 20 March 2018, §175 (although conceding that 'serious doubts may arise' as to whether the applicant's pre-trial detention was foreseeable, 'in view of its findings ... concerning the necessity of the interference, the Court considers that it does not have to settle this question').
[249] IACtHR, *Norín Catrimán v. Chile* (Series C, no. 279), 29 May 2014, §§162–163.

warranted because of the harsh prison sentences and the restrictions on fundamental rights that flow from terrorist offences.[250] The Court has also stated that the 'special intent or purpose of instilling "fear in the general population"' should be a 'fundamental element to distinguish conduct of a terrorist nature from conduct that is not, and without which the conduct would not meet the definition'.[251]

Certain soft law instruments have also sought to articulate contours of the definition of the physical conduct amounting to a terrorist act which in turn impacts speech-related offences. For example, the UN Special Rapporteur on terrorism has developed a model definition of terrorism as 'an action or attempted action' where the action constitutes 'intentional taking of hostages', is 'intended to cause death or serious bodily injury' or involves 'lethal or serious physical violence' and is done with the 'intention of (a) [p]rovoking a state or terror in the general public' or (b) '[c]ompelling a Government or international organization to do or abstain from doing something'.[252] While this offence does not incorporate speech, the Special Rapporteur on terrorism has also created a model incitement to terrorism offence, which 'must be limited to the incitement to conduct that is truly terrorist in nature' as defined in the model definition of terrorism.[253] Similarly, a number of UN and regional Special Rapporteurs on free speech adopted a 2008 joint declaration which held that the definition of terrorism 'at least as it applies in the context of restrictions of freedom of expression, should be restricted to violent crimes that are designed to advance an ideological, religious, political or organised criminal cause and to influence public authorities by inflicting terror on the public'.[254]

An overboard definition of terrorism is not the only manner in which terror laws may fail legality requirements: international bodies have also criticized laws that include only a vague causal link to terrorism on these grounds.[255] The UN High Commission for Human Rights has observed that 'it is important that vague terms of an uncertain scope such as *glorifying* or *promoting* terrorism are not used when restricting expression'.[256] The Human Rights Committee has stated that the offences of 'praising', 'glorifying' or 'justifying' terrorism should be 'clearly defined to ensure that they do not lead to unnecessary or disproportionate interference with freedom of expression'.[257] And the 2008 joint declaration of UN and regional Special Rapporteurs also criticized 'the criminalisation of speech' based on 'vague notions such as providing

---

[250] Ibid., §163.
[251] Ibid., §171.
[252] The action must also correspond to the 'definition of a serious offence in national law, enacted for the purpose of complying with international conventions and protocols relating to terrorism or with resolutions of the Security Council relating to terrorism' or '[a]ll elements of a serious crime defined by national law': UN Special Rapporteur Martin Scheinin, *Report on ten areas of best practices in countering terrorism* (2010) UN Doc. A/HRC/16/51, §28.
[253] Ibid., §§31–32. See s. III.3. (Necessity).
[254] UN Special Rapporteur, OSCE Representative on Freedom of the Media, OAS Special Rapporteur, ACmHPR Special Rapporteur on Freedom of Expression and Access to Information, *Joint Declaration on Defamation of Religions, and Anti-Terrorism and Anti-Extremism Legislation* (10 December 2008). See s. III.3. (Necessity) for how the Declaration addresses the requirements of causality and harm.
[255] See s. III.3.2.1. ('Glorification', 'justification' and 'apology' offences).
[256] OHCHR, *Human Rights, Terrorism and Counter-terrorism: Fact Sheet No. 32* (1 July 2008).
[257] HRC, General Comment No. 34 (2011), §46.

communications support to terrorism or extremism, the "glorification" or "promotion" of terrorism or extremism, and the mere repetition of statements by terrorists, which does not itself constitute incitement".[258]

1.2. Definition of extremism

International bodies have expressed concern regarding vague laws that criminalize 'extremism' without a definition or clear link to violence or hate speech. For example, the Human Rights Committee has critiqued Russian law's definition of 'extremist activity' on the basis that it 'is too vague to protect individuals ... against arbitrariness in its application' and 'to give notice to persons concerned' of 'actions for which they will be held criminally liable'.[259] The Committee has expressed a similar concern about the use of Uzbekistan's Counter-Extremism Act 'to unduly restrict' freedom of expression, on the basis of terms such as 'extremism', 'extremist activity' and 'extremist materials'.[260]

Similarly, the UN Special Rapporteur on terrorism has stated that criminalizing 'extremist' acts, '[a]bsent the qualifier' of 'violent extremism conducive to terrorism', may impermissibly 'encroach on human rights'.[261] According to the UN Special Rapporteur, the 'term "extremism" has no purchase in binding international legal standards and, when operative as a criminal legal category, is irreconcilable with the principle of legal certainty'.[262]

At the European level, the Venice Commission has noted that the term '"extremist" activities' is 'too broad, lack[s] clarity and may open the way to different interpretations'.[263] Similarly, the European Court has decried the breadth of these laws in a case concerning the forced dissolution of local Jehovah's Witness organizations in Russia, the banning of their publications and the prosecution of their members.[264] The Court observed that the banning of Jehovah's Witnesses' publications solely on the basis of non-violent attempts to persuade others of the virtues of their religion 'in the absence of any statements advocating violence, hatred or intimidation, was only possible because the definition of "extremism" in Russian law was overly broad and could be, and has been, applied to entirely peaceful forms of expression'.[265] It thus fell short of the 'prescribed by law' requirement.[266]

---

[258] UN Special Rapporteur; OSCE Representative on Freedom of the Media; OAS Special Rapporteur; ACmHPR Special Rapporteur on Freedom of Expression and Access to Information, *2008 Declaration on Defamation of Religions, and Anti-Terrorism and Anti-Extremism Legislation* (9 December 2008).
[259] HRC, *Concluding Observations, Russian Federation* (2003) UN Doc. CCPR/CO/79/RUS, §20; HRC, General Comment No. 34 (2011), §46.
[260] HRC, *Concluding Observations, Uzbekistan* (2020) UN Doc. CCPR/C/UZB/CO/5, §20.
[261] See UN Special Rapporteur M. Scheinin, *Report on human rights impacts of policies and practices aimed at preventing and countering violent extremism* (2020) UN Doc. A/HRC/43/46, §14.
[262] Ibid.
[263] Venice Commission, *Opinion on the Federal Law on Combating Extremist Activity* (Opinion no. 660/2011), 15–16 June 2012, §31. See also ECtHR, *Ibragimov v. Russia* (App. nos. 1413/08 & 28621/11), 28 August 2018, §85.
[264] ECtHR, *Taganrog LRO and Others v. Russia* (App. nos. 32401/10 & 19 others), 7 June 2022.
[265] Ibid., §201.
[266] Ibid.

1.3. Definition of public order

International human rights bodies have consistently found that vaguely worded offences related to the 'social order' or 'public order' fail the test that they must be 'provided by law'. For example the Working Group on Arbitrary Detention has expressed concern at the 'vague, imprecise or sweeping elements' in Chinese criminal laws such as 'disrupting social order', 'endangering national security', 'violating the unity and integrity of the State' and 'subverting public order'.[267] And the UN Special Rapporteur on the promotion and protection of the right to freedom of opinion and expression has noted that 'States often treat national security or public order as a label to legitimate any restriction'.[268]

Similarly, the Inter-American Commission has made clear that 'any definition of crimes related to national security' must be 'carefully drafted, in precise, express, and exhaustive terms, to ensure that it cannot be invoked to limit the exercise of the right to freedom of expression or punish criticism of the government and its authorities'.[269] For example, the Commission found Cuba's offence of 'collaborating with foreign media' with the objective of 'disrupting public order' or 'destabilizing the country' to be incompatible with the right to freedom of expression enshrined in the American Declaration.[270] The Commission noted that these criminal laws are a 'means to silence ideas and opinions because they discourage any type of criticism' and that they 'affect not only the individuals punished with their application by the Cuban courts, but also the entire Cuban society'.[271]

2. Legitimacy

The second requirement to validly penalize speech under article 19(3) of the ICCPR and regional free speech treaties is that the penalty pursues one of the 'legitimate aims' set out in international treaties.[272] To justify speech restrictions arising from terrorism and public order laws, states have relied on the aims of 'national security' and the protection of 'public order'.[273] For example, the European Court has noted that the legitimate aims of national security, territorial integrity or public safety, and the prevention

---

[267] WGAD, *Gulmira Imin v. China* (Opinion no. 29/2012), 29 August 2012, §30. See also WGAD, *Sokhet v. Cambodia* (Opinion no. 75/2021) 18 November 2021, §55 (involving a conviction for 'incitement to disrupt social order').

[268] UN Special Rapporteur D. Kaye, *Report on Promotion and protection of the right to freedom of opinion and expression* (2016) UN Doc. A/71/373, §19.

[269] IACmHR, *Roca Antúnez v. Cuba* (Case 12.127) 24 February 2018, §98.

[270] IACmHR. *Biscet v. Cuba* (Case 12.476), 21 October 2006, §210.

[271] Ibid., §209.

[272] See s. III. (International Legal Standards).

[273] See s. III. (International Legal Standards). See, e.g., ECtHR (GC), *Sürek v. Turkey (No. 1)* (App. no. 26682/95), 8 July 1999, §§51–52 (the Court finding Turkey's Prevention of Terrorism Act 1991 as having the legitimate aims of 'the protection of national security and territorial integrity and the prevention of disorder and crime'). States sometimes also refer to 'the rights of others': ECtHR (GC), *Sürek v. Turkey (No. 2)* (App. no. 24122/94), 8 July 1999, §29 (considering a Turkish law which criminalized revealing the identity of officials mandated to fight terrorism and thus protected them 'from being targeted for terrorist attack' as 'taken in the interest of national security and territorial integrity and for the protection of the rights of others').

of disorder or crime are 'frequently invoked in combination'.[274] And the European Court has recognized the connection between these aims and terror offences, noting that 'measures taken by national authorities to maintain national security and public safety [are] part of the fight against terrorism', and that it must 'ascertain whether a fair balance has been struck between the individual's fundamental right to freedom of expression and a democratic society's legitimate right to protect itself against the activities of terrorist organisations'.[275]

A state's assertion that national security interests are at stake will be given considerable, but not unlimited, deference by international bodies.[276] The Human Rights Committee requires states to point to the 'precise nature of [a] threat' rather than a 'general situation' of uncertainty.[277] Similarly, 'even where national security is at stake', the European Court has held that 'measures affecting fundamental human rights must be subject to some form of adversarial proceedings before an independent body competent to review the reasons for the decision'.[278]

The legitimate aim of 'public order' as a basis for penalizing speech differs slightly to both the aims of protecting national security and 'the rights of others' in that there are textual nuances between the ICCPR and its regional equivalents. Article 19 of the ICCPR allows for restrictions for the protection of 'public order (*ordre public*)', whereas article 10(2) of the European Convention instead provides for 'the prevention of disorder or crime' as well as 'national security or public safety'.[279] However, the drafting history of the European Convention does not suggest that the drafters intended to cast a broader net over the type of speech that can be penalized.[280] And the Human Rights Committee has considered 'public order' to encompass a wide range of limits to speech, including the additional aims expressly listed in article 10 of the European Convention.[281]

---

[274] ECtHR, Guide on Article 10 of the Convention, 31 August 2022, §539. See, e.g., ECtHR, *Stomakhin v. Russia* (App. no. 52273/07), 9 May 2018, §§84–87; ECtHR (GC), *Sürek v. Turkey (No. 1)* (App. no. 26682/95), 8 July 1999, §52; ECtHR (GC), *Sürek v. Turkey (No. 3)* (App. no. 24735/94), 8 July 1999, §31.

[275] ECtHR (GC), *Zana v. Turkey* (App. no. 18954/91), 25 November 1997, §55.

[276] See, e.g., ECtHR (GC), *Janowiec v. Russia* (App. nos. 55508/07 & 29520/09), 21 October 2013, §213; ECtHR, *Liu v. Russia (No. 2)* (App. no. 29157/09), 26 July 2011, §85. See also ch. 5 (Speech Related to National Security: Espionage and Official Secrets Laws), s. III.1. (International Standards Related to Speech Affecting National Security).

[277] HRC, *Park v. Republic of Korea* (Comm. no. 628/1995), 20 October 1998, §10.3 (finding that a reference 'to the general situation in the country and the threat posed by "North Korean communists" was insufficiently precise'). See also, e.g., HRC, *Shin v. Republic of Korea* (Comm. no. 926/2000), 16 March 2004, §7.3 (holding that while the national courts 'identified a national security basis as justification' for the confiscation of the artist's painting and his conviction under the National Security Law, 'the State party must demonstrate in specific fashion the precise nature of the threat to any of the enumerated purposes caused by the author's conduct'); WGAD, *Xiyue Wang v. Iran* (Opinion no. 52/2018), 23 August 2018, §75 (holding that the Government 'did not establish a clear connection between this activity and contemporary national security interests provided under article 19(3)' of the ICCPR).

[278] ECtHR (GC), *Janowiec v. Russia* (App. nos. 55508/07 & 29520/09), 21 October 2013, §213.

[279] ICCPR Art. 19(3), ECHR Art. 10(2). Article 13 of the American Convention references 'public order' but this is not followed by the French term '*ordre publique*' in brackets: ACHR Art. 13(2)(b).

[280] See ch. 1 (Introduction), s. II.1.1.1. (Abuses by the state). Cf. ECtHR (GC), *Perinçek v. Switzerland* (App. no. 27510/08), 15 October 2015, §§146–147 (where the ECtHR compared the meaning of 'prevention of disorder' in articles 8(2),10(2) and 11(2) of the ECHR to the 'maintenance of *ordre public*' as provided by articles 2(3) of Protocol No. 4 to the ECHR).

[281] See HRC, *Lovell v. Australia* (Comm. no. 920/2000), 24 March 2003, §9.4; HRC, General Comment No. 34 (2011), §31 ('Contempt of court proceedings relating to forms of expression may be tested against the public

The Human Rights Committee has so far avoided providing an explicit definition of 'public order', with Committee members 'understandably reluctant to erect strict definitions that might hamper legitimate future application of Article 19, paragraph 3' of the ICCPR.[282] But both the Human Rights Committee and the European Court have considered protecting 'public order' or the 'prevention of disorder and crime' as legitimate aims that extend beyond the realm of protecting national security, encompassing for example the guaranteeing of fair elections,[283] speech-making in public places[284] and contempt of court proceedings.[285]

Unlike its European counterpart, the Inter-American Court of Human Rights has provided an explicit definition of 'public order' and its basic parameters. In its advisory opinion on whether Costa Rica's compulsory licensing of media associations violated the American Convention on Human Rights, the Court held that the term 'public order' should be understood as constituting 'the conditions that assure the normal and harmonious functioning of institutions based on a coherent system of values and principles'.[286] Two foundational principles were articulated: first, that 'public order' may 'under no circumstances be involved as a means of denying a right guaranteed by the Convention or to impair or deprive it of its true content', and secondly, that public order restrictions 'must be subjected to an interpretation that is strictly limited to' the 'just demands' of 'a democratic society', which 'takes account of the need to balance the competing interests involved and the need to preserve the object and purpose of the Convention'.[287]

Similarly, the Inter-American Commission has noted that:

---

order (*ordre public*) ground'); HRC, *Agazade and Jafarov v. Azerbaijan* (Comm. no. 2205/2012) 27 October 2016, §§7.4–7.5; HRC, *Aleksandrov v. Belarus* (Comm. no. 1933/2010) 24 July 2014, §7.4 (holding that Belarus had not explained how the actions of a protestor 'would have violated the rights and freedoms of others or would have posed a threat to public safety or public order (*ordre public*)').

[282] See M. O'Flaherty, 'Freedom of Expression: Article 19 of the International Covenant on Civil and Political Rights and the Human Rights Committee's General Comment No 34' (2012) 12(4) *Human Rights Law Review* 627, 652.
[283] HRC, *Kim v. Republic of Korea* (Comm. no. 968/2001), 27 July 2005, §§4.1, 8.3 (where the Human Rights Committee considered that a conviction and fine against a journalist for publishing opinion polls too close to an election did not violate article 19 of the ICCPR, noting Korea's argument that 'the guarantee of fair elections is an integral part of public order in a democratic society').
[284] See ch. 3(Hate Speech), s. III.2.2. (Legitimacy). Cf. ECtHR (GC), *Perinçek v. Switzerland* (App. no. 27510/08), 15 October 2015, §§13, 153–154 (finding that calling the Armenian genocide a 'lie' could not be restricted on the basis of preventing disorder).
[285] See, e.g., HRC, General Comment No. 34 (2011), §31. See also ECtHR, *Karapetyan v. Armenia* (App. no. 59001/08), 17 November 2016, §49 (where restricting civil servants' freedom to engage in political activities was considered necessary 'to ensure the consolidation and maintenance of democracy'); ECtHR, *Nix v. Germany* (App. no. 35285/16), 13 March 2018, §§39, 44 (public order laws which require that persons using Nazi symbols clearly distance themselves from Nazi ideology were found to be legitimate on the basis that they 'prevent the revival of prohibited organisations' and to 'maintain political peace').
[286] IACtHR, *Compulsory Membership in an Association Prescribed by Law for the Practice of Journalism*, Advisory Opinion OC-5/85 (Series A, no. 5), 13 November 1985, §64. The Court also recognized the 'difficulty inherent in the attempt of defining with precision the concepts of 'public order' and 'general welfare'' (§67), with the result that it may consider its own definition to be an imprecise one.
[287] Ibid., §67. Applying these principles, the Inter-American Court held that the public order may justify licensing of other professions but 'cannot be invoked in the case of journalism because they would have the effect of permanently depriving those who are not members of the right to make full use of the rights that Article 13 of the Convention grants to each individual', hence violating 'the basic principles of a democratic public order on which the Convention itself is based': §76.

for any penalty to be imposed in the name of defending public order (understood as public safety, health and morals), it is necessary to demonstrate that the concept of 'order' being defended is not authoritarian; rather, it must be a democratic order, understood as the existence of structural conditions for all persons, without discrimination, to be able to exercise their rights freely, vigorously, and without fear of being punished for doing so.[288]

Finally, the Siracusa Principles, developed by experts and adopted by the UN Economic and Social Council, provide soft law guidance on the interpretation of 'public order' under article 19(3), holding that this term 'may be defined as the sum of rules which ensure the functioning of society or the set of fundamental principles on which society is founded. Respect for human rights is part of public order'.[289]

3. Necessity

The third arm of the tripartite test under article 19(3) of the ICCPR and regional free speech treaties is whether a penalty for speech is 'necessary', and most cases that come before international and regional bodies turn on this issue.[290] Central elements to assess the necessity of a restriction to speech are: (a) the type of harm arising from speech;[291] (b) the causal link between speech and harm;[292] and (c) the intent of the speaker.[293] The requirement of 'necessity' also encompasses the proportionality of penalties, as any restrictive measure 'must be the least intrusive instrument amongst those which might achieve their protective function' and penalties must be 'proportionate to the interest to be protected'.[294] In addition, international human rights law recognizes a number of defences or exceptions to liability for speech that are of particular importance for terrorism and public order laws. These include whether speech relates to the public interest,[295] and the defences of truth and opinion.[296]

3.1. Harm
Under international standards, speech cannot be restricted unless a state can demonstrate a specific type of harm that may arise from it.[297] As articulated by the Human Rights Committee '[w]hen a State ... invokes a legitimate ground for [a] restriction of

---

[288] IACmHR, *Roca Antúnez v. Cuba* (Case 12.127), 24 February 2018, §103.
[289] Siracusa Principles. The Siracusa Principles were formally included in the work of the UN Commission on Human Rights at its 41st session. See also ch. 5 (Speech Related to National Security: Espionage and Official Secrets), s. III.1. (International Standards Related to Speech Affecting National Security).
[290] See, e.g., ECtHR, Guide on Article 10 of the Convention, 31 August 2022, §61; s. III.1.1. (Definition of terrorism) (discussing how few cases turn on the issue of legality).
[291] See s. III.3.1. (Harm).
[292] See s. III.3.2. (Causal link between speech and harm).
[293] See s. III.3.3. (Intent).
[294] HRC, General Comment No. 34 (2011), §34.
[295] See s. III.4.1. (Public interest).
[296] See s. III.4.3. (Truth and opinion).
[297] The causal link that is required is discussed at s. III.3.2. (Causal link between speech and harm).

freedom of expression, it must demonstrate in a specific and individualized fashion the precise nature of the threat' posed by the speech.[298]

But international and regional bodies differ slightly in the type of harm that will meet this threshold, particularly what harms beyond violence may qualify. Speech that incites violence can clearly be penalized, even through criminal sanctions (which terrorism laws typically apply).[299] For instance, the Working Group on Arbitrary Detention has held that 'expression ... cannot be punished as such, if there are no violent acts committed ... and there is no factual proof of resort to or *advocacy of violence*'.[300] And incitement to violence is one of the 'serious and very exceptional circumstances' in which the African Court will consider custodial sentences for speech to be compatible with freedom of expression.[301] The Inter-American Commission has also declared penalties for speech can be justifiable if a speaker had intent to promote 'lawless violence'.[302]

The European Court has also found that 'incitement to violence' is a prohibited harm and interprets this broadly to encompass implied rather than just express calls for such harm.[303] As the Court has found, states 'cannot rely on protecting territorial integrity and national security, maintaining public order and safety, or preventing crime' as a basis for restricting speech unless the speech constitutes 'incitement to violence'.[304] But according to the European Court, such incitement need not necessarily mean expressly 'advocat[ing] recourse to violent action or bloody revenge'; it can also mean words that can 'be interpreted as likely to encourage violence by expressing deep-seated and irrational hatred towards identified persons'.[305] Indeed, in the case of terrorist offences, the Court 'accepts that disseminating messages in praise of the perpetrator of an attack, denigrating the victims, calling for the financing of terrorist organizations or other similar conduct may constitute acts of incitement to terrorist violence' and 'Article 10 does not prohibit any restrictions as such' to this speech.[306] And the Court considers

---

[298] HRC, General Comment No. 34 (2011), §35, citing HRC, *Shin v. Republic of Korea* (Comm. no. 926/2000), 16 March 2004. See also HRC, *Ross v. Canada* (Comm. no. 736/1997), 18 October 2000, §11.5. See s. III.3.2. (Causal link between speech and harm).

[299] However, international and regional bodies will still holistically consider whether a restriction was necessary and proportionate to advance a legitimate aim.

[300] WGAD, *Dolma Kyab v. China* (Opinion no. 36/2007), 30 November 2007, §15 (writer and teacher sentenced to 10 years' imprisonment for allegedly seeking to publish separatist content regarding Tibet, including the number and location of Chinese military installations). On a number of occasions the Working Group has found a violation of article 19 if 'no evidence' is provided that a speaker 'incited acts of violence' or was 'involved in any violence or force': see, e.g., WGAD, *Al-Hawali v. Saudi Arabia* (Opinion no. 29/2023), 3 April 2023, §32; WGAD, *Van Kham v. Viet Nam* (Opinion no. 13/2022), 31 March 2022, §74; WGAD, *Hammouri v. Israel* (Opinion no. 13/2023), 29 March 2023, §61.

[301] ACtHPR, *Konaté v. Burkina Faso* (App. no. 4/2013), 5 December 2014, §165.

[302] IACmHR, *Report on the Violence Against LGBTI Persons* (2015) OEA/Ser.L/V/II. Doc.36/15 Rev.2, §235. See s. III.3.3 (Intent).

[303] See, e.g., ECtHR, *Rouillan v. France* (App. no. 28000/19), 23 June 2022, §71; see s. III.3.2.1. ('Glorification', 'justification' and 'apology' offences).

[304] ECtHR, *Dmitriyevskiy v. Russia* (App. no. 42168/06), 3 October 2017, §100. See also ECtHR, *Mehmet Hasan Altan v. Turkey* (App. no. 13237/17), 20 March 2018, §209.

[305] ECtHR, *Dmitriyevskiy v. Russia* (App. no. 42168/06), 3 October 2017, §100. See also ECtHR, *Mehmet Hasan Altan v. Turkey* (App. no. 13237/17), 20 March 2018, §209.

[306] ECtHR, *Yavuz and Yaylalı v. Turkey* (App. no. 12606/11), 17 December 2013, §51.

incitement to violence to be only one of 'several factors' that the Court will assess when determining whether penalties imposed on speech are 'necessary'.[307]

Conversely, the Court has also found, in applying its incitement to violence test, that even when speech '[t]aken literally' 'might be construed as inciting readers to hatred, revolt or the use of violence', penalties can be disproportionate in certain contexts, including if the speech is 'artistic in nature'.[308] For instance, the Court considered a case in which a poet was convicted and sentenced to over a year in prison for engaging in 'propaganda' by disseminating poems that called for self-sacrifice for 'Kurdistan' and included some 'aggressive passages directed at Turkish authorities'.[309] Even though the Court accepted that the poems might amount to literal incitement to 'hatred, revolt and the use of violence', it considered that poetry, as a medium, is 'addressed to a very small audience', which 'limited' the poems' 'potential impact' on national security and public order. The Court concluded that 'even though some of the passages from the poems seem very aggressive in tone and to call for the use of violence, the Court considers that the fact that they were artistic in nature and of limited impact made them less a call to an uprising than an expression of deep distress in the face of a difficult political situation'.[310]

Beyond incitement to 'violence', international and regional bodies have found that incitement to 'armed resistance', 'commission of criminal offences',[311] 'serious disturbances' of public order[312] and 'lawless violence or any similar action' are harms that can also justify criminal penalties.[313] For example, in a case when a politician received a one-year suspended sentence for a keynote speech paying tribute to a former member of the terrorist organization ETA, the European Court found a violation of article 10 because the speech 'read as a whole did not incite the use of violence or *armed resistance*'.[314] The Inter-American Commission found a violation of freedom of expression when Cuban citizens disseminated documents critical of the state but these were not

---

[307] These include 'whether the statements were made against a tense political or social background' and 'the manner in which the statements were made, and their capacity—direct or indirect—to lead to harmful consequences'. ECtHR (GC), *Perinçek v. Switzerland* (App. no. 27510/08), 15 October 2015, §§204–208. However, in some cases the Court has described this as an 'essential element': see, e.g., ECtHR, *Erkizia Almandoz v. Spain* (App. no. 5869/17), 22 June 2021, §39.

[308] ECtHR (GC), *Karataş v. Turkey* (App. no. 23168/94), 8 July 1999, §§49–52.

[309] Ibid., §49.

[310] Ibid., §52. Compare ECtHR (GC), *Zana v. Turkey* (App. no. 18954/91), 25 November 1997, §§26, 58–61 (reaching the opposite conclusion in a case where a mayor was sentenced to 12 months' imprisonment based on the type of speech and its timing, given the 'extreme tension' in the region).

[311] HRC, *Rabbae v. Netherlands* (Comm. no. 2124/2011) (Individual Opinion (Concurring) of Committee members Sarah Cleveland and Mauro Politi), §7. This decision relates to hate speech. See ch. 3 (Hate Speech), s. III.2.3.1. (Harm).

[312] See, e.g., ECtHR, *Leroy v. France* (App. no. 36109/03), 2 October 2008, §45 (finding no violation of article 10 on the basis that speech 'elicited reactions which *could have* stirred up violence' and 'could have affected public order in the region' (emphasis supplied); HRC, *Marchant Reyes v. Chile* (Comm. no. 2627/2015), 7 November 2017, §§2.7, 7.5 (finding a violation of article 19 where Chile could not demonstrate 'a reasonable clarification of the existence of a real and specific threat to public order'): see s. III.3.2. (Causal link between speech and harm).

[313] IACmHR, *Report on the Violence Against LGBTI Persons* (2015) OEA/Ser.L/V/II. Doc.36/15 Rev.2, §235. The question of harm is also closely linked to the legitimate aim that a state is pursuing, such as protection of national security, territorial integrity and public order: see s. III.2. (Legitimacy).

[314] ECtHR, *Erkizia Almandoz v. Spain* (App. no. 5869/17), 22 June 2021, §§46. The politican was a leading member of the Basque independence movement, and also received a seven-year ban from office for the crime of 'praise or justification' of terrorism. See also ECtHR, *Üçdağ v. Turkey* (App. no. 23314/19), 31 August 2021, §85.

found to 'pose a certain and credible threat of a potentially *serious disturbance of the basic conditions for the operation of democratic institutions*'.[315] The Commission considered that it would be insufficient to invoke 'mere conjecture about potential disturbances of order ... that do not clearly pose a reasonable risk of serious disturbances' and then defined such disturbances as 'lawless violence'.[316] This is consistent with article 13(5) of the American Convention, which requires states to penalize speech that constitutes 'incitement to lawless violence *or to any other similar action*'.[317] Though 'similar action' is not defined, the drafting history of the treaty suggests that the harm should be comparable in severity to violence.[318]

A further type of harm that can make a penalty 'necessary' under international human rights law is incitement to a serious criminal offence. The harm standard proposed by members of the Human Rights Committee in the context of hate speech incorporates both incitement to violence and '*the commission of criminal offences*'.[319] The UN and the Council of Europe have suggested that the appropriate test is that speech 'causes a danger' that 'terrorist offences ... may be committed'.[320] The UN Secretary-General also defined the appropriate parameters of incitement as 'a direct call to engage in terrorism'.[321] And the UN Special Rapporteur has observed that the threshold for inchoate terror crimes should be a 'reasonable probability that the expression in question would succeed in inciting a *terrorist act*'.[322]

However, international and regional bodies have not consistently required the high bar of incitement to violence or criminal offences. Incitement to 'hatred' has also been sufficient to curtail speech in some cases assessing the application of laws on terrorism.[323] For example, despite decisions by the Working Group on Arbitrary Detention that have suggested a requirement of 'proof of resort to or advocacy of violence', the

---

[315] IACmHR, *Roca Antúnez v. Cuba* (Case 12.127), 2 February 2018, §107 (emphasis added). See s. III.3.2. (Causal link between speech and harm).

[316] IACmHR, *Roca Antúnez v. Cuba* (Case 12.127), 24 February 2018, §107. See also IACmHR, *Biscet v. Cuba* (Case 12.476), 21 October 2006. Cf. ECtHR (GC), *Sürek v. Turkey (No. 4)* (App. no. 24762/94), 8 July 1999, Concurring Judgment of Judge Bonello (freedom of expression 'does not permit a state to forbid or proscribe advocacy of the use of force except when such advocacy is directed to inciting or producing *imminent lawlessness* and is likely to incite or produce such action' (emphasis added)): see s. III.3.2. (Causal link between speech and harm).

[317] ACHR Art. 13(5) (emphasis added), see ch. 3 (Hate Speech).

[318] Inter-American specialized conference on human rights, San José, Costa Rica, Minutes of the second plenary session (22 November 1969) Doc. 86, US Statement, 444. The original provision provided for violence as well as 'discrimination' and 'hostility', but the US delegate recommended that this wording be replaced with 'similar action' to ensure consistency with First Amendment jurisprudence. In addition the Spanish version of article 13(5) provides for 'similar *illegal action*' ('acción ilegal similar').

[319] HRC, *Rabbae v. Netherlands* (Comm. no. 2124/2011) Individual Opinion (concurring) of Committee members Sarah Cleveland and Mauro Politi, §7 (emphasis added).

[320] See s. III.3.2. (Causal link between speech and harm). COE Convention on the Prevention of Terrorism (2005) Art. 5; UN Special Rapporteur on terrorism Martin Scheinin, *Report on Ten areas of best practices in countering terrorism* (2010) UN Doc. A/HRC/16/51.

[321] UN Secretary-General, *Report on The Protection of human rights and fundamental freedoms while countering terrorism* (2008) UN Doc. A/63/337, §61. This test also requires that the speech occur 'in the context in which the call is directly causally responsible for increasing the actual likelihood of a *terrorist act* occurring (see s. III.3.2. (Causal link between speech and harm) and that it occur 'with the intention that this will promote terrorism' s. III.3.3. (Intent).

[322] UN Special Rapporteur on terrorism, *Impact of measures to address terrorism and violent extremism on civic space and the rights of civil society actors and human rights defenders* (2019) UN Doc. A/HRC/40/52, §37 (emphasis added).

[323] See ch. 3 (Hate Speech), s. III.2.3.1. (Harm).

Working Group has also found that incitement to 'hatred or violence' was sufficient.[324] In one case, an Egyptian blogger who encouraged attendance at a demonstration against civilians being tried in Egyptian military courts was convicted of a public order offence and sentenced to five years' imprisonment.[325] The Working Group held that 'a vague and general reference to public order ... is insufficient to convince the Working Group that the restrictions on the freedom of expression by way of deprivation of liberty are necessary'.[326] It emphasized instead that 'the peaceful, non-violent expression or manifestation of one's opinion ... *if it does not constitute incitement to national, racial or religious hatred or violence*, remains within the boundaries of the freedom of expression'.[327] The African Court also considers 'public incitement to hatred' to fall within the 'exceptional circumstances' that may warrant custodial sentences for speech.[328]

Like other international bodies, the European Court has in certain circumstances qualified incitement to 'hatred' as being sufficient to make a penalty for speech 'necessary'. But the Court has gone beyond this, and in a number of recent decisions adopted as its 'essential question' or 'salient issue' whether speech 'could ... be seen as a call for violence, *hatred or intolerance*'.[329] Although the parameters of the concept of 'intolerance' are more frequently addressed in the context of hateful speech rather than terrorism or public order,[330] it is clear that the Court's conception of hatred and intolerance means that speech does not need to 'involve an explicit call for an act of violence, or other criminal acts' for a penalty to be considered 'necessary'.[331] Instead, as the Court has put it, a broader array of 'expression that promotes or justifies violence, *hatred, xenophobia or another form of intolerance* cannot normally claim protection'.[332] This lower harm threshold—combined with a lack of a strict causation requirement linking the speech to objectively possible or actual harm—has resulted in a disconnect between the European Court's approach to hate speech and speech-based terrorism laws in comparison to other international bodies.[333]

A further factor that sets the Court's jurisprudence apart is that in a small number of cases terrorism-related speech has been found to be unprotected under article 17 of

---

[324] WGAD, *Dolma Kyab v. China* (Opinion no. 36/2007), 30 November 2007, §15. See also WGAD, *Umbetaliyev v. Kazakhstan* (Opinion no. 33/2021), 8 September 2021, §43.

[325] WGAD, *Alaa Ahmed Seif al Islam Abd El Fattah v. Egypt* (Opinion no. 6/2016), 19 April 2016. The blogger was originally sentenced in absentia to 15 years' penal servitude, which was annulled and he was retried and sentenced to five years' penal servitude: §26.

[326] Ibid., §48.

[327] Ibid., §§48–49 (emphasis added). Cf. ch. 3 (Hate Speech), s. VI.4. (Recommendations) (recommending that hatred on the basis of sexual orientation, gender, political affiliation or other protected characteristics should be penalized in the same manner as discrimination based on race, ethnicity or religion).

[328] ACtHPR, *Konaté v. Burkina Faso* (App. no. 4/2013), 5 December 2014, §165.

[329] ECtHR, Guide on Article 10 of the Convention, 31 August 2022, §§554, 557 (emphasis added); ECtHR, *Ibragimov v. Russia* (App. nos. 1413/08 & 28621/11), 28 August 2018, §98. See also, e.g., ECtHR (GC), *Perinçek v. Switzerland* (App. no. 27510/08), 15 October 2015, §206; ECtHR, *Gündüz v. Turkey* (App. no. 35071/97), 4 December 2003, §§ 48, 51; ECtHR, *Féret v. Belgium* (App. no. 15615/07), 16 July 2009, §64.

[330] See ch. 3 (Hate Speech), s. III.2.2. (Case Study: International Standards on Blasphemy Laws), s. III.2.3.1. (Harm), and s. VI.3.3. (Recommendations).

[331] ECtHR, *Ibragimov v. Russia* (App. nos. 1413/08 & 28621/11), 28 August 2018, §94. See also ECtHR, *Vejdeland v. Sweden* (App. no. 1813/07), 9 February 2012, §55.

[332] ECtHR (GC), *Perinçek v. Switzerland* (App. no. 27510/08), 15 October 2015, §230 (emphasis added).

[333] See s. III.3.2. (Causal link between speech and harm).

the Convention. Article 17 provides that '[n]othing in th[e] Convention may be interpreted as implying ... any right to engage in any activity ... aimed at the destruction of any of the rights and freedoms' set out in the treaty. This means that in some cases speech is not analysed using the balancing exercise provided by article 10(2) but held instead to be essentially unprotectable as a threshold matter.[334] Article 17 has therefore effectively operated as a guillotine provision which overrides the Court's usual analysis of necessity and proportionality.[335]

The Court has construed article 17 as preventing 'individuals or groups with totalitarian aims from exploiting ... the principles enunciated in the Convention'.[336] And the Court has, on this basis, refused to consider claims involving 'speech [that] is incompatible with the values' of the Convention or 'contrary to' its 'text and spirit'.[337] Although the Court has stated that article 17 sets a 'high threshold'[338] and should only be applied 'on an exceptional basis and in extreme cases',[339] the Court has found a number of hate speech cases inadmissible on this basis.[340] And the Court has found 'terrorism' to be one of the values that is contrary to the Convention's text and spirit.[341]

Although article 17 has sweeping reach—and could potentially apply to all cases involving terrorism-related speech that incites 'hatred' as well as violence—it has been applied by the Court in a relatively small number of cases involving terrorist-related speech. For instance, the Court considered a case in which a Danish television company was convicted, fined and deprived of its licence to broadcast on the basis it promoted the PKK's terror operation over a four-year period.[342] The Court observed that the 'decisive point when assessing whether statements, verbal or non-verbal, are removed from the protection of Article 10 by Article 17' is whether statements are directed 'against the Convention's underlying values, for example by stirring up hatred or violence'.[343] Applying this principle to the company's broadcasting, the Court attached 'significant weight' to the Danish court's finding that the company's 'one-sided coverage

---

[334] See ECtHR, 'Factsheet—Hate Speech', September 2023, 5.
[335] See ch. 3 (Hate Speech), s. III.2. (Discretionary Restrictions on Hate Speech).
[336] ECtHR, *Hizb Ut-Tahrir v. Germany* (App. no. 31098/08), 12 June 2012, §72, citing ECtHR (GC), *Paksas v. Lithuania* (App. no. 34932/04), 6 January 2011, §§87–88.
[337] ECtHR, *Ivanov v. Russia* (App. no. 35222/04), 20 February 2007, §1; ECtHR, *Roj TV A/S v. Denmark* (App. no. 24683/14), 17 April 2018, §30.
[338] ECtHR, *Lilliendahl v. Iceland* (App. no. 29297/18), 12 May 2020, §§25–26.
[339] Ibid., §25. See also ECtHR (GC), *Perinçek v. Switzerland* (App. no. 27510/08), 15 October 2015, §114.
[340] See ch. 3 (Hate Speech); s. III.2.2. (Legitimacy). See, e.g., ECtHR, *Ivanov v. Russia* (App. no. 35222/04), 20 February 2007; ECtHR, *Norwood v. United Kingdom* (App. no. 23131/03), 16 November 2004; ECtHR, *Belkacem v. Belgium* (App. no. 34367/14), 27 June 2017.
[341] See UK Department of Digital, Culture, Media & Sport and Department of Science, Innovation & Technology, 'Policy paper: Online Safety Bill: European Convention on Human Rights Memorandum' (18 January 2023) ('The [European] Court has held that content expressing support for terrorism does not, by virtue of Article 17, attract the protection afforded by Article 10', citing ECtHR, *Roj TV A/S v. Denmark* (App. no. 24683/14), 17 April 2018. See also ECtHR, *Orban v. France* (App. no. 20985/05), 15 January 2009, §35 (providing that 'statements unequivocally aimed at justifying war crimes such as torture or summary executions' violate Art.10). In some cases, the Court has involved a value related to combatting terrorism: the 'peaceful settlement of international conflicts and the sanctity of human life': see ECtHR, *Kasymakhunov and Saybatalov v. Russia* (App nos. 26261/05 & 26377/06), 14 March 2013, §106.
[342] ECtHR, *Roj TV A/S v. Denmark* (App. no. 24683/14), 17 April 2018. The company was convicted under article 114e of the Danish Penal Code which penalized 'any person who promotes ... the activities' of a terrorist person or group and fined approximately 670,000 EUR.
[343] ECtHR, *Roj TV A/S v. Denmark* (App. no. 24683/14), 17 April 2018, §31.

with repetitive incitement to participate in fights and actions' amounted 'to propaganda for the PKK'.[344] The Danish court found that the channel 'unilaterally showed the views of the PKK' without any alternative voices or any 'effort on behalf of the applicant company to distance itself' from the inciting language.[345] As the programmes included 'incitement to violence and support for terrorist activity' they were found not to attract the protection of article 10.[346]

Similarly, the Court found that article 17 applied when German authorities confiscated assets and shut down activities of Hizb Ut-Tahrir, a self-described 'global Islamic political party and/or religious society' that advocated for the overthrow of governments and the installation of an Islamic Caliphate.[347] Although the group argued that it 'did not accept violence to achieve its religious and political objectives',[348] the Court observed that German authorities had concluded—based on statements published in magazines, flyers and transcripts of public statements—that Hizb Ut-Tahiri had 'called for the violent destruction' of the State of Israel and for the 'banishment and killing of its inhabitants'.[349] On that basis, the Court considered that article 10 could not protect the group's speech.[350] The Court came to the same conclusion in a different case concerning two members of Hizb Ut-Tahrir who were 'engaged in spreading its ideology by distributing its literature and recruiting new members'.[351] In that case the Court argued that Hizb ut-Tahrir had published 'anti-Semitic and pro-violence statements', in particular 'repeated statements justifying suicide attacks in which civilians are killed'.[352] This was considered 'clearly contrary to the values of the Convention, notably the commitment to the peaceful settlement of international conflicts and the sanctity of human life'.[353]

And when a Russian citizen was convicted and sentenced to one year imprisonment for disseminating 1,500 communist newspapers, the European Court also found that article 17 applied.[354] The Court observed that the articles in the newspapers 'went far beyond simply criticising the current President' of Ukraine and instead 'openly called for an armed civil conflict with the country aimed at the seizure of State power by the proletariat'.[355] In the Court's opinion, such speech 'constituted a threat to public order and to democracy which is a fundamental feature of the European public order', thereby running 'counter to the fundamental ideas and values underpinning the Convention'.[356]

---

[344] Ibid., §46.
[345] Ibid., §9. The channel was also financed in part by the PKK: §46.
[346] Ibid., §47. See also ECtHR, *Belkacem v. Belgium* (App. no. 34367/14), 27 June 2017, §§33–37.
[347] ECtHR, *Hizb Ut-Tahrir v. Germany* (App. no. 31098/08), 12 June 2012.
[348] Ibid., §67.
[349] Ibid., §§73–75.
[350] Ibid., §§73–78. The Court found that Arts 9, 10 and 11 did not apply to protect the group.
[351] ECtHR, *Kasymakhunov and Saybatalov v. Russia* (App. nos. 26261/05 & 26377/06), 14 March 2013, §106.
[352] Ibid., §106.
[353] Ibid., §106.
[354] ECtHR, *Romanov v. Ukraine* (App. no. 63782/11), 16 July 2020. The applicant, who conceded he had manufactured and detonated an explosive device, was sentenced to a total of 10 years' imprisonment for dissemination of printed material calling for an armed revolt against the constitutional order and a range of other offences, including terrorism and unlawful possession of firearms and explosives: §§27–44.
[355] Ibid., §163.
[356] Ibid., §164.

3.2. Causal link between speech and harm

In the terrorism context, numerous national laws criminalize speech based on its content, without any requirement as to its actual or potential impact.[357] Such laws violate international standards, which provide that states must demonstrate a causal link between speech and specific types of harm before speech can be restricted.[358]

The Human Rights Committee requires states to establish a 'direct and immediate connection between the expression and the threat' before speech can be penalized.[359] For example, when Chilean police removed a public work of art depicting human rights abuses in Santiago on the grounds that this was necessary to 'prevent[] potential disruption to public order arising out of the burning' of the work, the Committee observed that such harm was 'merely speculative' and found that Chile had violated article 19 of the ICCPR as it had not provided 'a reasonable clarification of the existence of a real and specific threat to public order'.[360]

The Working Group on Arbitrary Detention also requires a causal link between speech and harm, though its exact parameters are unclear. The Working Group has referenced the Human Rights Committee's causation standard in a number of national security cases.[361] In other decisions, it has required a state to show 'cause and effect' between speech and harm. For instance, the Working Group considered a case involving a Venezuelan politician from an opposition group who was charged with property damage and incitement to public disorder after speaking at a protest where violence broke out.[362] The Working Group found a violation of his freedom of speech on the basis that there was 'no evidence to suggest that there is a cause and effect relationship between the organization of a political demonstration, the speech made in the course of that demonstration and the deaths, injuries and material damage that occurred on the fringes of the demonstration'.[363]

Although Inter-American and African regional bodies have had limited opportunities to consider causation in the context of terrorism, they have adopted high causation requirements for other types of speech.[364] The Inter-American Commission has, for example, found a violation of the right to free speech in the American Convention when Cuban citizens who disseminated documents critical of the state were convicted

---

[357] See s. II.1.1.3. (Harm).

[358] For an analysis of which harms qualify, see s. III.3.1. (Harm).

[359] HRC, General Comment No. 34 (2011), §35, citing HRC, *Shin v. Republic of Korea* (Comm. no. 926/2000), 16 March 2004. See also HRC, *Ross v. Canada* (Comm. no. 736/1997), 18 October 2000, §11.5.

[360] HRC, *Marchant Reyes v. Chile* (Comm. no. 2627/2015), 7 November 2017, §§7.5, 9. The Committee ordered the police to locate the banners and return them and publicly acknowledge the violation of rights: §9.

[361] See ch. 5 (Espionage and Official Secrets Law), s. III.4.2.2. (Causation). See, e.g., WGAD, *Gulmira Imin v. China* (Opinion no. 29/2012), 29 August 2012, §28; WGAD, *Ziyuan Ren v. China* (Opinion no. 55/2014), 21 November 2014, §28; WGAD, *Zhen Jianghua v. China* (Opinion no. 20/2019), 1 May 2019, §71.

[362] He was also charged with incitement to arson: WGAD, *López Mendoza v. Venezuela* (Opinion no. 26/2014), 26 August 2014, §32.

[363] WGAD, *López Mendoza v. Venezuela* (Opinion no. 26/2014), 26 August 2014, §54 (the WGAD also noted that the demonstration had 'already ended'). Although this reasoning suggests that the Working Group requires actual violence to have occurred before it will find a restriction to speech valid, in other decisions the Group has indicated that 'incitement to hatred' may be sufficient cause to restrict speech: see s. III.3.1. (Harm) (discussing WGAD, *Alaa Ahmed Seif al Islam Abd El Fattah v. Egypt* (Opinion no. 6/2016), 19 April 2016).

[364] See ch. 3 (Hate Speech), s. II.1.2. (Harm) and ch. 5 (Speech Related to National Security: Espionage and Official Secrets Laws), s. III.4.2. (Harm).

of sedition. The Commission noted that any alleged 'violation of public order ... must arise' from speech or other causes that 'pose a certain and credible threat of a potentially serious disturbance of the basic conditions for the operation of democratic institutions'.[365] And it considered it insufficient to invoke 'mere conjecture about potential disturbances of order, or hypothetical circumstances derived from the authorities' interpretations of facts that do not clearly pose a reasonable risk of serious disturbances ("lawless violence")'.[366] Similarly, the OAS Rapporteur has declared that, in order to justify restrictions on freedom of expression to protect the rights of others, those rights must 'be clearly harmed or threatened'.[367] A speaker must have had both intent to 'promot[e] lawless violence or ... similar action' and 'the *capacity* to achieve this objective and create an *actual risk* of harm'.[368] Likewise, the Declaration of Principles of Freedom of Expression and Access to Information in Africa requires 'a close causal link between the risk of harm and the expression' to justify penalties on speech imposed on public order or national security grounds.[369]

The UN and the Council of Europe have suggested that the appropriate causation test is that speech 'causes a danger' that 'terrorist offences ... may be committed'.[370] The Council of Europe's Convention on the Prevention of Terrorism provides for the offence of 'public provocation to commit terrorist offences', prohibiting 'the distribution, or otherwise making available, of a message to the public, with the intent to incite the commission of a terrorist offence' where such speech '*whether or not directly advocating* terrorist offences, *causes a danger that* one or more such offences may be committed'.[371] The Explanatory Report of the Convention further explains that 'when considering whether such danger is caused, the nature of the author and of the addressee of the message, as well as the context in which the offence is committed shall be taken into account'.[372] The former UN Special Rapporteur on terrorism has tweaked this definition by stating that the caveat 'whether or not *directly* advocating terrorist offences' should be revised to 'whether or not "*expressly*" advocating' such offences.[373] This was intended to 'cover the situation of using coded language', but not to 'reduce the requirement to prove both a subjective intention to incite as well as an objective danger that a terrorist act will be committed'.[374] The current Special Rapporteur has also suggested that the

---

[365] IACmHR, *Roca Antúnez v. Cuba* (Case 12.127), 24 February 2018, §107.
[366] Ibid. See also IACmHR. *Biscet v. Cuba* (Case 12.476), 21 October 2006.
[367] IACmHR, *Annual Report of the Inter-American Commission on Human Rights: Report of the Special Rapporteur for Freedom of Expression* (2009) OEA/Ser.L/V/II., Doc. 51, 250.
[368] IACmHR, *Report on the Violence Against LGBTI Persons* (2015) OEA/Ser.L/V/II. Doc.36/15 Rev.2, §235 (in the context of mandatory restrictions on speech).
[369] ACmHPR, Declaration of Principles of Freedom of Expression and Access to Information in Africa (2019), Principle 22 (5).
[370] COE Convention on the Prevention of Terrorism (2005) Art. 5; UN Special Rapporteur on terrorism, Martin Scheinin, *Report on Ten areas of best practices in countering terrorism* (2010) UN Doc. A/HRC/16/51.
[371] COE Convention on the Prevention of Terrorism (2005) Art. 5 (emphasis added). The Convention has been signed and ratified by 42 states (including Russia) as well as the European Union. For a discussion of the intent requirements provided by Art. 5: see III.3.3 (Intent).
[372] COE, *Explanatory Report to the Council of Europe Convention on the Prevention of Terrorism* (2005) CETS 196, §100.
[373] UN Special Rapporteur on terrorism, Martin Scheinin, *Report on Ten areas of best practices in countering terrorism* (2010) UN Doc. A/HRC/16/51, §30 (emphasis added).
[374] Ibid. See s. III.1 (Legality).

causation requirement in the context of speech-related terrorism offences should be a *'reasonable probability that the expression in question would succeed in inciting a terrorist act*, thus establishing a degree of causal link or *actual risk* of the proscribed result occurring'.[375]

The European Court has imposed a lower causation threshold than its counterparts. Establishing a link to specific harm that speech may cause is not a requirement but one of many factors 'taken into account' when the Court considers the necessity of restricting speech.[376] And it appears that the Court may not have been consistent in the causation test it has applied. On some occasions, the Court has considered whether speech is 'capable of inciting' violence,[377] 'liable to incite to violence',[378] or that 'could have stirred up violence' and 'could have affected public order in the region'.[379] More recent decisions have coalesced around a single, albeit broad, standard: whether statements 'could, when read as a whole and in their context, be seen as a call for violence, hatred or intolerance'.[380]

Early iterations of the European Court's conception of causation were articulated in a number of Turkish cases in the late 1990s in which journalists, media professionals or politicians were charged under counterterrorism provisions for publishing material deemed to be supportive of the Kurdistan Workers' Party or 'PKK'. For example, the owner of a weekly publication was convicted and fined for the crime of 'propaganda' after publishing news articles referring to Turkish territory as 'Kurdistan', describing the fight for liberation as a 'war directed against the forces of the Republic of Turkey' and stating that 'we want to wage a total liberation struggle'.[381] While the Court held that the references to 'Kurdistan' and a 'national liberation struggle' cannot 'be deemed sufficient to regard the interference [with speech] as [being] necessary', the references to waging war 'must be seen as *capable of* inciting to further violence in the region', and therefore found the interference with speech proportionate.[382]

Some European Court judges have however criticized the Court's application of this 'capable of' or 'liable to' incite violence causation test on the basis this approach pays 'insufficient attention to the general context in which the words were used and their likely impact'.[383] In a leading case, *Surek (No. 4) v. Turkey*, the majority of the Court

---

[375] UN Special Rapporteur on terrorism, *Impact of measures to address terrorism and violent extremism on civic space and the rights of civil society actors and human rights defenders* (2019) UN Doc. A/HRC/40/52, §37 (emphasis added). See ch. 3 (Hate Speech), s. III.2.3.1. (Harm).

[376] These factors include 'the context in which the impugned statements were made, their nature and wording, their potential to lead to harmful consequences', whether 'the statements were made against a tense political or social background' and whether they 'could be seen as a direct or indirect call for violence or as a justification of violence, hatred or intolerance'. ECtHR, *Atamanchuk v. Russia* (App. no. 4493/11), 11 February 2020, §50. See also ECtHR, *Ibragimov v. Russia* (App. nos. 1413/08 & 28621/11), 28 August 2018, §99. See ch. 3 (Hate Speech), s. III.2.3.1. (Harm).

[377] ECtHR (GC), *Sürek v. Turkey (No. 3)* (App. no. 24735/94), 8 July 1999, §40.

[378] ECtHR (GC), *Sürek v. Turkey (No. 4)* (App. no. 24762/94), 8 July 1999, §58.

[379] ECtHR, *Leroy v. France* (App. no. 36109/03), 2 October 2008, §45.

[380] See s. III.3.1. (Harm); ECtHR (GC), *Perinçek v. Switzerland* (App. no. 27510/08), 15 October 2015, §§206, 240. ECtHR, Guide on Article 10 of the Convention, 31 August 2022, §557. See, e.g., ECtHR, *Gündüz v. Turkey* (App. no. 35071/97), 4 December 2003, §§ 48, 51; ECtHR, *Féret v. Belgium* (App. no. 15615/07), 16 July 2009, § 64.

[381] ECtHR (GC), *Sürek v. Turkey (No. 3)* (App. no. 24735/94), 8 July 1999, §10 (emphasis added).

[382] Ibid., §§40–42. The owner of the publication was sentenced to approximately 2.9 million EUR.

[383] ECtHR (GC), *Sürek v. Turkey (No. 4)* (App. no. 24762/94), 8 July 1999, Joint Concurring Opinion of Judges Palm, Tulkens, Fischbach, Casadevall and Greve.

applied this test and found a violation of article 10 after the owner of a publication was convicted of engaging in 'propaganda' for publishing news commentary about the Kurdish cause that stated that 'the real terrorist is the Republic of Turkey', and was fined approximately 2.9 million Euros.[384] The majority considered that 'State authorities enjoy a wider margin of appreciation' where 'remarks incite to violence', but found that on the whole, 'the content of the articles cannot be construed as being capable of inciting to further violence' or as 'liable to incite to violence'.[385] The Court stated that '[a]dmittedly', the commentary stated that 'it is time to settle accounts', but took the view that this reference 'must be seen in the context of the overall literary and metaphorical tone of the article and not as an appeal to violence'. It also described the reference to Turkey as 'the real terrorist' to be 'more of a reflection of the hardened attitude of one side to the conflict, rather than a call to violence' against it.[386]

But in a concurring judgment, five other judges argued that the majority's reasoning was faulty because, although the correct result was reached, the majority 'attaches too much weight to the form of words used in the publication'.[387] The concurring opinion stated that an 'approach which is more in keeping with the wide protection afforded to political speech ... is to focus less on the inflammatory nature of the words employed and more on the different elements of the contextual setting in which the speech was uttered'.[388] They considered that the Court should ask questions such as: '[w]as the language *intended to* inflame or incite to violence? Was there a *real and genuine risk* that it might actually do so?', as well as examining other contextual factors such as the position of influence of the author, the prominence of the newspaper or whether the words were 'far away from the centre of violence or on its doorstep'.[389]

Another concurring judgment in the same decision went a step further and advocated that the Court adopt the 'clear and present danger' test as articulated by US courts as the required causal link between speech and harm.[390] Judge Bonello held that the Court's existing causation threshold—described as justifying restrictions to speech that '*supported or instigated* the use of violence'—was an 'insufficient' yardstick.[391] He argued instead that freedom of expression 'does not permit a state to forbid or proscribe advocacy of the use of force except when such advocacy is directed to inciting or producing *imminent* lawlessness and *is likely to incite or produce* such action', which is a 'question of proximity and degree'.[392] And he concluded that the news commentary in that case did not have the 'potential of imminently threatening dire effects on the national

---

[384] ECtHR (GC), *Sürek v. Turkey (No. 4)* (App. no. 24762/94), 8 July 1999, §58. He was charged under a provision which criminalized 'written and spoken propaganda ... aimed at undermining the territorial integrity of the Republic of Turkey or the indivisible unity of the nation' and penalized any person 'who engages in such an activity' and fined 83,333,333 Turkish lira: §24.

[385] Ibid., §§57–58.

[386] Ibid., §58.

[387] Ibid., Joint Concurring Opinion of Judges Palm, Tulkens, Fischbach, Casadevall and Greve.

[388] Ibid., Joint Concurring Opinion of Judges Palm, Tulkens, Fischbach, Casadevall and Greve.

[389] Ibid. (emphasis added). See s. III.3.3. (Intent).

[390] See ch. 3 (Hate Speech), s. II.2.3.2. (United States).

[391] ECtHR (GC), *Sürek v. Turkey (No. 4)* (App. no. 24762/94), 8 July 1999, Concurring Judgment of Judge Bonello.

[392] Ibid. (emphasis added).

order', meaning that the sanctions imposed on the speaker were inappropriate.[393] These two concurring positions were replicated in similar terrorism cases handed down around this time.[394]

In decisions that postdate these concurring judgments, the European Court has continued to adopt broad causation requirements and attach considerable weight to the inflammatory nature of speech rather than its potential impact.[395] A leading example is the case of *Leroy v. France,* which involved a cartoon published in a Basque weekly newspaper depicting the attacks of September 11, two days after those attacks, with the caption 'We have all dreamt of it ... Hamas did it'.[396] Pursuant to France's 'apology for terrorism' offence, the cartoonist and publisher of the newspaper were convicted and each fined 1,500 Euros.[397] The Court took the view that the cartoon expressed 'support and moral solidarity' for the perpetrators of the attacks, and since it was printed two days after the attacks, 'when the whole world was reeling from the news' and 'in a politically sensitive [Basque] region' of France, that the cartoon 'elicited reactions which *could have* stirred up violence' and 'could have affected public order in the region' and therefore that article 10 had not been violated.[398]

Commentators have criticized the Court's decision in *Leroy,* arguing that 'it is hard to maintain that the drawing in question created a "credible" danger that more terrorist offences would be committed', in light of the relatively small circulation of the weekly [newspaper] and the differences between terrorist attacks taking place in the United States and differently-motivated attacks in the Basque region'.[399] According to this view, the case demonstrates that the 'capable of' or 'liable to' incite violence test 'is a vague one that allows judges considerable scope to prohibit speech merely because they consider it to be highly offensive', reflecting the concerns of the concurring judges from *Surek* and other earlier cases.[400]

In applying this contested approach to causation, the European Court considers a number of factors, including the identity of the speaker and the audience, the tone of the speech and the timing and location of the speech, including whether this overlaps with ongoing terrorist violence.[401] In practice, the Court's approach has resulted in a patchwork of jurisprudence from which it is difficult to draw patterns and predict when

---

[393] Ibid.
[394] See ECtHR, *Sürek v. Turkey (No. 1)* (App. no. 26682/95), 8 July 1999; ECtHR (GC), *Sürek v. Turkey (No. 3)* (App. no. 24735/94), 8 July 1999; ECtHR (GC), *Sürek and Özdemir v. Turkey* (App. nos. 23927/94 & 24277/94), 8 July 1999.
[395] See, e.g., ECtHR, *Z.B. v. France* (App. no. 46883/15), 2 September 2021.
[396] See ch. 3 (Hate Speech), s. III.2.3.1. (Harm).
[397] ECtHR, *Leroy v. France* (App. no. 36109/03), 2 October 2008.
[398] Ibid., §45 (emphasis added).
[399] S. Sottiaux, 'Leroy v. France: apology of terrorism and the malaise of the European Court of Human Rights' free speech jurisprudence' (2009) 3 *European Human Rights Law Review* 415, 424. See also A. Dyer, 'Freedom of Expression and the Advocacy of Violence: Which Test Should the European Court of Rights Adopt?' (2014) 33/1 *Netherlands Quarterly of Human Rights* 78–107.
[400] See Dyer (n 399) 97.
[401] Cf., Rabat Plan of Action, §29 (providing a six-part threshold test to determine if hate speech can be restricted by criminal penalties, including 'context'; 'speaker' and 'content and form'); HRC, General Comment No. 34 (2011), §34 ('The principle of proportionality must also take account of the form of expression at issue as well as the means of its dissemination').

the Court will or will not allow a restriction to speech on the basis of terrorism or public order laws.

3.2.1. 'Glorification', 'justification' and 'apology' offences

One consequence of the need for a causal link between the speech and proscribed harm is that crimes such as the 'glorification', 'justification' and 'apology' of terrorism have been deemed to violate international law.[402] These have been distinguished from 'incitement' to terrorism, on the basis that incitement provisions generally incorporate higher intent and causation requirements than these crimes: intent to incite a terrorist offence as well as causing a 'danger that a terrorist act will be committed'.[403] The former UN Secretary-General Ban Ki-moon denounced the 'troubling trend' of criminalizing 'glorifying' terrorism, insisting that 'incitement must be separated from glorification' and that 'the first may be legally prohibited, the second may not'.[404] The Secretary-General also defined the appropriate parameters of incitement as 'a direct call to engage in terrorism, with the intention that this will promote terrorism, and in a context in which the call is directly causally responsible for increasing the actual likelihood of a terrorist act occurring'.[405] The UN has also stated that '[s]uch offences as "encouragement of terrorism" and "extremist activity" as well as offences of "praising", "glorifying" or "justifying" terrorism' should be 'clearly defined to ensure that they do not lead to unnecessary or disproportionate interference with freedom of expression'.[406] In the words of the UN High Commission for Human Rights:

> A troubling trend has been the proscription of the glorification (*apologie*) of terrorism, involving statements which may not go so far as to incite or promote the commission of terrorist acts, but might nevertheless applaud past acts. While such statements might offend the sensibilities of individual persons and society, particularly the victims of terrorist acts, it is important that vague terms of an uncertain scope such as *glorifying* or *promoting* terrorism are not used when restricting expression.[407]

The UN Human Rights Committee has also highlighted that such laws, for example Ethiopia's 'criminalization of encouragement and inducement of terrorism through publication', can 'lead to abuse against the media'.[408] And the Working Group on Arbitrary Detention has found violations of freedom of speech in assessing laws that

---

[402] These have also been criticized or struck down on the ground of vagueness. See s. III.1. (Legality).
[403] UN Special Rapporteur on terrorism, Martin Scheinin, *Report on Ten areas of best practices in countering terrorism* (2010) UN Doc. A/HRC/16/51, §30. Although not all incitement provisions in state practice have high intent and causation bars: see s. II.1.1.1. (Inciting or encouraging terrorism).
[404] UN Secretary-General, *Report on The protection of human rights and fundamental freedoms while countering terrorism* (2008) UN Doc. A/63/337, §61.
[405] Ibid.
[406] HRC, General Comment No. 34 (2011), §46.
[407] OHCHR, *Human Rights, Terrorism and Counter-terrorism: Fact Sheet No. 32* (1 July 2008). See also CTED, *Global survey of the implementation of Security Council resolution 1624 (2005) by Member States* (2021) UN Doc S/2021/973 (Annex), §§19, 39 (observing that 'measures criminalizing glorification of acts of terrorism could lead to human rights violations').
[408] HRC, *Concluding Observations, Ethiopia* (2011) UN Doc. CCPR/C/ETH/CO/1, §15.

criminalize 'advocating' terrorism or 'encouragement of terrorism' due to the overbroad nature of such provisions.[409]

Similarly, a Joint Declaration published by a number of UN and regional Special Rapporteurs also criticized 'the criminalisation of speech' based on 'vague notions such as providing communications support to terrorism or extremism, the "glorification" or "promotion" of terrorism or extremism, and the mere repetition of statements by terrorists, which does not itself constitute incitement'.[410] It concluded that, instead, criminal penalties should be restricted to instances of 'intentional incitement to terrorism', which should be 'understood as a direct call to engage in terrorism which is directly responsible for increasing the likelihood of a terrorist act occurring, or to actual participation in terrorist acts'.[411] Recent reports of the UN Special Rapporteur on terrorism have also criticized offences of 'glorification, justification, advocacy, praising or encouragement of terrorism, and acts relating to "propaganda" for terrorism'.[412] The Special Rapporteur has described the problematic 'element common to these offences' as liability arising 'based on the content of the speech, rather than the speaker's intention or the actual impact of the speech'.[413] The Inter-American Commission has similarly taken the view that 'laws that broadly criminalize the public defense (apologia) of terrorism or of persons who might have committed terrorist acts, without considering the element of incitement "to lawless violence or to any other similar action" are incompatible with the right to freedom of expression'.[414]

In contrast, the European Court's expanded conception of harm and causation has seen the Court approve of offences that capture speech on a much broader basis than incitement to terrorism, such as 'engag[ing]' in separatist 'propaganda' or 'apology of terrorism'.[415] This is because the Court has 'accepted that certain forms of identification with a terrorist organization' and 'glorification' may be regarded as 'support for terrorism and incitement to violence and hatred', and deemed this to be sufficient harm to justify criminal penalties.[416] And the Court has considered that 'disseminating messages in praise of the perpetrator of an attack, denigrating the victims, calling for the financing of terrorist organizations or other similar conduct' can itself 'constitute acts of incitement to terrorist violence'.[417]

---

[409] See, e.g., WGAD, *Saber Saidi v. Algeria* (Opinion no. 49/2012), 16 November 2012, §§17–19 (finding that 'invoking loose definitions of offences that allow for a broad interpretation' of the charge of 'advocating terrorism' meant that 'the law is not in conformity with international law'); WGAD, *Eskinder Nega v. Ethiopia* (Opinion no. 62/2012), 21 November 2012, §§32, 40 (citing the Human Rights Committee's concern as to the scope of Ethiopia's encouragement of and inducement to terrorism offences, and holding that the 'application of the overly broad offences in the current case constitutes an unjustified restriction on the rights to freedom of expression and to a fair trial'). See s. III.1. (Legality).

[410] UN Special Rapporteur; OSCE Representative on Freedom of the Media; OAS Special Rapporteur; ACmHPR Special Rapporteur on Freedom of Expression and Access to Information, Declaration on Defamation of Religions, and Anti-Terrorism and Anti-Extremism Legislation (2008).

[411] Ibid.

[412] UN Special Rapporteur on terrorism, *Impact of measures to address terrorism and violent extremism on civic space and the rights of civil society actors and human rights defenders* (2019) UN Doc. A/HRC/40/52, §37.

[413] Ibid. See s. III.3.2. (Causal link between speech and harm).

[414] IACmHR, *Report on Terrorism and Human Rights* (2002) OEA/Ser.L/V/II.116 Doc. 5 rev. 1, §323.

[415] See, e.g., ECtHR, *Leroy v. France* (App. no. 36109/03), 2 October 2008; ECtHR (GC), *Sürek v. Turkey (No. 3)* (App. no. 24735/94), 8 July 1999; ECtHR (GC), *Zana v. Turkey* (App. no. 18954/91), 25 November 1997.

[416] ECtHR, *Yavuz and Yaylalı v. Turkey* (App. no. 12606/11), 17 December 2013, §51.

[417] Ibid. See s. III.3.1. (Harm).

For instance, in a case concerning France's 'apology for terrorism' provision, the European Court considered a radio broadcast of a former member of an extreme left-wing terror group who had spent 25 years in prison for terrorist-related murders.[418] When asked to comment on more recent terrorist attacks committed in France, he said that 'we can't say that these kids are cowards' and that he 'found them very brave'.[419] He was sentenced to 18 months' imprisonment.[420] The Court observed that states have a 'wider margin of appreciation' when 'remarks incite the use of violence', but also when 'statements ... glorify violence and thereby *indirectly* incite its use'.[421] Finding that even if the applicant 'did not express support for Islamist ideology', he 'presented the terrorist method of action, for which he himself had twice been sentenced to life imprisonment, in a romantic light by using positive and glorious images of the perpetrators'.[422] In light of this, and the fact his comments were made less than a year after the ISIS attacks, the Court determined they amounted to 'indirect incitement to the use of terrorist violence'.[423]

In another recent case, the European Court approved of a 'glorification' offence even though it accepted that the speaker was intending to be humorous rather than incite violence. In this case, an uncle gave his three-year-old nephew a T-shirt to wear to school which read 'I am the bomb!' and 'Jihad, born on 11 September', and was sentenced to two months' suspended imprisonment and a fine for 'glorify[ing]' serious crimes.[424] The nephew only wore the T-shirt for one afternoon in his kindergarten class and the wording was only viewed by two people—both adults—who were helping to dress the child.[425] In finding that this penalty was compatible with the right to free speech, the European Court took into account 'the importance and weight' of the 'general context', being that the incident took place 'only a few months after other terrorist attacks ... which caused the death of three children in a school'.[426] The fact that the uncle 'has no links to any terrorism movement' and 'has not subscribed to a terrorist ideology' but rather was intending to be humorous did not change this conclusion.[427] The Court also held that even appreciating the 'importance of the absence of publicity' in the context of only two individuals having viewed the message, the uncle 'could not have been unaware of the particular resonance' of the message in a school, and the national courts were in a 'privileged position to apprehend the need for a [criminal] sentence' in the case.[428] Media freedom group Article 19, which intervened in the case,

---

[418] ECtHR, *Rouillan v. France* (App. no. 28000/19), 23 June 2022. See s. III.5. (Penalties).
[419] Ibid., §5.
[420] Including 10 months' probation served at home, and a fine.
[421] ECtHR, *Rouillan v. France* (App. no. 28000/19), 23 June 2022, §66 (emphasis added).
[422] Ibid., §69.
[423] Ibid., §71. However, in light of its 'nature' and 'severity', the Court held his prison sentence was disproportionate to the aim pursued, and found a violation of article 10 'with regard to the severity of the criminal sanction imposed': §§75–77. See s. III.5. (Penalties).
[424] ECtHR, *Z.B. v France* (App. no. 46883/15), 2 September 2021, §11. His sister was also convicted and sentenced to a one-month suspended sentence and a fine, and they both were required to pay damages in a civil action.
[425] Ibid., §§8, 62.
[426] The European Court considered, but ultimately dismissed, an argument by France that Art. 17 of the Convention applied: ibid., §§18–27.
[427] Ibid., §§57–60.
[428] Ibid., §§62–66.

observed that 'it is clear that the inscriptions on the child's T-shirt were unlikely to incite violence', and that the Court 'consistently fails to heed international standards on freedom of expression accordingly to which the mere "praise", "glorification" or "support" of violence or terrorism are overly vague legal standards' bound to criminalize lawful speech.[429]

This view has more recently been advocated by a judge of the European Court, Judge Lemmens, who has suggested that the Court should explicitly hold that making it an offence to 'praise or justify terrorism, without requiring that the opinion expressed can be considered incitement to violence or hate speech' should be considered a violation of article 10 of the European Convention.[430] In that case, a politician spoke at an event honouring the ETA terrorist group and was charged with 'praise or justification' of terrorism.[431] The majority decision did not opine on the validity of the law itself, but concluded that the speech 'did not incite the use of violence or armed resistance, either directly or indirectly' as it advocated 'embarking on a democratic path' to achieve 'political objectives'.[432] As a result, the politician's one-year suspended prison term and seven-year ban on running for office could not qualify as 'necessary'. In a concurring decision finding a violation of article 10, Judge Lemmens held that Spain's provision was 'too broad in scope', because it 'makes it an offence to praise or justify terrorism, without requiring the opinion expressed be considered incitement to violence or hate speech'.[433] As a result, he 'would have preferred the Court to state explicitly that the problem of the disproportionate nature of the interference is rooted in the law itself'.[434]

3.3. Intent

International bodies have outlined a minimum 'intent' requirement for speech-based terrorism laws when assessing offences such as 'glorification', 'justification' or 'apology' of terrorism, now common across Europe and other parts of the world.[435] For example, the Human Rights Committee has critiqued the United Kingdom's 'encouragement of terrorism' offence for being 'broad and vague' and capturing speech even when a person 'did not intend members of the public to be directly or indirectly encouraged by

---

[429] Article 19, 'European Court of Human Rights: Contradictory rulings in two key free expression and terrorism cases' (2 September 2021).
[430] ECtHR, *Erkizia Almandoz v. Spain* (App. no. 5869/17), 22 June 2021 (Concurring opinion of Judge Lemmens), §7.
[431] ECtHR, *Erkizia Almandoz v. Spain* (App. no. 5869/17), 22 June 2021. See s. III.3.1. (Harm).
[432] ECtHR, *Erkizia Almandoz v. Spain* (App. no. 5869/17), 22 June 2021, §§46–52.
[433] Ibid. Concurring Opinion of Judge Lemmens, §7. Judge Lemmens also considered this to apply generally, not just in the case of Spain: 'the 'mere' fact of praising terrorism or justifying acts of terrorism without such remarks being considered as calls to violence or hate speech, is not sufficient to exempt such opinions from the protection of Article 10'): §9.
[434] Ibid. Concurring opinion of Judge Lemmens, §7.
[435] See s. III.3.2.1. ('Glorification', 'justification' and 'apology' offences); see also s. II.1.1.2. (Glorification or justification of terrorism). See, e.g., UN Special Rapporteur on terrorism, *Impact of measures to address terrorism and violent extremism on civic space and the rights of civil society actors and human rights defenders* (2019) UN Doc. A/HRC/40/52, §37 ('The element common to these offences is that liability is based on the content of the speech, rather than the speaker's intention or the actual impact of the speech').

his or her statement to commit acts of terrorism' but was nonetheless 'understood by some members of the public as encouragement to commit such acts'.[436]

In contrast, some 'incitement' to terrorism offences, which incorporate an intent requirement, have been found to comply with international standards. The UN Secretary-General has defined permissible incitement to terrorism offences as those encompassing 'a direct call to engage in terrorism, with the intention that this will promote' terrorism.[437] The Security Council's Counter-Terrorism Committee considers that 'United Nations human rights mechanisms have been clear that the offence of incitement to commit terrorist acts must apply only to those communications that are actually *directed at* inciting violence.'[438] And the UN Special Rapporteur's model offence of incitement of terrorism criminalizes those who 'intentionally distribute' a message 'with the intent to incite the commission of a terrorist offence'.[439] This model offence requires an express reference to two elements of intent: 'intent to communicate a message and intent that the message incite the commission of a terrorist act'.[440] The Council of Europe Convention on the Prevention of Terrorism requires the same double intent standard: that the offence is committed 'unlawfully and intentionally', and that the impugned speech is made or distributed 'with intent to incite the commission of a terrorist offence'.[441]

Other bodies have developed intent standards that are applicable in the context of terrorism and public order offences. The Inter-American Commission on Human Rights, adopting a position similar to U.S. domestic law,[442] has held that penalties for hate speech can only be justified when a speaker was 'not simply issuing an opinion' but also had 'intent' to 'promot[e] lawless violence or similar action'.[443] The Inter-American Court has also addressed offences penalizing physical acts of terrorism that were applied to speech, and held that 'the special intent or purpose' of instilling 'fear in the

---

[436] HRC, *Concluding observations, United Kingdom of Great Britain and Northern Ireland* (2008) UN Doc. CCPR/C/GBR/CO/6, §26. The Human Rights Committee recommended the United Kingdom consider amending this offence to ensure that 'its application does not lead to a disproportionate interference with freedom of expression'. The Committee also recommended that Morocco revise its terrorism-related offences so that they were defined 'on the basis of their objective', expressing concern as to 'reports that charges have been brought under these provisions without proper cause against journalists who were fulfilling their duty to inform the public'. HRC, *Concluding Observations, Morocco* (2016) UN Doc. CCPR/C/MAR/CO/6, §§17–18.

[437] UN Secretary General, *Report on the The protection of human rights and fundamental freedoms while countering terrorism* (2008) UN Doc. A/63/337, §61. See also CTED, *Global survey of the implementation of Security Council resolution 1624 (2005) by Member States* (2021) UN Doc. S/2021/973 (Annex), §10 (summarizing best practices outlined by UN human rights bodies as recommending incitement to terror offences 'expressly include both a subjective element (intent that a terrorist act be committed as a result) and an objective element (creation of a danger that this will in fact happen)').

[438] CTED, *Global survey of the implementation of Security Council resolution 1624 (2005) by Member States* (2016) UN Doc. S/2016/50, §11 (emphasis added).

[439] UN Special Rapporteur on terrorism Martin Scheinin, *Report on Ten areas of best practices in countering terrorism* (2010) UN Doc. A/HRC/16/51, §32.

[440] Ibid., §§30–31.

[441] COE Convention on the Prevention of Terrorism Art. 5; COE, *Explanatory Report to the Council of Europe Convention on the Prevention of Terrorism* (2005) CETS 196, §99.

[442] See ch. 3 (Hate Speech), s. II.2.3.2. (United States) and ch. 2 (Insulting Speech), s. II.1.2. (Intent) (regarding the adoption of the 'actual malice' standard in the Inter-American context).

[443] IACmHR, *Violence against LGBTI Persons* (2015) OAS/Ser.L/V/II.Doc.36/15 Rev.2, §235. See also OAS Special Rapporteur, *Inter-American Legal Framework regarding the Right to Freedom of Expression* (2009) OEA/Ser.L/V/II CIDH/RELE/INF. 2/09, §58.

general population' is a fundamental element to distinguish conduct of a terrorist nature from conduct that is not ... without which the conduct would not meet the definition'.[444] And in the African context, the Declaration of Principles on Freedom of Expression in Africa provides that when determining if any type of speech falls into the exceptional category of warranting criminal sanctions, states should take into account the 'existence of a clear intent to incite'.[445]

The European Court of Human Rights will also consider the intent of the speaker as a relevant factor in determining necessity, but sets a lower bar.[446] For example, the European Court held that 'the mechanical repression of media professionals' under a Turkish law which criminalized anyone who 'publish[ed] statements or leaflets by terrorist organizations' 'without taking into account their purpose ... cannot be reconciled with the freedom to receive or impart information or ideas'.[447]

However, in a number of cases the European Court has, even in the criminal context, allowed convictions without requiring a clear showing of intent to incite terrorism or even without reaching a conclusion as to the speaker's intent.[448] For example, in *Leroy v. France,* a cartoonist argued that he did not intend to encourage terrorism but to express his anti-American sentiment.[449] The Court, however, found his conviction compatible with his right to free speech, noting that the drawing could 'in itself demonstrate the intention of the author' to 'support[] and glorif[y] ... violence'.[450] And the Court ultimately concluded that 'the applicant's intentions are unrelated to the prosecution', given that his intent to critique American imperialism had only been expressed retroactively and could not 'in view of the context ... erase [his] positive assessment of the consequences of a criminal act'.[451]

Similarly, the Court found no violation of the right to free speech when an uncle was convicted of 'glorify[ing]' serious crimes when his nephew wore a T-shirt to school which read 'I am the bomb!' and 'Jihad, born on 11 September'.[452] Before the Court, the uncle argued that 'neither the domestic courts nor even the Government dispute that

---

[444] IACtHR, *Norín Catrimán v. Chile* (Series C, no. 279), 29 May 2014. §§171–174. However the Court found that the application of a presumption of such intent when certain explosives were used violated both the principle of legality and right to the presumption of innocence.

[445] ACmHPR, Declaration of Principles of Freedom of Expression and Access to Information in Africa (2019), Principle 23(2)(c).

[446] See, e.g., ECtHR (GC), *Jersild v. Denmark* (App. no. 15890/89), 23 September 1994 ('the object of the programme was to address aspects of the problem, by identifying certain racist individuals and by portraying their mentality and social background. There is no reason to doubt that the ensuing interviews fulfilled that aim. Taken as a whole, the feature could not objectively have appeared to have as its purpose the propagation of racist views and ideas'); ECtHR (GC), *Perinçek v. Switzerland* (App. no. 27510/08), 15 October 2015, §§238–240.

[447] See, e.g., ECtHR, *Gözel and Özer v. Turkey* (App. nos. 43453/04 & 31098/05) 6 July 2010, §63. This includes cases where the Court has allowed criminal penalties for offences that require speech that does not rise to the level of 'incitement' to terrorism: §61. Cf. HRC, *Kurakbaev and Sabdikenova v. Kazakhstan* (Comm. no. 2509/2014), 19 July 2021, §11.3 (providing that 'a ban on a particular publication' is not permissible 'unless specific content, that is not severable, can be legitimately prohibited under article 19(3)').

[448] See s. III.3.2.1. ('Glorification', 'justification' and 'apology' offences).

[449] ECtHR, *Leroy v. France* (App. no. 36109/03), 2 October 2008, §42. See s. III.3.1. (Harm); ch. 3 (Hate Speech), s. III.2.3.1. (Harm).

[450] ECtHR, *Leroy v. France* (App. no. 36109/03), 2 October 2008, §43.

[451] Ibid., §43. See also ECtHR (GC), *Sürek v. Turkey (No. 1)* (App. no. 26682/95), 8 July 1999, §62.

[452] ECtHR, *Z.B. v. France,* App. no. 46883/15 (2 September 2021), §11. See s. III.3.2. (Causal link between speech and harm).

he had a humorous intention when he wrote the disputed message'.[453] But the French government maintained that a humorous intention 'could not erase the presentation in a favourable light of attacks that had caused thousands of deaths'.[454] And the European Court agreed that despite 'the fact that the [uncle] has no links with any terrorist movement, or has not subscribed to a terrorist ideology', he 'could not have been unaware of the particular resonance' of the message shortly after attacks at another school and that this reflected 'a deliberate intention to valorize criminal acts'.[455] And although the Court recognized that only two adults had seen the message on the child's shirt, it decided not to 'speculate on the exact nature of the applicant's intentions' as to how widely he thought the message would be disseminated or the impact this would have.[456]

A number of judges of the European Court have criticized this approach and argued in favour of a higher intent standard. In a series of concurring judgments in 1990s cases concerning the PKK,[457] European Court judges advocated for the Court to consider whether speech was 'intended to inflame or incite to violence'.[458] This standard would bring the Court into line with the 'intent to incite' harm standards articulated by the Council of Europe and UN Special Rapporteur on terrorism.[459]

The Court's approach to intent has serious consequences for those who report on terrorism. Like the Human Rights Committee, which has stated that the 'media plays a crucial role in informing the public about acts of terrorism' and that 'journalists should not be penalized for carrying out their legitimate activities',[460] the European Court's starting point is that 'news reporting based on interviews or declarations by others, whether edited or not, constitutes one of the most important means whereby the press is able to pay its vital role of "public watchdog"'.[461] The Court has held as a result that punishing a journalist 'for assisting in the dissemination of statements made by another person could seriously hamper the contribution of the press to the discussion of matters of public interest'.[462] So where Turkish journalists were convicted and fined for publishing declarations of an illegal organization,[463] the Court found a violation of article 10, noting that a 'blanket ban' on such statements is unjustified, and regard

---

[453] ECtHR, *Z.B. v France*, App. no. 46883/15 (2 September 2021), §32.
[454] Ibid., §45.
[455] Ibid., §§57, 63.
[456] Ibid., §62.
[457] See s. III.3.2. (Causal link between speech and harm); ECtHR (GC), *Sürek v. Turkey (No. 4)* (App. no. 24762/94), 8 July 1999, Joint Concurring Opinion of Judges Palm, Tulkens, Fischbach, Casadevall and Greve. See also ECtHR, *Sürek v. Turkey (No. 1)* (App. no. 26682/95), 8 July 1999; ECtHR (GC), *Sürek v. Turkey (No. 3)* (App. no. 24735/94), 8 July 1999; ECtHR (GC), *Sürek and Özdemir v. Turkey* (App. nos. 23927/94 & 24277/94), 8 July 1999.
[458] ECtHR (GC), *Sürek v. Turkey (No. 4)* (App. no. 24762/94), 8 July 1999, Joint Concurring Opinion of Judges Palm, Tulkens, Fischbach, Casadevall and Greve.
[459] COE Convention on the Prevention of Terrorism Art. 5; COE, *Explanatory Report to the Council of Europe Convention on the Prevention of Terrorism* (2005) CETS 196, §99; UN Special Rapporteur on terrorism Martin Scheinin, *Report on Ten areas of best practices in countering terrorism* (2010) UN Doc. A/HRC/16/51, §§30–31.
[460] HRC, General Comment No. 34 (2011), §46.
[461] ECtHR, *Demirel v. Turkey (No. 3)* (App. no. 11976/03), 9 December 2008, §23.
[462] Ibid.
[463] Ibid. See s. III.4.1. (Public Interest).

must be had to whether the article, 'taken as a whole, can be considered an incitement to violence'.[464]

Similarly, the Court found a violation of article 10 when Turkey criminalized media professionals 'solely on the grounds that they had published statements by terrorist organizations, without carrying out any analysis of the content of the disputed writings or the context in which they were set'.[465] In this case, two editors-in-chief of monthly magazines were fined under a law that penalized anyone who 'prints or publishes statements or leaflets by terrorist organizations'.[466] The Court held that 'the mechanical repression of media professionals [under this law] without taking into account their purpose ... or the public's right to be informed from another point of view about a conflict situation, cannot be reconciled with the freedom to receive or impart information or ideas'.[467]

The Court came to the same conclusion when a newspaper received a caution under Russian anti-extremist legislation for publishing an article which contained statements and images from an ultra-right wing political organization that could allegedly incite social, racial or ethnic 'discord'.[468] The Court found that the article, written on the anniversary of the murder of two individuals allegedly by members of the organization, in fact 'aimed to uncover the true nature' of the organization as 'essentially fascist' and sought to 'draw the attention of the public and the authorities to matters of public interest, namely the existence and the activities' of the extremist organization.[469] According to the Court, the impugned quotations, 'when considered in the context of the journalistic and interview parts of the article, did not appear from an objective point of view to have had as their purpose the promotion of extremist ideals'.[470] The caution therefore ran counter to article 10 and did not answer any pressing social need.[471]

But the European Court has not always applied these principles consistently. In the cases in which the Court has found article 17 to apply to terrorist speech the Court does not always address the intent of the speaker.[472] And the Court has allowed the conviction of a media professional who provided an 'outlet' for terrorist speech that may have been intended to incite to violence, but without holding such intent themselves.[473] In this case, in which the owner of a weekly publication was convicted for disseminating separatist 'propaganda' after publishing readers' pro-Kurdish letters, the Court held that was 'a clear intention to stigmatize the other side to the conflict' by the use of phrases

---

[464] ECtHR, *Demirel v. Turkey (No. 3)* (App. no. 11976/03), 9 December 2008, §27.
[465] ECtHR, *Gözel and Özer v. Turkey* (App. nos. 43453/04 & 31098/05), 6 July 2010, §61.
[466] Ibid., §23. The fine was less than 200 EUR each.
[467] Ibid., §63.
[468] ECtHR, *RID Novaya Gazeta v. Russia* (App. no. 44561/11), 11 May 2021, §89.
[469] Ibid., §93. The fact the quoted interviews were accompanied by 'text amounting to an editorial statement' demonstrated that the newspaper 'considered the views expressed [by the organization] unacceptable': ECtHR, *RID Novaya Gazeta v. Russia* (App. no. 44561/11), 11 May 2021, §96.
[470] Ibid., §97. The Court also found that the public display of symbols indistinguishable from Nazi symbols in the article 'were intended to contribute to a public debate': ECtHR, *RID Novaya Gazeta v. Russia* (App. no. 44561/11), 11 May 2021, §107.
[471] Ibid., §99.
[472] See s. III.3.1. (Harm); ECtHR, *Roj TV A/S v. Denmark* (App. no. 24683/14), 17 April 2018. See also s. III.3.2. (Causal link between speech and harm); s. III.3.3. (Intent).
[473] ECtHR, *Sürek v. Turkey (no. 1)* (App. no. 26682/95), 8 July 1999, §63.

such as 'the fascist Turkish army' and 'the hired killers of imperialism' alongside references to 'massacres', 'brutalities' and 'slaughter' in the letters.[474] The Court accepted that the owner of the publication 'did not personally associate himself with the views contained in the letters', but held that 'he nevertheless provided their writers with an outlet for stirring up violence and hatred' and thereby found that his conviction and fine did not breach article 10.[475] As the owner of the publication, the Court considered he was 'vicariously subject to the "duties and responsibilities" which the review's editorial and journalistic staff undertake in the collection and dissemination of information to the public and which assume an even greater importance in situations of conflict and tension'.[476] This case, decided decades ago, should however be considered an outlier, as was recognized by a number of judges who dissented at the time on the basis that the Court's rationale was 'inconsistent' with a number of its other decisions.[477]

The European Union's decision to sanction Russian state media is an example of the challenges of applying these principles in practice. In 2022, the EU prohibited the 'broadcasting' of 'any content' by Russian outlets Russia Today (RT) and Sputnik.[478] The European Commission justified the ban on the basis of the 'massive propaganda and disinformation' on these outlets that was a 'significant and direct threat to the Union's public order and security'.[479] And the Commission declared it applied to 'all means for transmission and distribution, such as via cable, satellite, IPTV, platforms, websites and apps'.[480] The ban was put in place until the end of the Russian aggression in Ukraine or when Russia and its media outlets 'cease to conduct propaganda'.[481] Despite the global condemnation of Russia's invasion of Ukraine, and the deterioration of media freedom in Russia since that time,[482] this decision has also received strong criticism from groups that promote press freedom. The European Federation of Journalists opposed the decision as a 'complete break' from 'democratic guarantees', and the 'first time in modern

---

[474] Ibid., §62.
[475] Ibid., §§63–65. See also ECtHR, *Sürek and Özdemir v. Turkey* (App. no. 23927/94 & 24277/94), 8 July 1999, §61 (when determining whether a journalist should be penalized for reporting the statements of a terrorist, the European Court will examine whether the reporting 'taken as a whole' can be considered 'to incite to violence or hatred').
[476] ECtHR, *Sürek v. Turkey (no. 1)* (App. no. 26682/95), 8 July 1999, §63.
[477] Ibid., Joint Partly Dissenting Opinion of Judges Tulkens, Casadevall and Greve and Partly Dissenting Opinion of Judge Palm. See also ECtHR (GC), *Jersild v. Denmark* (App. no. 15890/89), 23 September 1994, §31; ECtHR (GC), *Bladet Tromsø v. Norway* (App. no. 21980/93), 20 May 1999, §63; ECtHR (GC), *Zana v. Turkey* (App. no. 18954/91), 25 November 1997.
[478] Council Regulation (EU) 2022/350 of 1 March 2022 amending Regulation (EU) No 833/2014 concerning restrictive measures in view of Russia's actions destabilizing the situation in Ukraine. The ban was later extended to three other Russian media outlets: IRIS Legal Observations of the European Audiovisual Observatory, 'Three additional Russian media outlets added to list of banned media in the EU'.
[479] See, e.g., B. Baade, 'The EU's "Ban" of RT and Sputnik' (Verfassungsblog, 8 March 2022).
[480] European Commission, 'Ukraine: Sanctions on Kremlin-backed outlets Russia Today and Sputnik' (2 March 2022). The United States, in a similar act, seized thirteen web domains belonging to the Lebanese Hizballah. Under US law, the domains were subject to seizure as assets of 'entities and organizations engaged in planning or perpetrating acts of terrorism'. According to the US Justice Department, the seizure 'disrupt[ed] terrorist activity by blocking one avenue these groups and individuals use to gather support and influence'. See US Attorney's Office for the Eastern District of Virginia, 'EDVA Seizes Thirteen Domains Used by Lebanese Hizballah and its Affiliates' (11 May 2023).
[481] Council Regulation (EU) 2022/350 of 1 March 2022 amending Regulation (EU) No 833/2014 concerning restrictive measures in view of Russia's actions destabilising the situation in Ukraine.
[482] See, e.g., Freedom House, 'Freedom on the Net: Russia' (2022).

history' that 'Western European governments are banning media'.[483] Others have critiqued the total banning of a platform as likely to be inconsistent with the European Court's harm and proportionality thresholds.[484] And free speech group Article 19 argued that 'any justification on the basis of public order and security' is unlikely to be convincing, given the EU is 'not directly engaged in armed conflict with Russia' and in light of the 'limited distribution and impact' of these channels in EU countries.[485] In 2022 a Dutch journalists' union filed multiple challenges to the ban before the EU's Court of Justice.[486]

4. Exclusions, Exceptions and Defences

4.1. Public interest

The requirement that a speaker should only be penalized under terrorism laws if they intend to incite terrorism means that, as a starting point, journalists merely reporting on terrorist speech should not be subject to criminal penalties.[487]

In addition, 'political' speech, or speech concerning a matter of 'public interest' is entitled to higher protection than speech that is not, even if it relates to national security.[488] The Human Rights Committee has stated that a 'public interest in the subject matter of a criticism' should be recognized as a defence'[489] and that it is not permissible to use national security laws 'to suppress or withhold from the public information of legitimate public interest that does not harm national security or to prosecute journalists, researchers, environmental activists, human rights defenders, or others, for having disseminated such information'.[490] The Human Rights Committee has also noted that the 'media plays a crucial role in informing the public about acts of terrorism and its capacity to operate should not be unduly restricted', meaning that 'journalists should not be penalized for carrying out their legitimate activities'.[491]

---

[483] European Federation of Journalists, 'Fighting disinformation with censorship a mistake' (1 March 2022).
[484] See, e.g., D. Voorhoof, 'EU silences Russian state media: a step in the wrong direction' (Columbia Global Freedom of Expression, 9 May 2022); Article 19, 'Response to the consultation of the UN Special Rapporteur on Freedom of Expression on her report on challenges to freedom of opinion and expression in times of conflicts and disturbances' (19 July 2022). Cf. HRC, *Kurakbaev and Sabdikenova v. Kazakhstan* (Comm. no. 2509/2014), 19 July 2021, §11.3 (providing that 'a ban on a particular publication' is not permissible 'unless specific content, that is not severable, can be legitimately prohibited under article 19(3)').
[485] Article 19, 'Response to the consultation of the UN Special Rapporteur on Freedom of Expression on her report on challenges to freedom of opinion and expression in times of conflicts and disturbances' (19 July 2022). See also Article 19, 'UN: Statement on propaganda for war and free expression' (22 September 2023). See also ch. 1 (Introduction), II.1.3.1.2. (ICCPR: Article 20) and ch. 3 (Hate Speech), s. III.1. (Mandatory Restrictions on Hate Speech) for a discussion of 'propaganda for war' in article 20(1) of the ICCPR.
[486] T. Sterling, 'Dutch journalists, rights group file lawsuit challenging EU ban on RT, Sputnik' (Reuters, 25 May 2022). See also NVJ, 'Tweede klacht over blokkade Russiche nieuwzenders bij Europees Hof' (7 September 2022). The EU Court of Justice dismissed a similar challenge on 27 July 2022, commenced by RT France: 'Russian anger after EU court upholds ban on RT' (France24, 27 July 2022).
[487] See s. III.3.3. (Intent); ECtHR (GC), *Sürek and Özdemir v. Turkey* (App. nos. 23927/94 & 24277/94), 8 July 1999, §61; ECtHR, *Gözel and Özer v. Turkey* (App. nos. 43453/04 & 31098/05), 6 July 2010, §63.
[488] See ch. 5 (Espionage and Official Secrets Laws), s. III.5.1. (Public interest defence).
[489] HRC, General Comment No. 34 (2011), §47 (in the context of defamation laws).
[490] Ibid., §30.
[491] Ibid., §46. See s. III.1.3.2.1. ('Glorification', 'justification' and 'apology' offences) (regarding the Committee's response to Ethiopia's 'encouragement of terrorism' offences); s. III.5. (Penalties).

Similarly, the European Court of Human Rights has held that there is 'little scope' for restrictions on free speech 'in two fields, namely political speech and matters of public interest'[492] and that 'public interest' extends beyond political speech.[493] The Court has found that a 'particularly narrow margin of appreciation' will be accorded to states regulating speech when remarks 'concern matters of the public interest',[494] meaning that the 'punishment of a journalist for assisting in the dissemination of statements made by another person would seriously hamper the contribution of the press to the discussion of matters of public interest, and should not be envisaged unless there are particularly strong reasons for doing so'.[495]

But the European Court has also found that where 'remarks incite to violence against an individual or a public official or a sector of the population, the State authorities enjoy a wider margin of appreciation when examining the need for an interference with freedom of expression'.[496] And the Court has emphasized that although 'a prison sentence imposed for an offence committed in the context of political debate is compatible with freedom of expression only in exceptional circumstances', such circumstances include when 'the speech exhorts the use of violence or constitutes hate speech'.[497]

Terrorism cases illustrate the balancing of these competing values. For example, the European Court considered the case of a Turkish journalist placed under pretrial detention for 'attempting to overthrow the constitutional order' after the 2016 attempted military coup that Turkish authorities alleged was instigated by US-based cleric Fethullah Gülen.[498] Turkish authorities argued that the journalist had visited Gülen at his home and made comments in news articles and a television broadcast 'serving the interests' of the terrorist organization linked to Gülen.[499] But the journalist claimed that his comments had instead warned against further coups, and that he had only interacted with Gülen in his professional capacity as a journalist.[500] The European Court indicated that it was 'prepared to take into account the circumstances' surrounding the Turkish cases brought before it, including that the 'coup attempt and other terrorist acts have clearly posed a major threat to democracy'.[501] However, 'the Court considers that one of the principal characteristics of democracy is the possibility it offers of resolving problems

---

[492] ECtHR (GC), *Bédat v. Switzerland* (App. no. 56925/08), 29 March 2016, §49. See, similarly, ECtHR (GC), *Sürek v. Turkey (No. 2)* (App. no. 24122/94), 8 July 1999, §34, citing ECtHR, *Wingrove v. United Kingdom* (App. no. 17419/90), 25 November 1996, §58; ECtHR, *Castells v. Spain* (App. no. 11798/85), 23 April 1992, §43.

[493] See ECtHR, *Lingens v. Austria* (App. no. 9815/82), 8 July 1986, §41: 'Whilst the press must not overstep the bounds set, inter alia, for the "protection of the reputation of others", it is nevertheless incumbent on it to impart information and ideas on *political issues just as on those in other areas of public interest*' (emphasis added).

[494] And it requires 'very strong reasons justifying restrictions on political speech', ECtHR (GC), *Bédat v. Switzerland* (App. no. 56925/08), 29 March 2016, §49; ECtHR, *Dmitriyevskiy v. Russia* (App. no. 42168/06), 3 October 2017, §95; ECtHR, *Alekhina v. Russia* (App. no. 38004/12), 17 July 2018, §212.

[495] ECtHR, *Demirel v. Turkey (No. 3)* (App. no. 11976/03), 9 December 2008, §23. And the Court in 'no way consider[s] the personality of the author of a piece of writing to be the sole determining factor in punishing the publication in question'. ECtHR, *Gözel and Özer v. Turkey* (App. nos. 43453/04 & 31098/05), 6 July 2010, §54.

[496] ECtHR (GC), *Sürek and Özdemir v. Turkey* (App. nos. 23927/94 & 24277/94), 8 July 1999, §60. See s. III.3.2. (Causal link between speech and harm).

[497] ECtHR, *Erkizia Almandoz v. Spain* (App. no. 5869/17), 22 June 2021, §39.

[498] See, e.g., 'Turkey's failed coup attempt: All you need to know' (Al Jazeera, 15 July 2017).

[499] ECtHR, *Mehmet Hasan Altan v. Turkey* (App. no. 13237/17), 20 March 2018, §25.

[500] Ibid., §25.

[501] Ibid., §210.

through public debate'.[502] In this context, 'criticism of governments and publication of information regarded by a country's leaders as endangering national interests should not attract criminal charges for particularly serious offences such as belonging to or assisting a terrorist organisation, attempting to overthrow the government or the constitutional order or disseminating terrorist propaganda'.[503] And the Court found a violation of the journalist's right to free speech as a result.[504]

The European Court also weighed whether public interest speech could be prosecuted as 'incitement to violence' when the owner and editor of a weekly newspaper were convicted and fined for 'publishing declarations of an illegal organisation' in an article by Abdullah Öcalan, the former leader of the PKK.[505] The Court examined the article and held that it could not be construed 'on any reading, as encouraging violence, armed resistance or an uprising' and was instead 'newsworthy content since it provided, however one-sided, historical information about an organisation which has since 1985 waged armed opposition against the State'.[506] The Court held that, when a publication cannot be categorized as 'incitement to violence', states cannot 'with reference to national security or territorial integrity restrict the right of the public to be informed by bringing the weight of the criminal law to bear on the media'.[507] As a result, the conviction under criminal law violated article 10.[508]

The Court came to the same conclusion when a leading politician in the Basque independence movement was sentenced to a one-year suspended sentence and a seven-year ban from office for the crime of 'praise or justification' of terrorism, following a keynote speech in which he paid tribute to a former member of a terrorist organization.[509] The European Court determined that the 'question of the Basque Country's independence', and 'the debate about whether or not to use armed violence to achieve independence' were 'a public debate of general interest'. However, the Court noted that 'the fact that this is a matter of general interest does not mean that the right to freedom of expression in this area is unlimited'.[510] Instead, it was necessary to determine 'whether the speech exhorts the use of violence or constitutes hate speech'.[511] The Court found that, '[a]lthough the speech was delivered as part of an act of homage' to a member of a terrorist group, 'it was clear from the applicant's words that he was advocating reflection with a view to embarking on a new democratic path' and that the speech 'read as a whole did not incite the use of violence or armed resistance'.[512]

---

[502] Ibid., §210.
[503] Ibid., §211. The Court also held that, even where such charges are brought, pre-trial detention 'should only be used as an exceptional measure of last resort'.
[504] Ibid., §214.
[505] ECtHR, *Demirel v. Turkey (No. 3)* (App. no. 11976/03), 9 December 2008.
[506] Ibid., §26.
[507] Ibid., §27.
[508] Ibid., §§27–30.
[509] ECtHR, *Erkizia Almandoz v. Spain* (App. no. 5869/17), 22 June 2021. See s. III.3.1. (Harm).
[510] ECtHR, *Erkizia Almandoz v. Spain* (App. no. 5869/17), 22 June 2021, §44.
[511] Ibid., §39. The Court noted that one of the 'factors that must be taken into account' when deciding whether hate speech has taken place is where the speech 'could be construed as a direct or indirect call to violence or as a justification for violence, hatred or intolerance': §40(ii). See s. III.3.1. (Harm).
[512] ECtHR, *Erkizia Almandoz v. Spain* (App. no. 5869/17), 22 June 2021, §§46–49.

The Inter-American Court and Commission and the African Court have also consistently provided a high level of protection for speech in the public interest or relating to public officials.[513] In one case, the Inter-American Commission found that charges against Cuban citizens who had disseminated documents criticizing Cuba's socio-economic problems violated the right to freedom of expression, and held that the test 'for the necessity of limitations [on speech] must be applied more strictly whenever dealing with expressions concerning the State, matters of public interest, public officials in the performance of their duties, candidates for public office, private citizens involved voluntarily in public affairs, or political speech and debate'.[514]

4.2. Truth and opinion

Although the defences of opinion and truth are less likely to arise in the context of terrorism laws than in contexts such as defamation, they remain applicable. The Human Rights Committee has made clear that, at least in the context of criminal laws that penalize defamatory speech, courts should recognize a 'defence of truth' and that such criminal laws 'should not be applied with regard to those forms of expression that are not, of their nature, subject to verification'.[515] The European Court and the Inter-American Court also consider that truth should be an exemption or defence from liability in defamation laws.[516] The UN Special Rapporteur has recommended a number of limits on hate speech laws, including that 'no one should be penalized for statements that are true'.[517] Similarly, the Declaration of Principles on Freedom of Expression in Africa provides that, at least in relation to defamation laws, '[n]o one shall be found liable for true statements'.[518] The truthfulness of a statement is relevant to the analysis of intent and reasonableness of conduct of speakers who have violated espionage or official secrets laws.[519] And the OAS Special Rapporteur on Freedom of Expression has similarly observed that the imposition of sanctions for incitement to violence 'must be backed up by actual, truthful, objective and strong proof that the person was not simply issuing an opinion (even if that opinion was hard, unfair or disturbing)'.[520]

An example of the European Court's approach to these defences in a case of 'extremist' speech is when the Court found Russia had violated article 10 by convicting feminist band Pussy Riot for performing their song *'Punk Prayer—Virgin Mary, Drive Putin Away'* in cathedrals in Moscow and uploading videos of these performances to

---

[513] See, e.g., IACtHR, *Herrera-Ulloa v. Costa Rica* (Case 12.367), 2 July 2004, §101(2)(c); ACtHPR, *Konaté v. Burkina Faso* (App. no. 4/2013), 5 December 2014, §155. See also OAS Special Rapporteur, *Inter-American Legal Framework regarding the Right to Freedom of Expression* (2009) OEA/Ser.L/V/II CIDH/RELE/INF. 2/09, §§37–38.

[514] IACmHR, *Roca Antúnez v. Cuba* (Case 12.127), 2 February 2018, §86.

[515] HRC, General Comment No. 34 (2011), §47.

[516] See ch. 2 (Insulting Speech), s. III.4.1. (Truth); IACtHR, *Herrera-Ulloa v. Costa Rica* (Series C, no. 107), 2 July 2004, §132; ECtHR, *Castells v. Spain* (App. no. 11798/85), 23 April 1992, §48.

[517] UN Special Rapporteur F. La Rue, *Promotion and protection of the right to freedom of opinion and expression* (2012) UN Doc. A/67/357, §50 (citing the UN Special Rapporteur, the OSCE Representative on Freedom of the Media and the OAS Special Rapporteur, Joint Statement on Racism and the Media (2001)).

[518] ACmHPR, Declaration of Principles of Freedom of Expression and Access to Information in Africa (2019), Principle 21.

[519] See ch. 5 (Espionage and Official Secrets Laws), s. III.5.3. (Truth).

[520] OAS Special Rapporteur, Inter-American Legal Framework regarding the Right to Freedom of Expression (2009) OEA/Ser.L/V/II CIDH/RELE/INF. 2/09, §58.

YouTube.[521] The band members were convicted of 'hooliganism for reasons of religious hatred and enmity' for the performances and Russian courts found that their website contained 'extremist' material and banned access to it.[522] In its reasoning, the European Court noted that it has previously found breaches of article 10 in cases 'where under the domestic law an applicant was unable effectively to contest criminal charges brought against him, as he was either not allowed to adduce evidence of the truth of his statements, or to plead a defence of justification'.[523] This meant that the Russian court did not provide 'relevant and sufficient reasons' to interfere with the band's free expression.[524]

5. Penalties

The proportionality of a penalty imposed on speech is a central factor in assessing whether it is 'necessary' and therefore compatible with international standards.[525] International human rights bodies have generally found criminal sanctions to be a disproportionate response to speech, including in the national security and terrorism context, although incitement to violence and even 'hatred' are notable exceptions in the jurisprudence of the European Court.[526]

The Human Rights Committee's jurisprudence demonstrates that it has exercised 'great caution in the imposition of criminal penalties that punish speech', to the point that a term of imprisonment has *never* been found to be an appropriate penalty to speech in individual cases that have come before the Committee.[527] The Committee has also criticized counterterrorism laws in nations such as Cameroon and Bangladesh that are punishable by the death penalty.[528] And the Counter-Terrorism Committee 'considers that the imposition of the death penalty in cases of incitement to commit acts of terrorism may run afoul of the requirements of international human rights law'.[529]

Similarly, the Working Group on Arbitrary Detention has asserted that 'a vague and general reference to the interests of national security or public order, without being

---

[521] The band uploaded multiple videos to YouTube, one in which they perform the song without incident, and another in which they do not manage to perform the song in full, but members of the band stood in front of a cathedral altar wearing brightly coloured dresses and balaclavas before security stopped them. At points the band members sung, knelt and crossed themselves. ECtHR, *Alekhina v. Russia* (App. no. 38004/12), 17 July 2018, §§11–16.

[522] Ibid., §§48, 231.

[523] Ibid., §266.

[524] Ibid., §267.

[525] See, e.g., HRC, General Comment No. 34 (2011), §§34–35; ECtHR, *Guja v. Moldova* (App. no. 14277/04), 12 February 2008, §78; IACtHR, *Palamara-Iribarne v. Chile* (Series C, no. 135), 22 November 2005, §85; ACtHPR, *Konaté v Burkina Faso* (App. no. 4/2013), 5 December 2014, §145.

[526] See ch. 1 (Introduction), s. II.3.2.6. (Criminal penalties for speech); ch. 5 (Espionage and Official Secrets Laws), s. III.5.5. (Penalties).

[527] HRC, *Rabbae v. Netherlands* (Comm. No. 2124/2011), 14 July 2016, Individual Opinion (concurring) of Committee members Sarah Cleveland and Mauro Politi, §7. See ch. 1 (Introduction), s. II.3.2.6. (Criminal penalties for speech).

[528] HRC, *Concluding Observations: Cameroon* (2017) UN Doc. CCPR/C/CMR/5, §§11–12; HRC, *Concluding Observations: Bangladesh* (2017) UN Doc. CCPR/C/BGD/CO/1, §§9–10.

[529] CTED, *Global survey of the implementation of Security Council resolution 1624 (2005) by Member States* (2016) UN Doc. S/2016/50 (Annex), §22; see s. I. (Introduction (describing the mandate of the UN Counter-Terrorism Committee)).

properly explained and documented, is insufficient to convince the Working Group that ... restrictions ... by way of deprivation of liberty are necessary'.[530] For example, the Working Group has criticized the proportionality of article 105 of China's Criminal Law, which includes fixed-term prison sentences of up to life imprisonment for 'subverting state power or overthrowing the socialist system'.[531] The Working Group, observing that this provision can apply to criminalize the 'exercise of fundamental freedoms, including those of expression and association', considered it to be 'neither necessary to protect public or private interests against injury nor proportionate to guilt'.[532]

Although the European Court of Human Rights considers the 'imposition of a prison sentence for a press offence' or for public interest speech to be compatible with free speech 'only in exceptional circumstances', it classifies 'incitement to violence' or 'dissemination of hate speech' as constituting such circumstances.[533] So while the Court will generally find that states should 'display restraint in resorting to criminal proceedings',[534] in a number of instances the European Court has allowed criminal convictions and punishment—even imprisonment—for speech that was related to terrorism.[535]

One of the few cases in which a prison term was found compatible with free speech by the Court was when a former Turkish mayor was sentenced to 12 months' imprisonment for suggesting he supported the PKK national liberation movement.[536] In an interview published in a newspaper, the mayor said: 'I support the PKK national liberation movement; on the other hand, I am not in favour of massacres' and suggested that the PKK kill women and children 'by mistake'.[537] The Court found that the comments—even though 'both contradictory and ambiguous' and liable to being 'interpreted in several ways'—should be viewed in the context of 'murderous attacks carried out by the PKK' in south-east Turkey, and the 'extreme tension' at that time.[538] In those circumstances, comments from a former mayor in a daily newspaper 'had to be regarded as *likely* to exacerbate an already explosive situation', and the Court held that the penalty imposed 'could reasonably be regarded as answering a 'pressing social need' that was justified under the European Convention.[539] This was despite the fact that the

---

[530] WGAD, *Gulmira Imin v. China* (Opinion no. 29/2012), 29 August 2012, §29.
[531] WGAD, *Chen Shuqing and Lü Gengsong v. China* (Opinion no. 76/2019), 21 November 2019, §7 ('Article 105 (1) of the Criminal Law of China ("subversion of state power") stipulates a fixed term of imprisonment of not more than three years for participants, three to 10 years for active participants, and not less than 10 years or life imprisonment for those who organize, plot or carry out the scheme of subverting State power or overthrowing the socialist system').
[532] Ibid., §46. Before the Working Group, Chinese authorities did not contest the claim that the applicants in the case, both freelance writers and political dissidents, had been 'charged, tried and imprisoned for their online and offline political activities and their role in the banned Democracy Party of China': §§49–50.
[533] ECtHR (GC), *Cumpănă v. Romania* (App. no. 33348/96), 17 December 2004, §115; ECtHR, *Rouillan v. France* (App. no. 28000/19), 23 June 2022, §74 See ch. 1 (Introduction), s. II.3.2.6. (Criminal penalties for speech).
[534] ECtHR (GC), *Incal v. Turkey* (App. no. 22678/93), 9 June 1998, §54.
[535] See, e.g., ECtHR, *Sürek v. Turkey (No. 1)* (App. no. 26682/95), 8 July 1999, §64. See also ECtHR, *Altintas v. Turkey* (App. no. 50495/08) 10 March 2020, §31–36; ECtHR (GC), *Sürek v. Turkey (No. 3)* (App. no. 24735/94), 8 July 1999, §31.
[536] The court noted that only one-fifth of his sentence was served in prison: ECtHR (GC), *Zana v. Turkey* (App. no.18954/91), 25 November 1997, §61. See s. III.3.2. (Causal link between speech and harm).
[537] Ibid., §12.
[538] ECtHR (GC), *Zana v. Turkey* (App. no. 18954/91), 25 November 1997, §§58–59.
[539] Ibid., §§60–62.

mayor argued that he had told journalists he supported a 'national liberation movement but was opposed to violence', that he was not a member of the PKK and had advocated for non-violent action as a political figure for many years.[540]

The European Court applied a similar focus to the timing and context in a case involving an uncle who dressed his nephew in a T-shirt which read 'I am the bomb!' and 'Jihad, born on 11 September'.[541] The nephew only wore the T-shirt for one afternoon in his kindergarten class and the wording was only viewed by two adults who were helping dress the child.[542] The uncle was sentenced to two months' suspended imprisonment and a fine for 'glorify[ing]' serious crimes.[543] In finding that the penalty was acceptable,[544] the European Court took into account that the incident took place 'only a few months after other terrorist attacks, which caused the death of three children in a school' and held that the French courts were in a 'privileged position to apprehend the need for a sentence' in the case and to better appreciate the 'specific societal problems in particular communities'.[545]

But the European Court will not always uphold criminal penalties even when speech incites violence. For example, in a recent case a former member of an extreme left-wing terror group active in the 1980s—who had spent 25 years in prison for acts of terrorist murder—was interviewed by journalists in a radio broadcast which was also uploaded to a website. When asked about terrorist attacks that had been committed in France in 2015, he said that even though 'we can say we're absolutely against their reactionary idea', 'we can't say that these kids are cowards' and that he 'found them very brave' as they know 'there are two or three thousand cops around them'.[546] He was sentenced to a fine and eight months' imprisonment which was increased on appeal to 18 months' imprisonment, including 10 months' probation, which he served in his home.[547]

The Court determined his interview amounted to 'indirect incitement to the use of terrorist violence' as he 'presented the terrorist method of action ... in a romantic light by using positive and glorious images of the perpetrators'.[548] And the Court held that domestic courts had taken care to justify 'not only the principle of the penalty imposed, but also its nature and quantum'.[549] However, in light of its 'nature' and 'severity', the Court held his prison sentence was disproportionate to the aim pursued, and found a violation of article 10 with specific 'regard to the severity of the criminal sanction imposed'.[550]

---

[540] Ibid., §52.
[541] ECtHR, *Z.B. v France* (App. no. 46883/15), 2 September 2021, §11. See s. III.3.2. (Causal link between speech and harm).
[542] ECtHR, *Z.B. v France* (App. no. 46883/15), 2 September 2021, §§8, 62.
[543] The boy's mother was also convicted and sentenced to one month suspended sentence and a fine, and they both were required to pay damages in a civil action.
[544] The European Court considered, but ultimately dismissed, an argument by France that article 17 of the Convention applied: ECtHR, *Z.B. v France* (App. no. 46883/15) 2 September 2021, §§1827.
[545] Ibid., §§62–66.
[546] ECtHR, *Rouillan v. France* (App. no. 28000/19), 23 June 2022, §5. See s. III.3.2.1 ('Glorification', 'justification' and 'apology' offences).
[547] For approximately 6 months of the 10-month probation period he was placed under electronic surveillance.
[548] ECtHR, *Rouillan v. France* (App. no. 28000/19), 23 June 2022, §§69, 71.See s. III.3.2.1. ('Glorification', 'justification' and 'apology' offences).
[549] Ibid., §75.
[550] Ibid., §§75–77. See s. III.5. (Penalties).

The Inter-American Court of Human Rights has held that a penalty for speech 'must be proportionate to the right affected and to the responsibility of the perpetrator, so that it should be established based on the different nature and seriousness of the acts'.[551] In one of the only terrorism cases before the Inter-American Court, the Court found that penalizing speakers by disqualifying them from using social media was disproportionate.[552] In this case, leaders of the Mapuche indigenous people were convicted under Chile's Counter-terrorism Act for acts of protest and unrest, including threats of terrorist arson.[553] They were sentenced to five years' imprisonment, 'absolute and permanent disqualification from public office and positions' and disqualification for 15 years 'from operating a social communications media outlet' or performing functions 'connected with the broadcast or dissemination of opinions or information'.[554] Although the Inter-American Court held that the convictions ultimately violated the principle of legality and procedural guarantees, the Court also noted that it considered the penalties restricting the freedom of expression of the Mapuche leader 'contrary to the principle of the proportionality of the punishment'.[555] In circumstances where the defendants played a 'decisive role in communicating the interests' of their communities, this penalty limited their right to expression 'in the exercise of their functions as leaders or representatives', and in turn 'could have instilled a reasonable fear in other members' of these communities who participate in lawful protests.[556] The Court therefore considered the restriction to have a 'negative impact on the social dimension of the right to freedom of thought and expression' as the Court had established in its case law, and found a violation of article 13.[557]

The African Court has also held that custodial sentences for violations of the laws of freedom of speech are generally inappropriate, and will only be lawful in 'serious and very exceptional circumstances' such as 'incitement to international crimes, public incitement to hatred, discrimination or violence or threats against a person or group of people, because of specific criteria such as race, colour, religion and nationality'.[558]

---

[551] IACtHR, *Norín Catrimán et al. v. Chile* (Series C, no. 279), 29 May 2014, §374.
[552] Ibid., §374. See s. III.3.3. (Intent).
[553] IACtHR, *Norín Catrimán v. Chile* (Series C, no. 279), 29 May 2014.
[554] Ibid., §117. This sentence was handed down against three of the applicants in this case. There were five other applicants in the proceedings who received different sentences: §§120–152.
[555] Ibid., §§374–376.
[556] Ibid.
[557] Ibid., §§375–378.
[558] ACtHPR, *Konaté v. Burkina Faso* (App. no. 4/2013), 5 December 2014, §165. Although this case grapples with criminal defamation laws, it reflects the Court's reluctance to consider criminal penalties for expression proportionate in any circumstances. Cf. ECOWAS CCJ, *Federation of African Journalists v. Gambia* (Suit no. ECW/CCJ/APP/36/15), 13 February 2018, where the Community Court of Justice of ECOWAS held that the practise of imposing criminal sanctions for sedition, defamation and false news publication has a chilling effect that may unduly restrict journalists' freedom of expression.

6. Approach of Private Companies to Online Incitement to Terrorism

Technology and social media companies play a critical role in responding to incitement to terrorism. As ISIS rose to power in Iraq and Syria, an estimated 40,000 foreign fighters travelled to the region to support them, many recruited through social media.[559] In 2019, attacks on two mosques in Christchurch, New Zealand, which led to the deaths of 51 people, were livestreamed on Facebook for 17 minutes and viewed 4,000 times before being removed.[560]

A number of technology and social media companies have committed to ensuring that they address hateful and violent speech in a manner consistent with international human rights standards.[561] For example, Twitter's Rules reference freedom of expression grounded in 'the United States Bill of Rights and the European Convention on Human Rights', and informed by 'works such as United Nations Principles on Business and Human Rights'.[562] Meta's policy declares that it is 'committed to respecting human rights as set out in ... the International Covenant on Civil and Political Rights' and other treaties.[563] It also has Community Standards stating that it 'look[s] to international human rights standards to make ... judgments' about content moderation.[564] And the Global Network Initiative, an alliance of internet companies that includes Meta, Microsoft and other tech giants, recognizes that such companies 'have the responsibility to respect and promote the freedom of expression', and 'should comply with ... internationally recognized human rights' including the rights set out in the ICCPR.[565] The Initiative also provides that the scope of article 19(3) to be 'read within the context of further interpretations issued by international human rights bodies, including the Human Rights Committee and the Special Rapporteur on the promotion and protection of the right to freedom of opinion and expression'.[566]

---

[559] See, e.g., US Department of State, 'Country Reports on Terrorism (2019)'.
[560] Christchurch Call, 'Christchurch Call story'.
[561] UN Special Rapporteur D. Kaye, *Report of the Special Rapporteur on the promotion and protection of the right to freedom of opinion and expression* (2018) UN Doc. A/HRC/38/35, §70. See also E.M. Aswad, 'The Future of Freedom of Expression Online' (2018) 17 *Duke Law & Technology Review* 26, 34. See ch. 3 (Hate Speech), s. V. (Approach of Private Companies to Online Hate Speech).
[562] Twitter (known as X since July 2023), 'Defending and respecting the rights of people using our service'; @jack, 'Tweet dated 10 August 2018'. In November 2022, after Elon Musk laid off the entire human rights team at Twitter, the UN High Commissioner for Human Rights sent an open letter to Musk urging that 'human rights are central to the management of Twitter under your leadership' and noting 'Twitter's responsibility to respect human rights ... set out in more detail in the UN Guiding Principles on Business and Human Rights': V. Türk, 'Open letter from Volker Türk, United Nations High Commissioner for Human Rights, to Mr. Elon Musk, Chief Executive Officer at Twitter' (5 November 2022).
[563] Meta, 'Corporate Human Rights Policy'.
[564] Meta, 'Facebook Community Standards'. See also TikTok, 'Upholding human rights' ('Our philosophy is informed by the International Bill of Human Rights ... and the United Nations Guiding Principles on Business and Human Rights'); Meta Newsroom, 'Hard Questions: Where Do We Draw the Line on Free Expression?' (9 August 2018) ('We look for guidance in documents like Article 19 of the International Covenant on Civil and Political Rights (ICCPR), which set standards for when it's appropriate to place restrictions on freedom of expression').
[565] GNI, 'GNI Principles on Freedom of Expression and Privacy' (2017).
[566] GNI, 'GNI Principles on Freedom of Expression and Privacy' (2017), n 7. The GNI Principles have also 'been drafted with reference to' the Johannesburg Principles: n 9. And Facebook, Google, Microsoft and Twitter also

An additional commitment was made regarding terrorist speech by 55 governments, the European Commission, 14 online service providers and numerous civil society organizations in the Christchurch Call.[567] Established by France and New Zealand in the aftermath of the 2019 Christchurch attacks, the Christchurch Call includes commitments made by tech companies and governments, as well as joint commitments. The companies that have joined the Christchurch Call—which include Facebook (Meta), Twitter, Microsoft and Google—have committed to taking transparent measures to prevent the upload and dissemination of 'terrorist and violent extremist content ... in a manner consistent with human rights and fundamental freedoms'.[568] These providers have also committed to (a) 'greater transparency in the setting of community standards and terms of service'; (b) regular public reporting 'on the quantity and nature' of terrorist content being detected and removed and (c) providing 'an efficient complaint and appeals process for those wishing to contest the removal of their content'.[569] In addition, the Christchurch Call requires companies to conduct a review of the operation of algorithms that may drive or amplify terrorist content. This includes using algorithms that direct users to 'credible, positive alternatives or counter-narratives'.[570]

While many human rights and media freedom organizations expressed broad support for the key values of the Christchurch Call,[571] a coalition of civil society organizations expressed some concerns in response to the Call.[572] So far the Call does not define 'terrorism and violent extremism' and does not distinguish between the obligations of user-generated content platforms—such as Facebook and YouTube—and those of internet access providers, including search engines such as Google. Some civil society actors have argued that '[e]fforts to restrict content should be limited to the level of user-generated content platforms and should not reach the infrastructure level' on the basis that broadening the 'scope of the Call beyond social media platforms can endanger the global and open nature of the Internet'.[573]

Two recent decisions of the US Supreme Court—decided on the same day—have also established the limits of technology companies' responsibility for the consequences of terrorist speech. In *Twitter v. Taamneh,* the US Supreme Court considered a case in which victims of terror attacks attempted to sue three of the largest social media

---

have policies in place to engage with human rights experts and civil society organizations to ensure they are correctly implementing these standards. See, e.g., Meta, 'Facebook Community Standards'.

[567] Christchurch Call, 'Support'.
[568] Ibid.; Christchurch Call, 'Christchurch Call text'.
[569] Ibid.
[570] Ibid.
[571] See also UN Counter-Terrorism Committee, 'Delhi Declaration on countering the use of new and emerging technologies for terrorism purposes' (2022), which '[n]otes the importance of continuing discussions on the challenges posed by emerging technologies being used for terrorist purposes ... including ... the Christchurch Call' and expressing an 'intention to develop ... a set of non-binding guiding principles' with a view to assisting states to 'counter the threat posed by the use of new and emerging technologies for terrorist purposes, including by compiling good practices on the opportunities offered by the same set of technologies to counter the threat, consistent with international human rights'.
[572] F Badii et al., 'Civil Society Positions on Christchurch Call Pledge' (Electronic Frontier Foundation).
[573] Ibid., 3. See, e.g., Article 19, 'New Zealand: Christchurch Call, violent extremism and human rights' (14 May 2021).

companies in the world—Facebook, Twitter and Google (which owns YouTube)—for aiding and abetting ISIS.[574] The case was brought by the family members of a victim of an ISIS terrorist attack in Istanbul, who accused the companies of 'knowingly allowing ISIS and its supporters to use their platforms and benefit from their "recommendation" algorithms, enabling ISIS to connect with the broader public, fundraise, and radicalize new recruits'.[575] But the Court found against them, holding that ISIS' use of these platforms was insufficient to fulfil the aiding and abetting standard of 'a conscious, voluntary, and culpable participation in another's wrongdoing'.[576] Justice Thomas, delivering the Court's unanimous opinion, held the companies' algorithms were 'agnostic as to the nature of content, matching any content (including ISIS' content) with any user' more likely to view it.[577] To find otherwise, the Court considered, would 'necessarily' hold the companies liable 'as having aided and abetted each and every ISIS terrorist act committed anywhere in the world'.[578]

In the companion case of *Gonzalez v. Google,* the Supreme Court was asked to consider the scope of section 230 of the Communications Decency Act, which protects an 'interactive computer service' such as YouTube, Google, Facebook or Twitter from liability arising from the speech of their users.[579] The plaintiffs, family members of 23-year-old Nohemi Gonzalez who was killed in a 2015 ISIS attack in Paris, argued that these companies lose section 230 immunity when they 'recommend' certain content to users by way of algorithms.[580] Google strongly contested this interpretation, as did a number of technology companies and free speech advocates who filed amicus briefs in the case.[581] Arguing that the plaintiffs' interpretation might 'threaten the basic organizational decisions of the modern internet', Google observed that platforms such as YouTube have to 'make constant choices about what information to display and how' to ensure that the vast amount of data online can be consumed by users.[582] And as

---

[574] US Supreme Court, *Twitter, Inc v. Taamneh* 591 U.S. 471, 18 May 2023. The plaintiffs argued that these companies had aided and abetted ISIS in violation of 18 U.S.C §2333(a) (which provides that US nationals who have been 'injured ... by reason of an act of international terrorism' may sue for damages) and §2333(d)(2) (which imposes civil liability on 'any person who aids and abets, by knowingly providing substantial assistance').
[575] Ibid., 5. The plaintiffs also had a specific set of allegations against Google, namely that it was gaining revenue from advertisements that were placed on ISIS videos.
[576] Ibid., 493.
[577] Ibid., 499.
[578] Ibid., 501. See also, ACLU, 'ACLU Comments Supreme Court Decisions Allowing Free Speech Online to Flourish' (18 May 2023). In a short concurring decision, Justice Jackson noted that both *Twitter v. Taamneh* and *Google v. Gonzalez* were 'narrow' decisions. She observed that to the extent the Court drew on 'general principles of tort and criminal law' to 'inform its understanding of §2333(d)(2)' these propositions 'do not necessarily translate to other contexts': US Supreme Court, *Twitter, Inc v. Taamneh* 598 U.S. 471, 18 May 2023, Concurring Opinion of Jackson J.
[579] US Supreme Court, *Gonzalez v. Google LLC* 598 U.S. 617, 18 May 2023. Section 230 of the Communications Decency Act provides 'No provider or user of an interactive computer service shall be treated as the publisher or speaker of any information provided by another information content providers': 47 U.S.C. §230(c)(1).
[580] See US Court of Appeals, Ninth Circuit, *Gonzalez v. Google LLC,* 2 F.4th 871, 881 (22 June 2021) ('The Gonzalez Plaintiffs' theory of liability generally arises from Google's recommendations of content to users', alleging that 'Google "has recommended ISIS videos to users"').
[581] See, e.g., US Supreme Court, *Gonzalez v. Google LLC* 598 U.S. 617, 18 May 2023, Brief of Amici Curiae Article 19: Global Campaign for Free Expression and the International Justice Clinic at the University of California, Irvine School of Law in Support of Respondent (19 January 2023); US Supreme Court, *Gonzalez v. Google LLC* 598 U.S. 617, 18 May 2023, Brief of Microsoft Corp. as Amicus Curiae in support of the Respondent (19 January 2023).
[582] US Supreme Court, *Gonzalez v. Google LLC* 598 U.S. 617, 18 May 2023, Brief in Opposition (5 July 2022), 22.

an amicus brief filed by the former UN Special Rapporteur on freedom of expression contended, if section 230 protections were removed, websites would face 'potentially crushing liability' and be forced to 'err on the side of caution by removing or blocking any content that might even remotely touch on illegal behaviour'.[583]

In a short *per curiam* decision, the Supreme Court declined to address the application of section 230, leaving its protections in place. In light of its decision in *Twitter v. Taamneh*, the US Supreme Court held that the complaint had 'little, if any, plausible claim for relief' on the merits, and remanded the case for reconsideration on the basis of *Twitter v. Taamneh*.[584] However, US lawmakers have called for law reform, with Democrats arguing that platforms should be responsible for taking down more content and Republicans arguing the opposite view.[585]

IV. Recommendations

The following recommendations draw on minimum international standards applicable to speech-related terrorism and public order laws. Where there is a divergence or lacunae in such standards, this chapter suggests a best practice approach based on national jurisprudence or emerging international standards. These recommendations are addressed to states as signatories to the international treaties that underlie such standards. However, they are also intended to guide private companies seeking to apply them.[586] And these recommendations are intended to be cumulative: they should *all* be implemented to ensure that terrorism and public order laws comply with minimum international standards.

International standards governing terrorism and public order laws are closely related to other types of speech—in particular the wider body of jurisprudence governing the interplay between speech and national security (of which terror-related speech is a subset), as well as hate speech that incites to violence. The lines between hateful speech that incites violence and speech that incites *terrorist* violence are often blurred, particularly in light of the contested definition of what physical conduct amounts to terrorism.[587] In light of this, these recommendations correlate with and should be read alongside recommendations with respect to hate speech and espionage and official secrets laws.[588]

---

[583] US Supreme Court, *Gonzalez v. Google LLC* 598 U.S. 617, 18 May 2023, Brief of Amici Curiae Article 19: Global Campaign for Free Expression and the International Justice Clinic at the University of California, Irvine School of Law in Support of Respondent (19 January 2023), 3.
[584] US Supreme Court, *Gonzalez v. Google LLC* 598 U.S. 617, 18 May 2023, 622.
[585] See, e.g., A. Liptak, ' Supreme Court Won't Hold Tech Companies Liable for User Posts' (The New York Times, 18 May 2023).
[586] See ch. 3 (Hate Speech), s. V. (Approach of Private Companies to Online Hate Speech).
[587] See Introduction (discussing the contested definition of terrorism).
[588] See ch. 3 (Hate Speech), s. VI. (Recommendations); ch. 5 (Espionage and Official Secrets Laws), s. IV. (Recommendations).

1. States must provide clear definitions of the violent conduct defined as 'terrorism' in their laws.

The lack of an internationally agreed definition of terrorism does not discharge a state's obligation to fulfil the principle of legality,[589] which means that terrorism laws must be 'formulated with sufficient precision to enable people to regulate their conduct' and to 'foresee, to a degree that is reasonable in the circumstances, the consequences which a given action may entail'.[590] This is particularly critical as terrorism laws often subject speech to heavy criminal penalties.[591]

The same requirements apply to criminal laws that regulate speech in the name of 'public order'.[592] Such offences should never penalize speech that is merely critical of a political party or government of the day, and peaceful protest and dissent must be lawful as restrictions cannot 'put in jeopardy the right itself'.[593]

Consistently with soft law guidance, criminalizing 'extremism' without a clear link to serious unlawful conduct is 'irreconcilable with the principle of legality'.[594] And laws that penalize 'glorification', 'justification' and 'apology' of terrorism are similarly likely to fail minimum legality requirements.[595]

2. States' terrorism laws should only criminalize speech if the speaker intends to incite an act of terrorist violence.

For all penalties imposed on speech, states must 'demonstrate in specific and individualized fashion the precise nature of the threat' caused by the speech.[596] International bodies have observed that speech that incites violence can clearly be penalized, as can incitement to a serious criminal offence, 'armed resistance' and 'serious disturbances' of public order.[597] In the *Rabbae* case, members of the Human Rights Committee

---

[589] See s. III.1. (Legality).
[590] ECtHR, *Alekhina v. Russia* (App. no. 38004/12), 17 July 2018, §254. States should also clearly define national security in their terrorism laws: See ch. 5 (Espionage and Official Secrets Laws), s. IV.2. (Recommendations).
[591] IACtHR, *Norín Catrimán v. Chile* (Series C, no. 279), 29 May 2014, §163. Terror laws, like all criminal laws, must also be non-discriminatory and non-retroactive. UN Special Rapporteur on terrorism Martin Scheinin, *Report on Ten areas of best practices in countering terrorism* (2010) UN Doc. A/HRC/16/51, §27.
[592] See s. III.1.3. (Definition of public order).
[593] HRC, General Comment No. 34 (2011), §21.
[594] See s. III.1.2. (Definition of extremism); UN Special Rapporteur on terrorism, *Report on Human rights impact of policies and practices aimed at preventing and countering violent extremism* (2020) UN Doc. A/HRC/43/46, §14.
[595] See s. III.1.1. (Definition of terrorism). Such laws may also fail on the basis of insufficiently stringent intent or causation requirements. See s. III.3.2.1. ('Glorification', 'justification' and 'apology' offences); See also s. IV.5. (Recommendations).
[596] HRC, General Comment No. 34 (2011), §35.
[597] See s. III.3.1. (Harm); HRC, *Rabbae v. Netherlands* (Comm. no. 2124/2011) Individual Opinion (concurring) of Committee members Sarah Cleveland and Mauro Politi, §7; HRC, *Marchant Reyes v. Chile* (Comm. no. 2627/2015), 7 November 2017; ECtHR, *Leroy v. France* (App. no. 36109/03), 2 October 2008, §45; ECtHR, *Erkizia Almandoz v. Spain* (App. no. 5869/17), 22 June 2021, §46.; IACmHR, *Roca Antúnez v. Cuba* (Case 12.127) 24 February 2018, §107; ACHR Art. 13(5).

suggested that speech should only be criminalized if it 'incites the commission of criminal offences or acts of violence'.[598] And when speech is criminalized on the basis that it is likely to incite a serious terrorist offence, that offence must itself comply with international human rights standards.[599] For example, offences such as criticizing a state's leaders or institutions—themselves incompatible with international human rights law—cannot be used as a legitimate basis to penalize speech likely to incite such a 'crime'.[600] And any terror offence that discriminates against a particular religion is similarly incompatible with international standards.[601]

A stringent harm requirement—such as requiring incitement to acts of violence or serious criminal offences that risk serious physical injury or endanger human life—is required to avoid overbroad criminalization that may result from the European Court's malleable conception of harm.[602] The Court interprets 'incitement to violence' to include implied calls for violence, and to be only one of 'several factors' it will consider in its assessment of whether (even criminal) penalties imposed on speech are 'necessary'.[603] And the Court allows penalization of speech if it 'could be seen as a call for violence, *hatred or intolerance*', meaning that speech does not need to 'involve an explicit call for an act of violence, or other criminal acts' for a penalty to be considered 'necessary'.[604]

But allowing criminal laws to target speech that promotes 'intolerance' casts an overbroad net over speech.[605] And authoritarian regimes are well placed to manipulate terms such as 'intolerance' and argue they were following international standards by doing so. Nor is the Court's analysis of speech under article 17—which obviates the need to consider intent, harm and causation altogether—compatible with the balancing test required under international treaties.[606] A strict harm standard such as that articulated by members of the Human Rights Committee in the *Rabbae* case is a better approach, minimizing the risk that non-dangerous speech will be penalized.[607]

---

[598] See s. III.3.1. (Harm); HRC, *Rabbae v. Netherlands* (Comm. no. 2124/2011) Individual Opinion (concurring) of Committee members Sarah Cleveland and Mauro Politi, §7.

[599] See, e.g., HRC, General Comment No. 34 (2011), §26 (laws restricting speech 'must also themselves be compatible with the provisions, aims and objectives of the Covenant').

[600] See ch. 2 (Insulting Speech), s. III.3.3.1.1. (Statements about public officials including heads of state or government). See also ch. 4 (False Speech), s. IV.4. (Recommendations).

[601] See, e.g., HRC, General Comment No. 34 (2011), §26 ('Laws must not violate the non-discrimination provisions of the Covenant').

[602] See s. III.3.1. (Harm).

[603] See s. III.3.1. (Harm). See, e.g., ECtHR, *Rouillan v. France* (App. no. 28000/19), 23 June 2022; ECtHR (GC), *Perinçek v. Switzerland* (App. no. 27510/08), 15 October 2015, §§204–208.

[604] ECtHR, Guide on Article 10 of the Convention, 31 August 2022, §§554, 557 (emphasis added); ECtHR, *Ibragimov v. Russia* (App. nos. 1413/08 & 28621/11), 28 August 2018, §§94–98; ECtHR, *Vejdeland v. Sweden* (App. no. 1813/07), 9 February 2012, §55.

[605] See, e.g., ECtHR, *Erkizia Almandoz v. Spain* (App. no. 5869/17), 22 June 2021, Concurring Opinion of Judge Lemmens (finding it 'somewhat ambiguous as to the types of remarks, in connection with terrorism' that authorities may restrict), §1. International standards on incitement to 'hatred' are dealt with in Chapter 3: See ch. 3 (Hate Speech), s. III.2.3.1. (Harm).

[606] See ss III.3.1. (Harm) and III. (International Legal Standards) (setting out the tripartite test pursuant to Art. 19 of the ICCPR); ECtHR, *Roj TV A/S v. Denmark* (App. no. 24683/14), 17 April 2018; ECtHR, *Hizb Ut-Tahrir v. Germany* (App. no. 31098/08), 12 June 2012; ECtHR, *Kasymakhunov and Saybatalov v. Russia* (App. nos. 26261/05 & 26377/06), 14 March 2013.

[607] HRC, *Rabbae v. Netherlands* (Comm. no. 2124/2011) Individual Opinion (concurring) of Committee members Sarah Cleveland and Mauro Politi, §7.

3. There should be an objective probability that the harm the speaker intended to incite would imminently occur as a direct result of the speech.

International standards provide that states must demonstrate a causal link between speech and harm before speech can be penalized.[608] National terrorism and public order laws that do not do so violate international law. Consistent with recommendations for criminal hate speech and espionage and official secrets laws,[609] it is recommended that states should only criminalize speech under terror or public order laws if it is objectively probable that an act of violence or serious criminal offence would imminently occur as a direct result of the impugned speech.[610] This standard accords with the Human Rights Committee's position that states must establish a 'direct and immediate' causal link between speech and harm if it is to be penalized.[611] And it is consistent with the UN-approved Rabat Plan of Action, which recommends 'a *reasonable probability* that the speech would succeed in *inciting actual action* against the target group, recognizing that such causation should be rather direct'.[612]

The European Court's relatively weak and inconsistent causation tests of whether speech is 'capable of' or 'liable to' or 'could' be 'seen as a call for violence, hatred or intolerance',[613] and its disregard of causation when assessing cases under article 17,[614] leave too much speech unprotected or subject to viewpoint-based restrictions.[615] As articulated in a number of concurring judgments handed down by European Court judges, these tests have seen the Court place 'too much weight' on the 'form of words' used by speakers, or its 'offensive' nature[616] when it should instead focus on the speaker's intent and the words' 'likely impact'.[617] Like hate speech, speech endorsing terrorism may be particularly abhorrent but, as judges of the Court have argued, the focus should be on whether there was a 'real and genuine risk' that language would 'incite to violence' and whether there was an intention to do so.[618] In practice, the flexibility of the

---

[608] See s. III.3.2. (Causal link between speech and harm).
[609] See ch. 3 (Hate Speech), s. VI.3. (Recommendations) and ch. 5 (Speech Related to National Security: Espionage and Official Secrets Laws), s. IV.3. (Recommendations).
[610] Objective probability meaning more probable than not. See s. IV.2. (Recommendations).
[611] HRC, General Comment No. 34 (2011), §35; UN Special Rapporteur on the right to freedom of opinion and expression F. LaRue, *Report of the Special Rapporteur on the Promotion and Protection of the Right to Freedom of Opinion and Expression* (2013) UN Doc. No A/68/362, §§52–53.
[612] Rabat Plan of Action, §29(f) (emphasis added). See also UN Special Rapporteur on terrorism, *Impact of measures to address terrorism and violent extremism on civic space and the rights of civil society actors and human rights defenders* (2019) UN Doc. A/HRC/40/52, §37.
[613] See, e.g., ECtHR (GC), *Sürek v. Turkey (No. 3)* (App. no. 24735/94), 8 July 1999, §40; ECtHR (GC), *Sürek v. Turkey (No. 4)* (App. no. 24762/94), 8 July 1999, §58; ECtHR, *Ibragimov v. Russia* (App. nos. 1413/08 & 28621/11), 28 August 2018, §98; ECtHR (GC), *Perinçek v. Switzerland* (App. no. 27510/08), 15 October 2015, §207.
[614] See, e.g., ECtHR, *Lilliendahl v. Iceland* (App. no. 29297/18), 12 May 2020, §46. See s. III.3.2. (Causal link between speech and harm); See also ch. 3 (Hate Speech), s. VI.3. (Recommendations).
[615] For example, blasphemy or denialism laws which prohibit speech on the basis of content rather than harm or intent: See ch. 3 (Hate Speech), s. VI.1. (Recommendations).
[616] Dyer (n 399) 78, 94, 97107.
[617] ECtHR (GC), *Sürek v. Turkey (No. 4)* (App. no. 24762/94), 8 July 1999, Joint Concurring Opinion of Judges Palm, Tulkens, Fischbach, Casadevall and Greve.
[618] Ibid.

Court's varied causation standards has seen it develop a patchwork of jurisprudence from which it is difficult to draw patterns and predict what speech will be lawful.[619]

4. Terrorism laws should incorporate a dual intent requirement: intent to communicate the impugned message and intent to incite the commission of a terrorist act.

Terrorism laws should incorporate a dual intent requirement: intent to communicate the impugned message and intent to incite the commission of a terrorist act.[620] Intent should not be presumed.[621] Stringent intent standards are particularly important to protect those who report on terrorism. Journalists should never be punished 'solely on the grounds that they had published statements by terrorist organizations'.[622] Penalization for media reporting of terrorism should only take place in the exceptional circumstances where media intend to incite violence or a serious offence and there is an objective probability this imminently occurs as a direct result of the reporting.[623] If a journalist repeats what a speaker has said in order to report the news, and that speaker's words amount to incitement to terrorism, this does not mean that the journalist's reporting amounts to incitement. Instead, like all speakers, a journalist should expect their speech to be protected if they did not intend to incite terrorism.

The European Court has not always adhered to this high bar. For instance, the Court allowed a conviction for a media professional who provided an 'outlet' for terrorist speech by way of published letters from readers, even though he 'did not personally associate himself with the views contained in the letters'.[624] This case, rightly considered an outlier and criticized by judges on the Court, does not accord with international intent standards or the bulk of the Court's jurisprudence.[625] And the Court should abandon its practice of analysing terrorism laws' application to speech under article 17 since, even if there are some cases that would be appropriately dealt with under article 17, this application of article 17 is akin to content-based regulation that bypasses an analysis of intent—as well as harm and causation—altogether.[626]

---

[619] See s. III.3.2. (Causal link between speech and harm).
[620] See s. III.3.3. (Intent); see, e.g., UN Special Rapporteur on terrorism, Martin Scheinin, *Report on Ten areas of best practices in countering terrorism* (2010) UN Doc. A/HRC/16/51, §§30–31; COE Convention on the Prevention of Terrorism Art. 5; COE, *Explanatory Report to the Council of Europe Convention on the Prevention of Terrorism* (2005) CETS 196, §§99–100; UN Secretary General, *The protection of human rights and fundamental freedoms while countering terrorism* (2008) UN Doc. A/63/337, §61.
[621] IACtHR, *Norín Catrimán v. Chile* (Series C, no. 279), 29 May 2014, §171.
[622] ECtHR, *Gözel and Özer v. Turkey* (App. nos. 43453/04 & 31098/05), 6 July 2010, §61. See s. III.3.3. (Intent).
[623] See s. III.4.1. (Public Interest).
[624] ECtHR, *Sürek v. Turkey (no. 1)* (App. no. 26682/95), 8 July 1999, §§63–65; see s. III.3.3. (Intent).
[625] ECtHR, *Sürek v. Turkey (no. 1)* (App. no. 26682/95), 8 July 1999, Joint Partly Dissenting Opinion of Judges Tulkens, Casadevall and Greve and Partly Dissenting Opinion of Judge Palm. See also ECtHR (GC), *Jersild v. Denmark* (App. no. 15890/89), 23 September 1994, §31. See s. III.3.3. (Intent).
[626] See s. III.3.1. (Harm); ECtHR, *Roj TV A/S v. Denmark* (App. no. 24683/14), 17 April 2018; ECtHR, *Hizb Ut-Tahrir v. Germany* (App. no. 31098/08), 12 June 2012; ECtHR, *Kasymakhunov and Saybatalov v. Russia* (App. nos. 26261/05 & 26377/06), 14 March 2013.

5. 'Glorification', 'justification' and 'apology' of terrorism laws that are not compatible with requirements of intent, harm and causation under international human rights law should be repealed.

Crimes such as 'glorification', 'justification' and 'apology' of terrorism which do not provide minimum intent, harm and causation requirements are incompatible with freedom of speech and should be reformed or repealed.[627] The key question is not the name of the offence but whether a state seeks to restrict speech without demonstrating either the connection between speech and serious harm or a speaker's intent to harm.[628] It is possible that vague or overbroad *incitement* to terror offences may also fail minimum causation and intent standards for this reason.[629] In a similar manner to blasphemy or denial laws, any terrorism offence which allows criminal penalties to be meted out against speakers on the basis of the *content* of speech, rather than the intent of the speaker and probable or actual harm caused by the speech sets a worrying precedent whereby a state or court decides which viewpoint is or is not acceptable.[630]

The European Court's approach to 'glorification', 'justification' and 'apology' of terrorism laws contradicts other international bodies and should be reconsidered.[631] It diverges from the Council of Europe's formulation under the Convention on the Prevention of Terrorism, which provides that speech should be prohibited if the speaker has the 'intent to *incite* the commission of a terrorist offence' where such speech '*whether or not directly advocating* terrorist offences, *causes a danger that* one or more such offences may be committed'.[632] A push to reconsider this jurisprudence was recently articulated by a judge on the Court, who observed that the offence of 'praising or justifying terrorism' without 'incitement to violence or hatred' was contrary to article 10 and that the 'disproportionate nature of the interference' was rooted in the law itself.[633]

6. States should provide additional protection to political speech or 'public interest' speech.

Speech in the public interest or of a political nature should only lead to liability if there are 'very strong reasons' for doing so.[634] This applies even if the speech concerns

---

[627] See s. III.3.2.1. ('Glorification', 'justification' and 'apology' offences).
[628] See s. III.3. (Necessity).
[629] See s. III.1. (Legality).
[630] See ch. 3 (Hate Speech), s VI.1. and VI.2. (Recommendations).
[631] See, e.g., Article 19, 'European Court of Human Rights: Contradictory rulings in two key free expression and terrorism cases' (2 September 2021) (arguing that the European Court 'consistently fails to heed international standards on freedom of expression accordingly to which the "praise", "glorification" or "support" of violence or terrorism are overly vague legal standards').
[632] COE Convention on the Prevention of Terrorism (2005) Art. 5 (emphasis added).
[633] See s. III.3.2.1. ('Glorification', 'justification' and 'apology' offences); ECtHR, *Erkizia Almandoz v. Spain* (App. no. 5869/17), 22 June 2021, Concurring Opinion of Judge Lemmens, §7.
[634] See s. III.4.1. (Public Interest).

matters related to national security.[635] Political or public interest speech should not be subjected to criminal sanction unless rising to the level of intentional incitement of acts of violence or serious criminal offences that may cause serious physical injury or endanger human life.[636]

The wide berth given to public interest speech is particularly important for journalists reporting on political issues. The media plays a 'crucial role in informing the public about acts of terrorism and its capacity to operate should not be unduly restricted'.[637] In particular, international bodies have made clear that journalists disseminating the statements of others—including in the form of interviews—is a key facet of the role of the press in a democratic society.[638] Such speech should be protected by way of strict intent and harm requirements but may also be subject to additional protections in national laws.[639]

7. States can only impose penalties for speech under terrorism laws to the extent that the penalty is necessary and proportionate to advancing a legitimate aim. Criminal sanctions should only be used in exceptional circumstances.

International standards regulating free speech mandate that any penalty imposed on speech must be proportionate.[640] Although the majority of terrorism and public order laws that restrict speech are criminal in nature,[641] international standards dictate that criminal penalties for speech should only be resorted to in exceptional circumstances.[642] Custodial sentences will rarely be justified for speech, unless, for instance, the speech intentionally incites death or serious physical injury.[643] And although the European Court has allowed terms of imprisonment in a small number of cases related to speech-based terror offences, the Court recognizes that the 'imposition of a prison sentence for a press offence' will be compatible with article 10 of the Convention 'only in exceptional circumstances',[644] 'incitement to violence' being one of them.[645]

---

[635] HRC, General Comment No. 34 (2011), §30. See s. III.4.1. (Public interest) and ch. 5 (Speech Related to National Security: Espionage and Official Secrets Laws), s. IV.3.3. (Recommendations).
[636] See s. IV.2. (Recommendations). In some legal systems this may include recklessness as to such harm being created: see ch. 3 (Hate Speech), s. VI.3.1. (Recommendations); see ch. 4 (False Speech), s. IV.6. (Recommendations).
[637] HRC, General Comment No. 34 (2011), §46.
[638] See s. III.3.3. (Intent).
[639] See s. III.4.1. (Public interest).
[640] See, e.g., HRC, General Comment No. 34 (2011), §§34–35; ECtHR, *Guja v. Moldova* (App. no. 14277/04), 12 February 2008, §78.
[641] See s. III.5. (Penalties); CTED, *Global survey of the implementation of Security Council resolution 1624 (2005) by Member States* (2021) UN Doc S/2021/973 (Annex), §2.
[642] See, e.g., IACtHR, *Álvarez Ramos v. Venezuela* (Series C, no. 380) 30 August 2019, §§119, 120; ACtHPR, *Konaté v Burkina Faso* (App. no. 004/2013), 5 December 2014, §165; HRC, General Comment No. 34 (2011), §47 (in the context of defamation); CERD, General Recommendation No. 35 (2013), §12.
[643] See s. III.5. (Penalties).
[644] ECtHR (GC), *Cumpănă v. Romania* (App. no. 33348/96), 17 December 2004, §115. See ch. 1 (Introduction), s. II.3.2.6. (Criminal penalties for speech).
[645] See s. III.5. (Penalties); ECtHR (GC), *Cumpănă v. Romania* (App. no. 33348/96), 17 December 2004, §115.

Consistently with the principle of proportionality, states should consider non-punitive responses to speech that may sometimes be appropriate, for instance where speech may promote non-violent harms such as 'intolerance'. As noted by the UN Security Council's Counter-Terrorism Committee, 'the law enforcement approach may in some instances prove to be less effective than other actions and even counter-productive'.[646] Effective counter-messaging, developing strategies to address the underlying conditions contributing to marginalization and intolerance—which may in turn contribute to extremist sentiments—and partnerships with media, civil and religious community groups may be less intrusive responses to speech than criminal sanctions.[647]

8. Tech companies should recognize international human rights standards as a floor, not a ceiling, of free speech protection.

Social media and technology companies should uphold the commitment to regulating speech in line with the Global Network Initiative principles, which recognize that international human rights law including article 19 of the ICCPR should be respected and 'read within the context of further interpretations issued by international human rights bodies'.[648] International human rights standards are a floor—rather than a ceiling—of protection for speech, and should be treated as such by private companies that have a role in regulating speech.[649]

---

[646] CTED, *Global survey of the implementation of Security Council resolution 1624 (2005) by Member States* (2016) UN Doc. S/2016/50 (Annex), §10.
[647] Ibid., §§13–14.
[648] GNI, 'GNI Principles on Freedom of Expression and Privacy' (2017), n 7.
[649] See ch. 3 (Hate Speech), s. VI.5. (Recommendations).

Index

For the benefit of digital users, indexed terms that span two pages (e.g., 52–53) may, on occasion, appear on only one of those pages.

accreditation schemes 11–12
actual malice standard
    defamation or insulting speech 75–76, 105–6, 109, 114, 143–44, 249–50
    false speech 249–50
    public officials 57–58, 82, 143, 249–50
artistic expression 93, 114, 126–27, 384

bans on work as a journalist 91, 139–40, 152
blasphemous speech 156–57, 163–64, 166, 191–93
    margin of appreciation 46
    see generally **hate speech**

capital punishment *see* **death penalty**
causation
    direct and immediate harm 107, 145–46, 248, 351, 389, 390–91, 417–18
    espionage and official secrets laws 309, 324, 340, 341–42
    false speech 230–31, 234, 251, 259, 263, 272–73
    harm 245, 248–49, 264, 266–67
    hate speech 167–68, 181–82, 193
        foreseeability 156
        harm 193, 196, 218, 266
    incitement to violence 391–93, 394, 395–97, 419
    insulting speech 105, 107–8
        harm 77–78, 105, 107–8, 145–46, 211
    intent 267, 394–97, 417–18
    necessity requirement 382, 391
    political speech 392
    proportionality 391, 397
    terrorism laws *see* **terrorism laws**
    blasphemous speech 161
    disinformation 251–52
    espionage and official secrets laws 325
    false speech 234–35, 238, 239, 250, 251–52
    hate speech 161
    insulting speech 92, 106, 135–36, 143–44
    political speech 161, 269, 271–72
    public interest defence 251–52
    terrorism laws 349, 360–61

civil penalties
    bans or restrictions on work as a journalist 91, 139–40, 152
    civil liberties, loss of 233
    costs 67, 89, 91, 137, 139, 164, 308–9
    damages *see* **damages**
    espionage and official secrets laws 279, 308–9
    false speech 232–34, 237, 259–60, 273, 275
    hate speech 160, 164, 173, 175–76, 204
    injunctions 91, 138–39, 151
    insulting speech 81, 89–91, 135–39
        decriminalization 140, 141–42
        defining elements of a civil wrong 142–49
        injunctions 91, 138–39, 151
    media outlets, banning, suspension or closure of 37, 40, 91, 139–40, 160–61, 227, 233–34, 402–3
    public office, bans on or suspension from running for 93–94, 205–6, 336, 363–64, 397, 405
    travel bans 100, 172
classified information 281–82, 283, 310, 319–20, 338–40
companies *see* **online speech**
confidential information, disclosure of
    espionage and official secrets laws 280–81, 282, 293, 300, 319
    harm 277, 322
    legitimacy requirement 315
    manner of obtaining information 329–30
    opinion 334
    public interest defence 285, 290, 325–26
    responsible journalism doctrine 332–33
    truth, defence of 333
    see also **whistleblowing**
    hate speech 183
    insulting speech 120–21, 124
    sources, protection of 1–13
corrections 152, 233–34, 244, 259–60, *see also* **rectification**
costs 66, 67
    espionage and official secrets laws 308–9
    hate speech 164
    insulting speech 89, 91, 137, 139
    SLAPPs 94, 95

Covid-19
  anti-vaccination activists 241
  arrest or detention of journalists 221
  chilling effect 234–35
  civil penalties 259
  derogations in time of emergency 40
  false speech 32, 40, 220–22, 228–29, 237
    anti-vaccination activists 241
    chilling effect 234–35
    civil penalties 259
    criminal penalties/criminalization 221, 223, 247–48
    derogations in time of emergency 40
    harm 247–48
    intent 229, 268
    ulterior purposes 264–65
    vagueness and overbreadth of legislation 235
  social media 3, 235, 237, 261–62
  ulterior purposes 264–65
  vaccine hesitancy 220–21
  vagueness and overbreadth of legislation 235
criminal penalties/criminalization
  causation 272–73
  Covid-19 221, 223, 247–48
  correctional labour 92
  death penalty *see* **death penalty**
  defamation 64–65, 91, 128–29, 130, 245, 259
  discrimination 17, 18
  elections 53, 93, 243–44, 246
  espionage and official secrets laws 287–88, 340–41
  false speech 231–32, 234–37, 257–59, 267, 272–73
  harm
    false speech 247–48, 266–67
    hate speech 156–57, 194, 215–17
    terrorism laws 357, 383–85
  hate speech 160–61, 163–64, 204–8
    blasphemous speech 157, 186, 212–13
    imprisonment 162–63, 165–66, 170–71, 200–1, 214–15
    incitement to violence 214–17
    religious hatred 163–76
  Holocaust denial 53, 70, 166–67, 184
  imprisonment *see* **imprisonment**
  insulting speech 72–74, 85–89, 128–35
  intent 156–57, 215–16
  necessity
    espionage and official secrets laws 307, 313–14, 315, 330–31
    false speech 262, 266, 272
    hate speech 164, 204–5, 206–7, 214–15
  insulting speech 101, 102–3, 105, 107, 126, 128
  terrorism laws 407–8, 409–10, 420–21
  political speech 72–73, 404, 419–20
  proportionality 45, 345–46
    espionage and official secrets laws 307, 313–14, 315, 330–31
    false speech 262, 266, 272
    hate speech 164, 204–5, 206–7, 214–15
    insulting speech 101, 107, 126, 128
    terrorism laws 407–8, 409–10, 420–21
  terrorism laws 359–60, 407–10
    incitement to terrorism 347–48, 359–60, 362, 372–73, 395
    incitement to violence criminal penalties/criminalization 373–74, 407, 408–9, 415–16
custodial sentences *see* **imprisonment**; *see also* **criminal penalties/criminalization**,
customary international law 4, 41–43
  derogations in time of emergency 36, 38, 42–43
  hate speech 43, 179–80
  insulting speech 101
  international standards 41–43
  non-parties to treaties, as binding on 4, 5, 36, 41
  opinio juris 41
  reservations 26, 42, 43
  state practice 41, 42, 43
cybercrime 230, 232–33

damages 89–90, 97–98, 99–100, 150–52
  actual malice standard 75–76
  chilling effect 89, 135–36
  civil penalties *see* **civil penalties**
  defamation 67, 75–76, 91, 100, 150–51
    actual malice standard 75–76
    large awards 89–90, 135–37
    means of the speaker 72–73, 139, 150–51
  journalists, relevance of speakers being 61–62
  means of the speaker 72–73, 139, 150–51
  nominal damages 89
  punitive or exemplary damages, abolition of 150–51
death penalty
  espionage and official secrets laws 287, 335
  false speech 231–32
  hate speech 157, 160, 166
    blasphemous speech 157, 166
  terrorism laws 359, 367, 407
declarations in treaties 1, 5–13, 35–36, 177, 179–80; *see* **reservations to treaties**

INDEX   425

interpretive declarations 1
reservations 5–13, 30–1, 32–33, 35–36, 177, 217
defamation see Chapter 2
actual malice standard 249–50
civil defamation 259
damages 67
false speech 222, 249–50, 259
   harm 245–46
   reputation 222, 237, 245
harm 245–46
hate speech 198–99, 201
public interest defence 76, 81–83
public officials
   actual malice test 249–50
reputation 222, 237, 245
responsible journalism doctrine 61–62
retractions 61
truth, defence of 253–54
deference to states
espionage and official secrets laws 48, 308–9, 315
jurisprudence of international bodies and courts 45–46
terrorism laws 380
denial laws
climate change 174
criminal penalties/criminalization 157–59, 200–1, 214
divergences in interpretation 55, 62–63, 70, 114–16, 207
historical facts 55–56, 157–58, 198–201, 213–14, 243–44
Holocaust see **Holocaust denial**
margin of appreciation 46
memory laws 157–58
opinion 198–201
repeal of laws 213–14
derogations from treaties in times of emergency 36–41
Covid-19 37, 38, 40
customary international law 36, 38, 42–43
extent required by exigencies of the situation, only to the 36–37, 38
international treaties 1–39
regional treaties 1–41
suspensive effect 36
time-limited derogations 40
discretionary restrictions on hate speech 183–207
discrimination see **incitement to discrimination**
disinformation see **false speech**
drafting history 13–26, 70

international treaties 1–22
regional treaties 1–26

economic coercion by states 3, see also **media outlets, banning, suspension or closure of**
elections
disinformation 227
false speech 3, 221–22, 227, 242, 243–44, 264
   harm 227–28, 246, 261–62, 265–66
   intent 230
   vagueness and overbreadth of legislation 224–25, 262–63
harm 227–28, 246, 261–62, 265–66
hate speech 162, 170–71, 204
intent 230
proportionality 264
terrorism laws 381
vagueness and overbreadth of legislation 224–25, 262–63
emergencies see **derogations from treaties in times of emergency**
espionage and official secrets laws see Chapter 5
deference to the state 48
truth, defence of 254
exclusions, exceptions and defences
espionage and official secrets laws 280, 285–86, 325–37, 339–40
false speech 231, 253–57, 261, 269, 271–72
good faith see **good faith**
hate speech 160, 167–68, 198–203
insulting speech 74, 76, 79, 81–85, 114–28
neutral reportage, defence of 148
opinion see **opinion**
public interest defence see **public interest defence**
reasonable publication defence see **reasonable publication defence**
responsible journalism doctrine see **responsible journalism doctrine**
terrorism laws 355–56, 358–59, 382, 403–7
truth see **truth, defence of**
existence of the state see **territorial integrity or existence of the state, threats to**
extremism laws 348, 364–65, 374, 421
vagueness or overbreadth of legislation 378, 379

fair and accurate reporting of official documents 71–84, 114, 124–25, 148
fair comment 76, 84–85, 114, 116, 147 see also **opinion**
fair trial, right to a 101, 119–20, 127–28, 268, 298

426 INDEX

fake news *see* **false speech**
false speech *see* Chapter 4
   Covid-19
      derogations in time of emergency 40
   public health 3
   recklessness 60–61
freedom of expression, definition of 5, 172–73
frivolous, vexatious or trivial claims 95–96, 146, 150

gender identity, hate speech based on 181, 182, 218
good faith
   espionage and official secrets laws 325, 331–32, 340–41
      manner of obtaining information 329–30
      necessity requirement 316–17
      public interest defence 286, 326–27
      truth, defence of 333–34
   false speech 249, 250, 256
   hate speech 160, 203
   insulting speech 82, 121, 123–24
   intent 325, 340–41
   necessity requirement 316–17
   public interest defence 286, 326–27
   responsible journalism doctrine 59–60
   terrorism laws 358–59
   truth, defence of 333–34

harm
   artistic expression 384
   causation
      espionage and official secrets laws 324
      false speech 245, 248–49, 264, 266–67
      hate speech 193, 194, 196, 218
      insulting speech 77–78, 105, 107–8, 211
      terrorism laws 358, 386, 389–97
   defamation 245–46
   espionage and official secrets laws 280, 283–84, 320–25, 337
      causation 324
      confidential information, disclosure of 283, 322
      intent 325, 340
      necessity requirement 319–25
      proportionality 321, 322–23, 324
      public interest defence 312–13, 322, 344
      serious harm, objective likelihood of 341–43
   false speech 221–22, 225–29, 244–53, 260
      causation 245, 248–49, 264, 266–67
      direct harm 265–67
      penalties 225, 237, 245–48, 261–62
      severity of harm 245–48, 265–66

hate speech 154–55, 156, 158–59, 165, 181–82, 341–42
   causation 193, 194, 196, 218
   definition 178, 182
   necessity requirement 193–96
   proportionality 195–96
   substantial harm 167
   vagueness and overbreadth of legislation 159
imminence of harm *see* **likelihood or imminence of harm or violence**
incitement to hatred 385–86, 387
incitement to violence 265–66, 383–86, 387–88
insulting speech 105, 108–14
   causation 77–78, 105, 107–8, 211
   direct, immediate and serious harm 145–46
   state practice 74, 77–80
   type and level of harm 105, 108–14
intent 218, 245, 249–53, 266–67, 325, 340, 395, 397–403
likelihood or imminence of harm *see* **likelihood or imminence of harm or violence**
necessity requirement 244–49, 319–25
   hate speech 193–96
   terrorism laws 382–88
objective likelihood of direct and serious harm 265–66
proportionality 195–96, 321, 322–23, 324
public interest defence 312–13, 322, 344
public officials 324
serious harm, objective likelihood of 341–43
severity of harm 320–23
state practice 74, 77–80
terrorism laws 348, 352, 357–58, 382–403
   apology 120–71
   glorification of terrorism 120–71
   incitement to terrorism 357–58, 383–86, 387–88, 395, 397–403, 416
   justification for terrorism 419
   reporting terrorism 420
type of harm 320–23, 382–88
vagueness and overbreadth of legislation 159, 358
hate speech 24–25 *see also* Chapter 3
   blasphemous speech *see* **blasphemous speech**
   customary international law 43
   denial laws *see* **denial laws**
   derogations in time of emergency 39–40
   incitement to hatred
      racial hatred 20
      terrorism laws 385–86, 387

incitement to violence 9, 18–20, 24–25
    objective approach 17–18
  online hate speech *see* **online speech**
  political speech 153–63, 201–2, 216–17, 218
  racial hatred
    incitement 20
  terrorism laws 373–74, 385–86, 387, 414
heads of state or government, insulting 5–13, 72–73, 85, 110–11, 210–11
Holocaust denial 55–56
  false speech 243–44, 252
  hate speech 157–58, 189, 202, 214
    opinion 199–200
  opinion 199–200
  public interest defence 202
hostility *see* **incitement to hostility**

imminence of harm or violence *see* **likelihood or imminence of harm or violence**
imprisonment 2, 3
  espionage and official secrets laws 280, 281, 292, 294, 298–99
    harm 320–21, 323
    manner of obtaining information 329–31
    opinion 335–37
    types of speech 280–81
  exceptional circumstances 53–54, 63–64
    espionage and official secrets laws 336–37
    false speech 247, 257–58
    hate speech 63–64, 201, 204–5, 206–7
    insulting speech 133–34
    terrorism laws 383, 385–86, 404, 408, 410, 420–21
  false speech 248–49, 267
  hate speech 160, 162–63, 165–66, 170–71, 200–1, 214–15
    exceptional circumstances 204–5
    religious hatred 164, 165, 171–72, 204–5
  insulting speech 145
  opinion 200–1, 335–37
  political speech 404
  religious hatred 164, 165, 171–72, 204–5
  terrorism laws 360, 363–64, 407–9, 410
    exceptional circumstances 420–21
    extremism laws 365
    harm 383–86
    justification for terrorism 364
    material support for terrorism 369–70, 372–73
    political speech 404
incitement *see* **incitement to discrimination; incitement to hatred; incitement to hostility; incitement to terrorism; incitement to violence**

incitement to discrimination
  blasphemous speech 213
  hate speech 154, 161–62, 175–76, 177–78, 213
    mandatory restrictions 173–74
    racial hatred 39–40, 173
    religious hatred 38, 39–40, 173, 209–10
incitement to hatred
  racial hatred 20, 154, 175–76, 177–78
  religious hatred 161–62, 174, 175–76
  terrorism laws 385–86, 387
incitement to hostility 2, 17, 64
  blasphemous speech 213
  denial laws 114
  derogations in times of emergency 38, 39–40
  hate speech 154, 158–59, 173, 196–97, 216–17
    mandatory restrictions 173–74, 175–76
    online hate speech 209–10
    religious hatred 171, 195–96
  hostility, definition of 18
  positive obligations 17
incitement to terrorism
  causation 391–93, 394, 395–97, 419
  harm 357–58, 383–86, 387–88, 395, 397–403, 416
  hate speech 414
  intent 356–57
  online incitement to terrorism 411–14
  proportionality 419
  public interest defence 403, 404, 405, 419–20
  type of speech 351–53
  vagueness and overbreadth of legislation 416, 419
incitement to violence
  causation 391–93, 394, 395–97, 419
  mandatory restrictions 154, 174–75, 180–82
  online incitement 411–14
  political speech 419–20
  public interest defence 403, 404, 405, 419–20
  racial hatred 20–21
  terrorism laws 362, 372–73, 419
    causation 391–93, 394, 395–97, 419
    harm 357–58, 383–86, 387–88, 416
    hate speech 414
    intent 356–57, 398–99, 400, 401–2, 419
    online incitement to terrorism 411–14
    political speech 419–20
    public interest defence 403, 404, 405, 419–20
    types of speech 351–53
    vagueness and overbreadth of legislation 416, 419

independent and impartial courts 6, 183, 263, 270, 273
injunctions 91, 124–25, 138–39, 151
insulting speech *see* Chapter 2; *see also* defamation; sedition
intent / *mens rea*
  actual malice standard *see* **actual malice standard**
  espionage and official secrets laws 280, 284–85, 325, 340–41, 342–43, 344
  false speech 224, 225, 229–31, 234, 237, 266–67, 268–69, 271
    causation 267
    imprisonment 272–73
    penalties 272–73
  harm 218, 245, 249–53, 266–67, 340
  hate speech 154–55, 159–60, 165, 169, 174, 176, 177, 181, 196–98
    harm 218
    knowledge test 160
    necessity requirement 193, 196–98
    religion or religious beliefs, insulting 165
  insulting speech 73–74, 75–77, 81, 105–7, 142, 143, 147
  necessity requirement 193, 196–98
  public interest defence 271
  recklessness *see* **recklessness**
  religion or religious beliefs, insulting 165
  responsible journalism doctrine 59–61, 62
  terrorism *see* **terrorism laws**

judicial proceedings, reporting on 84, 114, 148
judiciary
  independent and impartial courts 6, 183, 263, 270, 273
  insulting speech 72, 83, 106–7, 112, 119–20, 223

legality
  discretionary restrictions 185–87
  espionage and official secrets laws 313–15, 340–41
  extremism 378, 415
  false speech 238–40
  hate speech 175, 178, 181, 183–84, 185–88, 210, 216–17
  insulting speech 101–3
  terrorism laws 373, 374–79, 415
legitimacy requirement
  discretionary restrictions 187–93
  espionage and official secrets laws 312–13, 315, 317, 319
  false speech 238, 240–44, 264–65

hate speech 175, 181, 183–84, 187–93, 204, 207, 210
insulting speech 101, 104
soft law 382
terrorism laws 373, 379–82
lèse-majesté laws 92, 96–97, 102, 104, 140, 141–42, 226–27
licensing 11, 12, 28–29, 35, 233–34, 381
likelihood or imminence of harm or violence
  espionage and official secrets laws 311–12, 319–20, 324, 341–43
  false speech 245–48, 265–67
  hate speech 156, 158–59, 176, 194, 196, 214–17
    imminent lawless action 168–70
    incitement 176, 180, 182, 194, 207–8
    intent 177
    mandatory restrictions 174
    necessity requirement 207–8
  terrorism laws 356–57, 372–73, 374, 394, 395, 417–18

malice *see* **actual malice standard**
mandatory restrictions on hate speech 173–82, 184
  racial hatred 154, 174, 177–78, 181, 182
media outlets, banning, suspension or closure of 37, 40, 91, 139–40, 160–61, 227, 233–34, 402–3
media pluralism 1–12
military, insulting the 223
misinformation *see* **false speech**

national flags and emblems, insulting 83
national security 2, 6, 15, 16, *see also* **espionage and official secrets laws; terrorism laws**
  false news 226, 228, 264
  hate speech 187, 191, 212
  insulting speech 101, 104, 108
necessity requirement 45–46
  causation 382, 391
  espionage and official secrets laws 279, 307, 313–14, 316–25, 344–45
    confidential information, disclosure of 316, 317
    objective basis for designating information as secret 318–20
    public interest defence 295, 316–17, 319, 328, 344–45
    truth, defence of 333
  false speech 238, 244–53
    harm 244–49
    proportionality 238, 244, 245

INDEX 429

public health 264
harm 193–96, 382–88
hate speech 175, 181, 183–84, 187–88
  discretionary restrictions 193–98
  harm 193–96
  intent 193, 196–98
  legitimacy requirement 190
  online hate speech 210
insulting speech 101, 105–14
intent 193, 196–98
opinion 382
proportionality 183, 193
  false speech 238, 244, 245
  terrorism laws 373, 382, 420–21
public health 264
public interest defence
  espionage and official secrets laws 295, 316–17, 319, 328, 344–45
  terrorism laws 382
terrorism laws 373, 382–403
  criminal penalties/criminalization 420–21
  harm 382–88
  proportionality 373, 382, 420–21
  terrorism, definition of 376
truth, defence of 333, 382
negligence
  espionage and official secrets laws 284, 286
  insulting speech 77, 105–6, 120, 142–44
neutral reportage, defence of 148

official proceedings, fair and accurate reports of 71–84, 114, 124–25, 148
official secrets *see* **espionage and official secrets laws**
online speech
  internet
    continuous or multiple publication in the digital age 73–74
    cybercrime 230, 232–33
    cyberlibel 74, 97–99
    false speech 223, 227, 232–34, 260, 274, 275–76
    intermediaries 160–61
  shutdowns 3
  social media
    artistic expression 93
    Covid-19 3, 235, 237, 261–62
    espionage and official secrets laws 292–93, 298
    false speech 221, 235, 236–37, 261–62
    hate speech 165
    imprisonment 92
    insulting speech 92, 93
    terrorism laws 236, 410

  technology and social media companies
    aiding and abetting 412–13
    algorithms 412, 413–14
    Christchurch Call 412
    civil penalties 160–61
    civil society organizations 412
    complaints and appeals 412
    false speech 274–76
    hate speech 208–11, 218–19
      legality, legitimacy, and necessity requirements 210
      political speech 210–11
      proportionality 210
      public interest defence 210
opinion
  espionage and official secrets laws 334–37
  false speech 224, 253, 254–55, 271
  hate speech 181, 198–201
  insulting speech 76, 84–85, 125–27, 147–48
  mixed statements of opinion and fact 255
  terrorism laws 382, 406–7
overbreadth of legislation *see* **vagueness or overbreadth of legislation**

pandemic *see* **Covid-19**
penalties
  administrative penalties 173, 175–76, 259–60, 273
  blasphemous speech 157, 212–13
  civil penalties *see* **civil penalties**
  criminal penalties *see* **criminal penalties/criminalization**
  culpability, degree of 272–73
  defamation 237
  deprivation of other rights 71–140
  elections 242, 246
  espionage and official secrets laws 279, 287–88, 308–9, 334–37, 338–40
  false speech 231–34, 242–44, 257–60
    administrative penalties 259–60, 273
    civil penalties 232–34, 237, 259–60, 273, 275
    culpability, degree of 272–73
    defamation 237
    harm 225, 237, 245–47, 261–62
    licences, suspension of publication or broadcast 233–34, 273
    necessity requirement 244, 245
    proportionality 237, 242, 257, 258–59, 260, 272–73
  harm 225, 237, 245–47, 261–62
  hate speech 155, 156, 160–61, 173, 175–76, 204–7
  insulting speech 74–75, 85–92, 128–52

penalties (*cont.*)
  proportionality 204–5, 206–7
  legitimacy requirement 242–44
  licences, suspension of publication or broadcast 233–34, 273
  necessity requirement 244, 245, 420–21
  proportionality
    false speech 237, 242, 257, 258–59, 260, 272–73
    terrorism laws 420–21
  responsible journalism doctrine 61–62
  terrorism laws 420–21
pluralism *see* **media pluralism**
political speech
  application of national laws 97–99
  chilling effect 161
  espionage and official secrets laws 325–26, 332–33
  exclusions, exceptions and defences 114
  false speech 236–37, 241, 255–56, 269, 271–72
  hate speech 153–63, 201–2, 210–11, 216–17, 218
  insulting speech 72–73, 140, 141–42, 143–44
    application of national laws 97–99
    opinion 114
    public interest defence 114, 118, 120
    truth, defence of 114
  opinion 114
  public interest defence 114, 118, 120, 403–4, 420
  responsible journalism doctrine 60–61
  terrorism laws 361, 371, 415
    additional protection, recommendation for states to provide 419–20
    causation 392
    public interest defence 403–4, 420
  truth, defence of 114
prevent abuse by others, obligation of states to 1–13
prior restraint 6, 138–39, 151, 183–84
proportionality
  civil liability, imposition of 140, 141–42
  costs 139
  damages 135–36, 137, 150–52
  espionage and official secrets laws 307, 313–14, 315, 330–31
    harm 321, 322–23, 324, 343
    public interest defence 325–26, 328–29, 344–45
    serious harm, objective likelihood of 343
  fair hearing, right to a 128
  false speech 262, 266, 272
    penalties 237, 242, 257, 258–59, 260, 272–73
    public interest defence 255–56, 273
  harm 321, 322–23, 324, 343
  hate speech 167, 168, 184, 190, 218
    penalties 164, 204–5, 206–7, 214–15
    necessity requirement 183, 193
    online hate speech 210–11
  injunctions 138
  insulting speech 140, 141–42, 152
    costs 139
    damages 135–36, 137, 150–52
    fair hearing, right to a 128
    injunctions 138
    necessity requirement 101
    penalties 128, 150–51
    prior restraints 151
  international standards 420
  necessity requirement 101, 183, 193, 373, 382
  non-pecuniary remedies 152
  penalties 128, 150–51, 420–21
  prior restraints 151
  public, extent to which the speech is 71–114
  public interest defence
    espionage and official secrets laws 325–26, 328–29, 344–45
    false speech 255–56, 273
  serious harm, objective likelihood of 343
  terrorism laws 373, 391, 397
    penalties 407–8, 409–10, 420–21
    necessity requirement 373, 382
protecting the press, importance of 47, 50–53, 59, 69
public domain, information in the
  espionage and official secrets laws 292, 293, 300, 320, 338–39
  insulting speech 82, 110–11
public health 2, 6
  Covid-19 *see* **Covid-19**
  false speech 3, 220–22, 228–29, 230–31, 241, 244, 261–62, 264
  hate speech 187, 212
  insulting speech 101, 104
public morals 101, 104, 187–91, 212
public interest defence
  chilling effect 251–52
  civil liability, imposition of 141–44, 148–49
  criminal penalties/criminalization 272–73, 403–5, 408, 419–20
  defamation 140–41
  espionage and official secrets laws *see* **espionage and official secrets laws**
  fair comment 116
  false speech 253, 255–57, 261, 271–72

chilling effect 251–52
  proportionality 255–56, 273
 harm 109, 110–11, 112
 hate speech 153–202, 210
 incitement of terrorism 403
 incitement of violence 405, 419–20
 insulting speech 73–74, 79, 81–83, 116–20
  civil liability, imposition of 141–44, 148–49
  defamation 140–41
  fair comment 116
  harm 109, 110–11, 112
  opinion 76, 85, 126, 148
  prior restraints 151
  public officials 116–17, 130–31, 140–41, 143–44
  reasonable publication defence 81, 83, 116, 144–45
  truth, defence of 114
 necessity requirement 382
 opinion 76, 85, 126, 148
 political speech 403–4, 420
 prior restraints 151
 proportionality 255–56, 273
 public officials 116–17, 130–31, 140–41, 143–44
 reasonable publication defence 81, 83, 116, 144–45
 responsible journalism doctrine 60–62
 terrorism laws 358–59, 400–1, 403–6
  additional protection, recommendation for states to provide 419–20
  necessity requirement 382
  political speech 403–4, 420
 truth, defence of 114
public office, bans on or suspension from running for 93–94, 205–6, 336, 363–64, 397, 405
public officials
 actual malice test 57–58, 249–50
 espionage and official secrets laws 282, 286, 288, 324, 326–29, 334
 false speech 224–25, 255, 271–72, 274
 hate speech 169–70, 184–85, 201
 heads of state or government, insulting 210–11
 insulting speech *see* public officials, insulting speech against
 margin of appreciation 46
 misfeasance in public office 224–25
 reservations 28, 35
 terrorism laws 404, 406, 410
public officials, insulting speech against
 actual malice test 82, 143, 249–50

 civil penalties 150–51
 defamation 73–74, 77, 81, 82–83, 85
  actual malice test 82, 143, 249–50
  intent 105–6
 harm 109–10
 heads of state or government 72–73, 85, 110–11
 imprisonment 93–94, 133–34
 intent 75–76, 105–6
 media pluralism 99–100
 opinion 127
 public interest defence 116–17, 130–31, 140–41, 143–44
 reasonable publication defence 120
 silencing criticism 94–95, 99–100, 109
 SLAPPs 94–95
 statements about public officials including heads of state 110–11
public order laws *see* **terrorism laws**

racial hatred 154, 156–57, 176, 180–81, 218
 definition 178
 incitement 161–62, 175–76
 political speech 161
reasonable publication defence
 espionage and official secrets laws 325, 329–33
 insulting speech 76, 79, 81, 83, 114, 116, 120–24, 144–45
 terrorism laws 358–59
recklessness
 espionage and official secrets laws 332–33, 340, 341
 false speech 60–61, 229, 249–50, 252, 268
 hate speech 176, 215–16
 insulting speech 105, 106, 143, 147
 necessity requirement 57
 terrorism laws 353, 357
rectification 94–95, 99–100, 130, *see also* corrections
religion *see* blasphemous speech; religious hatred
religious hatred 176, 180–81, 218
 contempt of religion 172
 incitement 161–62, 171, 175–76
 insulting/disparaging religious doctrines 163–64, 165–66
reply, right of 24, 33, 114, 137, 152
reputation *see* reputation of states, endangering the;
reputation of states, endangering the
 espionage and official secrets laws 338–40
 false speech 226–27, 265–66
 heads of state 110
 terrorism laws 350, 375–76

432 INDEX

reservations and declarations to treaties 26–36
    categories 32
    constitutions, reference to 28, 29, 30, 32, 34, 35
    customary international law 26, 42, 43
    declarations 5–13, 30–1, 32–33, 35–36
    due process clauses 32
    general reservations 5–41
    hate speech 177, 179–80
    interpretation compatible with other rights 32
    modification to obligations, identification of extent of 26–27
    object and purpose, compatibility with 26–27, 28, 34
    objections 26–27, 34
    scope 26, 28
    state practice 42
    status 26
    war propaganda 29–31
responsible journalism doctrine 59–62
    corrections 61
    defamation 61–62
    espionage and official secrets laws 325, 331–33
    false speech 253, 256–57
    good faith 59–60
    hate speech 153–203
    insulting speech 114, 120–22, 123–24, 144, 145
    intent 59–61, 62
    non-journalists, application to 60–61
    objective approach 59–60, 62
    penalties 61–62
    political speech 60–61
    presentation of speech, manner of 60
    public interest defence 60–62
    reasonableness, test for 60–61
    replies, failure to publish 61–62
    verify information, steps taken to 60, 62
    watchdog function
        false speech 253, 256–57
        hate speech 112
        insulting speech 119, 120–21, 122, 145
        responsible journalism doctrine 60–61
        social media 52–53
        terrorism laws 400–1
retractions 61, 107, 152

sedition 72–73, 96–97
    application of national laws 92, 97
    civil liability, imposition of 142–49
    colonial-era laws 97
    Covid-19 97
    damages, proportionality of 150–51
    intent 77
    legality requirement 103
    legitimacy requirement 104
    objective approach 142–44
    opinion 147–48
    public interest defence 82
    truth, defence of substantial 146–47
    vagueness or overbreadth of legislation 142
sexual orientation, hate speech on grounds of 181, 182, 218
SLAPPs 73–74, 94–96
    abuse of rights 94–96
    anti-SLAPP legislation 95
    costs 94–95
    forum shopping 95
    frivolous claims, dismissal of 95–96
    libel tourism 71–96
    public interest defence 96
    serious harm threshold 96
sources, protection of journalists' 1–13
standards *see* international standards
state officials *see* public officials
state practice
    customary international law 41, 42, 43
    derogations in times of emergency 36
    espionage and official secrets laws 280, 325
    false speech 223–37, 264–65
    hate speech 156–73
    insulting speech 74–100
status of speakers as journalists 59–62, 69, 114–27
strategic litigation against public participation *see* SLAPPs
strict liability
    espionage and official secrets laws 284
    false speech 229–30, 249, 268
    hate speech 177–78, 215–16
    insulting speech 143
summaries of rulings, publication of 152
symbols, protection of 83, 113

territorial integrity or existence of the state, threats to 6, 28
    espionage and official secrets laws 339
    false speech 221–22
    hate speech 183, 188
    insulting speech 106–7
    terrorism and public order laws 350, 358, 366–67, 379–80, 405
terrorism laws *see* Chapter 6; *see also* 6–7, 16, 347–421 extremism laws
    blasphemous speech 212
    false speech 225, 228–29, 230, 236, 264

incitement to terrorism *see* **incitement to terrorism**
insulting speech 101, 104, 108
justification for terrorism 63
travel bans 100, 172
truth, defence of
defamation 253–54
espionage and official secrets laws 254, 333–34
false speech 253–54, 270–71
hate speech 198
insulting speech 81, 114–16, 125
  falsity, requirement for truth of 146–47
  post-publication facts and events, proof of 146
  substantial truth 146–47
terrorism laws 382, 406–7

ulterior purposes, use of misinformation laws for 234, 241–42, 264–65

vagueness or overbreadth of legislation *see* **legality**
blasphemous speech 157
Covid-19 235
espionage and official secrets law 311, 338–39
false speech 224–25, 235, 262–63
hate speech 155, 157, 159, 161, 216–17
incitement to violence 419
insulting speech 75, 102–3
state practice 224–25
terrorism laws 354, 358, 361, 395
  harm 358
  incitement to violence 419

verify information, steps taken to
espionage and official secrets law 316, 329–30, 333–34
false speech 231, 268–69
hate speech 198
insulting speech 71–122, 123–24, 125, 147
reasonable publication defence 83
responsible journalism doctrine 60, 62
terrorism laws 406

whistleblowing
confidential information, disclosure of 302, 325–26, 334
culpability 342–43
espionage and officials secret laws 295, 306–7, 328–29, 340–41
  confidential information, disclosure of 302, 325–26, 334
  good faith 333–34
good faith 333–34
internal channels, efforts made to report wrongdoing using 329, 330–31
last resort, publication as a 330–31
necessity requirement 316–17, 325
public interest defence 328–29
reasonable publication defence 330–31
retaliation, protection from 331
serious harm, objective likelihood of 342–43
truth, defence of 333–34
verify information, steps taken to 333–34